1-37

CRC Handbook of Environmental Radiation

Editor

Alfred W. Klement, Jr.
Environmental Scientist
Private Consultant
Kensington, MD

CRC Series in Radiation Measurement and Protection

Editor-in-Chief

Allen Brodsky
Certified American Board of Health Physics
American Board of Radiology
American Board of Industrial Hygiene

CRC Press, Inc.
Boca Raton, Florida

Library of Congress Cataloging in Publication Data
Main entry under title:

CRC handbook of environmental radiation.

(CRC series in radiation measurement and protection)
Bibliography: p.
Includes index.
1. Radiation—Safety measures—Handbooks, manuals, etc. 2. Radiation dosimetry—Handbooks, manuals, etc. I. Klement, Alfred W. II. Title: C.R.C. handbook of environmental radiation. III. Title: Handbook of environmental radiation. IV. Series.
QC795.32.S3C7 1982 363.1'79s [363.1'79]
ISBN 0-8493-3761-5 82-1169

This book represents information obtained from authentic and highly regarded sources. Reprinted material is quoted with permission, and sources are indicated. A wide variety of references are listed. Every reasonable effort has been made to give reliable data and information, but the author and the publisher cannot assume responsibility for the validity of all materials or for the consequences of their use.

Direct all inquiries to CRC Press, Inc., 2000 Corporate Blvd., N.W., Boca Raton, Florida, 33431.

International Standard Book Number 0-8493-3761-5

Library of Congress Card Number 82-1169

Printed in the United States

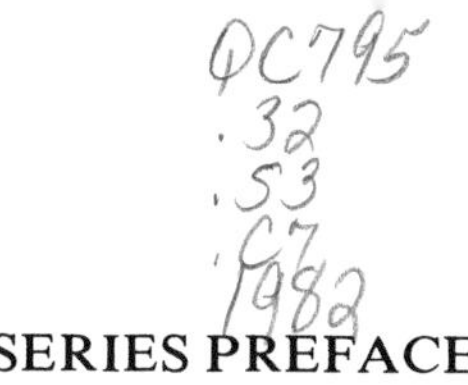

SERIES PREFACE

The purpose of this handbook series is to provide data and methods for dealing with the design and evaluation of radiation measurement instruments; monitoring and survey methods; selection of protective facilities, equipment and procedures for handling radioactive materials; effluent control and monitoring; radioactive waste disposal; transportation of radioactive materials; and many other related subjects. Aspects of these subjects involve not only all of the sciences but also management, legal, insurance, and public information considerations. The sciences themselves include the entire range of basic scientific and engineering methods, as broad a range as in the entire field of public health itself. This series of volumes will be divided as far as possible into logical groupings that hopefully will tend to maximize the usefulness of each volume, as well as the series of volumes, to its users.

The primary aim of the handbook series will be to include as much useful data as possible for the specialist needing ready access for the solution of problems most likely to arise in the radiation protection professions. However, some selected review of fundamental concepts is also included to enable persons with a basic science or engineering background to acquire the necessary knowledge to solve a majority of problems in especially important aspects of radiation protection. Also, since the profession is broad in discipline, an attempt has been made to fulfill the frequent need of professionals for a refresher course in some of the more important fundamentals needed to utilize data included in the handbook. Principles of management, organization, and procedures related to radiation safety will also be summarized in later volumes, with attention to presentation of methods for establishing new radiation safety programs based on the accumulated experience of others.

This series of volumes should, therefore, be useful in industrial, academic, medical, and governmental institutions and to scientists carrying out both applied and basic research in subjects related to radiation protection, to engineers designing protective facilities and equipment, to applied health physicists establishing radiation safety programs, to physicians involved with caring for patients exposed to radiation or radioactive materials, to public health and other government officials concerned with regulating radiation safety and developing national standards, to professors and students studying and synthesizing a broad base of knowledge in radiation protection, and to practically every other type of professional involved in radiation protection problems. The editor and publisher hope that the many users will offer continued suggestions for improving these volumes and for including data that will make them more useful.

A general acknowledgement of gratitude must be made to the advisory board, to the contributors, and to the authors and publishers who have granted permission to include material in this series. Contributors of the sections in this series have been selected for their professional knowledge in the respective subject areas, and in most cases have generously devoted their own personal time to this effort without monetary compensation. Material included in this handbook series was selected according to the professional opinions of authors, compilers, and editors and does not necessarily reflect any official sanction of the agencies or companies with which the contributors are employed. Addresses indicated for the contributors are for identification and correspondence purposes only. The collective responsibility for the total content lies, of course, with the editor, who is solely responsible for any omissions either from inadvertence or neccessity.

On the other hand, the editor has purposely built in some redundancy of certain important types of data, since it is advisable to cross-check values obtained from different literature sources or approaches. The editor has also, to some degree, allowed repetition of similar data in different sections of the handbook where it was deemed advisable for the continuity of individual sections or for the convenience of the user due to the need for frequent cross reference between text and data. In cases where the users intend to rely on a tabulated or calculated value for the protection of humans, it is, of course, necessary to arrive at values in different ways in order to not only avoid inadvertent mistakes but also to ensure better understanding of the degree of reliability or range of uncertainty of the end result. Frequently, in radiation protection design as in general engineering practice, factors of safety must be included that are based on knowledge of the ranges of uncertainty in estimated risks. A further purpose of the redundance of sources is also to include older as well as newer approaches in cases where the changes themselves may be of interest in evaluating the need for protective actions or changes in regulations or policies.

The editor is grateful to CRC Press for generally providing an outstanding facility and staff for the publication of data and reference sources currently needed in science and technology. The publishers, Bernard, Florence, and Earl Starkoff have also given invaluable guidance in determining the philosophy, scope, and organization of this handbook series. Their continued enthusiasm and encouragement has been an inspiration to the editor. Gerald A. Becker, Editorial Director when the project began, also provided early inspirational leadership in developing the concepts and format of this series. Kay Harter was helpful in the initial administration of this series. The editor would also like to acknowledge the invitation of Professors Niel Wald and Yen Wang to contribute to the *CRC Handbook of Radioactive Nuclides;* reprinting of some of the editor's sections from the above handbook ultimately inspired the development of this handbook series. Special mention should be made to the able assistance of Eileen M. Haycraft in initiating and carrying through so much of the detailed work necessary in Bethesda in compiling, drafting, and editing many of the sections of this series.

Allen Brodsky
Editor-in-Chief
Bethesda, Maryland
November 1978

PREFACE

The purpose of this volume is a continuation of the Handbook series stated in the Editor-in-Chief's preface to Volume I, Section A of the *CRC Handbook of Radiation Measurement and Protection.* This volume deals with principles of estimation and measurement of exposures to environmental radiation and radioactivity. Two major sections (''Protection of the Environment'' and ''Environmental Sampling, Monitoring, and Analysis'') of the volume deal with this both generally and specifically. The section entitled ''Radioactive Waste Disposal'' deals with radioactive waste disposal. This area involves specific and perhaps nonroutine and interesting current problems in the field of radiation protection.

Previous volumes in this Handbook series provide many of the basic data and methods, and much information applicable to the protection of the environment. Future volumes provide more specific information with regard to some important sources of environmental radioactivity. Reference should be made to these volumes. For coherence, some pertinent information is repeated briefly in this volume. An attempt is made here to provide basic information required in the protection of man due to radiation exposure through radioactivity in the environment. Because of the wide range of environmental radiological problems, the approach to the presentation is to include in the various subsections and chapters as much of the current methods of evaluation of, and sources of information on, radiation in the environment as possible through a variety of means. Since radiological protection problems range from apparently minor ones to very complex ones, and since a very common radiological protection problem deals with estimates and predictions of radiation exposures *before* the fact, emphasis has been placed here with examples of real problems. In general, the techniques used in these predictions are also indicative of the measurements that must be made to assess a situation during and after the fact.

Various techniques and methods are described in this volume. Some mathematical models are discussed in some detail. Some models are quite sophisticated, some are quite simple. The problem and the result required in a given situation should determine the ''sophistication'' of the model to be used, and the quality and quantity of data available are very important. All of the *types* of methods presented are in current use, modified as needed, and they reflect the fact that many radiological situations dealing with the environment cannot be handled too simply if one wants to perform an adequate assessment. On the other hand, where statistically adequate measurements are available, relatively simple models are adequate. So, here the gamut is discussed in the various chapters, with different approaches taken to different problems intentionally in order to provide both broad and narrow problem methods. The methods of both predictions and measurements emphasize the necessity for the use of adequate statistical planning and instrument selection commensurate with the problem.

Alfred W. Klement, Jr.
Kensington, Maryland
September 1980

THE-EDITOR-IN-CHIEF

Dr. Allen Brodsky has a broad professional background and interest in the scientific, engineering, and management aspects of radiation protection. After graduation with a B.E. in Chemical Engineering (Johns Hopkins University) and 1 year of postgraduate study in Radiological Physics at the Oak Ridge National Laboratory, his broad career in health physics and radiation measurements pinpointed the need for further study, which led to the degrees of M.A. in Physics (Johns Hopkins University) and Sc.D. in Biostatistics and Radiation Health (University of Pittsburgh), followed by board certifications from the American Board of Health Physics, the American Board of Industrial Hygiene, and the American Board of Radiology.

In addition to his education, positions as Physicist and Health Physicist, Naval Research Laboratory; Radiological Defense Officer, Federal Civil Defense Administration: Health Physicist, U.S. Atomic Energy Commission: Associate Professor of Health Physics, University of Pittsburgh: Radiation Therapy Physicist and Radiation Safety Officer, Mercy Hospital; and Adjunct Research Professor, School of Pharmacy, Duquesne University stimulated his interest in the need for readily available data to solve radiation measurement and protection problems, and to design facilities, equipment, and procedures for the safe handling of radiation sources and radioactive materials.

The Editor's research interests include the development of radiation measurement and dosimetry methods, hazard evaluation, facility design, methodology for health and mortality follow-up of radiation workers, and the theory of cancer induction by environmental agents. His present position at the U.S. Nuclear Regulatory Commission involves the development of guides for radiation protection in medical institutions, industry, and universities.

The editor welcomes suggestions or offers of further contributions of data for the handbook series at the following address:

Dr. Allen Brodsky
P. O. Box 34471
West Bethesda, MD 20817

THE EDITOR

Mr. Alfred W. Klement, Jr., has a broad background in engineering, radiobiology, physical sciences, and environmental sciences. His undergraduate training was conducted at Texas A&M University and the U.S. Military Academy, West Point, where he received his B.S. degree and commission in the U.S. Regular Army Artillery. His Army experience included command and staff positions and special military schooling. His graduate training included a year at the U.S. Naval Postgraduate School, Annapolis, followed by 2 years at the University of California, Berkeley, where he received a degree of M. Bioradiology, which instruction included summer courses in radiological defense at the Army Chemical Center and Health physics at the Oak Ridge National Laboratory — an Armed Forces program.

Following a tour of duty in research activities in health physics and physiology at the Army Chemical Center, Maryland, Mr. Klement attended the 1-year course of advanced training at the Army Artillery and Guided Missile School at Ft. Sill, Oklahoma, and Ft. Bliss, Texas. After further assignments in command and staff positions in an armored division, in 1957 he left the Army to join the U.S. Atomic Energy Commission's Division of Biology and Medicine as a health physicist involved with nuclear weapons testing and weapons effects. In 1959 he joined the new Fallout Studies Branch, analyzing environmental fallout data and later administering research programs in the environmental field and assisting in other biomedical research programs.

Shortly after becoming an assistant branch chief, Mr. Klement was assigned to direct and administer the AEC's environmental program in the Las Vegas office, conducted under the auspices of the U.S. Atlantic-Pacific Interoceanic Canal Study Commission. On completion of this study in 1970, he retired from Federal service, but soon was brought back to represent the AEC on an interagency special study of radiation exposures from all sources 1960—2000. During this period he also assisted in preparing and editing Environmental Statements for nuclear power facilities. He returned to retired status on completion of the special study in 1972. Since that time he has continued writing and editing articles and books in the environmental field, as well as doing consulting work for the U.S. Nuclear Regulatory Commission and the Department of Energy. He is also writing fiction as a sideline.

DEDICATION

This volume is dedicated to the following who have greatly contributed to a number of scientific fields and especially to the protection of the environment:

L. Joe Deal
Gordon M. Dunning
Edward E. Hardy, Jr.
S. Allan Lough*
Lester Machta
Allyn H. Seymour
G. Hoyt Whipple
John N. Wolfe*

* Deceased

ADVISORY BOARD MEMBERS

Dr. Walter S. Snyder
Deceased

Dr. J. Newell Stannard
Professor Emeritus
Department of Radiation Biology and Biophysics
The University of Rochester
17441 Plaza Animado
Apt. 132
San Diego, California 92128

Dr. Conrad P. Straub
2330 Chalet Drive
Minneapolis, Minnesota 55421

Dr. Niel Wald, Chairman
Department of Radiation Health
Graduate School of Public Health
University of Pittsburgh
130 DeSoto Street
Pittsburgh, Pennsylvania 15261

CONTRIBUTORS

Sanford G. Bloom
Principal Scientist
Columbus Laboratories
Battelle Memorial Institute
505 King Avenue
Columbus, Ohio 43201

Frank J. Bradley
Principal Radiophysicist
Radiological Health Unit
Division of Industrial Hygiene
New York Department of Labor
80 Centre Street
New York, New York 10013

Bernard L. Cohen
Professor
Department of Physics
University of Pittsburgh
Pittsburgh, Pennsylvania

Dale H. Denham
Senior Research Scientist
Battelle, Pacific Northwest Laboratories
P.O. Box 999
Richland, Washington 99352

James A. Duke
Chief
Economic Botany Laboratory
U.S. Department of Agriculture
Beltsville, Maryland 20705

Gilbert J. Ferber
Research Meteorologist
Air Resources Laboratory
National Oceanographic and Atmospheric Administration
8060 13th Street
Silver Spring, Maryland 20910

Jerome L. Heffter
Research Meteorologist
Air Resources Laboratory
National Oceanic and Atmospheric Administration
8060 13th Street
Silver Spring, Maryland 20910

Alfred W. Klement, Jr.
Environmental Scientist
Private Consultant
10105 Summit Avenue
Kensington, Maryland 20895

Arthur A. Levin (Deceased)
Health Physicist

William E. Martin (Deceased)
Ecologist

Thomas J. Overcamp
Associate Professor
Environmental Systems Engineering
College of Engineering
Clemson University
Clemson, South Carolina 29631

Gilbert E. Raines
Project Manager
Office of Nuclear Waste Isolation
Battelle Memorial Institute
505 King Avenue
Columbus, Ohio 43201

Vincent Schultz
Professor
Department of Zoology
Washington State University
Pullman, Washington 99164

David A. Waite
Staff Project Manager
Office of Nuclear Waste Isolation
Battelle Memorial Institute
505 King Avenue
Columbus, Ohio 43201

F. Ward Whicker
Professor
Department of Radiology and Radiation Biology
Colorado State University
Fort Collins, Colorado 80523

TABLE OF CONTENTS

Protection of the Environment

INTRODUCTION

Alfred W. Klement, Jr.

Previous sections in other volumes in this series have provided many of the basic data and much information applicable to the protection of the environment; therefore, reference should be made to those sections. For coherence, some pertinent information is repeated briefly in this section. An attempt is made here to provide basic information required for the protection of man from radiation exposure through radioactivity in the environment. Because of the very wide range of environmental radiological problems, and the limitation of such a handbook, the various subsections and chapters include as much as possible of the current sources of radiation and methods of estimating radiation exposure through a variety of means. Since radiological protection problems range from apparently minor to very complex, and since a very common radiological protection problem deals with estimates and predictions of radiation exposure *before* the fact, emphasis is placed here on examples of real problems. In general, the techniques used in these predictions are also indicative of the measurements that must be made to assess a situation during and after the fact. Today, the techniques are much more advanced than a few years ago, and they will become more sophisticated as studies continue.

Various techniques and methods are described in this section. Mathematical models are discussed in some detail. However, these are the methods in current use, with modifications in many cases, and reflect the fact that many radiological problems dealing with the environment cannot be handled too simply if one wishes to perform an adequate assessment. Therefore, the gamut is discussed in the various chapters, with different approaches intentionally taken to different problems in order to provide methods for solving both narrow and broad problems. The methods of both prediction and measurement emphasize the necessity for the use of adequate statistical planning and instrument selection commensurate with the problem.

Mathematical models are presented in such a way that they also assist in the understanding of the environmental pathways to man and the movement of radioactivity in the environment. They also indicate procedures that can be followed to reduce the work required in radiological assessments while at the same time provide a reasonably adequate assessment using whatever data are available.

NATURAL SOURCES OF ENVIRONMENTAL RADIATION

Alfred W. Klement, Jr.*

INTRODUCTION

Man is exposed in varying degrees, depending on his activities and location, to sources of radiation found in nature. Cosmic radiation entering the earth's atmosphere and crust is one source. Nuclear interactions of cosmic rays with matter produce radionuclides to which man is exposed. Other sources of natural radiation are elements found in the earth's crust that are composed of one or more radioisotopes.

COSMIC RADIATION

A number of reviews and data on cosmic radiation have been published.[3] Cosmic-ray dose rates vary[2] with latitude and geomagnetic latitude up to about 50°. For example, the whole-body dose rates at sea level from Alaska to Florida range from about 45 to 30 mrem/year. At 45°N from sea level to 8000 ft altitude the range is about 40 to 200 mrem/year. Based on these relationships, estimates of dose can be made for any population.

NATURAL RADIONUCLIDES

Primordial Radionuclides

A number of naturally occurring radionuclides are primordial, i.e., associated with the formation of the earth. The heaviest elements are composed entirely of radioisotopes, and all of these may be placed in one of four long-decay series; the important ones are the uranium, thorium, and actinium series. The neptunium series is of lesser interest. Decay schemes of the major long-decay series are shown in Figures 1 to 3. The primordial radionuclides are shown in Table 1.

Cosmogenic Radionuclides

Some radionuclides are produced through nuclear reactions between cosmic rays and nuclei in the atmosphere, soil, and water. Of the many radionuclides produced through these reactions, only a few are present at any time in detectable concentrations, and some of these require very tedious procedures for collection and analysis. Even when detected, some concentrations are available with large uncertainties. Those detectable and reported are listed in Table 2.[1]

Other cosmogenic nuclides, spallation products, thorium, uranium, and ^{40}K have been reported in meteoritic material; these include ^{10}Be, ^{14}C, ^{26}Al, ^{36}Cl, ^{37}Ar, ^{53}Mn, ^{60}Co, and others. Another group found in very small quantities and concentrations results from the natural fission of uranium and thorium.[4] Estimates of neutron-activated nuclides in air, soil, and water indicate the great variety of nuclides that are possible from cosmic ray reactions and natural fission.[5]

Some ranges of estimates of production rates of cosmogenic radionuclides are given

* This chapter was adapted from Klement, A. W., Jr., Natural radionuclides in foods and food source materials, in *Radioactive Fallout, Soils, Plants, Foods, Man,* Fowler, E. B., Ed., Elsevier, Amsterdam, 1965, 113. With permission. It is taken in part from Klement, A. W., Jr., Miller, C. R., Minx, R. P., and Shleien, B., Estimates of Ionizing Radiation Doses in the United States 1960—2000: Report ORP/CSD 72-1, U.S. Environmental Protection Agency, Washington, D.C., 1972, 7. Reference 3 provides additional references.

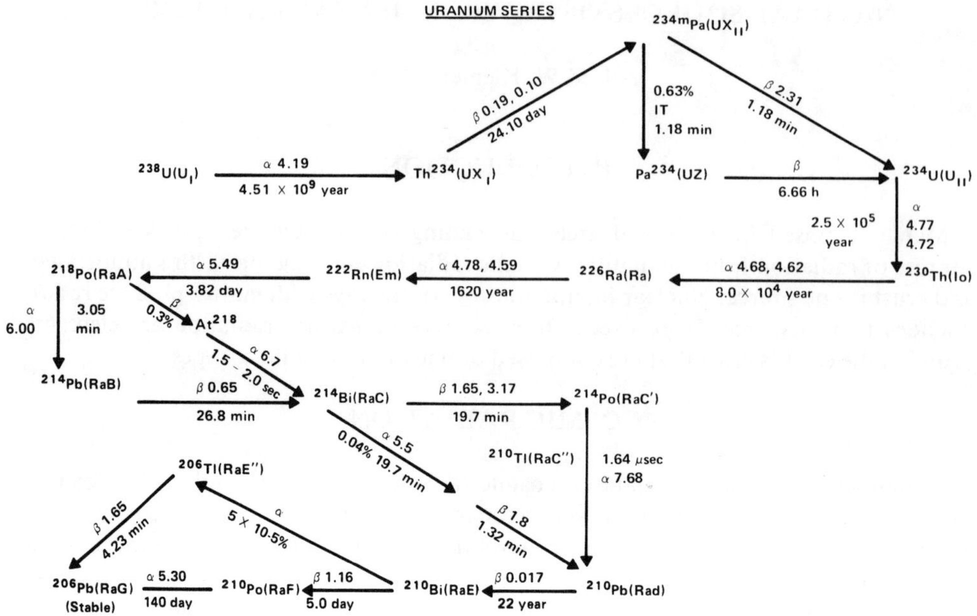

FIGURE 1. Uranium series decay scheme (α and β energies in megaelectronvolts). (From Klement, A. W., in *Radioactive Fallout, Soils, Plants, Foods, Man,* Fowler, E. B., Ed., Elsevier, Amsterdam, 1965, 113. With permission.)

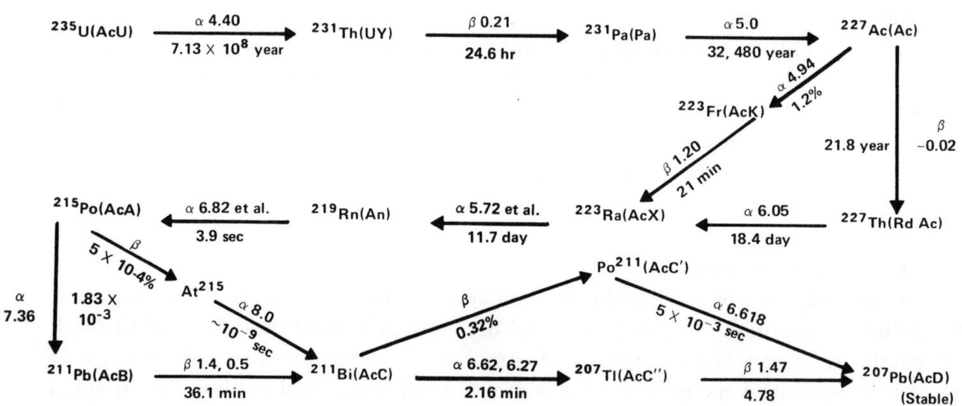

FIGURE 2. Actinium series decay scheme (α and β energies in megaelectronvolts). (From Klement, A. W., Jr., in *Radioactive Fallout, Soils, Plants, Foods, Man* Fowler, E. B., Ed., Elsevier, Amsterdam, 1965, 113. With permission.)

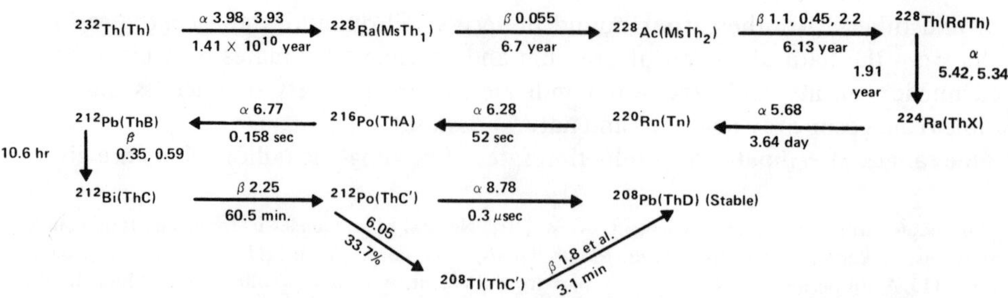

FIGURE 3. Thorium series decay scheme (α and β energies in megaelectronvolts). (From Klement, A. W., Jr., in *Radioactive Fallout, Soils, Plants, Foods, Man,* Fowler, E. B., Ed., Elsevier, Amsterdam, 1965, 113. With permission.)

Table 1
PRIMORDIAL RADIONUCLIDES

Nuclide	Half-life (years)	% isotopic abundance	Emissions, decay	Energy of primary emission (MeV)	Specific activity (Ci/g element)
^{40}K	1.3×10^{-9}	0.0118	$\beta, \gamma, \varepsilon$	1.32	8.3×10^{-10}
^{50}V	$\sim 6 \times 10^{-14}$	0.24	$\beta, \gamma, \varepsilon$	—	$\sim 2.8 \times 10^{-14}$
^{87}Rb	4.7×10^{10}	27.85	β	0.27	2.5×10^{-8}
^{115}In	6×10^{-14}	95.72	β	0.6	5.0×10^{-12}
^{138}La	1.1×10^{11}	0.089	$\beta, \gamma, \varepsilon$	0.205	2.1×10^{-12}
^{142}Ce	5×10^{-15}	11.07	α	1.5	5.7×10^{-14}
^{144}Nd	$\sim 5 \times 10^{-15}$	23.85	α	1.8	$\sim 1.2 \times 10^{-13}$
^{147}Sm	1.06×10^{11}	14.97	α	2.24	3.38×10^{-9}
^{148}Sm	1.2×10^{13}	11.24	α	2.14	2.24×10^{-11}
^{149}Sm	$\sim 4 \times 10^{-14}$	13.83	α	1.84	$\sim 8.2 \times 10^{-13}$
^{152}Gd	1.1×10^{-14}	0.200	α	2.15	4.15×10^{-12}
^{174}Hf	4.3×10^{-15}	0.18	α	2.5	8.4×10^{-14}
^{176}Lu	3.6×10^{10}	2.59	β, γ	0.42	1.47×10^{-10}
^{187}Re	7×10^{10}	62.93	β	<0.008	1.73×10^{-8}
^{190}Pt	7×10^{11}	0.0127	α	3.11	3.33×10^{-13}
^{192}Pt	$\sim 10^{15}$	0.78	α	2.6	$\sim 1.4 \times 10^{-14}$
^{204}Pb	1.4×10^{17}	1.48	α	2.6	1.83×10^{-16}
^{238}U (series[a])					
^{235}U (series[a])					
^{232}Th (series[a])					

[a] See Figures 1 to 3.

From Klement, A. W., Jr., in *Radioactive Fallout, Soils, Plants, Foods, Man,* Fowler, E. B., Ed., Elsevier, Amsterdam, 1965, 113. With permission.

Table 2
MAJOR COSMIC-RAY-ACTIVATED RADIONUCLIDES

Nuclide	Half-life	Emission, decay	Energy of primary emission (MeV)	Production rate (atom/cm²-sec)
^{3}H	12.26 years	β	0.0181	0.12—1.3
^{7}Be	53 days	ε, γ	—	0.021—0.035
^{10}Be	2.7×10^{6} years	β	0.56	0.04—0.1
^{14}C	5760 years	β	0.156	2—2.6
^{22}Na	2.58 years	$\beta^{+}, \varepsilon, \gamma$	0.54	—
^{32}Si	~700 years	β	0.1 (to ^{32}P)	2×10^{-4}
^{32}P	14.3 days	β	1.71	1×10^{-4}
^{33}P	25 days	β	0.25	1×10^{-4}
^{35}S	86.7 days	β	0.168	2×10^{-4}
^{36}Cl	3×10^{5} years	β, ε	0.71	—
^{39}Cl	55 min	β, γ	1.91, 2.18, 3.43	—

From Klement, A. W., Jr., in *Radioactive Fallout, Soils, Plants, Foods, Man,* Fowler, E. B., Ed., Elsevier, Amsterdam, 1965, 113. With permission.

in Table 2. However, as mentioned above, cosmic ray intensities vary considerably around the earth. Also, the concentrations of nuclei available for reactions vary considerably. Except for very gross estimates of average concentrations on which very gross dose estimates may be made, such estimates are of little value unless they are the only estimates available or obtainable. Of course, the best estimates are based on actual measurements within a particular area of interest. Natural tritium may be used as an example. It has been estimated that tritium is produced in the range of 0.12 to 1.3 atoms/cm^2-sec (see Table 2), which includes a number of locations and sampling and analytical techniques, the use of various half-lives, etc. It has been suggested that the production rate of tritium as an average around the world is 1 atom/cm^2-sec.[6] Based on this figure, it was estimated that there are about 30 kg.[6] However, the concentrations of tritium in various media in various locations may differ by orders of magnitude. The situation is further compounded by the inhomogeneous physical, chemical, and biological processes coming into play. The compound uncertainties involved in such estimates are obvious. Further, when one attempts to superimpose the uncertainties of the effects of radiation on these uncertainties, it is doubtful that many arguments concerning such estimates have more than a trace of validity. For this reason, no attempt is made here to provide estimates of production rates in terms of curies. The discussion below provides estimates of more value in radiation protection; even so, the uncertainties are important considerations.

DISTRIBUTION OF NATURAL RADIONUCLIDES

Estimates of natural radionuclides in the earth's crust have been made; these are shown in Table 3.[1] These nuclides are found throughout the environment — soils, waters, and the atmosphere.

Soils

The concentration of natural radionuclides varies quite widely in soils, as may be expected. Geographic location and geological origin of soils as well as climatic, hydrological, and agricultural history are important in this regard. The uses of fertilizers in various agricultural situations have affected radionuclide concentrations to a large extent. For example, ^{40}K is increased in soils when potassium fertilizers are used. It has been reported[7] that some virgin soils (under cultivation 1 to 2 years) had concentrations of 2.0 mg K_2O/100 g,* while soils under cultivation for 20 years had concentrations of 28.8 mg K_2O/100 g.* Some fertilizers have been used that have relatively high concentrations of other natural radionuclides, particularly isotopes of radium. Also, fertilizers may affect the chemical form of natural radionuclides in soils and, thus, their physical transport and biological uptake.

Table 4 is a summary of a number of estimates of natural radionuclides in various soils.[1] Tables 5 and 6 provide additional estimates.[1] There are few data with regard to concentrations of nuclides found at very low concentrations.

Radionuclides in soils are internal and external sources of radiation exposure to man and the environment. However, it has been estimated that only about 1% of total soil potassium is exchangeable, so that the availability to plants depends on a number of factors such as cropping practice, leaching, erosion, irrigation waters, fertilizing, etc.[8] Although the availability mechanisms may be quite different, the same would perhaps be true for other radionuclides also. It should be kept in mind, however, that the external dose rates are not dependent on chemical form except as it is affected by some transport mechanism.

Natural Waters

Natural radionuclides in the seas and marine sediments were subjected to detailed study more recently than soils, but a large amount of data have been reported in the

* Concentrations of potassium in soils are usually given in terms of K_2O equivalents as normal practice by soil scientists. These could be easily converted to curies per gram of ^{40}K, but this would serve no purpose here.

Table 3
NATURAL RADIONUCLIDES IN THE EARTH'S CRUST (μg/g)

	Igneous rocks					Sedimentary rocks			Deep sea sediments	
			Granite							
Nuclide	Ultrabasic	Basaltic	High Ca	Low Ca	Syenites	Shales	Sandstones	Carbonates	Carbonate	Clay
^{40}K	0.0047	0.98	2.97	4.96	5.66	3.14	1.26	0.32	0.34	2.95
^{50}V	0.096	0.60	0.21	0.10	0.072	0.31	0.048	0.048	0.048	0.29
^{87}Rb	0.056	8.4	31	47	31	39	17	0.8	2.8	31
^{115}In	0.01	0.21	0.0x	0.25	0.0x	0.1	0.x	0.x	0.x	1.4
^{138}La	0.000x	0.013	0.040	0.049	0.060	0.082	0.03	0.000x	0.009	0.102
^{142}Ce	0.0x	5.3	9.0	10	17.8	6.5	10	1.27	3.9	38.2
^{144}Nd	0.0x	4.8	7.9	8.8	15.5	5.7	8.8	1.1	3.3	33
^{147}Sm	0.0x	0.79	1.3	1.5	2.7	0.96	1.5	0.19	0.57	5.7
^{148}Sm	0.0x	0.60	0.99	1.1	1.0	0.72	1.1	0.15	0.43	4.3
^{149}Sm	0.0x	0.73	1.2	1.4	2.5	0.89	1.4	0.13	0.53	5.3
^{152}Gd	0.00x	0.011	0.018	0.02	0.036	0.013	0.02	0.0026	0.0076	0.076
^{174}Hf	0.0011	0.0036	0.041	0.0070	0.020	0.0050	0.0070	0.00054	0.00074	0.0074
^{176}Lu	0.00x	0.016	0.028	0.031	0.054	0.018	0.031	0.0052	0.013	0.12
^{204}Pb	0.015	0.09	0.22	0.28	0.18	0.30	0.10	0.12	0.12	1.2
Th	0.004	4	8.5	17	13	12	1.7	1.7	x	7
U	0.001	1	3	3	3	3.7	0.45	2.2	0.x	1.3

Note: x = an order of magnitude.

From Klement, A. W., Jr., in *Radioactive Fallout, Soils, Plants, Foods, Man,* Fowler, E. B., Ed., Elsevier, Amsterdam, 1965, 113. With permission.

Table 4
ESTIMATES OF NATURAL RADIONUCLIDES IN SOILS (pCi/g)[a,b,c]

Location	Radium	Thorium	Uranium	^{40}K
Cambridge Gault	1	—	—	—
Dublin	5.2,2.8	—	—	—
U.S.	1.97	3.6—6.1	—	—
U.S. subsoils	1.52	—	—	—
U.S.S.R. central mountains	0.28—0.95	0.25—1.50	0.3—6.0	—
Poland	—	1.0—1.2	3.1—3.2	—
Germany	0.15—1.30	—	—	—
Colorado—New Mexico	1.2—2.0	—	—	—
U.S.	80—800 mCi/mi^2	—	—	—
Germany—North America	39—780 mCi/mi^2	—	—	—
Germany(^{226}Ra)	433—1,660 mCi/mi^2	—	—	—
U.S.	0.9—1.5	—	—	0.0025—0.0075
Spain	0—237	—	—	—

[a] Summarized from Klement.[1] This table merely shows the paucity of data, but more importantly that the variability is very wide and these data are of little use in health protection except in a gross way, so that detailed studies would be needed on a local or specific area basis to be of value where a problem in this regard appears significant.

[b] The values shown were mostly originally reported in units of grams per gram.

[c] It has been estimated that for U.S. soils the average ^{40}K concentrations are about 21.3 Ci/mi^2.

From Klement, A. W., Jr., in Radioactive Fallout, Soils, Plants, Foods, Man, Fowler, E. B., Ed., Elsevier, Amsterdam, 1965, 113. With permission.

Table 5
ESTIMATES OF NATURAL RADIONUCLIDES IN THE LITHOSPHERE AND SOILS (pCi/g)

Nuclide	Lithosphere	Soils
Uranium	1	0.33
Th	0.87	0.65
Ra	1×10^{-9}	0.8
^{40}K	2.5×10^{-3}	1.3×10^{-3}
^{87}Rb	2.15	0.425

Adapted from Klement, A. W., Jr., in *Radioactive Fallout, Soils, Plants, Foods, Man,* Fowler, E. B., Ed., Elsevier, Amsterdam, 1965.

last few decades. A number of extensive reviews are available that summarize much of the data of interest (see References 1 and 3). Tables 7 and 8 provide a summary of concentrations of natural radionuclides in oceans and sediments.[1] Concentrations vary quite widely in marine waters and sediments, as in soils, because of geographic location, mixing, additions from fresh waters and silt, etc.

Concentrations of radium in fresh waters are shown in Table 9.[1] Some measurements of cosmogenic radionuclide concentrations in precipitation have been made and are summarized in Table 10.[1]

As a result of the distribution of natural radionuclides discussed above, it would be expected that they would be found in drinking waters as well. Thus, drinking waters are a source of dietary intake of natural radionuclides. Generally, natural fresh waters are processed to some extent before being used as drinking water. The processing of

Table 6
POTASSIUM-40 AND RUBIDIUM-87 IN SOILS OF THE U.S.S.R.[a]

Soils	^{40}K (pCi/g × 10^{-3})	^{87}Rb (pCi/g)
Tundra	1.01—4.12	0.7
Podzolic	1.26—3.09	0.55, 0.52
Chernozems	1.73—2.47	0.40—0.65
Chestnut and serozems	1.74—2.23	0.13—0.50
Red	0.17—0.42	0.35
Forest	1.64—2.49	0.52

[a] For dry soil in A, B, and C horizons.

Adapted from Klement, A. W., Jr., in *Radioactive Fallout, Soils, Plants, Foods, Man,* Fowler, E. B., Ed., Elsevier, Amsterdam, 1965.

Table 7
ESTIMATED AVERAGE CONCENTRATIONS OF PRIMORDIAL RADIONUCLIDES IN THE OCEANS AND SEDIMENTS

Nuclide	Seawater (g/ℓ)	Surface sediments (g/g)	Nuclide	Seawater (g/ℓ)	Surface sediments (g/g)
^{238}U	3.0×10^{-6}	1×10^{-6}	^{216}Po	1.0×10^{-27}	1.7×10^{-24}
^{235}U	2.1×10^{-8}	7.1×10^{-9}	^{215}Po	$<8.1 \times 10^{-29}$	1.4×10^{-26}
^{234}U	1.6×10^{-10}	8.1×10^{-11}	^{214}Po	3.0×10^{-28}	1.1×10^{-27}
^{234}Pa	1.4×10^{-19}	4.7×10^{-20}	^{212}Po	1.2×10^{-32}	2.4×10^{-29}
^{231}Pa	$<2 \times 10^{-12}$	1×10^{-11}	^{211}Po	$<6.8 \times 10^{-29}$	1.2×10^{-26}
^{234}Th	4.3×10^{-17}	1.4×10^{-17}	^{210}Po	2.2×10^{-17}	8.8×10^{-16}
^{232}Th	$<2 \times 10^{-8}$	5.0×10^{-6}	^{214}Bi	2.1×10^{-21}	8.8×10^{-20}
^{231}Th	8.6×10^{-20}	2.9×10^{-20}	^{212}Bi	2.2×10^{-22}	3.7×10^{-24}
^{230}Th	$<3 \times 10^{-13}$	2.0×10^{-10}	^{211}Bi	$<5.6 \times 10^{-24}$	1.0×10^{-21}
^{228}Th	4.0×10^{-18}	7×10^{-16}	^{210}Bi	7.8×10^{-19}	3.1×10^{-17}
^{227}Th	$<7.0 \times 10^{-20}$	1.3×10^{-17}	^{214}Pb	2.9×10^{-21}	1.2×10^{-19}
^{228}Ac	1.5×10^{-21}	2.4×10^{-19}	^{212}Pb	2.4×10^{-21}	3.9×10^{-19}
^{227}Ac	$<1 \times 10^{-15}$	5.9×10^{-15}	^{211}Pb	$<9.0 \times 10^{-23}$	1.6×10^{-20}
^{228}Ra	1.4×10^{-17}	2.3×10^{-15}	^{210}Pb	1.1×10^{-15}	4.5×10^{-14}
^{226}Ra	1.0×10^{-13}	4.0×10^{-12}	^{204}Pb	4.4×10^{-8}	—
^{224}Ra	2.1×10^{-20}	3.4×10^{-18}	^{208}Tl	4.1×10^{-24}	6.7×10^{-22}
^{223}Ra	$<4.4 \times 10^{-20}$	8.5×10^{-18}	^{207}Tl	$<1.2 \times 10^{-23}$	2.1×10^{-21}
^{223}Fr	$<7.0 \times 10^{-24}$	1.4×10^{-21}	^{142}Ce	4.4×10^{-4}	—
^{222}Rn	6.3×10^{-19}	2.5×10^{-17}	^{138}La	2.7×10^{-10}	—
^{220}Rn	3.3×10^{-24}	5.4×10^{-22}	^{87}Rb	3.3×10^{-5}	—
^{219}Rn	$<1.7 \times 10^{-25}$	3.1×10^{-23}	^{50}V	4.8×10^{-9}	—
^{218}Po	3.4×10^{-22}	1.4×10^{-20}	^{40}K	4.2×10^{-5}	0.8—4.5×10^{-5}

From Klement, A. W., Jr., in *Radioactive Fallout, Soils, Plants, Foods, Man,* Fowler, E. B., Ed., Elsevier, Amsterdam, 1965, 113. With permission.

waters will usually reduce concentrations. However, the processing may either increase or decrease the availability of a radionuclide for uptake in biological systems through changes in its chemical form. Table 11 summarizes concentrations of natural radionuclides in drinking water.[1]

Table 8
ESTIMATED CONCENTRATIONS OF MAJOR COSMOGENIC RADIONUCLIDES IN THE OCEANS

Nuclide	Surface seawater (g/l)	Surface sediment (g/g)
^{35}S	$<1.8 \times 10^{-18}$	—
^{32}P	$<1.5 \times 10^{-18}$	—
^{33}P	$<3.1 \times 10^{-18}$	—
^{32}Si	5×10^{-19}	$0—2 \times 10^{-16}$
^{14}C	$2—3 \times 10^{-14}$	$0.1—1 \times 10^{-13}$
^{10}Be	$0.7—8 \times 10^{-17}$	$1—3 \times 10^{-13}$
^{7}Be	$<4.9 \times 10^{-17}$	—
^{3}H	$0.7—5 \times 10^{-16}$	—

From Klement, A. W., Jr., in *Radioactive Fallout, Soils, Plants, Foods, Man,* Fowler, E. B., Ed., Elsevier, Amsterdam, 1965, 113. With permission.

Table 9
CONCENTRATION OF RADIUM IN FRESHWATERS[a,b] (pCi/l)

Location	Concentration
Various rivers	0.01—0.1
U.S.S.R. (normal)	1
U.S.S.R.	0.2—4
Germany (rivers)	0.07—0.84
U.S. (average)	0.1
U.S. (drinking water supplies)	0—6.5
Western U.S.	0.04—440
U.S.S.R. (deep spring brines)	up to 1,000
Germany (springs)	up to 18.4
Maine-New Hampshire (maximum)	730 (^{226}Ra)
Illinois (maximum)	36 (^{226}Ra)
Illinois (sandstone wells)	up to 36.1 (^{226}Ra)
Spas	1×10^{5}
U.S.S.R.	$20—272 \times 10^{6}$ (^{224}Ra)

[a] Summarized from Reference 1. This table merely shows the paucity of data; more important, the variability is very wide and these data are of little use in health protection except in a gross way, so that detailed studies would be needed on a local or specific area basis to be of value where a problem in this regard appears significant.
[b] The values shown were mostly originally reported in units of grams per gram.

From Klement, A. W., Jr., in *Radioactive Fallout, Soils, Plants, Food, Man,* Fowler, E. B., Ed., Elsevier, Amsterdam, 1965, 113. With permission.

Table 10
CONCENTRATIONS OF COSMOGENIC RADIONUCLIDES IN PRECIPITATION (atoms/mℓ)

Nuclide	Concentration
^{3}H	5×10^{2}—1×10^{6}
^{7}Be	2×10^{3}—6×10^{3}
^{14}C	14.7 dpm/g C
^{22}Na	∼40
^{32}P	∼40, 26
^{33}P	−30, 55
^{35}S	∼400, 316
^{39}Cl	2.5

From Klement, A. W., Jr., in *Radioactive Fallout, Soils, Plants, Foods, Man,* Fowler, E. B., Ed., Elsevier, Amsterdam, 1965, 113. With permission.

Table 11
CONCENTRATIONS OF RADIUM IN DRINKING WATER (pCi/l)

Location	Concentration
U.S.	0—0.17
Joliet, Ill.	5.8
Chicago, Ill.	0.03[a]
Germany	0.02—0.62
London	0.1

[a] This includes ^{226}Ra only.

Adapted from Klement, A. W., Jr., in *Radioactive Fallout, Soils, Plants, Foods, Man,* Fowler, E. B., Ed., Elsevier, Amsterdam, 1965.

Foods

Obviously, the human diet is a source of intake of natural radioactivity and human exposure. A large amount of data is available with regard to concentrations of natural radionuclides in foods. Tables 12 to 19 provide summaries of concentrations in various categories, locations, and age groups.[1] While the concentrations of natural radionuclides vary widely with location and local situations, agricultural practices, exportation and importation, manufacturing and marketing procedures, and other factors tend to equalize concentrations except in situations where foods are mostly locally grown and eaten. Indications are that while individual samples may vary widely, composite diets and samples do not as far as the statistical aspects of sampling and analyses are concerned, at least in the U.S. and probably other industrialized nations.

There are few data on concentrations of natural radionuclides in nonagricultural environmental biota.[1,3] The range shown is extreme for the data available, indicating the local nature of the situation. Concentrations in soils, air, and water for local situations generally dictate the range of concentrations to be found.

Air

Most of the natural radionuclides are found in the atmosphere in some locations and some situations.[3] However, isotopes of radon (especially ^{222}Rn) and their daugh-

Table 12
RADIUM-226 IN FOOD GROUPS FOR ESTIMATION OF TOTAL DIETARY INTAKE[a,b]

Food groups	New York				Chicago				San Francisco			
	pCi ^{226}Ra/kg		pCi ^{226}Ra/year		pCi ^{226}Ra/kg		pCi ^{226}Ra/year		pCi ^{226}Ra/kg		pCi ^{226}Ra/year	
Whole wheat bread	3.2	1.2	36	13	3.5	2.9	38	33	2.8[b]	2.8	31[b]	31
White bread	3.2	1.5	118	54	3.3	2.0	123	76	2.9	2.5	106	94
Flour (white)	2.7	1.7	117	74	2.4	2.0	106	84	1.34	0.83	58	36
Milk (liquid)	0.25	0.24	56	54	0.24	0.22	53	49	0.22	0.20	49	44
Potatoes	2.0	2.5	90	113	1.4	0.77	64	35	1.0	2.0	46	91
Macaroni	2.1	1.8	6.2	5.3	1.6	1.9	4.8	5.8	1.2	1.7	3.5	5.1
Dried beans	6.1	3.2	18	9.7	7.0	2.5	21	7.5	2.3	4.1	6.8	12
Canned vegetables	2.2	0.54	44	11	1.8	1.1	37	22	0.91	1.0	18	20
Fresh vegetables	2.4	1.2	105	53	2.2	0.57	97	25	0.66	0.84	28	36
Root vegetables	3.4	2.3	57	39	2.0	1.8	34	31	2.6	2.4	44	40
Canned fruit	0.37	0.37	9.7	9.5	1.2	0.26	31	6.7	0.50	0.73	13	19
Fruit juices	1.6	0.49	31	9.3	0.68	0.86	13	16	0.71	0.62	14	12
Fresh fruit	1.5	2.8	99	192	1.4	0.57	92	39	0.91	0.65	62	44
Rice	1.5	1.0	4.6	3.1	0.70	0.37	2.1	1.1	0.63	0.80	1.9	2.4
Eggs	4.1	7.9	66	127	2.7	2.7[b]	44	44[b]	2.6	1.9	41	31
Fresh fish	1.2	0.68	9.6	5.4	0.71	1.0	5.7	8.3	0.80	1.2	6.4	9.2
Shellfish	1.2	1.1	1.2	1.1	2.5	1.7	2.5	1.7	2.0	1.0	2.0	1.0
Meat	0.44	0.47	32	34	0.45	0.64	32	47	0.81	0.55	59	40
Poultry	0.73	0.86	12	15	0.79	1.4	13	23	1.9	0.49	32	8.4

[a] Results of two samplings, 1960 to 1961.
[b] Only one sample, same value used for calculations.

From Hallden, N. A. and Fisenne, I. M., in Fallout Program Quarterly Summary Report, Hardy, E. P., Jr. et al., Report HASL-112. U.S. Atomic Energy Commission, New York, 1961, 90.

Table 13
RADIUM AND CALCIUM IN GERMAN FOODS

Food item	^{226}Ra concentration pCi/kg	pDi/g Ca
Meat	0.8—1.5	8.8—79.5
Milk	0.3	0.2
Eggs	3.1	6.9
Butter	0.3	0.55
Fish	2.8—6.3	0.7—19.0
Cod liver oil	4.9	2240
Flour and bread	1.7—3.3	2.4—13.8
Margarine	0.1	0.34
Carrots	1.6—6.1	4.9—22.9
Cabbage (2)	1.0, 2.4	1.3, 2.6
Apples	0.9	15.0
Potatoes (N. Germany)	1.0	23.8
Potatoes (S. Germany)	0.6	12.4

From Muth, H., Rajewsky, B., Hantke, H.-J., and Aurand, K., *Health Phys.*, 2, 239, 1960. With permission.

Table 14
RADIUM-226, THORIUM-228, AND ALPHA RADIOACTIVITY IN FOODS

Foods	Total α pCi/kg	^{226}Ra pCi/kg	^{228}Th pCi/kg
Breakfast cereals	9—580 (20)	25—68 (3)	5—61 (4)
Nuts	5—16,900 (10)	3—2730 (4)	3—1200
Brazil nuts	16,900 (1)	2730	1200
Peanuts	120 (1)	18	9
Confectionery	<1—2900 (11)	2.4—520	1.9—170
Beverages	<1—510 (12)	40—57 (4)	0.8—57
Meats and fish	<1—310 (17)	0.9—57 (9)	0.6—19 (9)
Cockles	310	57	19
Mussels	100	18.2	6.1
Sausages	16	2	1.7
Salmon (canned)	18	—	—
Veal, beef	7,5	0.9,—	0.6,—
Lamb	1	—	—
Fruits and vegetables	<1—23 (18)		
Pears	7	1.1	0.6
Milk products	<1—15 (9)	—	—
Cheese (4)	9—15	1.5 (1)	1.5 (1)
Bread and flour	8—147	—	—

From Turner, R. C., Radley, J. M., and Mayneord, W. V., *Health Phys.*, 1, 268, 1958. With permission.

ters are the only significant ones leading to widespread exposure through inhalation. Others, including the decay products of radon, contribute to radionuclides in soils and waters, as discussed above. Radon is released as a decay product from soils, rocks, waters, and building materials. It is also contained in natural gas and other fossil fuels. Radon concentrations vary considerably from place to place and from time to time.

Table 15
ESTIMATES OF POTASSIUM-40 CONTENT OF FOODS[a]

Food groups	Estimated ^{40}K (range) pCi/ kg food	Food groups	Estimated ^{40}K (range) pCi/ kg food
Dairy products	(770—1510)	Vegetables	
Cows milk	1180	Roots	(910—4450)
Cheese	800	Carrots(raw)	3400
Fats, oils, shortenings	(0—480)	Carrots (canned)	910
Butter	190	Sweet potatoes	4450
Margarine	480	White potatoes	3400
Fruits (fresh, raw)	(620—3700)	Leaf or stem	(1080—6500)
Assorted berries	(750—1510)	Cabbage (raw)	1900
Apples	620	Lettuce	1150
Bananas	3520	Spinach (raw)	6500
Peaches	1320	Spinach (canned)	2140
Oranges	1400	Celery	2490
Cantaloupes	1900	Beans and peas	(800—4640)
Grain products	(710—1900)	Lima beans (raw)	4640
Wheat flour	710	Lima beans (green, canned)	1740
Rice (white)	1070	Snap beans (green, raw)	2490
White bread	1500	Peas (green, raw)	3070
Whole wheat bread	1900	Peas (green, canned)	800
Nuts	(3500—6400)	Other	
Brazil nuts	5600	Tomatoes (raw)	1900
Coconut (dry, sweet)	6400	Cucumbers (raw)	1900
Peanuts (roasted, salted)	5820	Corn, sweet (raw)	(1990—3070)
Meats (cooked)	(2740—3320)	Miscellaneous	
Seafoods (raw)	(925—4540)	Sugar (cane)	4
Seafoods (cooked)	(925—2520)	Sugar (brown)	1900
Eggs	840	Beer	390
		Cola beverages	430

[a] Based on total K values.

From Klement, A. W., Jr., in *Radioactive Fallout, Soils, Plants, Foods, Man,* Fowler, E. B., ED., Elsevier, Amsterdam, 1964, 113. With permission.

Continuous monitoring records show that in many locations over extended periods of time air concentrations of radon vary both diurnally and seasonally.[15,16] Rainstorm and wind effects are also seen.[16] Further variations occur because of burning of fossil fuels both commercially and in dwellings. For example, the use of natural gas in dwellings increases ambient concentrations of radon in dwellings as well as the general environment, depending on the type of construction and ventilation, and perhaps other factors superimposed on the ambient atmospheric conditions.[17] While some studies have been conducted and some are in progress in this regard, insufficient data are available at present to provide a basis for a reasonable estimate of the natural gas contribution to population doses.

Because of the variations mentioned above, no meaningful list of concentrations of radionuclides in the atmosphere seems appropriate for this handbook. Even the gross estimate for *average* world-wide lung doses from radon differs by a factor of about 10. Realistic estimates of concentrations of radon and the resulting radiation doses must necessarily be made on a local or areal scale through detailed and continuous measurements over considerable time periods.

Some illustrative examples may be useful. Measurements made at Argonne National Laboratory in 1958 showed minima of 0.03 to 0.05 pCi Rn/ℓ at heights above ground

Table 16
RADIUM-226 AND CALCIUM IN INFANT FOOD GROUPS AND ESTIMATED INTAKE FOR THE FIRST YEAR OF LIFE

Food group	Diet (kg)	^{226}Ra (pCi/kg	Ca (g/kg)	pCi ^{226}Ra/g Ca	Estimated intake	
					pCi^{226}Ra/ year	g Ca/year
Cereals	8	14.3	8.22	1.74	114	66
Vegetables	23	0.59	0.29	2.0	14	7
Fruits	23	0.44	0.08	5.5	10	2
Meats	17	0.43	0.12	3.6	7.3	2
Nonmilk fraction of diet	—	—	—	1.9	145	77
Formula	37	0.39	0.95	0.41	14	35
Evaporated	137	0.39	1.56	0.25	53	214
Milk fraction of diet	—	—	—	0.27	67	249
Combined milk and non-milk fractions	—	—	—	0.65	212	326

From Engelmann, E., in Fallout Program Quarterly Summary Report, Hardy, E. P., Jr. et al., Report HASL-113, U.S. Atomic Energy Commission, New York, 1961, 95.

Table 17
AVERAGE DAILY INTAKE OF RADIUM, POTASSIUM-40, AND CALCIUM FOR CHILDREN IN 1961[a]

Sampling location	No. of months	Diet (kg)	Ca (g)	^{40}K (months) (pCi)	Total Ra (range) (pCi)	Radium	
						pCi/kg	pCi/g Ca
Los Angeles, Calif.	11	1.60	0.96	1730(6)	5.42 (2.1—11)	3.4	5.6
Denver, Col.	10	2.16	1.47	2860(5)	6.7(1.7—12.6)	3.1	4.6
Atlanta, Ga.	10	1.56	0.88	1660(4)	5.1 (2.9—7.9)	3.2	5.7
St. Louis, Miss.	10	2.67	1.40	4360(4)	10.2 (3.6—29.7)	3.8	7.2
New York, N.Y.	12	1.25	0.62	1600(4)	3.5 (<1—<6)	2.8	5.6
Austin, Tex.	11	2.47	1.51	2730(4)	8.7 (3.6—17.2)	3.5	5.7
Seattle, Wash.	11	2.32	1.31	2830(6)	7.7 (2.1—13.6)	3.3	5.9
Chicago, Ill.	3	1.23	0.77	1590(3)	<7.5 (<1.4—<7.9)	<5	<9.7
Palmer, Alaska	3	1.91	0.73	2380(3)	<4.9 (1.6—6.7)	2.6	6.7
Tampa, Fla.	2	1.83	1.17	1960(2)	7.8 (5.7—<10)	4.3	6.7
Honolulu, Hawaii	2	2.12	0.62	2520(2)	14.4 (4.6—24.3)	6.8	23.2
Boston, Mass.	2	2.16	1.66	2600(2)	<9.0(<7.9—<10)	<4.2	<5.4
Memphis, Tenn.	3	1.96	1.20	2340(3)	<8.9(<7.1—9.6)	<4.5	<7.4
Salt Lake City, Utah	2	2.12	0.76	2590(2)	10.2 (7.2—13.2)	4.8	13.4
Unweighted averages	—	1.96	1.08	2410	<7.8 (<1—29.7)	<4.0	<8.0

[a] Composite samples for 7 days each month taken at boarding schools for children under 18 years of age. Samples include all beverages and snacks, but not drinking water. The ranges shown are those for monthly composite samples, < values are considered at value in averages.

From U.S. Public Health Service, *Radiol. Health Data,* 3, 42, 1962 (and subsequent issues).

at about 1 m and above.[18] At a height of 0.32 cm the minimum was 0.22 pCi/ℓ and the maximum was 3.93 pCi/ℓ. At all levels minima occurred between 10:00 a.m. and 12:00 noon (CST). Maxima at about 1 m ranged from 0.445 to 0.960 pCi/ℓ. Another study[19] showed that radon in soil varied about 70-fold in different geological formations; variations of emanation rates into the atmosphere varied by 1000-fold among geographical regions, although they were quite uniform in Champaign County, Ill. at

Table 18
RADIUM-226, POTASSIUM-40, AND LEAD-210 CONTENT OF COMPOSITE DIET SAMPLES AT CITIES IN THE U.S.

Item analyzed	No. of cities	Average/day (range)	Average/kg (range)	Average/g Ca (range)
pCi ^{226}Ra	25	1.6 (nd—5.0)	0.44 (nd—1.4)	0.83 (nd—2.4)
pCi ^{226}Ra	5	3.02 (2.17—4.35)	0.76 (0.58—1.04)	1.85 (1.35-2.40)
pCi ^{40}K	9	3400 (2600—3800)	980 (800—1100)	—
pCi ^{210}Pb	9	2.4 (nd—5.3)	0.7 (nd—1.4)	—
gCa	25	1.87 (1.27—2.11)	0.52 (0.44—0.59)	—
gCa	5	1.64 (1.54—1.82)	0.42 (0.40—0.43)	—
kg diet	25	3.60 (2.89—4.10)	—	—

From Klement, A. W., Jr., in *Radioactive Fallout, Soils, Plants, Foods, Man,* Fowler, E. B., Ed., Elsevier, Amsterdam, 1965, 113. With permission.

$140 \pm 73 \times 10^{-18}$ Ci/cm^2-sec.* Some measurements of short-lived radon daughters have been reported from collections at some locations around the world.[20] These are shown in Table 20.

Natural Ecological Systems

Data are not available for natural radionuclide concentrations in natural ecological systems. A few data have been reported for some parts of some systems, mostly single species of plants and animals.[1,3,21] These are of little value in assessing radiation doses to wild organisms. Ecological factors are discussed in the chapter entitled "Ecological Factors in Dispersal of Radioactivity in the Biosphere."

* Note the confidence limits.

Table 19
COMPARISON OF DIETARY ^{226}Ra, ^{40}K, and ^{210}Pb BY INCOME AND AGE GROUPS

Sample groups	Sample weight			pCi ^{226}Ra/			pCi ^{40}K/		pCi ^{210}Pb/	
	Total kg	kg/day	g Ca/kg	kg	g Ca	day	kg	day	kg	day
Middle-income teenage diet										
San Francisco, Calif.	47.3	3.38	0.51	0.4	0.8	1.4	1100	3700	0.8	2.7
Chicago, Ill.	46.5	3.32	0.59	0.8	1.4	2.7	1000	3300	1.1	3.7
New York, N.Y.	41.0	2.93	0.48	0.4	0.8	1.2	900	2600	0.7	2.0
Low-income teenage diet										
San Francisco, Calif.	46.0	3.28	0.51	0.7	1.4	2.3	900	2900	1.2	3.9
Chicago, Ill.	46.4	3.31	0.50	0.7	1.4	2.3	900	3000	0.9	3.0
New York, N.Y.	44.6	3.19	0.52	0.4	0.8	1.3	1100	3500	nd	nd
Middle-income adult diet										
San Francisco, Calif.	39.2	2.80	0.26	0.4	1.6	1.1	—	—	—	—
Chicago, Ill.	42.2	3.01	0.28	nd	nd	nd	—	—	—	—
New York, N.Y.	42.6	3.04	0.28	0.1	0.4	0.3	—	—	—	—
Infant (1-year-old) diet										
San Francisco, Calif.	22.0	1.57	0.63	0.7	1.1	1.1	—	—	—	—
Chicago, Ill.	22.6	1.62	0.59	nd	nd	nd	—	—	—	—
New York, N.Y.	20.8	1.49	0.75	0.5	0.7	0.7	—	—	—	—

From Michelson, I., Thompson, J. C., Jr., Hess, B. W., and Comar, C. L., *J. Nutr.*, 78, 371, 1962. With permission.

Table 20
SUMMARY OF MEASUREMENTS OF NATURAL RADIOACTIVITY IN THE GROUND LEVEL AIR

Site	Period of observation	Radioactivity (pCi/m³) Lead-214	Radioactivity (pCi/m³) Lead-212	Activity ratio lead-214/lead-212
Wales, Alaska	1953—59	20	0.16	125
Kodiak, Alaska	1950—60	9.9	0.04	250
Washington, D.C.	1950—61	122	1.34	91
Yokosuka, Japan	1954—58	56	0.48	117
Lima, Peru	1959—62	42	1.33	28
Chacaltaya, Bolivia	1958—62	40	0.53	72
Rio de Janeiro, Brazil	1958—62	51	2.54	20
Little America V, Antarctica	1956—58	2.5	<0.01	(>250)
South Pole	1959—62	0.47	<0.01	(>50)

From Lockhart, L. B., Jr., in *The Natural Radiation Environment,* Adams, J. A. S. and Lowder, W. M., Eds., University of Chicago Press, Chicago, 1964, 331. With permission.

REFERENCES

1. **Klement, A. W., Jr.,** Natural radionuclides in foods and food source materials, in *Radioactive Fallout, Soils, Plants, Foods, Man,* Fowler, E. B., Ed., Elsevier, Amsterdam, 1965, 113.
2. **Klement, A. W., Jr., Miller, C. R., Minx, R. P., and Shleien, B.,** Estimates of Ionizing Radiation Doses in the United States 1960—2000. Report ORP/CSD 72-1, U.S. Environmental Protection Agency, Washington, D.C., 1972, 7.
3. **Klement, A. W., Jr.,** Natural Environmental Radioactivity — An Annotated Bibliography: Report WASH-1061, U.S. Atomic Energy Commission, Washington, D.C., 1965; Report WASH-1061 (Suppl.) U.S. Atomic Energy Commission, Washington, D.C., 1970.
4. **Kuroda, P. K.,** On the Stratospheric ^{90}Sr Fallout, Report ANL-5920, U.S. Atomic Energy Commission, Argonne National Laboratory, 1958.
5. **Klement, A. W., Jr.,** A Review of Potential Radionuclides Produced in Weapons Detonations, Report WASH-1024, U.S. Atomic Energy Commission, Washington, D.C., 1959.
6. **Begemann, F. and Libby, W. F.,** Continental water balance, ground water inventory and storage times, surface ocean mixing rates and world-wide water circulation patterns from cosmic-ray and bomb tritium, *Geochim. Cosmochim. Acta,* 12, 277, 1957
7. **Godlin, M. M. and Olinevich, V. A.,** Variations of available forms of nitrogen, phosphorus, and potassium in virgin and cultivated peat soils, *Agrokhimiya,* 2, 23, 1966.
8. **Reitemeier, R. F.,** Soil potassium and fertility, in *Soils,* Stefferud, A., Ed., U.S. Department of Agriculture, Washington, D.C., 1957, 101.
9. **Hallden, N. A. and Fisenne, I. M.,** Radium-226 in the diet in three U.S. cities, in Fallout Program Quarterly Summary Report, Hardy, E. P., Jr. et al., Eds., Report HASL-113, U.S. Atomic Energy Commission, New York, 1961, 90.
10. **Muth, H., Rajewsky, B., Hantke, H.-J., and Aurand, K.,** The normal radium content and the ^{226}Ra/Ca ratio of various foods, drinking water and different organs and tissues of the human body, Health Phys., 2, 239, 1960.
11. **Turner, R. C., Radley, J. M., and Mayneord, W. V.,** The naturally occurring α-ray activity of foods, *Health Phys.,* 1, 268, 1958.
12. **Engelmann, E.,** Estimate of the dietary intake of radium-226 for New York City infants, in Fallout Program Quarterly Summary Report, Hardy, E. P., Jr. et al., Report HASL-113, U.S. Atomic Energy Commission, New York, 1961, 95.
13. U.S. Public Health Service, Institutional diet sampling program, *Radiol. Health Data,* 3, 42, 1962 (and subsequent issues).

14. Michelson, I., Thompson, J. C., Jr., Hess, B. W., and Comar, C. L., Radioactivity in total diet, *J. Nutr.*, 78, 371, 1962.
15. Lockhart, L. B., Jr., Radioactivity of the radon-222 and radon-220 series in the air at ground level, in *The Natural Radiation Environment*, Adams, J. A. S. and Lowder, W. M., Eds., University of Chicago Press, Chicago, 1964, 331.
16. Gold, S., Barkau, H. W., Shleien, B., and Kahn, B., Measurement of naturally occurring radionuclides in air, in *The Natural Radiation Environment*, Adams, J. A. S. and Lowder, W. M., Eds., University of Chicago Press, Chicago, 1964, 369.
17. Struxness, E. D., personal communication, Oak Ridge National Laboratory, Oak Ridge, Tenn., 1971.
18. Moses, H., Stehney, A. F., and Lucas, H. F., Jr., The effects of meteorological variables upon the vertical and temporal distributions of atmospheric radon, *J. Geophys. Res.*, 65(4), 1223, 1960.
19. Pearson, J. E. and Jones, G. E., Soil concentrations of emanating ^{226}Ra and emanation from ^{222}Rn from soils and plants, *Tellus*, 18, 655, 1966.
20. Lockhart, L. B., Jr., Radioactivity of the radon-222 and radon-220 series in air at ground level, in *The Natural Radiation Environment*, Adams, J. A. S. and Lowder, W. M., Eds., University of Chicago Press, Chicago, 1964, 331.
21. Osborne, W. S., Primordial radionuclides: their distribution, movement, and possible effects within terrestrial ecosystems, *Health Phys.*, 11, 1275, 1965.

MAN-MADE SOURCES OF ENVIRONMENTAL RADIATION

Alfred W. Klement, Jr.

INTRODUCTION

The various sources of environmental radiation exposure caused by man's use of radiation and radioactive materials are discussed in this section. Among these sources are natural radioactivity manipulated by man for various purposes: nuclear explosives for various purposes; the electrical power production processes; and other governmental, industrial, medical, and research uses of radionuclides and radiation sources. Because of the nature of existing radiation protection procedures and practices, some sources are of minor or no importance with regard to general environmental radiation exposures,[1] although they are quite important with regard to occupational exposures discussed in other sections of this handbook. Emphasis here is given to those sources of most importance with regard to exposure to the general population.

The considerable differences in the amounts and types of radiation and radioactivity associated with the various man-made sources are discussed in connection with dose estimation in later chapters.

GLOBAL FALLOUT FROM NUCLEAR WEAPONS TESTS

Fallout from nuclear weapons tests is another source of environmental radioactive material. Large-scale, high-yield atmospheric test series in the past (e.g., U.S. and Soviet tests, 1961 to 1962) introduced radioactive material into the stratosphere; this was later deposited worldwide. The last such test series was conducted in 1962. A portion of the small amount of material remaining in the stratosphere continues to be deposited annually. During the last several years, a few atmospheric tests have been conducted by other nations; these have been sufficient to maintain a relatively constant annual fallout rate.[2] Past and current tests have also injected material into the troposphere; this is deposited relatively quickly within a few degrees of the latitude of the tests. Local fallout is discussed in other sections below. Also, long-lived radionuclides which were deposited as local, tropospheric, or stratospheric fallout from nuclear weapons tests still constitute sources of radiation exposure in the environment, even though they decrease in time because of decay, dilution, and other chemical and physical processes.

PEACEFUL APPLICATIONS OF NUCLEAR EXPLOSIVES

A number of possible uses of nuclear explosives have been suggested for industrial applications. These include excavation, gas stimulation, recovery of oil from oil shale, mineral recovery, underground storage, waste and waste management, use of geothermal energy, and others.[3-5] Experimental programs in these areas have progressed to some extent. This is especially true of excavation and gas stimulation: which lack relatively little additional experimentation for complete development of capabilities and proven economic advantage.

With regard to the amount of environmental radioactivity involved in peaceful uses of explosives, excavation projects are the most extensive. Also, such projects include examples of the types of situations that may be encountered in other applications. For this reason, separate discussions are given in a later section, based on the very extensive and complex studies made for a proposed sea level canal in Central America under

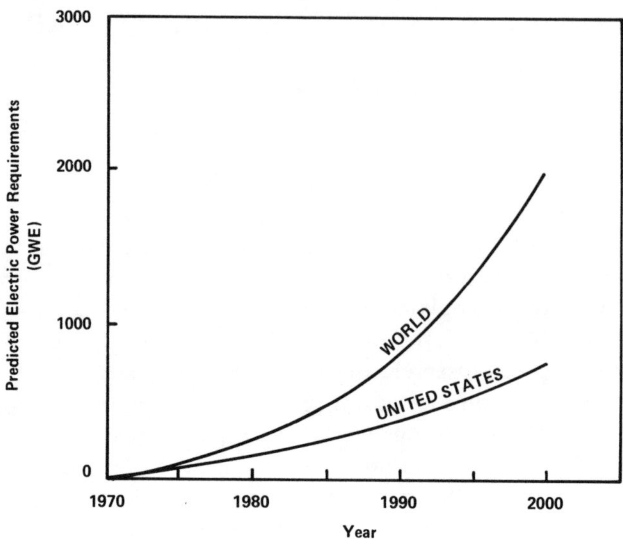

FIGURE 1. Predicted world and U.S. nuclear electric power requirements. (Adapted from References 6 and 7).

the auspices of the U.S. Atlantic-Pacific Interoceanic Canal Study Commission from 1966 to 1970.

NUCLEAR ELECTRIC POWER FACILITIES

The nuclear electric power industry has grown rapidly during the last decade and is expected to grow considerably more in the future. The various facilities involved in the production of nuclear power are potential sources of environmental radioactivity. These facilities are discussed below, as are projections for growth of the industry.

Estimates have been made of world-wide nuclear electric power requirements. A special study was conducted for the U.S. up to 1990.[2] The world nuclear generating capacity was predicted to increase from about 20 to 2000 billion watts electric[3] (GWE) between 1970 and 2000 (see Figure 1). The generation of this power will give rise to radioactive effluents that will be spread world-wide. These should be considered in addition to local radiation doses in the vicinity of nuclear power plants. The projections for the U.S. were made for each of the six National Power Survey Regions (see Figure 2); these provide a basis for projecting results on a realistic basis from past and current experience. These projections are shown in Table 1.

Estimates of requirements for uranium oxide indicate that uranium mining and milling will increase by about a factor of 25 between 1970 and 2000. While the number of uranium mines decreased after 1960, it increased later, although open-pit mines continued to decrease. Along with increased mining, the number of uranium mills has increased, and the production by mills is expected to increase by a factor of about 15 by the year 2000. One fuel reprocessing plant began operation in 1966, but was closed after several years of operation. A few other fuel reprocessing plants have applied for licenses. All of these plants are expected to be in operation within several years.

GOVERNMENT FACILITIES

Many types of government facilities are sources or potential sources of environmen-

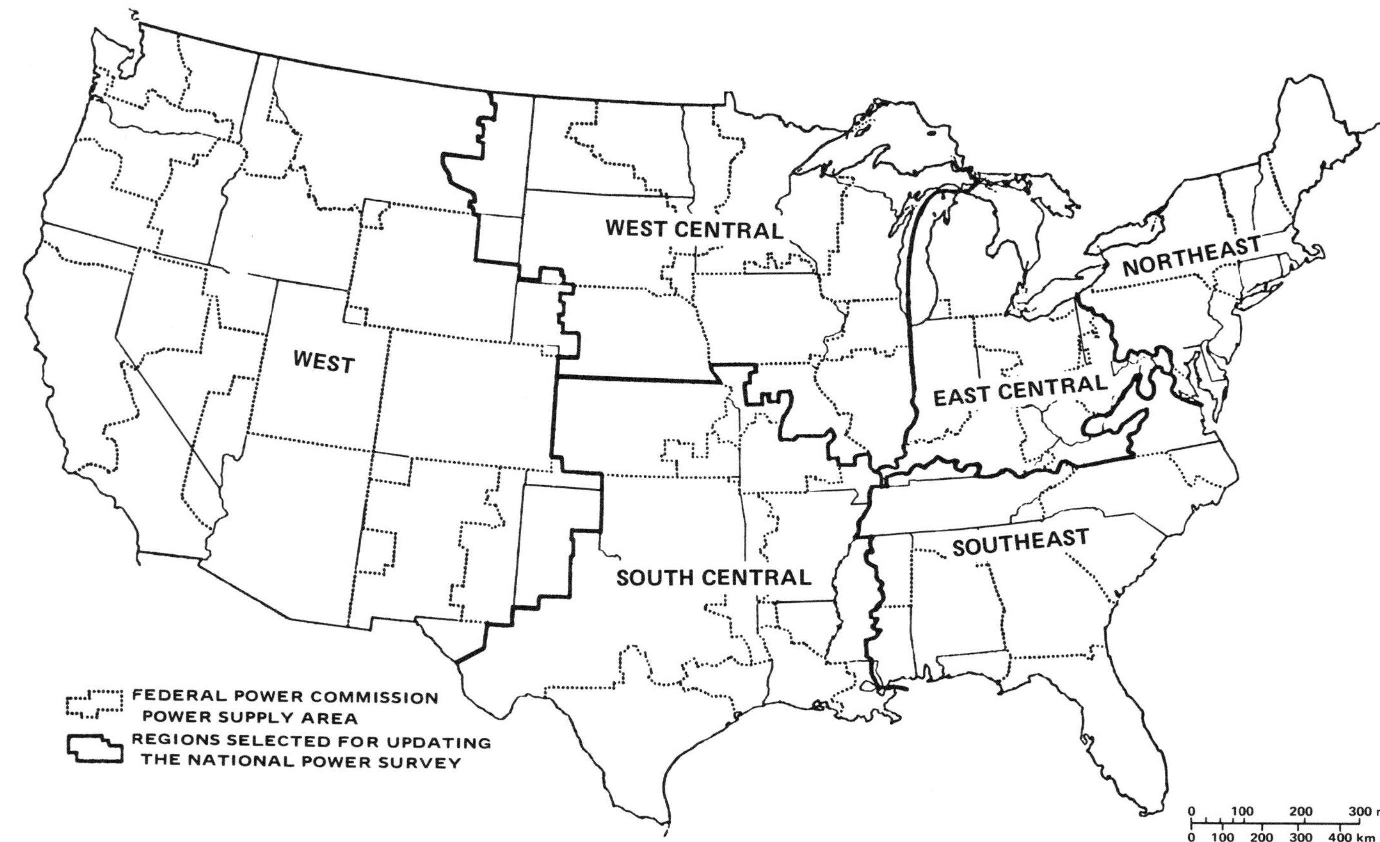

FIGURE 2. National electric power survey regions. (From Considerations Affecting Steam Power Plant Site Selection, Office of Science and Technology, Washington, D.C., 1968.)

Table 1
ESTIMATED NUCLEAR GENERATING PLANT SITES — 1990

Region[a]	Nuclear plants by capacity (MW electric) 500—1000	1000—2000	2000—4000	>4000	Total
Northeast	7	19	17	2	45
Southeast	10	22	21	7	60
East central	1	10	8	2	21
South central	3	9	9	1	22
West central	3	6	9	1	19
West	4	7	9	13	33
Total	28	73	73	26	200

[a] See Figure 2.

From *Considerations Affecting Steam Power Plant Site Selection,* Office of Science and Technology, Washington, D.C., 1968.

tal radioactivity. Some are operated on a somewhat intermittent basis. These include nuclear explosives testing for military and civilian purposes which give rise to environmental radioactivity, most of which is confined to the test site; however, some tests have caused off-site radiation exposure. In recent years all tests have been conducted at the Nevada Test Site northwest of Las Vegas. Some specific tests conducted elsewhere in the past are discussed in the following sections. This is true also for the Nuclear Rocket Development Station, which is currently inactive, adjacent to the Nevada Test Site.

Other Energy Research and Development Administration facilities involve a wide variety of activities in the Atomic Energy Program and a large number of contractor activities. Most of these facilities involve multiple-purpose activities, although a few are concerned with only certain phases of nuclear materials production or manufacturing. Most are concerned with research in one or more areas. The majority of the facilities are of research contractors at universities and private, commercial, and governmental installations. Most of these facilities involve the use of radioactivity and constitute a source of environmental radioactivity through airborne or liquid release of wastes. A few emit radiation inside the facility that is measurable outside the facility (see Reference 1).

PRIVATE FACILITIES

Many of the major private facilities utilizing radioactivity or radiation sources are involved in the nuclear power industry mentioned above. Others are operated under contract with government agencies, also mentioned above. The remainder of private facilities include research and medical organizations and those concerned with commercial applications similar to those of government agencies. These and others are concerned with use of radiation sources or radionuclide preparation as radiation sources, tracers, pharmaceuticals. Important sources of exposure to radiation to the general public are medical and dental radiology, diagnostic use of pharmaceuticals, and radiation therapy. These medical aspects of radiation exposure will be discussed in another volume in this series.

Television receivers emit ionizing radiation. In recent years improved design and development of television sets have reduced radiation emmission rates. Other consumer products are sources of radiation exposure, often unknown to the consumer.

These include fire detection devices, static eliminators, gauges, electronic tubes, and laboratory balances. In recent years tritium and ^{147}Pm have been used as radiation sources in self-luminous devices; radium compounds have long been used for such purposes. Further discussion of these sources is included in the chapter entitled "Estimation of Dose from External Radiation."

The use of radionuclides in other consumer products has been proposed. This includes the use of ^{60}Co in spark-gap igniters in fuel oil burners,[9] the use of thorium in personnel neutron dosimeters,[10] and the use of ^{237}Np as a power source in timepieces.[11]

Another incidental source of radiation exposure is related to air transport. Passengers and crew of aircraft are subjected to increased rates of exposure during high-altitude flight from galactic cosmic radiation, as well as fallout material (which is relatively minor compared to cosmic radiation) from nuclear explosive tests. Obviously, flight crews are subjected to this source of exposure to a greater extent than passengers in general. For further discussion of this source, see the chapter mentioned above.

REFERENCES

1. **Klement A. W., Jr., Miller, C. R., Minx, R. P., and Shleien, B.,** Estimates of Ionizing Radiation Doses in the United States 1960—2000, Rep. ORP/CSD 72-1, U.S. Environmental Protection Agency, Washington, D.C., 1972.
2. **Hardy, E. P., Jr.,** Sr^{90} and Sr^{89} in monthly deposition at world land sites, in Fallout Program Quarterly Summary Report, Rep. HASL-242, U.S. Atomic Energy Commission, New York, 1971.
3. Annual Report to the Congress for 1970, U.S. Atomic Energy Commission, Washington, D.C., 1971.
4. Interoceanic Canal Studies 1970, U.S. Atlantic-Pacific Interoceanic Canal Study Commission, Washington, D.C., 1970.
5. Engineering with Nuclear Explosives, Symp., January 14—16, 1970, Las Vegas, U.S. Atomic Energy Commission, 1970.
6. Siting of Fuel Fabrication Plants and Waste Management Facilities, Report ORNL-4451, U.S. Atomic Energy Commission, Oak Ridge National Laboratory, 1970.
7. **Pannetier, R.,** Distribution, Transport Atmospherique et Bilam du Krypton-85, Commissariat à l'Énergie Atomique, Report CEA-R-3591, Paris, 1968.
8. Considerations Affecting Steam Power Plant Site Selection, Office of Science and Technology, Washington, D.C., 1968.
9. Draft Environmental Statement, Exemption from Licensing Requirements for Spark-Gap Irradiators that Contain Cobalt-60, Report NUREG-75/086, Docket No. PRM 30-54, U.S. Nuclear Regulatory Commission, Washington, D.C., 1975.
10. **Wheeler, R. V., Landauer, R. S., Jr. and Company,** letter to R. F. Barker, October 22, 1973, (petition for rule making, to exempt from licensing personnel dosimeters containing thorium), U.S. AEC Docket No. 40-19, Washington, D.C., 1973.
11. **Neiman, L. M.,** Petition for change of Parts 30 and 32 of the Atomic Energy Commission Rules and Regulations, Bulova Watch Co., April 2, 1971 (to exempt from licensing timepieces containing neptunium-237), U.S. AEC Docket No. 30-50, Washington, D.C., 1971.

METEOROLOGICAL DISPERSION OF RELEASED RADIOACTIVITY*

Gilbert J. Ferber, Jerome L. Heffter, and Alfred W. Klement, Jr.

INTRODUCTION

Reference 1 serves as an extensive handbook and discussion of meteorological dispersion of radioactivity with regard to very local releases of radioactivity, which is too detailed for repeating here. It describes the wind-rose techniques commonly used in point-source releases of radioactivity for estimation or prediction of radionuclide concentrations and close-in radiation exposures. In many such releases of radioactivity into the atmosphere, longer range estimates or predictions of exposures are desirable or necessary for an adequate radiological protection analysis. In this section, the evaluation of atmospheric dispersion of radioactivity in the environment is discussed within the framework of a specific model, currently in use for such evaluations, to illustrate the methodology.

A REGIONAL-CONTINENTAL SCALE TRAJECTORY MODEL

A computerized post-facto trajectory model intended primarily for use in calculating the transport, diffusion, and deposition of effluents on regional and continental scales has been developed.[2-4] The trajectory model is described here. The diffusion and deposition model is described further in this chapter.

The computer model was designed to efficiently calculate the large number of trajectories needed to evaluate specific problems and to be used as a research tool to investigate long-range transport and diffusion mechanisms. A continuing program of research and field experiments is in progress to verify and improve the model.

In its present form, a month, season, or year of trajectories may be calculated: (1) from any origin in the Northern Hemisphere, (2) at 6-hr time intervals, (3) from 1 to 10 days in duration, and (4) forward or backward in time.

Trajectory computations use winds at any desired altitude above sea level or winds averaged through any desired layer above average terrain, up to about 5 km. The wind input is obtained from observed winds at reporting pibal or rawinsonde stations or analyzed wind fields at grid points. The types of output now available are

1. Tables giving details of trajectory computations
2. A listing or punched data cards giving trajectory end points at selected durations
3. Trajectories plotted on any desired map scale for either mercator or polar stereographic projections
4. Maps showing percent fequency of trajectory traverses over grid squares during a month, season, or year
5. Maps showing long-term average surface air concentrations
6. Maps showing long-term average surface air concentrations depleted by dry and wet deposition and maps of surface deposition amounts
7. Short-term average surface air concentrations at a point (or several points) including a tabulation of the plumes that contributed to each concentration and the amount contributed

* This section was adapted from several publications by the Environmental Research Laboratories, Air Resource Laboratories, National Oceanic and Atmospheric Administration, particularly from References 2 to 4.

Items 1 through 4 are described in this section and Items 5 through 7 are described later.

Input Data

The user has the option to select as input either observed winds, analyzed winds, or both. Observed winds are recommended as the basic input. However, in areas of sparse wind observations, such as over the oceans, analyzed winds should be used. The use of both types of wind input is often desirable where trajectories are expected to traverse land and ocean areas.

The observed winds used in the model are obtained from magnetic tapes. These tapes constitute a unique set of meteorological data organized by time sequence; worldwide and upper air reports for all reporting stations are grouped together for each observation time. For use in the model, data are extracted for a particular area of interest (e.g., 48 states and southern Canada) for all heights up to about 5 km.

Analyzed meteorological information, also available on magnetic tapes,[5] is in the form of two data analyses per day at each grid point of the Northern Hemisphere grid (4225 points) for standard pressure levels. The terrain heights used in the model are obtained from data tapes giving terrain height averages in 1° squares over the world.[6]

Transport Model

A trajectory is composed of a series of 3-hr segments. Each segment is computed assuming persistence of the winds reported closest to the segment time. The observed winds used in the computations are either those at a desired trajectory level or those averaged throughout a desired layer above the average terrain height. In practice, it is assumed that over regional-continental distances, an effluent released in the boundary layer (surface to about 2000 m) is transported by the average wind in the afternoon mixing layer. Seasonal values for the top of the afternoon mixing layer have been determined for the contiguous U.S. The base of the transport layer is usually assumed to be 300 m above average terrain to eliminate surface frictional effects that tend to slow down average transport speeds.

The average wind in a layer is computed from the reported winds linearly weighted with respect to the thickness between mid-levels. Each trajectory segment computed from observed winds is given by (see Figure 1)

$$TS_o = \frac{\sum^{R} DW_i AW_i TS_i}{\sum^{R} DW_i AW_i} \tag{1}$$

where TS_o is the trajectory segment computed from observed winds; $\sum^{R}$ indicates the summation over all observed winds within a radius R of the segment origin; $TS_i = (V_i)(\Delta t)$, the contribution to the trajectory segment from an observed wind V_i, and Δt is the segment time interval; $DW_i = f(dw_i)$, the distance weighting factor, a function of dw_i, the distance from an observed wind to the midpoint of TS_i; and $AW_i = f(\theta_i)$, the alignment weighting factor, a function of θ_i, the angle formed between TS_i and a line drawn from the segment origin to a wind observation point.

The user may select various parameter values to be used in the model. The following are parameter values currently used in the model:[2]

1. Time interval $\Delta t = 3$ hr.
2. Radius R = 300 nmi.
3. Distance weighting factor $DW_i = 1/dw_i^2$ (the closest observations receive the greatest weight)
4. Alignment weighting factor $AW_i = 1 - 0.5|\sin\theta_i|$.

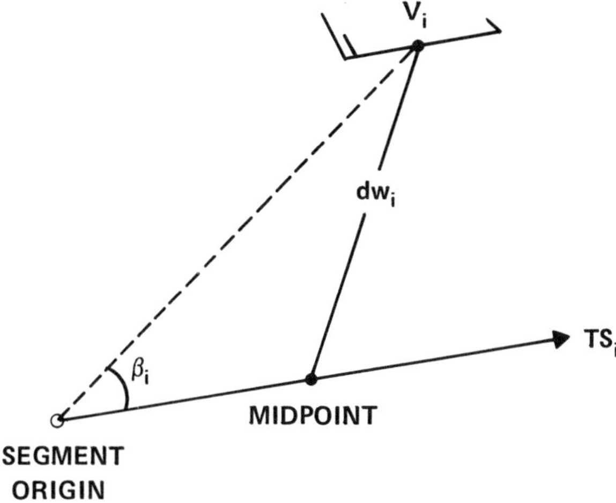

FIGURE 1. Configuration for determining a trajectory segment from observed winds.

For analyzed wind input the grid winds used in the computations are taken at the desired level or are averaged throughout any desired layer above the average terrain height. The average wind (V_i) in a layer at a grid point is determined the same way as an average observed wind in a layer. Each trajectory segment is computed using a wind at the segment origin as determined from bilinear interpolation between analyzed winds at the four corners of the grid square containing the segment origin.

Trajectory segments are linked together to produce a complete trajectory. Specifically, the first segment starts from the source and each following segment starts from the end point of the segment before it. Trajectories terminate after the desired duration or for lack of adequate input wind observations.

Further details and examples of the trajectory model are given in Reference 2. This trajectory model is primarily the basis for the remainder of this section.

DIFFUSION-DEPOSITION MODEL

The trajectory model discussed above combined with a plume model is the basis for calculations out to several thousand kilometers from the source. The model considers the fate of gaseous or particulate emissions from a uniform, continuous point source, treating local, regional, continental, and global scale dispersion in successive phases.[3] The model produces maps of mean monthly, seasonal, or annual air concentrations, deposition amounts, and population exposures. The current version does not provide detailed calculations in the immediate vicinity of the pollutant source. The model does include deposition by wet and dry removal processes. Resuspension of deposited material is not considered, but this feature could readily be incorporated.

The model can also be used to calculate short-term average air concentrations at specified locations, which is particularly useful for model verification where calculated concentrations from a known source, for specified sampling periods, can be tested against observed sample concentrations.

Trajectories are started from a source point four times per day, and diffusion-deposition calculations are made along each trajectory. Mean surface air concentrations and deposition amounts are accumulated at grid points covering a selected area for any desired time interval (e.g., a month, season, or year).

A plume is represented by a series of puffs (instantaneous point sources) traveling along the computed trajectories. Each puff undergoes diffusion according to

$$C = \frac{2\,Q}{(2\pi)^{3/2}\,\sigma_H^2\,(2K_z t)^{1/2}} \exp(-R^2/2\sigma_H^2) \qquad (2)$$

where C = surface air concentration (e.g., Ci/m^3); Q = emission rate (Ci/puff); σ_H = horizontal standard deviation (m); K_2 = vertical diffusion coefficient (m^2/sec); t = puff travel time (sec); and R = distance from puff center (m). The value of K_z may be specified by the user; at present K_z = $5m^2/sec$ is used as an average value for the lower troposphere. The model also uses the approximation that °H(m) = 0.5t, where t is travel time (sec). This appears to be a reasonable approximation for several days travel time based on a variety of diffusion data summarized by Heffter.[8]

In some applications, it may be preferable to assume that the effluent is uniformly dispersed through some specified mixing layer rather than assuming a Gaussian distribution in the vertical. If this option is chosen, surface air concentrations are calculated by

$$C = \frac{Q}{2\pi\sigma_H^2\,Z_m} \exp(-R^2/2\sigma_H^2) \qquad (3)$$

where Z_m, the thickness of the mixing layer (m), is an input parameter to be specified by the user.

This model is designed primarily for calculations from about 100 km to a few thousand kilometers from a source. The user is cautioned that several simplifications, incorporated to reduce computing time, might be undesirable for calculations in the immediate vicinity of a source. For example, stack height can be an important factor in determining air concentrations near a source, but it is not incorporated in Equations 3 and 4. A more detailed treatment of both horizontal and vertical diffusion as a function of atmospheric stability also would be desirable in this region. Development of a more sophisticated model for the region within 100 km of a source is in progress. It is expected that a trajectory model will prove superior to present techniques using stability-wind-rose data.

The concept of deposition velocity is used to calculate dry deposition amounts along a trajectory assuming

$$D_d = CV_d\,(\Delta t) \qquad (4)$$

where D_d is the amount deposited per unit area during the interval Δt; is the ground-level air concentration; V_d is the deposition velocity; and Δt is the time interval represented by each trajectory (e.g., 6 hr if trajectories are started four times per day).

Deposition velocity is dependent on particle size, wind speed, surface roughness, and other parameters. Most experimentally determined values are in the range of about 0.1 to a few centimeters per second. The user must specify an appropriate value for a particular situation.

Precipitation scavenging is a second mechanism for plume depletion and ground deposition. Wet deposition along a trajectory is assumed to be

$$D_w = C_w\,P\,(\Delta t) \qquad (5)$$

where D_w is wet deposition per unit area during the time interval. Δt; C_w is the concentration in rainwater at the ground, and P is the precipitation rate.

Model calculation of wet deposition is based on an empirically derived average scavenging ratio.[9]

$$E = C_w/\bar{C} \quad (6)$$

where $\bar{C}$ is the mean concentration in the column of air from the ground to the top of the rain-bearing layer.

With a Gaussian distribution in the vertical, it can be shown that

$$\bar{C} = C(\pi K_z t)^{1/2} (\Delta z_p)^{-1} \quad (7)$$

where Δz_p is the thickness of the precipitation layer. Substituting Equations 6 and 7 in Equation 5, we obtain

$$D_W = E\,P\,C(\pi K_z t)^{1/2} (\Delta z_p)^{-1} (\Delta t) \quad (8)$$

for deposition by precipitation scavenging.

The choice of an appropriate value for E is difficult since the scavenging ratio varies by more than a factor of ten, depending on rainfall rate, atmospheric stability, particle characteristics, and other variables, some of which have not yet been thoroughly explored. A value of 500 (mass ratio) was chosen as a reasonable average since it is approximately in the middle of the range of measured values. This is equivalent to a ratio of 4.2×10^5 by volume, which is currently used in the model. The user may substitute any other value thought appropriate.

The effects of wet and dry deposition are incorporated in the diffusion model as source depletion terms. The complete expression used to calculate surface air concentration depleted by deposition is

$$C_D = C \exp\left(-2V_d t^{1/2} (\pi K_z)^{-1/2}\right) \exp\left(-EPt\,(\Delta z)^{-1}\right) \quad (9)$$

where C is calculated from Equation 2. Typical deposition parameter values now being used in the model are $V_d = 3 \times 10^{-3}$ m/sec; $E = 4.2 \times 10^5$ (by volume); $P = 3.2 \times 10^{-8}$ m/sec; and $\Delta z = 400$ m.

Trajectories starting at a specified source point are printed on a gridded map, with grid spacing and area coverage selected by the user. Surface air concentration and deposition amounts are calculated for each grid box. Trajectories of duration up to 10 days may be started four times per day for a month, season, or year. Calculated concentrations from all trajectories are accumulated in each grid box and averaged over the chosen time period. A map is printed with coded mean air concentration values in each grid box, as illustrated in Figure 2 for an assumed source in South Carolina. The pattern of mean air concentrations is shown for December 1975 assuming the uniform emission rate of 800 Ci/day and no deposition. When deposition parameter values are supplied as input, a second air concentration map is plotted which takes depletion by wet and dry deposition into account. A third map provides the calculated surface deposition pattern (wet and dry deposition combined).

AN EXAMPLE — MEAN ANNUAL ^{85}Kr CONCENTRATIONS

As an example of the use of the models discussed above, a hypothetical nuclear fuel reprocessing plant in Illinois with a uniform emission rate of 1 Ci/year of ^{85}Kr is considered.[3,10] Krypton-85 disperses over the entire globe because of its long half-life and lack of significant sinks. In this example, air concentrations and population exposures resulting from 1 year of plant operation are calculated. Realistic estimates for an actual plant can be obtained by multiplying by the actual emission rate (Ci/year).

Phase I

The first phase of the model calculations deals with the first few hours of plume

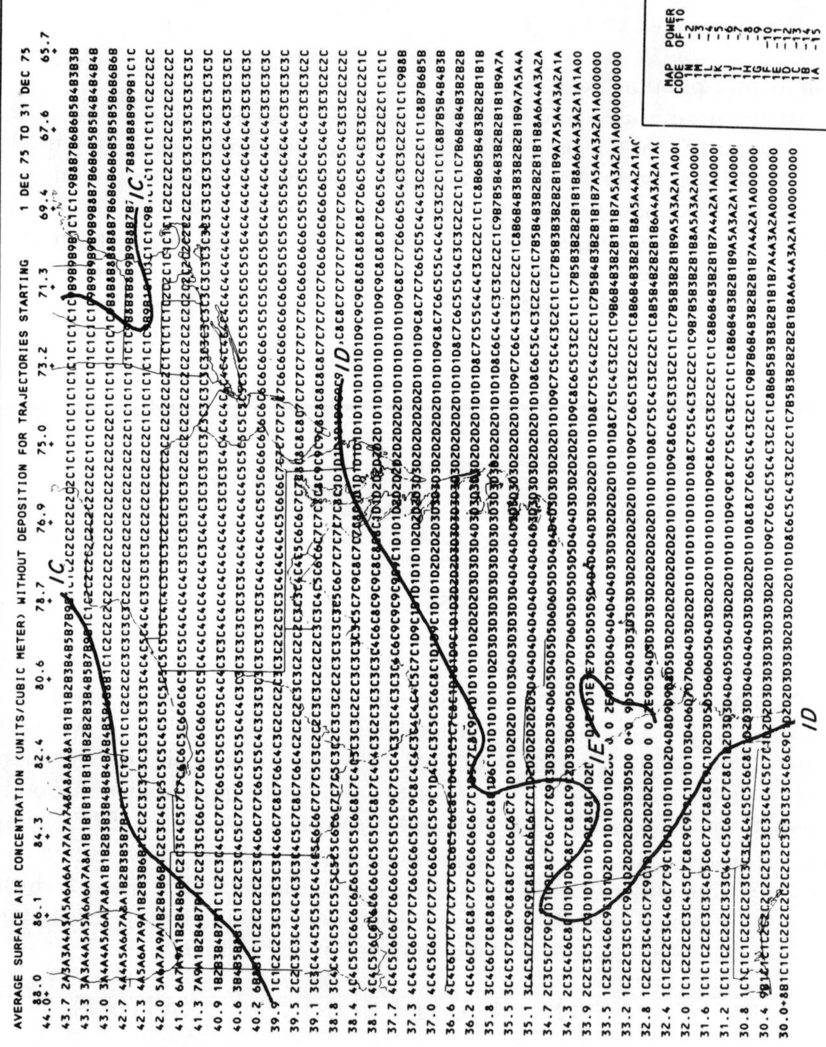

FIGURE 2. Map of coded mean surface air concentrations (pCi/m³) for December 1975 assuming an emission rate of 800 Ci/day at a site in South Carolina. (Zero values near the source indicate the area where calculations must be done on an expanded scale.)

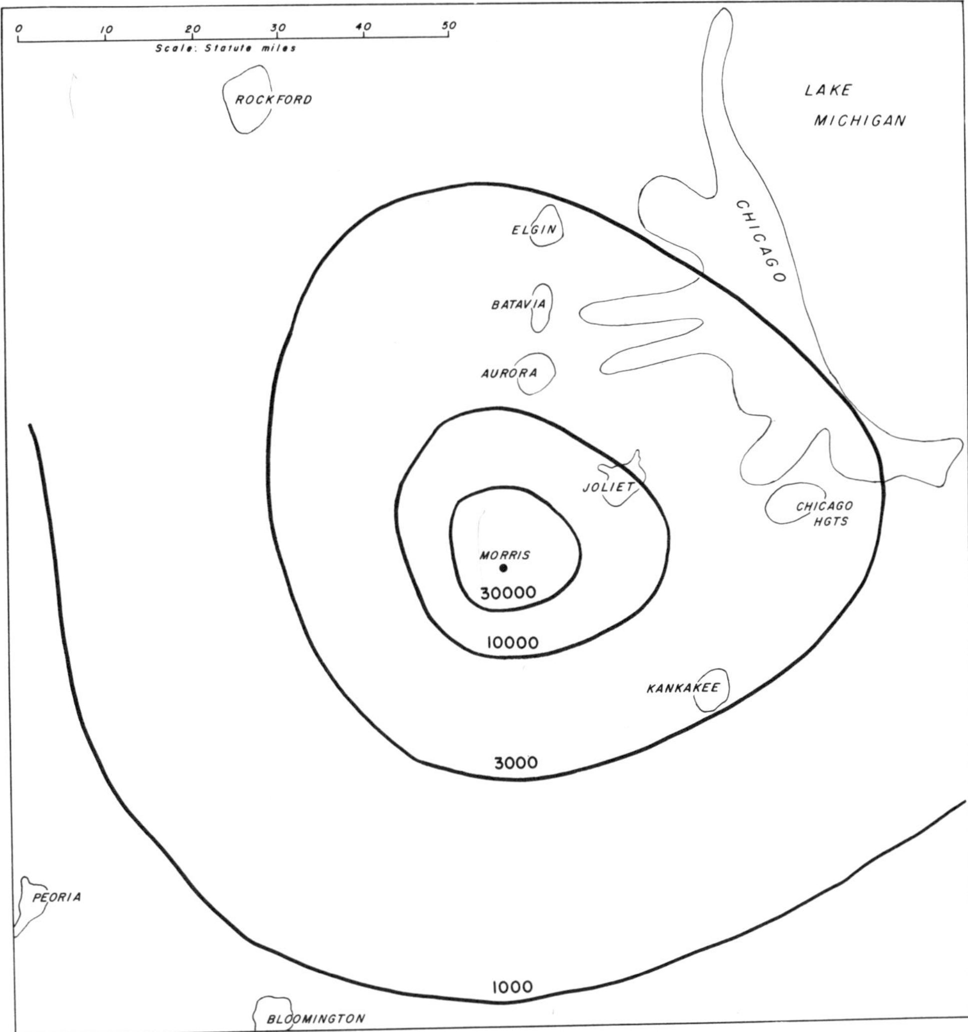

FIGURE 3. Mean annual surface air concentrations (10^{-20} Ci/m^3) for release of 1 Ci/year of ^{85}Kr at Morris, Illinois.

travel. A local wind-rose is used to assign material emitted during the year to directional sectors in proportion to the frequency with which the wind blows into each sector. The formula used for the mean air concentration, $\overline{C}$, at ground level from a continuous point source is

$$\overline{C} = \left(\frac{2}{\pi}\right)^{1/2} \frac{Q\,f}{\overline{u}\,\theta\,x\,\sigma_z} \tag{10}$$

where $\sigma_z = (2K_zt)^{1/2}$, K_z = vertical diffusion coefficient (5 m^2/sec); Q = emission rate (1 Ci/year = ½ × 10^{-8} Ci/sec); f = frequency of wind in sector; $\overline{u}$ = mean wind speed in sector (m/sec); θ = sector width (22½°); x = distance from source (m); and t = plume travel time (sec). The calculated air concentration pattern at Morris, Ill., located about 60 km southwest of Chicago, is shown in Figure 3. A more detailed stability-wind-rose model[11] may be used when local concentrations are of primary concern.

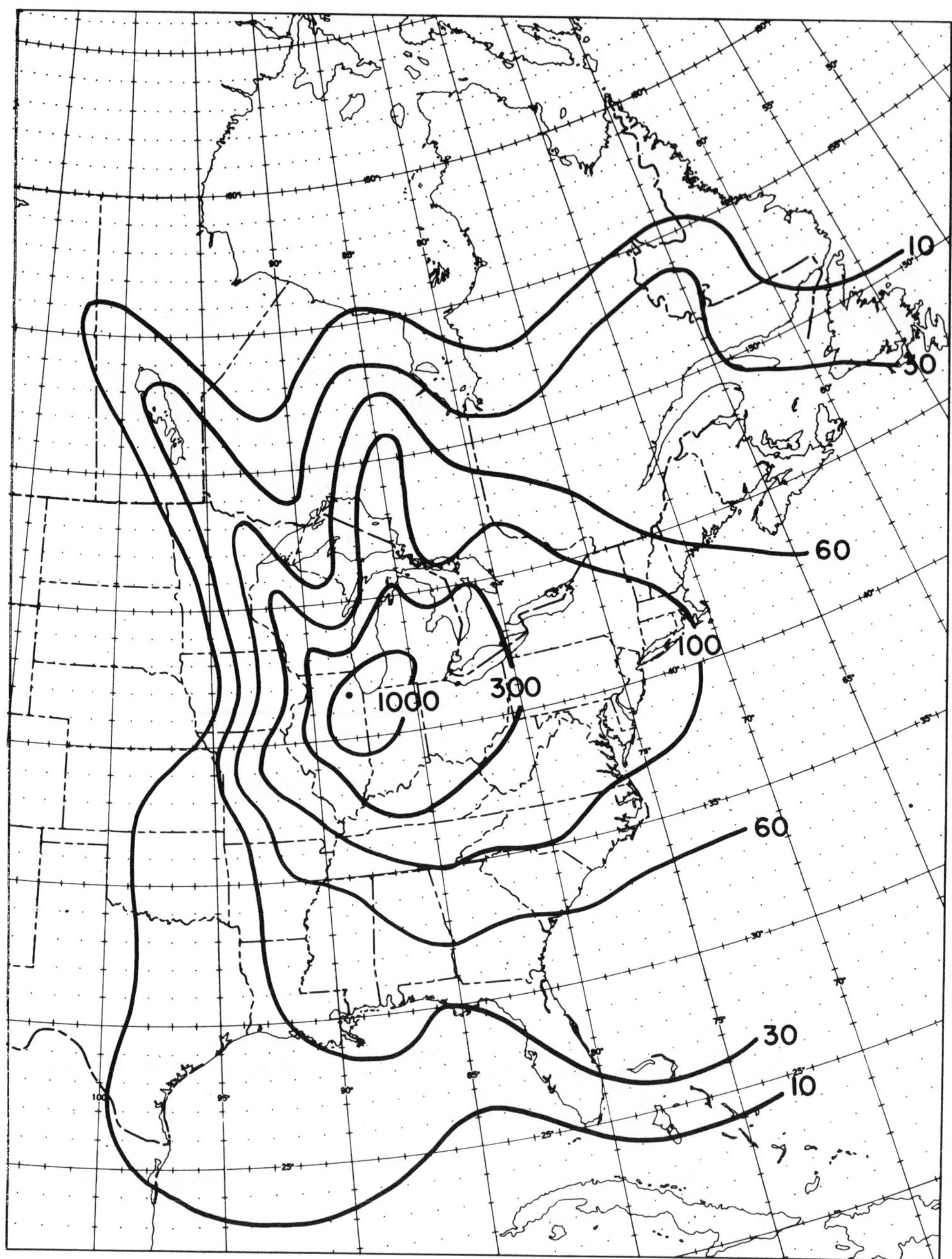

FIGURE 4. Mean annual surface air concentrations (10^{-20} Ci/m³) for Phase II.

Phase II

The second phase deals with plume dispersion at distances to a few thousand kilometers or several days travel time. At this range, single-station wind data are no longer applicable, and the trajectory model described earlier is used to estimate lateral dispersion and long-term concentrations.

For the illustration provided here, trajectories were calculated four times per day for 1 month out of each season to obtain an approximation of the average annual air concentration. Plume concentrations (Ci/m³) were calculated from Equation 2. The

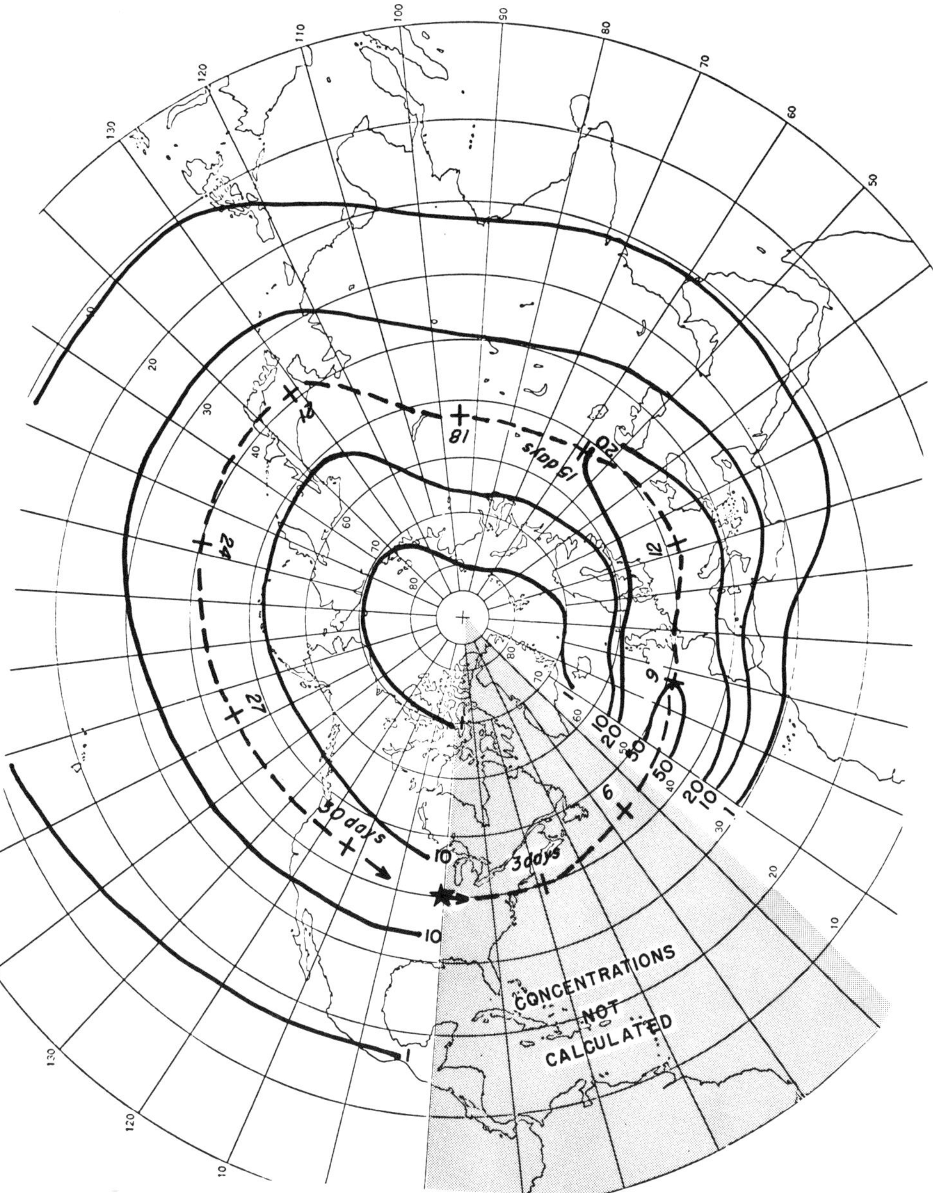

FIGURE 5. Mean annual surface air concentrations (10^{-20} Ci/m^3) from Phase III.

resulting mean annual concentration pattern over the eastern U.S. and Canada is shown in Figure 4. Concentrations within the contour of 1000 × 10^{-20} Ci/m^3 should be obtained from Figure 3, which provides more detail in that region.

Phase III

The third phase deals with the remainder of the first plume passage around the earth (about 30 days). In this phase, an effective diffusion coefficient (time dependent) is used to estimate the lateral spread of the plume about an average trajectory derived from climatological flow patterns in the lower atmosphere. The average trajectory carries the plume from the east coast of the U.S. across the Atlantic Ocean to Europe: Asia, the Pacific Ocean, and then back over North America, as shown by the dashed

Table 1
AVERAGE SURFACE AIR CONCENTRATIONS OF ^{85}K (1 Ci EMITTED UNIFORMLY OVER 1 YEAR IN 30° TO 50° LATITUDE BAND)

(10^{-20}Ci/m^{3}of aim)

Year	90—70° N	70—50° N	50—30° N	30—10° N	10° N—10° S	10—30° S	30—50° S	50—70° S	70—90° S
1[a]	23	25	23	19	11	6.3	5.1	4.3	3.8
2	32	31	30	27	22	22	20	19	19

All Latitudes

Year	10^{-20}Ci/m^3	Year	10^{-20}Ci/m^3	Year	10^{-20}Ci/m^3
3	22	12	12	25	5.0
4	20	13	11	30	3.7
5	19	14	10	35	2.6
6	18	15	9.6	40	1.9
7	17	16	9.0	45	1.4
8	15	17	8.5	50	1.0
9	14	18	7.9	55	0.73
10	13	19	7.4	60	0.53
11	13	20	7.0	65	0.38
—	—	—	—	70	0.28

[a] First-year values are actually the contributions to the mean annual concentrations from the end of the first month to the end of 1 year of plume dispersion. To obtain total mean annual concentrations for the first year, add the value from Figures 8, or 10.

From Machta, L., Ferber, G. J., and Heffter, J. L., *Proc. Symp. Physical Behavior of Radiactive Contaminants in the Atmosphere,* International Atomic Energy Agency, Vienna, 1974, 411.

Table 2
POPULATION-WEIGHTED CONCENTRATION AND TOTAL EXPOSURE (WORLD)

Phase	Plume travel period	Area affected	Annual concentration × population (10^{-10} man·Ci/m³)	Total exposure (10^{-10} man·Ci/m³)
1	0—6 hr	Illinois	2.7	—
2	6 hr to 3 days	U.S. and Canada (excluding Ill.)	2.5	—
3	30 to 30 days	Northern hemisphere	2.6	—
4	30 days to 1 year	World	7.5	—
1—4	1st year	World	15 (total)	15
4	2nd year	World	10	10
4	3rd—68th year	World	1.9 (average)	127
1—4	0—68th year	World	2.2 (average)	152

From Machta, L., Ferber, A. J., and Heffter, J. L., *Proc. Symp. Physical Behavior of Radioactive Contaminants in the Atmosphere,* International Atomic Energy Agency, Vienna, 1974, 411.

Table 3
WORLD POPULATION DISTRIBUTION[a]

Latitude band	Population (× 10⁶)
90—70°N	—
70—50°N	475
50—30°N	1210
30—10°N	1474
10°N—10°S	433
10—30°S	130
30—50°S	58
50—70°S	2
70—90°S	—
Total	3782

[a] Estimated 1972 population from Reference 13.

centerline in Figure 5. Concentrations in the shaded area of Figure 5 were calculated and shown in earlier phases.

Phase IV

In the fourth phase (beyond 30 days), concentrations are calculated using a global diffusion model.[12] During this period, concentrations are assumed to be uniform around the latitude circles and diffusion takes place only in the north-south and vertical directions. Resultant mean annual surface air concentrations for the source assumed in this example are shown in Table 1 for 20° latitude bands. As early as the second year, the north-south gradient is very small and, after that, latitudinal differences are too small to record. Virtually all of the decrease in concentration after 2 years is due to radioactive decay rather than dilution from vertical mixing through the model which extends to 40 km.

The mean annual concentration during the first year at a specific location is obtained by adding the value from Figures 3 through 5 to the appropriate first year value from Table 1. For succeeding years, only Table 1 is used.

Table 4
WORLD POPULATION-WEIGHTED CONCENTRATIONS FROM RELEASE OF 1 Ci OF ^{85}Kr

			Annual population × concentration (10^{-10} man·Ci/m³)				Cumulative exposure population × concentration × years (10^{-10} man·years·Ci/m³)		
Phase	Plume travel period	Region affected	Illinois site	South Carolina site	Simple model	Exposure period (years)	Illinois site	South Carolina site	Simple model
1, 2	0—3 days	U.S. and Canada	5.2	1.4	0.07 (world)	—	—	—	—
3	3—30 days	Northern hemisphere	2.6	2.6	0.66 (world)	—	—	—	—
4	30 days to 1 year	World	7.5	7.5	3.7	1	15.3	11.5	4.4
4	2nd year	World	10	10	8.4	2	25.3	21.5	12.8
4	3rd to 68th year (average)	World	1.9	1.9	1.9	68	152	148	137

From Macha, L., Ferber, C. J., and Heffter, J. L., *Proc. Symp. Physical Behavior of Radioactive Contaminants in the Atmosphere,* International Atomic Energy Agency, Vienna, 1974, 411.

Population Exposures

Population exposure estimates are obtained by multiplying the mean annual concentrations by the population affected. For simplicity, all calculations in this example assume that populations remain constant at the 1972 level. Table 2 provides the population multiplied by the average concentration (man-Ci/m^3) for the areas affected by each phase of plume travel. Annual values are also summed to provide the world-wide total exposure for periods up to 68 years (lifetime). The population distribution[13] is shown in Table 3.

The sensitivity of population exposures to plant location is illustrated by comparing results for a plant in South Carolina to those obtained for the Morris, Ill. site. In both cases, a total of 1 Ci of ^{85}Kr emitted uniformly over 1 year is assumed. The Illinois site is about 60 km upwind of a densely populated Chicago area, while the South Carolina site is remote from any large population center. Both sites affect the populous northeast coast of the U.S. during the second phase of plume dispersion. Table 4 summarizes calculations of population exposure for the two sites and also compares results with those obtained from a simple global dilution model (instantaneous dispersion and uniform concentration throughout the atmosphere).

The first 3 days of plume travel (Phases I and II) affect only the eastern U.S. and Canada with nearly a fourfold (5.2 to 1.4) difference in population exposure for the two sites. This is caused in part by differences in meteorology between the two sites producing different concentration patterns but the difference in population distribution is a much more significant factor. Population exposures during the later stages of plume dispersion are the same for both sites. Contributions from Phases I to IV are added to obtain the cumulative exposure for the first year. Cumulative world-wide population exposures are shown for periods of 1, 2, and 68 years (lifetime) on the right-hand side of Table 4. The cumulative world population exposures after 68 years differ by less than 3% (152 to 148) for the two sites.

The simple (uniform concentration) diffusion model greatly underestimates the population exposure from the early stages of plume travel. However, since most of the world population's lifetime exposure occurs after the second year when the ^{85}Kr surface air concentration is uniform over the globe, the difference in world-wide cumulative exposure estimates is only about 9% after 68 years. It is apparent that plant location and the early stages of plume dispersion can significantly affect population exposures on the local and regional scales, but world-wide population exposure is less sensitive to these factors for a long-lived nondepositing pollutant.

REFERENCES

1. Slade, D. H., Ed., *Meteorology and Atomic Energy 1968,* Report TID-24190, U.S. Atomic Energy Commission, Washington, D.C., 1968.
2. Heffter, J. L., Taylor, A. D., and Ferber, G. J., A Regional-Continental Scale Transport, Diffusion, and Deposition Model, Environmental Research Laboratories, NOAA Tech. Memo ERL-ARL-50, Air Research Laboratories, National Oceanic and Atmospheric Administration, Silver Spring, Md., 1975.
3. Machta, L., Ferber, G. J., and Heffter, J. L., Regional and global scale dispersion of ^{85}Kr for population-dose calculations, in *Proc. Symp. Physical Behavior of Radioactive Contaminants in the Atmosphere,* International Atomic Energy Agency, Vienna, 1974, 411.
4. Ferber, G. J., Elliott, W. P., Machta, L., and Heffter, J. L., Deposition parameters in a continental-scale dispersion model, in *Symp. Atmosphere-Surface Exchange of Particulate and Gaseous Pollutants,* Symp. Series, 38, U.S. Energy Research and Development Administration, Washington, D.C., 1974.

5. NMC Archives, Office Note 108, National Meteorological Center, National Oceanographic and Atmospheric Administration, National Weather Service, Camp Springs, Md., 1975.
6. **Smith, S. M., Menaerd, H. W., and Sharmin, G.**, World Wide Ocean Depth and Land Elevations Averaged for One Degree Squares of Latitude and Longitude, Scripps Institute of Oceanography, La Jolla, Calif., 1966.
7. **Holzworth, G. C.**, *Mixing Heights, Wind Speeds, and Potential for Urban Air Pollution Throughout the Contiguous United States*, Office of Air Programs, Report No. AP-101, U.S. Environmental Protection Agency, Washington, D.C., 32, 1972.
8. **Heffter, J. L.**, The variation of horizontal diffusion parameters with time for travel periods of one hour or longer, *J. Appl. Meteorol.*, 4(1), 153, 1965.
9. **Engelmann, R. J.**, Scavenging prediction using ratios of concentrations in air and precipitation, in *Proc. Symp. Precipitation Scavenging*, Symp. Series 22, U.S. Atomic Energy Commission, Washington, D.C., 1970, 475.
10. National Council on Radiation Protection, *Krypton-85 in the Atmosphere — Accumulation, Biological Significance, and Control Technology*, Report No. 44, Appendix A, National Council on Radiation Protection, Washington, D.C., 1975.
11. **Turner, D. B.**, *Workbook of Atmospheric Dispersion Estimates*, Office of Air Programs, Report No. AP-101, U.S. Environmental Protection Agency, Washington, D.C., 1972, 32.
12. **Machta, L.**, Global scale atmospheric mixing, in *Turbulent Diffusion in Environmental Pollution*, Frankiel, F. N. and Munn, R. E., Eds., *Advances in Geophysics Series*, Vol. 186, Landsberg, H. E. and Van Miegham, J., Eds., Academic Press, New York, 1974, 33.
13. United Nations Population Division, Working Paper No. 34 ESA R/WP34, New York, 1970.

ECOLOGICAL FACTORS IN DISPERSAL OF RADIOACTIVITY IN THE BIOSPHERE*

F. Ward Whicker and Vincent Schultz

INTRODUCTION

When introduced into the atmosphere or surface waters, radionuclides become dispersed and diluted, are transported over varying distances, and are usually concentrated in specific living and nonliving components of the environment. The environmental fate of radionuclides is governed by a highly complex mosaic of physical, chemical, and biological factors. The fact that nearly all environmental components contain at least traces of natural and man-produced radioactivity has stimulated considerable interest in radionuclide dispersion, transport, and concentration in most major ecosystems deemed important to man. Of primary interest are rates of movement of radionuclides within and between ecosystem components, mechanisms responsible for such movements, and degree of concentration of radionuclides within components, particularly biotic components.

Inasmuch as it is largely the nature and function of an ecological system which controls environmental behavior of radionuclides, observed behavior of radionuclides can elucidate these aspects of ecosystems, particularly the dynamic functional processes. For example, a considerable portion of our knowledge on atmospheric motions, ocean currents, and mineral transport has been developed through the measurement of radioactive contaminants.

GENERAL CONCEPTS

An ecosystem may be viewed as a set of compartments having functional connections to one another. Each compartment has unique characteristics and more or less defined boundaries containing organic and/or inorganic matter, i.e., a compartment may be biotic, abiotic, or both. Examples of ecosystem components that may be considered compartments include air, water, soil, primary producers (green plants), primary consumers (herbivores), secondary consumers (predators), and decomposers (bacteria, fungi, etc.). The major compartment green plants may be divided into cryptophytes, herbs, shrubs, and trees, and each of these categories might be subdivided into species, which in turn could be divided on the basis of age, class, size, and so on.

Compartments of a given ecosystem are physically linked by interchanges of water, minerals, and energy. For example, mineral nutrients are transferred between compartments by processes such as adsorption, absorption, inhalation, ingestion, excretion, dissolution, etc. Thus, a given compartment continually gains and loses minerals through various processes such as those just mentioned. When gains equal losses over a reasonable length of time, the compartment is said to be in "dynamic equilibrium" or "steady state," and the total mass of material of interest within the compartment is relatively constant through time. Obviously, if gains exceed losses, the compartmental content increases with time; if losses exceed gains, the compartment content decreases.

Ascertaining structure and function of an ecosystem is to determine kinds and sizes

* This section was adapted from portions of Schultz, V. and Whicker, F. W., Radiation ecology, *CRC Crit. Rev. Environ. Control,* 4(4), 423, 1974. With permission. Bibliographies are listed which provide additional references on this subject, as well as other notable bibliographies.[2-4]

of compartments and to elucidate and quantify the physical transfers and other relationships among compartments. It should be emphasized that ecological compartments and intercompartmental relationships are highly complex, variable in time and space, and subject to internal and external stimuli. The concept of compartment models has proven useful in the study of radionuclide behavior.[5-7]

Radionuclide behavior in an ecosystem is essentially controlled by the basic structure and function of the system itself and the physical and chemical properties of the radionuclide. As previously mentioned, those radionuclides that are in soluble form and are chemically analogous to essential nutrient elements will tend to follow ecological pathways in a fashion similar to their nutrient analogues. For example, radionuclides such as ^{90}Sr, ^{89}Sr, ^{140}Ba, ^{226}Ra, and ^{45}Ca will behave like calcium; ^{137}Cs, ^{86}Rb, and ^{40}K will generally follow the movement of potassium; ^{131}I and ^{133}I will resemble movement of stable iodine; tritium will qualitatively behave like hydrogen. Not only does the study of radionuclides provide insight into the movement of stable elements within the system, but the converse is also true.[8]

Some important radionuclides possess physical and chemical characteristics that are quite unique and whose behavior cannot be inferred from common nutrient elements. Some examples of these radionuclides are ^{144}Ce, ^{106}Ru, ^{95}Zr, ^{85}Kr, and ^{239}Pu.

As pointed out, a host of different radionuclides are of potential ecological significance, and each radionuclide displays essentially unique behavior, with only a few exceptions. This, coupled with the complex nature of ecosystems and the external variables imposed by man, results in the complexity of this subject. In spite of this complexity, a considerable amount of research has established a basis upon which a number of generalities can be formulated. Furthermore, behavior of several radionuclides in several kinds of ecosystems is rather well known, even though detailed mechanisms may not be completely understood.

Introduction of a radionuclide into the environment is generally followed by physical dispersion and/or concentration and biological accumulation and transfer. Prior to incorporation with biological or other solid materials large enough to be affected significantly by gravity, radionuclides in air or water are dispersed and diluted according to the motions of air and water. Turbulent media such as a mountain stream, an ocean surf, or wind on a mountain ridge would cause rapid movement and dilution of small radioactive particles. On the other hand, the hypolimnion of a lake or stagnant air would represent examples of media in which radionuclide dispersion would be very slow.

The radionuclide ^{137}Cs tends to attach very strongly to many materials, especially clay minerals and organic detritus,[9,10] as do many other nuclides. Radionuclides such as ^{3}H and ^{85}Kr are noteworthy exceptions in that they generally do not attach to solid objects or surfaces. Tritium may be found largely in the form of water (HTO), the cycle of which is well known, while ^{85}Kr (an inert gas) tends to remain in the atmosphere until it physically decays. Radon and radioiodine (in the form of I_2) also tend to remain in the gas phase.

In general, soil materials accumulate most radionuclides to equilibrium concentrations that are considerably higher than in the surrounding air or water medium. Soil properties are very important characteristics to consider.[11-14] A kilogram of fine sediment will accumulate more radioactivity from a given aqueous medium than a kilogram of course gravel because of greater surface area, assuming that other surface properties are alike. Similarly, finely branched, hairy vegetation generally accumulates airborne radioactivity more efficiently than smooth-surfaced, large-diameter vegetation.

Whether a surface increases or decreases in radioactivity over a span of time depends essentially on relative magnitudes of rates of income and loss. The rate of income increases with radionuclide concentration in the media and many other factors. Losses of radionuclides from adsorbing surfaces are caused by phenomena such as physical decay, leaching, resuspension or dissolution, or spatial reallocations of the adsorbing surfaces themselves. Rainfall, light, temperature, ecosystem structure, and conditions imposed by man are but a handful of the spectrum of factors that control income and loss rates (e.g., see References 15 and 16).

Once absorbed into a living system, the radionuclide may emulate the physical behavior of a nutrient analogue (if it has one) or it may exhibit unique behavior and locate in specific tissues or organelles. Further, a radionuclide incorporated with a biotic constituent is subject to food web transfer. This is true whether the radionuclide is merely attached to a biological surface by physical forces or whether it is physiologically incorporated within tissues.

In an aquatic system a radionuclide such as ^{137}Cs might be expected to move rapidly from the water compartment to sediments and to autotrophs such as sessile vegetation and phytoplankton.[17] Herbivorous consumers such as zooplankton and larger invertebrates in the system will then ingest ^{137}Cs incorporated into the diet of these autotrophs. Secondary consumers such as small fish will receive ^{137}Cs through ingestion of these primary consumers. Large predatory fish will then take in the radionuclide with their prey and possibly pass it on further to a terrestrial form such as a raptor, bear, or fisherman. Biologically incorporated ^{137}Cs may be returned to inorganic parts of the system by any biotic components through excretion, secretion, or death and subsequent decay and leaching. Radiocesium contained in the detritus and sediment compartments undergoes continuous physical exhange with the aqueous phase, and some ^{137}Cs passes into detritus feeders[18] and from there into higher order consumers.

In essence then, behavior of ^{137}Cs in an aquatic system is similar to behavior of those nutrient elements that are shared by all components of the system and which may be cycled or used repeatedly, enabling life processes to persist. Radiocesium may persist within the aquatic system for varying lengths of time, depending on its flushing characteristics and other mechanisms that remove components. Eventually, much of it may be buried by siltation. In any case, ^{137}Cs will decay with a 30-year physical half-life; this is one of the few things of which we can be certain.

A few radionuclides will frequently be found in increased concentrations at higher trophic levels,[19,20] but the majority of radionuclides in the environment do not increase in concentration with trophic level ("feeding level").

In general, readily solublized radionuclides having mineral nutrient counterparts are extensively and rapidly transferred in food webs. Persistence of radionuclides in ecological systems is directly related to physical half-life, biological half-life, and persistence of the system's components per se. Individual ecosystem components that have maximum income and minimum loss rates will have maximum radionuclide concentrations over long periods of time. A consumer organism within a food web will ingest radionuclides at a rate that is proportional to its food consumption rate and the average radionuclide concentration in the food.

Factors that affect the degree of radionuclide accumulation and concentration in biotic compartments may be described in relation to properties of the radionuclide, the organism, and the ecosystem.[21] The physical half-life of a radionuclide has an important bearing on the extent to which it will accumulate in plants and animals. If the radionuclide is extremely short-lived, as many are (i.e., half-life of less than 1 hr or so), it is likely to decay before significant biological concentration is possible. If extremely long-lived (i.e., half-life greater than 10^5 years or so), the specific activity of the radionuclide may be so low that the rate of energy release from a signficant concentration in terms of mass may be very small.

As mentioned previously, radionuclides that possess chemical characteristics closely similar to essential nutrient elements are most readily assimilated by and concentrated in living tissues, for example ^{32}P.[22] One of the most remarkable concentration processes involves accumulation of ^{131}I in thyroids of herbivores following contamination of foliage.[23-25] The radionuclide behaves chemically analogous to stable iodine, which is used by the thyroid for the synthesis of thyroxine and related compounds. The thyroid may concentrate ^{131}I up to 10^4-fold higher than the foliage. Chemically similar to calcium, ^{90}Sr is a radionuclide that may reach significant concentrations in bony tissues. In general, ^{90}Sr is replaced or otherwise removed from bone at a slow rate; thus, if it is chronically ingested over a long period of time, it may accumulate to concentrations that are very high relative to prevailing environmental concentrations.

It is clear from these and many other examples that uptake, retention, and hence, accumulation of a radionuclide by a biotic or abiotic entity are governed to a large extent by chemical properties of the radionuclide. To repeat, properties that enhance uptake, such as solubility and similarity to nutrients, and minimize elimination through strong chemical or physical bonding to compartments in question, will lead to maximal radionuclide accumulation. The physiological nature of an organism is also of concern because active processes involved in radionuclide behavior within the organism help determine the extent of transfer across biological membranes, rates of transfer between compartments, and retention within specific compartments.

Behavioral aspects of animals may have a strong bearing on radionuclide accumulation. Of utmost importance are patterns of movement and habitat selection that can place animals in proximity to contaminated areas. Different components of an animal's food base accumulate radionuclides to varying degrees; thus, it is obvious that food predilection and availability are important factors regulating radionuclide intake.[21,26] Furthermore, diet is important in that its composition may affect the degree of uptake and retention of radionuclides. For example, a diet high in calcium will tend to reduce radiostrontium accumlation in bone[27] by reducing both absorption and retention. One of the most classic examples demonstrating the importance of food habits is the study which shows the seasonal fluctuations in ^{137}Cs burdens in caribou according to their intake of lichens.[28]

Life span of an organism and longevity of its various tissues play a significant role in accumulation of radionuclides, particularly the longer lived ones. Persistent, long-lived plants such as lichens and mosses can accumulate radionuclides from the environment over long periods of time and after some years can achieve concentrations that are much higher than shorter-lived plant tissues. Deciduous trees and shrubs may be relatively long lived; however, much of their radioactivity is lost annually during leaf fall[11,29] and consequent incorporation into litter consumer-decomposer microcosms.[15,30] Further, newly formed leaves of such plants have only a limited period in which to accumulate environmental radionuclides.

Many inherent ecosystem properties have a pronounced effect on the overall accumulation of radionuclides in the system and on the movement and distribution of radioactive materials within the system. In terms of local contamination problems, proximity of ecosystems to the source of contamination is of obvious importance. Somewhat less obvious is the fact that some ecosystems, although remotely situated from the source of contamination, can receive considerable contamination as a result of dispersion patterns, climate, terrain, and physiognomy.

While some ecosystems tend to concentrate environmentally dispersed radionuclides, other systems are "flushed" continually by turbulent air or water motions which help to prevent radionuclide build-up by dispersion away from the system. Examples of such ecosystems are mountain tops or high ridges exposed to strong wind action, river channels periodically scoured by turbulent water and suspended debris, and seacoasts exposed to violent wind and water action. Some systems, such as the ocean, have a tremendous capacity for dilution of dissolved radionuclides through sheer volume.

On the other hand, ecosystems that have evolved in quiet, protected areas will tend to accumulate radioactive (and other) debris. Lee sides of mountain peaks and ridges are usually protected to some extent from winds, which allows suspended airborne debris or snowflakes to settle on the ground. A large fraction of atmospheric radioactivity is frequently attached to larger suspended particles and thus finds its way to the ground through this mechanism. Terrestrial ecosystems located in topographic depressions accumulate relatively large quantities of airborne and waterborne debris.[31] Quiet pools, bays, and sounds provide examples of aquatic systems that undergo long-term accumulation of suspended debris and in turn accumulate waterborne radionuclides.

Movement and concentration of radionuclides within an ecosystem are very complex but frequently predictable, at least qualitatively, from the nature of the system. A major question of very practical importance is partitioning of radioactivity between the biotic and abiotic substances. With rare exceptions, a system is likely to be in greater jeopardy if the radionuclide preferentially concentrates in biota than if it were "to seek" nonliving material. Furthermore, a vector to man or other organisms may be established in cases where biotic concentration occurs. A major factor that appears to govern partitioning of radionuclides between the biotic and abiotic components is mineral nutrient availability within the system.

Certain components of ecosystems act as reservoirs or even as "sinks" for some radionuclides and thus prevent movement of the radionuclide into organic tissues. A good example of this is a terrestrial system having soil with a high clay content. A radionuclide, such as ^{137}Cs, will eventually find its way to the soil; because of high affinity between the clay mineral lattices and the radionuclide, this radionuclide becomes immobilized in clay particles and is no longer subject to leaching or biological uptake. In such a system, several years after contamination the soil may contain high concentrations of the radionuclide, whereas very small or no detectable amounts of radioactivity may be found in plants growing on the soil. Apparently, ^{137}Cs in soils that are moist, sand, low in clay, and fairly acidic is readily taken up by plant roots and is thus biologically recycled through the system.

Ecosystem diversity relates to movement and accumulation of radionuclides within the system. A diverse array of plant and animal species is likely to constitute a relatively complex matrix of food web relationships with many pathways and alternative pathways.* Flow of minerals, energy, and radionuclides through such a system will be subdivided and partitioned to an extent commensurate with system diversity. In systems of relatively low diversity, a large fraction of the total energy, nutrient, and radionuclide flux will tend to flow through certain species since the total number of species is less and also because a few species or groups of species may exercise a high degree of functional dominance. This concept is strengthened by numerous observations of radionuclide behavior, particularly of radionuclide passage through arctic food webs, which provides one of the better examples of systems that are of relatively low biotic diversity.*

* Reference 1 provides a detailed discussion of an arctic system and intermediate systems.

REFERENCES

1. **Schultz, V. and Whicker, F. W.**, Radiation ecology, *CRC Crit. Rev. Environ. Control*, 4, 423, 1974.
2. **Klement, A. W., Jr. and Schultz, V.**, Terrestrial and Freshwater Radioecology: a selected bibliography, Report TID-3910, U.S. AEC, 1962; TID-3910 (Suppl. 1), 1963; TID-3910 (Suppl. 2), 1964; TID-3910 (Suppl. 3), 1965; TID-3910 (Suppl. 4), 1966; TID-3910 (Suppl. 5), 1968; TID-3910 (Suppl. 6), 1970; TID-3910 (Suppl. 7), 1971; TID-3910 (Suppl. 8), 1972; TID-3910 (Suppl. 9), 1974; TID-3910-S10, 1975; Report TID-3910-S11, U.S. Environmental Research and Development Agency, 1975.
3. **Klement, A. W., Jr., Lytle, C. F., and Schultz, V.**, Russian Radioecology: a bibliography of Soviet publications with citations of English translations and abstracts, Report TID-3915, U.S. AEC, 1968; TID-3915 (Suppl. 1), 1972; Report TID-3915 (Suppl. 2), U.S. Environmental Research and Development Agency, 1976.
4. **Edmundson, E., Jr., Schultz, V., and Klement, A. W., Jr.**, Marine Radioecology: a selected bibliography of non-Russian literature, Report TID-3917, U.S. Atomic Energy Commission, 1969; TID-3917 (Suppl. 1), 1972; TID-3917 (Suppl. 2), 1974.
5. **Olson, J. S.**, Analog computer models for movement of nuclides through ecosystems, in *Radioecology*, Schultz, V. and Klement, A. W., Jr., Eds., Reinhold, New York, 1963, 121.
6. **Olson, J. S.**, Equations of cesium transfer in a *Liriodendron* forest, *Health Phys.*, 11, 1385, 1965.
7. **Patten, B. C. and Witkamp, M.**, Systems analysis of ^{134}Cs kinetics in terrestrial microcosms, *Ecology*, 48, 813, 1967.
8. **Alexakhin, R. M. and Ravikovich, M. M.**, On the behavior of alkaline-earth elements — calcium, magnesium and strontium — in a forest biogeocoenosis (ecosystem), in *Radioecological Concentration Processes*,. Åberg, B. and Hungate, F. P., Eds., Pergamon Press, New York, 1967, 443.
9. **Davis, J. J.** Cesium and its relationships to potassium in ecology, in *Radioecology*, Schultz, V. and Klement, A. W., Jr., Eds., Reinhold, New York, 1963, 539.
10. **Dodd, J. D. and Van Amburg, G. L.**, Distribution of Cs^{134} in *Andropogon scoparius* Michx. clones in two native habitats, *Ecology*, 51, 685, 1970.
11. **Witherspoon, J. P., Jr.**, Cycling of cesium-134 in white oak trees, *Ecol. Monogr.*, 34, 403, 1964.
12. **Menzel, R. G.**, Soil-plant relationships of radioactive elements, *Health Phys.*, 11, 1325, 1965.
13. **Cline, J. F.**, The effects of substrate conditions on the uptake rate of ^{137}Cs by plants, in *Symposium on Radioecology*, Nelson, D. J. and Evans, F. C., Eds., U.S. Atomic Energy Commission Rep. CONF-670503, 1969, 547.
14. **Kalnina, Z. and Polikarpov, G. G.**, Strontium-90 concentration factors of lake plankton, macrophytes, and substrates, *Science*, 164, 1517, 1969.
15. **Witkamp, M. and Frank, M. L.**, Effects of temperature, rainfall, and fauna on transfer of ^{137}Cs, K, Mg, and mass in consumer-decomposer microcosms, *Ecology*, 51, 465, 1970.
16. **Wolfe, D. A. and Coburn, C. B., Jr.**, Influence of salinity and temperature on the accumulation of cesium-137 by an estuarine clam under laboratory conditions, *Health Phys.*, 18, 499, 1970.
17. **Pendleton, R. C. and Hanson, W. C.**, Absorption of cesium-137 by components of an aquatic community, *Proc. 2nd Int. Conf. on the Peaceful Uses of Atomic Energy*, Vol. 18, United Nations, Geneva, 1958, 419.
18. **Wilhm, J. L.**, Transfer of radioisotopes between detritus and benthic macroinvertebrates in laboratory microecosystems, *Health Phys.*, 18, 277, 1970.
19. **Pendleton, R. C., Lloyd, R. D., Mays, C. W., and Church, B. W.**, Trophic level effect on the accumulation of caesium-137 in cougars feeding on mule deer, *Nature*, 204, 708, 1964.
20. **Pendleton, R. C., Mays, C. W., Lloyd, R. D., and Church, B. W.**, A trophic level effect on ^{137}Cs concentration, *Health Phys.*, 11, 1503, 1965.
21. **Longhurst, W. M., Goldman, and Della Rosa, R. J.**, Comparison of the environmental and biological factors affecting the accumulation of ^{90}Sr and ^{137}Cs in deer and sheep, in *Radioecological Concentration Processes*, Åberg, B. and Hungate, F. P., Eds., Pergamon Press, New York, 1967, 635.
22. **Ball, R. C. and Hooper, F. F.**, Translocation of phosphorus in a trout stream ecosystem, in *Radioecology*, Schultz, V. and Klement, A. W., Jr., Eds., Reinhold, New York, 1963, 217.
23. **Hanson, W. C.**, Accumulation of radioisotopes from fallout by terrestrial animals at Hanford, Washington, *Northwest Sci.*, 34, 89, 1960.
24. **Hanson, W. C., Dahl, A. H., Whicker, F. W., Longhurst, W. M., Flyger, V., Davey, S. P., and Greer, K. R.**, Thyroidal radioiodine concentrations in North American deer following 1961—1963 nuclear weapons tests, *Health Phys.*, 9, 1235, 1963.
25. **Whicker, F. W., Farris, G. D., and Dahl, A. H.**, Radioiodine in Colorado deer and elk thyroids during 1964—65, *J. Wildl. Manage.*, 30, 781, 1966.
26. **Willard, W. K.**, Avian uptake of fission products from an area contaminated by low-level atomic wastes, *Science*, 132, 148, 1960.

27. **Goldman, M., Longhurst, W. M., Della Rosa, R. J., Baker, N. F., and Barnes, R. D.**, The comparative metabolism of strontium, calcium and cesium in deer and sheep, *Health Phys.*, 11, 1415, 1965.
28. **Hanson, W. C.**, Radioecological concentration processes characterizing arctic ecosystems, in *Radioecological Concentration Processes*, Åberg, B. and Hungate, F. P., Eds., Pergamon Press, New York, 1967, 183.
29. **Waller, H. D. and Olson, J. S.**, Prompt tranfers of cesium-137 to the soils of a tagged *Liriodendron* forest, *Ecology*, 48, 15, 1967.
30. **Reichle, D. E. and Crossley, D. A., Jr.**, Radiocesium dispersion in a cryptozoan food web, *Health Phys.*, 11, 1375, 1965.
31. **Plummer, G. L. and Helseth, F.**, Movement and distribution of radionuclides on granite outcrops within the Georgia Piedmont, *Health Phys.*, 11, 1423, 1965.

ESTIMATION OF DOSE FROM EXTERNAL RADIATION

Alfred W. Klement, Jr.

INTRODUCTION

The major sources of external environmental radiation were discussed in the chapters entitled "Natural Sources of Environmental Radiation" and "Man-Made Sources of Environmental Radiation". Natural sources include cosmic radiation and the terrestrial distribution of naturally radioactive nuclides. Man-made environmental sources include all those produced and distributed by artificial means, including the distribution and redistribution of natural radionuclides by man.

Generally, estimation of dose or exposure to external radiation sources is fairly straightforward. This does not imply that the information necessary is easy to obtain. The methods used follow basic physical facts or theories, or a combination, along with assumptions in most cases. The methods used are those deemed most applicable to a given situation, the degree of accuracy desired, and the degree of accuracy obtainable. The judgment made obviously must consider measurements and calculations, their extent and reliability. There are often controversial arguments among investigators with regard to both basic physical facts and theories.

When one is faced with estimating exposures in a real situation, the methods are quite simple. A statistically designed, properly instrumented, measurement program will provide a relatively sound basis for estimates of exposures. One method involves a simple averaging of measurements to obtain an average exposure for the area surveyed, considering the time factor. A similar average may be obtained for a potential or proposed situation where exposures are calculated from basic input data rather than measured. However, some system of integration of exposures over an area or a population may be desirable in order to specify estimates for a particular area or population. One simply integrates measured doses, by area and time, by population and time (man-rem) for actual or potential exposures. Occupational exposures in a real situation are, of course, best estimated by use of individual dosimeters or calculations for a specific person who will be potentially exposed. Occupational exposure is discussed elsewhere in this handbook, including a later section in which environmental and personnel monitoring and analysis are discussed. It is noted here that estimates of exposures due to a particular situation should consider and account for other ambient sources, including natural radiation.

Methods of prediction of exposures from atmospheric dispersion of radionuclides are discussed in the chapter entitled "Meteorological Dispersion of Released Radioactivity", as is ecological dispersion discussed in the chapter entitled "Ecological Factors in Dispersal of Radioactivity in the Biosphere." Other models are discussed in Chapter 6.4 in Volume II of the *CRC Handbook of Radiation Measurement and Protection.*

In this section **methods** of dose estimation are emphasized. They are discussed by way of examples that have been used, largely adapted from a study reported in Reference 1, primarily to suggest considerations of importance to specific situations. While the author is prepared to defend the selection of methods and the treatment of data used in the examples, it is intended for purposes of this handbook to indicate methods that may be used effectively, and not to imply that the results are "better" than those of others, although results of others and the methods used are referenced.

Estimates of exposures in the study used as an example below included doses or exposures to the entire U.S. population from most sources considered important. Estimates of doses for some very localized and specialized situations involving relatively small populations were not considered important and are not reported here. However, the sources are mentioned in the chapter entitled "Man-Made Sources of Environmental Radiation" and to some extent below. The methods used in the examples and discussion here can be applied equally as well to large areas and populations as to very small ones, although the latter are more suitable and practical for subjection to very detailed measurements or predictions. In these cases, as with occupational exposure, individual doses may be relatively high and warrant individual consideration with regard to measurements of exposure. It bears mention here that while present and future estimates of exposure may be made with a fair degree of accuracy when a monitoring program is planned, estimates of past exposures based on calculations, theories, and dated instrumentation for measurements cannot be made with a great deal of confidence. For very large-scale estimates, the degree of confidence may not be significant among past, present, and future estimates or predictions.

The selection of areal grids for integration of doses may vary widely. The availability of population data may be, and usually is, important. For broad-scale estimates, political units as a grid seems appropriate since reliable census data or estimates are readily available; e.g., natural radiation. In some cases, it seems more appropriate to use geographical or climatological units as a grid e.g., global fallout. For local situations it is possible to obtain a population census within preselected grids; e.g., nuclear power reactors often use a meteorological wind-rose as a grid, and a rectangular grid may be selected as convenient for a uranium mill site.

NATURAL RADIATION

Cosmic Radiation

Based on relationships of cosmic radiation dose to altitude and geomagnetic latitude,[2] estimates of dose at any geographical point can be made. For purposes of the example here,[1] the United Nations reference[2] was used. More "recent" data are shown in Figures 1 and 2.[3] The uncertainty in interpolation of the data can be seen. Estimates of altitude and latitude were made for each county or similar unit of the U.S. From these, dose rate estimates were made and along with population data[4-6] the average population dose rate in man-rem was obtained for each unit. The man-rem dose rate for each state or territory was obtained by summing the dose rates of the smaller political units and an average dose rate by the total population of the larger political units so that an average dose rate for the unit was obtained. Continuing this procedure, the average total man-rem and dose rate per person was obtained for the U.S. These are shown in Table 1, the average for the U.S. being 45 mrem/person/year. Another estimate gives an average of 28 mrem/year[3], using a shielding factor of 20% for buildings and a body shielding factor of 20% which were not used in the example study.[1] It is suggested that the differences in the results of the studies may not be significant with or without the use of shielding factors. Again, the important point here is that the example study[1] indicates a valid method of estimating dose in a systematic way.

While perhaps natural radiation is of little interest to some, this section is used here to describe general methods and an approach that may be applied to other situations discussed below. It is believed that the example approach may be more "sophisticated" than the data warrant if one merely wishes an overall average estimated dose. One could simply add the estimated average dose of all county-type units, or all states for that matter, ignoring the population, and arrive at an average for the U.S., or a particular state or territory. The results may not differ significantly. However, such an average may not provide the detail that may be desired by those concerned with the smaller unit and diverse population. Where sufficiently accurate population data are not available or easily obtainable, the areal approach may be the most adequate and applicable.

External Gamma Radiation

Based on several hundred reported measurements[7-10] with scintillation spectrome-

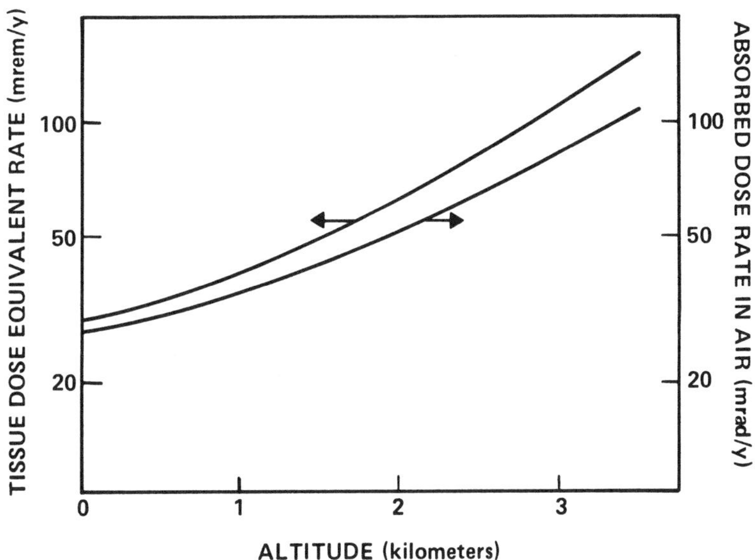

FIGURE 1. Long-term average dose from cosmic radiation. The charged particle absorbed dose rate in air or tissue is shown in the lower curve and the total dose equivalent rate (charged particles plus neutrons) is shown in the upper curve at 5 cm depth in a 30-cm thick slab of tissue. (From Natural Background Radiation in the United States, Rep. No. 45, National Council on Radiation Protection and Measurements, Washington, D.C., 1975. With permission.)

ters, estimates have been made in one study[10,11] of the range and "means" of whole-body dose rates by population and by areas for the U.S. This study showed that 90% of all areas fall in the range of 15 to 130 mrem/year, while 90% of the population falls in the range of 30 to 95 mrem/year. The estimated "mean" was given as 55 mrem/year.

In the example study,[1] the above referenced data were used to estimate average dose rates for counties where measurements were made. From these county measurements, an average was calculated for each state. These were then used to estimate the average man-rem per year and mrem per person per year for the U.S. population. For these estimates it was assumed that the variability within and among the various political units was the same as that of the reported measurements. Where measurements were made at different times in the same locations, the simple average was used to account for variations in time so far as the data permitted. Based on these assumptions and procedures, the overall U.S. average dose rate was estimated to be 60 mrem/year, which is near that estimated by other procedures referenced above. The averages for each state are shown in Table 2. In these estimates a factor of unity was used for conversion of open-field air-dose measurements to whole-body doses. Another study[2] showed an average gonad dose of 26 mrem/year assuming shielding factors mentioned above.

GLOBAL FALLOUT FROM NUCLEAR TESTS

Both current fallout and that deposited from past tests contribute to internal and external population doses. For the example study,[1] it was assumed that the rate and type of testing from 1965 to 1970 will continue for a number of years. Estimates were made for 1963, 1965, 1969, and subsequent decades to 2000. In 1963 the highest fallout occurred. The year 1969 was chosen as an example of the current situation at the time of the study.

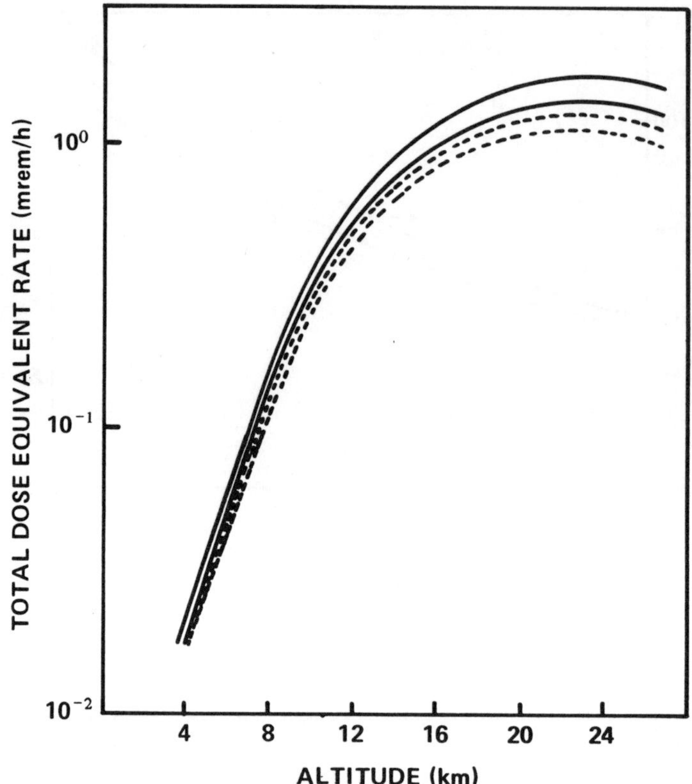

FIGURE 2. Total cosmic-ray dose equivalent rate at 5 cm depth in a 30-cm slab of tissue at latitude 55° N (—) and 43° N(-----) at solar minimum (upper curve) and solar maximum (lower curve). The quality factors for neutrons as a function of energy are included in the calculations. (From Natural Background Radiation in the United States, Rep. No. 45, National Council on Radiation Protection and Measurements, Washington, D.C., 1975. With permission.)

The accumulation of ^{137}Cs deposited from past nuclear tests is the major source of long-lived external gamma radiation from fallout. A number of short-lived radionuclides contribute significantly to doses within a few years of their production. Estimates of external gamma doses from fallout in the New York City area have been made which were verified by measurements.[12-14] Those values were the basis for the 1963 estimates in this study and an extension was used to estimate doses from short-lived nuclides in other years. Estimates of doses from ^{137}Cs for 1965 and 1969 were based on ^{90}Sr deposition data for New York City.[15] Two population areas were used for this purpose — "wet" and "dry" areas.[16,17] The average annual deposition of ^{90}Sr in "wet" areas is estimated to be 0.74 times that for New York City.[15,17] Based on measurements in 1963, deposition in "dry" areas was estimated to be 55% of that in "wet" areas (or 41% of that for New York City). The population in "dry" areas was calculated to be 15% of the U.S. population.

It was assumed that ^{137}Cs deposition was 1.6 times[18] that of ^{90}Sr, and that the factor[13] for conversion of ^{137}Cs deposition values to open-field exposure rate is 1.7×10^{-3} (μR/hr)/(mCi/mi^2). Exposure rates (μR/hr) are then converted to air dose rates (μrad/hr). A shielding factor[19] of 0.4 due to buildings and other structures and a screening factor[20] of 0.8 caused by body shielding were assumed for conversion of open-field air doses to whole-body doses. From these data, estimates, and assumptions, the man-rem was used to obtain average annual doses from this source.

Table 1
ESTIMATED ANNUAL COSMIC-RAY WHOLE-BODY DOSES (MREM/PERSON)

Political unit	Average annual dose	Political unit	Average annual dose
Alabama	40	New Jersey	40
Alaska	45	New Mexico	105
Arizona	60	New York	45
Arkansas	40	North Carolina	45
California	40	North Dakota	60
Colorado	120	Ohio	50
Connecticut	40	Oklahoma	50
Delaware	40	Oregon	50
Florida	35	Pennsylvania	45
Georgia	40	Rhode Island	40
Hawaii	30	South Carolina	40
Idaho	85	South Dakota	70
Illinois	45	Tennessee	45
Indiana	45	Texas	45
Iowa	50	Utah	115
Kansas	50	Vermont	50
Kentucky	45	Virginia	45
Louisiana	35	Washington	50
Maine	50	West Virginia	50
Maryland	40	Wisconsin	50
Massachusetts	40	Wyoming	130
Michigan	50	Canal Zone	30
Minnesota	55	Guam	35
Mississippi	40	Puerto Rico	30
Missouri	45	Samoa	30
Montana	90	Virgin Islands	30
Nebraska	75	District of Columbia	40
Nevada	85		
New Hampshire	45	Total U.S.	45

From Klement, A. W., Jr., Miller, C. R., Minx, R. P., and Shleien, B., *Estimates of Ionizing Radiation Doses in the United States 1960—2000,* Report, ORP/CSD 72-1, U.S. Environmental Protection Agency, Washington, D.C., 1972, 7.

Similarly, average dose estimates were made for short-lived radionuclides based on the study mentioned above.[12] There was no significant contribution from these nuclides in 1969.

The calculated total annual average external gamma radiation doses to the U.S. population for 1963, 1965, and 1969 were 5.9, 1.8, and 0.9 mrem/person, respectively. Annual doses from 1970 to 2000 were estimated to be about the same as those for 1969.

An alternative to the above method is possible. One could use individual local measurements of fallout to provide estimates for an integration grid of political units as was done for natural radiation discussed above. In the example study,[1] it appeared that the limited available measurements together with the important known climatological factors suggested that the climatological grid was adequate with regard to the obtainable reliability.

NUCLEAR POWER PLANTS

Here, another example from Reference 1 seems appropriate. As part of studies of

Table 2
ESTIMATED ANNUAL EXTERNAL GAMMA WHOLE-BODY DOSES FROM NATURAL TERRESTRIAL RADIOACTIVITY (MREM/PERSON)

Political unit	Average annual dose	Political unit	Average annual dose
Alabama	70	New Jersey	60
Alaska	60[a]	New Mexico	70
Arizona	60[a]	New York	65
Arkansas	75	North Carolina	75
California	50	North Dakota	60[a]
Colorado	105	Ohio	65
Connecticut	60	Oklahoma	60
Delaware	60[a]	Oregon	60[a]
Florida	60[a]	Pennsylvania	55
Georgia	60[a]	Rhode Island	65
Hawaii	60[a]	South Carolina	70
Idaho	60[a]	South Dakota	115
Illinois	65	Tennessee	70
Indiana	55	Texas	30
Iowa	60	Utah	40
Kansas	60[a]	Vermont	45
Kentucky	60[a]	Virgina	55
Louisiana	40	Washington	60[a]
Maine	75	West Virginia	60[a]
Maryland	55	Wisconsin	55
Massachusetts	75	Wyoming	90
Michigan	60[a]	Canal Zone	60[a]
Minnesota	70	Guam	60[a]
Mississippi	65	Puerto Rico	60[a]
Missouri	60[a]	Samoa	60[a]
Montana	60[a]	Virgin Islands	60[a]
Nebraska	55	District of Columbia	55
Nevada	40	Others	60[a]
New Hampshire	65	Total U.S.	60

[a] Assumed to be equal to the U.S. average.

From Klement, A. W., Jr., Miller, C. R., Minx, R. P., and Shleien, B., Estimates of Ionizing Radiation Doses in the United States, 1960—2000. Rep. ORP/CSD 72-1, U.S. Environmental Protection Agency, Washington, D.C., 1972, 7.

the long-range requirements and impacts of the nuclear power industry, computer models were developed to assess radiation doses from reactor effluents.[21,22] These models were tested with measurements made at 13 operating reactor sites.

The principal radionuclides in reactor effluents are ^{3}H, ^{58}Co, ^{60}Co, ^{85}Kr, ^{89}Sr, ^{90}Sr, ^{131}I, ^{131}Xe, ^{133}Xe, ^{134}Cs, ^{137}Cs, and ^{140}Ba. The amounts released as gaseous or liquid effluents depend on the type of reactor, and for a given type of reactor, the effluents vary widely because of the individual designs. Except for ^{85}Kr, ^{131}Xe, and ^{133}Xe, these radionuclides give rise to environmental contamination leading to potential internal doses. Krypton-85, ^{131}Xe, and ^{133}Xe emitted in gaseous effluents are the major contributors to external gamma doses as a result of immersion rather than surface deposition.

The external radiation dose model was designed to predict doses within several radii of a reactor site. It provides the average dose within each chosen radius, the total man-rem, and the average dose to the total exposed population.

The model involves the use of average wind data by 22.5° sectors around the reactor

Table 3
ESTIMATED EXTERNAL GAMMA WHOLE-BODY DOSES FROM REACTOR GASEOUS EFFLUENTS

Year	Man-years[a] at risk (millions)	Total U.S. population (millions)	Percent of U.S. population at risk	Annual man-rem	Annual average dose to population at risk (mrem/person)	Annual average dose to U.S. population (mrem/person)
1960	1.9	183	1.5	16.4	0.0085	0.0001
1970	47.6	205	22.3	430	0.0091	0.002
1980	275	237	100	6,080	0.026	0.026
1990	367	277	100	22,780	0.082	0.082
2000	670	321	100	56,000	0.17	0.17

[a] By 1980, a significant population would reside within 50 miles of more than one reactor site, indicated by the man-years/total U.S. population.

and the estimated population within each sector. Based on experience at 13 reactors, it was assumed that whole-body external gamma doses from atmospheric effluents were 5 mrem/year at site boundaries for each reactor unit. In general, actual levels were much less than this, so that dose estimates are quite conservative. Doses were calculated for populations between several radii, usually up to 50 miles, since at this distance or less, radiation doses were found to be at levels not distinguishable from background. Population estimates within each sector and radius were made for at least 2 years (e.g., 1960 and 1985) and computer calculations of doses were made.[21] From these, estimates were made for the years considered in this study by interpolation or extrapolation. This was done for each reactor site in operation or currently planned. As additional reactor units at a site became operable, simple multiples of the calculations provided estimates for each site in subsequent years.

After 1975 when currently unplanned reactors would become operable, (predictions, see the chapter entitled "Man-Made Sources of Environmental Radiation"), the calculated doses for the operable and planned reactors were averaged by capacity and National Power Survey Region to provide estimates up to 1990. This, in effect, assumes that the average dose, exposed population, and types of reactors in each region will be the same as that for existing or planned reactors. The prediction for 2000 was made by extrapolating from the 1960 to 1990 estimates which increased in a regular manner.

It is not expected that a significant number of liquid-metal fast-breeder reactors will be in operation by 1990, although there may be by the year 2000. Since these reactors operate with significantly lower effluents than current light water reactors,[23] the dose estimates for 1990 to 2000 may be too high. Also, other technological improvements in reactor subsystems would reduce doses below those estimated. The estimated external gamma whole-body doses are shown in Table 3. Skin doses were estimated to be about 10 times the whole-doses.

FUEL REPROCESSING PLANTS

As in the above, fuel reprocessing plants afford another source of external radiation and where an example of methods used[1] may be useful, both from the standpoint of being an important situation and one in which few reliable data are currently available. The methods used in the example study are based on calculations rather than measurements which may be applicable in principle to this and other health physics situations.

The calculated values depend on certain assumptions made and on values selected for various factors in the dose estimations. Therefore, they depend on the validity of

Table 4
PROJECTED QUANTITY OF REPROCESSED FUEL[a] (METRIC TONS/YEAR)

		Reactor fuel type		
		Lightwater		Fast breeder
Year	Total	U[b]	Pu[c]	Pu[c]
1970	200	200	—	—
1980	3,500	2,800	700	—
1990	10,000	3,000	4,000	3,000
2000	20,000	3,000	3,000	14,000

[a] Based on:
33,000 MWd burnup/metric ton,
0.30 thermal efficiency,
0.85 load factor,
MWE capacity 2 years before processing, and
fuel mixtures from Reference 24.

[b] Treated as LWR fuel.

[c] Treated as FBR fuel.

these assumptions and selected values. The calculated dose values will vary by as much as factors of 10 to 100 by changing the assumptions and selected values. Therefore, the methods of arriving at the dose values are presented so that future changes can be made as more accurate information becomes available, and as the applicability is pertinent to a situation.

Exposure to radiation from material released from the stack of a plant is considered. Local effects to a radius of 100 km (62 miles) around a plant are considered. While the example study considered the nation-wide buildup of ^{3}H and ^{85}Kr, this consideration is not discussed here. All exposures at a point of given distance from the plant are assumed proportional to the air concentration of radioactive material at that point. Therefore, air concentrations of radionuclides are calculated and from these, dose estimates are made.

The air concentration at a certain location depends on the amount of fuel processed per unit time, the amount of radioactivity of the various nuclides in the fuel, the release rates of the various radionuclides, and the dilution from the stack outlet to the location. Reference 24 was heavily relied upon to supply many of the factors needed.

Two types of fuel are considered in the calculations — light water reactor (LWR) fuel and fast breeder reactor (FBR) fuel. Light water reactor fuel consists of uranium or plutonium, while FBR fuel contains only plutonium. For the example study the LWR-Pu fuel was added with the FBR fuel since the amount of radioactivity produced per equal burnup is about the same. Table 4 gives a projection of the amount of each type of fuel to be processed up to the year 2000.

All fuel is assumed to be irradiated to a burnup of 33,000 MW-days/metric ton (t) with a thermal efficiency of 0.30. The LWR fuel is allowed to decay for 150 days before processing, and the FBR fuel is allowed to decay only 30 days because of the economics involved in plutonium recovery.[24] This difference in decay time causes a large difference in the amount of radioactivity present at fuel reprocessing time. Table 5 gives the radionuclide content of the fuel at the start of reprocessing.

Most of the radioactive material will go to waste storage but there will always be some fraction released depending on the element and process involved. In Table 6 are

Table 5
RADIONUCLIDE CONTENT OF LWR FUEL DECAYED 150 DAYS AND FBR FUEL DECAYED 30 DAYS

	Concentration (Ci/metric ton)			Concentration (Ci/metric ton)	
Nuclide	In LWR fuel	In FBR fuel	Nuclide	In LWR fuel	In FBR fuel
^{3}H	692	932	^{132}I	—	4,300
^{85}Kr	11,200	10,200	^{133}Xe	—	74,400
^{89}Sr	96,000	637,000	^{134}Cs	213,000	29,000
^{90}Sr	76,600	43,400	^{136}Cs	20.8	28,800
^{90}Y	76,600	43,500	^{137}Cs	106,000	109,000
^{91}Y	159,000	921,000	^{140}Ba	430	523,000
^{95}Zr	276,000	2,100,000	^{140}La	495	601,000
^{95}Nb	518,000	2,660,000	^{141}Ce	56,700	1,480,000
^{99}Mo	—	1,810	^{144}Ce	770,000	1,280,000
^{99m}Tc	—	1,730	^{143}Pr	694	644,000
^{99}Tc	14.2	14.9	^{144}Pr	770,000	1,280,000
^{103}Ru	89,100	1,760,000	^{147}Nd	51.0	185,000
^{106}Ru	410,000	1,290,000	^{147}Pm	99,400	353,000
^{103m}Rh	89,100	1,760,000	^{149}Pm	—	61.5
^{111}Ag	—	12,600	^{151}Sm	1,150	4,690
^{115m}Cd	44.3	269	^{152}Eu	11.5	10.5
^{124}Sb	86.3	76.7	^{155}Eu	6,370	79,400
^{125}Sn	20.0	6,720	^{160}Tb	300	9,460
^{125}Sb	8,130	19,600	^{239}Np	17.4	7,220
^{125m}Te	3,280	6,860	^{238}Pu	2,810	11,200
^{127m}Te	6,180	61,100	^{239}Pu	330	3,530
^{127}Te	6,110	61,800	^{240}Pu	478	4,260
^{129m}Te	6,690	181,000	^{241}Pu	115,000	600,000
^{129}Te	4,290	116,000	^{241}Am	200	1,570
^{132}Te	—	4,170	^{242}Cm	15,000	65,500
^{129}I	0.038	0.053	^{244}Cm	2,490	1,240
^{131}I	2.17	139,000			

From Siting of Fuel Reprocessing Plants and Waste Management Facilities, Rep. ORNL-4451, U.S. Atomic Energy Commission, Oak Ridge National Laboratory, 1970, 8—14.

shown the assumed fractional releases used in this study. All ^{3}H and ^{85}Kr is released through the stack while ^{133}Xe decays considerably because of holdup in the process. The halogen and particulate release rates are values that are assumed can be attained with advanced technology. The particulate release rate depends on the off-gas flow rate and on plant size, but the values given are used for all plants in this study.

A concentration factor of 5×10^{-7} (μCi/cm^3)/(Ci/sec released) was applied at a distance of 3000 m from the plant stack. This value was selected after comparison of values for several Atomic Energy Commission laboratories.[24,25] The ratios of the concentration factor at other distances to that at 3000 m are given in Table 7.

The average annual air concentration for individual or groups of radionuclides was then calculated by using the product of the radioactivity per metric ton (Table 5), the release fraction (Table 6), the concentration factor (5×10^{-7}), and a time factor assuming 1 t/da plant capacity is equivalent to 300 t processed per year.

Doses at 3000 m from a fuel reprocessing plant to the whole body and skin were calculated from the air concentrations. Whole-body gamma dose rates from most radionuclides in the plume were calculated using the equation

$$\frac{D(\text{nuclide i})}{D(^{137}\text{Cs})} = \frac{\Gamma_i C_i}{\Gamma_{Cs} C_{Cs}}$$

Table 6
ESTIMATED FRACTIONAL RELEASE OF RADIONUCLIDES PRESENT AT TIME OF REPROCESSING

Radionuclides	LWR fuel reprocessing plant	FBR fuel reprocessing plant
^{85}Kr	1.0	1.0
^{133}Xe	0.1	0.1
Tritium	1.0	1.0
Halogens	0.001	10^{-7}
Particulates	1.2×10^{-8}	8.5×10^{-10}

From Siting of Fuel Reprocessing Plants and Waste Management Facilities, Rep. ORNL-4451, U.S. Atomic Energy Commission, Oak Ridge National Laboratory, 1970, 8—12.

Table 7
AIR CONCENTRATION DISTANCE CORRECTION FACTORS[a]

Distance (m)	Air concentration correction factor[b]
1,000	10.0
3,000	1.0
5,000	0.50
10,000	0.20
50,000	0.026
100,000	0.010

[a] Adapted from References 24 and 25.
[b] Factor = Air concentration at selected distance/Air concentration at 3000 m

where C is the air radionuclide concentration in μCi/cm^3 and Γ is the gamma exposure rate constant for the radionuclides being considered. Its units are (R−cm^2)/(hr −mCi). (More details are discussed below.) Values of Γ were calculated for each radionuclide using Γ values for a specific gamma ray energy[26] and the number of gamma rays emitted per decay.[27] The ^{137}Cs dose was taken from a detailed calculation made for the Hanford, Washington area.[25] Krypton-85 dose values were taken from an extensive calculation[28] that gives a whole-body dose (from gamma energy) of 7 mrem/year for an air concentration of 3×10^{-7} μCi/cm^3. Results of these calculations are shown in Table 8.

Whole-body gamma dose rates from radioactive material deposited on the ground were determined by two methods. For the noble gases, calculations of others[24] were used for ^{85}Kr, and ^{133}Xe was compared to ^{85}Kr by the use of the Γ factor. All other nuclides were compared to calculated values for ^{131}I and ^{137}Cs using calculations for Hanford.[25] The nuclides were divided into two groups according to half-life since the half-life affects the maximum buildup on the ground. Those with a half-life less than

Table 8
ESTIMATED ANNUAL DOSE ACCRUED AT 3,000 METERS FROM A FUEL REPROCESSING PLANT PER 300 METRIC TONS OF FUEL REPROCESSED PER YEAR

Exposure pathway	Body organ	Annual dose accrued (mrem/person at 3000 m)[a] LWR fuel	FBR fuel
External gamma from plume passage			
^{85}Kr	Whole body	1.2	1.1
^{133}Xe	Whole body	—	9.1
All other nuclides	Whole body	$<10^{-3}$	$<10^{-3}$
^{3}H	Skin[b]	0.2	0.2
^{85}Kr	Skin[b]	53	48
^{133}Xe	Skin[b]	—	5.7
External gamma from surface deposition			
^{85}Kr	Whole body	0.09	0.08
^{133}Xe	Whole body	—	0.6
All other nuclides	Whole body	~0.04	~0.02

[a] Doses are received within 1 year of exposure.
[b] At 0.07 mm depth.

1 year were compared with ^{131}I and those with a half-life greater than 1 year were compared with ^{137}Cs. A ^{137}Cs buildup for 1 year was used. Assuming that ground deposition is proportional to air concentration, the dose rates were calculated using the Γ values and the ^{131}I and ^{137}Cs data from Hanford. A body shielding factor[20] of 0.82 and a structural shielding factor[19] of 0.4 were applied to correct air dose rates to body dose rates. More details of the calculations follow.

Whole-body gamma dose rate from a single radionuclide, due to immersion in a cloud of radioactivity can be determined from the equation:

$$D_i = \frac{2\pi}{10^3} \cdot \frac{\Gamma_i C_i}{\mu_i} \text{ rem/hr}$$

where μ is the linear attenuation coefficient for air, C is the average air radionuclide concentration in μCi/cm^3, and Γ is the gamma exposure rate constant in (R − cm^2)/(hr −mCi) for the radionuclide being considered. The above equation is obtained by taking half of an integration over an infinite sphere of radioactivity. Assuming μ is constant over the range of gamma energies of interest, each radionuclide can be related to ^{137}Cs by the following ratio:

$$\frac{D(\text{nuclide i})}{D(^{137}\text{Cs})} = \frac{\Gamma_i C_i}{\Gamma_{Cs} C_{Cs}}$$

The ^{137}Cs dose rate was taken from a detailed calculation for the Hanford, Washington, area[25] and multiplied by six since the dilution factor for Hanford is six times lower than the dilution factor used in this example.

Skin doses in the example were treated as follows:

- ^{3}H: Skin dose rate = $1.7 \times 10^3 \times$ rems/week[24] (Whole-body doses should be added to skin doses here for total skin doses),
- ^{85}Kr: Skin dose rate (0.07 mm depth) = $300\times/3 \times 10^{-7}$ mrem/year,[26,28]

- ^{133}Xe: Skin dose rate (surface) = 0.23 $\overline{E}X\Delta t$ (reference 25),
- ^{133}Xe: Skin dose (0.07 mm depth) = 0.20 × surface dose,[25] where X is the air concentration[24] in μCi/cm³, $\overline{E}$ = 0.112 Mev (the average beta energy of ^{133}Xe), and Δt = 3.15 × 10⁷ sec/year

The average annual dose accrued per person for the population around a reprocessing plant (out to a distance of 100 km) was determined using an average value of dose calculated for a specified population distribution. If the population density is uniform to a radius of 100 km around the plant, the average per capita dose for a specified dose at 3000 m is 0.027 times the dose at 3000 m. If the population density increases at a constant rate as the distance from the plant increases, the average dose factor is 0.015. The first value was chosen for this study.

Total man-rem was calculated by assuming a number for the population living within 100 km of the processing plant; 1.5×10^6 was chosen as the population value for 1970 and a 16% increase per decade was used. This value is reasonably representative of currently operating reactors, and the rate of population increase is the same as for the U.S.

REFERENCES

1. **Klement, A. W., Jr., Miller, C. R., Minx, R. P., and Shleien, B.**, Estimates of Ionizing Radiation Doses in the United States 1960—2000, Rep. ORP/CSD 72-1, U.S. Environmental Protection Agency, Washington, D.C., 1972, 7.
2. Report of the United Nations Scientific Committee on the Effects of Atomic Radiation, United Nations, New York, 1966.
3. Natural Background Radiation in the United States, Rep. No. 45, National Council on Radiation Protection and Measurements, Washington, D.C., 1975.
4. U.S. Census of Populations: 1960, U.S. Bureau of the Census, Washington, D.C., 1961.
5. U.S. Census of Populations: 1970 (Prelim. Rep.), U.S. Bureau of the Census, Washington, D.C., 1970.
6. Projections of the Population of the United States, by Age and sex (Interim Revisions), U.S. Bureau of the Census, Washington, D.C., 1970.
7. Lowder, W. M. and Solon L. R., Background Radiation, a Literature Search, Rep. NYO-4712 U.S. Atomic Energy Commission, New York, 1956.
8. **Beck, H. L., Lowder, W. M., Bennett, B. G., and Condon, W. J.**, Further Studies of External Environmental Radiation, Rep. HASL-170, U. S. Atomic Energy Commission, New York, 1966.
9. **Solon, L. R., Lowder, W. M., Shambon, A., and Blatz, H.**, Further investigations of Natural Environmental Radiation, Rep. HASL-73, U.S. Atomic Energy Commission, New York, 1959.
10. **McLaughlin, J. E.**, Unpublished data, U.S. Atomic Energy Commission, New York, 1970.
11. **Harley, J. H. and Lowder, W. M.**, Natural radioactivity and radiation, in Fallout Program Quarterly Summary Report, Hardy, E. P., Jr., Ed., Rep. HASL-242, U. S. Atomic Energy Commission, New York, I-2, 1971.
12. **Beck, H. L.**, Environmental gamma radiation from deposited fission products, 1960—1964, *Health Phys.*, 12, 313, 1966.
13. **Beck, H. L., Lowder, W. M., Bennett, B. G., and Condon, W. J.**, Further Studies of External Environmental Radiation, Rep. HASL-170, U.S. Atomic Energy Commission, New York, 1966.
14. **Lowder, W. M., Beck, H. L., and Condon, W. J.**, Dosimetric investigations of environmental gamma radiation from deposited fission products, in Radiactive Fallout from Nuclear Weapons Tests, Klement, A. W., Jr., Ed., Rep. CONF-765, U.S. Atomic Energy Commission, Washington, D.C., 233, 1965.
15. **Hardy, E. P., Jr., Ed.**, Sr^{90} and Sr^{89} in monthly deposition at world land sites, in Fallout Program Quarterly Summary Rep., U.S. Atomic Energy Commission, New York, Al, 1971.
16. Estimates and Evaluation of Fallout in the United States from Nuclear Weapons Testing Conducted Through 1962, Rep. No. 4, Federal Radiation Council, Washington, D.C., 1963.

17. Revised Fallout Estimates for 1964—1965 and Verification of the 1963 Predictions, Rep. No. 6, Federal Radiation Council, Washington, D.C., 1964.
18. **Hardy, E. P., Jr. and Chu, N.**, The ratio of Cs-137 to Sr-90 in global fallout, in Fallout Program Quarterly Summary Rep., Hardy, E. P., Jr., and Rivera, J., Eds., Rep. HASL-182, U.S. Atomic Energy Commission, New York, I-6, 1967.
19. External doses, in Report of the United Nations Scientific Committee on the Effects of Atomic Radiation, United Nations, New York, 41, 1964.
20. **Bennett, B. G.**, Estimation of gonadal absorbed dose due to environmental gamma radiation, *Health Phys.*, 19, 757, 1970.
21. **Waterfield, R. L.**, personal communication, U.S. Atomic Energy Commission, Washington, D. C., 1971.
22. **Rogers, L. and Gamertsfelder, C. C.**, U.S.A. regulations for the control of releases of radioactivity into the environment in effluents from nuclear facilities, in *Environmental Aspects of Nuclear Power Stations*, Proc. Symp., New York, August 10—14, 1970, International Atomic Energy Agency, Vienna, 127, 1970.
23. **Shaw, M.**, Statement, in Selected Materials on the Environmental Effects of Producing Electric Power, Joint Committee on Atomic Energy, U.S. Congress, Washington, D. C., 48, 1969.
24. Siting of Fuel Reprocessing Plants and Waste Management Facilities, Rep. ORNL-4451, U.S. Atomic Energy Commission, Oak Ridge National Laboratory, 1970.
25. **Slade, D. H., Ed.**, Meteorology and Atomic Energy, Rep. TID-24190, U.S. Atomic Energy Commission, Washington, D.C., 1968.
26. **Hine, G. J. and Brownell, G. L.**, *Radiation Dosimetry*, Academic Press, New York, 1956.
27. Radiological Health Handbook, U.S. Public Health Service, Washington, D.C., 1970.
28. **Hendrickson, M. M.**, The Dose from ^{85}Kr Released to the Earth's Atmosphere, Rep. BNWL-SA-3233A, U.S. Atomic Energy Commission, Battelle Northwest Laboratory, 1970.

MATHEMATICAL MODELS OF RADIONUCLIDE TRANSPORT IN ECOSYSTEMS*

William E. Martin, Gilbert E. Raines, Sanford G. Bloom, Arthur A. Levin, and James A. Duke

INTRODUCTION

Models for estimating external and internal radiation doses require input from source term and fallout prediction models. Models were developed for the complex situation illustrated in this section for external radiation doses from radioactive material deposited on the ground as well as atmospheric transport of the material.[3] The model for estimating potential internal radiation doses due to ingestion of contaminated food and water requires additional information concerning the probable rates of radionuclide intake by people living in or near areas contaminated by fallout or other radioactive debris. This information is provided by mathematical models designed to simulate transport of radionuclides from the biosphere to man. The quantitative data and other information required for model development and implementation of such models are obtained from the literature or are provided by ecological field studies.

FIELD STUDIES OF TRANSPORT PATHWAYS

The principal objectives of ecological field studies are (1) to determine which ecological pathways of radionuclide transport to man will account for a major part of the potential radionuclide intake by the reference population and (2) to collect quantitative data and other information required for development of mathematical models to simulate flow of radionuclides through those pathways.

Human Ecology Studies

Human ecology studies are required to determine dietary habits and to describe subsistence culture and demography of the reference population. Studies of dietary habits are designed to determine kinds, quantities, and sources of foods, water, and other materials in the diets of people comprising the reference population. Ideally, such information should be obtained by direct observation and measurements made in the field by experienced human ecologists. The results should indicate average amounts of different foods and water consumed per day by different age and culture groups. Studies of subsistence culture, i.e., methods of agriculture, hunting, fishing, etc., provide additional information concerning the relationship between the human populations and the ecosystems comprising its immediate environment. Demographic studies provide information concerning number and distribution of people in the study area, population structure as described by sex ratios and age distribution data, and population dynamics in terms of birth rates, death rates, population growth rates, immigration, etc. Such data are essential in planning for evacuation or other radiological protection

* This section was adapted from a previously published article of the same title and authors in Reference 1. It is included here as an example of a situation of a very complex environment and a very complex radiological protection problem and was developed during interoceanic sea-level canal studies in Panama and Colombia from 1966 to 1970.[2] This section is also included to illustrate the use of models in ecological transport of radionuclides as well as hydrological transport. While few situations are as complex, the methods illustrated here can be adapted to less complex situations, and they encompass most of the radiological problems encountered with regard to environmental radiation.

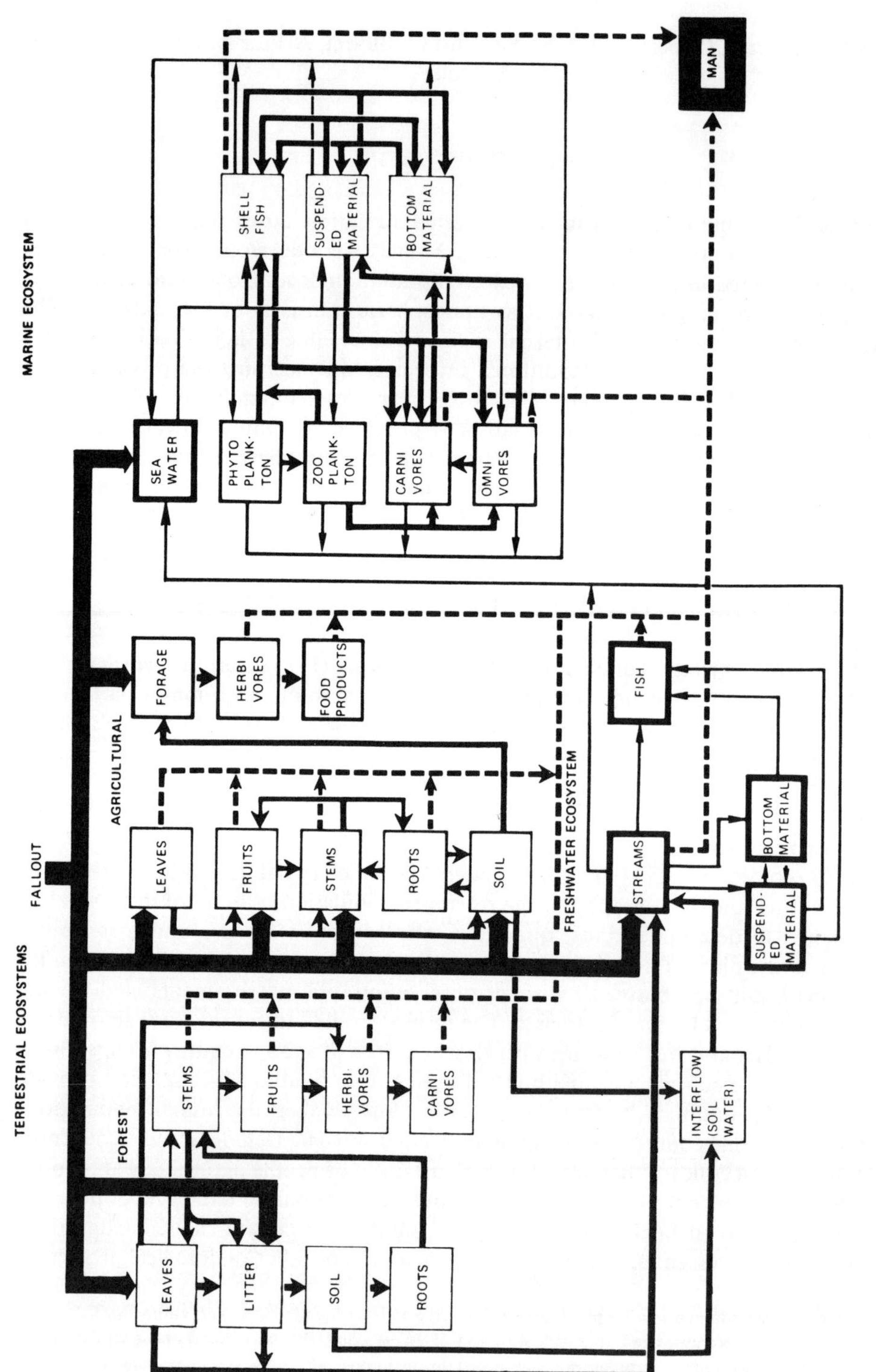

FIGURE 1. Generalized radionuclide transport diagram.

operations, and they provide additional clues to the relationship between the population and its environment. There are situations where, even in a relatively small area, a number of different cultures may exist with considerably different dietary habits.[4,5]

Once the dietary habits of the reference population have been determined, even in a preliminary fashion, one can trace the specific pathways leading to man back through the ecosystems from which they originate. Then, by analyzing the functional structure of the ecosystems involved, a network of interconnecting pathways can be diagrammed; and this provides a basis for planning field studies to obtain specific kinds of data required for development of mathematical models to simulate flow of radionuclides through the network.

Principal Pathways

Pathways of interest are those leading to man, but other pathways and various transport mechanisms may influence the flow of radionuclides through those specific pathways. Figure 1 shows a generalized radionuclide transport system for an area in which people obtain food and water from forest, agricultural, freshwater, and marine ecosystems. Each compartment represents a part of an ecosystem. The solid lines and arrows indicate principal pathways of fallout input and principal pathways of redistribution within and between different kinds of ecosystems; dotted lines indicate the materials contributing to man's diet.

Ecosystem Studies

Ecosystem studies are designed to determine the structure, composition, and mineral cycling dynamics of ecosystems contributing to man's diet. They are usually organized along the lines indicated in Figure 1. Most ecological field studies should begin with a general reconnaissance of the study area to determine the kinds of forest or other vegetation types present, the common systems of agriculture, drainage patterns, and other features.

Since radionuclides deposited in the biosphere generally are assumed to follow the same pathways as their stable element counterparts, it is not difficult at this stage of the study to determine the major compartments and intercompartmental transport pathways that characterize a particular ecosystem. As indicated in Figure 1, the principal transport mechanisms are usually (1) physical transport of dissolved or suspended inorganic material by water; (2) physical movement of organic material, i.e., litterfall in forests, mulching or other fertilizer applications to agricultural ecosystems, settling of dead organisms to the bottom of the sea, and movement of plant materials into a stream; (3) uptake of water and minerals from soil or water by plants, or direct contamination of plants by fallout; and (4) animal food chains.

Once major ecosystem compartments, intercompartmental transfer pathways, and principal transport mechanisms have been identified, specific sites or collection stations are established for more detailed studies to obtain quantitative data required for development of mathematical models to simulate flow or cycling of stable elements and radionuclides in different ecosystems. Detail of these studies will vary in relation to the ecosystems of reference. The particular kinds of data required to implement different kinds of transport models will be discussed later, but the basic kinds of information required are (1) chemical composition of each compartment and (2) flow rates or transfer coefficients for each intercompartmental or interecosystem transfer path.

The chemical composition of ecosystem compartments can be determined by collecting samples of soil, water, plants, animals, etc., from sites chosen to represent each kind of ecosystem and analyzing samples to determine the concentration and/or amount of specific elements in different ecosystem compartments. Early in the modeling program an effort is made to identify potentially critical radionuclides and chemical analyses are made especially for the stable element counterparts of those radionuclides.

DIFFERENTIAL EQUATIONS FOR RADIONUCLIDE TRANSPORT

Usually the transport of radionuclides through a food chain or a network such as shown in Figure 1 can be described by a mathematical model consisting of a system of first order, ordinary differential equations. This type of model is a logical extension of the radionuclide decay chains and is used by the ICRP[6] to estimate maximum permissible concentrations of radionuclides in air and water. It has also been used for more general descriptions of ecosystems by ecologists.[7-9]

General Equation

The general equation for this model is based on the following assumptions: (1) the functional components or compartments of ecosystems are large enough that the average radionuclide or stable element content of the compartment can be described by continuous mathematics, (2) the radionuclide or stable element flowing into a compartment is completely mixed with the radionuclide and/or stable element already present in the compartment, and (3) the rate of radionuclide or stable element transfer from one compartment to another is given by the product of a transfer coefficient and the amount of radionuclide or stable element in the transmitting compartment.

Upon equating the rate of change of the amount of radionuclide or stable element within a compartment to the rates of transfer to and from the compartment, one arrives at the following system of equations:

$$\frac{dy_i}{dt} + \lambda_{ii} y_i = \sum_{\substack{n=1 \\ n \neq i}}^{N} \lambda_{in} y_n$$

$$i = 1,2,\ldots N \qquad (1)$$

where y_i is the amount of the radionuclide in the ith compartment, y_n is the amount of the radionuclide in the nth compartment, λ_{in} is the transfer rate coefficient from the ith to n^{th} compartment, λ_{ii} is the elimination rate coefficient from i^{th} compartment, and N is the total number of compartments in the system.

Usually the λ_{ii} and λ_{in} values can be treated as constants (or as cyclical functions of time) and this simplifies Equation 1 to a system of linear differential equations.

There are many arguments for and against this approach to the problem. The arguments in favor of nonlinear transfer equations, partial differential equations, and statistical methods depend on interpretations of experimental data, but usually the amount and accuracy of data available will not be great enough to support such arguments. Furthermore, in a preliminary model designed to simulate radionuclide transport through several kinds of ecosystems, it is not practical to assemble enough experimental data to warrant the added mathematical sophistication.

Derivation of Differential Equations

Each equation of the system of differential equations given by Equation 1 can be derived in different ways. The most direct method of derivation is possible if (1) the stable element content of each compartment of the ecosystem is known, (2) all intercompartmental flow rates of the stable element are known, and (3) it can be assumed that the biological behavior of each radionuclide is identical to that of the corresponding stable element. An example of this method is referenced[10] for a model to simulate the transport of tritium through a tropical rain forest. A material balance for the element is given by

$$\frac{dy_i}{dt} = \sum_{\substack{n=1 \\ n \neq i}} \frac{F_{in} y_n}{C_n} - y_i \left(\frac{1}{C_i} \sum_{\substack{n=1 \\ n \neq i}}^{N} F_{ni} + \lambda_R \right)$$

$$i = 1,2,\ldots N \qquad (2)$$

where

$$y_i \left(\frac{1}{C_i} \sum_{\substack{n=1 \\ n \neq i}}^{N} F_{ni} + \lambda_R \right)$$

is the radionuclide loss rate from the ith compartment to all other compartments plus the loss rate due to radioactive decay,

$$\sum_{\substack{n=1 \\ n \neq i}}^{N} \frac{F_{in} y_n}{C_n}$$

is the radionuclide flow rate into the ith compartment from all other compartments, C_i is the total element content, both stable and radioactive of the ith compartment, λ_R is the radioactive decay rate coefficient, F_{in} is the total element flow rate, both stable and radioactive, from the nth to i^{th} compartment, F_{ni} is the total element flow rate from the ith to n^{th} compartment, and dy_i/dt is the rate of change of the radionuclide content of the ith compartment.

Upon comparing Equation 2 with Equation 1 it can be seen that

$$\lambda_{in} = \frac{F_{in}}{C_n} \text{ for } n \neq i \text{ and } \lambda_{ii} = \frac{1}{C_i} \sum_{\substack{n=1 \\ n \neq i}}^{N} F_{ni} + \lambda_R$$

The λ_{in} are constants if the stable element flow rates and the stable element contents are constants. This means that the flow rate of the stable element into the compartment must be equal the loss rate of the stable element from the compartment in order to keep the element content constant. Therefore, when the λ_{in} are constants,

$$\sum_{\substack{n=1 \\ n \neq i}}^{N} F_{in} = \sum_{\substack{n=1 \\ n \neq i}}^{N} F_{ni}$$

This, of course, implies an ecological steady state condition in which biomasses and concentrations of various elements in each compartment are more or less constant during the time interval considered. Such conditions would prevail, for example, in a climax community where the annual community photosynthesis and community respiration are approximately equal and the biomasses of plant and animal populations are more or less constant. Seasonal or other cyclic fluctuations of these or other parameters could be considered in the model, if necessary, by treating the transfer coefficients as cyclical functions of time. While this would provide a more accurate model of dynamic equilibrium, the necessary data are usually lacking.

Effect of Growth on Equilibrium

The kind of steady state equilibrium described above would not occur if the biomass and element content of one or more ecosystem compartments were to change radically during the time interval considered, and such changes are a normal consequence of growth. It is therefore necessary to consider the effects of growth with respect to most agricultural crops especially nonplantation species, secondary vegetation, and growing animal populations. In fact, any ecosystem in which one or more compartments and their stable element contents are increasing or decreasing during the time interval considered, will not exhibit the kind of steady state equilibrium which is a characteristic of climax communities. There is, however, another form of steady state condition which occurs when the total stable element content of a compartment can change but remains a constant fraction of the weight of that compartment. In this case the flow rate of the element into the compartment must equal the sum of the loss rates plus the rate of increase of element content due to growth of the compartment. Equations based on this form of steady state have been derived[11] and the following equation is a generalization of that derivation:

$$\frac{dy_i}{dt} = \left(\frac{dC_i}{dt} + \lambda_{Bi} C_i + \lambda_R \delta y_i\right) \sum_{\substack{n=1 \\ n \neq i}}^{N} \frac{f_{in}\, y_n}{C_n} - (\lambda_{Bi} + \lambda_R) y_i$$

$$i = 1,2,\ldots N \qquad (3)$$

where

$$\lambda_{Bi}$$

is the biological elimination rate coefficient of the element from the ith compartment,

$$\frac{dC_i}{dt}$$

is the increase of total element content per unit time due to the growth of the ith compartment,

$$f_{in}$$

is the fraction of the input of the element to the ith compartment which comes from the nth compartment, and

$$\delta$$

is a factor which converts activity units to mass units, and

$$\sum_{\substack{n=1 \\ n \neq i}}^{N} f_{in}$$

is unity.

Upon comparing Equations 3 and 1, it can be seen that the λ values are

$$\lambda_{in} = \frac{f_{in}}{C_n}\left(\frac{dC_i}{dt} + \lambda_{Bi}C_i + \lambda_R \delta y_i\right) \text{ for } n \neq i$$

$$\text{and } \lambda_{ii} = (\lambda_{Bi} + \lambda_R)$$

If δy_i is much smaller than C_i (and it usually is), Equations 2 and 3 can be compared to show

$$F_{in} = f_{in}\left(\frac{dC_i}{dt} + \lambda_{Bi}C_i\right) \text{ and } \sum_{\substack{n=1 \\ n \neq i}}^{N} F_{ni} = \lambda_{Bi}C_i$$

Furthermore, if the organism is not growing

$$\sum_{\substack{n=1 \\ n \neq i}}^{N} F_{in} = \sum_{\substack{n=1 \\ n \neq i}}^{N} f_{in}\lambda_{Bi}C_i = \lambda_{Bi}C_i$$

Determination of Transfer Coefficients

One of the principal objectives of ecological studies for radiological safety evaluation is to determine transfer coefficients for use in Equation 1. These can be determined by either direct or indirect methods.

(a) Direct measurements of transfer rates can be made by means of tracer experiments. Plants and animals may be placed in an environment containing the desired tracer (or the tracer may be added to a particular ecosystem compartment). Then measurements are made to determine the rate of tracer buildup while the organism is in the contaminated environment or the rate of decline after it is removed to a noncontaminated environment.

The rise and decline of the tracer in the compartment (organism or environmental medium) is plotted as a function of time, and in many cases the declining portion of the curve may be expected to fit an equation of the form

$$y_i = y_{Mi} \exp(-\lambda_{ii} t)$$

where y_{Mi} is the maximum content of the tracer of the ith compartment. For this declining portion of the curve, a plot of $\ln(y_i)$ versus t may yield a straight line whose slope is $-\lambda_{ii}$ and is given by

$$-\lambda_{ii} = \frac{\ln[\bar{y}_i(t_2)] - \ln[\bar{y}_i(t_1)]}{t_2 - t_1} \qquad (4)$$

where $\bar{y}_i(t)$ is the y value of the point on the straight line corresponding to time t.

The rising portion of the curve is usually more difficult to analyze. However, if the transfer into the receiver compartment is kept constant, the rising concentration of the tracer in the receiver compartment should fit an equation of the form

$$y_i = K[1 - \exp(-\lambda_{ii} t)]$$

or a plot of y_i versus $1 - \exp(-\lambda_{ii}t)$ should yield a straight line with slope K. The λ_{ii} value is the one obtained from Equation 4 and the value can be derived from the value of K by

$$\lambda_{in} = \frac{K\lambda_{ii}}{y_n}$$

where y_n is the constant tracer content in the nth (contributor) compartment, and λ_{in} is the transfer coefficient which describes the transfer rate of the tracer from the nth to the i_{th} (receiver) compartment. If the uptake experiment is conducted for a sufficient length of time, y_{Mi} will approach K.

If the transfer coefficients are not constants, the suggested plots will show deviations from straight lines, in which case more sophisticated analyses may be necessary to determine the functional form of the transfer coefficients.

(b) Indirect methods of determining transfer coefficients are usually based on measurements or estimates of stable element flow rates from one compartment to another and on the assumption that the ecological behavior of a radionuclide is essentially the same as that of the corresponding stable element. In the discussion following Equation 2 it was shown that

$$\lambda_{in} = \frac{F_{in}}{C_n} = \frac{F_{in}}{X_n W_n}$$

and

$$\lambda_{ii} = \frac{1}{C_i} \sum_{\substack{n=1 \\ n \neq i}}^{N} F_{ni} + \lambda_R = \frac{1}{X_i W_i} \sum_{\substack{n=1 \\ n \neq i}}^{N} F_{ni} + \lambda_R$$

where X_n and X_i are the concentrations of an element, both stable and radioactive, in the nth and i^{th} compartments, and W_n and W_i are the weights of the nth and i^{th} compartments.

If X_i and W_i are constant, the ith compartment is in equilibrium with its environment.

This relationship could be applied to an adult herbivore, for example, by determining the amount of each type of food ingested daily, the concentration of the element in each food, and the fraction of ingestion element which is assimilated. Then,

$$F_{in} = I_{in} X_n a_i$$

where I_{in} is the ingestion rate of a given food, and a_i is the fraction of ingested element, both stable and radioactive, assimilated in the ith compartment. Then,

$$\lambda_{in} = \frac{I_{in} a_i}{W_n}$$

If the herbivore is an adult and is not growing, it can be assumed to be in equilibrium with its environment and

$$\sum_{\substack{n=1 \\ n \neq i}}^{N} F_{ni} = a_i \sum_{\substack{n=1 \\ n \neq i}}^{N} I_{in} X_n$$

Therefore,

$$\lambda_{ii} = \frac{a_i}{X_i W_i} \sum_{\substack{n=1 \\ n \neq i}}^{N} I_{in} X_n + \lambda_R$$

If the elimination rate from the ith compartment (E_i) can be measured, then

$$\sum_{\substack{n=1 \\ n \neq i}}^{N} F_{ni} = E_i X_i$$

and

$$\lambda_{ii} = \frac{E_i}{W_i} + \lambda_R$$

As shown in the discussion following Equation 3, the elimination rate is related to the biological elimination rate coefficient and is

$$E_i X_i = \sum_{\substack{n=1 \\ n \neq i}}^{N} F_{ni} = \lambda_{Bi} C_i = \lambda_{Bi} X_i W_i$$

or

$$\lambda_{Bi} = \frac{E_i}{W_i}$$

If the equilibrium condition exists, the λ_{in} values may be determined from λ_{Bi} (or E_i) as shown in the discussion following Equation 3, i.e.,

$$\lambda_{in} = \frac{F_{in}}{X_n W_n} = \frac{f_{in} \lambda_{Bi} X_i W_i}{X_n W_n} = \frac{f_{in} X_i E_i}{X_n W_n}$$

Some of the above expressions for transfer coefficients are valid whether the organism is growing or not. Estimates of λ_{in} based on measurements of ingestion rates are valid whether or not the organism is in equilibrium with its diet. However, estimates of λ_{in} based on measurements of elimination rates require the equilibrium assumption. A similar argument should be applied to estimates of λ_{ii} based on estimates of elimination rates. If the organism grows in such a way that the concentration of element (X_i) remains constant, Equation 3 is applicable and the above expressions can be modified if the growth rate is known. Thus, to determine λ_{ii} from ingestion rate data when Equation 3 is applicable, the expression is

$$\lambda_{ii} = \frac{a_i}{X_i W_i} \sum_{\substack{n=1 \\ n \neq i}}^{N} I_{in} X_n + \lambda_R - \frac{1}{W_i} \frac{dW_i}{dt}$$

where dW_i/dt is the growth rate of the organism. Similarly, to determine the λ_{in} values from excretion rate data when Equation 3 is applicable, the expression is

$$\lambda_{in} = \frac{f_{in} X_i}{X_n W_n} \left[E_i + \frac{dW_i}{dt} \right]$$

HYDROLOGIC REDISTRIBUTION

Following initial fallback, ejecta, and fallout, radionuclides may be redistributed by either surface water or groundwater; therefore, many pathways of radionuclide redis-

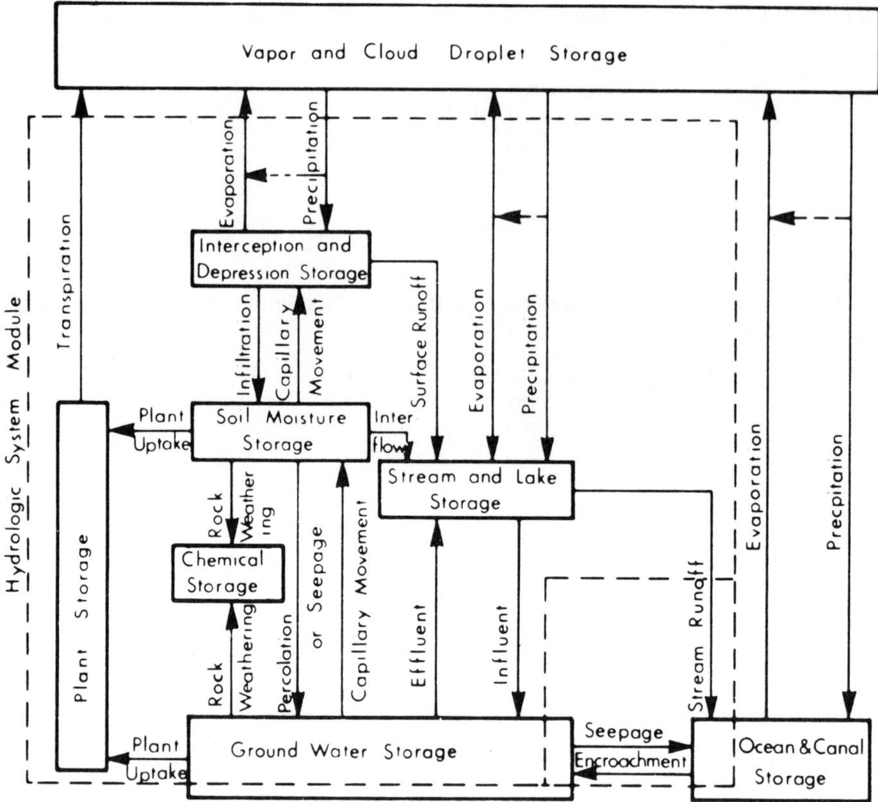

FIGURE 2. Diagrammatic model of the hydrologic cycle.

tribution within and between ecosystems will coincide with pathways of water movement in the hydrologic cycle. Differential equations have been derived[12,13] to describe hydrological movement of radionuclides in a fallout field and in the vicinity of a nuclear excavated sea-level canal. Much of the model would be applicable to a number of other kinds of radiological and nuclear situations.

The Hydrologic Cycle

Figure 2 is a diagrammatic model of the hydrologic cycle. Water moves from one part of the system to another in response to differences in potential of water in the two locations. Although most of tbe water in the system is continually in motion, the water in each phase or energy state can be assigned to storage compartments which are shown as boxes in Figure 2.

The largest reservoir in this model is the ocean-canal compartment from which water leaves by evaporation and is returned to the surface as precipitation. Water deposited on the land surface evaporates from vegetation or other surfaces, enters the soil moisture compartment and becomes available for plant uptake, finds its way to streams by surface runoff, is chemically combined with soil materials, or enters the groundwater. It returns from the land to the ocean either by runoff and groundwater flow or by evaporation and precipitation. In many heavily forested areas runoff does not normally occur overland but is confined to a layer near the surface called the interflow layer.

Figure 3 illustrates the corresponding movement and storage of radionuclides in volatile, soluble, or particulate form. Volatile radionuclides travel all paths of the hydrol-

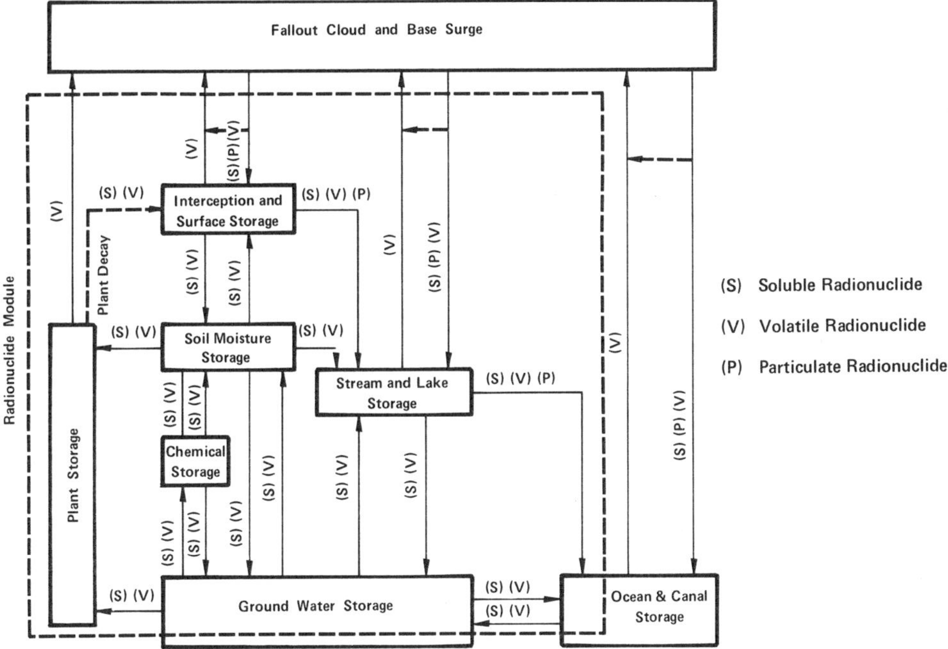

FIGURE 3. Diagrammatic model of radionuclide transport by water.

ogic cycle. Soluble radionuclides move with the water except during evaporation but may be retarded by plant uptake or adsorption on soil or rock particles. The filtering action of soil and rock restricts movement of particulate matter to surface water.

Nuclear excavation will alter the hydrologic system near the excavation site, but the major changes will be confined to a relatively small part of the total area affected. It is convenient to make separate analyses for the relatively small area close to the excavation site and the considerably larger area of the local fallout field. Generally, kinds and quantities of hydrologic data available for model development will make it impossible to consider all factors affecting hydrologic redistribution of radionuclides. Even if adequate data were available, it would be impractical to couple a detailed hydrologic model, accurate to within a few percent, with a biological model which, considering present knowledge, might be accurate to only a factor of two or three.

Fallout Zone Hydrologic Model

In modeling the redistribution of radionuclides deposited in the local fallout field, the primary objectives are to calculate the concentration of radionuclides in river water at some point (at any time) and the amount of radioactivity remaining (at any time) on the surface of the watershed. Because of variations in hydrologic conditions and initial radioactivity deposition, this can best be done by dividing the study area into a number of subwatersheds, each of which can be assumed to possess uniform hydrologic characteristics and initial distribution of radioactivity.

Within each watershed the amount of rain determines how much of a particular radionuclide is removed from fallout. Rainfall intensity and other watershed characteristics determine what fraction of precipitation leaves the basin as surface runoff and interflow and what fraction enters the ground. Some of the water which enters the ground is withdrawn by evaporation and transpiration; the rest becomes groundwater which eventually enters the stream outflow from the basin. At any use point contributions of radionuclide and water from all watersheds upstream are combined to deter-

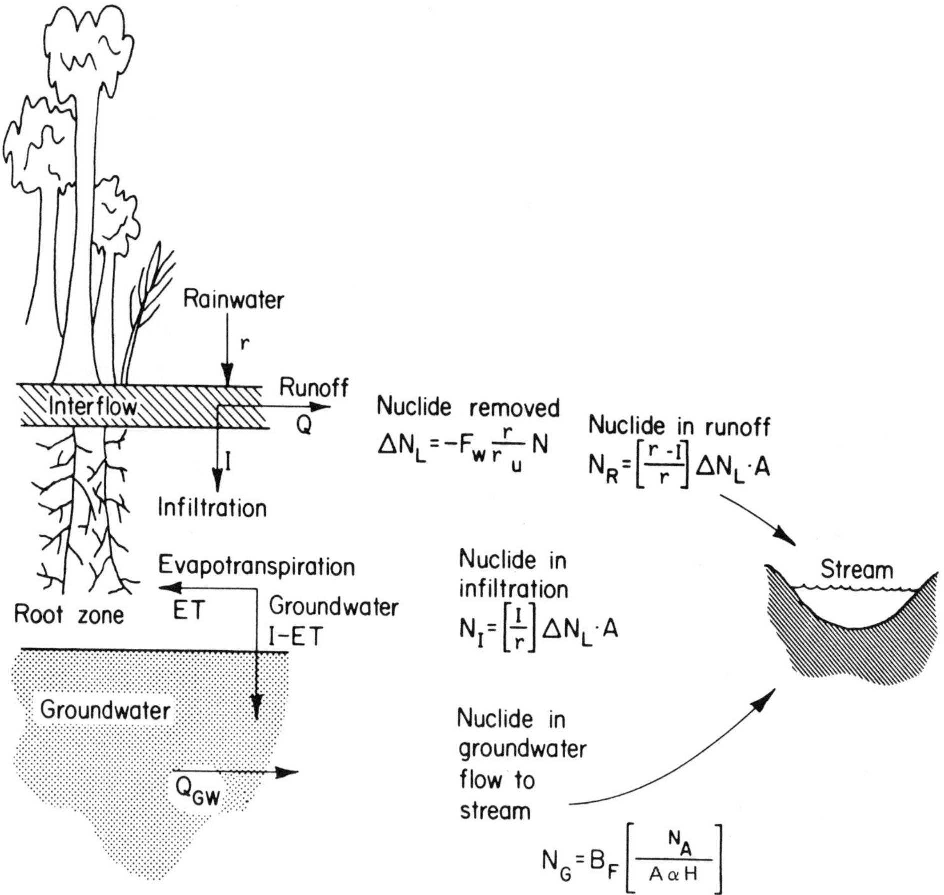

FIGURE 4. Diagrammatic representation of the fallout zone redistribution of radionuclides.

mine average concentration of nuclide in the river at that point. Figure 4 is a diagrammatic representation of the fallout zone redistribution or radionuclides.

The amount of radionuclide which is dissolved when rainwater comes in contact with fallout can be represented[14] by a distribution coefficient, K_d. The amount of rainwater needed just to fill the interflow layer is defined as the unit rain, r_u. It is assumed that this water is in contact with fallout long enough for equilibrium to be established. Since the amount removed is dependent upon a fraction of the total available at the start of the rain period, removal can be expressed as a simple rate reaction. The total amount of radionuclide removed from surface soil by leaching and radioactive decay during a time interval Δt is

$$\frac{\Delta N}{\Delta t} = -\left(\lambda + F_W \frac{r}{r_u}\right) N \tag{5}$$

where ΔN is the amount of radionuclide removed, Δt is the time interval, N is the amount of radionuclide on the soil surface, λ is the radioactive decay constant, r is the rainfall rate during the time interval t, r_u is the unit rain, F_w is the fraction of radionuclide leached from surface soil per unit rain,

$$\left[\frac{1}{1 + \left(\frac{1-\alpha}{\alpha}\right) K_d}\right]$$

K_d is the distribution coefficient, and α is the porosity of the interflow layer.

The amount of radionuclide dissolved during the time interval is carried with rainwater into the soil or stream; the proportion that follow each path depends upon the rate at which rainwater percolates below the interflow layer. In general, rate of infiltration varies with time and is dependent on precipitation history of the watershed. Following a dry period the infiltration rate is relatively high but it decreases during a storm, due to alleviation of soil moisture deficiency, swelling of colloids, and compaction and puddling of the surface by raindrops. In tropical forests the short term variation in infiltration capacity can be considered negligible. Infiltration capacity during the dry season will be greater than during the rainy season but during either season this value should remain fairly constant. The amount of radionuclide which enters the ground with infiltrated water is, therefore, a simple fraction of the total amount of radionuclide dissolved during the time interval. This fraction is the ratio of the infiltration rate (I) to the total rainfall rate (R) during the time interval (t). Rainfall in excess of infiltration leads to runoff through the interflow layer. The total amount of radionuclide removed in runoff is determined by the ratio of runoff to total rainfall

$$N_R = A\left(\frac{r - I}{r}\right)\Delta N_L \qquad (6)$$

where N_R is the total quantity of radionuclide in the runoff for the time interval Δt (Ci), A is the area of a watershed (cm^2), and ΔN_L is the amount of radionuclide removed per unit area by leaching alone (Ci/cm^2).

Water that does not run off becomes available for making up the soil moisture deficiency or groundwater recharge. Infiltrating water is subject to evaporation and uptake by plants. Radionuclide concentration in the water that is supplied to roots for plant uptake is the same as that in the rainwater which is percolated below the interflow layer. During the period when infiltration exceeds evapotranspiration the radionuclide in the infiltrating water can move directly to the groundwater. At times when evapotranspiration exceeds infiltration from the surface, the radionuclide flow to the groundwater is halted until the situation is reversed. When the soil moisture deficiency has been overcome, the radionuclide once again moves with water percolating to groundwater.

The groundwater system acts as a reservoir which delays water until it is eventually discharged into streams. Infiltrating water carries with it any dissolved radionuclide brought from the surface, but water and radionuclides do not usually travel at the same rates because migration of a radionuclide through the soil will be retarded due to ion exchange interaction. Radionuclides deposited on the surface follow a spectrum of path lengths through groundwater into the stream. During the first rainfall after fallout, radionuclides deposited on the stream edges may enter groundwater briefly and emerge almost immediately into the stream. In subsequent rainfalls radionuclides at increasing distances from the stream are moved into the stream.

The groundwater model replaces this complex system with a mixed reservoir that has an effective thickness, H: porosity α; and a constant retardation factor. Water input is by infiltration and output is the base flow into streams draining the watershed. Effective thickness is calculated from base flow, watershed geometry, and an estimate of mean groundwater velocity.

Mass balances are maintained for both groundwater and radionuclide in this reservoir. The total amount of radionuclide added to the stream during the time interval is determined from the ratio of total water loss from the reservoir by base flow to total water volume in the reservoir. This yields

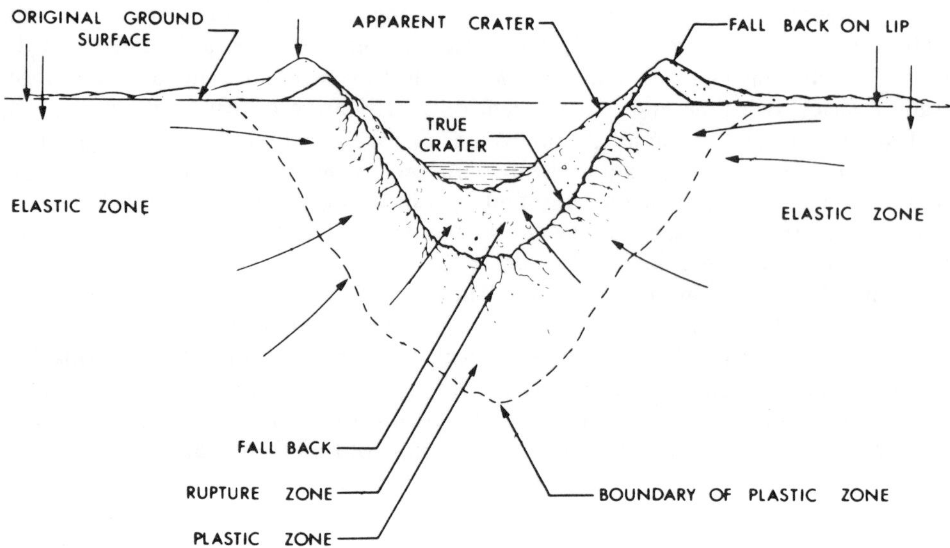

FIGURE 5. Hypothetical cross-section of a sea level canal showing direction of subsurface water flow (shown by unlabeled arrows).

$$\frac{\Delta N_g}{\Delta t} = B_F \left(\frac{N_A}{A\alpha H} \right) \tag{7}$$

where ΔN_g is the total amount of radionuclide added to the stream, B_F is the rate of base flow over the time interval, H is the effective thickness of the reservoir, and N_A is the total radionuclide present in the reservoir.

A cross section of a canal channel is illustrated in Figure 5. The lips of the craters will be composed of upturned, ruptured rock covered by several hundred feet of ejecta. The lips become drainage divides so that any surface water flow between the lips would be away from the canal. Flow within the canal will result from: (1) difference between mean sea level in the Atlantic and Pacific oceans, (2) tidal changes, (3) outflow of freshwater from the surface, and (4) groundwater flow into the canal.

Permeability and porosity of ejecta will depend upon the bulking ability of the original rock. One can expect an increase in fracture porosity and permeability in these materials for craters in most rock types, but permeability and porosity will decrease with depth because of compaction. Ejecta will have high porosity and permeability; its percolation rates will be high.

Rock structure in the excavation zone will be altered hydrologically. Porosity and permeability will be increased in ruptured rocks associated with the explosion. The water table will be lowered significantly and the canal will be effluent. Groundwater will then flow through fractured rocks in the explosion zone into and through the fallback and into the canal. Leaching of some trapped radionuclides will take place and water in the canal will be contaminated. The extent of contamination will depend upon the rate of leaching of radionuclides, rate of groundwater entry into the canal, and residence time of canal water.

Because of similarities between heat flow and groundwater flow, heat flow equations can be used to approximate the rate of water flow into the canal, provided adequate boundary conditions can be stated.[15] Flow into the canal is perpendicular to the channel. For a unit length of channel, the total steady-state flow into the canal (Q) for a time interval Δt can be expressed by

$$Q = (8hfK_hD_a)^{1/2}\Delta t \qquad (8)$$

where h is the height above sea level of the original water table (cm), f is the rate of infiltration from precipitation (cm/sec), K_h is the hydraulic conductivity (cm/sec), and D_a is the effective thickness of saturated aquifer (cm).

The volume of rubble produced per unit length along the channel can be obtained from the elementary considerations using empirical relationships.[16,17] Results of this determination[18] yield a volume of rubble per unit length equal to

$$V_r = W^{\frac{2}{3.4}}\left[\frac{\pi}{2}\left(\frac{C}{(\rho z)^{1/4}}\right)\left(\frac{C}{(\rho z)^{1/4}} + 90\right) + 6.11 \times 10^3\right] \qquad (9)$$

where V_r is the volume (ft^3/ft length), W is the yield of the device (kt), ϱ is the density of media (g/cm^3), z is the detonation depth (1000s of ft), and C is the media characteristic (47 for granite, 51 for alluvium, and 61 for tuff).

It is assumed that over the time span of interest, radioactivity that is not tightly bound will dissolve almost instantly. The amount of a radionuclide removed during time interval Δt can then be determined from the analogue to Equation 5, i.e.,

$$\frac{\Delta N_c}{\Delta t} = -\left(\lambda + F_c\frac{(8hfK_nD_a)^{1/2}}{\alpha_r V_r}\right)N \qquad (10)$$

where ΔN_c is the amount of nuclide removed from rubble, per unit length of canal channel, in time interval Δt (Ci),

F_c is

$$\left[\frac{1}{1 + \left[\frac{1-\alpha_r}{\alpha_r}\right]K_d}\right]$$

α_r is the rubble porosity, K_d is the distribution coefficient, and V_r is defined by Equation 9.

Summing $\Delta N_c/\Delta t$ over the length of the canal provides an estimate of the rate of radionuclide flow into the canal channel. This combined with estimates of the net flow rate of water out of the canal or from one ocean to the other through the canal, will provide a basis for calculating the amounts of radionuclides transferred from the canal to the marine environment.

Application of Hydrologic Models

The hydrologic redistribution models can be applied to specific field conditions by selecting proper values for the rate coefficients. The fallout zone subwatersheds must be characterized by dimensions for the interflow layer, groundwater reservoir, area, long-term infiltration rate, evapotranspiration rate, soil density, and porosity. Each radionuclide will have a specific distribution coefficient in each subwatershed, but variation in this coefficient is related primarily to the radionuclide species. For different segments of the canal channel, values must be found for groundwater potential, hydraulic conductivity, porosity, radionuclide distribution coefficient, and infiltration capacity. Methods of determining these values and of designing computer codes for making subsequent calculations have been described.[13]

If values are available for all parameters included in the model, calculations of radionuclide redistribution can be made for the entire hydrologic system. However, the calculations of greatest value to the overall ecological model are those which show the following quantities as a function of time:

1. Concentrations of radionuclides in river water at specified use points, i.e., the amounts available for uptake by man through drinking water or aquatic food chains;
2. Amounts of radionuclides remaining in different subwatersheds, and thus available for potential uptake by man through terrestrial food chains; and
3. Amounts of radionuclides entering oceans from rivers or the canal and thus potentially available for human uptake through marine food chains.

PHYSICAL REDISTRIBUTION IN THE MARINE ENVIRONMENT

Nuclear excavation may result in contamination of the marine environment by: (1) marine fallout, (2) terrestrial fallout, and (3) radionuclide transport from fallback and ejecta deposits. Marine fallout is a direct input which results in initially high levels of contamination that disperse rapidly. Marine inputs from terrestrial fallout, fallback, and ejecta occur at a relatively lower level but persist for a longer time. The pathways of radionuclide transport from terrestrial fallout to the ocean were discussed in relation to hydrologic redistribution. Obviously, the input of radionuclides from fallback and ejecta to the sea will be negligible unless the crater or craters are in contact with the sea. For the models discussed below, the craters are assumed to be part of a sea-level canal. The mathematical derivation of the models is similar to that given by Bloom and Raines.[18]

Physical Transport

Expressions for describing the physical transport of materials in the ocean are available in the form of partial differential equations in which: (1) time and distance are independent variables, (2) concentration of the material in the water is the dependent variable, (3) current velocities and turbulent diffusivities are parameters, and (4) rates of material addition to the ocean, land features, and bottom features are boundary and initial conditions. A simplified partial differential equation has been suggested[19] for dispersion based on the assumption that the spectrum of turbulence can be divided into two major parts which are sufficiently isolated from each other that the two parts act almost independently. These two parts are (1) large-scale eddies which produce a directed convection transport and (2) small-scale eddies which produce a random turbulent diffusion transport. The resulting partial differential equation for dispersion is

$$\frac{\partial C}{\partial t} + (V_o - yS_y - zS_z)\frac{\partial C}{\partial x} = A_x \frac{\partial^2 C}{\partial x^2} + A_y \frac{\partial^2 C}{\partial y^2} + A_z \frac{\partial^2 C}{\partial z^2} \tag{11}$$

where C is the concentration of the material in the water, t is the time, x is the horizontal coordinate axis in the direction parallel to the mean current, V_o is the time-dependent mean surface velocity, y is the horizontal coordinate axis in the direction perpendicular to the mean current, z is the vertical coordinate axis, S_y and S_z are the horizontal and vertical velocity gradients (assumed constant), and A_x, A_y, and A_z are the turbulent diffusivities (assumed constant).

The magnitude of vertical turbulent diffusivity is usually on the order of 0.01 to 0.001 that of the horizontal turbulent diffusivities. In the absence of a vertical velocity gradient, this would indicate that vertical dispersion can be neglected and a dispersion equation would need to consider only the horizontal components of diffusion. However, the vertical diffusion combined with a vertical velocity gradient in a horizontal flow can give rise to an effective horizontal dispersion larger than that due to the horizontal turbulent diffusivity. This effect was first shown by Taylor[20,21] for the case of dispersion in a tube, and the experimental results of Pritchard et al.[22] tend to confirm this effect for the marine environment.

Carter and Okubo[19] have given a solution to Equation 11 in an infinite medium for an instantaneous point source located at x = y = z = 0. The solution is

$$C(x,y,z,t) = K \exp \left\{ -\frac{[x - \bar{x} + \frac{t}{2}(yS_y + zS_z)]^2}{4A_x t g^2} - \frac{y^2}{4A_y t} - \frac{z^2}{4A_z t} \right\} \tag{12}$$

where g is

$$\left[1 + \frac{t^2}{12}\left(\frac{A_y S_y^2}{A_x} + \frac{A_z S_z^2}{A_x}\right)\right]^{1/2}$$

K is

$$\frac{M}{(4\pi t)^{3/2}\, g (A_x A_y A_z)^{1/2}}$$

$\bar{x}$ is

$$\int_0^t V_o(\tau)\, d\tau$$

and M is the strength of the source (μCi).

Equation 12 can be used to develop approximate mathematical models for sources other than an instantaneous point source. In the theory of heat conduction in solids[15] the solution for an instantaneous point source is regarded as a fundamental solution, and solutions for other sources or other boundary conditions can be readily developed from this fundamental solution. In the case of turbulent diffusion, the instantaneous point source solution is not a fundamental solution in the rigorous sense. However, if it is conceded that the model is only an approximation of the actual situation and that experimental data on currents, velocity gradients, and turbulent diffusivities do not usually warrant a precise model of dispersion, the instantaneous point source solution can be used, as if it were a fundamental solution, to construct models for other types of sources.

A General Model for the Distribution of Marine Fallout

Conservative source functions to describe a fallout input into the ocean would be an instantaneous plane source on a semi-infinite medium. This assumes the fallout is completely soluble in seawater and is therefore readily available for uptake by marine organisms. Since A_z is usually much smaller than A_x or A_y, the solution for a semi-infinite medium can be obtained by reflecting (see Reference 15) the solution for an infinite medium about the z = 0 plane. This corresponds to multiplying Equation 12 by two. If radioactive decay is considered in addition to dispersion, the concentration of a radionuclide resulting from a hypothetical, rectangular fallout pattern on the surface of the ocean is

$$C(x,y,z,t) = \frac{2\exp\left(\frac{-z^2}{4A_zt} - \lambda_Rt\right)}{(4\pi t)^{3/2}\, g(A_xA_yA_z)^{1/2}} \int_0^H \exp\left(\frac{-(y-y_0)^2}{4A_yt}\right) dy_0$$

$$\cdot \int_0^Z F_{AM}(x_0,y_0)\exp\left(\frac{-\left[x-\bar{x}-x_0+\frac{t}{2}(yS_y+zS_z)\right]^2}{4A_xtg^2}\right) dx_0 \tag{13}$$

where λ_R is the radioactive decay constant (day^{-1}), H is the width of the fallout pattern perpendicular to the current (cm), Z is the length of the fallout pattern parallel to the current (cm), and $F_{AM}(x_O,y_O)$ is the marine fallout per unit area ($\mu Ci/cm^2$).

A first approximation to the fallout input would be to make the source constant over a hypothetical rectangle. However, even with this simplification, the integration in Equation 13 is difficult to perform. Fortunately, the data of Pritchard et al.[22] indicate that $A_x \simeq A_y = A$ and $S_z >> S_y \simeq O$.

With the above approximations, Equation 13 becomes

$$C(x,y,z,t) = \frac{F_{AM}\exp\left(\frac{-z^2}{4A_zt} - \lambda_Rt\right)}{4(\pi A_zt)^{1/2}} \left[\xi\left(\frac{H-y}{2(At)^{1/2}}\right) + \xi\left(\frac{y}{2(At)^{1/2}}\right)\right]$$

$$\left[\xi\left(\frac{x-\bar{x}+tz\frac{S_z}{2}}{2g(At)^{1/2}}\right) + \xi\left(\frac{Z-x+\bar{x}-tz\frac{S_z}{2}}{2g(At)^{1/2}}\right)\right] \tag{14}$$

where $\xi(x)$ is the error function.[23]

Equation 14 is valid only if the depth to the thermocline (or bottom if the water is shallow) is very great or the time after fallout input is short. The rate at which material penetrates the thermocline is very small in comparison to the vertical transport in the upper layer of the ocean and therefore, the thermocline behaves almost as a solid boundary to this vertical transport. Since Equation 14 was derived on the basis of an infinite depth, it tends to underestimate the radionuclide concentrations near the thermocline for late times when the effect of the bottom boundary becomes significant. This boundary effect can be approximately included by reflecting Equation 14 about the bottom boundary. However, for the purpose of estimating radiation dose, the point-to-point variations of the radionuclide concentration are seldom necessary and some average concentration usually suffices. A conservative estimate of an average concentration is the maximum concentration derived from Equation 14.

The point of maximum concentration at any time is, according to Equation 14, located at $x = \bar{x} + (Z - tzS_z)/2$, $y = H/2$, and $z = 0$, and is given by

$$C_{max}(t) = \left[\frac{F_{AM}\exp(-\lambda_Rt)}{(\pi A_zt)^{1/2}}\right] \xi\left[\frac{H}{4(At)^{1/2}}\right] \xi\left[\frac{Z}{4g(At)^{1/2}}\right] \tag{15}$$

where C_{max} is the maximum concentration ($\mu Ci/cm^3$).

Equation 15 has the following limiting values:

$$C_{max}(t) \rightarrow \frac{F_{AM} \exp(-\lambda_R t)}{(\pi A_z t)^{1/2}} \quad \text{for } t \rightarrow 0 \text{ and} \tag{16}$$

$$C_{max}(t) \rightarrow \frac{3F_{AM} HZ \exp(-\lambda_R t)}{\pi^{3/2}(12A)^{1/2} A_z S_z t^{5/2}} \quad \text{for } t \rightarrow \infty \tag{17}$$

Because of the boundary effect, Equation 15 would tend to underestimate slightly the maximum concentration at late times. However, there is so much conservatism in the use of the *maximum* concentration as an estimate for an *average* concentration that Equation 15 still overestimates the average concentration.

An Alternative Model for the Redistribution of Marine Fallout

Equations 14 and 15 were based on the combination of diffusion and convection effects into one expression. However, Equation 16 indicates that vertical diffusion controls the spread of the material at early times, while Equation 17 indicates the importance of convective effects at later times. Therefore, an alternative model for estimating an average radionuclide concentration due to a fallout source would consist of one equation, based on vertical diffusion, for early times and another equation, based on convection effects, for later times.

The early-time equation can be considered as a solution to Equation 11 when $A_x = A_y = S_y = S_z = 0$. The resulting solution, including radioactive decay, is

$$C(z,t) = \frac{F_{AM} \exp\left(\frac{-z^2}{4A_z t} - \lambda_R t\right)}{(\pi A_z t)^{1/2}} \tag{18}$$

Equation 18 indicates that the concentration declines quite rapidly with increasing depth and the expression can be used to show that most of the radionuclide (79%) is contained in the region $0 < z < z_B$ where

$$z_B = (\pi A_z t)^{1/2} \tag{19}$$

When z_B is less than the depth to the thermocline (or bottom), z_B may be taken as a measure of the depth of water in which complete mixing takes place. Therefore, the average radionuclide concentration in this region is given by

$$C_{AV}(t) = \frac{0.79 F_{AM} \exp(-\lambda_R t)}{(\pi A_z t)^{1/2}} \tag{20}$$

or, as a conservative simplification,

$$C_{AV}(t) = \frac{F_{AM} \exp(-\lambda_R t)}{(\pi A_z t)^{1/2}} \tag{21}$$

where C_{AV} is the average radionuclide concentration ($\mu Ci/cm^3$).

When z_B becomes equal to the depth of the thermocline, convective effects become the controlling mechanism for the variation of radionuclide concentration. An expression for radionuclide concentration at this later time can be obtained as a solution to Equation 11 when $A_x = A_y = A_z = S_y$, and V_o is assumed constant. A simple approximation for S_z is V_o/D and, using this approximation, the required solution, including radioactive decay, is

$$C(x,z,t) = \frac{F_{AM}\exp(-\lambda_R t)}{B}\left[U_{-1}\left(x - V_o t + zV_o\frac{t}{B}\right) - U_{-1}\left(x - Z - V_o t + zV_o\frac{t}{B}\right)\right] \tag{22}$$

where B is the depth to the thermocline or bottom (cm), and U_{-1} is the unit step function defined by $U_{-1}(x) = 0$ for $x < 0$ and $U_{-1}(x) = 1$ for $x > 0$. According to Equation 22, $C = 0$ everywhere except within the region $0 < x < L + V_o t$. Within this region, the average concentration is given by

$$C_{AV}(t) = \frac{F_{AM}Z\exp(-\lambda_R t)}{(Z + V_o t)B} \tag{23}$$

Equations 21 and 22 both have the same value at the time given by

$$t_2 = \frac{\pi Z^2 A_z}{2B^2 V_o^2}\left[1 - \frac{2B^2 V_o}{\pi Z A_z} - \left(1 - \frac{4B^2 V_o}{\pi Z A_z}\right)^{1/2}\right]$$

$$\rightarrow \frac{B^2}{\pi A_z} \text{ for } 0 < \frac{4B^2 V_o}{\pi Z A_z} << 1 \tag{24}$$

The limiting value for t_2 in Equation 24 is identical to the value determined by setting z_B equal to B. If $4B^2V_o > \pi ZA_z$ when B is the depth to the thermocline or bottom, this is an indication that the convective effects become important when z_B is less than the depth to the thermocline or bottom. In this case the effective depth of mixing is given by

$$B = \left(\frac{\pi Z A_z}{4V_o}\right)^{1/2}$$

With a value of B given by the above expression, t_2 becomes Z/V_o.

Groundwater and Terrestrial Surface Water Input

Methods used by Charnell et al.[13] can be used to approximate radionuclide inputs to the marine environment from the canal channel, the groundwater, and terrestrial surface water. Using these methods the following expressions can be derived for these inputs:

$$N_s = \frac{f_r F_W r F_A A}{r_u}\exp\left[-\left(\frac{F_W r}{r_u} + \lambda_R\right)t\right] \tag{25}$$

and

$$N_c = \frac{B_c F_c Q}{V_c}\exp\left[-\left(\frac{B_c F_c}{V_c} + \lambda_R\right)t\right] \tag{26}$$

$$N_g = \frac{(1 - f_r)F_A A r F_W B_F F_g}{F_g B_F r_u - r F_W \alpha V_g}\left\{\exp\left[-\left(\frac{F_W r}{r_u} + \lambda_R\right)t\right] - \exp\left[-\left(\frac{B_F F_g}{\alpha V_g} + \lambda_R\right)t\right]\right\} \tag{27}$$

where N_c is the rate at which the radionuclide is added to the ocean from the canal channel, N_s is the rate at which the radionuclide is added to the ocean from terrestrial surface water, N_g is the rate at which the radionuclide is added to the ocean from groundwater, F_c is the ratio of the amount of radionuclide dissolved in the canal water to the total amount present in the canal channel and rubble, F_W is the ratio of the amount of radionuclide dissolved in the surface water to the total amount present on the soil surface, F_g is the ratio of the amount of radionuclide dissolved in the groundwater to the total amount present in the groundwater reservoir, r is the average rainfall, r_u is the unit rain as defined by Charnell, Zorich, and Holly,[13] F_A is the terrestrial fallout input per unit area, A is the area of the terrestrial surface-water drainage system, f_r is the ratio of runoff water to total rainwater, B_F is the flow rate of groundwater, B_c is the net flow rate of water through the canal channel, Q is the total amount of radionuclide initially present in the canal channel and rubble, α is the porosity of the groundwater reservoir, V_c is the volume of water in the canal channel, and V_g is the volume of the groundwater reservoir.

Equation 25 represents the input of surface water which is contaminated by terrestrial fallout. Equation 26 represents the direct contamination of the canal water due to contact with radionuclides in the canal channel and rubble formed by the explosion. Equation 27 represents the contribution from contaminated surface water which reaches the groundwater system through infiltration. By proper choice of parameters Equation 27 represents contamination both by direct groundwater flow into the sea and by the indirect route of groundwater to streams and the sea.

The contributions of these terrestrial inputs to the radionuclide concentration in seawater can be approximated by allowing these inputs to mix with water which contains the direct fallout input. This results in a conservatively high estimate for these terrestrial contributions. The mixing volume based on Equation 21 and 23 is

$$V_M = ZH(\pi A_z t)^{1/2} \text{ for } 0 < t < t_2$$

and

$$V_M = (Z + V_o t)\, HB \text{ for } t > t_2 \tag{28}$$

where V_M is the mixing volume of seawater.

Using these expressions, a material balance for the radionuclide in the mixing volume is

$$\frac{d}{dt}(V_M C_{AV}) = N_s + N_c + N_g - \lambda_R (V_M C_{AV})$$

$$V_M C_{AV} = F_{AM} ZH \text{ at } t = 0 \tag{29}$$

The solution to Equation 29 gives a conservatively high approximation to the total radionuclide concentration in seawater. This solution is

$$C_{AV} = \frac{\exp(-\lambda_R t)}{V_M}\Bigg[F_{AM}HZ + F_A A - f_r F_A A \exp\left(-F_W \frac{rt}{r_u}\right) - Q\exp\left(-\frac{F_c B_c t}{V_c}\right) + \frac{(1-f_r)F_A A F_W r\alpha V_g}{F_g B_F r_u - F_W r\alpha V_g}\exp\left(-\frac{F_g B_F t}{\alpha V_g}\right) - \frac{(1-f_r)F_A A F_g r_u B_F}{F_g B_F r_u - F_W r\alpha V_g}\exp\left(-\frac{F_W rt}{r_u}\right)\Bigg] \tag{30}$$

For many areas, especially areas which have clay soils and a large rainfall, infiltration flow is very small in comparison to runoff. For these areas groundwater terms in Equation 30 can be neglected and f_r can be set equal to unity to give

$$C_{AV} = \frac{\exp(-\lambda_R t}{V_M}\left[F_{AM}HZ + F_A A + Q - F_A A \exp\left(-\frac{F_W rt}{r_u}\right) - Q \exp\left(-\frac{F_c B_c t}{V_c}\right)\right] \tag{31}$$

The radionuclide concentration given by Equation 31 is the basis for developing conservative expressions to estimate the radionuclide content of seafood and the resulting radiation dose to man.

Laplace Transform of Concentration in Seawater

In order to derive expressions for the infinite internal radiation dose to man, it is useful to have the Laplace transform of variables which enter into these expressions. One of these variables is the average radionuclide concentration given by Equation 31. Since the transformation of the concentration given by Equation 31 is more difficult than most other variables, the details for obtaining this transform are given here.

The Laplace transform is defined by

$$\bar{C}_{AV}(p) = \int_0^\infty C_{AV}(t)\exp(-pt)dt \tag{32}$$

where $\overline{C_{AV}}(p)$ is the Laplace transform of $C_{AV}(t)$.
Equation 31 can be written in the general form

$$C_{AV} = \frac{K_s}{t^{1/2}}\sum_{n=1}^{3} K_n \exp(-k_n t) \quad \text{for } 0 < t < t_2 \tag{33}$$

and

$$C_{AV} = \frac{K_L}{K_o + t}\sum_{n=1}^{3} K_n \exp(-k_n t) \quad \text{for } t > t_2 \tag{34}$$

where

K_s is $\frac{1}{HZ(\pi A_z)^{1/2}}$ K_o is $\frac{Z}{V_o}$

K_1 is $F_{AM}HZ + F_A A + Q$ k_1 is λ_R

K_2 is $-F_A A$ k_2 is $\lambda_R + \frac{F_W r}{r_u}$

K_3 is $-Q$ and

K_L is $\frac{1}{HBV_o}$ k_3 is $\lambda_R + \frac{F_c B_c}{V_c}$

The Laplace transform of the general form of Equation 31 is

$$\bar{C}_{AV}(p) = K_s \int_0^{t_2} \frac{1}{t^{1/2}} \sum_{n=1}^{3} K_n \exp[-(k_n + p)t]\,dt$$

$$+ K_L \int_{t_2}^{\infty} \frac{1}{K_o + t} \sum_{n=1}^{3} K_n \exp[-(k_n + p)t]\,dt \qquad (35)$$

Upon making the substitution $x^2 = (k_n + p)t$ in the first integral of Equation 35 and $y = K_o + t$ in the second integral, Equation 35 becomes

$$\bar{C}_{AV}(p) = K_s \sum_{n=1}^{3} K_n \int_0^{[(k_n+p)t_2)]^{1/2}} \exp(-x^2) \frac{(k_n + p)^{1/2}}{x} \cdot \frac{2x}{(k_n+p)}\,dx$$

$$+ K_L \sum_{n=1}^{3} K_n \exp[(k_n + p)K_o] \int_{K_o+t_2}^{\infty} \frac{1}{y} \exp[-(k_n + p)y]\,dy$$

The integrals in Equation 36 can be compared with formulae in Abramowitz and Stegun[23] to show

$$\bar{C}_{AV}(p) = \pi^{1/2} K_s \sum_{n=1}^{3} \frac{K_n}{(k_n + p)^{1/2}} \xi \left\{ [(k_n + p)\,t_2]^{1/2} \right\}$$

$$+ K_L \sum_{n=1}^{3} K_n \exp[(k_n + p)K_o]\,E_1\,[(k_n+p)\,(K_o + t_2)] \qquad (37)$$

Substitution of the values for K and k terms into Equation 37 gives the final result which is

$$\bar{C}_{AV}(p) = \frac{1}{HZA_z^{1/2}} \left[\frac{F_{AM}HZ + F_A A + Q}{(\lambda_R + p)^{1/2}} \xi \left\{ \left[(\lambda_R + p)\,t_2 \right]^{1/2} \right\} \right.$$

$$- \frac{F_A A}{\left(\lambda_R + p + \frac{F_W r}{r_u}\right)^{1/2}} \xi \left\{ \left[\left(\lambda_R + p + \frac{F_W r}{r_u}\right) t_2 \right]^{1/2} \right\}$$

$$\left. - \frac{Q}{\left(\lambda_R + p + \frac{F_c B_c}{V_c}\right)^{1/2}} \xi \left\{ \left[\left(\lambda_R + p + \frac{F_c B_c}{V_c}\right) t_2 \right] \right\} \right]$$

$$+ \frac{1}{HBV_o} \left\{ (F_{AM}HZ + F_A A + Q) \exp\left[(\lambda_R + p) \frac{Z}{V_o} \right] E_1 \left[(\lambda_R + p) \left(t_2 + \frac{Z}{V_o} \right) \right] \right.$$

$$- F_A A \exp\left[\left(\lambda_R + p + \frac{F_W r}{r_u}\right) \frac{Z}{V_o} \right] E_1 \left[\left(\lambda_R + p + \frac{F_W r}{r_u}\right) \left(t_2 + \frac{Z}{V_o} \right) \right]$$

$$\left. - Q \exp\left[\left(\lambda_R + p + \frac{F_c B_c}{V_c}\right) \frac{Z}{V_o} \right] E_1 \left[\left(\lambda_R + p + \frac{F_c B_c}{V_c}\right) \left(t_2 + \frac{Z}{V_o} \right) \right] \right\} \qquad (38)$$

Equation 38 is the expression which is used, with p = 0, in the expressions for infinite radiation dose to man.

METHODS FOR SOLVING DIFFERENTIAL EQUATIONS

Methods for solving ordinary differential equations can usually be grouped under four categories: analytical, semianalytical, finite-difference, or analog computer methods. Analytical or closed-form solutions to Equation 11 are limited to the cases where the system is linear (i.e., the λ_{in} values are constants or functions of t only), or of some very special form which can be reduced to a linear system by a simple transformation. Also, there may be a practical limit on the size of the system, the limit being usually on the order of 5 to 10 equations. Finite-difference methods have no theoretical limitations as to the type or size of system which can be solved, but the expense and time involved in solving equations requiring small time steps can be limiting. Semianalytical solutions fall between analytical and finite-difference solutions in their relative merits. Their limitations as to size and linearity are slightly greater than finite-difference solutions, but they are much less limited than analytical solutions. Their chief advantage over finite-difference techniques is increased speed of solution.

The preceding three methods are applicable to either a hand solution or a digital computer solution. A distinct alternative to these methods is an analog computer solution. Solutions on an analog computer resemble analytical solutions but do not have the linearity restrictions or the same size restrictions as analytical solutions. The wiring diagram required for operation is almost identical to the elemental flow diagram for the ecosystem, but the size of the system of equations which can be solved is limited by size of the computer and the accuracy of the solution is limited by the number and accuracy of electronic components which must be used. Another limitation is that problems must be scaled down in order to keep electrical current and potentials within limits of the analog computer. Further information on analog computers and analog computer solutions is referenced.[24]

Analytical Solutions

Analytical solutions to linear, ordinary differential equations are usually obtained by either the "integrating factor" method or by use of the Laplace transform methods. It can be shown that an integrating factor for Equation 1, if all λ_{ii} are constants, is $\exp(\lambda_{ii}t)$ so that

$$\frac{d}{dt}\left[y_i \exp(\lambda_{ii}t)\right] = \exp(\lambda_{ii}t) \sum_{\substack{n=1 \\ n \neq i}}^{N} \lambda_{in} y_n$$

$$i = 1,2,\ldots N \qquad (39)$$

For many ecosystem problems the major flow of elements and radionuclides can be treated as if they were unidirectional. In Equation 1 this corresponds to setting the $\lambda_{in} = 0$ for $n > i$. If the $\lambda_{in} = 0$ for $n > i$, the solution for each y_i is readily obtained in a sequential manner. As an example, consider the system

$$\frac{dy_1}{dt} + \lambda_{11}y_1 = 0$$

$$y_1(0) = 1$$

$$\frac{dy_2}{dt} + \lambda_{22}y_2 = \lambda_{21}y_1$$

$$y_2(0) = 0$$

$$\frac{d}{dt}[y_1 \exp(\lambda_{11}t)] = 0$$

$$y_1 \exp(\lambda_{11}t) = 1$$

$$y_1 = \exp(-\lambda_{11}t)$$

$$\frac{d}{dt}[y_2 \exp(\lambda_{22}t)] = \lambda_{21} \exp[(\lambda_{22} - \lambda_{11})t]$$

$$y_2 \exp(\lambda_{22}t) = \frac{\lambda_{21}}{\lambda_{22} - \lambda_{11}} \left\{\exp[(\lambda_{22} - \lambda_{11})t] - 1\right\}$$

$$y_2 = \frac{\lambda_{22}}{\lambda_{22} - \lambda_{11}} [\exp(-\lambda_{11}t) - \exp(-\lambda_{22}t)]$$

If the $\lambda_{in} \neq 0$ for $n > i$, the solution to Equation 2 by integrating factor method becomes much more difficult. An alternative method, when the λ_{in} are constants, involves use of the Laplace transform. The Laplace transform is defined by

$$L\left\{y(t)\right\} = \bar{y}(s) = \int_0^\infty y(t) \exp(-st)dt$$

A useful property of the transform is

$$L\left\{\frac{dy}{dt}\right\} = s\bar{y}(s) - y(0)$$

This property converts Equation 1 into a system of algebraic equation given by

$$(s + \lambda_{ii})\bar{y}_i - \sum_{\substack{n=1 \\ n \neq i}}^{N} \lambda_{in}\bar{y}_n = y_i(0)$$

$$i = 1,2,\ldots N \qquad (40)$$

The algebraic solution of Equation 40 can be expressed in the form

$$\bar{y}_i = \sum_{n=1}^{N} A_n \prod_{m=1}^{N} \frac{1}{s + b_m}$$

$$1 = 1,2,\ldots N \qquad (41)$$

where A_n is a function of s and $y_n(0)$ and b_m is a constant for those cases where $\lambda_{in} = 0$ for $n > i$, $b_m = \lambda_{mn}$

The inverse transform of $\overline{y}$ gives y as a function of time. The inverse for the system given by Equation 41 for the case in which no two b_m are equal is

$$y_i(t) = \sum_{n=1}^{N} A_n \sum_{m=1}^{N} \exp(-b_m t) \prod_{\substack{j=1 \\ j \neq m}}^{N} \frac{1}{b_j - b_m} \tag{42}$$

The Laplace transform method applied to the preceding example gives

$$(s + \lambda_{11})\overline{y}_1 = 1$$

$$\overline{y}_1 = \frac{1}{s + \lambda_{11}}$$

$$(s + \lambda_{22})\overline{y}_2 = \frac{\lambda_{21}}{s + \lambda_{11}}$$

$$\overline{y}_2 = \frac{\lambda_{21}}{(s + \lambda_{22})(s + \lambda_{11})}$$

$$y_1 = \exp(-\lambda_{11} t)$$

and

$$y_2 = \frac{\lambda_{21} \exp(-\lambda_{11} t)}{\lambda_{22} - \lambda_{11}} + \frac{\lambda_{21} \exp(-\lambda_{22} t)}{\lambda_{11} - \lambda_{22}}$$

$$= \frac{\lambda_{21}}{\lambda_{22} - \lambda_{11}} \left[\exp(-\lambda_{11} t) - \exp(-\lambda_{22} t)\right]$$

Another feature of the Laplace transform method, one which makes it particularly attractive for radiation dose calculations, is the final value theorem[25] from which the following expression can be derived:

$$Y = \lim_{s \to 0} \overline{y}(s)$$

where Y is

$$\int_0^\infty y dt \tag{43}$$

Equation 43 is true only for those cases where y(s) is analytic (i.e., the derivative of y with respect to s exists) and the real part of s (s is a complex number having both a real and an imaginary part) is greater than zero. For cases where Equation 43 is not valid, infinite dose cannot be calculated because Y will not have a finite value but these cases are usually of no interest.

The infinite-time radiation dose is an upper limit of the actual lifetime dose. For Standard Man,[6] the infinite-time dose is given by

$$D_\infty = R \int_0^\infty y dt = RY = R \lim_{s \to 0} \overline{y}(s)$$

where D_∞ is the infinite-time dose to Standard Man and R is the dose rate per unit of the radionuclide deposited in the critical organ of Standard Man (constant for a given radionuclide and a given critical organ).

Using Equation 43, the value of Y_i can easily be determined from Equation 41 as

$$Y_i = \sum_{n=1}^{N} A_n \prod_{m=1}^{N} \frac{1}{b_m}$$

$$i = 1,2,\ldots N$$

In the example problem, the Y values for the two compartments are

$$Y_1 = \frac{1}{\lambda_{11}}$$

and

$$Y_2 = \frac{\lambda_{21}}{\lambda_{22}\lambda_{11}}$$

The direct integration of y_2 gives

$$\int_0^\infty y_2 dt = \frac{\lambda_{21}}{\lambda_{22} - \lambda_{11}} \int_0^\infty [\exp(-\lambda_{11}t) - \exp(-\lambda_{22}t)] \, dt$$

$$= \frac{\lambda_{21}}{\lambda_{22} - \lambda_{11}} \left(\frac{1}{\lambda_{11}} - \frac{1}{\lambda_{22}}\right) = \frac{\lambda_{21}}{\lambda_{11}\lambda_{22}}$$

Therefore, if compartment 2 represented man and Compartment 1 represented his environment, and approximate calculation of his finite-time dose due to a unit amount of radionuclide introduced into his environment would be

$$D_\infty = \frac{R\lambda_{21}}{\lambda_{11}\lambda_{22}}$$

Because infinite-time doses can be easily calculated by the Laplace transform method, this method can be used in a preliminary analysis of the ecosystem even if a finite-difference or semianalytical procedure will eventually be used. The preliminary analysis will screen all of the radionuclides which might be introduced into an ecosystem and can be used to eliminate those which will contribute only an insignificant infinite-time dose. Also, for each significant radionuclide, the relative hazard of each ecological pathway leading to man can be judged. Since the dose to man for each radionuclide is approximately proportional to the Y value of that radionuclide for man, those pathways which contribute only a negligible fraction of Y can be combined into simpler, more approximate pathways and need not be considered in detail. However, those pathways which contribute significantlty to Y must be considered in detail and, in fact, may require more detail than was used in the initial calculations for Y. The Laplace transform method can quantitatively show the contribution of each pathway to Y without the need for actually solving the system of differential equations.

Finite-Difference and Semianalytical Methods

There are many finite-difference techniques which can be used to solve Equation 1. In all of these techniques, the derivative is approximated by differences in y values. Two frequently used techniques are the Runge-Kutta-Gill method (e.g., Ralston and Wilf[26]) and the modified Hamming[27] method. In the Runge-Kutta-Gill method, the value of y at a new time is found from the value of y at the present time by the following sequence of steps:

(1) set $P_i(0) = 0$ for $i = 1,2,\ldots N$,

(2) set $k = 1$,

(3) set $i = 1$,

(4) $y_i(t + \Delta t) = y_i(t) + \alpha_k \Delta t[\dot{y}_i(t) - \beta_k P_i(t)]$,

(5) $P_i(t + \Delta t) = P_i(t) + 3\alpha_k[\dot{y}_i(t) - \beta_k P_i(t)] - \gamma_k \dot{y}_i(t)$

(6) repeat steps (4) and (5) for $i = 2, 3, \ldots N$,

(7) repeat steps (3) through (6) for $k = 2, 3$, and 4,

(8) repeat steps (2) through (7) for a new time

where P_i is an auxiliary variable,

$\dot{y}(t)$ is $\dfrac{dy}{dt}$,

Δt is the time step,

α_k is 0.5, $1 - (0.5)^{1/2}$, $1 + (0.5)^{1/2}$, and 1/6 for $k = 1, 2, 3$, and 4,

β_k is 2, 1, 1, and 2 for $k = 1, 2, 3$, and 4, and

γ_k is 0.5, $1 - (0.5)^{1/2}$, $1 + (0.5)^{1/2}$, and 0.5 for $k = 1, 2, 3$, and 4.

Since the Runge-Kutta-Gill method requires saving only a few intermediate values during a calculation step, it does not require much computer storage when used on a digital computer. However, it requires four evaluations of the derivative for each time step, and this can lead to an excessive amount of computer time. The modified Hamming method requires only two evaluations of the derivative for each time step to achieve the same accuracy, but the required computer storage may be twice that required for the Runge-Kutta-Gill method. The modified Hamming method proceeds in the following steps:

(1) set $i = 1$,

(2) $P_i(t + \Delta t) = y_i(t - 3\Delta t) + \dfrac{4\Delta t}{3}[2\dot{y}_i(t) - \dot{y}_i(t - \Delta t) + 2\dot{y}_i(t - 2\Delta t)]$,

(3) $M_i(t + \Delta t) = \dfrac{112}{121}[Q_i(t) - P_i(t)] + P_i(t + \Delta t)$,

(4) $Q_i(t + \Delta t) = \dfrac{1}{8}\left\{9y_i(t) - y_i(t - 2\Delta t) + 3\Delta t[M_i(t + \Delta t) - 2\dot{y}_i(t) - \dot{y}_i(t - \Delta t)]\right\}$,

(5) $y_i(t + \Delta t) = Q_i(t + \Delta t) - \dfrac{9}{121}[Q_i(t + \Delta t) - P_i(t + \Delta t)]$

(6) repeat steps (2) through (5) for $i = 1, 2, 3, \ldots N$

(7) repeat steps (1) through (6) for a new time

where P_i, M_i, and Q_i are auxiliary variables.

The modified Hamming method requires a starting method, usually the Runge-Kutta-Gill method, to calculate the first four time steps. The remaining points are then calculated by the modified Hamming method.

In contrast to finite-difference methods in which the derivative is approximated, semianalytical methods rely on an approximation to the solution. A very useful semianalytical method is the matrix exponential technique as given by Ball and Adams.[28] Equation 1 can be represented in matrix form as

$$\frac{d\vec{y}}{dt} = \Lambda\vec{y}$$

where $\vec{y}$ is a column vector of the y_i variables, and Λ is the matrix of all the λ_{in} and λ_{ii} values.

If the λs are constants, the solution to Equation 66 in matrix notation is

$$\vec{y}(t) = \exp(\Lambda t)\vec{y}(0) \tag{47}$$

The solution to Equation 46 can also be written in incremental form as

$$\vec{y}(t + \Delta t) = \exp(\Lambda\Delta t)\vec{y}(t) \tag{48}$$

Ordinarily, the reduction of Equation 47 or 48 to explicit expressions for each y_i can be very difficult. However, the Taylor Series expansion of the matrix exponential function is analogous to the scalar exponential function so that

$$\exp(\Lambda\Delta t) = I + \Delta t + \frac{(\Lambda\Delta t)^2}{2} + \ldots \tag{49}$$

where I is the identity matrix.

If Δt is small enough, the series converges very fast and only a few terms are needed in Equation 69. Once the matrix exponential function has been computed, it need not be computed again unless the Δt value is changed, and the solution for any time can be calculated in a stepwise fashion from Equation 48. Since only a simple matrix multiplication is required, the solution proceeds very rapidly.

As an example of the matrix exponential method, the preceding example problem can be written in matrix form as

$$\frac{d}{dt}\begin{bmatrix} y_1 \\ y_2 \end{bmatrix} = \begin{bmatrix} -\lambda_{11} & 0 \\ \lambda_{21} & -\lambda_{22} \end{bmatrix}\begin{bmatrix} y_1 \\ y_2 \end{bmatrix}$$

The formal solution is

$$\begin{bmatrix} y_1 \\ y_2 \end{bmatrix} = \exp\left\{\begin{bmatrix} \lambda_{11}t & 0 \\ \lambda_{21}t & -\lambda_{22}t \end{bmatrix}\right\}\begin{bmatrix} 1 \\ 0 \end{bmatrix}$$

and the incremental form is

$$\begin{bmatrix} y_1(t + \Delta t) \\ y_2(t + \Delta t) \end{bmatrix} = \exp\left\{\begin{bmatrix} -\lambda_{11}\Delta t & 0 \\ \lambda_{21}\Delta t & -\lambda_{22}\Delta t \end{bmatrix}\right\}\begin{bmatrix} y_1(t) \\ y_2(t) \end{bmatrix}$$

The series expansion for the matrix exponential function is

$$\exp\left\{\begin{bmatrix} -\lambda_{11}\Delta t & 0 \\ \lambda_{21}\Delta t & -\lambda_{22}\Delta t \end{bmatrix}\right\} = \begin{bmatrix} 1 & 0 \\ 0 & 1 \end{bmatrix} + \begin{bmatrix} -\lambda_{11}\Delta t & 0 \\ \lambda_{21}\Delta t & -\lambda_{22}\Delta t \end{bmatrix} + \ldots$$

Therefore, the expressions for y can be written as

$$\begin{bmatrix} y_1(t + \Delta t) \\ y_2(t + \Delta t) \end{bmatrix} = \begin{bmatrix} 1 - \lambda_{11}\Delta t + \ldots & 0 \\ \lambda_{21}\Delta t + \ldots & 1 - \lambda_{22}\Delta t + \ldots \end{bmatrix} \begin{bmatrix} y_1(t) \\ y_2(t) \end{bmatrix}$$

Some modification of the basic method is required when the λ_{in} are not constants; this is given by Ball and Adams.[28] For systems in which the λ_{in} are constants, the method is virtually exact while for other cases, the accuracy tends to be better than most finite-difference techniques. The big disadvantage of the matrix exponential method, when applied to a digital computer, is the large amount of storage required. This storage can easily be five times the storage required for the modified Hamming method and 10 times that required for the Runge-Kutta-Gill method. However, because of its accuracy and speed of solution, the matrix exponential method is preferred if the problem can fit on the computer.

APPLICATION TO NUCLEAR CRATERING EXPLOSIONS

A mathematical model designed to simulate the entire process of radionuclide distribution in a representative portion of the biosphere would be required to consider a large number of complex variables including (1) the 300 or more radionuclides produced by nuclear cratering explosions, (2) one to many fallout patterns, (3) an indefinite number of ecosystems and all material transport pathways that characterize them, (4) physical and/or biological transport mechanisms responsible for materials transfer through each of the pathways, (5) an indefinite number of population subgroups depending on ecological and cultural factors which determine dietary habitats, and (6) a variety of physiological parameters which are different for different radionuclides and may vary with respect to age and other characteristics of individuals or subgroups comprising the reference population.

It is obvious that a detailed model considering all of these parameters, and field-tested under realistic conditions to determine its accuracy, would provide an excellent basis for evaluating potential radionuclide intakes by people living in or near radionuclide contaminated environments. However, because of the complexities of situations such as nuclear excavation of a sea-level canal, it is neither practical nor is it necessary to consider all aspects of radionuclide redistribution by ecological processes. Many of the radionuclides produced by nuclear cratering explosions (or other nuclear activities) are produced in such small quantities or have such short lives that their potential contributions to internal radiation doses are negligible. Many possible redistribution pathways are of no direct concern because they do not lead to man, and many of those that do lead to man are inconsequential. Furthermore, experimental data from which parameter values could be derived for development of a detailed model are neither available, nor could they be obtained during the short time ordinarily available for a feasibility study. In any case, many of the mathematical sophistications involved in detailed models have very little effect on the final outcome of the modeling effort.

General Approach to Ecological Cycling

In a very complex nuclear situation a series of models should be used to identify the most important radionuclides and other factors affecting calculation of potential radiation doses to man. The simplest model in the series is based on conservative assumptions concerning the general behavior of radionuclides in the biosphere and is used to calculate the maximum possible contribution of each radionuclide to the internal radiation dose. Those radionuclides whose combined contributions add up to an insignificant dose (i.e., 1 rem infinite-time dose) are eliminated from further consideration. Those remaining are evaluated on the basis of a generalized transport model which is more realistic than the first-step model but still contains conservative assumptions concerning transport processes and makes use of parameter values which tend to overestimate the potential radiation dose due to each radionuclide. This process of elimination is repeated until only the most important radionuclides remain. Only these radionuclides are treated in the most detailed, most realistic ecological model, and this model is based on the best information available concerning the transport of specific radionuclides in particular transport pathways leading to man. The advantage of this approach is that the number of radionuclides to be considered at each step decreases as the complexity of the model increases; this allows both data collection and data interpretation programs to concentrate on the most important aspects of radionuclide redistribution and transport to man.

Modified Specific Activity Model

A simple two-compartment model is used for the second screening of radionuclides.* In this model, Compartment 1 represents a total diet and Compartment 2 represents a critical organ of Standard Man.[6]

Flow rates in and out of Compartment 2 are based on physiological data tabulated by ICRP.[6] For each element, the flow rate from Compartment 1 to Compartment 2 is the product of the element ingestion rate and the fraction of the element ingested that reaches the critical organ. Flow rates out of Compartment 2 depend on the amount of element present in the compartment, biological elimination rate coefficient of the element, and radioactive decay rate coefficient of the radionuclide. Metabolic discrimination between a radionuclide and its corresponding stable element is assumed to be negligible in this step.

Specific activity of each radionuclide in Compartment 1, i.e., the ratio of each radionuclide to the corresponding stable element, is assumed to be the same as that of the radioactive debris produced in the nuclear cratering explosion (or other situation). Estimates of specific activities of radionuclides are based on source-term predictions and chemical composition of the geological and other materials with which the radionuclides are mixed during the cavity-formation stage of the cratering process.

Using these specific activities to characterize Compartment 1, the solution to the two-compartment model, for all organs except the gastrointestinal tract, is as follows:

$$S_1 = S_1(0)\exp(-\lambda_R t) \text{ and}$$

$$y_2 = \frac{F_{21}S_1(0)\exp(-\lambda_R t)}{\lambda_B}[1 - \exp(-\lambda_B t)]$$

where $S_1(O)$ is the initial specific activity of the radioacive debris and F_{21} is the element flow rate into Compartment 2.

The movement of material through the gastrointestinal tract cannot be adequately

* Initial screening is based on source term predictions. Radionuclides considered in the second screening are those having an inventory of at least 1 Ci at 4 weeks after one or more of the releases considered.

described by a biological elimination rate because the material does not remain in one place long enough to allow for any significant mixing. A simple approximation for the average radionuclide content of a portion of the tract is the product of the rate at which the radionuclide enters the portion and the time it takes the material to traverse that portion. The resulting expression is

$$y_2 = F_{21} S_1(0)\tau_2 \exp(-\lambda_R t)$$

where τ_2 is the time it takes material to traverse the portion of the tract, and U_{-1} would appear in the differential equation. Here we give only the solution, and the case of x < O is of no interest.

If man is excluded from the contaminated area for a given time, the value of $S_1(O)$ to be used in the above expressions would be the initial value reduced by the radioactive decay during the exclusion time.

In addition to factors needed to calculate y_2, the ICRP has tabulated data needed to calculate the dose rate to a critical organ of Standand Man per unit of radionuclide.[6] This value is the R term in Equations 50 and 51 below, and is constant for a given radionuclide. The expression to calculate the internal dose for all organs except the gastrointestinal tract is

$$D = RF_{21}S_1(0)\left\{\frac{1}{\lambda_R(\lambda_B + \lambda_R)} - \frac{\exp(-\lambda_R t)}{\lambda_R\lambda_B} + \frac{\exp\left[-(\lambda_R + \lambda_B)t\right]}{\lambda_B(\lambda_B + \lambda_R)}\right\} \quad (50)$$

The equivalent expression for the gastrointestional tract is

$$D = \frac{RF_{21}S_1(0)\tau_2}{\lambda_R}\exp(-\lambda_R t) \quad (51)$$

where R is 51.1 ε/m, ε is the effective energy absorbed by the organ (MeV/dis.), and m is the mass of organ, if it is not part of the gastrointestional tract, or twice the mass of the contents of the reference portion of the gastrointestional tract (g).

Equations 50 and 51 are the expressions used in the initial screening of the radionuclides. Approximately 270 of the 300 or more radionuclides can be shown to produce an insignificant dose when the total dose is obtained by summing the contribution from each of the 270 radionuclides. As a conservative estimate, these 270 radionuclides can be assigned a dose contribution equal to this insignificant dose which can then be added to the doses determined for the other radionuclides by using more sophisticated models.

The specific activity model results in highly conservative overestimates of potential internal radiation doses because it ignores the dilution effects of several important processes. In the first place, the estimates of initial specific activity, $S_1(O)$, are based on the assumption that radionuclides produced are mixed only with the stable materials contained in the fireball volume. In the cratering process these materials are actually mixed with a considerable volume of rubble, and materials actually deposited in the fallout field have a lower specific activity than calculated for use in Equations 50 and 51. Furthermore, it is assumed that radionuclides and their stable element counterparts follow the same transport pathways and exhibit the same metabolic behavior, but the two-compartment model ignores the effects of environmental and biological dilution plus the time required for food chain transport on the specific activity in different environmental and biological compartments. Since exclusion of these factors from the specific activity model results in overestimates of dose, the radionuclides eliminated probably contribute less to the potential radiation dose than would be indicated by the model.

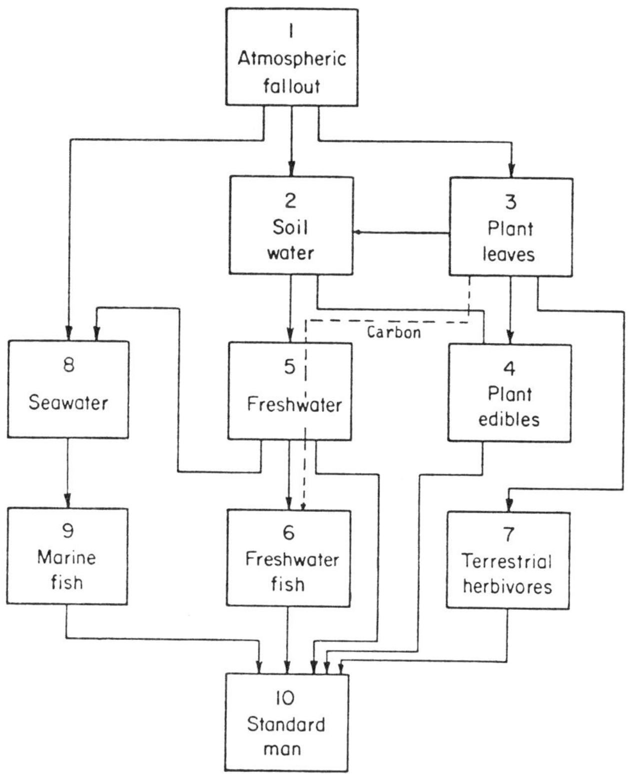

FIGURE 6. Ten-compartment food web.

Generalized Transport Model

The next step toward a more realistic evaluation considers a simple ecosystem model containing 10 compartments. A diagram showing these compartments and the main pathways leading to man is given in Figure 6. A calculation based on this model requires, in addition to ICRP data and estimates of initial specific activities, fallout predictions (e.g., Reference 3) and estimates of transfer coefficients for those radionuclides remaining after the first screening.

The food-web diagram shown in Figure 6 is a compromise between the hypothetical and ultraconservative two-compartment model described above and the extremely complex, more realistic, but mathematically unwieldy model that would result if all the ecological pathways and transport processes were to be included. It is intended to represent only the major kinds of food-web pathways in an area large enough to include one or more terrestrial, freshwater, and marine ecosystems, and to indicate a high degree of ecological coupling between man and environment, including food and water. The diet consists of wild or cultivated plants, wild or domesticated terrestrial animals (mainly herbivorous birds and mammals, but not excluding reptiles, amphibians, etc.), freshwater fish (and other freshwater animals), marine fish and other seafoods and water that is taken from streams. The transfer coefficients and other data used to represent the 10 compartment of the second-step model (Figure 6) are based on "average" or "typical" components of each compartment. Whenever there is uncertainty concerning which parameter values are most realistic, relatively high input rates and low output rates are selected to make the dose estimates conservatively high.

Since parameters used in the model are dependent not only on the kinds of ecosystems considered but also on their location in the fallout field, a method of indicating location is required. One convenient method of indicating the location of a terrestrial ecosystem is to divide the area into watersheds or larger drainage areas. This method is based on the assumption that most of the transfer of elements between watersheds is by rivers; and, except for rivers, each watershed behaves almost independently of others. In order to make dose calculations based on the 10-compartment model more conservative, the terrestrial ecosystems are located in the watershed which has the highest fallout input, and the lowest rate of radionuclide loss due to runoff; but calculations for the aquatic compartments make use of a higher runoff rate. Similarly, a conservatively high dose rate contribution is calculated for the marine ecosystems by arbitrarily locating it to maximize the fallout input to sea water, maximize the radionuclide input from surface water, and minimize the dilution due to dispersion and convection.

Fallout input is determined by a separate calculation which gives the amount of each radionuclide per unit area as a function of location at a given time. In order to apply the fallout results to the model, the fallout concentration for each watershed segment, i.e., areas between isodose contours, are weighted by area to provide an average concentration for the entire watershed. For example, if the area of the watershed is 2000 km², the area of the watershed enclosed by the 10 μCi/cm² and 1 μCi/cm² fallout contours is 100 km², that for the 1 μCi/cm² and 0.1 μCi/cm² is 900 km², and that by the 0.1 μCi/cm² and 0.01 μCi/cm² is 1000 km², the fallout input is given by

$$F_A = \frac{(10)(100) + (1)(900) + (0.1)(1000)}{2000} = 1\ \mu\text{Ci/cm}^2$$

where F_A is the average fallout concentration on a watershed. The results obtained by this method are about a factor of three higher for each contour interval than would be obtained by using the geometric means of the boundary contours.

The differential equations describing the specific activity in many of the compartments of Figure 6 can be derived from Equation 3 by using the definition

$$S_i = \frac{y_i}{C_i} \tag{52}$$

which gives

$$\frac{dS_i}{dt} = \frac{\frac{dy_i}{dt}}{C_i} - \frac{y_i}{C_i^2} \cdot \frac{dC_i}{dt} = \frac{\frac{dy_i}{dt}}{C_i} - \frac{S_i}{C_i} \cdot \frac{dC_i}{dt} \tag{53}$$

where S_i is the specific activity of the radionuclide in the ith compartment (μCi/g element).

These equations are as follows.

(a) Plant Edibles for All Elements Except Hydrogen

$$\frac{dS_4}{dt} = f_{43}\lambda_g S_3 + f_{42}\lambda_g S_2 - (\lambda_R + \lambda_g) S_4 \tag{54}$$

$$S_4(0) = 0 \tag{55}$$

where S_4 is the specific activity of the radionuclide in plant edibles (μCi/g element), S_2 is the specific activity of the radionuclide in the soil water (μCi/g element), S_3 is the specific activity of the radionuclide on plant leaves (μCi/g element), f_{43} is the fraction of the element in plant edibles which comes from leaves, f_{42} is the fraction of the element in plant edibles which comes from the soil, λ_g is the growth rate coefficient for plant edibles (day^{-1}), C_4 is the total element content, both stable and radioactive, of plant edibles (g element), and

$$\lambda_g \text{ is } \frac{\frac{dC_4}{dt}}{C_4}$$

(b) Freshwater Fish for All Elements Except Carbon (Neglecting Growth)

$$\frac{dS_6}{dt} = \lambda_{B_6} S_5 - (\lambda_R + \lambda_{B_6}) S_6 \quad (56)$$

$$S_6(0) = 0 \quad (57)$$

where S_6 is the specific activity of the radionuclide in freshwater fish (μCi/g dry weight), S_5 is the specific activity of the radionuclide in freshwater (μCi/g element), and λ_{B6} is the biological elimination rate of the element from freshwater fish (day^{-1}).

(c) Freshwater Fish for Carbon (Neglecting Growth)

$$\frac{dS_6}{dt} = \lambda_{B_6} S_3 - (\lambda_{B_6} + \lambda_R) S_6 \quad (58)$$

$$S_6(0) = 0 \quad (59)$$

(d) Animals (Terrestrial Herbivores, Neglecting Growth)

$$\frac{dS_7}{dt} = \lambda_{B_7} S_3 - (\lambda_R + \lambda_{B_7}) S_7 \quad (60)$$

$$S_7(0) = 0 \quad (61)$$

where S_7 is the concentration of radionuclide in animals (μCi/g element) and λ_{B7} is the biological elimination rate of the element from animals (day^{-1}).

(e) Marine Fish (Neglecting Growth)

$$\frac{dS_9}{dt} = \lambda_{B_9} S_8 - (\lambda_R + \lambda_{B_9}) S_9 \quad (62)$$

$$S_9(0) = 0 \quad (63)$$

where S_9 is the concentration of radionuclide in marine fish (μCi/g element), λ_{B9} is the biological elimination rate of the element from marine fish (day^{-1}), and S_8 is the specific activity of the radionuclide in seawater (μCi/g element).

The equation for freshwater fish (Compartment 6) for carbon is different from all other elements because the herbivorous fish obtain most of their carbon from leaves and other vegetation which fall into the streams rather than from carbon dissolved in the water.

(f) Plant Edibles for Hydrogen

The equation for plant edibles (Compartment 4) for hydrogen is derived from a combination of Equations 2 and 3. The evapotranspiration stream is a major transport mechanism for hydrogen and must be included in a hydrogen model. On the assumption that the loss of rainwater to groundwater is negligible, the flow rate of any element from soil water (Compartment 2) to plant edibles via the evapotranspiration mechanism is

$$F_{42} = (1 - f_r)rC_2 \tag{64}$$

where F_{42} is the element flow rate from soil to plant edibles via evapotranspiration (g element/cm^2/day), C_2 is the stable element concentration in soil water (g element/cm^3), r is an average rainfall rate (cm/day), and f_r is the ratio of runoff water to total rainwater.

It will be shown in the derivation of the equation for soil water that a suitable expression for C_2 is

$$C_2 = X_2 + \frac{F_A F_W}{S_{01} r_u} \exp\left(-\frac{rF_W t}{r_u}\right) \tag{65}$$

where F_W is the ratio of the amount of radinuclide dissolved in surface water to the total amount present on the soil surface, S_{01} is the initial specific activity of the radionuclide in the fallout (μCi/g element), r_u is the unit rain defined by Charnell, Zorich, and Holly[13] (cm), and X_2 is the normal concentration of the element in soil water (g element/cm^3).

Some of the element entering the plant edibles through the evapotranspiration mechanism goes toward maintaining the normal concentration of the element in the plant edibles during growth. Therefore, the loss rate of the element by evapotranspiration is less than the intake due to this growth. The elimination coefficient, including radioactive decay, then becomes

$$\lambda_{44} = \frac{(1 - f_r)(1 - X_{W_4})\rho_W r}{X_{W_4} W_4} - \lambda_g + \lambda_R \tag{66}$$

where λ_{44} is the elimination rate coefficient (day^{-1}), X_4 is the concentration of element in plant edibles dry weight), X_{W4} is the water content of plant edibles (g element/g) W_4 is the biomass of plant edibles (g dry weight/g wet weight), and ϱ_w is the density of water (g water/cm^3).

Note that the factor $(1 - X_{W4})$ is the ratio of dry weight to wet weight and is needed because biomass is usually expressed on a dry-weight basis.

Using the above expressions for F_{42}, C_2, and λ_{44}, the equation for plant edibles for hydrogen is

$$\frac{dS_4}{dt} = \frac{S_2 r(1 - f_r)\left[X_2 r_u + \frac{F_W F_A}{S_{01}} \exp\left(-\frac{rF_W t}{r_u}\right)\right]}{W_4 X_4 r_u} + f_{43}\lambda_g S_3 - S_4\left[\lambda_R + \frac{r\rho_W(1 - f_r)(1 - X_{W_4})}{W_4 X_{W_4}}\right] \tag{67}$$

$$S_4(0) = 0 \tag{68}$$

(g) Plant Leaves

The equation for plant leaves (Compartment 3) has a direct input from atmospheric fallout. The time required to deposit this fallout is small (less than 1 day) in comparison to the time of interest for dose calculations (several years). Therefore this input is treated as an initial condition to the plant leaves equation.

In addition to providing a non-zero initial condition, the direct fallout input complicates the plant leaves equation by contributing more stable element than that which normally appears on the leaves. This excess amount would be removed from the leaves by the same weathering process which removes the radionuclide. Therefore, a differential equation for this excess stable element can be written as

$$\frac{dC_{X3}}{dt} = -k_W C_{X3} \qquad (69)$$

$$C_{X3}(0) = \frac{f_I F_A}{S_{01} W_3} \qquad (70)$$

where C_{x3} is the concentration of excess stable element on leaves (g element/g dry weight), f_I is the fraction of fallout intercepted by plant leaves, W_3 is the biomass of plant leaves (g dry weight/cm^2), and k_w is a weathering elimination rate as defined by Miller and Lee[29] (day^{-1}).

Note that the term F_A/S_{O1} is the deposition of stable element, expressed as g element/cm^2, which accompanies the radioactive fallout.

The solution to Equation 69 with Equation 70 is

$$C_{X3} = \frac{f_I F_A}{S_{01} W_3} \exp(-k_W t) \qquad (71)$$

Combining Equation 71 with the normal concentration gives

$$C_3 = X_3 + \frac{f_I F_A}{S_{01} W_3} \exp(-k_W t) \qquad (72)$$

where C_3 is the stable element concentration on leaves (g element/g dry weight) and X_3 is the normal concentration of the element in leaves (g element/g dry weight).

Using Equation 72, the differential equation for the specific activity of a radionuclide on plant leaves is

$$\frac{dS_3}{dt} = -S_3 \left[\lambda_R + \frac{k_W X_3 W_3}{X_3 W_3 + \frac{f_I F_A}{S_{01}} \exp(-k_W t)} \right] \qquad (73)$$

$$S_3(0) = \frac{f_I F_A}{X_3 W_3 + \frac{f_I F_A}{S_{01}}} \qquad (74)$$

(h) Soil Water

The equation for soil water (Compartment 2) has the same complications arising from a direct fallout input as the equation for plant leaves. In addition, there are other complications arising from the fact that the soil water is in motion and, as such, is not a real storage compartment. It is the upper layer of soil which is the actual storage compartment. Using the simplifying assumption that rainfall and runoff are continuous, the methods used by Charnell et al.[12,13] can be used to derive a differential equation for the excess stable element in the soil compartment. This equation is

$$\frac{dC_{X2}}{dt} = k_W W_3 C_{X3} - \frac{r F_W C_{X2}}{r_u} \qquad (75)$$

$$C_{X2}(0) = \frac{(1 - f_I) F_A}{S_{01}} \qquad (76)$$

where C_{x2} is the areal concentration of excess stable element in the soil surface (g element/cm²).

The solution to Equation 75 with Equations 76 and 71 is

$$C_{X2} = \frac{F_A}{S_{01}}\left[\frac{f_I k_w r_u}{rF_W - r_u k_w}\exp(-k_w t) + \frac{rF_W(1-f_I) - r_u k_w}{rF_W - r_u k_w}\exp\left(-\frac{rF_W t}{r_u}\right)\right] \tag{77}$$

Existing evidence indicates that f_I is no greater than 0.3 even for very dense vegetation. Since the predictions from the 10-compartment model are probably no better than a factor of two, the coefficient of the second exponential function can be taken as one for a conservative approximation. Also, if k_w is small, the first term in Equation 77 will be negligible in comparison to the second. Conversely, if k_w is large, the first term may be significant initially (approximately 30% of the second term), but the exponential function will reduce it faster than the second term. From these considerations a simpler but adequate expression for C_{x2} is

$$C_{X2} \approx \frac{F_A}{S_{01}}\exp\left(-\frac{rF_W t}{r_u}\right)$$

The expression which gives the rate that the excess stable element is removed from the soil by the rain is the negative term in Equation 75. The corresponding flow rate of water from the soil is simply r (cm³/cm²/day). Therefore, the stable element concentration in soil water, including the normal concentration is

$$C_2 = \frac{rF_W F_A}{r_u S_{01} r}\exp\left(-\frac{rF_W t}{r_u}\right) + X_2$$

$$= \frac{F_W F_A}{r_u S_{01}}\exp\left(-\frac{rF_W t}{r_u}\right) + X_2 \tag{78}$$

A differential equation similar to Equation 75 can be written for the radionuclide in the soil. Multiplying this expression by (F_w/r_u) transforms it to the differential equation for the concentration of the radionuclide in soil water. Using Equations 78 and 53, this latter equation becomes the differential equation for the specific activity of soil water which is

$$\frac{dS_2}{dt} = \frac{X_3W_3 + \dfrac{f_I F_A}{S_{01}}\exp(-k_w t)}{X_2 r_u + \dfrac{F_W F_A}{S_{01}}\exp\left(-\dfrac{rF_W t}{r_u}\right)} F_W k_w S_3$$

$$\frac{dS_2}{dt} = \frac{X_3W_3 + \dfrac{f_I F_A}{S_{01}}\exp(-k_w t)}{X_2 r_u + \dfrac{F_W F_A}{S_{01}}\exp\left(-\dfrac{rF_W t}{r_u}\right)} F_W k_w S_3 - S_2\left[\lambda_R + \frac{rF_W X_2}{X_2 r_u + \dfrac{F_W F_A}{S_{01}}\exp\left(-\dfrac{rF_W t}{r_u}\right)}\right] \tag{79}$$

$$S_2(0) = \frac{(1 - f_I) F_W F_A}{X_2 r_u + \dfrac{(1 - f_I) F_W F_A}{S_{01}}} \quad (80)$$

(i) Freshwater

If it is assumed that the radionuclide concentration in freshwater is identical to that of soil water, the specific activity of freshwater is simply the product of the specific activity of soil water and the ratio of the stable element concentrations of soil water and freshwater. Therefore, the equation for freshwater is

$$S_5 = S_2 \frac{X_2 r_u + \dfrac{F_W F_A}{S_{01}} \exp\left(-\dfrac{r F_W t}{r_u}\right)}{X_5 r_u} \quad (81)$$

where X_5 is the concentration of the element in freshwater (g element/cm^3).

(j) Seawater

The physical transport of radionuclides in the marine environment is better described by a partial differential equation than by an ordinary differential equation. A mathematical model to describe this transport is based on a model derived by Bloom and Raines,[18] and it gives the concentration of a radionuclide in seawater, as a function of time, due to inputs from marine fallout, surface runoff and groundwater flow. By properly selecting the parameters, the term describing the direct contamination of groundwater can describe the contamination of water in the canal channel. The actual radionuclide input into the sea through groundwater is negligible in comparison to the surface water input. From these considerations, the equation for the specific activity in seawater is

$$S_8 = \frac{\left\{HZF_{AM} + AF_A\left[1 - \exp\left(-\dfrac{rF_W t}{r_u}\right)\right] + Q\left[1 - \exp\left(-\dfrac{B_c F_c t}{V_c}\right)\right]\right\}\exp(-\lambda_R t)}{V_M X_8 + \dfrac{HZF_{AM}}{S_{01}} + \dfrac{AF_A}{S_{01}}\left[1 - \exp\left(-\dfrac{rF_W t}{r_u}\right)\right] + \dfrac{Q}{S_{01}}\left[1 - \exp\left(-\dfrac{B_c F_c t}{V_c}\right)\right]} \quad (82)$$

where

V_M is $HZ(\pi A_z t)^{1/2}$ for $0 < t < t_2$,

V_M is $(Z + V_o t)HB_E$ for $t > t_2$,

t_2 is $\dfrac{\dfrac{0.5TZ}{V_o}}{1 - 0.5T + (1 - T)^{1/2}}$ for $T \leqslant 1$,

B_E is B for $T \leqslant 1$,

t_2 is $\dfrac{Z}{V_o}$ for $T \geqslant 1$,

B_E is $0.5\left(\dfrac{\pi A_z Z}{V_o}\right)^{1/2}$ for $T \geqslant 1$,

T is $\dfrac{4B_E^2 V_o}{\pi A_z Z}$

F_{AM} is the average fallout concentration on the marine fallout area (μCi/cm^2), Q is the total amount of radionuclide initially present in the canal channel and rubble (μCi), F_c is the ratio of the amount of radionuclide dissolved in canal water to the total amount present in the canal channel and rubble, B_c is the net flow rate of water through the canal channel (cm^3/da), H is the horizontal extent of the marine fallout area in the direction perpendicular to the current (cm), Z is the horizontal extent of the marine fallout area in the direction parallel to the current (cm), A is the area of the terrestrial watershed contributing the surface water to the ocean (cm^2), V_c is the volume of water in the canal channel (cm^3), V_M is the mixing volume in the ocean (cm^3), X_8 is the normal concentration of element in sea water (g element/cm^3), A_z is the turbulent diffusivity in the vertical direction (cm^2/day), V_o is the speed of the ocean current (cm/day), B is the depth to the thermocline (or bottom if the water is shallow) (cm), B_E is the effective mixing depth (cm), and t_2 is the maximum time for which a simple diffusion mechanism is applicable to describe the physical transport of a radionuclide in the sea (days).

(k) Standard Man

The equation for Standard Man (Compartment 10) depends on whether the critical organ is part of the gastrointestinal tract or not. The radionuclide intake by Standard Man depends on the ingestion rates of various food items and is

$$A_{10} = I_{104}X_4S_4 + I_{105}X_5S_5 + I_{106}X_6S_6 + I_{107}X_7S_7 + I_{109}X_9S_9 \tag{83}$$

where A_{10} is daily radionuclide intake by Standard Man (μCi/day), X_6 is the concentration of element in freshwater fish (g element/g dry weight), X_7 is the concentration of element in animals (g element/g dry weight), X_9 is the concentration of element in marine fish (g element/g dry weight), I_{104} is the ingestion rate of plant edibles by man (g dry weight/day), I_{105} is the ingestion rate of water by man (cm^3/day), I_{106} is the ingestion rate of freshwater fish by man (g dry weight/day), I_{107} is the ingestion rate of animals other than fish by man (g dry weight/day), and I_{109} is the ingestion rate of marine fish by man (g dry weight/day).

The radionuclide content of a critical organ of the gastrointestinal tract

$$y_{10} = \tau_2 f_w A_{10} \tag{84}$$

where y_{10} is the radionuclide content in a critical organ of Standard Man (μCi) and f_w is the fraction of ingested radionuclide which reaches the critical organs.

The radionuclide content of a critical organ other than the gastrointestinal

$$\frac{dy_{10}}{dt} = f_w A_{10} - y_{10}(\lambda_R + \lambda_B) \tag{85}$$

$$y_{10}(0) = 0 \tag{86}$$

Using either Equation 84 or the solution to Equation 85, the equation for internal radiation dose to a critical organ becomes

$$\frac{dD}{dt} = Ry_{10} \tag{87}$$

$$D(0) = 0 \tag{88}$$

where R is dose rate per unit radionuclide.

Approximations Leading to Infinite Dose Expressions

Many of the above differential equations for the 10-compartment model have coefficients which vary with time because the stable element concentration is a function of time. These coefficients present no problem in calculating time-varying doses by numerical techniques; but in order to use the Laplace transform technique to calculate infinite doses, it is desirable to have constant coefficients. Therefore, the following conservative approximations were made to some of the equations of the 10-compartment model in order to arrive at the expressions for infinite dose.

(a) Plant Leaves

$$g_3 = \frac{X_3 W_3}{X_3 W_3 + \dfrac{f_I F_A}{S_{01}}} \leqslant \frac{X_3 W_3}{X_3 W_3 + \dfrac{f_I F_A}{S_{01}} \exp(-k_W t)} \tag{89}$$

$$\frac{dS_3}{dt} \approx -S_3 \left(\lambda_R + k_W g_3\right) \tag{90}$$

(b) Soil water

$$g_2 = \frac{X_2 r_u}{X_2 r_u + \dfrac{F_W F_A}{S_{01}}} \leqslant \frac{X_2 r_u}{X_2 r_u + \dfrac{F_W F_A}{S_{01}} \exp\left(-\dfrac{r F_W t}{r_u}\right)} \tag{91}$$

$$\frac{dS_2}{dt} \approx S_3 \frac{X_3 W_3 F_W k_W}{X_2 r_u} - S_2 \left(\lambda_R + \frac{r F_W g_2}{r_u}\right) \tag{92}$$

$$S_2(0) \approx \frac{F_W F_A g_2}{X_2 r_u} \tag{93}$$

(c) Freshwater

$$S_5 = \frac{X_2}{X_5} \cdot \frac{S_2}{g_2} \tag{94}$$

(d) Plant Edibles (Hydrogen)

$$\frac{dS_4}{dt} \approx S_2 \frac{r X_2 (1 - f_r)}{W_4 X_4 g_2} + S_3 f_{43} \lambda_g - S_4 \left[\lambda_R + \frac{\rho_W r (1 - f_r)(1 - X_{W_4})}{W_4 X_{W_4}}\right] \tag{95}$$

(e) Seawater

$$V_M X_8 \leqslant V_M X_8 + \frac{HZF_{AM}}{S_{01}} + \frac{AF_A}{S_{01}} \left[1 - \exp\left(-\frac{r F_W t}{r_u}\right)\right] + \frac{Q}{S_{01}} \left[1 - \exp\left(-\frac{B_c F_c t}{V_c}\right)\right] \tag{96}$$

$$S_8 \approx \frac{\left\{HZF_{AM} + AF_A \left[1 - \exp\left(-\dfrac{r F_W t}{r_u}\right)\right] + Q \left[1 - \exp\left(-\dfrac{B_c F_c t}{V_c}\right)\right]\right\} \exp(-\lambda_R t)}{V_M X_8} \tag{97}$$

Infinite Dose Equations

The approximations given by Equations 89 through 97 reduce all the differential equations for the 10-compartment model to equations with constant coefficients. The Laplace transform technique can then be applied to these equations to form expressions for the infinite integral of the specific activity for each compartment. The Laplace transform of the specific activity of seawater is given by Bloom and Raines[18] and earlier in this chapter.

The infinite integrals of approximate compartment equations are

$$S_{\infty n} = \int_0^{\infty} S_n dt \quad (98)$$

where $S_{\infty n}$ is the infinite integral of S_n.

$$S_{\infty 3} = \frac{g_3 f_I F_A}{X_3 W_3 (\lambda_R + k_W g_3)} \quad (99)$$

$$S_{\infty 5} = S_{\infty 2} \frac{X_2}{X_5} \quad (100)$$

$$S_{\infty 2} = S_{\infty 3} \frac{X_3 W_3 F_W k_W}{X_2 r_u \left(\lambda_R + \frac{r F_W g_2}{r_u}\right)} + \frac{g_2 F_W F_A}{X_2 r_u \left(\lambda_R + \frac{r F_W g_2}{r_u}\right)} \quad (101)$$

For all elements except hydrogen:

$$S_{\infty 4} = S_{\infty 3} \frac{f_{43} \lambda_g}{\lambda_R + \lambda_g} + S_{\infty 2} \frac{f_{42} \lambda_g}{\lambda_R + \lambda_g} \quad (102)$$

For hydrogen:

$$S_{\infty 4} = \frac{(1 - f_r) \dfrac{r X_2 X_{W4}}{g_2 X_4}}{\lambda_R W_4 X_{W4} + (1 - f_r)(1 - X_{W4}) \rho_W r} + S_{\infty 3} \frac{f_{43} \lambda_g W_4 X_{W4}}{\lambda_R W_4 X_{W4} + (1 - f_r)(1 - X_{W4}) \rho_W r} \quad (103)$$

For all elements except carbon:

$$S_{\infty 6} = S_{\infty 5} \frac{\lambda_{B_6}}{\lambda_R + \lambda_{B_6}} \quad (104)$$

For carbon:

$$S_{\infty 6} = S_{\infty 3} \frac{\lambda_{B_6}}{\lambda_R + \lambda_{B_6}} \quad (105)$$

$$S_{\infty 7} = S_{\infty 3} \frac{\lambda_{B_7}}{\lambda_R + \lambda_{B_7}} \quad (106)$$

$$S_{\infty 8} = \left(HZF_{AM} + AF_A + Q\right)\left[\frac{\xi\left(\lambda_R t_2\right)}{X_8HZ\left(\lambda_R A_Z\right)^{1/2}} + \frac{E_1\left[\left(t_2 + \frac{Z}{V_o}\right)\lambda_R\right]\exp\left(\frac{\lambda_R Z}{V_o}\right)}{X_8HB_EV_o}\right]$$

$$- AF_A\left[\frac{\xi\left\{\left[\left(\lambda_R + \frac{rF_W}{r_u}\right)t_2\right]^{1/2}\right\}}{X_8HZ\left[\left(\lambda_R + \frac{rF_W}{r_u}\right)A_Z\right]^{1/2}}\right.$$

$$\left. + \frac{E_1\left[\left(t_2 + \frac{Z}{V_o}\right)\left(\lambda_R + \frac{rF_W}{r_u}\right)\right]\exp\left[\left(\lambda_R + \frac{rF_W}{r_u}\right)\frac{Z}{V_o}\right]}{X_8HB_EV_o}\right]$$

$$- Q\left[\frac{\xi\left\{\left[\left(\lambda_R + \frac{B_cF_c}{V_c}\right)t_2\right]^{1/2}\right\}}{X_8HZ\left[\left(\lambda_R + \frac{B_cF_c}{V_c}\right)A_Z\right]^{1/2}}\right.$$

$$\left. + \frac{E_1\left[\left(t_2 + \frac{Z}{V_o}\right)\left(\lambda_R + \frac{B_cF_c}{V_c}\right)\right]\exp\left[\left(\lambda_R + \frac{rF_W}{r_u}\right)\frac{Z}{V_o}\right]}{X_8HB_EV_o}\right] \tag{107}$$

where $\xi(x)$ is the error function, and $E_1(x)$ is one form of the exponential integral function (e.g., see Reference 23).

$$S_{\infty 9} = S_{\infty 8}\,\frac{\lambda_{B9}}{\lambda_R - \lambda_{B9}} \tag{108}$$

Using the above expressions for infinite integrals, the expressions for the infinite integral dose to a critical organ of the gastrointestinal tract are (see Equations 83 and 84):

$$D_{\infty 4} = \tau_2 Rf_W I_{104} X_4 S_{\infty 4} \tag{109}$$

$$D_{\infty 5} = \tau_2 Rf_W I_{105} X_5 S_{\infty 5} \tag{110}$$

$$D_{\infty 6} = \tau_2 Rf_W I_{106} X_6 S_{\infty 6} \tag{111}$$

$$D_{\infty 7} = \tau_2 Rf_W I_{107} X_7 S_{\infty 7} \tag{112}$$

$$D_{\infty 9} = \tau_2 Rf_W I_{109} X_9 S_{\infty 9} \tag{113}$$

where $D_{\infty 4}$ is the infinite dose contribution from eating plants (rem), $D_{\infty 5}$ is the infinite dose contribution from drinking water (rem), $D_{\infty 6}$ is the infinite dose contribution from eating freshwater fish (rem), $D_{\infty 7}$ is the infinite dose contribution from eating terrestrial animals (rem), and $D_{\infty 9}$ is the infinite dose contribution from eating marine fish (rem).

$$D = D_{\infty 4} + D_{\infty 5} + D_{\infty 6} + D_{\infty 7} + D_{\infty 9} \qquad (114)$$

The expressions for the infinite integral dose to a critical organ other than the gastrointestinal tract are identical to Equations 109—114 except the factor

$$\frac{1}{\lambda_{B10} + \lambda_R}$$

replaces τ_2.

Equation 114 is used in the third screening of the radionuclides in the same manner as Equations 50 and 51 were used in the second screening. The doses which are found to be significant through use of Equation 114 would be added to the sum of insignificant doses from Equations 50 and 51.

In addition to estimating doses for those radionuclides whose contributions to the total dose are insignificant, Equation 114 can be used to evaluate the pathways by which the more important radionuclides are transported to man. This is done for each reference radionuclide by calculating each pathway's contribution to the infinite dose. A pathway which contributes only a small portion to the infinite dose need not be considered in greater detail while a pathway making a large contribution should be considered in greater detail if possible.

The 10-compartment model described above was the one used[30] in the sea level canal feasibility studies. It makes use of all the information currently available concerning the potential pathways and mechanisms of radionuclide transport to man, stable element concentrations of ecosystem compartments, intercompartmental and interecosystem transfer coefficients, and human dietary habits. However, because of the complexity of the ecological and other processes involved and the limitations of time, the information at present is either incomplete or not detailed. Therefore, the 10-compartment model is a compromise between the specific activity model used for screening the radionuclide inventory and the more realistic but very complex model implied by Figure 1, a compromise made necessary by the incompleteness of input data. To compensate for uncertainties involved in calculating potential radionuclide intake rates and consequent radiaion doses, it was necessary to make a series of conservative assumptions and to select a variety of conservative parameter values. The result of this procedure is that dose estimates probably will be an upper limit for the specific situation considered. The only disadvantage of this result is that some problems associated with radiological safety may appear to be more serious than they actually are.

Further steps in the hierarchal development of ecological simulation models would be to consider separately some of the variables that have been lumped together in the implementation of the 10-compartment model, and the development of stochastic models in which frequency distributions are substituted for some of the parameter values now treated as constants. An obvious advantage of stochastic models is that the outputs are frequency distributions on which statistical analyses can be performed; and this would allow the addition of error terms to the predicted values. However, at present a great many more basic ecological studies are needed before such models can be implemented. Considering the present state of the art, it would be inadvisable to undertake a large program of the kind required to provide the necessary data until after the validity of some of the simpler ecological simulation models has been tested under realistic field conditions.

EDITOR'S NOTE

Several plans were proposed in the canal study for excavation of a sea level canal at different locations using conventional techniques, all-nuclear techniques, and conventional-nuclear techniques.[2] The Darien Isthmus route (Route 17) was proposed as an all-nuclear excavation plan. It would involve some 250 nuclear explosives ranging in yields from 100 kt to 3 mt detonated in about 30 groups in rows. The results of the study indicated that radiological safety could be maintained, i.e., with proper radiological measures being taken, radiation doses would be very small even with the highly conservative estimates made by the methods discussed above. The more serious uncertainties with regard to nuclear excavation dealt with engineering potentialities of nuclear explosives, since nuclear excavation experiments had not and have not proceeded as would be necessary for firm conclusions as to the size and dimensions of craters. With regard to safety, the uncertainties in the effects of airblast and ground shock (seismic) effects were far greater than those dealing with radiological safety.

In considering this very complex nuclear situation and very complex ecological environment, the discussion includes many considerations that may apply in any radiological safety situation. Most nuclear and ecological situations are complex, perhaps because of the lack of current knowledge. It seems only a matter of degree as to how any situation is considered by the health physicist. Waste disposal, accidents or earthquakes at nuclear power plants or reprocessing plants, and perhaps other situations may involve the same kind and degree of analysis.

REFERENCES

1. **Martin, W. E., Raines, G. E., Bloom, S. G., Levin, A. A., and Duke, J. A.,** Mathematical models of radionuclide transport in ecosystems, in *Nuclear Cratering Explosion Effects for Interoceanic Canal Feasibility Studies,* Klement, A. W., Jr., Ed., U.S. Atomic Energy Commission Rep. NVO-67, Las Vegas, 1970, 39. (Note: this publication was revised and reissued in 1971 without the knowledge of the editor who does not concur in or accept responsibility for the revisions made).
2. U.S. Atlantic-Pacific Interoceanic Canal Study Commission, *Interoceanic Canal Studies 1970,* Washington.
3. **Ferber, G. J. and Palmer, T. R.,** Nuclear cloud formation, transport, and deposition, in *Nuclear Cratering Explosion Effects for Interoceanic Canal Feasibility Studies,* Klement, A. W., Jr., Ed., U.S. Atomic Energy Commission Rep. NVO-67, Las Vegas, 1970, 11, (see Ref. 1).
4. **Torres de Arauz, R.,** Human ecology of Route 17 (Sasardi-Morti) region, Darien, Panama, bioenvironmental and radiological-safety feasibility studies, Atlantic-Pacific interoceanic canal, Battelle Columbus Labs., Columbus, Ohio, U.S. Atomic Energy Commission Rep. BMI-171-39, 1970.
5. Ecuador Instituto Ecuatoriano de Antropologia y Geografia, *Proyecto de Ecologia Humana, Ruta No. 25-Colombia,* Quito.
6. International Commission on Radiological Protection, *Report of Committee II on permissible dose for internal radiation,* Publ. 2, Pergamon Press, London, 1959. (Also: *Health Phys.,* 3, 1, 1960).
7. **Patten, D. C.,** Systems ecology: a course sequence in mathematical ecology, *BioScience,* 16, 593, 1966.
8. **Olson, J. S.,** Gross and net production of terrestrial vegetation, *J. Ecol.,* 52 (Suppl.), 99, 1964.
9. **Martin, W. E.,** Early food chain kinetics of radionuclides following close-in fallout from a single nuclear detonation, in *Radioactive Fallout from Nuclear Weapons Tests,* Klement, A. W., Jr., Ed., U.S. Atomic Energy Symp. Ser. 5, Rep. CONF-765, 758, 1965.

10. **Bloom, S. G.**, Mathematical formulation of the hydrogen budget model, in hydrogen budget and compartments in the rain forest at El Verde, Puerto Rico, pertinent to consideration of tritium metabolism, Odum, H. T., Puerto Rico Nuclear Center, Battelle Columbus Labs., U.S. Atomic Energy Commission Rep. BMI-171-002, A-1, 1967.
11. National Academy of Sciences — National Research Council, Disposal of low-level radioactive waste into Pacific coastal waters, Publ. 985, Washington, 1962.
12. **Charnell, R. L., Zorich, T. M., and Holly, D. E.**, Hydrologic redistribution of radionuclides around nuclear excavated sealevel canals in Panama and Colombia, Isotopes-Teledyne Co., Palo Alto Labs., Battelle Columbus Labs., U.S. Atomic Energy Commission Rep. BMI-171-016, 1968.
13. **Charnell, R. L., Zorich, T. M., and Holly, D. E.**, Hydrologic redistribution of radionuclides around a nuclear excavated sealevel canal, *BioScience*, 19, 799, 1969.
14. **Kaufman, W. J.**, An appraisal of the distribution coefficient for estimating underground movement of radioisotopes, groundwater study program, Hazelton-Nuclear Science Corp., Palo Alto, Rep. HNS-21, 1963.
15. **Carslaw, H. W. and Jaeger, J. C.**, *Conduction of Heat in Solids*, Oxford University Press, New York, 1959.
16. U.S. Army Engineer Nuclear Cratering Group, Isthmian canal plans — 1964, excavation with nuclear explosions, Livermore, Calif., Rep. PNE-2001, 1964.
17. **Cauthen, L. J., Jr., Karver, J. A., Nordyke, M. D., Preston, R. G., Reed, J. W., and Vortman, L. J.**, Isthmian canal plans — 1964, safety evaluation for airblast, groundshock, throwout, and dust, Lawrence Radiation Lab., Livermore, Calif. U.S. Atomic Energy Commission Rep. PNE-2003, 1964.
18. **Bloom, S. G. and Raines, G. E.**, A preliminary mathematical model for predicting the transport of radionuclides in the marine environment, Battelle Columbus Labs., U.S. Atomic Energy Commission Rep. BMI-171-123, 1969.
19. **Carter, H. H. and Okubo, A.**, A study of the physical processes of movement and dispersion in the Cape Kennedy area, Chesapeake Bay Institute, Johns Hopkins University, U.S. Atomic Energy Commission Rep. NYO-2973-1, 1965.
20. **Taylor, G.**, Dispersion of soluble matter in solvent flowing slowly through a tube, *Proc. Royal Soc. (London)*, A219, 186, 1953.
21. **Taylor, G.**, The dispersion of matter in turbulent flow through a pipe, *Proc. Royal Soc. (London)*, A223, 446, 1954.
22. **Pritchard, D. W., Okubo, A., and Carter, H. H.**, Observations and theory of eddy movement and diffusion of an introduced tracer material in the surface layers of the sea, in *Disposal of Radioactive Wastes into Seas, Oceans, and Surface Waters*, International Atomic Energy Agency, Vienna, 397, 1966. (STI/PUB/126).
23. **Abramowitz, M. and Stegun, I. A., Eds.**, *Handbook of Mathematical Functions: with Formulas, Graphs, and Mathematical Tables*, National Bureau of Standards, Washington, 1964.
24. **Johnson, C. L.**, Analog Computer Techniques, McGraw-Hill, New York, 1956.
25. **Gardner, M. T. and Barnes, J. L.**, *Transients in Linear Systems*, John Wiley & Sons, New York, 1942.
26. **Ralston, A. and Wilf, H. S.**, *Mathematical Methods for Digital Computers*, John Wiley & Sons, New York, 1960.
27. **Hamming, R. W.**, Stable corrector methods for ordinary differential equations, *J. Assoc. Comp. Math.*, 6, 37, 1959.
28. **Ball, S. J. and Adams, R. K.**, MATEXP, a general purpose digital computer program for solving ordinary differential equations by the matrix exponential method, Oak Ridge National Lab., U.S. Atomic Energy Commission Rep. ORNL-TM-1933, 1967.
29. **Miller, C. T. and Lee, H.**, Operation Ceniza-Arena: the retention of fallout particles from Volcan Irazu (Costa Rica) by plants and people, Stanford Research Institute, Stanford, Proj. No. MU-489, 1966.
30. **Bloom, S. G., Levin, A. A., Martin, W. E., and Raines, G. E.**, Mathematical methods for evaluating the transport and accumulation of radionuclides, Battelle Columbus Labs, U.S. Atomic Energy Commission Rep. BMI-171-030, 1970.

Environmental Sampling, Monitoring, and Analysis

INTRODUCTION

Dale H. Denham and David A. Waite

This section describes and discusses methods for conducting environmental radiation surveillance programs in the vicinity of nuclear facilities, including facilities devoted to all phases of the nuclear fuel cycle, radioisotope production and research installations, and accelerators.

Since radionuclides released with the effluents from nuclear installations become dispersed in the environment, and because external radiation sources at the sites of nuclear facilities cannot economically be totally shielded, some radiation dose to the local population in the vicinity of the nuclear installation can occur. Hence, environmental radiation surveillance programs conducted around nuclear installations should as a minimum provide data that may be used for (1) individual and population dose calculations that can be compared with Federal and State standards, (2) evaluation of radionuclide buildup in the environs, and (3) public information purposes.

Technical information for development of this section was obtained primarily from publications of recognized international (IAEA, ICRP)* and national (AIF, BRH, DOE, EPA, NCRP)** organizations and from the experience of the authors. In the latter context, liberal use has been made of the information gathered by the authors and others in developing "A Guide for: Environmental Radiological Surveillance at U.S. Department of Energy Installations"[1] and the Health Physics Society Committee report, "Upgrading Environmental Radiation Data."[2]

This section is divided into six areas of environmental surveillance protocol, ranging from program planning (both preoperational and operational), implementation (sampling and analytical methods and equipment) and data interpretation to suggested action guides and countermeasures. In the ensuing discussions, it will be helpful to remember the authors' use of certain terminology as listed in the Glossary that follows and the several definitions of measurement sensitivity shown in Table 1.

GLOSSARY

Aliquot — The fraction of a field sample taken for complete processing through an analytical procedure (a "laboratory sample" of a field sample).

Analytical detection limit — See Lower Limit of Detection.

Bias — An estimate of the absolute error of a measurement or calculated concentration as a deviation from the true value.

Continuous sampling — Both noninterrupted sampling and repetitive collection of a small sample obtained automatically at intervals short enough to yield a representative sample for the entire sampling period.

* International Atomic Energy Agency, International Commission on Radiological Protection. See the references of this section and the handbook bibliography.

** Atomic Industrial Forum, Bureau of Radiological Health, Department of Energy, Environmental Protection Agency, National Council on Radiation. National Protection and Measurement. See the references of this section and the handbook bibliography.

Table 1
MEASUREMENT SENSITIVITY

Terminology	Source	Definition
Minimum detectable limit	EPA-ORP[3] IAEA[4]	Defined only as "practical detection levels" with specified instrumentation.
Sensitivity	ANSI Standard[5]	A signal count rate associated with a specific nuclide detectable at the 95% confidence level in the presence of a specified background count rate $$n_s = 2\sqrt{n_b/2RC}$$ where n_s = signal count rate, 2 = constant associated with a 95% confidence level, n_b = background count rate, and 2RC = two times the instrument time constant associated with the background count rate.
Terms given in third column	Bureau of Radiological Health[6]	"A large enough sample must be taken to insure that the disintegration rate will be statistically significant and not primarily the result of counting error." $$E = Z\left(\frac{S}{t_s} + \frac{B}{t_b}\right)^{1/2}$$ where E = permissible counting error (cpm), Z = the constant associated with a given confidence level, S = gross count rate of the sample (cpm), B = background count rate (cpm), t_s = duration of sample count or sample counting time (min), t_b = duration of background count, or background counting time (min)

Critical pathway — The chain of environmental transfers from place to place and from one trophic level to another, which results in the greatest fraction of an applicable dose criterion to a population group and body organ (or whole body).

Critical population group (organ, nuclide) — The population group (organ, nuclide) showing the greatest fraction of an applicable radiation dose criterion as a result of site releases and environmental transfers.

Dose/dose equivalent — The term dose has been used throughout this section as a shorthand notation, where the term dose equivalent (calculated in mrem) is intended.

Environmental detection limit — The smallest concentration of a radioelement in an environmental medium that can be unambiguously distinguished at a given confidence level using a particular combination of sampling and measurement procedures, sample volume, analytical detection limit, and processing procedure.

Environmental medium — A discrete portion of the total environment, animate or inanimate, which may be sampled or measured directly.

Environmental surveillance program	— The complex of activities which has as its objective the measurement, interpretation, and reporting of environmental concentrations of selected trace materials. These activities include: design of sampling systems and specification of measurement techniques; the taking, preparation, and analysis of samples; the correlation of the measurements with other data and with concepts of health physics and the environmental sciences; and advisory services regarding the status, consequences, and forecasts of environmental impacts.
Less-than-detectable (LD)	— A measurement or calculated concentration which is not statistically different from the associated background or control value.
Lower limit of detection (LLD)	— The smallest amount or concentration of a radioelement that can be distinguished in a sample by a given measurement system in a preselected counting time at a given confidence level.
Minimum detectable limit or level (MDL)	— See Table 1.
Monitoring	— Continuous measurement of contaminant concentration or radiation intensity by direct or indirect means.
Precision	— A general term for the dispersion of values in a data set around some central value; for a homogeneous distribution, the measurement of precision is a selected multiple of the standard deviation.
Proportional sample	— A known and constant fraction of the medium for the time period covered by the sample.
Representative sample	— A sample with the same characteristics as the source at the time of sampling.
Sensitivity	— A general term for the detectability of an increment of measurement or concentration; a specifically defined measure of sensitivity is Lower Limit of Detection (also see Table 1).
Variability	— A general term for the dispersion of values in a data set; see Precision.

PLANNING ENVIRONMENTAL MONITORING PROGRAMS

Dale H. Denham

ENVIRONMENTAL SURVEILLANCE OBJECTIVES

Many valid statements of the objectives of an environmental surveillance program are available.[1-4,7,14,154-157*] The following list of objectives for routine radiological environmental monitoring programs is suggested. These are listed in approximate order of importance for protection of the public:

1. Assessment of the actual or potential exposure of people to radioactive materials or radiation released to the environment as a result of nuclear facility operations or the estimation of the probable limits of such exposure
2. Evaluation of long-term trends of concentrations in the environment, with the intent to detect failure or lack of adequate control of releases and to initiate appropriate actions
3. Determination of the fate of contaminants released to the environment, especially with the intent of discovering previously unconsidered mechanisms of exposure
4. Maintenance of a data base and capabilities for rapid evaluation and response to unusual releases of radioactivity
5. Detection and evaluation of radioactivity from off-site sources in order to distinguish and compare the results of site operations
6. Demonstration of compliance with applicable regulations concerning releases to the environment, for both legal and public relations purposes

The time lag and generally more diffuse effects inherent in most environmental measurements make primary reliance on any environmental measurement as an action signal unwise (other than for further investigation). With the exception of long-term accumulations of contaminants from source terms too dilute to be conveniently measured, all environmental measurements should be considered as supplementary insofar as action guides are concerned, with primary emphasis on effluent or other continuous facility measurements. When all knowledge regarding mechanisms of environmental dispersal is complete, one could, in fact, consider all environmental measurements as being theoretically redundant since complete and continuous control and monitoring of effluents, along with a complete knowledge of the fate of radionuclides in the environment, would make them unnecessary.

In practice, it is known that some environmental measurements are vital to achieve the objectives stated earlier. Measurements as near as possible to the actual exposure vectors of people should, therefore, provide a more accurate (if less precise) dose estimate. In fact, Regulatory Guide 4.1[8] states that " . . . it may not be necessary to extensively sample and measure grazing plants and fodder to keep track of iodine-131 cycling in the food chain, since sampling and measuring the milk produced by dairy cows in surrounding areas may be adequate." Those responsible for the environmental program at each site are, therefore, faced with frequent decisions as to the relative reliance for population dose estimates on environmental vs. effluent measurements, as well as to the points in the exposure pathways at which measurements are best made. In addition, environmental measurements included in the routine program for purposes other than dose estimation, e.g., trend evaluation or public interest, are needed

* All references are found starting on page 197.

(but should be clearly distinguished). Since these judgments are heavily weighted by site-specific factors, only a general discussion of pertinent factors is included.

The off-site environmental surveillance program should be established on the basis of an evaluation of radionuclide composition of the liquid and gaseous discharges from the facility (or facilities) and the local environmental parameters that could affect their dilution and dispersion in the environment. The recommended surveillance program consists of two phases: the preoperational and the operational. The preoperational phase provides data that can be used as a basis for evaluating increases in radioactivity or radiation levels in the vicinity of the site after the plant becomes operational. The evaluation must also determine whether an increase is attributable to plant operations or to a general increase in environmental radioactivity.

Preoperational environmental surveillance — This phase should be carried out for a minimum of 1 year, preferably 2, prior to facility operations. The preoperational program should consist of: (1) identification of probable critical exposure pathways and (2) the critical population groups, (3) selection of the sample media and sample site locations, (4) the collection and analysis of environmental samples, and (5) the interpretation of the data. The extent of preoperational surveillance depends upon the particular environment in which the nuclear installation is located.

The operational environmental surveillance — This program should begin at the time the plant becomes operational. Specific media to be monitored during the initial phase of the operational program should have been identified during the preoperational surveillance program. Since environmental conditions around nuclear facilities will vary, the program should be tailored to individual site characteristics as detailed in the balance of this section. Typical minimal sampling programs are outlined in the (EPA) Surveillance Guide.[3] These recommended minimum levels of surveillance are for nuclear power plants; however, the levels suggested should provide a reasonable guide for tailoring to any types of nuclear facilities. In any case, the recommended programs should include monitoring of four basic exposure pathways (air, water, food, and external radiation) and certain indicators of environmental trends.

PROGRAM PLANNING AND DESIGN PROCESS

In order to properly design an environmental monitoring program, a number of factors must be considered. Obvious factors that affect the relative level of surveillance, and to some extent the points at which measurements are to be made, are listed in the (DOE) Surveillance Guide[1] and are repeated here for ready reference:

1. The potential hazard of the materials released, considering both quantities and relative radiotoxicities (see the chapter entitled "Recommended and Regulatory Limits of Environmental Radioactivity")
2. The extent to which facility operations are routine and unchanging
3. The size and distribution of the exposed population
4. The cost-effectiveness of increments to the environmental program, since even a modest additional surveillance effort at a very small facility may represent a significant fraction of the total effort
5. The availability of measurement techniques that will provide adequate comparisons with applicable standards and "background" measurements

The procedural flow diagram of Figure 1 is provided as an aid to placing the needed data inputs and the environmental pathway analysis procedure in the proper relationship to program planning. In the figure, rectangles indicate data inputs and diamonds indicate procedural steps. The many different kinds of data that must be provided (or estimated) are apparent; the relationships are further illustrated in Figure 2 which de-

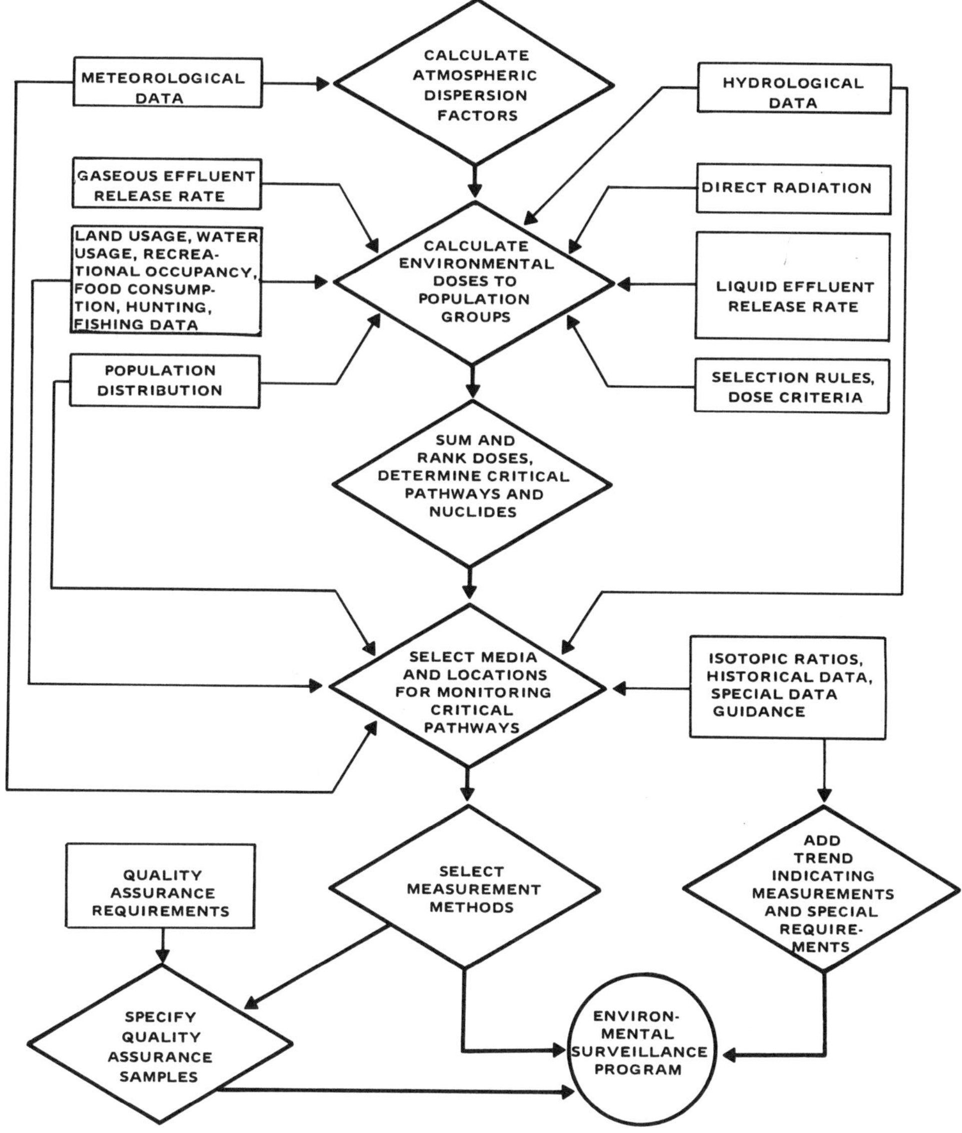

FIGURE 1. Environmental surveillance program design process.

tails the dose calculation procedure. The environmental dose calculation is, of course, an iterative procedure for each nuclide released.

Since the basic radiation standards are given in terms of dose to people, environmental program planning is addressed first to the sampling or direct measurement of critical environmental pathways that may contribute to the radiation exposure of the public. Selection of locations, media, frequency, nuclides to be measured, and measurement methods to be used for critical pathway surveillance provides the basic requirements for the environmental surveillance program. To these, any special monitoring requirements, including trend indicators and those additional samples or measurements required for quality assurance will be added. Criteria for selection of samples and measurements should be recorded so that the purpose and any limitations on interpretations of results will be clear.

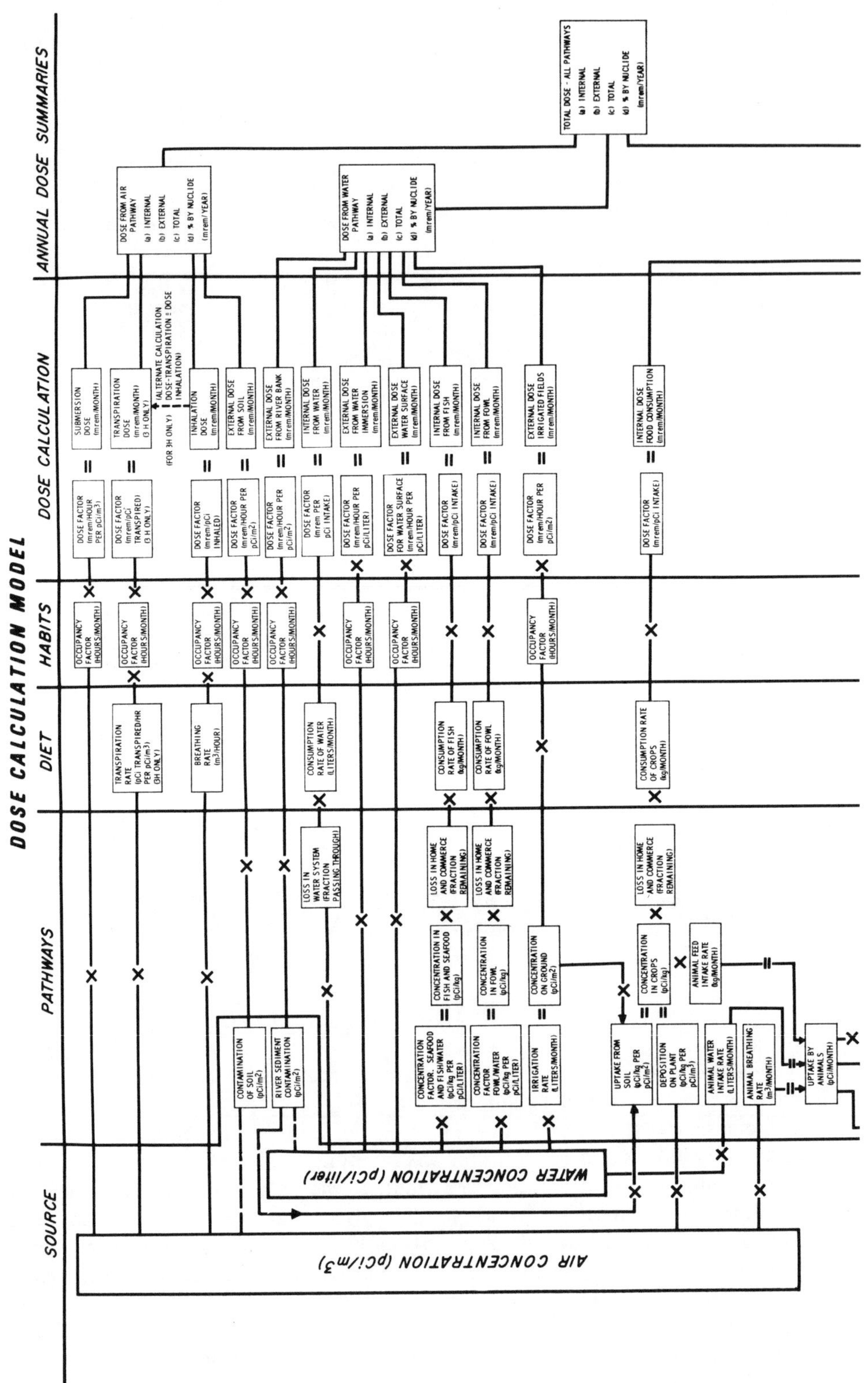
DOSE CALCULATION MODEL
SOURCE
PATHWAYS
DIET
HABITS
DOSE CALCULATION
ANNUAL DOSE SUMMARIES
AIR CONCENTRATION (pCi/m3)
WATER CONCENTRATION (pCi/liter)
TOTAL DOSE - ALL PATHWAYS (a) INTERNAL (b) EXTERNAL (c) TOTAL (d) % BY NUCLIDE (mrem/YEAR)
DOSE FROM AIR PATHWAY (a) INTERNAL (b) EXTERNAL (c) TOTAL (d) % BY NUCLIDE (mrem/YEAR)
DOSE FROM WATER PATHWAY (a) INTERNAL (b) EXTERNAL (c) TOTAL (d) % BY NUCLIDE (mrem/YEAR)
SUBMERSION DOSE (mrem/MONTH)
TRANSPIRATION DOSE (mrem/MONTH) (3 H ONLY)
(ALTERNATE CALCULATION DOSE-TRANSPIRATION ≡ DOSE INHALATION)
(FOR 3H ONLY)
INHALATION DOSE (mrem/MONTH)
EXTERNAL DOSE FROM SOIL (mrem/MONTH)
EXTERNAL DOSE FROM RIVER BANK (mrem/MONTH)
INTERNAL DOSE FROM WATER (mrem/MONTH)
EXTERNAL DOSE FROM WATER IMMERSION (mrem/MONTH)
EXTERNAL DOSE WATER SURFACE (mrem/MONTH)
INTERNAL DOSE FROM FISH (mrem/MONTH)
INTERNAL DOSE FROM FOWL (mrem/MONTH)
EXTERNAL DOSE IRRIGATED FIELDS (mrem/MONTH)
INTERNAL DOSE FOOD CONSUMPTION (mrem/MONTH)
DOSE FACTOR (mrem/HOUR PER pCi/m3)
DOSE FACTOR (mrem/pCi TRANSPIRED) (3 H ONLY)
DOSE FACTOR (mrem/pCi INHALED)
DOSE FACTOR (mrem/HOUR PER pCi/m2)
DOSE FACTOR (mrem/HOUR PER pCi/m2)
DOSE FACTOR (mrem PER pCi INTAKE)
DOSE FACTOR (mrem/HOUR PER pCi/LITER)
DOSE FACTOR FOR WATER SURFACE (mrem/HOUR PER pCi/LITER)
DOSE FACTOR (mrem/pCi INTAKE)
DOSE FACTOR (mrem/pCi INTAKE)
DOSE FACTOR (mrem/HOUR PER pCi/m2)
DOSE FACTOR (mrem/pCi INTAKE)
OCCUPANCY FACTOR (HOURS/MONTH)
TRANSPIRATION RATE (pCi TRANSPIRED/HR PER pCi/m3) (3H ONLY)
BREATHING RATE (m3/HOUR)
CONSUMPTION RATE OF WATER (LITERS/MONTH)
CONSUMPTION RATE OF FISH (kg/MONTH)
CONSUMPTION RATE OF FOWL (kg/MONTH)
CONSUMPTION RATE OF CROPS (kg/MONTH)
LOSS IN WATER SYSTEM (FRACTION PASSING THROUGH)
LOSS IN HOME AND COMMERCE (FRACTION REMAINING)
CONCENTRATION IN FISH AND SEAFOOD (pCi/kg)
CONCENTRATION IN FOWL (pCi/kg)
CONCENTRATION ON GROUND (pCi/m2)
CONCENTRATION IN CROPS (pCi/kg)
ANIMAL FEED INTAKE RATE (kg/MONTH)
CONTAMINATION OF SOIL (pCi/m2)
RIVER SEDIMENT CONTAMINATION (pCi/m2)
CONCENTRATION FACTOR, SEAFOOD AND FISH/WATER (pCi/kg PER pCi/LITER)
CONCENTRATION FACTOR FOWL/WATER (pCi/kg PER pCi/LITER)
IRRIGATION RATE (LITERS/MONTH)
UPTAKE FROM SOIL (pCi/kg PER pCi/m2)
DEPOSITION ON PLANT (pCi/kg PER pCi/m3)
ANIMAL WATER INTAKE RATE (LITERS/MONTH)
ANIMAL BREATHING RATE (m3/MONTH)
UPTAKE BY ANIMALS (pCi/MONTH)

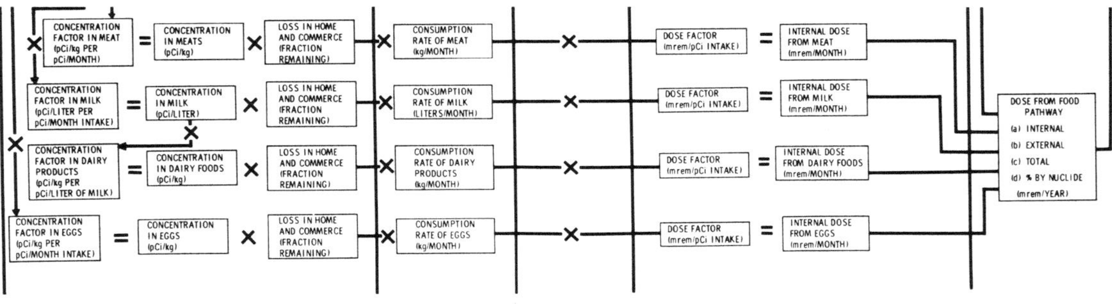

FIGURE 2. Dose calculation matrix.

A basic principle is that the environment is dynamic, showing both spatial and temporal variations of nearly all constituents. Some variations are highly deterministic, e.g., changes in river concentration with river flow. Others may be so complex that they require a form of randomized sampling, especially those associated with atmospheric movement. Some initial assumptions will generally be necessary concerning natural movements of air, water, and biota and their effect on distributions of effluent releases.

The "graded-effort" concept of adjusting the surveillance program intensity to the severity of environmental impact is generally accepted, with the support of the ICRP[7] and Federal Radiation Council (FRC).[9] The principle is embodied in most existing programs, even where not specifically documented. The underlying principle (and need) is flexibility — changing the program scope and intensity in response to changing facility processes, environmental parameters, and program results.

A history of stable operations, populations, and environmental results (especially if routinely less than detection level) will warrant a minimized program, provided that the program retains sufficient scope to detect fluctuations and especially persistent changes in environmental levels of radioactivity originating on site.

CRITICAL PATHWAY ANALYSIS

The importance of individual radionuclides depends on the physical and chemical forms that determine their movement in the environment and eventual uptake, deposition, and retention by people and on their differential metabolism by man. As a result, environmental measurements for dose evaluation should usually be specific for given radionuclides.

Establishing numerical transfer coefficients between different media in a given dose pathway is normally a function of research, and accurate assay of environmental media for effluent materials may require research techniques beyond the scope of routine monitoring programs. Monitoring programs, because they are selective and incomplete measures of the environment, may only indicate semiquantitative changes within the media sampled.

To determine the relative importance of medium/nuclide combinations in environmental surveillance, the experience at 19 major DOE (AEC) sites was reviewed.[11] Typical nuclides or nuclide groupings (tritium, noble gases, radioiodine, mixed fission or activation products, and transuranics), found or expected to be found in the effluent streams (air and/or water) were used to calculate doses to maximum individual using a standard dose model.[10] The individual (or critical group) doses were calculated for each effluent pathway/nuclide combination based on unit release. Secondarily, indirect dose pathways (e.g. soil, sediment, rainfall) were considered on a relative basis by comparing detection sensitivities for a given nuclide in the environmental media commonly sampled, resulting in the nuclide/medium combination that provides the greatest measurement sensitivity (including both short- and long-term contamination accumulation). By this scheme, it was possible to preferentially rank each nuclide/medium combination as a point of measurement for a given effluent pathway.

Table 1 presents the relative importance, so determined, of monitoring specific environmental media for a unit release of the given radionuclide(s) via each effluent pathway. The relative importance of a particular entry in the table is based on (1) the dose to a critical population group or maximum individual (population doses also were calculated, but were insignificant relative to the individual doses), and (2) the importance of that nuclide/medium combination as a trend indicator (i.e., the environmental medium in which the greatest detection sensitivity occurs). Combinations resulting in the highest dose or having the greatest detection sensitivity are listed in the table with

Table 1
RELATIVE IMPORTANCE OF ENVIRONMENTAL MEDIA AS A FUNCTION OF EFFLUENT PATHWAY AND RADIONUCLIDE(S)

Effluent Pathway—Atmosphere

	Tritium	Noble gases	Iodine (131)	MF & AP[a]	TRU[b]
1	Air	Direct radiation	Milk	Air	Air
	Vegetables	Air	Vegetables	Vegetables	
2	Honey		Air	Milk	Deposition
	Native grasses		Animal thyroids	Direct radiation	Terrestial biota
	Precipitation		Forage	Deposition	Soil
3				Forage	

Effluent Pathway—Hydrosphere

	Tritium	Iodine (131)	MF & AP[a]	TRU[b]
1	Drinking water	Drinking water	Fish, shellfish	Sediment
	Surface water	Milk		Fish
2	Vegetables	Surface water	Waterfowl	Surface water
	Groundwater	Vegetables	Surface water	Vegetation
	Honey	Forage	Milk	
3			Sediment	
			Drinking and ground water	
			Terrestial biota	

[a] Mixed fission and activation products.
[b] Transuranic nuclides, primarily ^{239}Pu.

a relative importance factor of one. Generally speaking, the change from an importance factor of one to two and from two to three indicates at least an order of magnitude decrease in dose or sensitivity. The differences between media at a given relative importance factor are not considered significant, although the medium shown first in each pathway/nuclide(s) column is considered to be the most important. When only one or two groups of media are shown for a particular effluent pathway/nuclide combination, all other media were considered to be unimportant for that pathway.

The exposure pathway concept is sufficiently understood; (see References 13, 45, 158-163), and documented that no extended treatment is given here. Although various graphical illustrations are available, a more complete analysis is provided by the dose calculation matrix of Figure 2; the diagram shown is for a single radionuclide and must be reiterated for each nuclide released, with organ doses summed for all nuclides. First prepared for the year 2000 regional dose study,[12] the procedure has been separately documented with calculation subroutines and lists of various standard parameters (see References 15, 18, 20, 164, 165).

It is not suggested by any means that every site need routinely go through the entire complex calculation for every potential nuclide released, especially since many of the pathways for a given nuclide will end up with zeroes. However, this does afford a useful basis for checking the completeness of the dose evaluation process, particularly for the omission of any potential critical pathway. Where local data indicate a difference from standard parameter listings, such data may be used. This possibility especially exists for such factors as growing season, irrigation practices, cattle feed sources, land productivity, and local fish and game consumption.

Summation of organ doses, comparison with environmental dose criteria, and intercomparison of calculated doses and fractions of dose criteria will indicate which of the nuclides released are the critical nuclides. For these nuclide(s), a retrace of the dose calculation procedure (as per Figure 2) will reveal both the critical pathways and the possibilities for measurement, as well as those other nuclides and pathways that will not require routine measurement for dose evaluation.

A review of historical surveillance records, expected isotopic ratios, special studies of the local environment, and possibly literature studies may show the availability of indicator measurements that can be reliably related to population dose or at least individual dose pathways. As noted in Regulatory Guide 4.1,[8] "Where practical, a suitable indicator medium or organism in each important pathway should be sampled and analyzed for the plant-contributed radionuclides released to the environment." The guide goes on to offer these cautionary statements, "When sampling organisms, an abundant, readily available species with known habits should be selected. Careful attention should be given to . . . avoid inducing serious stress on populations of important species."

SITE-SPECIFIC DATA REQUIREMENTS

For existing facilities, specific nuclide release data should be available; otherwise, it must be obtained. For planned new facilities or facility modifications, the design or operating groups should provide the needed release estimates. If adequate information is available, intermittent operation may be factored into the dose calculations where seasonal exposures occur, but only for postoperational dose evaluation. It may be possible, although some small risk of an oversight may be incurred, to make an initial elimination of some nuclides based on such information as chemical analogies, radiotoxicity, and half-life. Other nuclides may also be dropped from the analysis if estimates of pathway travel times make it evident that environmental exposure will not occur. The physical site characteristics — topographical, meteorological, and hydrological — require attention in the placement of monitoring locations.

Site topography is largely significant in its effect on local meteorology. Its importance has been generally recognized in the concentration of air sampling locations in the "prevailing downwind" direction. Several precautions are in order, however, since the prevailing wind direction is not always the direction of maximum exposure to airborne effluents. Dilution is also dependent on air mass stability.

There is no adequate substitute for on-site meteorological data. At the larger sites, more than one such record applicable to the actual release points is highly desirable. Where no on-site data are available, the nearest available records must be used; however, the necessary detailed data analysis will generally not be readily available. The meteorological records should be analyzed to provide stability class frequency for each wind direction in order to prepare atmospheric dispersion (χQ) tables or graphs. Ideally, where dose estimates must be made from effluent release data, this kind of measurement should be available for dose calculations for each year; otherwise, historical meteorological data may be used, introducing a probably small but unknown error.

Although an updating is in progress, *Meteorology and Atomic Energy — 1968*[16] is probably still the best reference for atmospheric dispersion calculations. Atmospheric dispersion models used in Regulatory Guides 4.8, 1.109, and 1.111[15,17,18] are also suggested for appropriate methodology. Regulatory Guide 1.23[19] may be used as a reference for meteorological instrumentation.

Surface hydrology data are needed where any direct or indirect release to a stream or larger body of water may occur. Dye studies or other means of determining dilution rates, travel times, and sedimentation areas may be needed for releases into tide-influenced water bodies, as well as streams whose hour-to-hour flow is heavily influenced by dam operations. The annual hydrographic cycle must be established for each stream site and taken into account, especially where operations or releases are intermittent. U.S. Geological Survey (USGS) historical stream-flow records are available for nearly all surface streams of any size. Tide tables are generally available by elevations but do not reflect actual flow regimes in streams or estuaries. For the latest guidance on estimating aquatic dispersion of effluent radionuclides, the reader is referred to Regulatory Guide 1.113.[20]

Ground water hydrology requires a major study program if radionuclide-containing liquids are discharged in quantity to covered liquid disposal sites (cribs), ponds, or solid waste burial grounds. Fortunately, many nuclides will be tightly held on the soil, at least for a period sufficiently long to permit radioactive decay. The greater problem lies in estimating flow paths and travel times to a surface stream or other potential point of population exposure. This will vary by several orders of magnitude between nuclides and must be separately estimated for each.

Demographic factors include the population distribution around a site, as well as land usage, recreational activities, and dietary habits of that population (which are required to determine intake and occupancy factors). Census data are readily available for all incorporated communities; frequently, the local chamber of commerce will be able to furnish both urban and suburban population sizes. For a rural population, county offices can often provide the data. In addition, the Bureau of the Census has divided the U.S. into Census Districts with reference coordinates. These data should be available in tabular form if needed.*

Agricultural land usage, including crop data, is usually available from the county agricultural agent. A special survey (usually a limited effort) may be necessary to discover locations and sizes of dairy herds and beef cattle, especially on those farms having only one or two dairy cows primarily for the family's own use.

Fishing and hunting activities which have been part of the most critical pathway at DOE installations such as Hanford, both from occupancy and consumption, may be addressable through local game wardens or state offices. Total collection data are usually fairly accurate, but individual success and consumption figures taken from hearsay must be treated skeptically. Estimating the fraction of sportsmen fishing or hunting locally but living outside the 80-km radius is difficult; for conservatism, inclusion of all exposure from consumption of local fish and game in the 80-km population dose is recommended.

In the absence of local data, ICRP Standard Man data may still be used for routine air and water consumption, supplemented by ICRP Publication No. 10[22] for inhalation exposures and FRC guidance for milk intake.[9] For diet data, Department of Agriculture Bulletins[23,24] should be used. Intake/dose factors may be calculated by direct ratio from ICRP data or from FRC guidance.

SAMPLE FREQUENCY AND SIZE

The environment is so large that no practical samples can represent it with better than poor statistical certainty. Thus, the need to take samples exceeding a definite size relates to analytical sensitivity, as indicated by the sampling equation below, rather than to environmental representivity. Potential methods of lowering the minimum detection limit of a nuclide in a sample of the environment for a given analytical lower limit of detection in the laboratory are indicated by the following sampling equation:

$$A = a \frac{(tC)}{Vfret} \tag{1}$$

where A = target concentration, the smallest concentration which will be quantita-

* The EPA has computerized population dose calculation from any given source using this system,[21] as has the Accident Analysis Branch of DOE.[1]

tively measured by the procedure; t = counting time devoted to a sample; C = minimum count rate measurable by the detector in time t; V = volume of the sample collected; f = the fraction of the sample collected which is carried into the purification and counting steps; r = fractional analytical recovery (efficiency) for the radionuclide of interest; e = counting efficiency of the detector (fraction of a count per disintegration); and a = unit conversion factor.

Values of the terms V, tC, e, and r are all affected by available hardware, technical training, and operating expenses. Obviously, a broad range of combinations of these four terms will satisfy the requirement for measuring a given value of A. In practice, several trial combinations and their implications should be evaluated in order to optimize the sampling and analytical procedures.

The target concentration, A, deserves careful selection to allow for action levels, natural background, variability in background, and statistical problems arising when detected radioactive transitions are few in number. For example, setting the target concentration equal to some action level implies that no knowledge of concentrations smaller than the action level will be obtained. Although it would be useful in some selected situations, the entire monitoring program should not be designed on a target concentration based on action levels.

The sampling equation can be rearranged to determine the nominal sample size (mass or volume), V, required. It can also be used in an audit function to judge the sensitivity of a sampling/analytical effort in terms of the smallest concentration, S (for a single sample), that can be reliably assessed. Obviously, S should be smaller than an action level (as noted above), but it may not be necessary for S to be smaller than background, as long as the background distribution provides some samples that have concentrations larger than S. A method described in the chapter entitled "Interpretation of Environmental Radioactivity Measurements," shows how the average and standard deviation may be obtained for truncated distributions. That method of treating less-than-detection values presumes that observed concentrations greater than S belong to the same statistical distribution as the concentrations smaller than S. Such a presumption could be supported by more sensitive temporary studies to determine that specific fact.

Aside from sample sensitivity requirements, the frequency of sample collection and measurement must take into account the half-life of the radionuclide being measured. Even though a decay correction can be made, a delay of two half-lives between sampling and analysis for an intermittent occurrence of a radionuclide in the medium being analyzed increases the probable error and thus the minimum detectable level (MDL) by a factor of at least two, and probably more depending on the time of arrival relative to the time of sample collection. For a sample analysis with a barely acceptable sensitivity in any case, such an increase may be unacceptable.

Since effluent releases and the environmental media they affect may both vary with time, nonproportional and periodic grab sampling risk bias by being synchronized with some cyclic feature of the process or the environment (e.g., a liquid effluent release schedule, tidal cycles, or daily fluctuations of stream flow). Synchronization (i.e., collecting an environmental sample either in or out of phase with effluent releases) may be desirable if the sensitivity of the monitoring system can be increased, but inadvertent synchronization should be avoided, because the resulting bias may lead to misinterpretation of the results.

Seasonal habits of people and animals can also result in irrelevant data from a uniform year-round program. Recreational exposures are an excellent example. Aquatic and terrestrial biota can be selective in what they eat, and they select differently according to availability. For example, assessing the dose impact via milk cattle requires sampling the forage species that cows eat in the season that it is eaten. The temptation to take either random or a complete series of samples of vegetation for such a purpose,

Table 2
GENERAL GUIDES FOR ENVIRONMENTAL SURVEILLANCE PROGRAMS[1]

1. Every exposure pathway should be routinely measured that, as determined by site-specific exposure pathway analysis and either predicted or historical release rates, may contribute more than 10% of a total environmental dose of site origin, if the total exceeds:
   a. 1 mrem/year to the whole body or specific organ dose of individuals or critical population groups; or
   b. 100 man-rem/year whole body dose per 1 million population within an 80 km(50 m) radius of the release point (or centroid of a cluster of release points).
2. For dose calculation, actual measurements need not be made on more than two media for each critical radionuclide/pathway combination, one of which may be the effluent stream.
3. If reasonably achievable, routine measurement techniques for dose calculation should have minimum detections limits no higher than those equivalent to the dose criteria given in item 1.
4. "Background" or "control" location measurements should be taken for every critical nuclide/pathway combination for which environmental measurements are used in the dose calculation.
5. Dose calculations from direct environmental measurements should be based only on statistically significant differences between the point of measurement and background or control data. For this purpose, statistical comparisons should be made at the 95% confidence level (a difference in mean values for the assumed statistical distributions of at least two times the pooled standard deviations of the data).
6. Gross activity analyses as such should be used only as trend indicators, with supporting analyses to relate results to specific nuclide concentrations or doses.
7. The exposure pathway anlaysis should be documented, with data references and local assumptions clearly distinguished, and with critical nuclides, pathways, and population groups described.
8. Sampling or measurement intervals for each critical nuclide/medium combination should not exceed twice the half-life of the nuclide to be measured.
9. Where significant periodic variations in environmental concentrations may be expected, samples or measurements should be either continuous or at an interval less than half the expected peak-to-peak interval.

based solely on an arbitrary schedule, e.g., every 6 months, should be resisted, because the data may well be of no value in pathway analysis. Although such data may be suggestive, they are not likely to be reliable.

GENERAL SURVEILLANCE PROGRAM CRITERIA

Routine environmental dose estimation are taken from the DOE Guide[1] and are included in Table 2. Application of these to an individual site or facility requires that an adequte study be made of expected releases and potential exposure pathway networks therefrom. It is believed that these guides can be applied to the broad spectrum of nuclear facilities in question while supplying adequate data to satisfy members of the public and regulatory agencies with legitimate concerns. The proposed dose evaluation criteria do not define "as low as practicable" for environmental doses or needed controls, but suggest the dose levels of interest that reflect current NRC regulations. In the final analysis, however, judgment must be exercised to select the appropriate media and measurements to be included in the environmental program upon which future dose calculations are to be based. The EPA's "recommended minimum level environmental surveillance program"[3] and the NRC's Regulatory Guide 4.1,[8] "Programs for Monitoring Radioactivity in the Environs of Nuclear Power Plants," should be consulted for detailed methods of choosing sampling locations. The programs suggested therein must be supplemented by on-site measurements where appropriate, mainly in the stacks and in the liquid effluent streams.

The proper design of a sampling program is perhaps more important than the measurements made on the samples; if a key item is not even sampled, then its significance is totally unrecognized. In the chapter entitled "Sampling Instruments and Methods," some considerations are outlined for each medium requiring sampling. The sampling program must, of course, include consideration of the analytical and instrumentation capabilities (see the chapter entitled "Analysis of Environmental Samples by Chemical and Physical Means").

SAMPLING INSTRUMENTS AND METHODS

Dale H. Denham

INTRODUCTION

This section provides guidance on the selection of sampling methods and measurement techniques for environmental media, including not only those commonly found to be important from the standpoint of radiation dose to people, but also those noted as a site for accumulation of radionuclides and commonly used as trend indicators. Substantial information has been published and is available on sample collection equipment. Detailed descriptions of the methods and equipment appropriate to the particular contaminant and environmental medium are provided in the references, especially the four-volume Lawrence Berkeley Laboratory (LBL) manual, *Instrumentation for Environmental Monitoring*,[25]* the American Public Health Association (APHA) manuals, *Methods of Air Sampling and Analysis*[26] and *Standard Methods for the Examination of Water and Wastewater*[27] and the more recent handbooks of the NCRP, Environmental Radiation Measurements,[166] Instrumentation and Monitoring Methods for Radiation Protection,[167] and A Handbook of Radioactivity Measurements Procedures.[168] Those collection and measurement criteria that must be considered to provide meaningful and comparable interpretation of environmental surveillance data are noted in the appropriate subsections that follow.

In a routine surveillance program, a number of trade-offs must be made to obtain adequate measurement sensitivity and accuracy with minimum cost. For example, to increase the sensitivity of air sampling, larger volumes can be sampled (implying purchase of more air samplers or larger capacity pumps) or longer counting times can be used (implying purchase of more counting equipment). Some compromises are inevitable either because completely satisfactory measurement techniques are not available or because the best techniques are far too expensive for routine use over large geographical areas. Fortunately, high precision is seldom necessary for environmental data at the radiation levels normally encountered and is a controlling factor only when it is necessary to distinguish small fractional differences between numbers.

ELEMENTS OF GOOD PRACTICE

Consistent good practice in environmental measurement and sampling is necessary to achieve satisfactory results. Major sources of controllable error include nonrepresentative sampling, differences in individual sampling techniques, and losses in sampling lines and containers. The following general considerations are supplemented by further discussion in the sections addressed to specific measurements. For additional discussion on collection and preparation of environmental samples for laboratory analysis, including sampling and analytical considerations, and problems in sampling, the reader is referred to the NCRP recommendations on environmental radiation measurements.[7a]

Representative Sampling

The key to correct evaluation of environmental impacts is the procurement of data truly representative of the environmental media of interest. Selection of approximate sampling and measurement locations is based on air and water circulation patterns,

* All references are found starting on page 197.

population distribution, land and water usage, and availability. Just as important for correct interpretation of results is the correct selection of exact locations and procedures, which is also quite difficult.

Before final placement of any environmental station, an initial (preoperational if possible) on-the-spot survey for existing or potential sources of anomalies is essential. Examples of placement situations to be avoided if possible are listed here; some ingenuity may be needed to foresee other potential inferences.

1. Local concentrations of natural radioactivity
2. Building wake effects
3. Dripping and puddling and precipitation
4. Heavy dust-raising activities
5. Backwater areas in streams
6. Riverbank springs (unless the influent is the sample desired)
7. Atypical vegetation pattern

In practice, compromises are sometimes necessary between location desirability and availability. One general solution to the problem of selecting representative sampling sites is to add more stations; although this does not eliminate anomalous results, their occurrence will be more readily distinguished. Subsequent periodic inspection and audit of nearby activities is also required as insurance against changing local conditions. Caution is especially needed in cultivated areas because of the potential changes in data that may result from tillage, irrigation, growth, and harvesting of crops. Control of access to environmental sampling sites and of nearby activities is desirable but often not available.

Field Sampling Procedures

Consistency in taking samples or measurements requires mandatory detailed procedures, including such instructions as the specified height of an instrument measurement, the taking of a stream sample below the surface while avoiding stirred-up sediments, and the use of a specific container. Comparable results may indeed be obtained with knowledgeable departures from routine procedures, but additional risk is involved. These detailed procedures should also include needed precautions to avoid either the loss or inadvertent contamination of a sample during handling and transport.

All samples must be accompanied by information that identifies the sample site, date of collection, type of sample, and the collector. It may be desirable to assign a sample number in order to follow the sample through a series of analyses. Perishable samples that must be saved for later analysis should be frozen or chemically preserved, making certain that the treatment will not subsequently affect the radiochemical analysis. An excellent reference on sample preservation methods is included in the EPA Manual on Water and Wastewater Analysis.[28] Sealable plastic bags or polyethylene bottles are generally recommended for collection and storage of samples.

The selection of background or control sampling/monitoring locations must be made with care. They should be located so that they will be beyond measurable influence by the nuclear installation in question or by other nuclear facilities. State fallout networks are good sources of control data for some sample media, especially if the sampling and analyses are done on the same basis, i.e., with the same type of equipment (or better yet, as split samples), the same media, and the same decay time. If possible, more than one control or background location should be used for most media; a notable exception might be for surface water. Ease of access and, if possible, control of access to background stations is desirable.

Sample Lines and Containers

A common problem in collecting and storing samples is the loss of radionuclides to apparatus and container surfaces through chemical, physical, and/or biological action. Selection of relatively nonreactive and nonretentive materials and the minimization of areas of sample contact (especially sampling lines), sample storage, and transit times are of some value, as is flushing of containers with the sample stream before final collection of grab samples. Information on the magnitude and rate of uptake by surfaces is widely scattered and qualitative, and no materials appropriate to the entire spectrum of encountered radionuclides is known. Pretreatment of sample containers with aqueous solutions of the same element as the radionuclide of interest has been successful in some cases. Samples of open waters will always show continued biological activity if left standing. Hence, these must be preserved as noted above.

In the following subsections, sampling and measurement techniques have been divided into the three natural environmental categories: atmospheric, terrestrial, and aquatic. Each grouping includes a brief discussion of the basis, methods, radionuclides, locations and frequency for sampling.

ATMOSPHERIC ENVIRONMENT

Air

Since air is a primary exposure pathway to people from radionuclides released to the atmosphere, environmental air sampling is conducted to evaluate potential exposures from inhaled or ingested radionuclides or from external radiation. The inhalation route of atmospheric radionuclides, either from the source (facility) or from resuspension following deposition, may result in their absorption through the lung, GI tract, or skin. Absorption and subsequent distribution in the human body depends on the particle size and the physical (and probably chemical) state of the inhaled radionuclide. Some airborne radionuclides, notably tritium, may enter the body by transpiration through the skin. Three types or airborne radionuclides normally require measurement: particulates; noble gases, and halogens, principally iodine. A fourth, airborne tritium, also should be measured at specific sites.

The measurement of airborne particulates can provide a means of evaluating the inhalation exposure from particulate radionuclides. In addition to the potential inhalation hazard, the measurement of airborne particulates can be used to predict surface deposition levels from which people may be exposed to direct gamma radiation or via the contamination of fruits and vegetables that may later be consumed. Noble gases are treated under External Radiation, since it is generally more feasible to measure the potential dose impact of noble gases directly rather than through air sampling. Sampling and measurement of airborne halogens is performed primarily for the eight-day ^{131}I, which can enter milk via the air-pasture-cow pathway. Airborne tritium measurements provide a useful means of evaluating exposure to that radionuclide because (in HTO form) it can be inhaled as well as absorbed through the skin in approximately equal proportions.

Important guides to air sampling of radioactive materials are ANSI N13.1-1969,[29] in which the methods are said to be "generally acceptable and adequate bases for the design and conduct of monitoring programs for airborne effluents" at nuclear power stations,[30] and the APHA manual.[26] The collection and analysis of air samples for radioactivity must be related to the monitoring objectives discussed in the chapter entitled "Planning Environmental Monitoring Programs".

The usual "sampling train" consists of a collection device or devices, an air mover, and an airflow measuring system. Each component of interest is removed from the air by a sample collection device or by a series of devices to collect different components, e.g., a filter for particulates followed by a charcoal cartridge for radioiodines followed by a molecular sieve for tritium followed by a cold trap for noble gases. The airstream being sampled may also be split to accommodate different sampling rates for different collectors. Since each collector has unique characteristics and is designed for one of the four general types of radioactivity in air, they will be treated separately in the subsections that follow.

The joint requirements of sufficient volume (for the required concentration sensitivity) and frequency of sample collection (for the desired speed of data retrieval) may impose unrealistic demands on a sampling system. The sample volume is the product of sampling time and flow rate; the available flow rate is a function of pump capacity and pressure drop across the sample collector; and the pressure drop and collection efficiency are functions of the collecting medium, linear flow rate, and total volume sampled. A common solution to the problem of obtaining greater sensitivity with an existing system is to make only indicator measurements on individual samples, then to group samples over time or location for additional analysis. Potential pressure drop across the filter medium and collection efficiency impose constraints on linear air velocity at the collector face if comparable results are to be achieved from site to site.

Measurement of the volume of air sampled is important since the accuracy of the calculated radioactivity concentration can be no better than the accuracy of the measured volume. A flow measuring system should be included to indicate the volume of air sampled by either direct (total volume, such as through the use of a total gas flow meter) or indirect (flow-rate times elapsed time, using a flow-rate meter) methods. The volume of air sampled should be measured with an accuracy of at least ±10%. If flow-rate measurement is used, power outages or other factors that affect the data should be automatically recorded. A running-time meter is commonly used.

Although there are a number of applicable air monitoring systems commercially available,[31,32] their sensitivity is generally much lower than the collection-laboratory analysis method. In addition, equipment cost and field maintenance can be prohibitive if an adequate number of stations are established. A suggested list of air sampler performance criteria is presented as follows from the DOE Guide.[1]

1. The system should be designed to take a representative sample of the ambient air on a continuous basis. The preferred sampling height is approximately 1.5 m above ground level, in a location free from unusual micrometeorological or other conditions (e.g., proximity of large buildings, vehicular traffic) that could result in artificially high or low air concentrations.
2. The linear flow rate across particulate filters and charcoal cartridges should be maintained between 0.3 and 1.0 m/sec.
3. A fixed sampling rate should be used, constant to within ±20% during normal operation and expected filter-loading. Total airflow or total running time should be indicated.
4. The assembled sampling system should be leak-tested and flow-calibrated in the field.
5. The entire system should be inspected and tested at least quarterly and recalibrated and maintained when indicated.
6. The air-sampling system should be protected from the weather, and should be housed in a locked facility to afford a measure of security from accidental or willful damage or tampering.

Particulate air sampling techniques include filtration, electrostatic precipitation, impingement, and impaction. By far, the most popular air sampling method and the method of choice here for air particulates is filtration. With appropriate filter media, samples can be collected in almost any form or quantity. Handling problems are usually minimal, and several radioactivity measurements can be performed directly on the filter.

Correct use of the newer ICRP lung model, as described by the Task Group on Lung Dynamics,[33] requires a knowledge of the chemical state and the particle size distribution. If inhalation is potentially significant in terms of population dose, measurements of the radioactivity associated with each particle size should be made at least on an occasional basis. The need for particle size measurements is especially important at those sites where resuspension of previously deposited material is or can be a significant factor in environmental air concentrations. Such particle size measurements may also be useful in distinguishing resuspended material from that of current emissions.

Several methods, including the impactors (e.g., multistage cascade impactor) and electrostatic precipitators referred to above, can be used to classify particle size. Waite and Nees[34] and Kotrappa et al.[35] discuss techniques for particle sizing based on the flow discharge perturbation method and the HASL cyclone, respectively. These techniques are not recommended here for routine environmental surveillance of airborne particulates, although their use for special studies or for the evaluation of effluent streams should not be overlooked. A wide variety of particulate filters (cellulose, cellulose-asbestos, glass fiber, membrane, for example) is available. The type of filter is selected according to needs such as high collection efficiency, particle-size selectivity, retention of alpha emitters on the filter surface, and the ease of radiochemical analysis. Any filter used should retain a minimum of 99% of diocytl phthalate (DOP) particles with an aerodyanmic mean diameter of 0.3 μm at the linear air velocity and pressure drop expected in use.[31] Specific data on various filter materials, especially retention efficiencies, have been reported by several authors,[36-39] and additional information is available from manufacturers. Table 1 gives relative collection efficiencies for a number of filter media at different flow rates.

Pure cellulose papers are useful for samples to be dissolved and analyzed radiochemically, but the analytical filter papers used to filter solutions are inefficient collectors for aerosols and clog easily. Cellulose-asbestos filter papers combine fairly high efficiency, high flow rates, high mechanical strength, and low pressure drops when loaded and are very useful for collecting large samples but present difficulties in dissolution and their manufacture is diminishing because of the asbestos. Fiberglass filters can function efficiently at high flow rates but require fluoride treatment for dissolution and generally contain sufficient radioactive nuclides to complicate low-activity analysis. Polystyrene filters are efficient and capable of sustaining high air flow rates without clogging. They are readily destroyed for analysis by ignition (~300°C) or by wet washing with oxidizing agents and are also soluble in many organic liquids. They have the disadvantage of low mechanical and tensile strength and must be handled carefully. Membrane filters are excellent for surface collection efficiency and can be used for direct alpha spectrometry on the filter. They are, however, fragile and suffer from environmental dust loading. Presently, the filters of choice for radionuclides in the environment are glass fiber and polystrene.

The monitoring of airborne radioiodine is complicated by the probable existence of several species, including particulate iodine or iodine bound to foreign particles, gaseous elemental iodine, and gaseous nonelemental compounds. A well-designed monitoring program should be capable of distinguishing all possible iodine forms. While it may not always be necessary to differentiate between the various species, care should be taken so that no bias can result by missing one or more of the possible species.

In addition to the problems noted above, charcoal cartridges (canisters) for the collection of radioiodine in air are subject to channeling. Hence, they should be carefully checked before operation in the field (analogous to DOP testing of high efficiency particulate air (HEPA) filters *in situ*), or several should be mounted in series to prevent

Table 1
FLOW RATE AND COLLECTION EFFICIENCY CHARACTERISTICS OF SELECTED AIR FILTER MEDIA

At indicated face velocity		mm Hg Pressure drop			Percent Penetration of 0.3 μm DOP				Flow Reduction Due to Loading
Filter type	Filter	53[b]	106[b]	211[b]	26.7[b]	53[b]	106[b]	211[b]	%/m³/cm²
Cellulose	Whatman 1	86	175	350	7	0.95	0.061	0.001	17.9
	Whatman 41	36	72	146	28	16	2	0.30	5.0
	Whatman 541	30	61	123	56	40	22	9	10.4
	IPC 1478	1.5	3	5.5	90	90	90	85	<<0.1
Cellulose-asbestos	HV-70 (9 mil)	64	127	254	1.8	0.8	0.20	0.05	1.7
Cellulose-glass	Type 5-G	5	10	21	32	32	26	16	0.20
Glass	MSA 1106BH	30	61	120	0.068	0.048	0.022	0.005	0.43
	Gelman A	33	65	129	0.019	0.018	0.011	0.001	0.50
	Gelman E	28	57	114	0.036	0.030	0.014	0.004	0.53
	Hurlbut 934AH	37	74	150	0.010	0.006	0.003	0.001	0.47
	Whatman GF/A	29	60	118	0.018	0.015	0.008	0.001	0.37
Polystyrene	Microsorban	44	89	176	0.45	0.40	0.20	0.05	0.29
Membrane	Millipore AA (0.8 μm)	142	285	570	0.015	0.020	—	—	1.6
	Polypore AM-1 (5 μm)	23	46	95	12	8	5	2	2.4
	Polypore Am-3 (2 μm)	84	190	380	0.36	0.22	0.090	0.015	3.1

Data extracted from NRL Report No. 6054

[a] Table 4.2 from Reference 1 as extracted from the original NRL Report No. 6054[36]
[b] Indicated face velocities in centimeters per second.

loss of iodine. Too high a sampling rate reduces both the collection efficiency and retention time of charcoal filters, especially for the nonelemental forms of iodine.[40,41] The retention of iodine in charcoal is dependent not only on charcoal volume but also the length of the charcoal bed. Typical air flow rates for particulate sampling of 30 to 90 ℓ/min (1 to 3 ft^3/min) are quite acceptable for environmental concentrations of radioiodine, even in organic form, if larger cartridges than those recommended by the Intersociety Committee[26] are used. The method proposed by the Intersociety Committee[26] for ^{131}I concentrations in the atmosphere involves collecting iodine in its solid and gaseous states with an "absolute" particulate filter in series with an activated charcoal cartridge followed by gamma spectrometric analysis of the filter and cartridge. The Intersociety-recommended charcoal cartridges are 5/8-in. diameter by 1.5-in. deep containing 3 g of 12 to 30 mesh KI-activated charcoal. The minimum detectable level using the Intersociety method is 0.1 pCi/m^3. Larger cartridges will improve retention, permitting longer sampling periods. A more sensitive system has been described by Baratta et al.[42] in which concentrations as low as 0.01 pCi/m^3 of air are attainable.

Compound filter canisters of several designs (for an example, see Reference 43) have been used to distinguish the several chemical forms of radioiodine that may be present in the atmosphere. They will generally contain a particulate filter and silver wire or mesh plus charcoal, each of which is analyzed separately. Although the resulting data may be valuable enough to warrant special studies, the additional analytical cost is seldom warranted on a routine basis.

Because of the extremely long half-life and normally low environmental concentrations, ^{129}I determinations must usually be performed by neutron activation analysis after chemical isolation of the iodine. For concentrations above 3×10^{-10} μCi/ml, liquid scintillation counting can be used after solvent extraction.[44] For the short-lived radioiodines (mass numbers 132, 133, 135), environmental sampling is complicated by the need to obtain a sufficient volume for analysis while, at the same time, retrieving the sample soon enough to minimize decay (with half-lives ranging from 2 to 31 hr). Short period (grab) sampling with charcoal cartridges is possible, with direct counting of the charcoal as soon as possible for gamma emissions, but radon and thoron will affect detection levels. Presently, routine environmental surveillance for the noble gases is most commonly performed by external radiation measurements or laboratory analysis of occasional grab samples of ambient air.[11] Because of the limitations of current state-of-the-art systems and techniques, it is recommended that effluent monitoring coupled with occasional environmental sampling (and subsequent laboratory analyses) be utilized for routine environmental surveillance for the noble gases. It is expected that any significant contributions to external penetrating radiation dose from noble gases will be detected by environmental external radiation monitoring systems. Where ^{85}Kr is the only source of external exposure, a skin dose estimate for its beta emission may also be required. Experience has shown that calculation of environmental concentrations of the noble gases can be reasonably made from effluent measurements, concurrent meteorological parameters, and atmospheric dispersion techniques.[16,46-48]

Radioactive gas sampling, either grab or continuous, is based on collection in an evacuated chamber by adsorption in a medium such as charcoal, by cryogenic collection, or by a combination of these.[48-50] Low volume (<1 m^3) grab samples can be collected with a hand pump, while larger volumes must be collected in metal tanks by pumping to pressures of 10 to 30 atm.[50] Data on atmospheric stability and wind speed and direction during the period when the samples were collected should be noted. The naturally-occurring radioactive gases, ^{222}Rn and ^{220}Rn, may interfere with the eventual analyses. Johns[50] has suggested a continuous sampling method capable of operating up to 2 weeks without attention, followed by laboratory analysis of the collected gases.

For other methods, the reader is referred to the works of several authors[48,51,52] and the Lawrence Berkeley Laboratory Manual.[32]

The literature on environmental tritium measurements is extensive, including proceedings of symposia in 1961[53] and 1971[54]. References 55 to 61 and 171 are a partial listing of individual publications on the subject.

In air, tritium occurs primarily in two forms: as water vapor (HTO) and as hydrogen gas (HT). Tritiated organic compounds in the vapor phase or attached to particulate matter occur only occasionally. There are two common approaches to the measurement of tritium in air: ionization chambers or gas proportional counters with filtered air introduced for internal counting and removal of HTO vapor from the air with a bubbler, condenser, or desiccant, followed by counting of the resulting tritiated water with liquid scintillation techniques. To measure tritium as HT or in tritiated organics, the gas phase can be oxidized, converting the tritium to HTO before desiccation and counting. For dosimetric purposes, the fraction present as HT can usually be neglected, since the relative dose for a given activity concentration of HTO is 400 times that for HT.

The use of silica gel as a desiccant to remove moisture (H_2O, HTO) from air before liquid scintillation counting is a common technique for tritium determinations in air[11] and is the method proposed by the Intersociety Committee.[26] Its main advantage is its extremely high sensitivity. The Intersociety procedure is to use a 12-in. long by 1¼-in. diameter aluminum cylinder filled with silica gel (180 g). Air is pumped at 100 to 150 cm^3/min through the silica gel column, which collects essentially all of the moisture. Following sample collection (up to 2 weeks), the gel is heated to remove the moisture and the distillate is counted using standard liquid scintillation techniques. A somewhat less sensitive system than the desiccant method has been described by Osborne.[59] Tritium gas (HT) is totally excluded by these systems. Brown et al.[60] have reported a method for measuring and differentiating HT and HTO concentrations in ambient air. Additionally, Jacobs[55] and Iyengar et al.[61] have shown that water vapor for tritium analyses may be condensed on a cold surface. As with other air sampling methods, the largest source of error is uncertainty in the volume of air sampled. Other uncertainties include the prevailing temperature, pressure, and relative humidity of the air (essential parameters for concentration calculations).

Measurement of the specific activity of tritium in atmospheric moisture using a passive device, such as a container of silica gel suspended in air to collect tritiated water vapor, may be satisfactory as a detection device. Retention efficiency must be tested under operating conditions, and possible adverse effects on the collection efficiency by other gases at various concentrations should be tested. The chemical form of the radionuclide especially influences the collection efficiency. Considerable judgment must be used to appropriately deploy air sampling sites in the environment. For example, knowledge of a variety of site meteorological and demographic parameters is important in order to understand how stack-measured activities relate to dose to persons in the general environment. Regulatory Guides 1.21[30], 4.1[8], and 4.8[17], and the EPA Guide[3] contain detailed discussions on this issue. Another good reference is the technique suggested by Waite[62] which is based on average meteorological conditions and existing population distributions. When no population centers exist within 10 miles of the installation, air sampling should be established at locations where historical sampling information exists or at locations justified by topography and meteorology.

In general, the frequency of collection for air samples is adjusted to take into account sample collector limitations, air mover capabilities, and the physical problem of retrieving samples from each location on a fixed frequency. Experience has shown that sampling rates of 30 to 120 ℓ/min can be used with moderate power requirements and acceptable dust loading for 47-mm diameter air particulate filters changed on a weekly basis. However, the sensitivity of state-of-the-art counting equipment (with typical <100 min counting times) is often inadequate to permit analysis for some of the more toxic radionuclides (e.g., ^{90}Sr, ^{239}Pu) at levels well below the concentration guides for exposures of the general public.

The common practice has been to composite filters (monthly, quarterly, etc.) for subsequent analysis from several locations and successive time periods, taking advantage of the larger volume of air sampled to achieve the desired sensitivity with lower analytical costs. Use of this practice implies that the concentration of a given nuclide at the locations composited is sufficiently constant for the end use of the data. For dose calculation purposes, this practice is deemed acceptable; the annual average concentration for a location or for a group of locations can still be compared against an annual average for a background location as an indication of potential plant impact during the year in question. Averages for successive years can also be compared for detection of general trends. However, compositing does not permit a ready correlation of environmental concentrations with the releases from a given facility nor a reliable indication of an unusual release (because of dilution with potentially uncontaminated samples). Thus, individual samples should be measured before they are composited. It must be emphasized, however, that for air sampling of other than particulates, factors other than dust loading and air mover capacity are overriding. Of particular importance is the fact that "breakthrough" can occur with the charcoal cartridges, silica gel, and molecular sieves used for radioiodine, noble gas, and tritium collection. The "breakthrough" phenomena can be flow rate, total volume, or activity dependent, or a combination of them. Utilizing the sampling techniques suggested in this section and at typical environmental concentrations, these problems should be minimal.

Deposition Assessment

Deposition assessment refers to those techniques that utilize natural or artificial surfaces or open containers for collection of particulate pollutants by natural forces. The advantage of deposition sampling over other particulate sampling methods is simplicity. Not only is the sampling equipment easy to handle, but no power supply or auxiliary equipment is required in the field. With simple devices, it is possible to set up a collection station for a minimal cost.

Deposition sampling does not measure the concentration of a contaminant in the ambient atmosphere, only the amount deposited from the ambient atmosphere. This is a most pertinent measurement where the objectives of environmental surveillance include the evaluation of long-term accumulation trends and the estimation of environmental radionuclide inventories. Specialized media sampled to meet these objectives may not be directly related to exposure pathway analysis.

In addition to radionuclides that are specific to a particular operation or facility, naturally occurring (uranium and thorium series, ^{7}Be, and others) and fallout radionuclides can be expected in deposition samples. The relative importance of these contributors is somewhat dependent on site geography, geology, and meteorology.

The methods recommended here for measuring deposition are (1) direct instrument measurements for "quick-sort" objectives, where determining the presence or absence of recent deposition is of the greatest importance; (2) deposition collectors for intermediate time periods and for long-term evaluation where naturally integrating media (e.g., perennial grasses) are not available; and (3) surface soil sample collection for meeting long-term objectives, with core sampling for inventory purposes. The use of "control plots" with direct instrument measurement requires the establishment of typically 3-m by 3-m "control plots" which are entirely surveyed with a beta-gamma and/or alpha survey instrument on a monthly or quarterly basis to detect incremental changes in radionuclide contamination. Plots should be located in the immediate vicinity of air and soil/vegetation sampling sites.

The common portable Geiger-Mueller (G-M) survey instrument is highly useful for making spot checks for trends of radiation in the environment.[63,64] It may be necessary to specify a slower response time than normally supplied to reduce spurious meter movements. For known measurement techniques and mixtures of radionuclides, a dose-rate conversion factor may be experimentally obtained, but this is usually a supplementary or emergency response technique for dose-rate estimation.

The need to survey large surface areas for possible plutonium contamination resulted in the development of the FIDLER.[65,66] Consisting of a 12.7-cm (5-in.) diameter by 0.16-cm (1/16-in.) thick NaI(Tl) detector optically coupled to a 12.7-cm (5-in.) photomultiplier tube, it is designed to be carried over the terrain at about 30 cm above the surfaces. The battery-powered electronics package separates and counts two energy windows (normally 17 and 60 keV) which are related to the presence of plutonium and americium. Along with the soil parameters, the Pu/Am ratio must be known to translate survey results to soil concentrations if measuring the 60 keV photon only.

Although the equipment is expensive, direct gamma spectrum measurement and analysis is an excellent method of documenting environmental radioactivity resulting from natural sources, weapons testing fallout, and nuclear facilities operations.[67,68] Large-volume germanium detectors of the lithium-drifted [Ge(Li)] and intrinsic [IGE] types, with their inherent excellent-energy resolution, suitably mounted for *in situ* field spectrometry, have been shown to be especially useful in identification of radionuclides in the environment.[69,70,169,170] From such identification, the originating source can be inferred and radionuclide concentrations and external exposure rates calculated. The typical field [Ge(Li)] spectrometer system consists of a 50 to 70 cm^3 [Ge(Li)] detector (usually a downward-looking detector supported 1 m above the ground surface), a cryogenic mount and liquid nitrogen supply, a preamplifier, pulse-height analyzer, and magnetic tape data storage. A portable generator or battery converter is needed for power.

A number of different devices may be used for collection of deposition samples. These range from simple pail-like devices to complex wind-directional type units. Three common deposition collectors are the dustfall jar, coated surfaces, and precipitation collectors.[11]

The equipment recommended here is a combination precipitation/particulate deposition-collection device similar to one presently in use[71] at Hanford and designed to maximize the utility of the data generated. The collector consists of a funnel of 25-cm (10-in.) diameter. Clamped into the top of the funnel is a 0.6-cm (0.25-in.) thick disc of fibermat ventilation filter material. Normally, no support grid is needed beneath this filter material. Attached to the stem beneath the funnel is a plastic bag to collect any precipitation that occurs. The volume of this bag should be selected to contain any anticipated amount of rainfall that might occur between sample collections.

The height of the collector mount can be varied to emphasize either vertical deposition (including precipitation) or resuspension, depending on the sampling objective. For deposition only, the height of the opening should be at least 1.5 m above ground. In this case, a rigid support to fix the upright orientation of the device should be provided at each sampling site. For collection of resuspended material, as well as deposition, these collectors may be set at approximately ground level by inserting the support in the ground. To prevent collection of massive particles and debris and inhibit removal of collected material, a raised lip around the filter disc is necessary.

It may be sufficient for some purposes to survey the collection media *in situ* with portable instruments. Otherwise, sample collection with this device involves returning the fiber mat and precipitation reservoir to the laboratory and replacing them with clean components. The filter is leached and any liquid in the plastic bag is decanted and added to a water rinse of the collector. The two solutions may then be combined or analyzed separately. The collected samples are evaporated to dryness and counted. The analysis of deposition samples may vary from a gross alpha or beta count to a specific radionuclide analysis. Data may be presented in terms of activity per unit area or as deposition rate (e.g., μCi/m^2-day).

Samples of vegetation not directly part of an exposure pathway may be taken to measure either current or accumulated contamination levels in a given locality, dependent on whether the sample is of brush, fresh growth, or litter. The preferred sample will vary from site to site but will generally consist of the entire vegetative cover over the prescribed surface area. Data is generally reported in μCi/g dry weight.

As pointed out in the "Summary of Selected AEC Contractor Environmental Surveillance Techniques and Capabilities,"[11] there is perhaps the greatest diversity between sites in the techniques used for sampling and analyzing soil. Part of this diversity arises from different purposes of soil analysis. The limitations of sampling and analysis of plutonium in soil are clearly stated in Regulatory Guide 4.5[72] Although useful in special cases involving unexpected releases or long-term accumulations, soil analysis is a poor technique for assessing small incremental releases and is therefore not recommended as a method of choice for monitoring routine releases of radioactive material on a current basis.

Even though the presence of naturally occurring emitters and world-wide fallout (and potentially any facility-released radionuclides) are to be expected in soil samples, recent emphasis has been on plutonium in soil. Basic conflicts in philosophy and methodology of soil sampling and analysis have pointed to the need for the establishment of basic standards in this area. Several proposed standards are available and can be used as guidance in sampling, preparing samples and analyzing soil for plutonium,[17,72-74] and in comparing observed concentrations to allowable concentrations.[75]

Choices of procedure are given for both core and surface samples. It is recommended that routine sampling under normal plant operating conditions should emphasize the determination of trends in local environmental nuclide levels. In keeping with this objective, surface soil sampling to 5 cm depth[72] is recommended. The procedure calls for collection of 10 samples of approximately 10-cm diameter from an array within a 5- by 5-m square sample plot, compositing all of the samples from a given plot. Details of plot size, sample diameter and array, and number and (within limits) depth of samples are probably not nearly as significant as the nonreproducibility from plot to plot of amount and type of vegetative cover, gravel sizes, and effective surface roughness. Every effort should be made to select sampling plots and individual sample cuts as homogenous as possible and to avoid tilled areas or areas of unusual wind influence. However, good reproducibility of sample results should not be expected because of the nonhomogenous particulate distribution.

Coring methods are also described[72,76] involving the use of metal jigs from which slices can be taken at successive depths. The primary value of coring is to establish an inventory value for a nuclide in the environment based on random sampling of a predetermined grid pattern. In view of the large number of samples required to establish a valid estimate, this is not recommended for routine programs.

For all deposition sampling, gross alpha and beta analyses are of questionable usefulness, and primary emphasis should be given to isotopic analysis. This is especially true of soil samples. Deposition-precipitation collectors should be placed at selected air-sampling locations such as those that correspond to the plant boundary and in areas of anticipated maximum ground-level concentrations in the prevailing downwind directions. Other sampling locations might include points of suspected buildup and the nearest identifiable points of individual and population exposure. Background determinations should be made at points corresponding with background air sampling locations. Soil and vegetation sampling locations are usually selected to coincide with air and deposition collector sites, since the comparability of data may be important in achieving the objectives of sampling these nonpathway media.

Deposition collectors should be changed on a monthly or quarterly basis depending on the need. For undisturbed soils and perennial vegetation, an annual sampling frequency is sufficient.

Direct Radiation

The exposure of environmental population groups to direct radiation from nuclear facility operations includes that from cloud passage of airborne effluents; on-site sources, such as waste storage and transportation; and that from previous radionuclide deposition on soil, vegetation, or sediments. External exposure from radionuclides in water should be insignificant during normal operations at most nuclear facilities, although unique situations may still arise where recreational, commercial, or industrial use of a receiving body of water may incur some direct exposure. In addition, radiation generating facilities, especially the high-energy accelerators (but also industrial X-ray equipment and large isotopic sources), will have external radiation as the most probable critical pathway if the exclusion area is relatively small. For the high energy machines, not only gamma but also neutron flux may need to be measured.

For most facilities, the whole body (or gonad) exposure will be the significant measurement. Exceptions may be fuel reprocessing facilities, where release of ^{85}Kr will give a predominant beta dose to the skin during cloud immersion, or in areas of predominant deposition of beta-emitters. In general practice, the gamma exposure (or exposure rate) is measured or calculated, any significant skin dose from airborne beta emitters calculated from effluent measurements, and beta doses from deposition determined by intermittent measurements with beta-responsive portable instruments or by calculation from analysis of deposition samples.

The feasibility of distinguishing an annual incremental exposure, even as low as 5 mR at a given location, with the best of available dosimetry is highly questionable in view of the variability of background radiation. Gamma spectrometry in the field on a continuing basis is available, yet expensive, and may provide sufficient discrimination to distinguish incremental exposures of a few milliroentgens per year.

Direct radiation measurement devices may be either integrating dosimeters or rate devices. Either of these may be used on a continuous or intermittent basis, but some continuous measurements should always be part of an environmental program. Integrating dosimeters include thermoluminescent dosimeters (TLD), film, and ionization chambers. TLD is the dosimeter of choice on the basis of demonstrated sensitivity, reproducibility, reliability, and long-term stability. The individual dosimeters are relatively inexpensive, although a complete dosimeter/reader system can be costly.

A number of thermoluminescent materials are available commercially; activated lithium fluoride (LiF), calcium fluoride (CaF_2), and calcium sulfate ($CaSO_4$) are the most commonly employed. Various forms and packaging configurations are available as shown in Table 2, derived from References 77 to 82 and data on commercially available TLD systems given in "Instrumentation for Environmental Monitoring."[25] The list of literature references on TLD is extensive and still increasing. An American National Standards Institute (ANSI) standard[83] and a Nuclear Regulatory Commission Reg. Guide[172] give performance, testing, and procedural specifications for TLDs in environmental use, as well as suggested techniques for making corrections. Their use as standard references is recommended.

With careful handling and annealing procedures, the precision of measurement of a presorted batch of dosimeters should fall within ±5% at the 95% confidence level in the range of 1 to 100 mR.[78] Under less carefully controlled conditions in field use, precision of ±10% is still attainable with consistent annealing, calibration, readout,

Table 2
COMPARISON OF TLDs FOR ENVIRONMENTAL RADIATION MEASUREMENT[a]

TLD Phosphor	Form	Package	Exposure range	Minimum photon energies[b]	Energy dependence to 1 MeV[b]	Comments
LiF	Extrusion	None	<5 mR to 10^5 R	15 keV	±25%	High triboluminescence; requires careful annealing; may be neutron sensitive; relatively energy - independent; neutron sensitive in natural form; depleted form available
CaF_2:Mn	Powder on wire, extrusion	Glass capsule, metal case and shield	1 mR to 10^4 R	25 keV	±25%	Less stringent annealing requirements; capsule may cause self-dosing; some energy dependence; some room temperature fading
CaF_2:Dy	Extrusion	Tantalum and lead shield	0.5 mR to 10^4 R	50 keV	±20%	Low triboluminescence; high initial fading; careful shielding and annealing required
$CaSO_4$:Tm	Powder			30 keV	±40%	High sensitivity; low fading; high energy dependence
$CaSO_4$:Dy		Capsule and metal shield	<0.1 mR to 20 R	30 keV	±40%	
$CaSO_4$:Mn	Powder	Capsule and metal shield	<0.1 mR to 20 R	15 keV	±25%	High sensitivity; rapid fading; high energy dependence
BeO	—	Capsule	2 mR to 200 mR	15 keV	±25%	Some fading

[a] Table 4.3 from Reference 1.
[b] For packaging indicated; may be altered by additional shielding.

storage, and exposure periods. Accuracy of the measurements, especially with those materials most subject to fading, is less certain (Reference 80 specifies ±30%). Unless valid documentation is already available for the system in use, accuracy should be verified by independent measurement. Exchange and readout of at least some dosimeters on a monthly schedule is suggested as at least a partial answer to long-term fading. Irradiation of calibration dosimeters at the beginning or at least early during the period of field measurements also helps to minimize fading errors. Postexposure annealing is especially helpful in dealing with long-term fading, although some sensitivity is sacrificed for the sake of accuracy.

Ideally, calibration procedures for both dosimeters and exposure-rate instruments should be based on the nuclide mixture to be measured in use. Since, for environmental measurements, there will generally be a mixture of unknown nuclides (including those from natural radioactivity), no ideal source is available. The most commonly used have been radium, ^{137}Cs, and ^{60}Co. It is suggested that an aged radium source be used since it gives a spectrum of gamma energies, and standardization by the National Bureau of Standards is readily available.

For the monitoring of intermittent or unplanned releases and for better identification of source terms, exposure-rate instrumentation should be available. Several types of instruments suitable for measurement of environmental exposure rates are available commercially, as shown in Table 3.

The argon-filled ion chamber listed is capable of continuous unattended operation and exposure rate measurements down to 1 μR/hr and has excellent energy response characteristics. In addition to a chart record, an optional tape cassette readout can provide computer-compatible data for detailed computer analysis.

Low-level portable exposure-rate instruments using either GM tubes or scintillator materials are capable of exposure rate measurements down to 5 μR/hr and are relatively inexpensive compared to the pressurized argon-filled ion chamber. However, stability and reproducibility of measurements are much less satisfactory.

For neutron monitoring, the moderated BF_3 tube in several commercially available models is generally satisfactory, either as a fixed monitor or semiportable instrument. Dose-rate estimates based on these measurements require a knowledge of the neutron energy spectrum, as is also the case where measurements are made with a "rem-meter." Although paired TLDs, including one enriched in ^6Li, are used for personnel monitoring for neutron exposure, the sensitivity of this technique is not adequate for environmental measurements.

Periodically (e.g., biennially), *in situ* quantitative gamma spectrometric measurements should be performed to characterize any increases in environmental levels. The spectra should be analyzed to apportion the total gamma dose rate among the various contributing radionuclides. The routine environmental surveillance program should be evaluated at this time to determine if the program needs modification. This evaluation should be made on the basis of: (1) changes in quantity or characteristics of discharges as compared to predicted or actual circumstances on which the previous program was based; (2) analyses of samples of media that are not routinely monitored but which, on the basis of research or experience, have potential for population exposure or long-term buildup of radioactivity; and (3) experience with the existing program, which may indicate that deletion of certain media or modification of the frequency, type of analysis, or sampling techniques would not compromise the program.

As with air sampling, a sufficient number of dosimeter locations must be established to provide reliable estimates of external doses to key population groups, as well as the 80-km (50 mi) population dose. For convenience, therefore, integrating dosimeters may be placed at all off-site air sampling stations, including control or background locations. Because of the nonspecific nature of the measurements, it may be desirable

Table 3
EXPOSURE RATE INSTRUMENTS[a]

Type	Detector	Radiation	Exposure rate range	Energy range	Accuracy	Graph readout	Power	Operation period	Relative Cost
Movable	Pressurized argon chamber	γ	1 μR/hr to 150 μR/hr	50 keV to 5 MeV	±5%	Option	Line or Battery	Continuous (200 hr) on battery	High
Stationary	GM	γ or β, γ	10 μR/hr to 100 mR/hr	100keV to 2.5 MeV	±20%	Option	Line	Continuous	Moderate
Portable	Scintillator	γ	5 μR/hr to 50 mR/hr	—	—	Option	Battery	100—300 hr	Moderate
Portable	Air ionization	β, γ	10 μR/hr to 1000 mR/hr	40 keV to 1.3 MeV	±20%	—	Battery	100 hr	Moderate
Portable	GM	β, γ	5 μR/hr to 2000 mR/hr[b]	45 keV to 3 MeV	±20%	—	Battery	4 hr continuous 50 hr intermittent	Low

[a] Table 4.4 from Reference 1.
[b] Selected ranges available within these limits.

to add dosimeter locations for better area discrimination or to monitor specific continuing activities.

Where integrating dosimeters are used, three or more dosimeters should be provided at each location (if possible in the same package) to permit averaging and rapid detection of faulty dosimeters. Alternatively, it is possible to use dosimeters at each location for long-term exposure in addition to others changed monthly. Different exchange periods are acceptable as long as precision and accuracy are not sacrificed. Integrating dosimeters should be read without undue delay, but above all, at a consistent time following collection.

The recommended height for placement of dosimeters is at 1 m above the surface. If another height is used, the relationship to the 1-m height should be established for the site. Special care must be used in mounting dosimeters to avoid partial shielding by buildings, trees, or posts. Suspension from a fence wire or from a thin metal post at minimum of 50 m from the nearest building is recommended. Some compromise may be necessary for protection of the dosimeters because of the susceptibility of dosimeter packages to pilferage and vandalism.

TERRESTRIAL ENVIRONMENT

The specific media which fall under this general category are food crops (fruits and vegetables), milk (cow and goat), domestic animals (meat and poultry), animal products (eggs, cheese), game animals (deer, rabbits, squirrels), and game birds (pheasant).

Samples of food, milk, and certain terrestrial animals are of greatest importance in environmental surveillance because they provide the most direct basis for assessing the radiation dose to man. The principal pathways for radionuclide contamination of food and plants are atmospheric deposition from airborne releases and crop irrigation from rivers, ponds, or lakes receiving liquid effluents.

In sampling food, milk, and biota, there are generally two different goals: the definition of direct and indirect pathways leading to dose to man, and the determination of long-term radionuclide accumulation in the environment. Milk analyses for certain nuclides can be used for evaluation of short- or long-term trends as well as direct dose calculation. As a direct dose contributor, ^{131}I may be the critical nuclide for nuclear power plant effluents, via the air-forage-cow-milk pathway, to infants consuming the milk. This same pathway may also be important for certain longer-lived materials, notably ^{90}Sr. Milk is particularly important because it is one of the few foods commonly consumed soon after production. To a lesser degree, the same applies for some home-grown garden products, such as lettuce and spinach. However, for many adults, meat — either from domestic or game animals — will provide the major intake of local foods.

Animal feeds may provide important data for determining radionuclide concentrations in the food chain. Foods may be categorized according to the U.S. Department of Agriculture scheme as leafy vegetables, grains, treegrown fruits, etc. and representative samples from each group selected for analysis.

Milk

As noted above, particular attention should be given to milk sampling, whether from dairy herds or "family" cows. No particular milk sampling techniques are required, other than preservation of the sample from souring or curdling, except that excessive dilution of samples with milk from unaffected areas should be avoided. Raw milk should be obtained for determining individual (infant) dose impact as close as possible to the site boundary. Samples from the major milksheds should be processed milk. Commercial sources of processed milk are adequate. At least a 4-ℓ sample of cow's milk should be collected in a polyethylene container. For goat's milk, a 1-ℓ sample may be the maximum available, especially from a single goat. Liquid milk should be refrigerated or otherwise preserved as noted in the literature[84-86] prior to analysis. Analytical procedures for milk are well documented[6,44,84-87] and should be considered when deciding upon a sample preservation method.

Since animal metabolism discriminates against many of the radionuclides from plant sources and world-wide fallout, only a few radionuclides are expected to have a significant dose impact via the milk pathway, notably ^{89,90}Sr, ^{131}I, ^{137}Cs, and ^{140}Ba-La. The foregoing should be considered in the collection, preparation, and analysis of milk samples.

Milk will commonly be the food product of greatest potential dose significance. However, when fresh milk is not available (because of physical location of the plant site or lack of milk cows or goats), it is suggested one or more of the following samples be used instead: animal thyroids (livestock, deer), fresh forage, or fresh leafy vegetables. Animal thyroids (a veterinarian or qualified biologist should be consulted to assure collection of the proper organ) are a most sensitive measure of environmental ^{131}I contamination; however, the data are useful primarily as indicators, not for dose calculations. For dose calculations, leafy vegetable samples should be taken when milk is not available.

The frequency of milk sampling should be based on the nuclides of interest. For ^{131}I analyses, this would be at least biweekly just during the grazing season; for ^{90}Sr analyses, quarterly sampling may be adequate unless this is the critical exposure pathway and site releases are highly variable. For such conditions, monthly sampling is recommended during the grazing season.

Vegetation

Several kilograms of a vegetation sample may be needed, depending upon analytical sensitivities for the radionuclides of interest. The choice of species and sample type must be guided by factors such as species availability, seasonal growth patterns, soil types, and farming practices. The pathways of radionuclides to the analyzed fractions, such as surface deposition, root uptake, translocation from other parts of the plant, must also be considered.

As in all terrestrial samples, naturally occurring ^{40}K and the uranium and thorium series contribute to the radiation observed. Deposition of such cosmic-ray-produced nuclides as ^{7}Be and of nuclear-weapons-test fallout may also be present. Properly selected processed items from commercial sources may be helpful in providing background data.

Wildlife

Animals whose meat is eaten by man are of greatest interest for dose calculation. Other animals may be collected as indicators of plant-released activity, because they concentrate certain radionuclides, consume foods of special interest, forage over wide areas, or inhabit particular locales. However, the data from small numbers of samples of wild animals or game birds should not be casually used for trend indication because of their great variation in mobility, age, and diet. A possible exception could be small rodents.

Wildlife samples can be trapped as suggested by Maletskos, et al.,[89] acquired from hunters, collected after accidental road kills, or obtained by request to the appropriate state game agency. Wildlife that is relatively rare locally should not be taken as environmental samples. Since the choice of species sampled may be crucial to the usefulness of the results, local ecologists and biologists should be consulted prior to sample collection to insure consideration of factors that affect animal radionuclide uptake and retention, such as size, age, sex, feeding locus, and food consumption. An estimate of the radionuclide intake of the animal just before its death may be provided by analyzing the stomach content, especially the rumen in cattle, sheep, and deer. However, the sample must be collected within a brief period (2 to 4 hr) after death.

In sampling deer and other animals, it is important not to contaminate the meat sample by whatever nuclides may have been deposited on the animal's fur or may be present in the gut. Washing or dipping in paraffin are advisable, and special care for the cleanliness of tools used to open the animal is necessary.

Meat and Produce

Meat, poultry, eggs, fresh produce, and other foodstuffs may be procured from local farmers. Meat samples may also be collected at a slaughterhouse if the origin of the animals can be documented. Local health departments may also be able to provide or assist in getting samples. Samples should be placed in sealed plastic bags and appropriately labeled and preserved prior to delivery to the analytical laboratory. All foodstuff samples should be reduced to edible portions for analysis in a manner similar to that for human consumption (i.e., remove cores, bones, seeds, other nonedible parts) and weighed as received from field (i.e., wet weight) within 24 hr. Wet weights are desired since consumption data is generally on that basis.

For fresh produce, other crops, and domestic food animals, a local land-use study will almost certainly be necessary to determine what crops and animals are important in the local diet and where they are produced with regard to the site. Fruit and vegetable samples should be collected near the point of maximum predicted annual ground concentration from airborne releases and from areas that may be contaminated by water into which liquid plant wastes have been discharged (e.g., irrigated crops). Local land usage should be periodically reviewed as well as current farming and stock-feeding practices at sampling locations.

Samples of meat, poultry, and eggs produced in the area should be collected from appropriately located commercial producers or "family farms" in the area. The samples should represent animals fed on crops grown within 25 km (15 miles) of the site in the prevailing downwind direction, again including both the nearest source and the source with the highest predicted air concentration from routine releases. Samples from animals that drink from a source downstream of the discharge or forage on crops irrigated from such a source should also be included where available.

The suggested frequency of sampling is annually for domestic food animals and fresh produce, specifically at the local time of slaughter or harvest, as well as for poultry and eggs. Eggs may represent a critical pathway for several nuclides, in which case monthly sampling is recommended.

Game birds and mammals that are hunted locally should be sampled during the hunting season in the vicinity of the site (within 25 km). If no such biota are normally used or available as food stuffs, smaller mammals may be substituted for trend indication.

AQUATIC ENVIRONMENT

The principal exposure pathways to individuals or groups of individuals in the environment from waterborne radionuclides are ingestion of drinking water; consumption of fish, ducks, or other aquatic species; and consumption of irrigated crops. Of secondary importance are external radiation from surface water (swimming, boating, water skiing), sediment deposits along the shoreline, or deposits on an irrigated field. The radiation doses from these external sources are generally several orders of magnitude less important than from pathways[11,13] leading to ingestion.

Experience at most ERDA (now DOE) facilities[90] indicates that the waterborne radionuclide releases consist mostly of fission and activation products associated with reactor and supporting fuel cycle operations. The same can be said for nuclear power plant facilities. Thus, sampling should include surface and groundwater supplies as well as drinking water, taking into account both the waste management practices and regional water usage at a specific site. The sampling of sedimentary material from streams or ponds can provide an indication of the accumulation of undissolved radionuclides that may lead to exposure of man through aquatic species, resuspension into drinking water supplies, or as an external radiation source to fishermen, waders, etc. Sediment sampling is particularly appropriate for most of the transuranics (especially ^{239}Pu); such activation products as ^{54}Mn, ^{58}Co, ^{60}Co, and ^{65}Zn; and several fission products, e.g., ^{95}Zr-Nb, ^{134}Cs, and ^{137}Cs.

Water and Sediment Sampling

The major concerns in sampling are the collection of representative samples and the maintenance of radionuclides in their original concentrations prior to analysis. The general problem of the measurement of radioactivity in environmental water has been discussed by Kahn[91]; Perkins and Rancitelli[92] have discussed nuclear techniques for determining radionuclides in natural waters. Standardized water sampling procedures are also discussed in Standard Methods[27], an EPA Manual[28], and the American Society for Testing and Materials (ASTM) Water Manual.[93] Sediment sampling is less standardized with samples being collected manually by dredging and coring methods. Portions of the detailed HASL[6] and Nuclear Regulatory Commission (NRC)[72] procedures for preparing soil samples for analysis are equally applicable to sediment samples.

Sample collection should be coordinated with waste management practices for liquid wastes. For example, grab samples collected downstream from nuclear facilities at fixed time intervals may be of little value if the liquid wastes are discharged periodically or in batches, rather than continunously. Ideally, a continuous proportional sampling device should be used. A number of DOE sites[11] are successfully using battery-operated or line-powered continuous water samplers. However, in the absence of a significant direct population exposure pathway from surface water (e.g., drinking water supplies taken directly from the stream), continuous sampling may not be needed. As an alternative, one may collect frequent grab samples and include a record of the effluent discharge rate from the site at the times samples are taken. The following factors should be considered when selecting water sampling equipment: (1) probability for significant fluctuations in concentration of the water sampled, (2) potential for significant human impact (dose), and (3) applicability to radionuclide(s) of interest.

The recommended practice for surface and drinking water samples is automated continuous sampling followed by analysis of the unfiltered sample. A known volume (10 to 100 mℓ) should be automatically diverted from a flowing line (sampling the surface stream or drinking water supply) into a treated container on a time frequency of about 30 min, providing a composited sample for weekly analysis. These samples should be taken with timing proportional to flow rate if the data therefrom is to be used for radionuclide transport or inventory purposes. When the data are to be used for dose calculations, the method should utilize a fixed-time sampling frequency, similar to that by which water is withdrawn for human consumption. When circumstances prohibit this type of automated continuous sampling (e.g., power restrictions, prohibitive pumping requirements, freezing temperatures, etc.), a suggested alternative is to take weekly grab samples of surface water composited for monthly analyses and daily grab samples of drinking water composited for weekly or monthly analyses.

The collection and preparation of representative environmental water samples for analysis present a number of unique problems for which clearly defined answers are not always available. In addition to the general problems of avoiding interferences and of finding sampling locations representative of the stream or body of water at points of interest, natural waters are frequently two-phase systems, i.e., solid materials are suspended in or floating on the water. All routine water samples should be carefully taken from beneath the water surface to avoid both floating debris and any sediments or growths on the bottom.

Appropriate caution should be exercised to assure that water samples are not cross contaminated by reuse of sampling containers for collecting samples. When obtaining surface water grab samples, the sample container should be rinsed twice with the water being sampled prior to taking the actual sample. When aliquoting from a larger water sample, extra effort is required to make the aliquot representative of the entire sample. A proportional part of the suspended material should be included in the aliquot either by mixing the solution vigorously during sampling or, if possible, by dissolving suspended or wall-collected material. A tritium dial watch worn by the sample collector may affect the tritium concentration observed in the sample.[94] Other potential sources of sample contamination may be less obvious.

Sample preservation techniques are applied to limit biological and chemical action in the sample during and after collection. Known phenomena include the following:

1. Cations, at very low concentrations, can be lost from solution, e.g., cesium can exchange with potassium in the container (glass).
2. Radionuclides can be absorbed by algae or slime growths in sample lines or on container walls, especially in sample containers that remain in the field for extended periods.
3. Hydrolysis and sorption on container walls or on particles in the water can occur at low acidities (typical of many natural waters).
4. Radiocolloidal phenomena may result in large flocculant particle formation or additional plate-out on container walls.
5. Pretreatment may induce change in nuclide distribution, e.g., acidification can leach suspended particles in the original sample so that more radioactivity appears in solution.
6. Acids used as biocides can oxidize iodide to iodine, resulting in its volatilization.
7. Acids may quench standard liquid scintillation cocktails, invalidating tritium analysis.
8. A change in counting geometry may occur for gamma-ray counting if finely-divided particulate activity settles out or if soluble species become fixed on the container walls during counting.

Reference 28 lists various preservative methods and permissible storage times for water samples according to chemical species and is recommended as a basic reference. Current practice at most nuclear installations is to predose the sample container with an acid (typically 2 to 3 $m\ell$ concentrated H_2SO_4/ℓ of sample), which inhibits both biological growth and plate-out of dissolved ions on the container wall. Pretreatment of the sample container with a salt solution of the same chemical species as the nuclide to be measured can assist in minimizing wall adsorption. Keeping the sample container refrigerated inhibits biological growth. Filtration during sample collection may be effective for some situations. The radioanalytical procedures to be used and the purpose of the measurements will govern which, if any, pretreatment may be used, since the procedures may be adversely affected by additives used to preserve other nuclides. Radioiodines especially should not be analyzed on an acidified sample. It is recommended that the optimum preservation procedure be determined by local testing.

Surface water background samples should be collected routinely at a representative unaffected location to provide control data for comparison with data from downstream stations. Care should be taken to avoid any immediate groundwater inflow or effluent being moved upstream by tides or large eddies. If the receiving stream originates on-site, a counterpart stream in the vicinity may be substituted if investigation shows it to be independent of local radioactivity. The other recommended off-site sampling sites for surface water are at the edge of the effluent mixing zone and at the nearest down-current point of withdrawal for domestic or other uses. Where experience and operating design can be used to assure that no release will be made to surface waters that could cause the dose criteria of Table 2 to be exceeded, this portion of the surveillance program may be reduced. Multiple sampling points, based on diffusion and transport studies of the mixing zone, may be necessary to obtain a reliable estimate for that location. Sampling at the first downstream point of withdrawal for public use provides an upper estimate of the amount of radioactivity in the water supply (for drinking or irrigation) of any population group. Usually, this will be the first farm or town downstream from the site. However, transport anomalies may result in greater concentrations of radionuclides at some other location. Special studies should be made to confirm sample representativeness and relationship to maximum concentrations. A suggested method of performing this analysis is to perform traverse sampling at a number of points along a line perpendicular to the stream flow. Samples on the traverse should be taken at more than one depth and at least four to six equally spaced points across the streamflow. It is further suggested that traverse studies be repeated whenever significant change occurs either in the types and quantities of radionuclides (actual or expected) in the effluent released or in the flow regime of the stream.

The recommended sampling location for downstream drinking water is at the withdrawal point of maximum probable effluent concentration in surface water. This practice will tend to maximize the dose estimates made therefrom. Samples of untreated water at the same location should also be taken to determine any removal by water treatment and to improve the accuracy of dose estimates.

It is unlikely that groundwater will accumulate radioactivity from nuclear facilities, except for those facilities that discharge liquid effluents to the ground. The soil acts as a filter and ion exchange medium for most radionuclides. However, tritium especially has a substantial potential for seeping through the soil into the groundwater, as do the halogens and certain chemical states of a few other radionuclides (notably ^{106}Ru).

Periodic grab sampling is the method of choice for groundwater since the flow rate of most groundwater systems is several orders of magnitude less than that of surface streams. Groundwater grab sampling is usually done by dipping or bailing, but more reliable results can be obtained by pumping with either a pressure air lift or a submersible pump. In either case, it is desirable to pump sufficiently long to obtain "clear" samples or to dip several times to assure adequate mixing and a representative sample.

Filtration of well samples is recommended since suspended material is usually an artifact of the sampling process (well casing particles, dirt near water-soil interface) and is not representative of the groundwater.

The frequency and location of wells to be sampled routinely should be determined from available knowledge of local groundwater conditions. In this regard, the experience of local well drillers and hydrologists can be of great assistance in planning and evaluating a groundwater program. Experience at Hanford[95] has shown that, even though past waste management practices included the routine release of large and varying volumes of liquids to the ground, changes in groundwater concentrations from wells away from the disposal sites did not change rapidly with time. Using that experience as a guide, groundwater sampling on a quarterly basis is recommended only for wells nearest disposal sites to which liquid discharges are made. For more remote wells, yearly sampling is suggested. As a minimum, the nearest well down-gradient of potential site influence in the water table should be sampled.

If no release is made to the ground, no groundwater is consumed, and no evidence of plant sources in the nearest well is found, no other samples should be necessary.

Samples of deposited sediments in water can be collected by scoop or trowel, by dredge, or by core sampler. The manual methods are most useful because location and depth can be well defined. The dredge and coring methods utilize a sampling device dropped from a boat. When the device contacts the sediment (benthos), the sampling mechanism is activated.

With a dredge (a number of types are available), sediment is collected without exact knowledge of the location or the depth. The manual and dredge methods provide primarily surface sediment samples, whereas the coring device provides sample separation (with depth) of sediment. Water depth and stream flow data at the time of sampling are of interest. Characteristics of the sample, such as particle-size distribution, soil type, ion-exchange capacity, and organic content, may be useful for proper interpretation of the analytical results.

Sediment samples are usually taken to detect the buildup of radionuclides by sedimentation. Therefore, the most favorable times for sampling are prior to and just after the spring freshet. Suggested sampling locations include an upstream site beyond any possible plant influence and two downstream locations, one preferably near the discharge site and the other in an area which favors sedimentation, e.g., the inner bank of a bend (see the EPA guide[3] for further suggestions). Precipitation and flocculation of the suspended sediments occur at fresh salt-water interfaces and at dam impoundments, creating primary areas for measurement of radionuclide levels in the sediments. If liquid effluents from a nuclear facility are discharged to a lake or pond, a sediment sample should be taken near the outfall but beyond the turbulent area created by the effluents. An annual frequency for sediment sampling is recommended since sediments are usually not in a critical exposure pathway.

Aquatic Organisms

Aquatic organisms may concentrate radionuclides from their environment or from their food.[96-98] For this reason, and because fish, shellfish, and waterfowl may be consumed in relatively large quantities by people, these organisms must be considered in the routine environmental surveillance program.

Aquatic plants and animals as discussed here are any species which derive all or substantial portions of their nourishment from the aquatic ecosystem, are part of a human food chain, and show significant accumulation of radioactivity. Fish and invertebrates as well as aquatic mammals and game birds are of the most practical interest.

Flora

Aquatic biota such as algae, seaweed, and benthic organisms are indicators and concentrators of radionuclides — especially ^{59}Fe, ^{60}Co, ^{65}Zn, ^{90}Sr, and ^{137}Cs — and can be vectors in the water-fish-man food chain. As such, they may be sampled upstream and downstream at locations similar to those described for sediment. Because of their high water content, several kilograms (wet weight) should be collected per sample. Both algae, obtained by filtering water or by scraping submerged substrates, and rooted aquatic plants should be sampled. These organisms should only be a part of the periodic surveillance program if higher organisms (fish, waterfowl) are not available.

Fish and Shellfish

Fish and shellfish may be purchased from local sources if the origin can be determined. Samples can also be obtained by pole fishing, netting, or electric shock devices. Samples should include each of the principal edible types in local catches. Several kilograms of each fish sample are usually required; this may be one large fish, but preferably a composite of a number of small ones. Analysis of the edible portions of food fish as prepared for human consumption is of major interest. The whole fish is analyzed if it is used for the preparation of fish meal for consumption or if only trend indication is required. In a program where fish are the critical pathway, fish are analyzed by species; if less detail is required, several species with similar feeding habits (such as bottom feeders, insectivores, or predators) may be collected and the data grouped.

In large bodies of water, samples at several stations are desirable because of the difficulty in knowing whether a fish caught at a given location had lived there for an extended period. Thus, the presence or absence of a radionuclide in a specific fish does not permit any definite conclusion concerning the presence of the radionuclide in water at that location. For some fish, more specific information concerning their usual location may be available; for example, dams, salinity gradients, and temperature gradients can be effective barriers to their movement. Expert guidance and information on fish age, feeding habits, and the quality of the aquatic environment are desirable to evaluate the significance of any findings.

The frequency of sampling for fish should make it possible to define any changes in concentration expected on a cyclical basis, such as that observed at one time for ^{32}P in Columbia River whitefish.[99] A suggested minimum frequency would be quarterly for those edible species available all year long or monthly for those available only portions of the year.

Shellfish such as clams, oysters, and crabs are collected for the same reasons as fish but have the advantage as indicators of being relatively stationary. This restricted mobility contributes substantially to the interpretation and application of analytical results to environmental surveillance needs. Edible and inedible portions of these organisms can be analyzed separately.

In fresh water, the principal nuclides to be expected in fish or shellfish (in addition to the naturally occurring ^{40}K and uranium) include ^{3}H, ^{137}Cs, and ^{90}Sr, although any nuclide present in the water will be present in the fish. In salt or brackish water, the expected nuclide mixtures will be more apt to reflect accumulated fallout nuclides. One might also expect greater concentrations of ^{40}K.

Waterfowl

Waterfowl such as ducks and geese, may also concentrate radionuclides from their food sources in the aquatic environment. The migratory patterns and feeding habits of waterfowl vary widely. Some species are bottom feeders and, as such, tend to concentrate those radionuclides associated with sediments such as ^{60}Co, ^{65}Zn, and ^{137}Cs. Others feed predominantly on surface plants, insects, or fish.

Waterfowl should be collected (most commonly by hunting, but Maletskos et al.[89] used a trapping procedure for wild birds) from the public hunting areas nearest the site, or on-site for those species known to migrate to and from lakes, ponds, or streams within the site boundaries. Sampling should coincide with the local hunting seasons for dose estimations, but additional quarterly samples are desirable as trend indicators for a waterfowl population resident at on-site waters. An important consideration in collecting a sample from waterfowl is that their exterior surfaces, especially feathers, may be contaminated. It is important to avoid contaminating the "flesh" sample during handling. As with other biota samples, analyses on only the edible portions are

Table 4
ENVIRONMENTAL SURVEILLANCE PROGRAM ALTERNATIVES[a]

	Advantages	Disadvantages
Atmospheric		
Particulates		
Constant air monitors	Real-time readout, chart record	Cost, maintenance, sensitivity, interference (Rn, Tn)
Pump and filter	Sensitivity, cost	Time delay in obtaining results
Electrostatic precipitators	Sensitivity	Cost, variable efficiency
Noble Gases		
Evacuated chamber	Portability	Sensitivity, not continuous
Compressed air	Sensitivity	Not continuous
Cryogenic	Sensitivity	Cost
Direct radiation (TLD)	Cost, integrator, direct dose measurement	Sensitivity, high background, not nuclide specific
Ion chamber	Real-time readout, chart record, sensitivity, direct dose rate measurement	Cost, maintenance
Halogens		
Charcoal	Cost, all forms collected	Not nuclide specific
Molecular sieves		Cost, capacity, not nuclide specific
Bubblers	Sensitivity, cost	Maintenance
Tritium		
Cryogenic	No sample preparation	Not ^3H specific, cost, portability, HT not collected
Bubblers	Cost, no sample preparation	Maintenance, sensitivity, HT not collected, not ^3H specific
Molecular sieves	Portability, ^3H specific (with distillation)	Sample preparation needed, HT not collected, capacity varies with ralative humidty
Drierite	Portability, ^3H specific (with distillation)	HT not collected, poor water capacity, sample preparation needed
Silica Gel	Portability, ^3H specific (with distillation)	Sample preparation needed, HT not collected, capacity varies with relative humidity
Terrestrial		
Milk	Dose vector, nuclide specific, case of data interpretation,	Availability
Foodstuffs	Dose vector, case of data interpretation	Availability, weathering
Wildlife	Dose vector	Mobility, availability, data interpretation
Vegetation	Availability, multiple accumulation modes	Not nuclide specific, data interpretation, weathering
Direct instrument	Cost, fast	Sensitivity, not nuclide specific
Deposition collection	Defined time span for sampling period, area and collection factors known	Weathering
Soil sampling	Time integrator	Cost, representativeness, time delay in obtaining results, data interpretation

Table 4 (continued)
ENVIRONMENTAL SURVEILLANCE PROGRAM ALTERNATIVES[a]

	Advantages	Disadvantages
	Aquatic	
Surface water	Availability	Data interpretation
Ground water	Indicator for waste management	Availability, data interpretation
Drinking water	Dose vector	Sensitivity
Aquatic plants	Sensitivity	Data interpretation
Sediment	Sensitivity, integrator	Data interpretation
Fish	Sensitivity, dose vector	Availability, mobility, data interpretation
Waterfowl	Dose vector	Availability, mobility, data interpretation

[a] Taken from Table 4.5 of Reference 1.

the most meaningful and should be reported on a "wet" weight basis. Local game officials or aquatic ecologists should be consulted to aid in choosing the proper species.

Caution is advisable with selection of background or control locations for all biota (terrestrial and aquatic) sampled, at least for those species whose mobility and feeding habits may significantly affect the results obtained. Since this mobility makes it difficult to establish upstream/downstream sampling locations for biota in a manner analogous to those for air, water, or plants, it is recommended that the expert advice and direction of ecologists and fish and game personnel be used in planning the sampling programs. Samples from the background locations should be from an ecosystem identical to that of those collected near the site, but unaffected by site effluents.

SUMMARY OF PROGRAM ALTERNATIVES

The necessity of adjusting surveillance techniques to meet established objectives is a principle widely recognized yet sometimes ignored. Many environmental measurements will indeed serve more than one purpose (for example, both trend evaluation and ecological study), but seldom optimally for more than one purpose. For example, a total inventory estimate for a given radionculide will usually require a rigid three-dimensional sampling scheme; simple trend evaluation will permit much more flexibility and simplicity. Table 4 is intended to afford some guidance on the relative advantages and disadvantages of alternative means of achieving the same surveillance objectives. By no means complete, it should at least provide a framework for the staff at each site to use where alternative techniques appear to be equally useful.

ANALYSIS OF ENVIRONMENTAL SAMPLES BY CHEMICAL AND PHYSICAL MEANS

Dale H. Denham

Specific radioanalytical methods are omitted from this section, except for generic procedures which are noted as they affect sample collection, handling, and preparation. Many of the principles, methods, and techniques used in the measurement of radionuclides in environmental samples are common to all low-level radioanalysis and applicable to other environmental contaminants. A monograph by Korenman[100]* discussed many of the factors and considerations that apply to all analyses at low concentrations. References 14, 26-28, 101-105, and 168 also provide detailed discussions of low-level radioanalytical techniques and measurements. Current procedures from HASL-300[6] may be used as standard references.

Evaluation of population doses from the "as low as reasonably achievable" viewpoint has created pressure for increasingly sensitive radiation measurement and evaluation techniques. As a result, at most commercial laboratories, radioanalytical detection levels for the more common analyses, using practicable sample size and counting times, are available equivalent** to annual organ doses of less than 5 mrem (for most analyses less than 1 mrem). Detection levels of this magnitude for direct measurement of incremental external radiation in the environs are not readily available because of the comparatively large variability of natural radiation levels.

ANALYTICAL CONSIDERATIONS AND GOALS

Gross radioactivity measurements alone are generally not adequate for radiological monitoring. However, gross radioactivity measurements may be useful to indicate the concentration of a specific radionuclide when such measurements are shown to be truly indicative of the actual quantity or concentration of that radionuclide. Gross activity measurements in air (particulates) and water (fresh) can and should play a major role in environmental monitoring procedures as trend indicators or for a given site as indicators of specific nuclides (from experimental determinations.)

Detection Capabilities

The detection capabilities associated with measuring and analyzing radioactivity levels should be established primarily on the basis of potential human dose. These detection capabilities will vary according to the instrumentation and analytical techniques used. (See Table 3 in Regulatory Guide 4.8[17] and Table 1 (included) from the EPA Guide[3]). Because of the need for a preoperational monitoring program, detection capabilities for a particular program should be determined during that time and for those radionuclides observed in that particular environment and/or expected there following plant operation. Every reasonable effort should be made to achieve detection capabilities that are the most sensitive and practicably achievable for measuring plant-contributed radionuclides in the environment.

Confusion and noncomparability of reported data have resulted both from differing terminology for the measure of analytical sensitivity and from differing mathematical

* All references are found starting on page 197.

** Table 2 of Reference 3 gives dose equivalents for stated analytical levels. The detection capabilities given in that 1972 document and included here are readily lowered by most laboratories, especially for ^{90}Sr and ^{131}I.

Table 1
TYPICAL ANALYTICAL DETECTION LEVELS FOR ENVIRONMENTAL RADIOACTIVITY SURVEILLANCE[a]

Media and Isotope	Sample Size	Minimum Detectable Levels[b]
	Air-particulates	
Gross beta	300 m^3	3×10^{-3} pCi/m^3
^{89}Sr	1200 m^3	5×10^{-3} pCi/m^3
^{90}Sr	1200 m^3	1×10^{-3} pCi/m^3
^{134}Cs	1200 m^3	1×10^{-2} pCi/m^3
^{137}Cs	1200 m^3	1×10^{-2} pCi/m^3
^{140}Ba-La	1,200 m^3	1×10^{-2} pCi/m^3
	Air-gases and vapors	
^{3}H (HTO)	10—15 mℓ of condensate	2 pCi/m^3
^{85}Kr	1 m^3	1 pCi/m^3
^{131}I	300 m^3	4×10^{-2} pCi/m^3
	Not applicable	20 mrem/year
	Short-lived gases	
	Water, Milk	
^{3}H	4—5 mℓ	200 pCi/ℓ
^{14}C	200 mℓ	30 pCi/ℓ
^{54}Mn	3.5 ℓ	10 pCi/ℓ
^{58}Co	3.5 ℓ	10 pCi/ℓ
^{60}Co	3.5 ℓ	10 pCi/ℓ
^{59}Fe	3.5 ℓ	10 pCi/ℓ
^{65}Zn	3.5 ℓ	20 pCi/ℓ
^{89}Sr	1 ℓ	5 pCi/ℓ
^{90}Sr	1 ℓ	1 pCi/ℓ
^{95}Zr-Nb	3.5 ℓ	5 pCi/ℓ
^{131}I	10 ℓ	0.4 pCi/ℓ
^{134}Cs	3.5 ℓ	10 pCi/ℓ
^{137}Cs	3.5 ℓ	10 pCi/ℓ
^{140}Ba-La	3.5 ℓ	10 pCi/ℓ
	Fish and Shellfish	
^{54}Mn	200g	80 pCi/kg
^{55}Fe	100 g	20 pCi/kg
^{59}Fe	200 g	160 pCi/kg
^{58}Co	200 g	80 pCi/kg
^{60}Co	200 g	80 pCi/kg
^{65}Zn	200 g	160 pCi/kg
^{89}Sr	200 g	25 pCi/kg
^{90}Sr	200 g	5 pCi/kg
^{134}Cs	200 g	80 pCi/kg
^{137}Cs	200 g	80 pCi/kg

[a] Data excerpted from table 2 of Reference 3.

[b] The minimum detectable levels (MDL) are practical detection levels, rather than theoretical detection levels and are characteristic of the analytical procedure and the counting instrumentation in use. The MDL's listed assume the following instrumentation: (1) low background beta counter, (2) standard gamma scan-400 to 512 multichannel analyzer — 4×4-inch NaI(Tl) detector, and (3) for tritum and ^{14}C — liquid scintilla-

Table 1 (continued)
TYPICAL ANALYTICAL DETECTION LEVELS FOR ENVIRONMENTAL RADIOACTIVITY SURVEILLANCE[a]

tion counter. The detection limits listed are those practically obtained with the concentrations and mixtures of radionuclides normally encountered with environmental samples. If only a single radionuclide is present in a sample to be analyzed by gamma spectrometry, the detection limits listed could probably be reduced. The detection limits for specific nuclides would be considerably greater than those listed when complicated mixtures are encountered and in particular when certain constituents are present in relatively high concentrations.

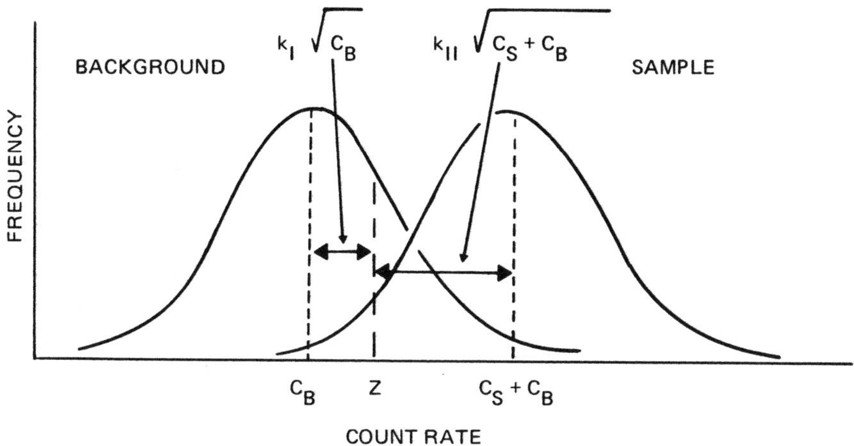

FIGURE 1. Intersecting distributions for background and sample count rates.

definition. Frequently, as in the EPA *Environmental Radioactivity Surveillance Guide,*[3] "minimum detection limit" or a similar term has been used without definition. Several current usages taken from frequently used documents are listed in the glossary in the Introduction to this section.

The minimum detection limit, or minimum detectable level (MDL) as commonly used, refers to a minimum incremental concentration or exposure rate based only on analytical or instrument sensitivity. In order to lessen confusion, the HASL usage[6] of lower limit of detection (LLD) is recommended for the minimum detectable increase in sample counting rate. The LLD can be converted to an MDL by specification of an acceptable error factor and conversion to sample concentration. Note that an LLD for measurement of external radiation can be calculated in exactly the same way as the counting of samples; for such measurements, the LLD and the MDL are identical.

An MDL for either a sample concentration or a direct measurement can be translated to an equivalent minimum detectable dose by carrying it through the environmental pathway matrix of Figure 2 in the chapter "Planning Environmental Monitoring Programs".

The basic problem is illustrated in Figure 1. Since both the background and sample counts (and count rates) represent distributions rather than points, preselecting a lower limit of detection [equivalent to $(C_S + C_B)$] as some multiple of C_B implies the acceptance of a certain probability of error in evaluating a sample count. The total error probability is the sum of probabilities of Type I decision error (accepting the presence of radioactivity in the sample when none is present) and Type II error (failure to recognize the presence of radioactivity when it is present). For direct counting of a sample with no interferences, several reasonable assumptions permit the following derivation. Assume:

1. Poisson counting statistics: standard error $= \sqrt{C}$
2. Similar counting times for determination of $(C_S + C_B)$ and standard error of C_B
3. Standard error of $(C_S + C_B) \cong$ standard error of C_B for small increments of C_S

$$C_S = (C_S + C_B) - C_B$$

then,

$$S.E._{C_S} = \sqrt{S.E.^2_{(C_S + C_B)} + S.E.^2_{C_B}} = \sqrt{2 \times C_B}$$

Let C_S = LLD, which can be set to some factor K times the standard error of C_S, that is,

$$LLD = K\sqrt{2C_B}$$

and

$$K = k_I + k_{II}$$

where K values are taken from the standardized normal variate probability tables for one-sided errors. It is the Health and Safety Laboratory (now the Environmental Measurements Laboratory, EML) practice to use the term lower limit of detection for the quantity here defined, that is: The lower limit of detection (LLD) is the smallest true sample net count rate which, using a given measurement process, will be detected $100p_{II}\%$ of the time and the risk of falsely concluding sample activity is present when it is not is $100p_I\%$. A tabulation of values of K for common probability combinations of Type I and Type II errors is provided in the DOE Guide.[1] Johnston,[106] addressing the equivalent of an MDL directly and incorporating other sources of variability in the overall sampling/analysis scheme, derived an "Index of Adequacy" equivalent to this combined probability factor.

It has been the practice at several sites to assign to the factor K a value of two (an approximation of 1.96) for a claimed 95% confidence level of detection. This may be standardized in a definition of LLD and by the implication of the MDL for reporting purposes but with the recognition that a continued probability of 95% detection of positive results has a corollary of false positive reporting for as many as one out of three determinations.

Pasternack and Harley[107] have extended the derivation to the much more complex problem of gamma spectrum analysis, pointing out that, for such analyses, the LLD for a given nuclide varies not only with the other nuclides present but also with the list of nuclides assumed to be present. No attempt is made here to provide standard MDLs and, for gamma emitters, comparability between laboratories will undoubtedly remain questionable.

Potential methods of lowering the minimum detection limit for a given analytical lower limit of detection are indicated by the sampling equation presented in Chapter 19.1 and repeated here with the same meaning of terms:

$$A = a\frac{(tC)}{Vfret} \tag{1}$$

The value of making improvements in counting statistics depends on the precision of the rest of the sampling-measurement system. For example, the volume of air

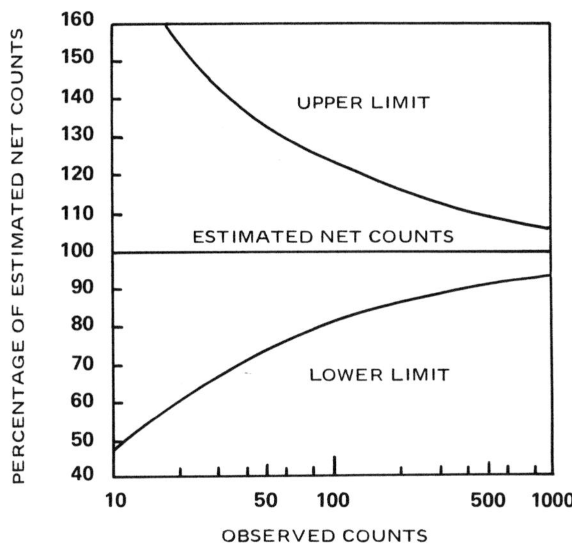

FIGURE 2. 95% Confidence intervals as percent of estimated net counts.

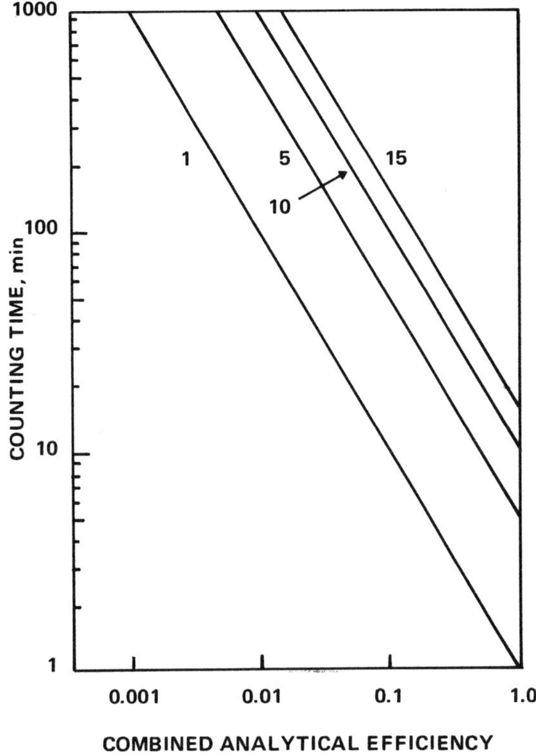

FIGURE 3. Performance index efficiency-time product given by the analytical procedure.

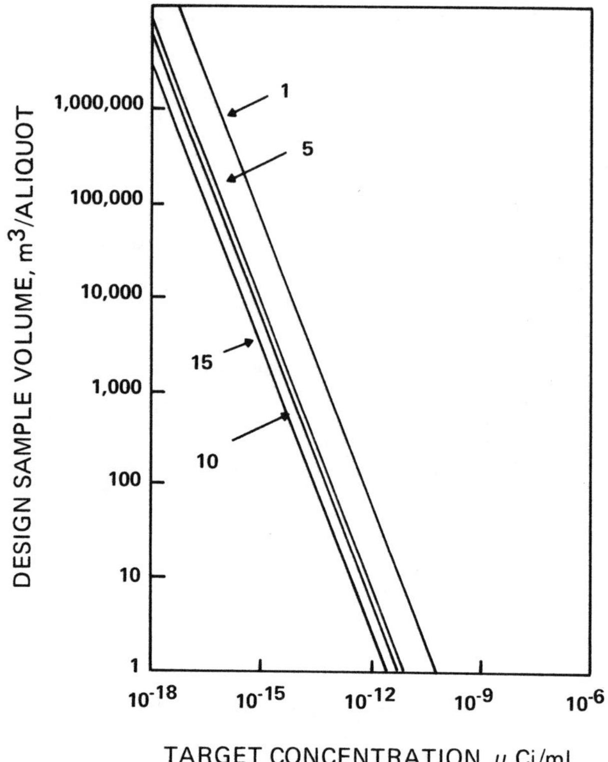

FIGURE 4. Efficiency-time product to satisfy the concentration-volume conditions and yield ±10% analytical reliability.

pumped may not be known more precisely than ±10%. In this case, there may be little merit in incurring significant costs to make the counting procedure much more precise than ±10%. Figure 2 illustrates the possible variation of an estimated concentration due solely to the randomness of radioactive decay.

A graphical solution to the sampling equation can be obtained from Figures 2 to 4. In Figure 2, a counting precision of ±10% corresponds to about 400 detected counts. Substituting 400 counts into the numerator of the sampling equation (in place of the product $t \times C$) yields a simple relation between volume and target concentration which, with suitable values for f, r, and e, could be used for preliminary program design. A performance index is obtained from Figure 3; the index is the product of counting time (t) and overall efficiency of the counter and analytical procedure ($f \times r \times e$). Figure 4 is entered with the performance index and the target concentration so that the design sample volume may be determined.

Use of these figures may be illustrated for the case of plutonium in air, frequently observed at concentrations of about 10^{-16} μCi/mℓ in ambient air. Some alpha spectrometers involve counting efficiencies of about 0.06, which would require a 250-min count to yield an index of 15 (Figure 3). That index requires a sample volume of more than 120,000 m^3 in order to determine plutonium concentrations to precisions of ±10% (Figure 4). Since $10^5 m^3$ corresponds to a pumping rate of nearly 2.3 m^3/min (100 cfm) for a 30-day period, a technically possible but awkward condition, one might instead consider changing the procedures affecting the counter efficiency or counting time. Alternatively, one might decide that the costs involved with measuring plutonium to precisions of ±10% at the 10^{-16} μCi/ml level are excessive compared to the local need to know.

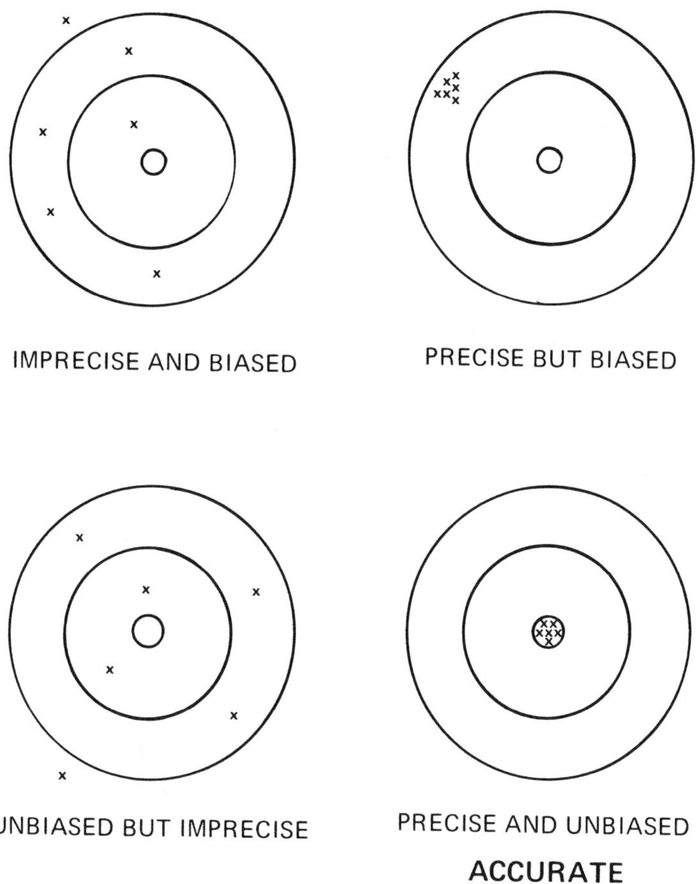

FIGURE 5. Precision and bias with respect to a target concentration.

Analytical Criteria: Acceptable Standard Deviation[108]

In any program of environmental surveillance, the validity of the analytical data is a vital factor in the significance of the final product. Analytical validity is measured by the accuracy of the data. Accuracy includes both repeatability (precision) and freedom from systematic error (bias). Figure 5 shows the combinations of precision and freedom of bias required for accuracy. The accuracy necessary in a given set of data is determined primarily by the use to be made of the data. For a set of data to be considered valid, it must be possible to document their accuracy. A statistical analysis of the results is required for documentation.

There is a cost-benefit trade-off between the quality of the results produced and the effort necessary to obtain this quality. It is impossible, therefore, to arbitrarily state that a given determination should be made within any preestablished set of criteria. A laboratory must have its own criteria for precision and accuracy in order to determine whether or not its results meet its own goals. One basic criterion is the acceptable standard deviation of a determination. The following paragraphs and equations suggest a procedure for the establishment of the acceptable standard deviation as a function of radionuclide concentration based on laboratory-accepted values for counting statistics and manipulative error. These standard deviations can then be used for various quality control purposes.

There is little guidance for the establishment of criteria for analytical measurements in radiological environmental surveillance as judged by the two primary bodies promulgating standards. The Nuclear Regulatory Commission (NRC) states: "Procedures shall be prepared for ensuring the quality of program results, including analytical measurements . . . " but does not give any requirements for precision and accuracy other than required lower limits of detection. The EPA Guide[3] provides a section on analytical quality control methods but gives only a list of "Practical Detection Levels" characteristic of specific analytical procedures and counting instrumentation in use presumably in Environmental Protection Agency laboratories. The Environmental Protection Agency intercomparison program[109] gives acceptable standard deviations but does not give a source for these values. In 1968, the Public Health Service[110] gave estimates of precision for the determination of five nuclides in milk. These values, all at the sigma level, were: Strontium-89, ±5 pCi/ℓ or ±10%; Strontium-90, ±2 pCi/ℓ or ±10%; and Gamma Emitters, ±10 pCi/ℓ or ±10%. In each case, the larger of the two errors, the picocurie values below a certain level and the percentage error above that value, was used.

In any analytical measurement, the standard deviation can be considered to be the combination of two contributing standard deviations, s_1, and s_2;

$$s^2 = s_1^2 + s_2^2 \tag{2}$$

where s_1 is the standard deviation associated with signal-to-noise problems, and s_2 is the standard deviation associated with manipulations and nonsignal measurements (e.g., weighing). At low concentrations, s_1 becomes controlling; at high concentrations, s_2 becomes controlling. In radionuclide measurements, s_1 measures the counting statistics variability. The precision terms given by the Public Health Service and those used in the EPA intercomparison program are essentially s_1 and s_2 as defined above.

In its intercomparison programs, EPA indicates that a 1-sigma standard deviation of 5% is to be expected. At least such a precision would also be expected in general in analytical chemistry when signal-to-noise ratios were not limiting. Therefore, a high level criterion of ±5.0% at the one-sigma level is taken here. This is expressed as: $S_2(R) = 0.05\ R$, where R is a net counting rate.

In low-level determinations, counting variations are controlling. The actual variability of the background is more appropriate for calculating low-level precision than the counting statistics (Poisson) variability of that background. The variability of interest is the variability that can be obtained on a given instrument over the period of time for which a single blank measurement is used. Thus, if measurements are made every day, it is the variability over a day; if measurements are made over a week, it is the variability over a week. In any case, it is not the variability over a long period of time, e.g. 6 months. This last variability (i.e., over periods of months) is affected by long-term changes in instrument response and is largely corrected by the use of many short-period background values.

The concept of an "equivalent background counting rate" R_b' is useful for introducing actual background variability instead of counting statistics background variability. It is the background counting rate which would give the observed background (or blank) variability when counted for the specified time, and it can be calculated from the observed standard deviation and the counting time regularly used in the determination. Thus, if the sample and background counting times are equal and $R = R_s - R_b = (R + R_b) - R_b$ (the observed net count rate), then the counting statistics error, including non-Poisson variability, can be calculated as follows:

$$s_1^2(R) = \text{Var}(R + R'_b) + \text{Var } R'_b = \left(\frac{R}{t} + \frac{R'_b}{t}\right) + \frac{R'_b}{t}$$

$$= \frac{R + 2R'_b}{t} \qquad (3)$$

The total variance s^2 is then given by

$$s^2(R) = \frac{R + 2R'_b}{t} + (0.05\ R)^2 \qquad (4)$$

The counting rate at which the standard deviation is a stated fraction f is given by

$$s^2(R) = \frac{R + 2R'_b}{t} + (0.05\ R)^2 = f^2R^2 \qquad (5)$$

which can be written as

$$R + 2R'_b = t(f^2 - 0.05^2)\ R^2 \qquad (6)$$

Since R'_b and t are known, R can be calculated for any desired f. The counting rates can be converted to picocuries per unit volume or unit weight using appropriate values for efficiency and sample size.

The application of Equations 2 through 6 to gross beta and tritium analyses are discussed in the following paragraphs and are shown on the graphs of Figures 6 and 7.

Consider a gross beta measurement, with the following parameters:

1. Background counting rate = R_b = 1 cpm
2. Counting time devoted to sample = 30 min
3. Volume of aliquot removed from sample = V = 0.25ℓ
4. Counting efficiency of detector (fraction of a count per disintegration) = e = 0.40

Then

$$1\text{ cpm} = \frac{1}{(0.25)(0.40)(2.22)} = 4.50\text{ pCi/l}$$

Assume that the actual background standard deviation does not exceed the Poisson variability. Then $R_b = R'_b$, and Equation (6) becomes:

$$R + 2 = 30\left[f^2 - (0.05)^2\right] R^2 \qquad (6a)$$

The desired acceptable standard deviations calculated from Equation 6a are graphed as Figure 6.

Now consider a tritium determination, with these parameters:

1. Background counting rate = R_b = 10 cpm
2. Counting time devoted to sample = t = 400 min
3. Volume of aliquot removed from sample = v = 8 mℓ
4. Counting efficiency of detector (fraction of a count per disintegration) = e = 0.20

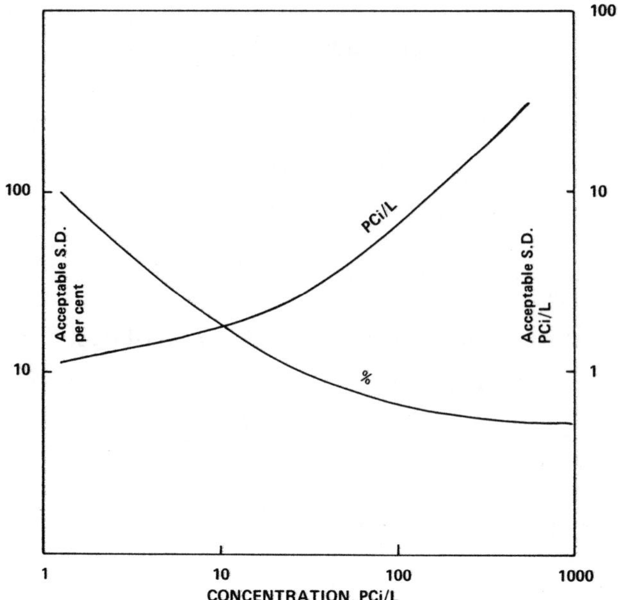

FIGURE 6. Example of acceptable standard deviations, gross beta in water, assuming t = 30 min for background and for background + sample counting times, a counting efficiency of 0.40, and R_b = 1 cpm.

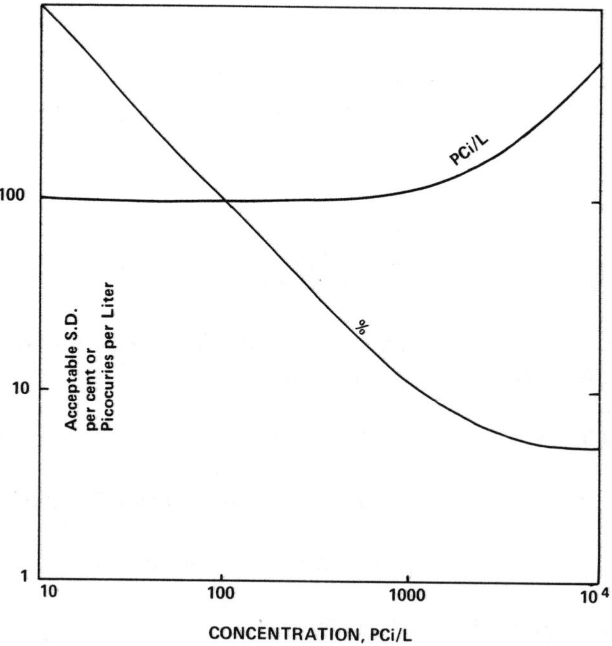

FIGURE 7. Example of acceptable standard deviations, tritium in water, for R_b' = 25 cpm, t = 400 min, efficiency = 0.20 (see example in text).

Then

$$1 \text{ cpm} = \frac{1}{(0.008)(0.20)(2.22)} = 280 \text{ pCi/l}$$

Equation (6), if applied to these data, would give

$$R + 20 = 400\left[f^2 - (0.05)^2\right] R^2 \quad (6b)$$

However, suppose experimental data indicate that the standard deviation of repeated blank counts is actually 0.25 cpm rather than the 0.16 cpm that correspond to the background and counting time. The equivalent background rate corresponding to a variability of 0.25 cpm can be calculated as follows:

$$(0.25)^2 = \frac{R'_b}{400}$$

$$R'_b = 25$$

Equation (6) then becomes:

$$R + 50 = 400\left[f^2 - (0.05)^2\right] R^2 \quad (6c)$$

which gives the acceptable standard deviations plotted in Figure 7.

LABORATORY PROCEDURES

One general goal in sample handling and preparation is to minimize both the number of preparation steps and the number or complexity of radiochemical procedures. Each additional procedure introduces additional risk of error, including inadvertent contamination of the sample. Since only part of the sample is used in some procedures, a nonhomogenous sample may give very different results on different portions of the sample.

Choices are not always straightforward. For example, soil samples taken to measure particulate contamination (e.g., plutonium dioxide) often contain large pebbles or rocks. Sieving is quicker, cheaper, and easier than grinding; the concentration of plutonium in the fines fraction is larger, effectively improving the sensitivity of the analysis. On the other hand, the raw analytical results (in units of activity per unit weight) does not describe the intact sample. Any adjustment of the raw data to allow for the mass of the discarded fraction should depend on the uses to which the data subsequently will be put, e.g., exposure potential or total inventory.

A similar problem arises with regard to suspended sediments in water samples. The difficulty in obtaining a truly representative aliquot for analysis usually makes filtration of the sample desirable, with separate analyses of both filter and filtrate, if the filtered material is apt to show a major fraction of the radioactivity being measured.

The radioactivity content, from both natural and man-made sources, of chemical reagents, materials of construction for radiation detectors and shields,[111] laboratory and sampling supplies (such as filter paper), and laboratory air (when precipitates are filtered) must be considered and evaluated by referenced data or actual measurement. If a problem exists that cannot be eliminated by change of procedure or source of supply, correction factors must be determined. Suggested sources of information are the multivolume LBL manual,[25] the HASL procedures manual,[76] and several others.[27,103-105]

The quantitative effects of handling procedures may require special studies to establish the accommodations that are most appropriate. Elimination of, rather than compensation for, bias is generally preferable, but exceptions occur either when the cost of elimination is comparatively large or when elimination of one bias introduces another that is difficult or expensive to accommodate. From the laboratory point of view, one of the most difficult and tedious, but important, aspects of dealing with environmental materials for radiological examination is sample preparation for analysis. Depending on the type of analysis required, pretreatment may range from essentially no treatment to laborious and time consuming ashing or fusing processes. Sample handling is further complicated by the large sample frequently needed. Associated problems in the laboratory include heat and humidity control and, especially with certain samples, odor and smoke. Unless the laboratory is carefully planned and operated it may easily become a visual and olfactory nuisance.

Preparation of Solid Samples

In the sample preparation laboratory, a variety of operations are encountered unlike those in a standard analytical chemistry lab. For example, if food samples are to be prepared, they are usually separated into edible and nonedible portions prior to homogenization and reduction. Thus, fruits may be peeled, nuts shelled, shellfish shucked, eggs cracked, meat deboned, etc. These operations require an assortment of kitchen knives, chopping blocks, and the like. Similarly, other solid samples such as soil, vegetation, and some other media require assorted pulverizers, blenders, meat grinders, etc.

If efforts are made to evaluate the reduction in radioactivity by normal domestic food preparation, equipment and space must also be available for such things as washing of leafy vegetables, carrot paring, potato peeling, etc. Sample pretreatment may also be facilitated by steaming or partial cooking. Shucking shellfish and deboning meat are especially simplified by preliminary heating. For this purpose, a large pressure cooker or conventional autoclave is convenient.

Following the preliminary steps outlined above, the solid sample or an aliquot is ready for reduction, usually to a dry ash. For this purpose, large drying ovens are necessary, one drying at about 110°C followed by partial carbonization at 250°C, and then dry ashing in a muffle furnace at a temperature of not more than 550°C. At higher temperatures, loss of alkali metals, particularly cesium, may be significant.

The selection of containers for drying and ashing is important. Although platinum dishes would generally be applicable, the high cost makes platinum ware out of reach for most laboratories. Possible substitutes such as stainless steel (for drying), fused silica, or nickel (for ashing) are not always free from difficulty. Probably the most used substitutes are pyroceramic materials such as Vycor® or Corningware®.[6] In any case, it is important to remember that most slurried samples can form hard glazes that may adhere to the drying pan and make quantitative transfer of the sample difficult and time consuming.

Among the foodstuffs giving the most trouble in drying and ashing are those materials that are high in fat, i.e., nuts and meats, or high in sugar. If the carbonized sample is soaked with a saturated ethanol solution of ammonium acetate and ignited before ashing in a muffle furnace, the resultant ash is white and fluffy as contrasted to a hard incompletely-ashed material obtained by direct ashing. For eggs (with high fat and sulfur contents), freeze-drying results in a light easily-dealt-with cake that can be readily ashed. The butterfat content of milk is also a problem in ashing. This can be eliminated by changing the method of milk analysis so that ashing is unnecessary.

Freeze-drying is an excellent but expensive method for drying all types of large samples, especially those containing considerable organic matter. This technique avoids the spattering and frothing that may occur during heating. After samples have been dried, they should be reduced to a small particle size by grinding and homogenized by mixing. Commercially available grinders, mills, pulverizers, mixers, and blenders are suitable provided loss of fines is prevented. To prevent cross-contamination, thorough cleaning of equipment between samples is necessary. Portions of the detailed HASL procedures[6] for preparing soil samples for analysis can be equally applicable to other solid samples.

Preparation of Liquid Samples

By contrast with the foregoing, the preparation of liquid samples for radiological samples is simplicity itself. The basic need is to reduce sample volume or to prepare completely dried water residues. Occasionally, it may be necessary to separately measure suspended and dissolved radioactivity. This separation can be accomplished by the use of membrane filters or filters that have a minimum ash. The two basic methods of volume reduction are the use of ion exchange columns (used even in the field for sampling streams and precipitation)[11] and evaporation techniques.

Because of the relatively large volumes of water that can be sampled, significant gains in radioanalytical sensitivity can be achieved by the use of ion exchange techniques to concentrate radionuclides from the water sampled. Tritium is an exception but can be determined on a collected fraction of the water leaving the column. Nearly all radionuclides other than tritium may be removed from water by astute selection of ion exchange media. Sample concentration on ion exchange resins is readily feasible for fresh water sources,[112] but in brackish and/or sea water, the salt content inhibits retention of radionuclides except with specially prepared resins. The efficiency of any system or combination of systems chosen must be tested under operating conditions to determine the effects of flow rate, volume, chemical form of the radionuclide, stable isotopes of the radionuclide, and other material in the water. Also, radioanalysis of milk usually involves ion-exchange techniques (especially for ^{131}I) followed by beta or gamma counting or, at very low levels, beta-gamma coincidence techniques.

The U.S. Public Health Service[101] usually calls for filtering surface water samples (unless it is drinking water, in which case the total activity is desired) prior to volume reduction to obtain the distribution of activity within the sample. It is suggested here that, if some useful information can be obtained, such as soluble/insoluble nuclide ratios that can be related back to effluent data, soluble and insoluble forms should be measured. Otherwise, total activity measurements should be adequate. Generally, evaporation of large volumes (several gallons) is accomplished by heating the sample in an open beaker on a hot plate (an infrared lamp may be placed above the beaker as an additional heat source). As the volume decreases, additional sample is added until the entire sample has been concentrated. The sample container should be rinsed with distilled water containing a few drops of concentrated HCl to insure quantitative transfer. Depending on subsequent radiochemical analysis and organic content, the sample may be dried in a counting planchet or simply adjusted to a convenient volume. A second evaporative technique makes use of the chick feeder principle and works on smaller samples (1ℓ or less). In this case, the sample is measured in a volumetric flask which is inverted over a counting planchet on a hot plate. Loss of solids to the inner walls of the flask may be reduced to negligible levels by addition to the sample of a solution of a chelating agent, ammonia, and a wetting agent prior to evaporation.

Preparation of Air Samples

The treatment required for air-particulate filters depends largely on the type of filter used and the analyses required. As noted in the chapter entitled "Sampling Instruments and Methods" under Air Sampling, pure cellulose and membrane filters are readily dissolved for radiochemical analyses (e.g., ^{90}Sr, ^{239}Pu), but the more practical filter media (from air collection properties and mechanical strength) present difficulties in dissolution — either high ash content or the need for fluoride treatment for dissolution. Most air-particulate filters are counted directly for gross activity. Often, however, state-of-the-art counting equipment is not sufficiently sensitive with typical (100 min) counting times to permit evaluation for some of the more toxic radionuclides (e.g., ^{90}Sr, ^{239}Pu) at levels well below the concentration guides for exposures of the general public. Hence, for sensitivity, annual average concentration, and dose calculation, it is recommended that air filters be composited for subsequent analysis on a location-by-location basis over time. Experience has shown that monthly compositing of weekly filters provides adequate sensitivity for ^{90}Sr determinations; however, less frequent compositing (such as quarterly or semiannually) is desirable for ^{239}Pu. The latter is especially true when one attempts to distinguish the facility impact (if any) from the concentrations due to world-wide fallout. As composited, however the filters need to be dissolved or otherwise treated to reduce the sample to that suitable for counting. Gamma spectral analysis can be performed directly on a canned group of composited filters without any additional steps. This is frequently done prior to the dissolution for ^{90}Sr and ^{239}Pu analyses.

In the case of charcoal cartridges, they are generally canned and analyzed by gamma spectrometry. Tritium samples are collected on a desiccant such as silica gel, followed by heating the gel to remove the tritiated moisture and counting of the distillate using standard liquid scintillation techniques.

INSTRUMENTATION REQUIREMENTS

Routine laboratory determinations usually include gross beta, tritium, radiostronitium, and gamma spectrometry according to the nuclides released from the site and other potential sources. Gross alpha and alpha spectrometry may also be included. In addition to total activity analyses, it may be desirable to measure the distribution of activity between soluble and suspended materials, the volatile nuclides, or the chemical form of a radionuclide.

Airborne noble gases such as ^{41}Ar, ^{85}Kr, and $^{133-138}Xe$ are often detected through the use of dosimeters or other external measurements described in detail in Chapter 19.2 or through analysis of short-term gas samples returned to the laboratory in evacuated chambers. While ^{41}Ar and the radioxenons can be detected through gamma emission, the measurement of ^{85}Kr is essentially based on detecting its beta decay (less than 1% gamma emission occurs).

The detection of tritium is made difficult by the low energy of the tritium betas (E_{max} = 18.6 keV) to which only a few detectors are sensitive. Various interferences may be present depending on where, when, and how the tritium is sampled and subsequently measured. In the gas detectors, the higher energy betas from the reactor-produced noble gases (Kr, Xe) or the radioactivity of naturally occurring gases (radon and thoron) can provide a significant interfering background. In the vapor phase, beta emitters such as ^{131}I or ^{90}Sr may interfere.

Direct measurement of radioactivity in liquids is not uncommon, although the generally limited sensitivity and nonspecific (for individual nuclides) measurements make such techniques more useful for direct measurement of extended exposure or as secondary alarm devices. Among the techniques used are suspension over the water of dosimeters, low-level dose-rate meters, or gamma scintillators.[113] Dosimeters and gamma scintillators may also be immersed in the water[114-116] to improve sensitivity. Flow-through chambers with several different sensors, although more common for effluent monitoring, have been used with some success.

Given this large number and variety of radiological measurement tasks in the environment around nuclear facilities, the instrumentation and analytical requirements may be beyond the capability of the local site. In actual fact, this is often the case, especially for nuclear power plants; many utilities have contracted out some or all of their measurement needs to commercial laboratories. It is not our place here to judge the merits of each but to merely present an overview of the types of equipment needed to do the very best job of measurement and analysis. Detailed discussions of instruments are found in many of the references cited, but especially in References 5, 25, 119, 122, and 167.

Laboratory equipment begins with a gamma spectrometer. There are two kinds in common use: NaI(Tl) crystal spectrometers with high efficiency and low energy resolution; and anticoincidence shielded Ge(Li) and/or IGe semiconductor spectrometers with superb energy resolution, but lower efficiency. A well-equipped analytical laboratory would need one of each type: the Ge(Li) or IGe system for "peak-hunting" to determine all of the various gamma-emitting isotopes in an unknown sample, and a NaI(Tl) system for the ultimate in single nuclide sensitivity. An added beta-coincidence feature inside a NaI(Tl) well is required for ^{131}I sensitivity below the limits in Regulatory Guide 4.8.[17] Unfortunately, the systems noted above are all very expensive since they all must include electronic accessories such as multichannel analyzers and data-recording devices. These systems are also not easy to operate at maximum sensitivity, and may require computer analysis of the data for ultimate performance. If a choice has to be made, perhaps the better instrument for this set of requirements would be a Ge(Li) system for "peak-hunting"; in that case, some very low-activity samples would have to be measured on a NaI(Tl) system elsewhere.

The second key laboratory instrument is the low-background beta internal gas proportional counter. This instrument, useful for gross-beta as well as beta-spectrometry measurements, is much easier to operate and maintain than the gamma spectrometry equipment. It can also be used with minor changes for gross-alpha measurements.

An alternative or supplement to the beta proportional counter is a silicon surface-barrier detector for alpha and beta spectrometry. This instrument has superb resolution but cannot accommodate as large a number of samples as the gas counter. Either type must be accompanied by a multichannel analyzer system.

Tritium measurements are performed with a liquid scintillation/photomultiplier set-up. These are available commercially as complete units and can also be used for other low energy beta emitters such as ^{14}C.

Dosimetry is performed either with thermoluminescent dosimeters (TLD reader systems are commercially available), or pressurized ion chambers (also available commercially) for field deployment. Portable and mobile equipment includes possible mobile gamma-spectrometry for *in situ* measurements and any of a long list of portable hand-held meters (Geiger-Muller counters, ion chambers, proportional counters, etc.). Calibration sources, shielding, reagents, and other items must also be included. The list could go on and on and yet not be complete. The reader should understand that all of this equipment is necessary only for a complete, self-sustaining laboratory. More likely, as mentioned above, at least some of the required measurements will be made by shipping samples off-site for analysis by an independent laboratory.

A wide variety of analytical-chemical instruments also must be available for the individual measurement problems, ion-exchange columns, wet- and dry-ashing apparatus, organic chemistry supplies, and so on.

QUALITY ASSURANCE

Although details may differ, the elements of an adequate quality assurance program[173] for environmental surveillance should include: (1) process quality control (to test the consistency of sample preparation and analysis); (2) instrument quality control (to ensure that appropriate equipment is procured, tested, and is operating properly); (3) interlaboratory cross-check analysis (e.g., participation in one or more programs such as the EPA and IAEA sample cross-check programs); and (4) comprehensive data review (to assure the integrity of the reported values).

The percentage of the environmental surveillance effort devoted to the routine quality assurance program will vary from site to site and from year to year dependent upon the stability of the program, past and current variability experience, and the variety and type of measurements included in the routine program. Dedication of between 5 and 15% of all measurements to quality assurance purposes appears to be appropriate.

The environmental surveillance staff should provide appropriate performance specifications for the equipment and analyses performed. To the extent applicable, national standards (e.g., References 29 and 117 to 120) may be used or referenced. Reference 121 gives useful lists of general specifications for several types of instrumentation, although the performance specifications pertain to emergency instrumentation. Reference 25 is especially useful as a compilation of vendor-supplied performance specifications.

Routine Calibrations

The distinction between true calibrations and operational performance tests is sometimes blurred. Actual calibration to a known quantity of radioactivity or radiation flux is required infrequently after initial calibration if a reliable, convenient, and inexpensive operational test is available. The usual response check is an operational test procedure.

It is standard practice to make periodic source checks on all continuous radiation monitoring devices with either built-in or portable radiation sources. Fixed instrument source checks are recommended on no less than a weekly frequency, portable instrument source checks before each use, and sampler flow rates on no less than a semiannual frequency. In addition, rechecks after replacement of components or nonroutine maintenance procedures should be required. Sometimes overlooked is the need for periodic verification of a field-check device against a known standard or direct measurement. Reference 122 provides a useful discussion of instrument calibrations under various radiological and environmental conditions.

Analytical Quality Control

Although the variances due to analytical uncertainties should not exceed (and will usually be smaller than) other variances associated with environmental radioactivity measurements, the maintenance of auditable quality control records should be mandatory. Matuszek[123] has emphasized the need for periodic review of quality control in the laboratory.

Analytical quality control is commonly tested by processing a series of audit samples, the concentrations in which are unknown to the laboratory staff. These control checks and tests should be applied to the analytical process by the use of blind duplicate analyses of selected samples and by cross-check analysis of selected samples with an independent laboratory (here it is suggested that the lab consider participation in the EPA cross-check program). Quality controls should also be applied to the entire sample-collection procedure to ensure that representative samples are obtained and that samples are not changed, cross-contaminated, or otherwise affected by handling or their storage environment prior to their analysis.

Replicate Sampling

Replicate sampling, along with replicate analyses on split samples, are the means of assessing several sources of variability as noted in earlier sections. Splitting a sample involves obtaining two identical samples from a single collected volume with one sample being analyzed by the laboratory and the other by a control laboratory and subsequent comparison of the results. When splitting samples for interlaboratory comparison, it is vital that both samples are representative of the media in question. Splitting procedures for the most common sample types are listed below by media:

1. Air particulate filter paper should contain a symmetric distribution of deposition and may be cut exactly in half; prior to cutting, the filter should be sprayed lightly with a plastic coating to prevent loss of the sample to the container.
2. To obtaing a split of a direct radiation measurement, the sampling procedure must utilize multiple dosimeters. The exposures should be made side by side for exactly the same length of time and the dosimeters must be treated as similarly as possible, e.g., similar annealing or charging of dosimeters and similar exposure during storage or transit. Splitting the sample with a control laboratory may be impractical for short duration (1 quarter) exposures due to variable exposure in transit.
3. When milk samples are being taken at local farms, the collection should take place after milk has mixed thoroughly in the bulk storage tank, or the individual samples should be mixed in the laboratory and then split into two separate containers.
4. Solid organic samples, such as fish, meat, and vegetables should be collected in a quantity equal to twice the normal sample. The sample should then be mixed thoroughly (blended where practical) and divided into separate containers.
5. Radioactive material in water samples may deposit on sample container walls and therefore it is desirable to obtain duplicate samples simultaneously in similar containers rather than split one large sample.
6. Sediment samples should be taken in duplicate. The total sample should be thoroughly mixed, halved, and bagged for shipment. The samples should be as uniform as possible, taking care to avoid having larger particles concentrated in one sample.

Reporting Procedures

Reporting of data generated by the programs suggested herein should be done following a clear and uniform format suitable for automatic data processing. The reported information should generally include the following information:

1. Geographic location of sample site
2. Sample type (media)
3. Sample number (optional)
4. Identification of organization or person collecting the sample
5. Identification of organization analyzing the sample
6. Time and date sample was taken (include duration of sample period for integrated samples)
7. Sample preparation as appropriate (e.g., concentration or wet vs. dry)
8. Type of analysis performed
9. Value and units for each analysis and associated 2-sigma error
10. Parameters needed to calculate decay of sample prior to analysis where short-lived radionuclides are involved.
11. Any known events that may have affected the analytical results.

Much of the above information, such as sample site location and organization identification, can be coded to reduce the record volume.

Procedural Audits

Validity of interpretation of much of the data from the environmental surveillance program will depend on specific procedural requirements, embodied in a set of routine procedures. Compliance of staff with these procedures should be audited and documented on a routine basis by qualified staff, which is not part of the direct supervisory function. All parts of the routine program should be audited during the year, but this effort may be divided into partial, more frequent efforts.

The results of these internal audits are primarily for the benefit of the program planner and manager. Skilled auditors will not only detect departures from recommended procedures but provide useful recommendations for procedural improvements.

Documentation for quality assurance program purposes should include:

1. Routine environmental surveillance procedures
2. Routine enviornmental surveillance schedule
3. Quality assurance
4. Audit, calibration, and test records.

The routine environmental procedures may be embodied in a health physics manual, or a separate environmental manual. Procedures for each environmental procedure should include not only the vital details of size, instrument, container, etc. but also the important elements of good practice applicable to that measurement or sample and locations at which the procedure is used. With the use of the manual or procedures referred to above, an auditor should be able to determine that all important procedural requirements are complied with. Environmental emergency procedures may be included or documented separately.

The routine surveillance schedule should be included in the procedure manual but may also be documented separately. The purpose of each measurement included should be identifiable whether for dose calculation, trend evaluation only, or other.

The quality assurance program description may also be included in the environmental procedures manual. Included here are required performance specifications for equipment, procured services and calibration checks, a current listing of analytical audit samples and any cross-check programs, the current schedule for replicate sampling and procedural audits, and a description of the documentation and records system.

INTERPRETATION OF ENVIRONMENTAL RADIOACTIVITY MEASUREMENTS

D. A. Waite

INTRODUCTION TO PROBLEM AND POTENTIAL SOLUTIONS

Finding average concentrations or radiation levels in the environment is the most basic purpose of environmental surveillance programs. Because all environmental compartments are dynamic and nonuniformly contaminated, data tend to be scattered and ambiguous; the fraction of the environment that can be analyzed is small compared to the size of environmental compartments, making statistical representivity a problematic issue. (However, samples representative of the entire environment are not always needed, as discussed previously.) Consequently, masses of raw data must be sorted, adjusted, combined, and interpreted in order to yield the simple numerical values that are given in summary reports, used in pathway calculations, extended to estimates about dosage to humans, and offered as evidence about legal compliance. Several methods are available for finding these averages. The classical method of summing data and dividing by the number of data used in the sum provides the best estimate of the mean only for the immediate items sampled. However, for severely skewed data, the sum is dominated by the largest few data. Hence, the uncertainty about whether the calculated average is close to the environmental average is dominated by the unrepresentivity of the few largest data, and the estimated mean in this case is not a useful parameter for describing the population distribution.

Skewed data, downward environmental contaminant concentration trends, and increased demands on environmental surveillance data have made it necessary for data treatment to become more sophisticated than merely calculating averages in the classical way. The detection and assessment of facility releases, quantification of background levels, systemization of normal background level variations, assessment of estimate errors, and establishment of estimate confidence intervals require much more than the determination of arithmetic averages for meeting programmatic objectives.

The extreme variability of environmental compartment behavior probably makes it necessary at one time or another to use both parametric and nonparametric statistical techniques in data treatment and interpretation. Selected alternative techniques within these major categories are listed in Table 1. Details of these methods are documented elsewhere.[124-133*]

The need met by all of these procedures is the induction of general characteristics of data sets from a limited number of environmental surveillance data.

DISTRIBUTION ANALYSIS

The technique of preference generally selected for applicability testing in meeting this inductive reasoning need in the environmental surveillance data analysis, as well as many other data analysis areas, is distribution analysis. The skewness of most environmental surveillance data limits the variety of distribution types available for use to the log-normal, Weibull, gamma, and extreme value. Regulatory demands that distribution parameters in summary reports be — or be related to — the average and standard deviation of the unskewed normal distribution further narrows the set of applicable distribution types to the log-normal and gamma distributions, with the log-normal being the most commonly used.

* All references are found starting on page 197.

Table 1
ALTERNATIVE STATISTICAL TECHNIQUES

Parametric
- Calculation of μ and σ
- Students "t" test
- χ^2
- F test

Distribution analysis
- Normal
- Lognormal
- Gamma
- Extreme value
- Weibull

Non parametric
- Range statistics
- Order statistics
- Rank statistics

The advantage of handling environmental surveillance data as distributions instead of individual datum points, and graphically instead of numerically, is that these distribution plots yield, with the same or less effort, average values and standard deviations that are the same as those obtained by numerical methods. These plots also quickly show whether the distribution choice was correct and whether the data belong to two statistical sets.

Characteristics of special importance in the use of log-probability curves are linearity (denoting data from a common source), geometric standard deviation (GSD) (indicating variability in time or space) and geometric mean ($\overline{X}_g$). Even though the GSD of environmental contaminant concentration curves must be experimentally determined, many sets of media background concentrations have GSD values near two. GSD values greater than two or nonlinearity usually denote the presence of a source-related concentration distribution. Quoting with confidence an $\overline{X}_g$ value less than the environmental detection limit is uniquely possible by means of distribution analysis and overcomes the divisive problem of how to deal with such results. In summary, the analysis of data changes from a task of evaluating the relationship of one datum entry to adjacent entries to an assessment of the entry's fit in the governing distribution, by distribution analysis.

Mechanics of Distribution Analysis

Figure 1 shows four ways to describe the same data, but the four are not equally useful. The graph in the upper left represents a typical set of analytical data. The data contain an excess of large values over what a normal distribution would contain. Actually, nonnormal distributions for the analytical values should be expected for trace materials anywhere in the environment, since negative concentrations are physically impossible. If the data are truly homogeneous then some mathematical transformation exists for which the transformed values are distributed normally. Finding that proper transformation is essential. The graph in the lower left corresponds to data after the proper transformation has been made. Thus transformed, the data are distributed normally and then (but only then) our notions about averages and standard deviations become appropriate. Trying to plot a Gaussian curve from empirical data is expensive, since several tens to hundreds of data are required for precise definition of the curve. However, by adjusting the scales of our plots, we can get along with fewer data. The

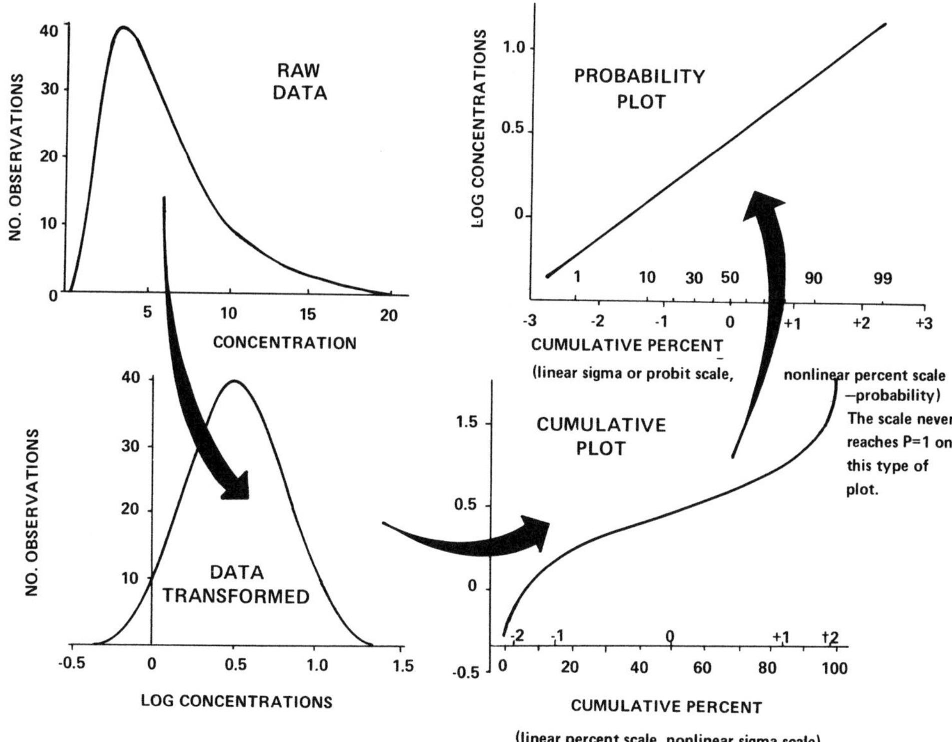

FIGURE 1. Data transformation.

graph in the lower right involves cumulative percent, and a few tens of data points will define it nicely.

The graph on the upper right is derived from the lower right graph by replacing the cumulative percent axis with a probability scale. There are four advantages to using this kind of plot. First, the plot will be linear when the transformation of the data yields a normal distribution. Second, the question of linearity may become answerable with as few as 10 or 12 data points. Third, the geometric mean value (and median) for the data is given by the 50th cumulative percent intercept. Fourth, the standard deviation (or geometric standard deviation, GSD) can be determined from the 84% and 50% intercepts. Some convenient graph papers are available commercially that have a Gaussian probability scale along the horizontal axis, and the vertical axis is variously linear or logarithmetic. The objective is to find the combination of distribution type and data transformation that yield a straight line. (See Chapter 6.2 in Volume II of the *CRC Handbook of Radiation Measurement and Protection* for a summary of mathematical relationships betweeen parameters of the log-normal distribution, the arithmetic mean, and the estimated intervals, including various percentages of the data.)

Distribution Plotting Procedure

In this section, we have chosen a set of typical data for air particulate samples collected at a given location as a function of time to demonstrate the log-normal data handling technique. The data so chosen are from biweekly samples in which the observed concentrations ranged from <0.015 to 0.1 pCi/m^3 (Table 2). In this case, as in any others, the complete set of data to be analyzed are arranged chronologically (or over space) as typically entered into data record books.

To construct a cumulative frequency plot, first, the raw data entries (Column I,

Table 2
DATA ORGANIZATION MECHANICS

Column I Raw data (pCi/m³)	Column II Ranked data (pCi/m³)	Column III Cumulative percent
0.060	<0.015	2
0.031	<0.015	6
0.040	<0.020	10
0.045	<0.020	14
0.062	0.024	18
<0.020	0.026	22
0.037	0.027	26
<0.015	0.031	30
0.033	0.031	34←
<0.015	0.031	38
0.024	0.033	42
0.031	0.037	46
0.051	0.037	50←
0.051	0.037	54
0.043	0.040	58
0.026	0.043	62
0.027	0.043	66←
0.031	0.045	70
0.037	0.051	74
0.078	0.051	78←
<0.020	0.051	82
0.100	0.060	86
0.037	0.062	90
0.051	0.078	94
0.043	0.100	98

Table 2) are arranged in order from smallest to largest (ranked data, Column II).* Less-than-detection limit values may occur in the data to be plotted. In some cases, this will result in the occurrence of observed values smaller than the largest "less than" value. In these circumstances, the largest less-than-detection limit value should be identified and all data with smaller values should be considered less than this largest value. All entries are included even though repetition of the same values may occur. Thus, $X_{(1)}, X_{(2)}, ---, X_{(n)}$ are arranged such that $X_1 \leqslant X_2 \leqslant X_1 \ . \ . \ . \leqslant X_n; \ i = 1,2 \ . \ . \ . \ n$. The second step in preparing the distribution plot is calculating the cumulative percent for the X_is by using the equation of Hahn and Shapiro.[134]

$$\text{cumulative percent} = 100(i - 1/2)/n$$

The cumulative percent (column III) of a ranked datum point (Column II) is the estimated probability that a value sampled from the underlying distribution will be less than or equal to the ranked datum value.

In the Table 2 example, there are 25 data points. Therefore, the first datum point represents a 100(1 − 0.5)/25 or 2% chance that data obtained from the same distribution will have a value less than that value. It should be noted that this cumulative percent calculation is done without regard to the numerical value of the ranked data

* Often it is quite sufficient (and simpler) just to count the number of values less than or equal to each of a chosen set of X and simply plot "percent of values $\leqslant$X" on the probability scale vs. X on the log scale.[136,137]

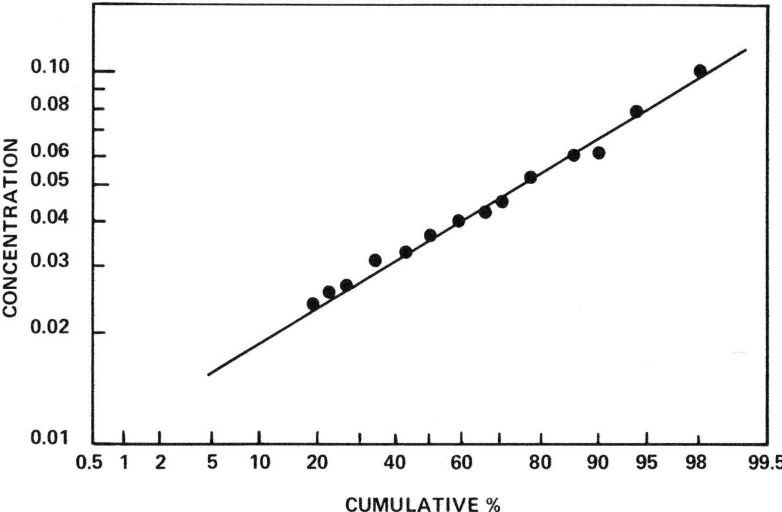

FIGURE 2. Probability plotting mechanics.

(Column II). Unique characteristics of less-than-detection-limit values and multiple entries are disregarded at this stage of the process.

The data are now ready to be plotted on log-probability graph paper. In plotting the ranked data vs. cumulative percent, one must first designate the values and units of the y-axis; the x-axis (Figure 2) is designated in probability (cumulative percent) values as purchased. The calculated values in Column III of Table 2 are to be plotted on the x-axis. (Other forms of commercial graph paper are available on which concentration may be plotted horizontally on the logarithmic x-axis, and cumulative percent may be plotted conventionally on the y-[probability or probit] axis.) The environmental concentration values (Column II, Table 2) are plotted on the logarithmic scale y-axis. There are no zero or negative concentration possibilities on this plot. Any such values that might result from counting idiosyncrasies properly should have been placed in the less-than-detection-limit category during the data ranking process. Also, the probability scale never reaches 0 or 1; however, data on the extreme ends of the probability scale are not usually of interest, nor are the points plotted statistically precise.

Since plotting every entry in Column II vs. every entry in Column III yields horizontal traces whenever single concentration values recur (Column II), only the average percent corresponding to the percent of the total data group with the same or less value of the data point being considered is plotted. For example, the concentration value of 0.031 is plotted vs. 34%. The data shown on Figure 2 as a result of this selection rule are emphasized by arrows in Column III of Table 2.

When data are plotted on probability paper, some variation about a straight line exists because of statistical fluctuations. From the best straight line drawn through the data, values for the geometric mean and geometric standard deviation (GSD) can be readily obtained. The geometric mean is given by the 50th cumulative percent intercept, while the GSD is obtained from the ratio of the 84.1% and 50% intercepts (i.e., the ratio between values for cumulative percent intercepts that correspond to any whole unit of standard deviation, here and most commonly chosen as 1 standard deviation).

For the example plot in Figure 2, the geometric mean concentration ($\overline{X}_g$) is 0.036 and the GSD is 1.6. The linearity of the data as plotted in Figure 2 indicates adherence of this data group to the log-normal distribution. Experience has shown that a wide variety of concentration levels and GSD values are possible for similar plots of envi-

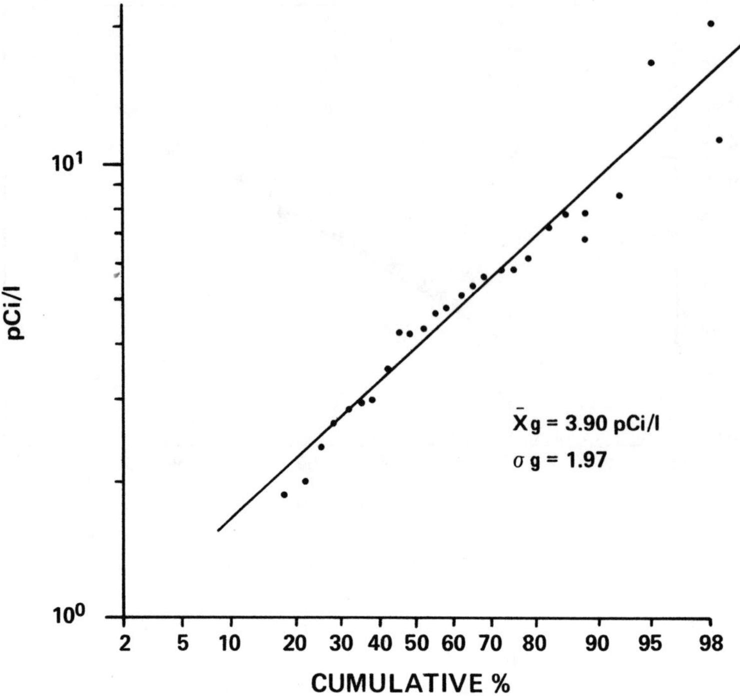

FIGURE 3. Sr-90 in milk, 1975.

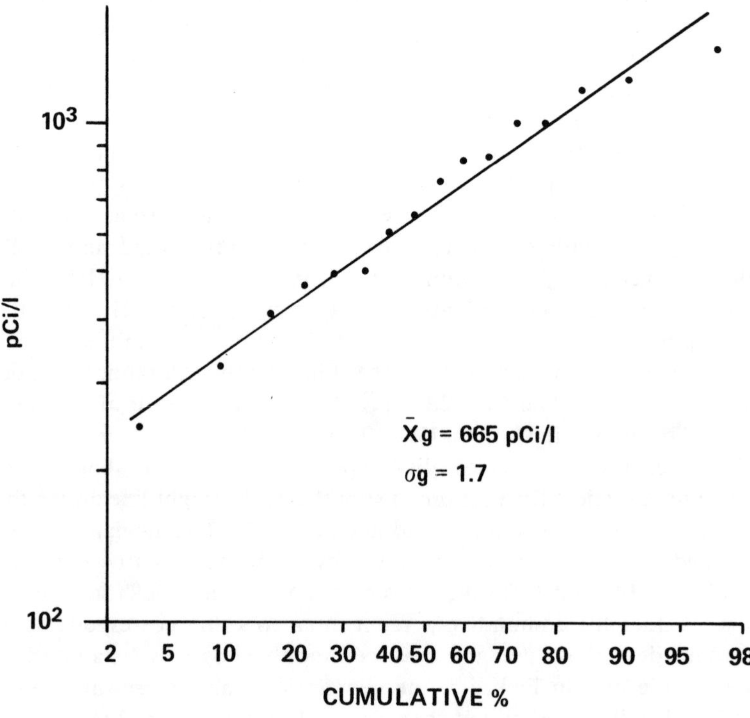

FIGURE 4. Tritium in soil water — Facility Area, 1973—1975.

ronmental surveillance data. Examples of this type of plot from a recent nuclear power reactor environmental surveillance report[135] are shown in Figures 3 and 4.

APPLICATIONS OF DISTRIBUTION ANALYSIS

Handling of Less-Than Values

Because environmental monitoring programs sometimes require state-of-the-art technology applied to vanishingly small amounts of contaminants, some analyses do not detect the substance sought. For many environmental measurements, particularly those from which a chemical or instrumental background must be subtracted, it is possible to obtain net values that are lower than the minimum detection limit of the system; it is not uncommon for individual measurements to result in values of zero or negative numbers. In spite of the fact that a negative value for an environmental measurement does not represent a physical reality, a valid long-term average (e.g., annual average environmental concentration) of many measurements can be obtained only if all of the values (both the very large and the very small, including zero and negative values) are included.

If a large fraction of the data group indicates environmental concentrations below the detectable limit, i.e., the data are less than the environmental detection limit (EDL), special considerations are needed to determine the long-term average concentration and the standard deviation. A number of methods have been devised and are commonly used[11] to deal with this problem. These include the assumptions that all less-than values are (1) at the EDL, (2) are zeroes, or (3) are at some value, such as one half of the EDL. Another method of averaging is to use the actual net counting data, adjusted for sample size, etc., including the smallest or negative values with the larger positive values. The assumption that all EDL samples actually had concentrations equal to the detection limit or equal to zero can severely bias the computed average and should be avoided. The classical method of summing data and dividing by the number of data used in the sum always provides an unbiased estimate of the population mean. However, for severely skewed data (a common feature in log-normal distributions) the sum is dominated by the few largest values; thus, the arithmetic average is not a good measure of central tendency (i.e., it is not a parameter in the log-normal function). Hence, the uncertainty about whether the calculated average is close to the environmental average is dominated by the (statistical) unrepresentivity of those few largest data. A preferred choice of handling values at or below the EDL involves probability plotting. As described earlier, the data are ranked by size, assigned to percentile values, and plotted on probability paper. The EDL values span the range of percentile values in accord with the fraction of the group they represent, as shown in Table 3 and Figure 5. The larger values are plotted in their respective percentile positions, and a best straight line is fitted through them ignoring the misfit to the EDL values. As before, the ratio of the 84%/50% intercepts (as read from the concentrations plotted on the logarithmic scale) from the visual fit straight line yields the geometric standard deviation (GSD), while the geometric mean is obtained from the intersection of the 50th percentile with the fitted line (for Figure 5, GSD = 2.1 and $\overline{X}g$ = 0.062, respectively). This method succeeds even when more than half of the data are less than EDL, since the fitted line can be extrapolated to the 50th percentile in any case, as done in Figure 5. The method is valid so long as a few data exceed the detection limit although, as a practical matter, the confidence interval about the estimated mean may be wide if fewer than ten values above the EDL are involved with the fitting.

In Table 4, we have compared the results of several averaging methods for the data presented in Figure 5.

When data of one kind are fewer than approximately 10 in number, no method of

Table 3
RANKED DATA FOR PROBABILITY PLOTTING AND DETERMINATION OF ANNUAL AVERAGE CONCENTRATION

Ranked concentration (pCi/m^3)	Cumulative percent
<0.066	2.6
<0.066	7.9
<0.066	13
<0.066	18
<0.066	24
<0.066	29
<0.066	34
<0.066	40
<0.066	45
<0.066	50
0.070	55
0.074	61
0.093	66
0.100	71
0.110	76
0.130	82
0.154	87
0.170	92
0.210	97

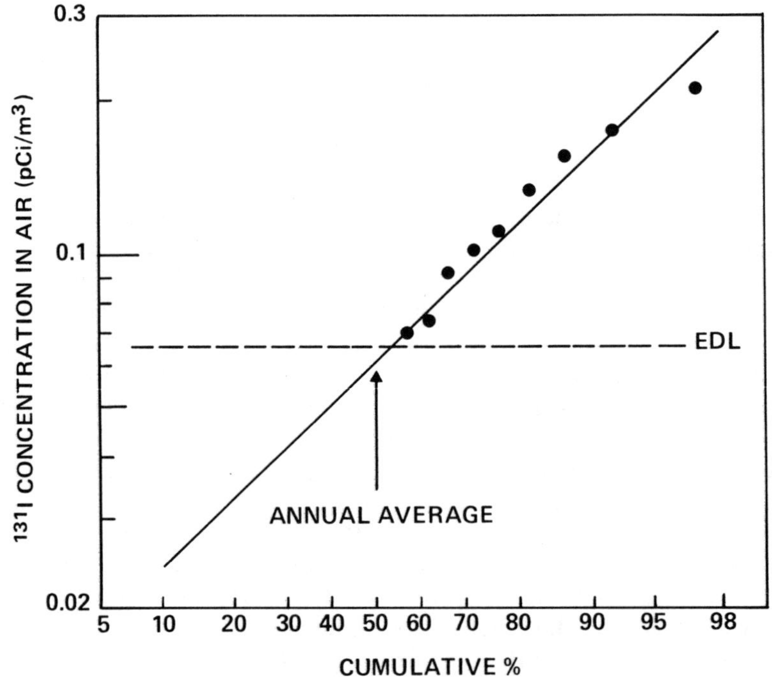

FIGURE 5. Handling "less-than" values.

Table 4
CALCULATION OF ANNUAL AVERAGES FROM LESS-THAN EDL DATA

Method 1:	Utilize EDL values for all less-than numbers; quote result as less than. Result: $\overline{C} < 0.093$
Method 2:	Utilize EDL values and zeroes for all less-than values and state result as range. Result: $0.058 \leqslant \overline{C} \leqslant 0.093$
Method 3:	Utilize actual net counting data for all numbers. Result: $\overline{C} = 0.075$
Method 4:	Utilize log-normal plot in Figure 5 to determine geometric mean. Result: $\overline{C} = 0.081$, ($\overline{C} = \overline{X}_g \exp(^{ln\ SGD_2{}^2})$ — see Section 6.2 in Volume II of the *CRC Handbook of Radiation Measurement and Protection*)

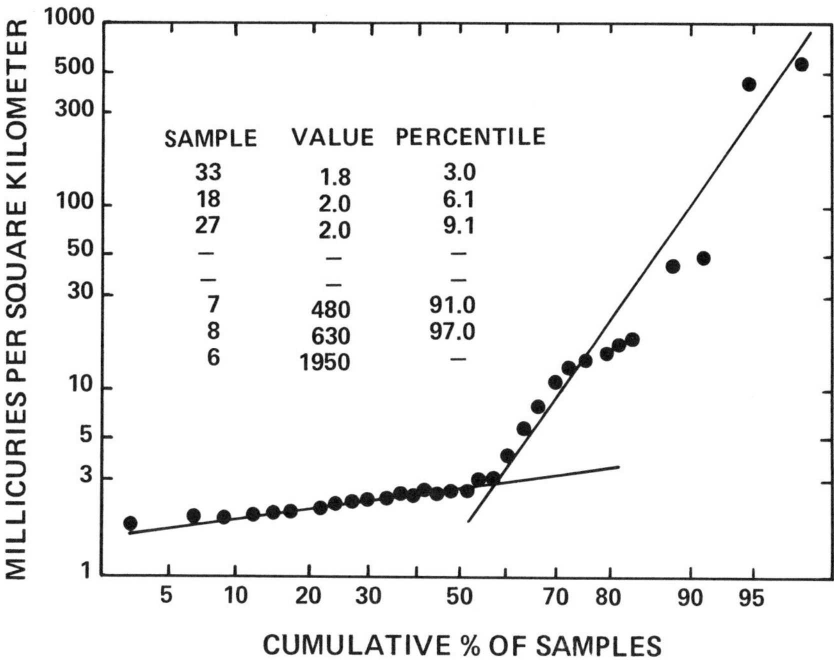

FIGURE 6. Superimposed distributions.

When data of one kind are fewer than approximately 10 in number, no method of handling them is likely to be superior to another as judged solely on the data; for example, the choice of treating the data as distributed normally or log-normally is unlikely to have a high confidence level for either choice. Additionally, suggested division of the group into subgroups may also be associated with still lower levels of confidence. Averages and standard deviations for small numbers of data may best be obtained on the basis of distributional assumptions derived from the experience of treating small groups in ways most appropriate for larger groups of data.

Questions may be raised about whether two data distributions are involved, such that some or all of the EDL values belong to a background distribution; the higher values might then represent effluent impact, perhaps a process out of control. Such contention would be realistic if all the data above detection limit were very much above that limit. In other situations, such questions cannot be answered solely from the data involved. However, other independent data can usually be found to help resolve that

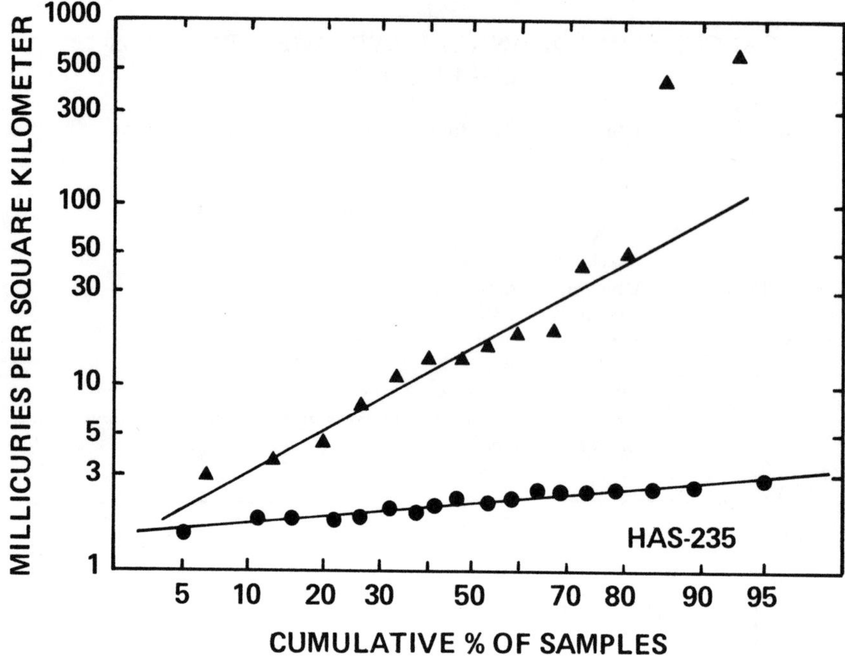

FIGURE 7. Two constituent distributions.

issue. These might include measures of background concentrations determined by a more sensitive system of sampling and analysis.

Assessing Facility Releases

The data shown in Figure 6 are from Health and Safety Laboratory (HASL) Report 235 and involve 33 soil samples taken in the Denver area. On the plot, we see two distinct legs and conclude that either the data are not distributed log-normally or are not a homogeneous collection. From the plot, we see that the two legs intersect near the value of 3 mCi/km^2. Using the 3 mCi/km^2 value as the criterion, the 33 data points can be segregated into two subgroups, each of which can be tested for homogeneity by replotting as two independent distributions. The linear plots in Figure 7 affirm that both the log-normal plot is appropriate and the two groups are homogeneous. After groups or subgroups of data have been arranged so they are separately homogeneous, medians, averages, and geometric standard deviations may be obtained from the graphs. The logarithmically transformed concentrations may in turn be described and treated statistically by use of normal distribution theory, as required.

RECOMMENDED AND REGULATORY LIMITS OF ENVIRONMENTAL RADIOACTIVITY

D. A. Waite

Recommended and regulatory limits for environmental radioactivity have been promulgated by a number of agencies at all levels of government. Details of the regulations and the environmental radioactivity regulatory structure are discussed in the literature.[137,138]* In general, the current regulations issued in Title 10, Part 20, of the Code of Federal Regulations are based on recommendations by the National Council on Radiation Protection and Measurements and the International Commission on Radiological Protection (ICRP).[140] In addition, the Environmental Protection Agency (EPA) promulgates regulations under Title 40, Protection of Environment, of the Code of Federal Regulations. The most recent issues by the EPA have been concerned with drinking water[141] and the uranium fuel cycle.[142]

The relative significance of radiation protection standards on the basis of applicability is illustrated in Figure 1 by Morgan.[143] In the figure, standards relating to environmental surveillance emanate upward from the primary standards into the internal exposure category. Some specific recommendations or standards that have been issued, other than the primary regulations, are mentioned in the following paragraphs.

The latest concept in limits relating to annual dose restrictions is "as-low-as-reasonably-achievable" (ALARA), which is an adaptation of previous ICRP and NCRP concepts of minimizing unnecessary exposure to radiation. Numerical criteria for this concept as applied to nuclear power reactors are contained in 10 CFR 50, Appendix I.[144] Table 1 provides a listing of the design objective dose limits to meet Appendix I. Similar guidance has been published by the EPA as noted in the following paragraphs from the Federal Register.[145]

Subpart B — Environmental Standards for the Uranium Fuel Cycle

§ 190.10 Standards for normal operations.

(a) The annual dose equivalent shall not exceed 25 millirems to the whole body, 75 millirems to the thyroid, and 25 millirems to any other organ of any member of the public as the result of exposure to planned discharges of radioactive materials, radon and its daughters excepted, to the general environment from uranium fuel cycle operations and radiation from these operations.

(b) The total quantity of radioactive materials entering the general environment from the entire uranium fuel cycle, per gigawatt-year of electrical energy produced by the fuel cycle, shall contain less than 50,000 curies of krypton-85, 5 millicuries of iodine-129, and 0.5 millicuries combined of plutonium-239 and other alpha-emitting transuranic radionuclides with half-lifes greater than one year.

Recommendations in terms of permissible body burdens and maximum permissible concentrations have been derived (as indicated on Figure 1)** from the basic dose criteria (10 CFR 20) that preceded the Appendix I adoption. A portion of the text discussing radioactivity release limits to the environs[146] and a portion of the referenced "Appendix B Table II" (Table 2) are presented below to illustrate the qualitative and quantitative aspects of recommendations at this level of guidance.

§ 20.106 Radioactivity in effluents to unrestricted areas.

(a) A licensee shall not possess, use, or transfer licensed material so as to release to an unrestricted area radioactive material in concentrations which exceed the limits specified in Appendix "B", Table II of this part, except as authorized pursuant to § 20.302 or paragraph (b) of this section. For purposes of this section, concentrations may be averaged over a period not greater than one year.

* All references are found starting on page 197.

** Adoption of ICRP 26 and 30 methods and nomenclature would necessitate minor revisions in this Figure.

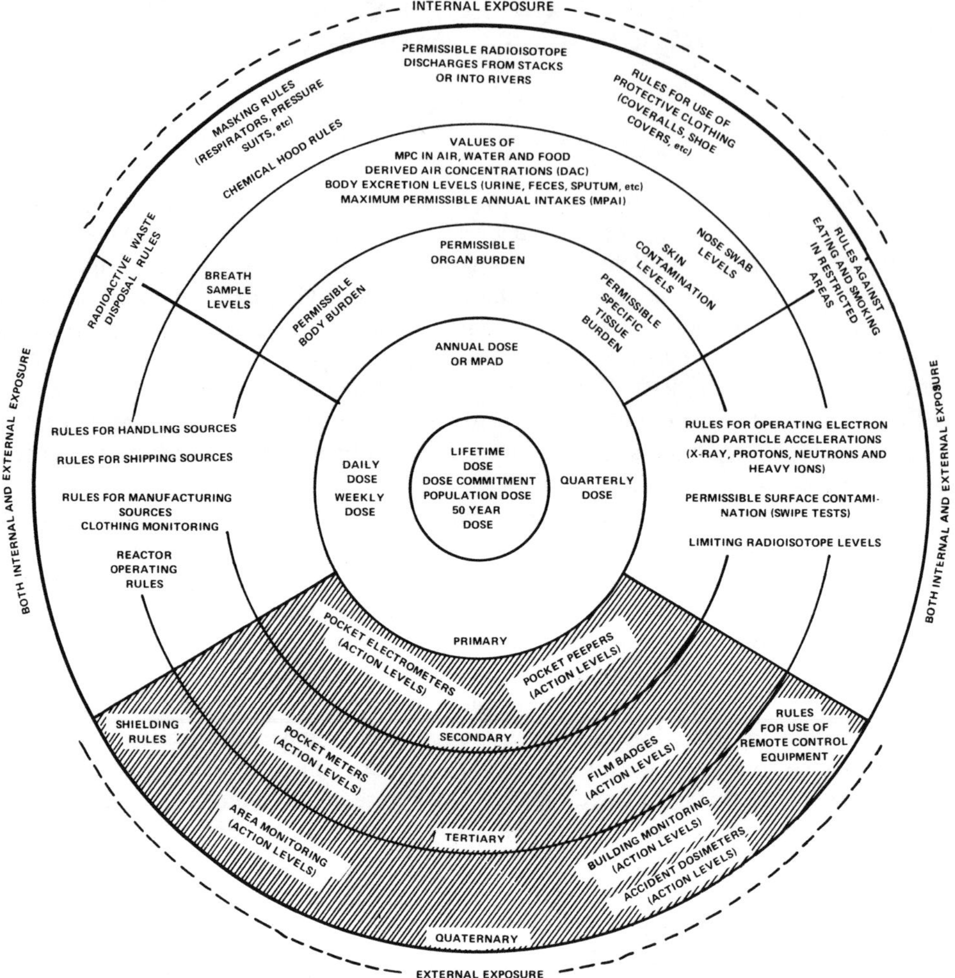

FIGURE 1. Relative significance of radiation protection standards.

(b) An application for a license or amendment may include proposed limits higher than those specified in paragraph (a) of this section. The Commission will approve the proposed limits if the applicant demonstrates:

(1) That the applicant has made a reasonable effort to minimize the radioactivity contained in effluents to unrestricted areas; and

(2) That it is not likely that radioactive material discharged in the effluent would result in the exposure of an individual to concentrations of radioactive material in air or water exceeding the limits specified in Appendix "B", Table II of this part.

(c) An application for higher limits pursuant to paragraph (b) of this section shall include information demonstrating that the applicant has made a reasonable effort to minimize the radioactivity discharged in effluents to unrestricted areas, and shall include, as pertinent:

(1) Information as to flow rates, total volume of effluent, peak concentration of each radionuclide in the effluent, and concentration of each radionuclide in the effluent averaged over a period of one year at the point where the effluent leaves a stack, tube, pipe, or similar conduit;

(2) A description of the properties of the effluents, including:

(i) chemical composition;

(ii) physical characteristics, including suspended solids content in liquid effluents, and nature of gas or aerosol for air effluents;

(iii) the hydrogen ion concentrations (p^{14}) of liquid effluents; and

(iv) the size range of particulates in effluents released into air.

Table 1
SUMMARY OF STAFF POSITION — METHODS OF EVALUATING COMPLIANCE WITH APPENDIX I[15]

Type of Dose	Appendix I design objective	Point of dose evaluation
	Liquid effluents	
Dose to total body from all pathways	3 mrem/year per unit	Location of the highest dose offsite[a]
Dose to any organ from all pathways	10 mrem/year per unit	Same as above
	Gaseous effluents[b]	
Gamma dose in air	10 mrad/year per unit	Location of the highest dose offsite[c]
Beta dose in air	20 mrad/year per unit	Same as above
Dose to total body of an individual	5 mrem/year per unit	Location of the highest dose offsite
Dose to skin of an individual	15 mrem/year per unit	Same as above
	Radioiodines and particulates[d] released to the atmosphere	
Dose to any organ from all pathways	15 mrem/year per unit	Location of the highest dose offsite[e]

[a] Evaluated at a location that is anticipated to be occupied during plant lifetime or evaluated with respect to such potential land and water usage and food pathways as could actually exist during the term of plant operation.

[b] Calculated only for noble gases.

[c] Evaluated at a location that could be occupied during the term of plant operation.

[d] Doses due to carbon-14 and tritium intake from terrestrial food chains are included in this category.

[e] Evaluated at a location where an exposure pathway actually exists at time of licensing. However, if the applicant determines design objectives with respect to radioactive iodine on the basis of existing conditions, and if potential changes in land and water usage and food pathways could result in exposures in excess of the guideline values given above, the applicant should provide reasonable assurance that a monitoring and surveillance program will be performed to determine: (1) the quantities of radioactive iodine actually released to the atmosphere and deposited relative to those estimated in the determination of design objectives; (2) whether changes in land and water usage and food pathways which would result in individual exposures greater than originally estimated have occurred; and (3) the content of radioactive iodine and foods involved in the changes, if and when they occur.

(3) A description of the anticipated human occupancy in the unrestricted area where the highest concentration of radioactive material from the effluent is expected, and in the case of a river or stream, a description of water uses downstream from the point of release of the effluent.

(4) Information as to the highest concentration of each radionuclide in an unrestricted area, including anticipated concentrations averaged over a period of one year:

(i) In air at any point of human occupancy; or

(ii) In water at points of use downstream from the point of release of the effluent.

(5) The background concentration of radionuclides in the receiving river or stream prior to the release of liquid effluent.

(6) A description of the environmental monitoring equipment, including sensitivity of the system, and procedures and calculations to determine concentrations of radionuclides in the unrestricted area and possible reconcentrations of radionuclides.

Table 2
CONCENTRATIONS IN AIR AND WATER ABOVE NATURAL, BACKGROUND[a]

Element (atomic number)	Isotope[b]		Table I[c] Column 1 Air (μCi/mℓ)	Table I[c] Column 2 Water (μCi/mℓ)	Table II[d] Column 1 Air (μCi/mℓ)	Table II[d] Column 2 Water (μCi/mℓ)
Cesium (55)	^{134}Cs	S	4×10^{-8}	3×10^{-4}	1×10^{-9}	9×10^{-6}
		I	1×10^{-8}	1×10^{-3}	4×10^{-10}	4×10^{-5}
	^{137}CS	S	6×10^{-8}	4×10^{-4}	2×10^{-9}	2×10^{-5}
		I	1×10^{-8}	1×10^{-3}	5×10^{-10}	4×10^{-5}
Hydrogen (1)	^{3}H	S	5×10^{-6}	1×10^{-1}	2×10^{-7}	3×10^{-3}
		I	5×10^{-6}	1×10^{-1}	2×10^{-7}	3×10^{-3}
Iodine (53)	^{131}I	S	9×10^{-9}	6×10^{-5}	1×10^{-10}	3×10^{-7}
		I	3×10^{-7}	2×10^{-3}	1×10^{-8}	6×10^{-5}
Plutonium (94)	^{239}Pu	S	2×10^{-12}	1×10^{-4}	6×10^{-14}	5×10^{-6}
		I	4×10^{-11}	8×10^{-4}	1×10^{-12}	3×10^{-5}
Strontium (38)	^{89}Sr	S	3×10^{-8}	3×10^{-4}	3×10^{-10}	3×10^{-6}
		I	4×10^{-8}	8×10^{-4}	1×10^{-9}	3×10^{-5}

[a] Excerpted from Appendix B of § 20.601 of Standards for Protection Against Radiation, Code of Federal Regulations, Title 10, Part 20, 1975.

[b] Soluble (S); Insoluble (I).

[c] Table I values are limits for exposure of individuals to concentrations of radioactive material in restricted areas (i.e., radiation workers).

[d] Table II values are limits for radioactivity in effluents to unrestricted areas (i.e., permissible annual average environmental concentrations).

(7) A description of the waste treatment facilities and procedures used to reduce the concentration of radionuclides in effluents prior to their release.

(d) For the purposes of this section, the concentration limits in Appendix "B", Table II of this part shall apply at the boundary of the restricted area. The concentration of radioactive materials discharged through a stack, pipe or similar conduit may be determined with respect to the point where the material leaves the conduit. If the conduit discharges within the restricted area, the concentration at the boundary may be determined by applying appropriate factors of dilution, dispersion, or decay between the point of discharge and the boundary.

(e) In addition to limiting concentrations in effluent streams, the Commission may limit quantities of radioactive materials released in air or water during a specified period of time if it appears that the daily intake of radioactive material from air, water, or food by a suitable sample of an exposed population group, averaged over a period not exceeding one year, would otherwise exceed the daily intake resulting from continuous exposure to air or water containing one third the concentration of radioactive materials specified in Appendix "B", Table II of this part.

(f) The provisions of this section do not apply to disposal of radioactive material into sanitary sewerage systems, which is governed by § 20.303. [29 F.R. 14434, Oct. 21, 1964]

The objective of all these and other secondary through quaternary standards is to make comparisons, for compliance testing purposes, with operationally available data as straightforward and efficient as possible.

ACTION GUIDES AND COUNTERMEASURES

D. H. Denham and D. A. Waite

INTRODUCTION

The control of the intake of radioactive materials from the environment can involve many different actions. The character and import of these actions vary widely from those that entail little interference with usual activities, such as monitoring and surveillance, to those that involve a major disruption, such as condemnation of food supplies. Some control actions would require prolonged lead times before becoming effective, e.g., major changes in water supplies. For these reasons, control programs should be based upon appropriate actions taken at different levels of intake. In order to provide guidance in developing appropriate programs, this section describes the graded approach of the Federal Radiation Council[9]* for specific radionuclides, involving three ranges of transient rates of daily intake applicable to different degrees or kinds of action and gives specific numerical examples of emergency reference levels.

The objective of the graded scale of actions is to limit intake of radioactive materials so that specified concentration guides (CGs) will not be exceeded.[143] Daily intakes varying within the total extent of all three ranges of intake might result in annual doses not exceeding a single CG. A suggested graded system of actions is outlined below. For each of the three ranges of transient rates of daily intake, the general type of action appropriate for the range is outlined.

RANGE I

Under normal conditions, intake falling into this range would not be expected to result in any appreciable number of individuals in the population reaching a large fraction of the CG. Therefore, if calculations based upon a knowledge of the sources of release of radioactive materials to the environment indicate that intakes of the population are in this range, the only action required is surveillance adequate to provide reasonable confirmation of calculations.

RANGE II

Intakes falling into this range would be expected to result in average exposures to population groups not exceeding the CG. Therefore, such intakes call for active surveillance and routine control.

Surveillance — Surveillance must be adequate to provide reasonable assurance that efforts being made to limit the release of radioactive materials to the environment are effective. It must also be adequate to provide estimates of the probable variation in average daily intake in time and location. Detection of sharply rising trends is very important. In some cases, the complexities of the environment may require that surveillance data be sufficiently reliable to be used as a rough check on whether or not radioactive materials in the environment are behaving as expected. Not only must the radioactive materials in question be studied but the environment must also. Appropriate efforts might be made to obtain measurements in man as well as to study physical, chemical, and metabolic factors affecting uptake. Appropriate consideration should be given to other independent sources of exposure to the body (the same organs or different ones) to avoid exceeding CGs.

* All references are found starting on page 197.

Control — Routine control of useful applications of radiation and atomic energy should be such that expected average exposures of suitable samples of an exposed population group will not exceed the upper value of Range II. The sample should be taken with due regard for the most sensitive population elements. Control actions for intakes in Range II would give primary emphasis to three things: (1) assuring by actions primarily directed at any sharply upward trend that average levels do not rise above Range II, (2) assuring by actions primarily directed either at specific causes of the environmental exposure levels encountered or at the environment that a limit is placed on any tendencies of specific population segments to rise above the CG, and (3) reducing the levels of exposure to segments of the population furthest above the average or tending to exceed Range II.

RANGE III

Intakes within this range would be presumed to result in exposures exceeding the CG if continued for a sufficient period of time. However, transient rates of intake within this range could occur without the population group exceeding the CG if the circumstances were such that the annual average intake fell within Range II or lower. Therefore, any intake within this range must be evaluated from the point of view of the CG and, if necessary, appropriate positive control measures instituted.

Surveillance — The surveillance described for intakes in Range II should be adequate to clearly define with a minimum of delay the extent of the exposure (level of intake and size of population group) within Range III. Surveillance would need to provide adequate data to give prompt and reliable information concerning the effectiveness of control actions.

Control — Control actions would be designed to reduce the levels to Range II or lower and to provide stability at lower levels. These actions can be directed toward further restriction of the entry of radioactive materials into the environment or the control of radioactive materials after entry into the environment in order to limit intake by humans. Sharply rising trends in Range III would suggest strong and prompt action. The prompt actions suggested for Range III might range from decontamination to protective actions. Several typical protective actions are listed below from Report No. 5 of the Federal Radiation Council:[147]

1. Altering production, processing, or distribution practices affecting the movement of radioactive contamination through the food chain and into the human body. This action includes a storage of food and animal feed supplies to allow for the radioactive decay of short-lived nuclides.
2. Diverting affected products to uses other than human consumption.
3. Condemning foods.

Other possible types of action currently are judged to be less desirable for reasons of effectiveness, safety, or practicality. The use of additives in cattle rations, solid treatment, and the chemical removal of radionuclides from milk are not included among the types of actions listed.

Protective actions to reduce the intake of radioactive materials by special alterations of the normal diet are accomplished best on an individual basis under the supervision of medical authorities.

Guidelines for selection of decontamination methods are presented in Table 1[148] with specific decontamination method capabilities tabulated in Tables 2 and 3. As an example of application and reaction alternatives,[149] details of the prompt action strategy regarding the accident at Windscale No. 1 Pile, U.K., October 10, 1957, follow

The two original reactors at Windscale, known as No. 1 and No. 2 Piles, were essentially graphite-moderated, natural uranium fuelled reactors, cooled by a forced air draft. The coolant was exhausted through a filter bank fitted at the top of a 125-m stack. During a routine operation begun on 7th October 1957, to

Table 1
GUIDELINES FOR SELECTION OF DECONTAMINATION METHOD

	Fire hosing	Hand shoveling	Filling	Road[a] grader	Ploughing	Bulldozing	Motor[b] scraper
Unpaved area							
Cohesive soils (clays)	D	B	B	A	A	B	A
Noncohesive soils (sand and gravel)	B	B	B	B	A	B	A
Soils containing boulders	D	D	B	D	D	A	A
Exposed rock formations	C	D	B	D	D	D	D

	Vacuum sweeper	Mechanical sweeper	Street flusher	Firehose
Paved areas and all hard surfaces	A	A	B	B

Note: A — Applicable to large areas, B — Recommended for smaller areas, C — Applicable where little or no earth cover exists, D — Not applicable or recommended.

[a] Highway maintenance equipment used for road grading by spreading material or for light stripping.
[b] Heavy construction equipment pulled by tractor used to scrape several inches of soil and to carry removed material to dumping ground.

From *Evaluation of Radiation Emergencies and Accidents — Selected Criteria and Data,* Technical Reports Series, No. 152, International Atomic Energy Agency, Vienna, 1974, 79.

release Wigner energy from the graphite, excess nuclear heating was wrongly applied causing the failure of a number of fuel cartridges. The uranium caught fire and the fire spread until it involved about 150 channels. Fission-products were released to the atmosphere from the stack. From measurements of air-borne activity and of activity deposited upon the ground it has since been estimated that approximately 20,000 Ci ^{131}I, 12,000 Ci ^{132}Te, 600 Ci ^{137}Cs, 80 Ci ^{89}Sr, and 2 Ci ^{90}Sr were released. Some of this activity reached the continent of Europe.

The first indication of an abnormal release of activity came through routine air-sampling on the site. The air sample collected between 11.00 a.m. and 2.00 p.m. on 10th October at a point about 800 m from the stack indicated a contamination level of 3000 β-dis/min per cubic metre, about 10 times that normally resulting from the decay products of radon and thoron. The situation was confirmed by further air samples taken at other points on the site. The state of affairs in the reactor was discovered by visual inspection.

The first requirement was to determine gamma-radiation levels in the district around the Works. A survey vehicle was therefore sent out at 3.00 p.m. to make ground and air measurements in the down-wind direction (south-east). A second vehicle left at 5 p.m. to explore the area north of the site.

The radiation levels due to deposited activity were generally about 0.15—0.20 mR/h in the area 3—5 km south of the Works and much lower in other directions. There then appeared to be no significant external radiation hazard. Measurements continued during the period of release and it has been estimated that the integrated exposure to any member of the public did not exceed 75 mR.

Throughout the period of release some thousands of air samples were taken both on the site and in the nearby district. Although the air contamination rose on occasion to worrying, but not dangerous levels on the site, dilution resulting from wind variation considerably reduced the hazard in the district. After midday on 11th October air contamination levels both on and off site fell rapidly to well below the ICRP values for continuous exposure.

By the evening of 11th October it was clear that there was no significant external radiation or inhalation hazard. Further planning was based on the assumption that the release contained a normal distribution of mixed fission-products. The gamma-radiation survey results were therefore interpreted as indicating that there might be a marginal risk from contamination of milk with isotopes of iodine and strontium.

Milk samples were collected from local farms during the evening milking on 10th October and the morning and evening milkings on 11th October. However, the analytical results were not available until noon 12th October. The milk collected on the evening of the 10th and morning of the 11th, in fact, contained only traces of radioiodine but that obtained on the afternoon of 11th October contained 0.4—0.8 μCi/litre. The analyses revealed a higher proportion of radioiodine than would be present in a normal reactor fission-product mixture. It was evident that iodine vapour had passed through the stack filter but that the major part of the particulate material had been retained.

Table 2
DECONTAMINATION METHODS — COLD WEATHER CONDITIONS

Method	Rate (100 ft^2/hr)	DF
Bare sloped asphalt shingles		
Firehosing (lobbing)		
(25°F)	8	3
(0°F)	8	2
Undisturbed snow		
Snow plough (blade)	330	10—35
Grading	125	2—20
Scraping	72	5—7
Snow plough (rotary)	53	7—50
Packed snow		
Grading (0—30°F)	70	5—6
Mechanical sweeping (below 20°F)	60	15
Vacuum sweeping (10 to 30°F)	30	6
Firehosing (30°F)	13	10
(15°F)	13	5
(0°F)	13	4
Paved areas		
Mechanical sweeping	65	15
Firehosing (0°F)	20	10—15
Bare frozen ground		
Mechanical sweeping	70	10—35
Vacuum sweeping	70	8
Firehosing	20	2

From *Evaluation of Radiation Emergencies and Accidents—Selected Criteria and Data*, Technical Reports Series, No. 152, International Atomic Energy Agency, Vienna, 1974, 80.

Table 3
DECONTAMINATION — TEMPERATE WEATHER CONDITIONS

Method	Rate (100 ft^2/hr)	DF
Roofs		
Firehosing		
Composition shingle	12—60	10—35
Tar and gravel	7—35	8—100
Firehosing and scrubbing		
Tar and gravel	5	50
Composition shingle	5	50
Wood shingle	5	10
Corrugated sheet metal	5	100
Paved areas		
Motorized flushers	100—300	25—50
Street sweepers	25—100	6—25
Vacuumized sweepers	25—100	4—50
Firehosing	5—25	15—50
Unpaved land areas		
Grading (few in.)	60	15
Ploughing	25	5
Scraping (several in.)	9	50
Bulldozing (several in.)	8.5	15
Filling		
6-in. fill	4	7
12-in. fill	2	50

From *Evaluation of Radiation Emergencies and Accidents — Selected Criteria and Data*, Technical Report Series, No. 152, International Atomic Energy Agency, Vienna, 1974, 81.

Table 4
EMERGENCY REFERENCE LEVELS FOR EXTERNAL EXPOSURE

	Type of exposure		
Exposure group	Gamma radiation	Beta and gamma radiation[a]	Skin contamination[b]
Children up to 16 years pregnant women	20 R in free air	75 rads to superficial tissue	75 rads to superficial tissue
Other persons	30 R in free air	150 rads to superficial tissue	150 rads to superficial tissue

Note: A further 30 R may be permitted for essential duties by a special category comprising adult males (preferably in the older age group) or females above reproductive age.

[a] Subject to a limit of 15 rads gamma, corresponding to 20 R in free air, or 25 rads gamma corresponding to 30 R in free air.
[b] Limited to 1/10 of the body surface and in addition to footnote a.

From Reinig, W. C., Ed., *Environmental Surveillance in the Vicinity of Nuclear Facilities,* Charles C Thomas, Springfield, Ill., 1970, 153. With permission.

No permissible level for ^{131}I in milk existed at that time. A group of experts was convened in the afternoon of 11th October and by 9.00 p.m., the decision had been reached that distribution of milk should be prohibited if the ^{131}I concentration exceeded 0.1 μCi/litre. Arrangements were made to prevent milk deliveries that night from 12 milk producers within a 3-km radius of Windscale.

On Sunday, 13th October, a widespread monitoring programme was initiated to delineate the areas over which an embargo on the consumption and sale of milk would be necessary. By 14th October, this restriction finally covered a coastal strip about 50 km long and about 500 km^2 in area.

It was soon found that considerable use could be made of the gamma-survey as a guide to the area from which milk samples were required. The bulk of the survey work was done with portable scintillation gamma-monitors designed for geological prospecting. These were found to have many advantages over the conventional ionization chambers previously used for district surveys. Ground measurements, coupled with simple direct measurement of the ^{131}I level in milk made by placing the detector head of the instrument in contact with the side of a milk churn, provided a screening technique for deciding the farms or collecting centres from which milk should be sampled for more precise laboratory analyses.

Fifteen vehicles, each with a team of two men, were used to delineate the restricted areas and subsequently follow the trends of milk contamination until the restriction could be lifted. Altogether these teams collected over 2000 litres of milk , mainly in 250-ml samples. The analytical teams handled over 3000 samples.

In addition to milk, other footdstuffs were monitored and during the occurrence of the survey over 1 tonne of vegetables, about 700 eggs and about 50 kg of meat were handled. Drinking water supplies in Cumberland, Lancashire and North Wales were also analysed. In all cases it was found that the level of contamination was well below that which would constitute a hazard. In vivo monitoring of the thyroid glands of selected adults and children demonstrated the efficacy of the remedial measures; the highest dose to a child's thyroid was estimated as 16 rads and to an adult's thyroid, 4 rads. Thyroid glands from sheep, cows and pigs were also examined, the maximum dose to an animal's thyroid being estimated to be less than 1000 rads (incurred by grazing sheep).

By 4th November the only restricted area remaining was a coastal strip extending about 20 km southwards from Windscale. This area remained under restriction until 23rd November, by which time sufficient analyses of strontium in milk had been made for it to be certain that no restriction was necessary on account of ^{90}Sr.

In view of the possibility that some ^{90}Sr might reside in the root mat and soil and find its way to grass and thence to milk at some later time, it was decided to examine grass and milk for this nuclide for an extended period and measurements went on, in fact, until late 1958. The early fears were not realized and by the late summer of 1958 there was no evidence of any contribution to radiostrontium contamination of milk from the accident.

Twenty persons were employed in handling and recording the samples obtained during the period of intensive monitoring and assisting in the operation of a control centre where all information was recorded

Table 5
EMERGENCY REFERENCE LEVELS FOR IODINE 131 AND CAESIUM 137

Parameter	Iodine-131		Caesium-137	
	6-month old child[a]	Adult	6-month old child[a]	Adult
Critical organ	Thyroid	Thyroid	Whole body	Whole body
ERL of dose to critical organ	25 rad	25 rad	10 rad	10 rad
Dose per microcurie inhaled	15 rad/μCi	1.5 rad/μCi	0.049 rad/μCi	0.047 rad/μCi
Dose per microcurie ingested	20 rad/μCi	1.9 rad/μCi	0.066 rad/μCi	0.062 rad/μCi
ERL of cloud dosage	0.024[b]Ci sec/m³	0.075 Ci sec/m³	2.9 Ci sec/m³	0.93[c] Ci sec/m³
ERL in milk[d]	0.18 μCi/ℓ	2.5 μCi/ℓ	6.7 μCi/ℓ	9.8 μCi/ℓ
ERL on pasture[e]	1.3 μCi/M²	18 μCi/m²	22 μCi/m²	33 μCi/m²

[a] The values for the 6-month old child can be taken as typical of children in the first year of life.
[b] Where there is a dose contribution from other iodine isotopes and tellurium-132, the values for iodine-131 should be reduced by a factor of two or, in the case of a release of short-lived fission products from a criticality accident, by a factor of ten.
[c] The adult is the limiting case due to the much shorter half-life of cesium-137 in children than in adults.
[d] The tabulated values are for the maximum levels reached after a single deposition.
[e] The levels on pasture are the initial activities of the total deposits.

From Reinig, W. C., Ed., *Environmental Surveillance in the Vicinity of Nuclear Facilities,* Charles C. Thomas, Springfield, Ill., 1970, 153. With permission.

Table 6
ERL'S[a] FOR STRONTIUM 89 AND STRONTIUM 90

Parameter	Strontium 89		Strontium 90	
	6-month old child[b]	Adult	6-month old child[b]	Adult
Critical organ	Bone	Bone	Bone	Bone
ERL of dose to critical organ	15 rads	15 rads	1.5 rads/year	1.5 rads/year
ERL of cloud dosage	0.079 Ci s/m³	0.36 Ci s/m³	0.00083 Ci s/m³	0.0036 Ci s/m³
ERL in milk	0.2 μCi/g Ca	0.2 μCi/g Ca	0.002 μCi/g Ca	0.002 μCi/g Ca
ERL in pasture	10 μCi/m²	10 μCi/m²	0.1 μCi/m²	0.1 μCi/m²

[a] The basis for these emergency reference levels, i.e., the assumption that the criterion should be local dose to mineral bone, is being reconsidered and it is likely that the basis may be changed and the values of the reference levels increased.
[b] The values for the 6-month old child can be taken as typical of children in the first year of life.

From Reinig, W. C., Ed., *Environmental Surveillance in the Vicinity of Nuclear Facilities,* Charles C. Thomas, Springfield, Ill., 1970, 154. With permission.

and displayed on maps. Some 150 radiochemists, distributed between the various U.K.A.E.A. establishments, contributed to the analytical effort.

Several valuable lessons were learned from the accident which served to highlight the need for (a) authoritative and agreed exposure criteria for use in emergency situations, (b) portable, self-contained instruments of the required sensitivity for gamma-survey work, (c) means of obtaining assistance from outside sources to cope with the increased load on monitoring and, particularly, analytical facilities, and (d) a prepared plan of action with both local and central government organizations.

Table 7
RECOMMENDED INTERIM STANDARD FOR PLUTONIUM IN SOILS[75]

	In <100 μm particle Size fraction			Total[b]		
	dpm per g	μCi/g	μCi/m²	dpm per g	μCi/g	μCi/m²
Top 0.1 cm[a]	500	2×10^{-4}	0.4	1,000	4×10^{-4}	0.8
Any 1-cm layer	500	2×10^{-4}	4	10,000	4×10^{-4}	8

[a] For bare soil or areas with sparse vegetation. Where area is reasonably well vegetated (greater than 50% of the area is covered with low vegetation) and a reasonable root mat exists to hold the soil, the concentration listed can be applied to a 0.5-cm layer which would permit up to 2μCi/m² in this layer.

[b] With the provision that the fraction with particle sizes less than 100 μm is known not to exceed the limits given. If this is not known, the values for the < 100μm fraction should be applied to the total.

Table 8
SUMMARY OF INTERNATIONAL PERMISSIBLE ALPHA CONTAMINATION LEVELS WRITTEN INTO LAW [(151)]

Country	Maximum permissible alpha contamination (μCi/m²)	Application
Czechoslavakia	0.11	Workplaces, after decontamination
France	0.01	Skin
	0.1	Equipment and workplaces in "inactive" areas
	1.0	Equipment and workplaces in "active" areas
Poland	0.1	Laboratories restricted to 100 μCi
	1.0	Laboratories in which 100 μCi permitted
South Africa	0.1	Body, personal clothing, inactive areas, etc.
	1.0	Equipment and workplaces inside controlled areas

Table 8 (continued)
SUMMARY OF INTERNATIONAL PERMISSIBLE ALPHA CONTAMINATION LEVELS WRITTEN INTO LAW[151]

Country	Maximum permissible alpha contamination (μCi/m²)	Application
U.S.	0.02	Interstate Commerce Commission (Department of Transportation), pertains to interior of vehicles previously used for transportation of radioactive materials
U.S.S.R.	0.015	Work clothing and surfaces before cleaning
	0.002	Hands and work underclothing, before cleaning
	0.006	Work surfaces, after cleaning
	Background	Hands and work underclothing, after cleaning
United Kingdom	0.1	"Inactive" areas
	1.0	"Active" areas

Table 9
INTERIM MAXIMUM PERMISSIBLE SURFACE CONTAMINATION LEVELS FOR ENVIRONMENTAL PuO_2 [151]

	Average dpm/ 100 cm²	Maximum dpm/100 cm²
Urban, suburban, and recreation areas	10^3 (0.04 μCi/m²)	10^4 (0.4 μCi/m²), spread over ≤10% of the total area included
Rural: truck farming, annual food crops, grazing land, milkshed, etc.	10^4 (0.4 μCi/m²)	
Rural: deep root perennials (e.g., nuts, certain fruits)	10^5 (4 μCi/m²)	
Remote or controlled: desert, forest, fenced, or limited access areas	10^6 (40 μCi/m²)	

Table 10
PLUTONIUM DISPOSITION CRITERIA MATRIX[152]

	Surface Contamination		
	Fixed (dpm/100 cm²)	Smearable (dpm/m²)	Activity/mass concentration
Unrestricted	220	220	10 pCi/g
Conditional non-surveillance	2,200	220	100 pCi/g
Conditional surveillance	22,000	220	1 nCi/g
Restricted	>22,000	220	>1 nCi/g

Tables 4 to 6[150] show emergency fission product reference levels used in the U.K. Atomic Energy Authority. An emergency reference level is a dose or a derived quantity below which it is unlikely that countermeasures will be justified unless the countermeasures have exceedingly low impact on the community. Similar guidance for plutonium and alpha emitters has tended to take the form of permissible contamination levels. Interim recommended standards for plutonium in soils are shown in Table 7,[75] while such levels for surface contamination are shown in Tables 8 and 9.[151]

Surface and volumetric contamination limits have been derived as a function of the use of a facility or site; Table 10[152] shows the criteria so derived for a high exposure plutonium mixture. The same methodology[153] has also been used for mixtures of plutonium and transuranics and mixed fission products. All of these action guides and residual contamination limits have the rapid and reasonable response to abnormal environmental conditions as an objective.

REFERENCES

1. Corley, J. P., Denham, D. H., Jacquish, R. E., Michels, D. E., Olsen, A. R., and Waite, D. A., *A Guide for: Environmental Radiological Surveillance at U.S. Department of Energy Installations,* DOE/EP-0023, Office of Operational Safety, U.S. Department of Energy, Washington, D.C., July 1981.
2. Watson, J. E., Chairman, Health Physics Society Committee Report HPSR-1 (1980), *Upgrading Environmental Radiation Data,* EPA 520/1-80-012, U.S. Environmental Protection Agency, Washington, D.C., August 1980.
3. Office of Radiation Programs, *Environmental Radioactivity Surveillance Guide,* ORP/SID 72-2, Environmental Protection Agency, Washington, D.C., June 1972.
4. *Objectives and Design of Environmental Monitoring Programs for Radioactive Contaminants,* Safety Series No. 41, International Atomic Energy Agency, Vienna, 1975.
5. American National Standards Institute, *American National Standard Specification and Performance of On-Site Instrumentation for Continuously Monitoring Radioactivity in Effluents,* ANSI N13. 10-1974, Institute of Electrical and Electronics Engineers, New York, 1974.
6. Harley, J. H., *HASL Procedures Manual,* HASL-300, Health and Safety Laboratory, Atomic Energy Commission, New York, 1972 (revised annually; now Environmental Measurements Laboratory, U.S. Department of Energy).
7. International Commission on Radiological Protection, *Principles of Environmental Monitoring Related to the Handling of Radioactive Materials,* ICRP Publ. No. 7, Pergamon Press, New York, 1965.
8. Office of Regulatory Standards, *Programs for Monitoring Radioactivity in the Environs of Nuclear Power Plants,* Revision 1, Regulatory Guide 4.1, U.S. Nuclear Regulatory Commission, Washington, D.C., April 1975.
9. U.S. Federal Radiation Council, *Background Material for the Development of Radiation Protection Standards,* FRC Rep. No. 2, U.S. Government Printing Office, Washington, D.C., September 1961.
10. Soldat, J. K., Robinson, N. M., and Baker, D. A., *Models and Computer Codes for Evaluating Environmental Radiation Doses,* BNWL-1754, Battelle, Pacific Northwest Laboratories, Richland, Wash., February 1974.
11. Denham, D. H., Waite, D. A., and Corley, J. P., *Summary of Selected AEC Contractor Environmental Surveillance Techniques and Capabilities,* BNWL-B-384, Battelle, Pacific Northwest Laboratories, Richland, Wash., September 1974.
12. Fletcher, J. F. and Dotson, W. L., *HERMES — A Digital Computer Code for Estimating Regional Radiological Effects from the Nuclear Power Industry,* HEDL-TME-71-68, Hanford Engineering Development Laboratory, Richland, Wash., December 1971.
13. Soldat, J. K., *Modeling of environmental pathways and radiation doses from nuclear facilities,* BNWL-SA-3939, Battelle-Pacific Northwest Laboratories, Richland, Wash., October 1971.
14. *Environmental Radiation Measurements,* NCRP Rep. No. 50, National Council on Radiation Protection and Measurements, Washington, D.C., 1977.
15. Office of Standards Development, *Calculation of Annual Doses to Man from Routine Releases of Reactor Effluents for the Purpose of Evaluating Compliance with 10 CFR Part 50, Appendix 1,* Regulatory Guide 1.109, Rev. 1 U.S. Nuclear Regulatory Commission, Washington, D.C., October 1977.
16. Slade, D. H., Ed., *Meteorology and Atomic Energy — 1968,* U.S. Atomic Energy Commission, Division of Technical Information, Oak Ridge, Tenn., July 1968.
17. Office of Standards Development, *Environmental Technical Specifications for Nuclear Power Plants,* Regulatory Guide 4.8, U.S. Nuclear Regulatory Commission, Washington, D.C., December 1975.
18. Office of Standards Development, *Methods for Estimating Atmospheric Transport and Dispersion of Gaseous Effluents in Routine Releases From Light-Water-Cooled Reactors,* Regulatory Guide 1.111, Rev. 1, U.S. Nuclear Regulatory Commission, Washington, D.C., July 1977.
19. Division of Regulatory Standards, *On-Site Meteorological Programs,* Regulatory Guide 1.23, U.S. Atomic Energy Commission, Washington, D.C., February 1972.
20. Office of Standards Development, *Estimating Aqueous Dispersion of Effluents from Accidental and Routine Reactor Releases for the Purpose of Implementing Appendix I,* Regulatory Guide 1.113, Rev. 1, U.S. Nuclear Regulatory Commission, Washington, D.C., April 1977.
21. Athey T. W., Tell, R. A., and Janes, D. E., "The use of an automated population data base in population exposure calculations," in *Symp. Population Procedures, Proc. 8th Midyear Topical Symp. Health Physic Society,* Knoxville, Tenn., October 21—24, 1974, CONF 741018, East Tennessee Chapter, Health Physics Society, Knoxville, Tenn., October 1974, 29—36.
22. International Commission on Radiological Protection, *Report of Committee IV on Evaluation of Radiation Doses to Body Tissues from Internal Contamination due to Occupational Exposure,* ICRP Publ. 10, Pergamon Press, New York, 1968.

23. Agricultural Research Service, *Food Intake and Nutritive Value of Diets of Men, Women, and Children in the United States, Spring 1965 — A Preliminary Report,* ARS 62-18, U.S. Department of Agriculture, Washington, D.C., March 1969.
24. Economic Research Service, *National Food Situations,* NSF-151, U.S. Department of Agriculture, Washington, D.C., 1975.
25. Environmental Instrumentation Group, *Instrumentation for Environmental Monitoring,* LBL-1, Volumes 1—4, University of California, Lawrence Berkeley Laboratory, Berkeley, 1972.
26. Intersociety Committee for a Manual of Methods for Ambient Air Sampling and Analysis, *Methods of Air Sampling and Analysis,* American Public Health Association, Washington D.C., 1972.
27. *Standard Methods for the Examination of Water and Wastewater,* 13th ed., American Public Health Association, Washington, D.C., 1971.
28. Methods Development and Quality Assurance Research Laboratory, *Methods for Chemical Analysis of Water and Wastes,* EPA 625/6-74-003, U.S. Environmental Protection Agency, Washington, D.C., 1974.
29. *Guide to Sampling Airborne Radioactive Materials in Nuclear Facilities,* ANSI N13.1, American National Standards Institute, New York, 1969.
30. Directorate of Regulatory Standards, *Measuring, Evaluating, and Reporting Radioactivity in Solid Wastes and Releases of Radioactive Materials in Liquid and Gaseous Effluents from Light-Water-Cooled Nuclear Power Plants,* Regulatory Guide 1.21, Revision 1, U.S. Nuclear Regulatory Commission, Washington, D.C., June 1974.
31. *Air Sampling Instruments for Evaluation of Atmospheric Contaminants,* 4th ed., American Conference of Governmental Industrial Hygienists, Washington, D.C., 1972.
32. Environmental Instrumentation Group, *Instrumentation for Environmental Monitoring,* LBL-1, Vol. 1, University of California, Lawrence Berkeley Laboratory, Berkeley, 1972.
33. International Commission on Radiological Protection Task Group on Lung Dynamics, Deposition and retention models for internal dosimetry of the human respiratory tract, *Health Phys.,* 12, 173, 1966.
34. **Waite, D. A. and Nees, W. L.,** *A Novel Particle Sizing Technique for Health Physics Applications,* BNWL-SA-4658, Battelle, Pacific Northwest Laboratories, Richland, Wash., June 1973.
35. **Kotrappa, P., Dua, S. K., Bhanti, D. P., and Joshi, P. P.,** HASL Cyclone as an instrument for measuring aerosol parameters for new lung model, in *Proc. 3rd. Int. Cong. International Radiation Protection Association,* September 9—14, 1973, Washington, D.C., CONF-730907-P2, Atomic Energy Commission Technical Information Center, Oak Ridge, Tenn., September 1974, 12.
36. **Lockhart, L. B., Jr. and Patterson, R. L., Jr.,** *Characteristics of Air Filter Media Used for Monitoring Airborne Radioactivity,* NRL-6054, Naval Research Laboratory, Washington, D.C., 1964.
37. **Denham, D. H.,** Effectiveness of filter media for surface collection of airborne radioactive particulates, *Health Physics Operational Monitoring,* Vol. 2, Willis, C. A. and Handloser, J. S., Eds., Gordon & Breach, New York, 1972, 1093.
38. **Stafford, R. B.,** *Comparative Evaluation of Several Glass-Fiber Filter Media,* LA-5297, University of California, Los Alamos Scientific Laboratory, Los Alamos, N.M., June 1973.
39. **Smith, W. J. and Benson, A. L.,** Filter media for atmospheric sampling and analysis, in *Instrumentation for Monitoring Air Quality,* ASTM STP 555, American Society for Testing and Materials, Philadelphia, 1974.
40. **Keller, J. H., Thomas, T. R., Pence, D. T., and Maeck, W. J.,** An evaluation of materials and techniques used for monitoring airborne radioiodine species, in *Proc. 12th AEC Air Cleaning Conference,* U.S. Atomic Energy Commission, Washington, D.C., January 1973, 322—332.
41. **Bellamy, R. R.,** Elemental iodine and methyl iodide adsorption on activated charcoal at low concentrations, in *Nuclear Safety,* Vol. 15, U.S. Atomic Energy Commission Technical Information Center, Oak Ridge, Tenn., 1974, 711—723.
42. **Baratta, E. J., Chabot, G. E., and Donlen, R. J.,** Collection and determination of Iodine-131 in the air, *Am. Ind. Hyg. Assoc. J.,* 29, 159, 1968.
43. **Megaw, W. J. and May, F. G.,** *J. Nucl. Energy,* 16, 427, 1962.
44. **Gabay, J. J., Paperiello, C. J., Goodyear, S., Daly, J. C., and Matuszek, J. M.,** A Method for Determining Iodine-129 in Milk and Water, *Health Phys.,* 26, 89, 1974.
45. **Ng, Y. C., Burton, C. A., Thompson, S. E., Tandy, R. K., Kretner, H. K., and Pratt, M. W.,** *Prediction Of The Maximum Dosage To Man From The Fallout Of Nuclear Devices IV, Handbook For Estimating The Maximum Internal Dose From Radionuclides Released To The Biosphere,* UCRL-50163 Part IV, Lawrence Livermore Laboratory, Livermore, California, 1968.
46. **Alonso, A.,** Generalization of Holland's method to assess gamma-doses from radioactive clouds, *Health Phys.,* 13, 487, 1967.

47. **Schaeffer, R.**, Dose calculations in external exposure to inert gases, Paper No. 103, in Proc. 3rd Int. Cong. Int. Radiation Protection Assoc., September 9—14, 1973, Washington, D.C., CONF-730907-Pl, U.S. Atomic Energy Commission Technical Information Center, Oak Ridge, Tenn., September 1974, 659.
48. **Stanley, R. E. and Moghissi, A. R., Eds.**, Noble gases, Proc. Cong., Las Vegas, August 1972, Messenger Graphics, Phoenix, Ariz., 1974.
49. **Goldin, A. S.**, Adsorption of Fission Noble Gases on Charcoal, Paper No. in *Proc. 3rd. Int. Cong. International Radiation Protection Association,* September 9—4, 1973, Washington, D. C., U.S. Atomic Energy Commission Technical Information Center, Oak Ridge, Tenn., September, 376.
50. **Johns, F. B.**, Sampling and Measurement of the Noble Gases in the Environment, presented at 2nd Atomic Energy Commission Environmental Surveillance Workshop, U.S. Atomic Energy Commission, Albuquerque, N.M., April 1974.
51. **Magno, P. J., et al.**, *Calibration and Initial Field Testing of ^{85}Kr Detectors for Environmental Monitoring,* BRH/NERHL 70-4, Bureau of Radiological Health, Northeastern Radiological Health Laboratory, Mass., November 1970.
52. **Karches, G. J., et al.**, Field determination of dose from ^{133}Xe in the plume from a pressurized water reactor, in Rapid Methods for Measuring Radioactivity in the Environment, *Proc. Int. Symp.*, Neuherbert, July 5—9, 1971, International Atomic Energy Agency, Vienna, 1971, 515.
53. **Tritium in the Physical and Biological Sciences**, *Proc. IAEA Symp.*, International Atomic Energy Agency, Vienna, 1961.
54. National Environmental Research Center, Tritium, *Proc. Tritium Symp.*, August 30 to September 3, 1971, Las Vegas, Environmental Protection Agency, Las Vegas, 1972.
55. **Jacobs, D. B.**, *Sources of Tritium and Its Behavior upon Release to the Environment,* TID-24635, U.S. Atomic Energy Commission Division of Technical Information Extension, Oak Ridge, Tenn., 1968.
56. **Hanna, B. J. and Kershner, C. J.**, *Bibliography on Handling, Control, and Monitoring of Tritium, (December 1968 to June 1972),* MLM-1946, Mound Laboratory, Monsanto Research Corp., Miamisburg, Ohio, 1972.
57. **Rudolph, A. W., Carroll, T. E., and Davidson, R. S.**, *Tritium and Its Effects in the Environment — A Selected Literature Survey,* BMI-171-203, Battelle Memorial Institute, Columbus, Ohio, 1971.
58. **Ostlund, H. G.**, *A Rapid Field Sampling for Tritium in Atmospheric Hydrogen,* Report ML 70075, Rosenstiel School of Marine and Atmospheric Sciences, University of Miami, Fla., 1970.
59. **Osborne, R. B.**, Sampling for Tritiated Water Vapour, *Proc. 3rd Int. Cong. International Radiation Protection Association,* September 9—14, 1973, Washington, D.C., CONF-730907-P2, U.S. Atomic Energy Commission Technical Information Center, Oak Ridge, Tenn., September 1974, 1428—1433.
60. **Brown, R., et al.**, *A Ruggedized Ultrasensitive Field Air Sampler for HTO and HT,* MLM-2015, Mound Laboratory, Monsanto Research Corp., Miamisburg, Ohio, April 1973.
61. **Iyengar, T. S., Sadarangani, S. H., Somasundaram, S., and Vaze, P. K.**, A cold strip apparatus for sampling tritium in air, *Health Phys.*, 11, 313, 1965.
62. **Waite, D. A.**, *Analysis of an Analytical Technique for Distributing Air Sampling Locations Around Nuclear Facilities,* BNWI-SA-4676, Battelle, Pacific Northwest Laboratories, Richland, Wash., May 1973.
63. **Aten, A. H. W., Jr., Heertje, I., and Dejong, W. M. C.**, Measurements of low-level environmental radiation by means of Geiger-Muller Counters with observations in the Amsterdam region, *Physica,* 27, 809, 1961.
64. **Sommers, J. F.**, Sensitivity of instrument surveys for beta-gamma particulate contamination, Paper No. 163, presented at Health Physics Society 19th Annual Meeting, Houston, Tex., July 1974.
65. **Schmidt, C. T. and Koch, J. J.**, Plutonium survey with X-ray detectors, in Hazards Control Progress Rep. No. 26, UCRL-50007-66-2, Lawrence Radiation Laboratory, Livermore, Calif., 1966, 1—6.
66. **Tinney, J. F. and Koch, J. J.**, An X-ray survey meter for plutonium contamination, Hazards Control Progress Rep. No. 29, UCRL-50007-67-3, Lawrence Radiation Laboratory, Livermore, Calif., 1967, 6—15.
67. **Philipp, L. L. and Sheen, E. M.**, *Aerial and Ground Gamma Survey Monitors,* BNWL-62, Battelle, Pacific Northwest Laboratories, Richland, Wash., May 1965.
68. **Burson, Z. G., Boyns, P. K., and Fritzsche, A. E.**, Technical procedures for characterizing the terrestrial gamma radiation environment by aerial surveys, in *Proc. 2nd Int. Symp. Natural Radiation Environment,* CONF-720805-P2, Adams, J. A. S., Lowder, W. M., and Gesell, T., Eds., U.S. Atomic Energy Commission, Washington, D.C., 1974.
69. **Beck, H. L., Lowder, W. M., and McLaughlin, J. E.**, *In situ* external environmental gamma-ray measurements utilizing Ge(Li) and NaI(Tl) spectrometry and ionization chambers, Rapid Methods for Measuring Radioactivity in the Environment, *Proc. Int. Symp.*, Neuherberg, July 5—9, 1971, International Atomic Energy Agency, Vienna, 1971, 448—513.

70. **Anspaugh, L. R., Phelps, P. L., Gudiksen, P. H., Lindeken, C. L., and Huckabay, G. W.**, The *in situ* measurement of radionuclides in the environment with a Ge (Li) spectrometer, in *Proc. 2nd Int. Symp. Natural Radiation Environment,* Adams, J. A. S., Lowder, W. M., and Gesell, T., Eds., U.S. Atomic Energy Commission, Washington, D.C., 1974, 279—303.
71. **Waite, D. A.**, *Use and Interpretation of Particulate Deposition Collector Data,* BNWL-SA-4874, Battelle, Pacific Northwest Laboratories, Richland, Wash., July 1974.
72. **Directorate of Regulatory Standards,** *Measurements of Radionuclides in the Environment—Sampling and Analysis of Plutonium in Soil,* Regulatory Guide 4.5, Nuclear Regulatory Commission, Washington, D.C., May 1974.
73. **Fowler, E. B., Henderson, W., and Milligan, F., Eds.**, *Proc. Environmental Plutonium Symp.,* August 4—5, 1971, LA-4756, University of California, Los Alamos Scientific Laboratory, Los Alamos, N.M., December 1971.
74. **Sill, C. W. and Williams, R. L.**, Rapid identification and determination of alpha emitters in environmental samples, in *Rapid Methods for Measuring Radioactivity in the Environment,* International Atomic Energy Agency, Vienna, 1971, 201.
75. **Healy, J. W.**, *A Proposed Interim Standard for Plutonium in Soils,* LA-5483-MS, University of California, Los Alamos Scientific Laboratory, Los Alamos, N.M., January 1974.
76. National Council on Radiation Protection and Measurements, (NCRP), Report No. 62, NCRP, Washington, D.C., 1979.
77. **Hall, R. M. and LaRocca, J. P.**, Thermoluminescent dosimeters for environmental monitoring, *Health Phys.,* 12, 851, 1966.
78. **Hendee, W. R.**, Radiation response of LiF at low doses, *Health Phys.,* 13, 1235, 1967.
79. **Mejdahl, V.**, Measurement of environmental radiation intensity with thermoluminescent $CaSO_4$:Dy, *Health Phys.,* 18, 164, 1970.
80. **Hoy, J. E.**, Environmental radiation monitoring with thermoluminescent dosimeters, *Health Phys.,* 21, 860, 1971.
81. **Denham, D. H., Kathren, R. L., and Corley, J. P.**, *A CaF_2:Dy Thermoluminescent Dosimeter for Environmental Monitoring,* BNWL-SA-4191, Battelle, Pacific Northwest Laboratories, Richland, Wash., August, 1972.
82. **Burke, G. de P.**, *Investigation of a CaF_2:Mn Thermoluminescent Dosimetry System for Environmental Monitoring,* HASL-252, U.S. Atomic Energy Commission Health and Safety Laboratory, New York, April 1972.
83. *Performance, Testing, and Procedural Specifications for Thermoluminescence Dosimetry: (Environmental Applications),* ANSI N545-1975, American National Standards Institute, New York, December 1975.
84. **Porter, C. and Kahn, B.**, Improved Determination of Strontium-90 in Milk by an Ion Exchange Method., *Anal. Chem.,* 36, 676, 1964.
85. **Kahn, B.**, Determination of Picocurie Concentrations of Iodine-131 in Milk, *Agric. and Food Chem.,* 13, 21, 1965.
86. **Lamanna, A., Yancik, V., Abbot, T. P., and Holmes, J.**, Thimerosal, a preservative for milk to be tested for radioactivity, *Health Phys.,* 11, 586, 1965.
87. **Johns, F. B.**, *Southwestern Radiological Health Laboratory—Handbook of Radiochemical Analytical Techniques,* SWRHL-11, U.S. Environmental Protection Agency, National Environmental Research Center, Las Vegas, Nev. 1970.
88. **Morton, J. S., Halford, D. K., and Parker, D.**, A confinement device for the determination of whole-body radiouclide concentrations in live ducks, *Health Phys.,* 38, 234-236, 1980.
89. **Maletskos, C. J., Youngstrom, K. A., and Levy, C. K.**, Repetitive Nondestructive Assessment of Environmental Radionuclides in Re-Capturable Wild Birds, Paper No. 114, presented at the Health Physics Society 19th Annual Meeting, Houston, Tex., July 1974.
90. Division of Operational Safety, *Environmental Monitoring at Major U.S. Energy Research and Development Administration Contractor Sites—Caldendar Year 1974,* ERDA-54, U.S. Energy Research and Development Administration, Washington, D.C., 1975.
91. **Kahn, B.**, Determination of radioactive nuclides in the environment, water, in *Water and Waste Pollution Handbook,* Ciacco, L. L., Ed., Marcel Dekker, New York, 1972, chap. 25.
92. **Perkins, R. W. and Rancitelli, L. A.**, *Nuclear Techniques for Trace Elements and Radionuclide Measurements in Natural Water,* BNWL-SA-3993, Battelle-Pacific Northwest Laboratories, Richland, Wash., 1971.
93. *1980 Annual Book of ASTM Standards,* Part 31—Water, American Society for Testing and Materials, Philadelphia, 1980.
94. **Kim, S. M. and Vaughn, W. L.**, Low-level ^{3}H Measurement and Tritiated Luminous Dial Watches, *Radiochem. Radioanal. Lett.,* 8(2), 115—118, 1971.
95. **Kipp, K. L.**, *Radiological Status of the Groundwater Beneath the Hanford Reservation,* 1973, BNWL-1860, Battelle, Pacific Northwest Laboratories, Richland, Wash., 1975.

96. **Thompson, S. E., Burton, C. A., Quinn, D. J., and Ng, Y. C.,** *Concentration Factors of Chemical Elements in Edible Aquatic Organisms,* UCRL-50564 Rev. 1, University of California, Lawrence Radiation Laboratory, Berkeley, October 1972.
97. **Freke, A. M.,** A model for the approximate calculation of Safe Rates of discharge of radioactive wastes into marine environments, *Health Phys.,* 13, 743, 1965.
98. Panel on Radioactivity in the Marine Environment, *Radioactivity in the Marine Environment,* National Academy of Sciences, Washington, D.C., 1971.
99. **Essig, T. H. and Bhagat, S. K.,** *Age-Dependent Radiation Dose Estimates for Residents of the Hanford Environs,* 1945—968, BNWL-SA-3079, Battelle, Pacific Northwest Laboratories, Richland, Wash., June 1970.
100. **Korenman, I.,** *Analytical Chemistry of Low Concentrations,* Translated from Russian By J. Schmarak, (Israel Program for Scientific Translations, Jerusalem, 1968), 1966.
101. **Douglas, G. S., Ed.,** *Radioassay Procedures for Environmental Samples,* Public Health Service Publ. No. 999-RH-27, U.S. Department of Health, Education, and Welfare, Washington, D.C., 1967.
102. *Measurement of Low-Level Radioactivity,* ICRU Rep. No. 22, International Commission on Radiation Units and Measurements, Washington, D.C., 1972.
103. **Cooper, J. A., Wogman, N. A., Palmer, H. E., and Perkins, R. W.,** The Application of Solid State Detectors to Environmental and Biological Problems, *Health Phys.,* 15, 419, 1968.
104. **Brauer, F. P., Kaye, H. J., and Connally, R. E.,** "X-ray and beta-gamma coincidence spectromety applied to radiochemical analysis of environmental samples in *Advances in Chemistry Series,* No. 93, American Chemical Society, Washington, D.C., 1970, 231.
105. **Krieger, H. L. and Gold, S.,** *Procedures for Radiochemical Analysis of Nuclear Reactor Aqueous Solutions,* EPA-R4-73-014. U.S. Environmental Protection Agency, Washington, D.C., May 1973.
106. **Johnston, J. W.,** *An Index of Adequacy and Some Other Statistical Considerations for an Environmental Monitoring System,* BNWL-B-250 Battelle, Pacific Northwest Laboratories, Richland, Wash., February 1973.
107. **Pasternack, B. S. and Harley, N. H.,** Detection limits for radionuclides in the analysis of multicomponent gamma ray spectrometer data, *Nucl. Instrum. Methods,* 91, 533, 1971.
108. **Goldin, S.,** Analytical Criteria I; Acceptable Standard Deviation, presented at Bioassay Conference, Philadelphia, October 1976, Radiation Management Corporation, Philadelphia.
109. National Environmental Research Center, Environmental radioactivity laboratory intercomparison studies program 1975, EPA-680/4-75-002b, U.S. Environmental Protection Agency, Las Vegas, 1975.
110. Public Health Service, *Milk Surveillance,* Radiol. Health Data Rep., 730—746, 1968.
111. **Lloyd, R. D.,** Gamma-ray emitters in concrete, *Health Phys.,* 31, 71—73, 1976.
112. **Montgomery, D. W., Krieger, H. L., and Kahn, B.,** Monitoring low-level radioactive aqueous discharges from a nuclear power station in a seawater environment, IAEA-SM-180/41, in *Environmental Surveillance around Nuclear Installations, Proc. Symp.,* Warsaw, 5—9 November, 1973, International Atomic Energy Agency, Vienna, 1974, 243—256.
113. **Stringer, J. L.,** *Radiological Monitor for the Columbia River,* HW-79186, General Electric, Richland, Wash., Wash., 1963.
114. **Fix, J. J.,** *Environmental Surveillance at Hanford for CY-1974,* BNWL-1910, Battelle, Pacific Northwest Laboratories, Richland, Wash., 1975.
115. **Fisher, W. L.,** *Use and Calibration of the Automatic Columbia River Monitoring Station Iodine Monitor,* BNWL-B-41, Batelle, Pacific Northwest Laboratories, Richland, Wash., 1970.
116. **Cate, J. L., Jr. and Hoeger, T. O.,** Radioisotope monitoring system for sewage effulent, *Am. Ind. Hyg. Assoc. J.,* 33, 10, 1972.
117. **Blakely, J. P.,** *Compilation of United States Nuclear Standards,* 9th ed., ORNL-NSIC-112, Oak Ridge National Laboratory, Oak Ridge, Tenn., 1973.
118. *Specification of Portable X- or Gamma-Radiation Survey Meters,* American National Standard N13.4, American National Standards Institute, New York, 1971.
119. *Installation, Inspection and Testing Requirements for Instrumentation and Electrical Equipment during the Construction of Nuclear Power Generating Stations,* American National Standard N45.2, American National Standards Institute, New York, 1972.
120. **Costrell, L.,** *Standard Nuclear Instrument Modules,* TID-20893, revision 4, U.S. Atomic Energy Commission Division of Technical Information Extension, Oak Ridge, Tenn., 1974.
121. **Selby, J. M., et al.,** *Technological Considerations in Emergency Preparedness: Phase II-A,* BNWL-1635, Battelle, Pacific Northwest Laboratories, Richland, Wash., 1972.
122. *Handbook on Calibration of Radiation Protection Monitoring Instruments,* Tech. Rep. Ser. No. 133, International Atomic Energy Agency, Vienna, 1971.
123. **Matuszek, J.,** Quality control in a radiochemistry laboratory — the need for periodic review, Paper No. 116, presented at 20th annual meeting Health Physics Society, Buffalo, July 1975.

124. **Snedecor, G. W. and Cochran, W. G.,** *Statistical Methods,* Iowa State University Press, 1968, 124.
125. **Natrella, M. G.,** *Experimental Statistics,* Handbook No. 91, National Bureau of Standards, Superintendent of Documents, U.S. Government Printing Office, Washington, D.C., 1963.
126. **Gilbert, R. O.,** *Recommendations Concerning the Computation and Reporting of Counting Statistics for the Nevada Applied Ecology Group,* BNWL-B-368, Battelle, Pacific Northwest Laboratories, Richland, Wash., September 1975.
127. **Aitchison, J. and Brown, J. A. C.,** *The Lognormal Distribution,* Cambridge University Press, 1963.
128. **Hollander, M. and Wolfe, D. A.,** *Nonparametric Statistical Methods,* John Wiley & Sons, New York, 1973.
129. **Waite, D. A. and Denham, D. H.,** *Log-Normal Statistics Applied to the Planning, Collection and Analysis of Preoperational Environmental Surveillance Data,* BNWL-SA-4840, Battelle, Pacific Northwest Laboratories, Richland, Wash., February 1974.
130. **Speer, D. R., and Waite, D. A.,** Statistical distributions as applied to environmental surveillance data, in Operational Health Physics, Proc. 9th Midyear Topical Symp. of the Health Physics Society, Health Physics Society, Rocky Mountain Chapter, Denver, Colo., February 1976, 693—700.
131. **Denham, D. H. and Waite, D. A.,** Some practical applications of the log-normal distribution for interpreting environmental data, presented at the Health Physics Society 20th Annual Meeting, Buffalo, New York, July 1975.
132. **Brodsky, A., Specht, R. P., Brooks, B. G., and Cool, W.,** Log-normal distributions of occupational exposure in medicine and industry, in Operational Health Physics, Proc. 9th Midyear Topical Symp. of the Health Physics Society, Health Physics Society, Rocky Mountain Chapter, Denver, Colo. February 1976, 373—379.
133. **Schubert, J., Brodsky, A., and Tyler, S.,** The log-normal function as a stochastic model of the distribution of strontium-90 and other fission products in humans, *Health Phys.,* 13, 1187—204, 1967.
134. **Hahn, G. J. and Shapiro, S. S.,** *Statistical Models in Engineering,* John Wiley & Sons, 1967, chap. 8.
135. **Johnson, J. E.,** Environmental Radiation Surveillance conducted in the vicinity of the Fort St. Rain Nuclear Generating Station — Summary Rep. July—December, 1975, Department of Radiology and Radiation Biology, Colorado State University, January 1976.
136. **Michels, D. E.,** Log-normal analysis of data for plutonium in the outdoors, *Proc. Environmental Plutonium Symp.,* LA-4756, Los Alamos Scientific Laboratory, Los Alamos, N.M., August 1971, 105—111.
137. **Rogers, L. and Gamertsfelder, C. C.,** USA Regulations for the Control of Releases of Radioactivity into the Environment in Effluents from Nuclear Facilities, Environmental Aspects of Nuclear Power Stations, *Proc. Symp.,* New York, August 1970, 10—4, International Atomic Energy Agency, Vienna, 1971, 127—146.
138. **Roberts, I. C.,** *Effluent Monitoring and Evaluation — A Power Reactor Design Guide,* BNWL-251, Battelle-Pacific Northwest Laboratories, Richland, Wash., December 1966.
139. *Basic Radiation Protection Criteria,* NCRP Report No. 39, National Council on Radiation Protection and Measurements, Washington, D.C., 1971.
140. International Commission on Radiological Protection, *Recommendations of the International Commission on Radiological Protection,* Publ. No. 9, Pergamon Press, Oxford, 1966, International Commission Radiological Protection.
141. U.S. Environmental Protection Agency, Drinking Water Regulations 40 CFR 141, Federal Register Vol. 41, No. 133, Office of the Federal Register, National Archives and Records Service, General Services Administration, Washington, D.C., July 9, 1976, 28, 402—428, 409.
142. U.S. Environmental Protection Agency, Radiation Protection Standards for the Uranium Fuel Cycle, 40 CFR, Federal Register Vol. 42, No. 9, Office of the Federal Register, National Archives and Records Service, General Services Administration, Washington, D.C., January 13, 1977, 2858—2861.
143. **Morgan, K. Z.,** Proper use of information on organ and body burdens of radioactive material, in Assessment of Radioactive Contamination in Man., *Proc. Symp.,* Stockholm, November 22—26, 1971, International Atomic Energy Agency, Vienna, 1972, 3—23.
144. U.S. Nuclear Regulatory Commission, Code of Federal Regulations Title 10, Part 50, Licensing of Production and Utilization Facilities, Appendix I, Numerical Guides for Design Objectives and Limiting Conditions for Operation to Meet the Criterion "As Low As Reasonably Achievable" for Radioactive Material in Light-Water-Cooled Nuclear Power Reactor Effluents, Office of the Federal Registry, National Archives and Records Service, General Services Administration, Washington, D.C., December 1975.
145. U.S. Environmental Protection Agency, Radiation Protection for Nuclear Power Operations — Proposed Standards, 40 CFR 190, Federal Register Vol. 40, No. 104, Office of the Federal Register, National Archives and Records Service, General Services Administration, Washington, D.C., May 29, 1975.

146. U.S. Nuclear Regulatory Commission, Code of Federal Regulations, Title 10, Part 20, Standards for Protection Against Radiation, Office of the Federal Register, National Archives and Records Service, General Services Administration, Washington, D.C., 1975.
147. Federal Radiation Council, Background Material for the Development of Radiation Protection Standards, Rep. No. 5, July 1964.
148. *Evaluation of Radiation Emergencies and Accidents — Selected Criteria and Data,* Tech. Rep. Series, No. 152, International Atomic Energy Agency, Vienna, 1974.
149. *Environmental Monitoring in Emergency Situations,* Safety Series, No. 18, International Atomic Energy Agency, Vienna, 1966, 109—12.
150. **Howells, H. and Dunster, H. J.**, Environmental monitoring in emergencies, in Environmental Surveillance in the Vicinity of Nuclear Facilities, *Proc. Symp. Health Phys. Soc.*, Augusta, Ga., 1968, Reinig, W. C., Ed., Charles C Thomas, Springfield, Ill., 1970, 151—161.
151. **Kathren, R. L.**, *Towards Interim Acceptable Surface Contamination Levels for Environmental PuO,* BNWL-SA-1510, Battelle-Pacific Northwest Laboratories, Richland, Wash., March 1968.
152. **Waite, D. A., and Jenkins, C. E.**, *Development of Disposition Criteria Derivation Methodology for Commercial Fuel Cycle Facilities,* BNWL-SA-5501, Battelle, Pacific Northwest Laboratories, Richland, Wash., August 1975.
153. **Waite, D. A., Jenkins, C. E., Faust, L. G., and Hoenes, G. R.**, *Disposition Criteria for Decontamination and Decommissioning of a Mixed Oxide Fuel Fabrication Plant,* BNWL-2008, Battelle, Pacific Northwest Laboratories, Richland, Wash., March 1976.
154. Operational and Environmental Safety Division, *Environmental Protection, Safety, and Health Protection Reporting Requirements,* DOE Order 5484.1, U.S. Department of Energy, Washington, D.C., February 1981.
155. Office of Standards Development, *Radiological Effluent and Environmental Monitoring at Uranium Mills,* Regulatory Guide 4.14, Revision 1, U.S. Nuclear Regulatory Commission, Washington, D.C., April 1980.
156. Office of Standards Development, *Measuring, Evaluating, and Reporting Radioactivity in Releases Of Radioactive Materials In Liquid And Airborne Effluents From Nuclear Fuel Processing and Fabrication Plants,* Regulatory Guide 4.16, U.S. Nuclear Regulatory Commission, Washington, D.C., March 1978.
157. **Denham, D. H., Eddy, P. A., Hawley, K. A., Jacquish, R. E., and Corley, J. P.**, *Technology, Safety and Costs of Decommissioning a Reference Low-Level Waste Burial Ground-Environmental Surveillance Programs,* NUREG/CR-0570 Addendum, Office of Nuclear Regulatory Research, U.S. Nuclear Regulatory Commission, Washington, D.C., July 1981.
158. **Killough, G. G. and McKay, L. R.**, *A Methodology for Calculating Radiation Doses From Radioactivity Released To The Environment,* ORNL-4992, Oak Ridge National Laboratory, Oak Ridge, Tennessee, 1976.
159. International Commission on Radiological Protection (ICRP), *Radionuclide Release into the Environment—Assessment of Doses to Man,* ICRP-29, Pergamon Press, New York, New York, 1979.
160. **Gallegos, A. F., Garcia, B. J., and Sutton, C. M.**, *Documentation of TRU Biological Transport Model (BIOTRAN),* LA-8213-MS, Los Alamos National Laboratory, Los Alamos, New Mexico, January 1980.
161. **Nelson, R. W., and Schur, J. A.**, *PATHS Groundwater Hydrologic Model,* PNL-3162, Battelle, Pacific Northwest Laboratories, Richland, Wash., April 1980.
162. Science Applications, Inc., *Tabulation of Waste Isolation Computer Models,* ONWI-78, Office of Nuclear Waste Isolation, Battelle Memorial Institute, Columbus, Ohio, August 1981.
163. **Hoffman, F. O., Shaeffer, D. L., Miller, C. W. and Garten, C. T., Jr.**, *Proc. Workshop Evaluation of Models Used For The Environmental Assessment of Radionuclide Releases, Gatlinburg, Tennessee, September 6—9, 1977.* CONF-770901, National Technical Information Service, April 1978.
164. **Napier, B. A., Roswell, R. L., Kennedy, W. E., Jr., and Stenge, D. L.**, *ARRRG and FOOD - Computer Programs for Calculating Radiation Dose to Man From Radionuclides In The Environment,* PNL-3180, Battelle, Pacific Northwest Laboratories, Richland Wash., June 1980.
165. **Napier, B. A., Kennedy, W. E., Jr., and Soldat, J. K.**, *PABLM — A Computer Program to Calculate Accumulated Radiation Doses From Radionuclides In The Environment,* PNL-3209, Battelle, Pacific Northwest Laboratories, Richland, Wash., March 1980.
166. National Council on Radiation Protection and Measurements (NCRP), *Environmental Radiation Measurements.* NCRP Report No. 50, NCRP, Washington, D.C., December 1976.
167. National Council on Radiation Protection and Measurements (NCRP), *Instrumentation and Monitoring Methods for Radiation Protection,* NCRP Report No. 57, NCRP, Washington, D.C., 1978.
168. National Council on Radiation Protection and Measurements (NCRP), *A Handbook of Radioactivity Measurements Procedures,* NCRP Report No. 58, NCRP, Washington, D.C., November 1978.

169. **Ahlquist, A. J., Umbarger, C. J., and Stoker, A. K.,** Recent Developments for field monitoring of alpha-emitting contaminants in the environment, *Health Phys.*, 34, 489—498, 1978.
170. **Crites, T. R., Denham, D. H., and Barnes, M. G.,** The effect of plowing on $_{241}$Am contamination in sandy soil, *Health Phys.*, 38, 699—703, 1980.
171. **Kelly, J. J. (ed.),** Effluent and Environmental Radiation Ssurveillance, *Proc. Symp.*, Johnson, Vermont, 9—14 July 1978, ASTM Special Technical Publication 698, American Society for Testing and Materials, Baltimore, Md., 1980.
172. Office of Standards Development, *Performance, Testing, and Procedural Specifications For Thermoluminescence Dosimetry: Environmental Applications,* Regulatory Guide 4.13, Revision 1, U.S. Nuclear Regulatory Commission, Washington, D.C., July 1977.
173. Office of Standards Development, *Quality Assurance for Radiological Monitoring Programs (Normal Operations) — Effluent Streams And The Environment,* Regulatory Guide 4.15, Revision 1, U.S. Nuclear Regulatory Commission, Washington, D.C., February 1979.

Radioactive Waste Disposal

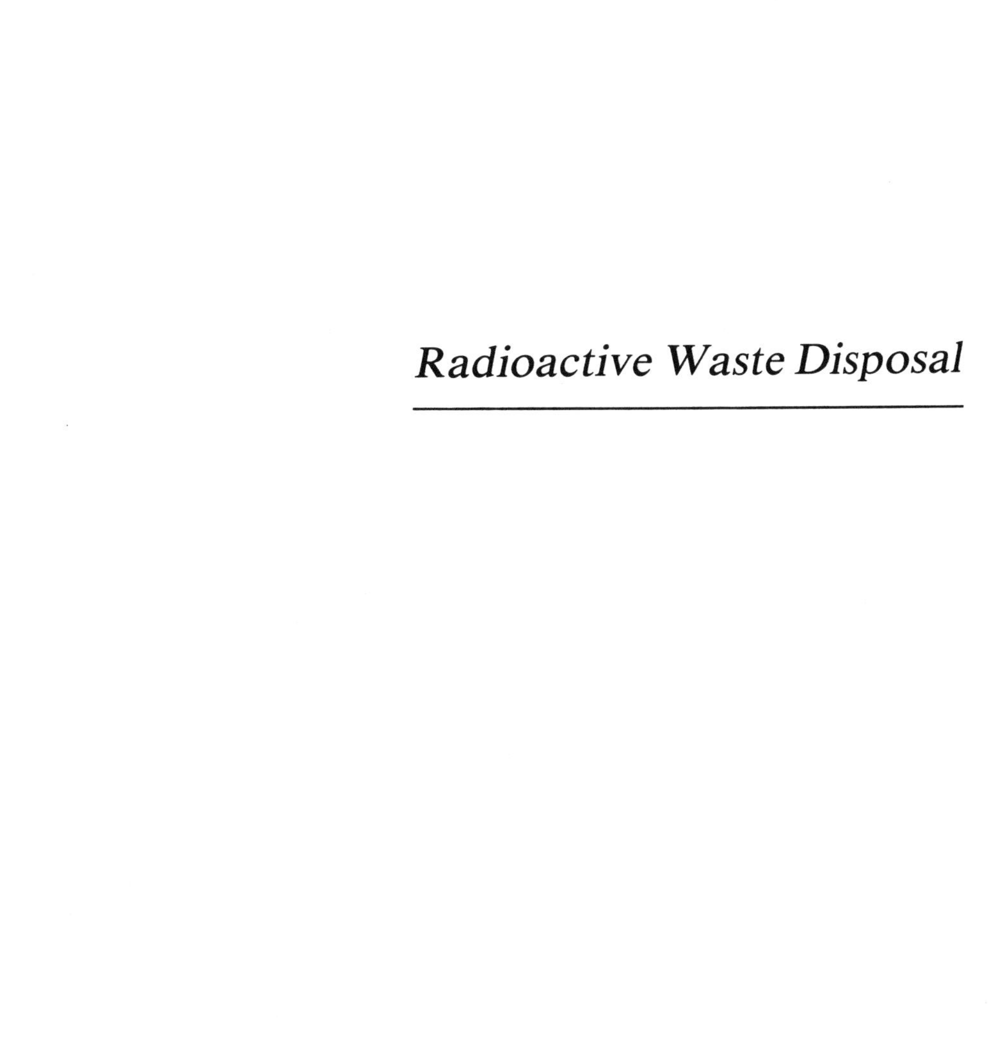

LOW-LEVEL RADIOACTIVE WASTE DISPOSAL BY SHALLOW LAND BURIAL

Thomas J. Overcamp

INTRODUCTION

In the routine operation of nuclear power and research reactors, nuclear fuel facilities, research laboratories, hospitals, and certain industries, substantial volumes of low-level, solid and liquid radioactive wastes are produced. Unlike the widely publicized and controversial high-level wastes from reprocessing spent nuclear fuel, many of these wastes may not require heavy shielding and may decay in the course of months, years, or decades. These wastes typically include solidified liquids, ion exchange resins, and filters from nuclear reactors; contaminated equipment and tools from the nuclear industry; scintillation fluids, paper products, labware, and clothing from laboratories and hospitals; and putrescible materials such as the carcasses of animals used in radiotracer experiments. In the U.S., these wastes are currently being generated at an annual rate of nearly 10^5 m^3/year with total activities of about 1 million curies (Ci). Depending primarily on the future of commercial nuclear power, the waste generation rates have been projected to increase by a factor of from 3 to 20 by the year 2000.[1]

These wastes must be properly treated and disposed of in a manner to prevent contamination of the environment and increased exposure of the public to ionizing radiation. A variety of methods have been used for disposal in various parts of the world, including incineration followed by burial of the ashes, burial at sea, burial in abandoned mine sites, and shallow land burial. In the U.S. and Canada, shallow land burial is now the predominant practice due to its relatively low cost and potential for minimizing contamination of the biosphere.

Much of the U.S. federal government low-level wastes is buried in one of five sites operated for the Department of Energy. Commercial low-level wastes from nuclear power reactors, research laboratories, hospitals, and industry are sent to commercial burial grounds licensed to accept low-level radioactively contaminated wastes. The first of these sites were at Beatty, Nev., and Maxey Flats, Ky., which were opened in 1962 and 1963 respectively. Additional commercial burial sites were established near West Valley, N.Y., Richland, Wash., Sheffield, Ill., and Barnwell, S.C.[1]

In Canada there are five areas for subsurface radioactive waste disposal. The largest is at the Chalk River Nuclear Laboratories in northern Ontario. There are sites at the Whiteshell Nuclear Research Establishment in southeastern Manitoba and the Defense Research Establishment near Suffield, Alberta. Commercial disposal sites are at the Bruce Nuclear Power Development of Ontario Hydro and the Gentilly Nuclear Power Development of Quebec Hydro. At these sites both low- and medium-level wastes are buried.[2]

When shallow land burial was adopted, it was generally assumed that the radionuclides in the wastes would either be contained within their burial trenches or readily sorbed by the soil surrounding the trenches. These engineered and natural barriers were felt to be sufficient to contain the wastes for a sufficient time to allow their decay to innocuous levels of activity.

In recent years, this assumption has come under question. There have been small, but detectable, migrations of radionuclides from several of the U.S. Department of Energy's burial sites and from the commercial sites at Maxey Flats, Ky., and West Valley, N.Y. Although the releases from these sites are generally not felt to present a hazard to public health, they have raised questions with respect to burial site engineering, the location of future sites, and the viability of shallow land burial for certain types of wastes.

These problems have brought about Congressional hearings that dealt with the environmental and economic problems at Maxey Flats,[3] West Valley,[4] and Sheffield.[5] The U.S. General Accounting Office has called for a new policy with respect to future siting, has recommended site-specific information that should be determined at both the federal and commercial burial grounds, and has requested new policies for the long-term care and funding for these sites.[6] The National Research Council reviewed the operations of the federal burial sites.[7] Because of the potential of groundwater contamination, they recommended that future sites be built exclusively in arid climates with deep groundwater tables. If new sites are established in humid areas, they recommended the use of engineered containers that will isolate the wastes for hundreds of years. Considering the large volume of commercial wastes produced, these recommendations, applied to commercial sites, would result in significantly higher costs for waste burial.

In the last few years the sites at Maxey Flats and West Valley were closed due to environmental and related economic difficulties. The Sheffield site was filled to capacity and has not been permitted to expand on to adjoining land. These closings shifted the wastes to the three remaining sites. Since the Barnwell site was the only site remaining in the eastern U.S., it received most of the wastes that would have gone to the three closed sites. To prevent the Barnwell site from being filled too rapidly, the state of South Carolina restricted the types of wastes it could accept and ordered it to reduce the future volume of wastes accepted for burial.[1] In 1979, the Beatty and Richland sites were temporarily closed because of the arrival of poorly packaged wastes.[8,9]

The controversy over low-level wastes has resulted in the re-examination of the regulations for the siting and operation of shallow land burial sites. The U.S. Nuclear Regulatory Commission is revising its policy[10,11] and the U.S. Environmental Protection Agency is proposing criteria for developing environmental standards for radioactive waste burial.[12]

This subsection of the handbook will consider the problems of the operation and siting of low-level waste disposal by shallow land burial with a primary focus on the commercial sites in the U.S. It will discuss the sources of low-level wastes, the operation of disposal sites, and the potential for environmental contamination from these sites. It will present various siting criteria that have been proposed and make recommendations for research that should be conducted to resolve controversies concerning low-level waste disposal.

LOW-LEVEL WASTES

Low-level wastes encompass a wide range of materials contaminated with radionuclides. In the nuclear fuel cycle the wastes generated include filters, ion exchange resins and sludges from the air and water treatment systems, activated materials removed from nuclear reactors, and laboratory wastes. Low-level wastes also come from hospitals, research laboratories, and certain industries. These wastes include scintillation vials, animal carcasses, and laboratory wastes.

Some of the wastes require shielding. Other wastes, only suspected of being contaminated, are classified as low-level wastes because it is frequently more convenient to dispose of them than assay them for radioactivity. The potential hazards of these wastes depends on their activity, the half-lives of their radionuclides, their physical form, and their chemical form.

Classification of Radioactive Wastes

Many systems have been proposed for classifying radioactive wastes. These have been based on various criteria such as the origin of the waste, its isotopic composition, or its level of activity. At present there is no universally accepted classification scheme. The following definitions are consistent with present usage and regulations in the U.S.,[13]

1. By-product material — radionuclides produced in a nuclear reactor including fission products.
2. Source material — unenriched uranium or thorium.
3. Special nuclear material (SNM) — plutonium, ^{233}U or ^{235}U or materials artificially enriched with these nuclides.
4. Transuranium-contaminated wastes (TRU) — wastes contaminated with greater than 10 nCi/g of transuranic nuclides. These are nuclides that have an atomic number greater than 92.
5. Spent nuclear fuel — unreprocessed fuel elements from a nuclear reactor. It is considered to be high-level waste.
6. High-level wastes — the waste from the first cycle extraction of the reprocessing of spent nuclear fuel or equivalent. These wastes contain both fission products and transuranic nuclides.
7. Nonhigh-level wastes — those other than high-level wastes or transuranium-contaminated wastes. Frequently these are further subdivided into the following categories:

   a. Intermediate-level wastes — wastes requiring shielding to protect personnel from ionizing radiation.
   b. Low-level wastes — wastes containing radionuclides of sufficiently low concentration that shielding is not required.

Since most U.S. commercial burial sites accept both low- and most intermediate-level wastes, this chapter will refer to all nonhigh-level wastes as low-level wastes.

Half-Lives of Principal Nuclides in Low-Level Wastes[14]

In evaluating the potential environmental impact of a specific radionuclide at a burial site, a major factor is the rate of decay or half-life of that nuclide. If this rate of decay is fast compared to the rates of migration and uptake, that radionuclide cannot pose a significant threat to public health.

The rate of decay can be described by the exponential decay law

$$C = C_o\, e^{-0.693t/T_{1/2}} \qquad (1)$$

in which C is the activity at time t, C_o is the activity at zero time and $T_{1/2}$ is the half-life of the radionuclide. For a given radionuclide, it takes one half-life to decay to 0.5 C_o, about 6.6 $T_{1/2}$ to decay to 0.01 C_o and about 10 $T_{1/2}$ to decay to 0.001 C_o.

Figure 1 shows how radionuclides decay as a function of their half-lives over a 1000 year period. Nuclides with half-lives in the order of 1 year or less rapidly decay. In a decade, their activities are less than 0.1% of their initial activities. A 100 year half-life nuclide will have 0.1% of its original activity after the 1000 year period shown.

Table 1 gives the half-lives of selected radionuclides found in wastes including source material, special nuclear material, and transuranic elements. Nuclides with half-lives of less than 1 year were not included because they can only cause potential exposure offsite if they are migrating from the site almost immediately after disposal. This could

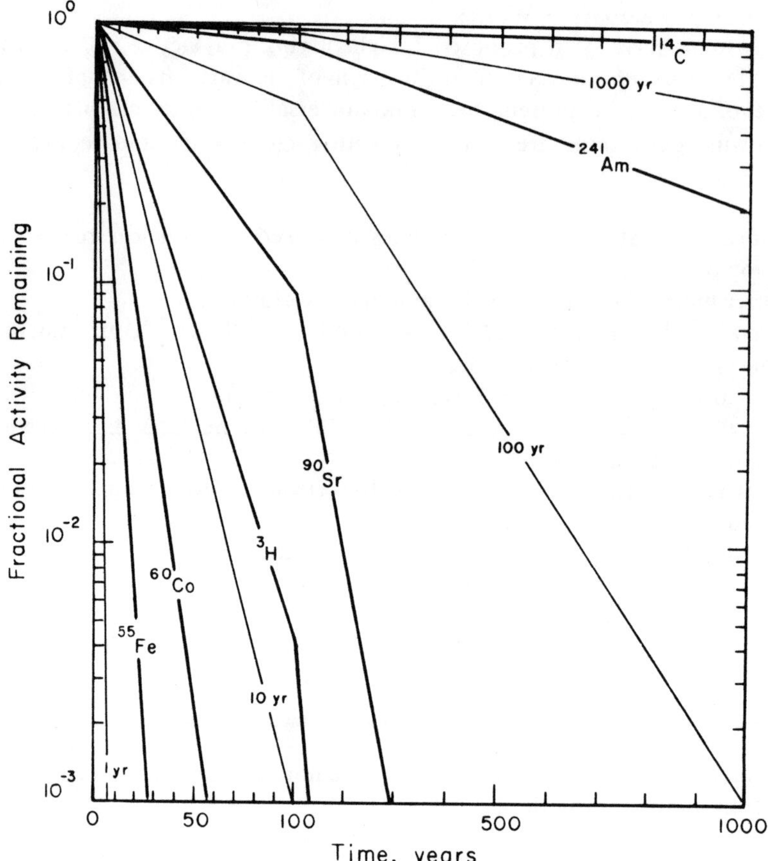

FIGURE 1. Fraction of radioactivity remaining after burial

occur by fires, theft, or spills with subsequent surface runoff or suspension into the air.

Figure 1 also shows the rates of decay for several of the shorter-lived nuclides in Table 1. The nuclides ^{55}Fe, ^{60}Co, and ^{3}H are usually the most abundant nuclides in existing disposal sites. To decay to 0.1% of their initial activities requires approximately 29, 53, and 123 years respectively. It takes approximately 300 years for the fission products ^{90}Sr and ^{137}Cs to decay to the 0.1% level.

FUEL-CYCLE LOW-LEVEL WASTES

The nuclear fuel cycle for light water reactors, from the mine through enrichment, fuel fabrication, use in a reactor, to its reprocessing or final disposal, produces a variety of low-level radioactive wastes. In the U.S., the fuel-cycle wastes currently account for about 60% of the volume and nearly all of the activity of the low-level wastes sent to commercial burial grounds. These wastes come from the fuel production processes, the nuclear reactor, and from spent fuel storage, or reprocessing. To examine the environmental problems faced at low-level disposal sites, the sources, activity, physical form, and packaging of the wastes from the fuel cycle must be understood. These factors will determine their potential hazards and how soon they may be able to migrate from the burial trenches.

Table 1
SELECTED RADIONUCLIDES WITH HALF-LIVES GREATER THAN 1 YEAR

Radionuclide	Common name	Half-life (years)	Specific activity (Ci/g)
^{3}H	Tritium	1.2×10^{1}	9.7×10^{3}
^{14}C	Carbon-14	5.7×10^{3}	4.5
^{22}Na	Sodium-22	2.6	6.3×10^{3}
^{55}Fe	Iron-55	2.7	2.4×10^{3}
^{59}Ni	Nickel-59	8.0×10^{4}	7.6×10^{-2}
^{63}Ni	Nickel-63	1.0×10^{2}	5.7×10^{1}
^{60}Co	Cobalt-60	5.3	1.1×10^{3}
^{85}Kr	Krypton-85	1.1×10^{1}	3.9×10^{2}
^{90}Sr	Strontium-90	2.9×10^{1}	1.4×10^{2}
^{99}Tc	Technetium-99	2.1×10^{5}	1.7×10^{-2}
^{129}I	Iodine-129	1.6×10^{7}	1.7×10^{-4}
^{134}Cs	Cesium-134	2.1	1.3×10^{3}
^{135}Cs	Cesium-135	2.3×10^{6}	1.2×10^{-3}
^{137}Cs	Cesium-137	3.0×10^{1}	8.7×10^{1}
^{147}Pm	Promethium-147	2.6	9.4×10^{2}
^{154}Eu	Europium-154	8.6	2.7×10^{2}
^{226}Ra	Radium-226	1.6×10^{3}	9.9×10^{-1}
^{235}U	Uraniun-235	7.1×10^{8}	2.1×10^{-6}
^{238}U	Uranium-238	4.5×10^{9}	3.3×10^{-7}
^{238}Pu	Plutonium-238	8.8×10^{1}	1.7×10^{1}
^{239}Pu	Plutonium-239	2.4×10^{4}	6.2×10^{-2}
^{241}Am	Americium-241	4.3×10^{2}	3.4

Adapted from *Chart of the Nuclides,* 11th ed., General Electric Company, San Jose, Calif.

Low-Level Wastes in Fuel Production[15-18]

In the U.S., the present uranium fuel production process involves (1) mining an ore containing very small amounts of uranium; (2) milling of the ore which involves crushing and chemical extraction to produce "yellowcake" powder containing about 75% by weight of U_3O_8; (3) conversion of the yellowcake to uranium hexafluoride, UF_6; (4) enrichment of the ^{235}U fraction through gaseous diffusion; and (5) fuel fabrication by conversion of the UF_6 into uranium dioxide, UO_2, pelletizing the UO_2, and sealing it into cladded fuel elements.

The natural uranium and its shorter-lived decay products including radium, ^{226}Ra and radon gas, ^{222}Rn, are in the ore. In the mining and milling process, the gaseous radon trapped in the ore is released and the radium is separated from the uranium to produce yellowcake. This necessitates the mines and mills having adequate ventilation and careful management of the tailing piles and waste streams.

The U_3O_8 yellowcake is refined and converted to volatile uranium hexafluoride, UF_6, by either a dry hydrofluor or a wet solvent extraction process. The wastes from the dry process are ashes consisting of calcium and other fluorides contaminated with uranium. This waste is shipped to a low-level burial site. The wastes from the wet process are liquids and sludges. The liquids are held in ponds for evaporation. The sludges are presently stored or buried onsite.[17,18]

In the gaseous diffusion enrichment process, the ^{235}U content of the UF_6 is increased from the 0.7% found in natural uranium to the 2 to 4% required for light water reactors. The wastes are mainly liquids that are treated and discharged into holding ponds.

The sludges from the water treatment systems and holding ponds are usually buried onsite.[16]

In fuel fabrication, the UF_6 is converted to uranium dioxide, UO_2, which is sealed in zircaloy clad fuel elements. As with the enrichment process, the wastes are primarily liquids which are discharged into holding ponds. The sludges from these ponds are buried onsite or shipped to a low-level burial ground.[16-18]

Sources of Low-Level Wastes in Light Water Reactors[15-18]

In the U.S., commercial power reactors presently produce a large fraction of the waste volume shipped to low-level burial sites. The volume of these wastes will grow as more nuclear plants are placed into operation and as emission limits for the release of radionuclides into the atmosphere and surrounding waters are made more restrictive.

In light water nuclear reactors, the energy is obtained from the fissioning of ^{235}U in the enriched fuel and the ^{239}Pu that has been produced from ^{238}U by neutron capture. These fission reactions produced radionuclides called fission products. Although many of these nuclides decay quickly to form stable elements, significant amounts of longer-lived nuclides are produced, such as ^{3}H, ^{85}Kr, ^{90}Sr, and ^{137}Cs. Most of these fission products are contained within the fuel cladding and are retained in the spent fuel. A small fraction, normally much less than 1%, of the fuel claddings perforate or rupture. This releases some of the fission products to the cooling water. In addition "tramp" uranium residues on the surface of the fuel element undergo fission and contaminate the cooling water.

The second source of radionuclide production in reactors is the neutron activation of corrosion products and chemical additives in the cooling waters. The structural materials, fuel racks, control rods, and instruments placed in the reactor core also become highly activated. The principal activation products with half-lives of a year or more include ^{3}H, ^{55}Fe, ^{60}Co, ^{59}Ni, and ^{63}Ni.

The reactors operate water treatment systems to remove the radionuclides from the cooling water. The volatile radionuclides such as the ^{3}H, noble gases, ^{14}C, and the radioactive iodines are removed from the coolant by the steam deaerator. These gases are filtered through high efficiency (HEPA) filters to remove particulate matter, temporarily stored in tanks to allow for the decay of the shortest-lived nuclides, and finally released through a vent stack to the atmosphere. The newer plants have carbon adsorption beds for the removal of the radioiodines. The major nuclides released from the nuclear plant are ^{85}Kr, ^{3}H, ^{14}C, and possibly ^{131}I and ^{129}I. The used HEPA filters and spent carbon adsorption beds contain fission products and must be sent to low-level disposal sites.

The light water reactors have water treatment systems to remove fission and corrosion products from the cooling waters. The water is treated by filtration and ion exchange in demineralizers. The backwash water from the filters and demineralizers is sent to evaporators and additional demineralizers to remove its radioactive contaminants. The filter sludges and the evaporator concentrates or bottoms contain high concentrations of radionuclides. These wastes are solidified and shipped to a low-level waste disposal site.

When the fuel is removed from the reactor core, it is sent to a spent fuel storage pool to allow it to cool. This pool has a separate filter and demineralizer to remove the fission products that continue to leak from the leaky fuel elements. In addition, contaminated water from leaks, laundry, laboratory, and personnel showers must be treated to remove radionucludes.

Structural materials, control rod guides, control rods, and instruments removed from the core of the reactor can be highly activated and require shielding and special handling prior to shipment to a low-level burial site. There is also a significant volume of contaminated paper products and clothing used in clean-up reactor maintenance, and in the laboratory. There are other miscellaneous solid and liquid wastes generated in reactor maintenance and in the laboratory. These wastes must be treated and sent to a low-level burial site.

Packaging of Low-Level Wastes at Reactor Sites

The low-level wastes from light water reactors have a variety of physical forms, radionuclide content, and requirements for shielding. There are the sludges and aqueous wastes from the water treatment system, HEPA filters, a large volume of contaminated paper products and protective clothing, and wastes from the laboratory.[19] Although some of these wastes may be essentially free from radioactive contamination, it is frequently easier and less costly to dispose of any suspect materials than to survey them for radioactive contamination.

The dry wastes which are lightly contaminated are put into approved 210 ℓ (55 gal) drums, light metal bins, or wooden boxes for storage and shipping to the low-level burial site. At some sites compactors are used to reduce the volume of these wastes to reduce shipping and burial costs. Although incineration is not being used at U.S. reactor sites for volume reduction of combustible wastes, there is considerable interest in adapting incinerators used at U.S. government installations[20] in Canada[21] and Europe for these wastes at nuclear reactors.[22]

The highly activated materials removed from the core of the reactor require a shielded container or cask to protect the personnel from excessive exposure. If these items are large in size, such as control rod guides or control rods, they must either be sheared into pieces before being put into casks or put directly into special large casks for shipping to the low-level site.[23]

The aqueous wastes, spent ion exchange resins, evaporator bottoms, and filters from the reactor coolant treatment system have high activity. These wastes must be dewatered or solidified to aid in the containment of the wastes during shipping and after burial.

Several different systems are used for waste solidification. The simplest system is to mix the liquid wastes with adsorbents such as vermiculite. Since this does not produce a solid and since the radionuclides can be leached from the wastes, these adsorbed wastes from reactors are no longer accepted for burial at most commercial sites. The two most popular solidification agents in the U.S. are hydraulic cement and urea-formaldehyde (UF) resin. The waste and the hydraulic cement of the UF resin can be mixed in the storage drum or in an in-line mixer prior to putting it in the drum. In Europe, asphalt cement or bitumen is used for waste solidification. Other polymer systems such as vinyl ester-styrene resin have been proposed to solidify wastes.[22,24]

There are a number of problems with these solidification techniques. In some cases there is free standing water in the container after solidification. The wastes may appear to solidify, but they may have as much as 10% free water in the wastes. The free water problem is more common with the urea-formaldehyde resins than with hydraulic cement. The failure of the wastes to solidify is felt to be the results of wide variations in the pH of the aqueous wastes and from attempts to maximize the proportion of waste in the solidification media.[22,25] High boric acid concentrations and oily wastes can retard the setting of hydraulic cement.[24] Other problems include difficulties in capping drums and in instrumentation.[22,25]

Low-Level Wastes from Fuel Reprocessing Plants[15-18]

The spent fuel from nuclear reactors contains significant amounts of fissile ^{235}U and ^{239}Pu and fertile ^{238}U, as well as very large amounts of mixed fission products and transuranic elements. The uranium and the plutonium can be recovered from the spent fuel for uranium or uranium-plutonium mixed oxide fuel. The nonvolatile fission products and the transuranic elements recovered in fuel reprocessing are the high-level wastes. These wastes require heavy shielding, cooling, and permanent disposal. If the spent fuel is not reprocessed, it becomes a highly radioactive waste that must also eventually be sent to a permanent storage facility. At present, the only fuel reprocessing in the U.S. is for spent fuel from defense weapons programs and naval reactors.

In spent fuel reprocessing by the Purex process, the fuel elements are first chopped open. The spent fuel and its claddings and chopped fuel bundle hardware are put into concentrated nitric acid to dissolve the fuel and to leach most of the fuel and fission products from the claddings and miscellaneous hardware. This process releases large quantities of gaseous fission products such as ^{85}Kr, ^{129}I, and some ^{3}H. The uranium and plutonium are extracted from the aqueous nitric acid solution using an organic solution containing tributyl phosphate. Finally, the uranium and plutonium are chemically separated and purified.

There are numerous waste streams from the Purex process. The most significant are the high-level wastes consisting of the mixed fission products and transuranic elements left in the first nitric acid extract. The chopped fuel cladding hulls and fuel bundle hardware are contaminated with fuel and fission products and are activated by the neutron flux from the reactor. The off-gas treatment systems produce liquid, gaseous, or solid wastes which have high activities and are possibly contaminated with long-lived transuranic elements. Under proposed U.S. regulations to limit the concentration of transuranic elements in low-level wastes sent to commercial sites, these wastes are not acceptable for shallow land burial.[26]

The low-level wastes that can be shipped to commercial burial sites include the wastes produced in the spent fuel storage areas that hold the fuel prior to reprocessing, the highly activated fuel racks, control rods, and other fuel hardware that are not chopped with the fuel elements, wastes from the UF_6 dryer and several other waste streams that may qualify as nontransuranic wastes. At the proposed Allied-General Nuclear Services plant at Barnwell, S.C., these low-level wastes are projected to be about 1000 m^3/year.[27]

Decontamination and Decommissioning of Nuclear Facilities

The equipment and facilities built for the nuclear power cycle eventually wear out or become obsolete. At that point the facilities themselves become radioactively contaminated wastes that require proper disposal. For light water power reactors, the average service life has been estimated to range from 20 to 30 years[28] up to 40 years.[29]

For light water reactors one source of radioactive contamination of equipment can be surface contamination due to the deposition of activated corrosion products, fission products, and possibly transuranic elements. This surface contamination may be removed by steam cleaning, chemical cleaning agents such as acids, caustic solutions, organic solvents, and complexing agents, and by sand blasting. These operations produce liquid and solid contaminated wastes including the decontamination solutions, paper products used in cleaning, and protective clothing. Porous surfaces like concrete can be decontaminated by removing the surface layer.[28]

The other source of radioactive contamination in a light water reactor is the neutron activation of structural materials in the reactor core. The major nuclides activated are ^{60}Co (5.3-year half-life), ^{55}Fe (2.7-year half-life), ^{63}Ni (100-year half-life), ^{14}C (5730-year half-life), and ^{59}Ni (80,000-year half-life). Since the activity is distributed throughout the activated materials, they must either be removed or shielded to prevent unnecessary exposure.

When light water reactors are decommissioned, all spent fuel and radioactive wastes must be removed from the site for storage or disposal. U.S. regulations require that the reactor be put into protective storage, entombed, or dismantled. Each method has economic and environmental advantages and disadvantages.

Placing a facility in protective storage is the simplest and has the lowest initial costs of the alternatives. This option, which is frequently called mothballing, requires a continuing radiation monitoring program to determine if radionuclides are being released from the site. Certain services and equipment such as building ventilation may have to be operated. It will also require that the security of the site be maintained for centuries to prevent unauthorized entry. At present, there are at least ten mothballed reactors in the U.S. whose sizes range from small research reactors to demonstration and commercial reactors.[28]

Entombment of a reactor requires that the fuel assemblies and radioactive wastes be removed from the site and the pressure vessel be sealed with appropriate structural and biological shields. The surrounding site can be used for other purposes such as the construction of a new reactor. There would be a need for continued maintenance, monitoring, and surveillance as required to protect the public health. The potential disadvantages of entombment are lack of technology for maintenance-free containment of radionuclides and the potential difficulties in dismantling the reactor if this is required in the future.[28] There are several entombed experimental reactors in the U.S. These have been welded closed, covered in concrete, and weatherproofed.[28,29]

The third alternative is the dismantling of the reactor and restoration of the site for unrestricted use. This requires the removal of the reactor pressure vessel and its internals and the containment building. Since these are highly radioactive, the dismantling must be done behind heavy shielding. The tools that are used include plasma torches, power saws, portable shears, milling machines, and shaped explosive charges. These are needed to cut the metal structural parts of the reactor into small pieces for shipping in shielded casks and for demolition of the containment building.

The only power reactor in the U.S. that has been dismantled is the Elk River Reactor in Minnesota, which was a 58 MW (th) boiling water reactor built adjacent to a conventional steam electrical plant. After 4 years of commercial operation and an additional 4-year shutdown, it was dismantled and the site was restored to unrestricted use. The radioactive inventory of the reactor was nearly 10^4 Ci and the maximum contact radiation dosage was 8000 R/hr. Despite extensive shielding and other precautions, the workers received a total dose equivalent of 75 man-rems of whole body penetrating radiation with an average whole body dose equivalent of 0.8 rem.[28,30]

The Atomic Industrial Forum conducted a study on the decommissioning costs of 1100 MW(e) light water reactors. It projected that such reactors will have radioactive inventories as high as 15×10^6 Ci. The dismantling of such a reactor will produce approximately 9900 m^3 of radioactive waste to be shipped to a commercial low-level waste disposal site. In addition, there will be approximately 18,300 m^3 of nonradioactive solid wastes.[29]

The estimated occupational dose equivalent for the dismantling of a 1100 MW(e) reactor is 630 man-rems for a pressurized water reactor and 550 man-rems for a boiling water reactor. The study showed that mothballing or entombment of the reactor for 100 years prior to dismantling will reduce the total exposure to approximately half the exposure from immediate dismantling. The projected radiation dose equivalent for just mothballing or entombment of these reactors ranges from 80 to 160 man-rems.[29]

At the present time there are no decontamination standards that can be used to determine if facilities, equipment, and materials can be put into uncontrolled use. This encourages the shipment of all materials with induced activity above natural background levels to waste disposal sites. In addition, valuable metals with only slight contamination are buried instead of being salvaged for reuse. Decontamination standards will reduce the volume of low-level wastes and the costs of decommissioning.[31]

Fuel reprocessing plants and mixed oxide fuel fabrication plants will be contaminated with plutonium and other transuranic elements. The decontamination or dismantling of these facilities requires caution to avoid the dispersal of these long-lived nuclides. Much of the waste from these facilities is not acceptable for burial at U.S. commercial facilities. A recent study has estimated that the dismantling of a fuel reprocessing plant would produce 3100 m^3 of wastes that could be shipped to a low-level site.[32]

NONFUEL-CYCLE LOW-LEVEL WASTES

The nonfuel-cycle low-level wastes, which currently account for approximately 40% of the volume of wastes sent to commercial burial grounds in the U.S., come from thousands of institutions and industries throughout the country. These sources include medical schools, hospitals, medical and research laboratories, universities, and some industries. Unlike wastes from the nuclear fuel cycle, many of these wastes have very low activities, and the majority of their radionuclides have half-lives of a few months or less. On the other hand, these wastes have a wide range of physical forms including dry wastes from laboratories, sealed sources, scintillation vials and fluids, pathological wastes, animal excreta and carcasses from radiotracer experiments, and wastes from radiochemical manufacturers.

Institutional Wastes

Andersen et al.[33] and Beck et al.[34] have recently made surveys of the waste generation and disposal practices of large U.S. institutions including all medical schools, larger hospitals, and colleges and universities with over 5000 students. In 1975 these large institutions produced 11% of the volume of all wastes buried at low-level sites in the U.S.

Beck et al.[34] classified the institutional wastes as medical, biological research, and nonbiological research wastes. The medical sector produced 7% of the wastes from these institutions. The wastes included radiopharmaceutical wastes and laboratory wastes from clinical radioassays. The majority of these wastes were dry solids. The biological research sector produced 79% of the institutional waste volume. These wastes were primarily scintillation vials and fluids, dry solids, biological wastes, and absorbed liquids. The nonbiological research portion accounted for the remaining 14% of the institutional wastes. The wastes were mainly dry solids and absorbed liquids.

Table 2 gives the estimates of the total radionuclide content of the wastes shipped for burial in 1975 from the larger institutions. This excludes the wastes due to refueling of research reactors and high-activity ^3H targets used for neutron production in particle accelerators. Except for the longer-lived ^3H and ^{14}C, with half-lives of 12.3 years and 5700 years respectively, most of these wastes will decay in the first few years after burial. Medical schools, academic institutions, and teaching hospitals produce the majority of these two long-lived nuclides.

A significant fraction of the institutional waste was scintillation vials and fluids. In 1975 the survey population disposed of 28 million vials and more than 5×10^5 ℓ of scintillation fluids.[33] These fluids are organic solvents, such as toluene and xylene, containing scintillators. In general, they contain only very low concentrations of radionuclides. Andersen et al.[23] speculated that these fluids have a greater potential for chemical toxicity than for radiological damage. In 1979 the commercial site near Barnwell, S.C., ceased to accept these scintillation fluids because of their chemical composition.[35]

Table 2
RADIONUCLIDES SHIPPED FROM LARGE SURVEY INSTITUTIONS FOR COMMERCIAL SHALLOW LAND BURIAL IN 1975 (ACTIVITIES IN mCi)

Nuclide	Clinical hospital	Teaching hospital	Medical school	University/college	Total
^{3}H	1,313	13,788	46,659	23,516	85,276
^{14}C	214	1,523	19,585	4,788	26,114
^{32}P	41	2,085	11,256	2,024	15,407
^{35}S	0	360	4,426	1,149	5,935
^{51}Cr	113	438	3,495	612	4,658
^{67}Ga	21	264	33	0	318
^{99}Tc	9,021	76,614	4,813	0	90,448
^{125}I	174	4,998	23,564	2,816	10,342
^{131}I	105	15,324	1,310	561	17,300
Misc.	403	2,890	25,182	8,771	37,246

From Andersen, R. L., Cooley, L. R., Beck, T. J., and Strauss, C. S., *Institutional Radioactive Wastes*, Rep. NUREG/CR-0028, U.S. Nuclear Regulatory Commission, University of Maryland (Baltimore), 1978.

These institutions ship 62% of the low-level wastes in 210 ℓ (55 gal) steel drums and 30% in 115 ℓ (30 gal) steel drums which are easier to handle. The remaining 8% are shipped in other containers such as fiberboard drums, cardboard boxes, wooden crates, and paint cans.[33]

Alternative Disposal Methods for Institutional Wastes

Since the institutional wastes frequently have low concentrations of only short-lived nuclides, alternatives to shipment to commercial burial sites are used because of convenience or reduced costs. These methods include release to sanitary sewers, holding for decay and disposal with nonradioactive wastes, incineration, and onsite burial.[33,36-39]

Table 3 gives the principal disposal method of the majority of the activity by the large institutions as judged by Andersen et al.[33] The "no disposal" category is for those using only sealed sources or those just initiating radionuclide programs. The sanitary sewer is used as a disposal method for very-low-activity wastes and for radionuclides in human or animal excreta. Those institutions using larger quantities of the longer-lived nuclides such as medical schools, teaching hospitals, and universities, ship their wastes for burial. Incineration is the least common primary method of disposal, but it is used by some institutions for biological wastes and occasionally for scintillation fluids.[20,33,35,38] A few institutions operate their own burial sites for low-activity wastes.[39]

The institutional survey found interest in wider adoption of incineration for low-level wastes, but there have been difficulties in obtaining licenses.[35] Guidelines for the incineration of liquid scintillation wastes have been published recently.[38] Andersen et al.[33] suggest that the use of regional holding centers to store the wastes until they decay to insignificant levels would be a better alternative to shipment for burial. Beck et al.[34] recommend that most of the purely medical wastes be held for decay and then treated as ordinary refuse. Disposal of biological research wastes must take into consideration the chemical, biological, and radiological character of the wastes. In many cases the

Table 3
PRIMARY METHOD OF LOW-LEVEL WASTE DISPOSAL BY LARGE INSTITUTIONS IN 1975

	No disposal	Sewer-trash	Onsite burial	Incinera-tion	Ship for burial
Clinical hospitals	3	56	6	6	29
Teaching hospitals	2	37	5	2	54
Medical schools	0	2	4	11	83
Universities	29	31	11	1	28
Weighted average	13	34	7	4	42

From Andersen, R. L., Cooley, L. R., Beck, T. J., and Strauss, C. S., *Institutional Radioactive Wastes*, Rep. NUREG/CR-0028, U.S. Nuclear Regulatory Commission, University of Maryland (Baltimore), 1978.

activity of these wastes is so low that they recommend they be poured into the sewer system or sent to a sanitary landfill. Sealed sources and wastes with higher concentrations of long-lived radionuclides require burial at a low-level site. No economic or environmental analyses were given to support these recommendations.

Other Nonfuel-Cycle Wastes

Other nonfuel-cycle waste generators include radiopharmaceutical and radiochemical manufacturers, luminous dial manufacturers, and producers and users of sealed sources.[33,34] Rare metal and rare earth processors produce tailings that contain uranium, thorium, and radium.[40] Some of these wastes are shipped to low-level commercial burial sites. The U.S. Department of Energy and its contractors have shipped low-level wastes to commercial sites as well as to the federal burial sites. The majority of these wastes originate in its defense-related programs, including the decommissioning of surplus facilities.[1,41] In 1979 the Department of Energy wastes were estimated to be 18% of the total volume received at commercial sites.[8]

There is little published information on the sources, composition, radionuclide content, or volumes of these other nonfuel cycle wastes.

PROJECTIONS OF COMMERCIAL LOW-LEVEL WASTE VOLUMES

Estimates of the future generation of low-level wastes are important in planning for the expansion of existing burial sites, the opening of new sites, and commitments for research and development of new techniques for handling of the wastes or alternative disposal methods. Because these forecasts are sensitive to factors such as the future development of nuclear power, the use of radionuclides in medicine and research, and new waste disposal regulations, substantial differences exist in the published waste volume projections. This section will discuss waste projections in the U.S. and the factors that influence them.

Fuel-Cycle Waste Projections

The volume of fuel-cycle low-level wastes depends on the number and type of power reactors and their radioactive waste treatment systems; the volume reduction practiced in packaging the wastes; the costs of handling, shipping, and burying the wastes; and regulations on the disposal of low-level wastes. Since the volume of wastes shipped to commercial burial sites can be significantly affected by these factors, it is important to understand the basic assumptions underlying any projections.

Waste projections made in the early 1970s were based on the assumption that there

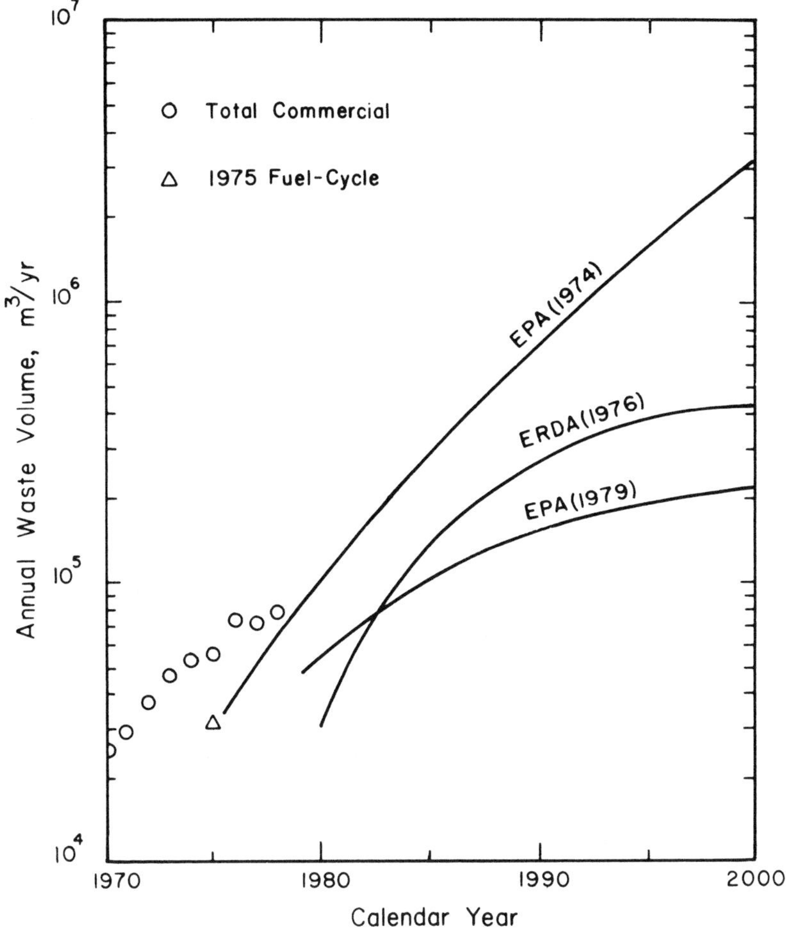

FIGURE 2. Fuel-cycle waste projections

would be a rapid transition to nuclear power for electrical power generation. Since there are fewer reactors in operation and under construction than were anticipated, fuel-cycle wastes will be correspondingly lower.

The volume of waste produced at each reactor depends on its size and type, its waste treatment systems, and its operations. Because of differences in individual reactors and their operations, no consistent relationship between the reactor power output and total wastes produced has been found. Boiling water reactors produce a larger volume and higher activity waste than pressurized water reactors.[18] Onsite incineration and further compaction have the potential to significantly reduce the volumes of these wastes.

The costs of shipping and burying low-level wastes influence the generation rates. High costs provide incentives to invest in equipment and personnel to reduce the volume of wastes shipped. On the other hand, relatively low disposal costs will discourage the development and application of new technologies to decrease waste volumes.

Other factors important in projecting future generation rates are changes in regulations governing the siting and operation of commercial disposal sites. Under proposed revisions to waste disposal regulation in the U.S., an upper limit of 10 nCi/g of transuranic elements will be established for wastes buried at commercial sites.[26] Wastes exceeding this limit will be sent to future federal waste repositories. This is currently

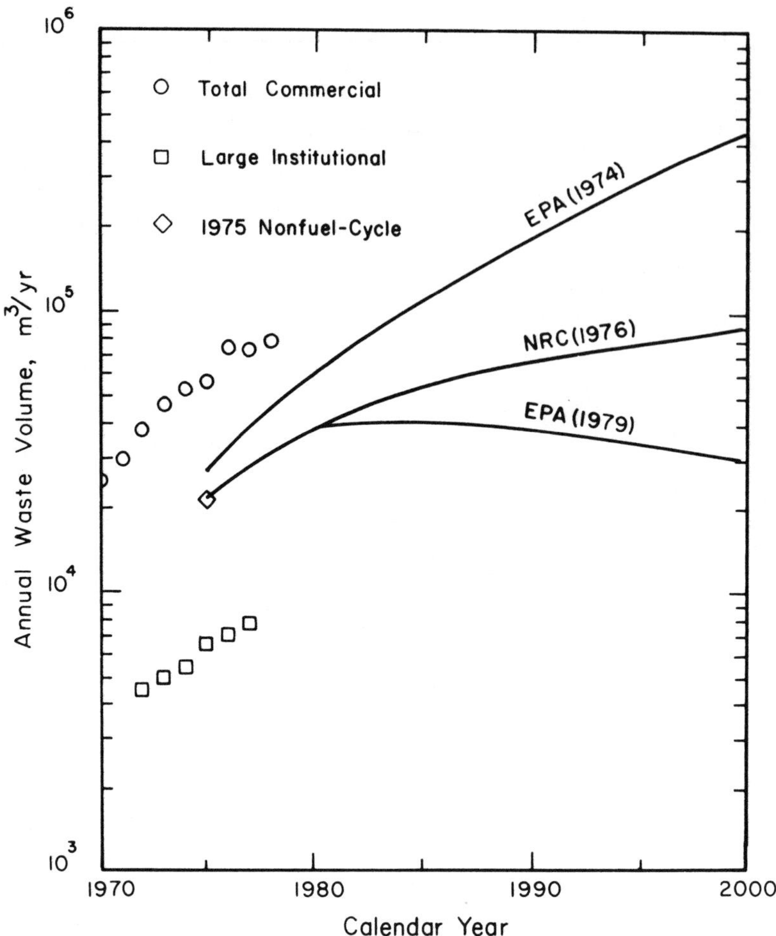

FIGURE 3. Nonfuel-cycle waste projections

the limit for wastes buried at all but one of the existing commercial sites. The U.S. Environmental Protection Agency has proposed new criteria that will affect the siting and operation of commercial burial grounds.[12] These will increase costs of disposal that could stimulate reactor operators to find methods to reduce their waste volumes.

Figure 2 shows three fuel-cycle waste projections for the rest of this century. It also indicates that total annual volume of wastes buried at all commercial sites from 1970 to 1978 and an estimate of the fuel-cycle portion in 1975.[42] The 1974 U.S Environmental Protection Agency fuel-cycle waste projections[43] were based on an extrapolation of historical data on total wastes and the assumptions of Blomeke[44] on the fraction of nonfuel-cycle wastes in this period.[1] The 1976 Energy Research and Development Administration[45] estimates of uncompacted waste volumes are significantly lower than the earlier EPA estimates. These are based on a moderate growth of nuclear power with a 638.6 GW(e) capacity in the year 2000, but they include the assumption that fuel will be reprocessed. The 1979 U.S. Environmental Protection Agency fuel-cycle waste projections[1] were based on an assumption of 0.78 m^3/MW(e)-year for the entire fuel cycle and an installed generating capacity of 330.7 GW(e) in the year 2000. The installed capacity in 1978 was about 50 GW(e).[1]

In view of uncertainties in the growth of nuclear power, the 1979 EPA fuel-cycle estimates probably represent an upper boundary to actual waste volumes in the remaining 2 decades of this century.

Nonfuel-Cycle Waste Projections

The nonfuel-cycle users of radionuclides include medical schools, hospitals, research laboratories, universities, and some industries. Figure 3 gives three estimates of the nonfuel-cycle wastes through the end of this century. It also shows the total annual volume of wastes buried at all commercial sites from 1970 to 1978,[1] and the estimate of the total 1975 nonfuel-cycle wastes and the wastes from the large institutions surveyed by Andersen et al.[33] The 1974 Environmental Protection Agency projections[43] were based on an extrapolation of total waste volume and Blomeke's[44] assumption of the percentage of nonfuel-cycle wastes. This fraction ranged from 44% in 1975 to 14% in the year 2000. The 1979 EPA estimates of the nonfuel-cycle wastes are based on the same fraction of nonfuel-cycle to total wastes.[1] The 1976 Nuclear Regulatory Commission predictions are staff estimates.[10] The latter two estimates show a low growth rate which is in conflict with the present growth of the institutional wastes.[33,34] The 1979 EPA estimate does not include Department of Energy wastes sent to commercial sites.

LOW-LEVEL BURIAL SITES

In the U.S. the problems of the treatment and disposal of large amounts of radioactive wastes were first faced in the defense nuclear programs. With little experience in dealing with radioactive wastes, it was decided to store the high-level wastes in steel tanks awaiting the development of technologies for their solidification and final disposal. The nonhigh-level wastes were treated and released to the environment in the ground, the surface waters, or the atmosphere. At some sites liquid wastes were discharged to surface ponds or underground cribs to allow the radionuclides to decay and to be diluted and dispersed in the groundwater. Solid wastes and some absorbed or solidified liquids were buried in shallow trenches. A relatively small amount of these solids was buried at sea.

In the early days of nuclear programs the civilian sector produced small amounts of wastes compared to the defense programs. At that time most of the civilian wastes were from nonfuel-cycle sources such as hospitals, research laboratories, and certain industries. These wastes were generally low in activity. They were buried at the AEC sites or at sea. As the volume of civilian wastes grew, the policy of encouraging the development of regional, commercial burial sites was adopted. The first of these sites were licensed in 1962 at locations near Beatty, Nev., and at Maxey Flats near Morehead, Ky. Over the next decade, sites were licensed near West Valley, N.Y., Sheffield, Ill., and Barnwell, S.C., to serve their respective regions of the country.

U.S. Department of Energy Burial Sites

Figure 4 shows the locations of the major federal burial sites, which are now operated by the Department of Energy. These are located at government nuclear research and production facilities. Wastes generated at other locations are shipped to one of these sites, buried at one of several smaller disposal sites, or sent to a commercial facility. Until 1962 these sites also accepted radioactive wastes from the civilian sector. These sites and their environmental impacts have been reviewed in recent reports by the National Academy of Sciences,[7] the General Accounting Office,[6] the U.S. Energy Research and Development Administration,[46] and the U.S. Nuclear Regulatory Commission.[41]

The federal sites are similar in their locations, design, and burial practices to the present commercial sites in the U.S. Table 4 gives the basic hydrogeological characteristics of these sites. The Savannah River and Oak Ridge burial sites are in humid regions of the country and have permanent groundwater at or near the bottom of the

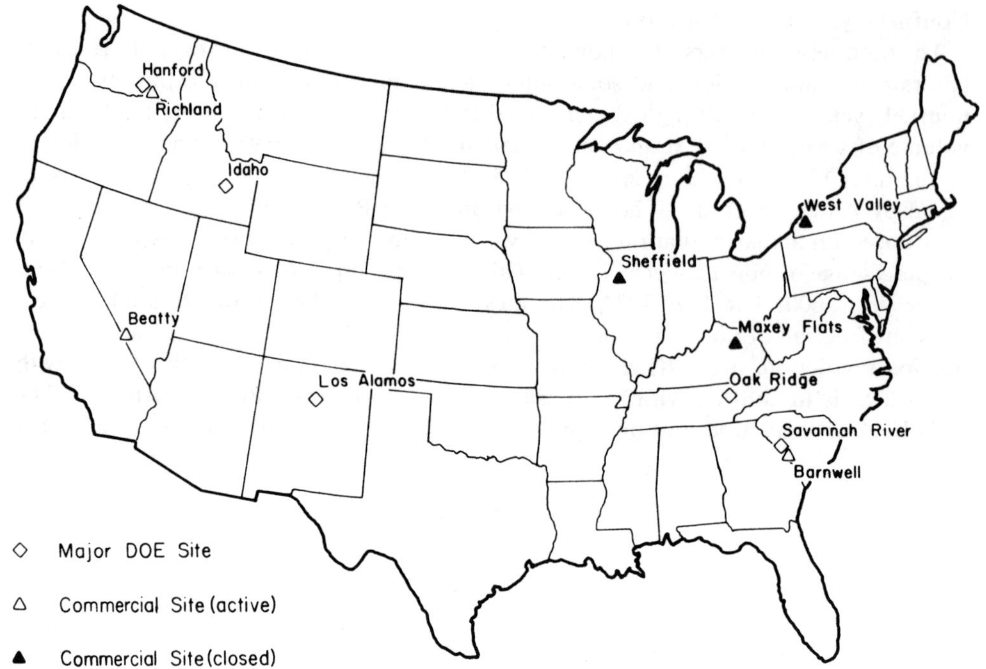

FIGURE 4. Major low-level burial sites in the U.S.

trenches. The three western sites at Los Alamos, Idaho, and Hanford are in semi-arid or arid regions with the saturated zone lying 50 to 300 m below the waste.

Table 5 gives a summary of the wastes buried at these sites. Although transuranic wastes have been buried at all these sites, wastes having transuranic concentrations exceeding 10 nCi/g are now temporarily stored above ground or buried in retrievable containers.

A summary of known migrations of radionuclides and potential causes of future problems at the shallow land burial grounds are given in Table 6. The two sites in humid areas, Oak Ridge and Savannah River, have had migrations of radionuclides from the burial site in the groundwater and also by surface runoff at Oak Ridge. The Hanford and Idaho sites have also had migration of radionuclides. The radionuclide concentrations are presently below permissible limits for release to the environment and are not generally considered to be a significant threat to public health.

At Oak Ridge National Laboratories[7,47,48] in southeastern Tennessee radioactive wastes have been buried at a number of sites. In the 1950s the wastes were buried in the Solid Waste Storage Area 4. This site was selected because it is in a formation of weathered shale that has a low permeability to the flow of groundwater and a high sorptive capacity for many radionuclides. The chief drawbacks to the site are that its groundwater table is close to the surface and it is near a creek.

The trenches were dug in the shale and the wastes were buried and covered with the original soil materials. At later periods portions of the site were covered with as much as 7 m of uncontaminated fill from building excavations.

The shallowness of the groundwater table led to a number of problems. During rainy periods it would rise to or near the surface in the lower elevations of the site. This limited the burials of wastes in these lower areas to the dry periods of the year. Since the fill materials covering the trenches were much more permeable than the underlying shale formation, water which percolated downward was held in the trenches. Gra-

Table 4
HYDROGEOLOGICAL CHARACTERISTICS OF THE MAJOR DEPARTMENT OF ENERGY BURIAL SITES

	Savannah River	Oak Ridge	Los Alamos	Idaho	Hanford
Mean annual precipitation (mm)	1100	1300	400	200	200
Surficial material type	Sand and claysand	Weathered shale and fill	Weathered tuff	Alluvial sand and gravel	Clay, sand, and gravel
Thickness (m)	0—10	0—10	0—2	1—10	Over 150
Interstitial permeability to water	Very low	Very low	Moderate	Moderate	Variable
Bedrock material type	Clay, sand, and sandstone	Shale	Volcanic tuff	Basalt	Volcanic
Structure	Flat-lying	Folded	Flat-lying	Flat-lying	Flat-lying
Ground water; depth to shallowest saturated zone (m)	10—20	0—5	200—400	60—300	100
Depth of continuous groundwater zone (m)	10—20	2—5	200—400	60—300	100
Depth to regional aquifer (m)	200	None present	200—400	60—300	100
Surface water proximity	On site	On site	1 km	3 km	10 km
Flow characteristics	Small, perennial	Small, perennial	Small, ephemeral	Small, ephemeral	Large, perennial (Columbia River)
Adsorptive or ion exchange capacity of material surrounding burial[a]	Moderate	High	High	Moderate	Moderate
Principal flow paths away from burial	Pore spaces in sand	Shale fractures and pores in fill	Fractures and pores in sand	Pores in sand	Pores in sand

[a] Interstitial permeability and adsorptive capacity can be bypassed by flow fractures or other high permeability zones.

From Alternatives for Managing Wastes from Reactors and Post-Fission Operations in the LWR Fuel Cycle, Rep. ERDA-76-43-U.S. Energy Research and Development Administration, Vol. 4, 24.1—24.49, 1976.

Table 5
WASTES INVENTORIES AT THE MAJOR DEPARTMENT OF ENERGY BURIAL SITES

	Hectares	Total volume buried (m^3)	Activity remaining (Ci)	Uranium (kg)	TRU (g)
Savannah River	38	279,000	4,410,000	79,000	7,000
Oak Ridge	24	179,000	60,000[b]	100	13,000
Los Alamos	23	225,000	160,000	251,000	13,000
Idaho	21	140,000	3,579,000	288,000	361,000
Hanford	98	199,000	810,000	600,000	365,000

[a] Data compiled from References 7 and 46. Waste Summary is through July, 1975.
[b] Estimated since some records were lost in a fire.

dually the trenches were flooded. The similarity of water being held in the trenches to water held in a bathtub has led to this phenomena being called the ''bathtub effect''.

Once the trench was flooded, the radionuclides began to be leached from the wastes. This leaching was apparently enhanced by the presence of organic chelating agents in some of the wastes. These chemicals may have inhibited the sorption of radionuclides such as ^{90}Sr by the shale.

The contaminated trench water slowly flowed laterally with the groundwater toward lower elevations and the creek. In some of the flooded trenches the water spilled over the downslope end and flowed to the surface in a spring of contaminated water which was carried to the creek by surface runoff. The total transport of ^{90}Sr to the creek is estimated to be 1 to 2 Ci/year.[47]

At the Savannah River Plant near Aiken, S.C.,[7,49] the solid radioactive waste storage site is a burial ground in a relatively level area underlain with sands and clays. The waste trenches are 6 m deep and the water table lies an average of 10 to 20 m below the surface. To determine if water collects in the trenches, 24 wells have been placed in the trenches. Although most of the wells are dry, water is found in some of the wells during at least part of the year. In these wells the water has been observed to be 1 to 2.5 m above the trench bottom. This perched water is felt to be a result of infiltration through the trench cap. No overflow from the trenches has been observed.

The only detectable radionuclide migration from the buried waste is ^{3}H as tritiated water. This has been observed to move downward toward the water table or saturated zone at a rate of 2 m/year. Then it flows laterally with the groundwater at a rate of 10 to 15 m/year.

As a result of transfer accidents and spills of the contaminated kerosene-tributyl phosphate solvent used in the separations facility, there are trace amounts of plutonium and fission products in the soil beneath the trenches. These are sorbed in a layer of soil at the water table and are moving laterally at a rate estimated to be less than 30 cm/year.[49]

The Los Alamos Scientific Laboratory is in a semi-arid region with the water table 200 m or more beneath the surface.[7,46] The site has observed onsite migration of ^{3}H as tritiated water vapor.[45]

The Hanford Reservation is in an arid climate with an average annual precipitation of 200 mm. The groundwater table is 100 m below the 98-ha used for shallow land burial of solid wastes.[7,45,50-52] There has been migration of radionuclides from these trenches and from the underground cribs used for disposal of liquid wastes. There is uptake of radionuclides by tumbleweeds that can be blown away after the plant dies.[51,52] In addition, rodents have ingested radionuclides. The rodent excreta and carcasses have spread the radionuclides away from the disposal area.[51-54]

Table 6
RADIONUCLIDE MIGRATION AT THE MAJOR DEPARTMENT OF ENERGY BURIAL SITES

	Savannah River	Oak Ridge	Los Alamos	Idaho	Hanford
Extent of tritium migration observed	Onsite ground water	On- and offsite surface water, onsite ground water	Onsite vadose zone	None	None from solid waste burial ground
Extent of other radionuclide migration	None detected	On- and offsite surface water, onsite ground water	None detected	On- and offsite surface water, resuspension by wind, rodents	Uptake by deep rooted plants (tumbleweeds) and by rodents
Transport mechanisms	None observed	Overflow from water filled trenches Ground water Surface water	None observed	Floods Wind-borne Rodent excreta and carcasses	Tumbling tumbleweeds Rodent excreta and carcasses
Potential causes for future problems	Surface water infiltrations of trenches	Continued uncontrolled surface and ground water	Dramatic climatic changes	Surface water infiltration and movement through fissured formations	Uncontrolled plant growth
Solutions or precautions	Surface water control	Engineered surface and ground water control Exhumation	None necessary	Surface water control	Plant species control

[a] Information taken from References 46, 52, and 55.

Table 7
U.S. COMMERCIAL LOW-LEVEL BURIAL GROUNDS LICENSING

	West Valley	Maxey Flats	Barnwell	Sheffield	Beatty	Richland
Site operator	Nuclear Fuel Services (NFS)	Nuclear Engineering Co. (NECO)	Chem-Nuclear (CNS Systems)	NECO	NECO	NECO
Site ownership	State, leased to NFS	State, leased to NECO	State, leased to CNS	State, leased to NECO	State leased to NECO	Federal, leased to state, leased to NECO
Year first licensed	1963	1963	1971	1967	1962	1965
Agreement state	Yes	Yes	Yes	No (pending)	Yes	Yes
Activities licensed directly by NRC	None	None	Handling and burial of SNM	All burial	Handling and burial of SNM	Handling and burial of SNM
Activities licensed by state	All	All	All other	None	All other	All other
Burial of plutonium >10 nCi/g	Restricted since 1974	Restricted since 1974	Never permitted	Restricted since 1975	Restricted since 1975	Pending restriction
Operational status	Closed	Closed	Open	Closed	Open, SNM license suspended in 1976.	Open

[a] Information taken from References 1 and 46.

The Idaho National Engineering Laboratory is in an arid region with an average annual precipitation of 200 mm. The groundwater table lies 200 m beneath the surface.[7,46] The burial site is in a shallow depression. Preliminary data indicate that radionuclides have been leached from the waste by infiltrating groundwater.[7] In 1962 and 1969 the burial site was flooded by water from melting snow. Radionuclides apparently were carried with the surface waters. Some were distributed further by rodents and by resuspension in strong winds. Flood control dikes have been constructed to avoid future flooding.[55]

In addition to the five major burial sites operated, there are a number of smaller active and inactive burial sites at Department of Energy facilities.[41]

U.S. Commercial Burial Sites

The locations of the six commercial burial sites are shown in Figure 4. The status of these sites is shown in Table 7. These sites are located on lands owned by the states or the federal government which are leased to their commercial operators. They are licensed by either their respective states under agreements with the Nuclear Regulatory Commission or by the Nuclear Regulatory Commission itself. Due to economic and environmental difficulties the West Valley and Maxey Flats sites are now closed. Since the Sheffield site is full, there are only three sites accepting significant quantities of wastes.

The hydrogeological characteristics of the sites are given in Table 8. The four eastern sites are in humid areas with the groundwater table 5 to 20 m below the surface. The two western sites are in arid regions with permanent water tables lying 80 to 100 m below the surface.

The size of the sites and a summary of their waste inventories are given in Table 9. The by-product material is given as the undecayed activity in curies. The source material, which is unenriched uranium and thorium, is given in kilograms. Much of this source material is felt to be in the wastes from UF_6 conversion plants and fuel fabrication plants. The special nuclear material, which includes ^{233}U, ^{235}U, and plutonium, is given in grams. Much of the special material now being buried is felt to be ^{235}U in sludges from fuel fabrication plants. The origin of the source and special nuclear material needs to be documented. Plutonium and other transuranic nuclides at concentrations greater than 10 nCi/g have been buried at all the commercial sites except Barnwell. The Sheffield site has buried only small amounts of plutonium.

Table 10 gives the known migration of radionuclides at the commercial sites. The West Valley, Maxey Flats, and Sheffield sites have had migration of ^{3}H as tritiated water and possibly other radionuclides in the surface or groundwater. At the other sites there is the possibility of ^{3}H migration from the trenches, but this has not been documented. The four eastern sites are considered to have the greatest potential for future problems with water causing the migration of radionuclides.

The first commercial site was opened in 1962 at a location near Beatty in southwestern Nevada. The operator of the 32-ha burial ground is the Nuclear Engineering Co. (NECO). The site is in an arid region with an annual average of 100 mm precipitation. The water table is 80 m below ground. This site has had no detected migration of radionuclides although it is possible that ^{3}H as tritiated water vapor is diffusing through the soil.[45]

In 1976 the site operator reported that a concrete mixer that had been used at the burial site to solidify liquid wastes had been used to pour concrete in the town of Beatty. A survey of the town found that some of the concrete slabs were contaminated. In addition, numerous items from the burial site were located in the town including tools, radium dial clocks and compasses, radioactive waste shipping containers, plywood, and equipment. The contaminated concrete and other items were taken to the

Table 8
HYDROGEOLOGICAL CHARACTERISTICS OF THE U.S. COMMERCIAL BURIAL SITES

	West Valley	Maxey Flats	Barnwell	Sheffield	Beatty	Richland
Mean annual precipitation (mm)	1000	1200	1100	900	100	200
Surficial material type	Glacial drift, silty clay/interbedded sand and gravel	Weathered shale; clay and sand	Sand and clay sand	Glacial drift; sand, silt and gravel	Alluvial sand and gravel	Clay, sand and gravel
Thickness (m)	20—30	3—5	0—10	20—30	Over 200	Over 150
Interstitial permeability to water (cm/day)	Low (0.5)	Very low (0.02)	Very low (0.02)	Variable (0.04—40)	Variable (0.02—0.1)	Variable
Bedrock material type	Shale	Shale	Clay, sand and sandstone	Shale, claystone and coal	Metamorphic and sedimentary	Volcanic
Structure	Flat-lying	Flat-lying	Flat-lying	Flat-lying	Folded	Flat-lying
Ground water depth to shallowest saturated zone (m)	Variable, 1—20	1—2	10—20	5—20	80—90	100
Depth of continuous groundwater zone (m)	20	10—15	10—20	5—20	80—90	100
Depth to regional aquifer (m)	None present	None present	200	100	80—90	100
Surface water proximity	On site	500 m	At site boundaries	At site boundaries	3 km	10 km
Flow characteristics	Small, perennial	Small, perennial	Small, perennial	Lake to north; small, perennial to south	Ephemeral, following storms	Large, perennial (Columbia River)
Adsorptive or ion exchange capacity, of material surrounding burial[a]	High	High	Moderate	Low	Moderate	Moderate

Principal flow paths aways from burial	Shale fractures and lens in drift	Shale fractures	Pore spaces in sand	Pore spaces in till	Unsaturated flow in pores	Unsaturated flow in pores

[a] Interstitial permeability and absorptive capacity can be bypassed by flow fractures or other high permeability zones.

From Alternatives for Managing Wastes from Reactors and Post-Fission Operations in the LWR Fuel Cycle, Rep. ERDA-76-43, U.S. Energy Research And Development Administration, Vol. 4, 24.1—24.49, 1976.

Table 9
WASTE INVENTORIES AT THE U.S. COMMERCIAL BURIAL SITES[a]

	Hectares	Total volume buried (m^3)	Undecayed by-product material (Ci)	Source material (Kg)	Special nuclear material (g)
West Valley	9	66,521	577,778	462,726	56,795
Maxey Flats	102	135,287	2,406,288	228,970	431,487
Barnwell	110	205,439	1,526,749	1,122,823	873,577
Sheffield	9	86,701	60,206	267,843	57,053
Beatty	32	67,365	160,819	129,094	695,939
Richland	40	23,659	711,837	19,603	101,947

[a] Data compiled from Holcomb, W. F., Inventory (1962—1978) and projections (to 2000) of shallow land burial of radioactive wastes at commercial sites, *Nucl. Saf.*, 21, 380—388, 1980. Wastes summary through 1978.

burial site.[56] Because of violations of the condition of the license, the State of Nevada suspended the license for 3 months. The Nuclear Regulatory Commission suspended the site license for special nuclear material pending the completion of an investigation. In 1979 the site was closed for a short period by the State of Nevada because of shipping irregularities.[8]

The second commercial site is at Maxey Flats, located near Morehead in eastern Kentucky. This area has an annual average of 1200 mm precipitation. The site operator is the Nuclear Engineering Company. The 102-ha site is located on a flat-topped ridge rising 100 m above the surrounding valleys. The burial grounds are underlain with shale, siltstone, and sandstone. The site was chosen because it was felt that the ridge had no known water table and that the shale formations were highly sorptive of radionuclides.[57] Later investigations have shown that, although the formations are aquitards, water moves readily along fractures and open joints within the formations.[58,59] Perched water tables within the ridge and natural seeps and springs from the lower formations of the ridge have been found.[59]

Burial commenced at Maxey Flats in 1963. As with the Beatty site, both solid and liquid wastes were received for disposal. The liquid wastes were stored in tanks and later solidified with newspapers, clay, and cement.[57] Over 2.25×10^6 ℓ of liquid wastes were solidified before this practice was discontinued in 1972.[43] Estimates of the total activities of individual radionuclides buried at this site have been given by Clark[60] and Gat et al.[61]

Since the burial trenches were dug into a relatively impermeable shale formation, water that percolated through the trench cap was held within the trench. This water accelerated the leaching of radionuclides from the waste and the decomposition of organic matter in the waste. In some cases the trenches overflowed, allowing contaminated trench water to run off the site. Also, trench water may have been able to flow along open joints in the underlying formation.[58,62]

Because of the infiltration of water, the site operator began an intensive water control program. Water was pumped from the trenches, stored in tanks, and evaporated in an evaporator. The evaporator bottoms were solidified and buried onsite. By 1976, more than 10^7 ℓ had been pumped from the trenches. A surface water control program was also begun. This included the compaction and reshaping of the trench caps to promote runoff, planting shallow rooted grasses to prevent erosion, and installation of a surface drainage system.[58]

Table 10
RADIONUCLIDE MIGRATION AT THE U.S. COMMERCIAL BURIAL SITES

	West Valley	Maxey Flats	Barnwell	Sheffield	Beatty	Richland
Extent of tritium migration observed	On- and offsite surface water; onsite ground water	On- and offsite surface water; on- and offsite ground water	None,[b] possible percolation of trench water	Onsite lateral migration of trench water	None[b] possible vapor diffusion in soil	None,[b] possible vapor diffusion in soil
Extent of other radionuclide migration observed	On- and offsite surface water	On- and offsite surface water; on- and offsite ground water	None observed	None observed	None observed	None observed
Transport media	Surface contamination carried by runoff Water infiltration of trenches and overflow Effluent from liquid waste treatment Possible ground water transport	Surface contamination carried by runoff Effluent from liquid waste treatment Ground water transport	None indicated	None indicated	None indicated	None indicated
Potential causes for future problems	Loss of surface water control Ground water infiltration	Loss of surface water control Ground water infiltration	Loss of surface water control Rise of water table	Loss of surface water control Rise of water table	Drastic climate change	Drastic climate change
Solutions or preventions	Surface water control Possible engineered ground water control	Surface water control Possible engineered ground water control	Surface water control	Surface water control	Natural conditions sufficient	Natural conditions sufficient

[a] Information taken from References 46 and 72.
[b] Environmental surveillance program may be insufficient for detection of all modes of migration

The State of Kentucky and the U.S. Environmental Protection Agency conducted radiological surveys both on site and in the adjacent areas. They found plutonium and other radionuclides in soil cores taken at depths of 75 cm and in the suspended solids and sediments of wells and surface waters. They found many cases in which the plutonium concentrations and the $^{238}Pu/^{239}Pu$ ratio significantly exceeded the regional background due to fallout. The concentrations were far below applicable state and federal standards.[58,63]

Meyer[58] proposed four potential pathways for the migration of plutonium and other radionuclides: (1) transport by surface runoff, (2) lateral migration with the water in the soil, (3) subsurface flow along open joints and bedding planes, and (4) dispersal in the vapor plume from the evaporator. He presented evidence to lend support to each of these pathways. Alternative explanations for these concentrations include the possibility of cross-contamination in sampling and surface runoff from minor spills.[64]

When an additional tax of 10¢/lb of waste was imposed by the State of Kentucky to obtain additional monies for monitoring and perpetual care, the waste volume buried at the site decreased dramatically.[42] In late 1977 the site was closed.[1]

The third commercial burial ground is at the Western New York Nuclear Center near West Valley, N.Y. This facility, which is operated by Nuclear Fuels Services (NFS), has a 9-ha low-level burial ground, a nuclear fuel reprocessing plant with high-level waste storage tanks, and another burial ground for fuel hardware and cladding hulls. From 1963 to 1972 the plant reprocessed high-burn spent fuel from commercial reactors and low-burn fuel from the NPR reactor at the Hanford Reservation. The plant closed in 1972 for modification and expansion. Because of changes in federal regulations, the plant has never reopened.[65]

The surficial material at the site is a 30 m layer of silty, clayey till interbedded with very fine sand and gravel. The till itself has low permeability and good sorption for radionuclides. The site has an annual average precipitation of 1000 mm.[46,66]

Burial of wastes at West Valley began in 1963. Within the first few years, water was observed in monitoring wells at the lower end of the trench. Because of continually rising water levels, programs to reduce infiltration of surface water and decrease erosion were instituted in 1968. The trench caps were reworked and the soil was mounded over individual trenches. This gradually stopped the water level from rising in the older trenches. At the same time, the design for future trenches was modified to incorporate greater separation between trenches, better surface preparation, increased depth of the cover, and compaction of the cover. After the new trenches were closed, the water level would initially rise but it would stabilize at low levels.[67]

In the period from 1969 to 1972 the State of New York found ^{3}H, ^{89}Sr, and ^{90}Sr concentrations above background levels in surface waters near the burial site.[68] In 1971 the water levels in the older trenches began to rise again. In 1975 trench water began to slowly seep through the cap on several of the older trenches. Attempts were made to divert this seepage into a holding lagoon. To reduce the water levels in the trenches, $8 \times 10^{5} \ell$ of water were pumped into a holding lagoon. The trench water was treated in the lagoon by pH adjustment and ferric hydroxide to precipitate some of the radionuclides. Then the water was treated at the low-level waste treatment plant at the fuel reprocessing plant. This treatment process removed about 99% of the cesium and 99.8% of the strontium. The ^{3}H was not removed from the water before it was discharged to a nearby creek.[67,69,70] The burial site was voluntarily closed in 1975.[1]

Studies of the site indicated that the water probably infiltrated into the older trenches through cracks in the trench cap. There is little lateral migration of ^{3}H. Due to improvements in their construction, the newer trenches have maintained their low water levels.[66] There is some concern about the long-term slope stability due to erosion and slumping.[67]

The fourth commercial burial site is located on the Department of Energy's Hanford Reservation on a 400-ha site that is leased to the State of Washington. This is located between the 200-E and 200-W Areas that are used for fuel reprocessing and waste storage in defense programs. In 1965 the State of Washington leased 40 ha to Nuclear Engineering Company for the commercial burial site. This site is commonly called the Richland site to distinguish it from the nearby Hanford burial grounds which are in the 200 Areas.[1,52]

The site characteristics are the same as the Hanford burial ground. The site is in semi-arid climate with an average of 200 mm annual precipitation. The ground water is over 100 m deep. Although there have been no detected migrations of radionuclides from the burial site, it is possible that this has occurred through uptake by vegetation as has happened at the adjacent Hanford sites. It is the last commercial site accepting wastes with transuranic concentrations exceeding 10 nCi/g. Burial of these transuranic wastes may cease in the near future.[42] In 1979 this site was closed for a short period by the State of Washington due to shipments of contaminated wastes.[8]

The fifth commercial site was opened in 1967 at a location near Sheffield, Ill. The operator is the Nuclear Engineering Company. The site is a small 9-ha site which is adjacent to an 18-ha hazardous chemical disposal site operated by NECO, coal strip mines, and farmland.[71,72] The surficial materials at the site are glacial drift, sand, silt, and gravel. The site has highly variable permeability and low sorptive capacity for radionuclides. The annual average precipitation is 900 mm. The water table lies 5 to 20 m below ground.[6,46]

Although the site is licensed by the Nuclear Regulatory Commission, the State of Illinois has placed a limit of 1 Ci/ft^3 of waste (35.3 Ci/m^3) on all wastes unless prior state approval is granted. Although burial of plutonium was permitted up to 1974, less than 15 kg of plutonium have been buried at the site. In 1975 the site adopted the 10 nCi/g limit for all transuranic elements.[72]

Although little water has been found in the trenches, tests have shown that ^3H has migrated laterally as far as 30 m from one trench. This rapid migration is felt to be due to a sand layer that intersects with the trench.[72]

All the land suitable for conventional burial trenches on the original 9-ha site has been utilized. To extend the capacity of this site, the last two trenches were built-up trenches that were made by compact-and-fill methods used in some conventional sanitary landfills. It was proposed by the operator that built-up trenches be used on the remaining area of the original site and on a portion of 75 ha adjacent to it. It was claimed that this method is superior to conventional trenches since the sidewall material can be selected in construction to avoid problems such as the sand layers found in some of the earlier trenches. Also, this method can make better use of the high and low areas of the site. The Nuclear Regulatory Commission has not approved continued use of the built-up trenches or expansion of the site.[71-73] The Sheffield site was closed in 1978.[1]

The last commercial burial site that has been established is near Barnwell, S.C. It is adjacent to the Savannah River Plant and the site of the Allied-General Nuclear Services Plant. The operator is Chem-Nuclear Systems, Inc. The 110-ha site, which opened in 1971, is currently the only operational site east of the Rockies.[1] The site currently handles the largest volume of wastes of any of the sites. To prevent the site from being filled too rapidly, the State of South Carolina has recently limited the site to burying no more than 6.8×10^4 m^3/year. At the current rate of growth of wastes sent to this site, it was anticipated that the site would have reached this limit in 1980. The site has also recently refused to accept scintillation fluids because they have a higher chemical than radiological toxicity.[35]

The characteristics of the site are similar to the nearby Savannah River burial grounds. It receives an average of 1100 mm of precipitation each year. The water table lies 10 to 20 m below the surface. The surficial soil materials are clayey sands that are interbedded with isolated lenses of gravel. Except for these pockets of coarse sand and gravel, these materials are only slightly permeable and have moderate sorptive capacities.[46,74] These sediments have numerous cracks, fissures, and clastic dikes similar to those found at the nearby Savannah River Plant where it has been shown that much of their migration of radionuclides has occurred through sandy lenses and sandy clastic dikes.[75] During very wet periods perched water tables have been observed in areas near the burial site.

Little or no water has been observed in the monitoring wells of the completed trenches. Sampling from a monitor well located very close to one trench has shown very limited migration of ^{3}H and organic chemicals.[76] This site is the only one in a humid area that has not had some difficulty with water accumulating in the trenches or lateral migration of radionuclides.

Design and Operation of Low-Level Burial Sites

Commercial low-level burial sites generally have two types of burial trenches. The first consists of large open trenches used for the majority of the wastes. The second type is of special trenches or dry wells used for that small volume of beta-gamma wastes that require shielding to protect the site personnel. These wastes included sealed sources of cobalt and other radionuclides and highly activated nonfuel bearing components from the core of a nuclear reactor.

The design of the large open trenches varies at different sites because of local soils, climate, and topography. They are typically 60 to 300 m long, 10 to 30 m wide, and 6 to 8 m deep. They may have sloped or nearly vertical trench walls. In humid areas the trench bottoms are usually sloped toward one end where a sump pump is installed in a gravel-filled sump. At several of these sites the bottoms are also sloped toward a gravel-filled trench or french drain which is along the centerline or one side of the trench. The french drains and the sump aid in the collection of any water that accumulates in the trench during burial and after the trench is closed.[46]

The newer trenches at the Barnwell site incorporate the most elaborate site and trench preparations of any of the commercial sites. First a 1 to 2 m layer of loose sand is stripped from the site of a new burial trench. It is replaced with clayey materials more suitable for trench walls. This clay layer extends 1.5 m beyond the sides of the new trench. Then a 300 m long, 30 m wide, and 6 m deep trench is excavated. The bottom of the trench is sloped toward one side and also toward one end. A gravel-filled french drain is installed along the lower side and a sump pump is installed at the lower end. At intervals along the length of the trench, sump pipes that extend from the french drain to the surface are installed. These allow for observation and sampling of any water that may be in the drain. Then the bottom of the trench is covered with a sand layer. Unless excessive amounts of water are allowed to accumulate in the trench, the sand should prevent the waste from being continuously immersed. Except for some minor difficulties with the earliest trenches, no water has accumulated in the trenches.[76,77]

The waste handling operations at all the commercial sites are similar. The wastes shipped in 210-ℓ barrels, cardboard boxes, and other small containers are usually dumped randomly in the trenches. Although this uses more of the trench volume than orderly stacking of the wastes, it tends to minimize exposure to radiation and also to reduce labor costs. Large items such as tanks of spent ion exchange resins, contaminated equipment, and large blocks of wastes solidified in concrete are placed in the trenches with a crane. If the wastes were shipped to the site in a reusable shipping cask, they are usually removed from the cask prior to burial.

At the sites in humid areas the wastes are covered daily with soil or with tarpaulins to keep them dry. At the two commercial sites in arid regions the wastes are left uncovered until the trench has been filled.[46]

The wastes are dumped to within 0.6 to 1 m of the surface. The final cover is either the excavated earth or clay materials. The final depth of the cover varies from 1 to 3 m at the commercial sites. At the humid sites the cover is compacted. At all the sites the cover is mounded slightly over the trench to promote surface runoff. At the closing of the trenches permanent markers are placed at the ends of the trench or at each corner to identify the trench. In humid areas the trench caps are seeded with shallow-rooted grasses to minimize erosion.[46]

At the Barnwell site the newer trenches are placed with their centerlines approximately 66 m apart. This allows another 30 m wide trench to be placed between the other two at a later time. Since the trenches have a 1.5 m wide clay surface layer on each side, the entire site eventually will be capped with relatively impermeable clay. The clay materials are covered with 0.9 to 3 m of earth to prevent the clay from drying and cracking.

Except for the two compact-and-fill trenches at Sheffield, the wastes are not mechanically compacted in place as in a sanitary landfill. At Barnwell sand is backfilled in the void spaces.[76] Since some of the wastes are decomposable materials packed in cardboard boxes, the waste will eventually settle. Because other wastes are solid objects, the settling will not be uniform over the entire area of the trench. As the trench cap slumps in places, surface water can collect and percolate into the wastes. This slumping may also cause the trench cap to crack, giving any surface water a direct pathway into the waste cell. To avoid these potential problems the trench caps must be regraded and reseeded as required.

Some high-activity beta-gamma wastes received at commercial burial sites require shielding to protect the site personnel. To minimize exposure these are frequently buried in special slit trenches or dry wells. The slit trenches are typically 1 to 2 m wide. These may be lined with poured concrete walls or stacked 210-ℓ steel drums filled with other wastes. The dry wells are constructed by boring holes 0.3 to 0.6 m in diameter. These may be lined with concrete or steel pipes. Another method of constructing a dry well is to place a steel pipe vertically in a conventional trench. Wastes are dumped around the pipe and covered in the usual manner, leaving the top of the pipe exposed. Then high-activity wastes are placed in the pipe at a later time.[76]

These high-activity beta-gamma wastes are shipped to the site in shielded casks. Normally they are removed and buried without shielding. To minimize occupational exposure special casks that unload from the bottom have been designed.[23] After the wastes are placed in the trench or well, they are covered with concrete or soil to provide shielding.[46]

Although no longer permitted, large volumes of liquid wastes have been shipped to several commercial sites for disposal.[43] At Maxey Flats these liquid wastes were mixed with clay, cement, and newspapers in a commercial cement mixer. The slurry was poured into a polyethylene-lined trench to solidify. It was then covered with clay.[57]

Gaseous wastes such as ^{85}Kr or ^{3}H are buried at low-level sites. They must be at a pressure of 1 to 1.5 atm or less. The cylinder containing the gas is normally sealed in a steel can filled with a dessicant. The can is coated with tar and placed in a pipe which is sealed in concrete. This pipe is then buried in a trench.[46]

Activity of Individual Radionuclides at Burial Sites

In order to make environmental assessments of the potential impact of a burial site, it is not sufficient to know only the total activity of all radionuclides at the site, such as given in Table 9. It is important to have additional information such as the activity of individual radionuclides, their physical and chemical form, and their method of packaging. Although the sites are required to record the total activity and radionuclide compositions when possible, the records have been summarized only at the Maxey Flats site.

Clark[60] reported a preliminary inventory of the Maxey Flats site that was developed from a manual compilation of the site radioactive shipping records. He gave the waste volume, the total activity of the by-product materials, and the total masses of special nuclear and source materials that were buried in each trench through 1971. He also gave the activities of ^{3}H, ^{60}Co, ^{90}Sr, ^{137}Ce, ^{226}Ra, and ^{239}Pu buried in two separate trenches. Clark noted that many irregularities were found in the records and that much of the total activity was listed as mixed fission products or as not specifically identifiable radionuclides. The totals for the entire site are the same as those given by O'Connell and Holcomb[43] and by Holcomb.[42].

After the Maxey Flats manual records were transfered to a computer data base, Gat et al.[61] summarized the inventories of individual radionuclides in individual trenches. They also found errors and inaccuracies in the original manual records and in their transfer to the computer data base. They attempted to correct the records and deleted any irreconcilable records from their calculations.

Despite these attempts it is apparent that there are substantial differences between this study and the earlier one by Clark[60] and the data given by Holcomb.[42] Several examples are given below so that care will be taken in any future use of these results. Although Holcomb[1] reports that the total by-product material buried through the end of 1972 is 1.37×10^{6} Ci, Gat et al. reported that in 1974 the present activity of the wastes buried through the end of 1972 was 1.9×10^{7} Ci. This value was based on the totals of their corrected records, including the decay since burial. Presumably their figure may include the activity of the special nuclear and source materials but, according to Cohen and Jow,[78] these total less than 1.6×10^{4} Ci.

In addition to questions raised by Gat et al.[61] and by Cohen and Jow[78] on the validity of the records for certain radionuclides such as ^{226}Ra, it is apparent that there are other errors. Although Gat et al. did indicate that several extremely large shipments were not included in their study, the omission of a single 6.55×10^{5} Ci shipment of ^{3}H that was specifically mentioned by O'Connell and Holcomb[43] and by Clark[60] resulted in an order of magnitude underestimate of the total ^{3}H buried at the site. On the other hand, Gat et al. reported that over 4.55×10^{5} Ci of ^{207}Bi were deposited in a single trench. This was not reported by Clark in either the summary of the total activity deposited in that trench or in a table listing special authorizations for burials exceeding the 5000 Ci limit for the site. Also there are inconsistencies between the results of Clark[60] and those of Gat et al.[61] in the total activity in several of the trenches and in their radionuclide composition.

Two other errors in their data are apparent. In the legend to several of their tables they state that the units for fissile material are grams and the units for special nuclear material are pounds instead of special nuclear material in grams and source material in pounds. Cohen and Jow[78] followed the latter interpretation when they converted these quantities to curies. Also, comparison of the values given in their tables for the total activity in the trench and for the radionuclide composition indicates that in some cases values in curies, grams, and pounds were added indiscriminately to give their estimates total activity in individual trenches.

The work by Clark[60] and by Gat et al.[61] does give an indication of how the wastes were buried at Maxey Flats. For example, a significant fraction of the ^{60}Co listed was buried in a small number of special hot wells which probably indicates that they were sealed sources or highly neutron-activated metal components. In either case the ^{60}Co would be much less mobile than if it were distributed throughout the wastes. The

Table 11
RADIONUCLIDE INVENTORIES AND AVERAGE CONCENTRATION AT LOW LEVEL BURIAL SITES

	Maxey Flats[a]		Reference facility[b]	
adionuclide	Total activity (Ci)	Average concentration (Ci/m³)	Total activity (Ci)	Average concentration (Ci/m³)
^{3}H[c]	7.18×10^{5}	7.3	2.7×10^{6}	4.3
^{14}C	2.52×10^{4}	0.3	9.4×10^{4}	0.15
^{55}Fe	1.30×10^{2}	1.5×10^{-3}	1.6×10^{5}	2.6
^{60}Co	1.05×10^{5}	1.2	4.8×10^{5}	0.77
^{90}Sr	7.80×10^{3}	0.09	1.8×10^{3}	2.9×10^{-3}
^{99}Tc	7	8.2×10^{-5}	12	1.9×10^{-5}
^{125}Sb	1.20×10^{3}	0.014	—	—
^{129}I	0.011	1.3×10^{-7}	2.4	3.8×10^{-6}
^{135}Cs	1.37×10^{-3}	1.6×10^{-8}	12.0	1.9×10^{-5}
^{137}Cs	2.43×10^{4}	0.29	3.2×10^{5}	0.51
^{147}Pm	1.23×10^{3}	0.014	—	—
^{154}Eu	1.57×10^{4}	0.18	—	—
^{207}Bi[d]	4.52×10^{5}	5.3	—	—
^{226}Ra[d]	4.8×10^{3}	0.056	—	—
MFP[e]	5.6×10^{5}	6.7	—	—
^{235}U	0.38	4.5×10^{-6}	20	3.5×10^{-5}
^{238}U	70.9	8.3×10^{-4}	450	7.1×10^{-4}
^{238}Pu	1.35×10^{4}	0.16	82	1.3×10^{-4}
^{239}U	1.47×10^{3}	0.017	11	1.7×10^{-5}
^{240}Pu	—	—	17	2.7×10^{-5}
^{241}Pu	46.9	5.5×10^{-4}	4.2×10^{3}	6.7×10^{-5}
^{241}Am	198.0	2.3×10^{-3}	8.2	1.3×10^{-5}
^{244}Cm	—	—	48	7.6×10^{-5}
Other TRU listed	0.04	4.7×10^{-7}	0.75	1.2×10^{-6}

[a] Based on Gat et al.[61] for the 1974 present value of wastes buried 1963—1972 with Holcomb's[1] 1972 accumulated waste volumes. Values not listed are unavailable. See text.
[b] Based on Reference 79. Values not listed are unavailable.
[c] 6.55×10^{5} Ci added to value of Gat et al. for Maxey Flats.
[d] See text. Quantities are especially questionable
[e] MFP includes totals for mixed fission products, not specifically identifiable, not otherwise specified, and low specific activity.

source material and most of the special nuclear material were buried in the large trenches.

Despite possible errors, these data are the available that indicate individual radionuclides buried at low-level sites. Table 11 gives the total activity and average concentrations for individual radionuclides for Maxey Flats. These are based on the 1974 present activity of the wastes buried from 1963 to 1972 as given by Gat et al. The accumulated volume of wastes through 1972 was from Holcomb.[42] The ^{3}H value was increased by 6.55×10^{5} Ci to account for a single shipment that was not included by Gat et al. The table also gives values used by the Nuclear Regulatory Commission in a generic impact study.[79] These values are for a reference facility with a waste capacity of 6.3×10^{5} m³. These average concentrations may have little significance for those radionuclides buried in a few high-activity packages.

Average concentrations of by-product material, special nuclear material, and source material for all six commercial sites are given in Table 12.

Table 12
AVERAGE CONCENTRATIONS AT COMMERCIAL BURIAL SITES THROUGH 1978

	By-product material (Ci/m^3)	Special nuclear material (g/m^3)	Source material (kg/m^3)
West Valley	8.7	0.9	7.0
Maxey Flats	17.8	3.2	2.1
Barnwell	7.4	4.3	5.5
Sheffield	0.7	0.7	3.1
Beatty	2.4	10.3	1.9
Richland	30.1	4.3	0.8

Adapted from Holcomb, W. F., Inventory (1962—1978) and projections (to 2000) of shallow land burial of radioactive wastes at commercial sites, *Nucl. Saf.*, 21, 380—388, 1980.

Integrity of Wastes and Waste Containers

Radioactive wastes that are held in their burial container or within the burial trench pose little environmental threat unless the wastes are uncovered or exhumed. In the past the assumption that the radionuclides would be readily sorbed and retained by the soil surrounding the trench led to a de-emphasis on the integrity of the waste packages in containing the wastes. Since radionuclides have migrated from the burial trenches at several commercial sites, there is renewed interest in improving the waste containers to improve the short-term containment of certain wastes.

A wide variety of waste forms and containers have been sent to commercial low-level burial sites. Most can be grouped into five general categories: (1) cardboard and wooden boxes and fiberboard drums, (2) thin-walled steel drums, (3) solidified wastes which may be in drums or metal boxes, (4) dewatered, spent ion exchange resins in steel containers, and (5) relatively immobile nonfuel bearing components and sealed sources.

The wastes in cardboard boxes, wooden boxes, and fiberboard drums are usually the dry wastes from fuel and nonfuel cycle generators such as contaminated paper products, clothing, labware, and tools. These containers may have a plastic bag liner. The wastes are the low specific-activity, low-beta-gamma wastes that are shipped without a shielded cask.

In the trench these containers have limited lives. They may be crushed in compacting the trench cap. In a humid area, trench moisture and soil bacteria will decompose both the container and the organic fraction of the wastes in a period of months to years. This will release radionuclides to the trench and produce organic decomposition products that may act as chelating and complexing agents for radionuclides. The decay will produce gaseous decay products that can carry away ^{3}H and ^{14}C. These gases can increase the pressure in a sealed container until it bursts or leaks. In arid areas the decomposition of the container will occur much more slowly.

In studies on the problems of exhuming buried wastes, containers were exhumed at the Idaho National Engineering Laboratory.[80,81] This site has a semi-arid climate with 200 mm annual average precipitation. Cardboard boxes buried for 7 years had disintegrated and the surrounding soil was contaminated with their wastes. Plywood boxes that had been buried for 5 to 8 years were in very poor condition. The ½-in. plywood lids could easily be torn off and the nominally 2 × 4 in. support members were rotten. The boxes could not be removed intact. In humid areas the containers should deteriorate more quickly.

A very popular container is the standard 210-ℓ (55-gal), light steel drum which may have a plastic bag liner. These are used for a variety of wastes including dry wastes, absorbed liquids, animal carcasses, scintillation vials, and solidified wastes from nuclear reactors.

The exhumation study at the Idaho burial grounds showed the condition of drums buried at a semi-arid site.[80,81] Drums that had been stacked in an orderly manner and buried were in good condition after 18 months. Very few had leaked and nearly all drum identification labels were legible. Stacked drums that had been buried for 12 years were in poor condition due to corrosion. The surrounding soil was contaminated with radionuclides. Drums that had been randomly dumped and buried for 3 to 7 years were much more difficult to exhume. Many of these drums had been physically damaged in the dumping and in the compaction of the trench.

A similar exhumation study was conducted at the Savannah River Plant which has 1100 mm average annual precipitation. This study showed that some containers buried for 7 years had substantially deteriorated and their wastes had contaminated the soil.[81] A review of the major factors in the corrosion of steel drums in soil has been given in Colombo and Neilson.[82]

If wastes are completely solidified in drums or metal boxes with hydraulic cement, urea formaldehyde, or bitumen asphalt, they should be contained for longer periods. If the metal container fails, the radionuclides must be leached from the wastes by water. Unless the trench is flooded, the total amounts of radionuclides released will be limited by the rate at which water percolates through the wastes and by the rate of leaching.

Experience has shown that the wastes may not be completely solidified. Free standing water can be present in the drum. Occasionally the wastes may not solidify and there have been problems with capping drums.[22,25] In these cases radionuclides may be released from the container shortly after burial.

Colombo and Neilson[82] have conducted tests on the solidification and free standing water for simulated reactor wastes and various solidification media. With portland cements, they found that the time to solidify and the product hardness depend on the waste/cement ratio. Boric acid wastes were especially difficult to solidify. Adjustment of the pH to 10 with sodium hydroxide, low waste/cement ratios, and the addition of proprietary agents were found helpful in some cases. Masonry cement had a greater ability to solidify boric acid wastes than portland cement. The tests showed that free standing water was present at higher waste/cement ratios. The radionuclide concentrations of this free standing water showed lower concentrations of ^{60}Co and ^{85}Sr and the same concentration of ^{137}Cs as in the waste. This was attributed to a selective ion-exchange process with the cement. The solidified wastes had average compressive strengths of 300 to 20,000 kPa (about 40 to 3000 psi). The solidified waste generally had improved strength at lower waste/cement ratios.

Tests with urea-formaldehyde showed that some free standing water was present for most simulated wastes. The amount of free standing water generally had a maximum at low waste/UF ratios and then decreased. The free standing water was acidic and had essentially the same concentration of ^{137}Cs, ^{85}Sr, and ^{60}Co as the wastes. The average compressive strength of the solidified waste was found to be 450 to 3000 kPa (about 60 to 400 psi).

Since the bitumen solidification systems should evaporate the water in the wastes, there should be no free standing water in the solidified wastes. Free standing water was not observed for vinyl ester-styrene solidification media.[82]

The rate at which radionuclides can be leached from a solidified waste depends on its physical and chemical properties, chemical reactions between the radionuclides and the solidification media, and the chemical nature of the leachate. For example, consider solidification with cement. The presence of salts such as chlorides and sulfates can lead to a rapid rate of decomposition of the cement, and organic matter may retard its solidification.[83] The radionuclides in the waste may participate in the hydration reactions with the cement or they may remain with the interstitial water in the concrete which slowly diffuses out of the cement. If the radionuclides react with the cement, the cement must be dissolved or destroyed to release the nuclides.[84] In either case the rate of release will depend on the chemical nature of the water in contact with cement. For example, acidic solutions can damage the cement to form soluble calcium sulfate or to form insoluble calcium sulfoaluminates that expand and weaken the concrete.[83] This dissolution and destruction of the cement will release radionuclides.

Colombo and Neilson[82] have reported leaching tests for different solidification media. The test was either a modification of the procedure proposed by the International Atomic Energy Agency in which the leachate was routinely replaced with fresh leachate or an equilibrium procedure that had no leachate replacement. The typical waste specimens were cylindrical with a 2.54 cm diameter and 5.08 cm length. Tests were conducted with a simulated BWR chemical regenerative waste containing ^{137}Cs, ^{85}Sr, and ^{60}Co. In the modified IAEA procedure with distilled water as the leachate, the release of ^{137}Cs and ^{85}Sr was high for UF and cement and much lower for vinyl ester-styrene. The leaching of ^{60}Co was very low for cement. Similar results were found for the equilibrium tests with the exception that the ^{85}Sr release rate from cement was very low. There was evidence that UF and cement media reabsorbed a small fraction of the ^{137}Cs released. Additional leaching tests for cement with different wastes have been reported by Colombo and Neilson.[85]

Tests were conducted using distilled water and a groundwater with bitumen for the BWR chemical regenerative waste and for boric acid wastes. The BWR waste-bitumen samples had a tendency to crack, swell, and break up during the test. This was caused by the hydration of the Na_2SO_4 in the waste which occupies a larger volume than the original anhydrous form. This degradation was not observed for the boric acid wastes. In these tests radionuclides were not added to the waste. For the BWR waste nearly all the sulfate was released from a 4.9 cm-diameter, 10-cm long specimen in 10 days. The release of boron from the boric acid waste specimen occurred much more slowly. In 100 days approximately 10% was released.[82]

Additional tests should be conducted using other wastes typical of those found in the nuclear power industry. Since the leaching rate could also change with the character of the leachate, tests should be conducted with water at various pH values and with synthetic or actual trench leachates.

Some nuclear plants dewater their ion-exchange resins and ship for burial without solidification. Colombo and Neilson[82] have reported data from leaching tests for ^{137}Cs and ^{85}Sr on a bead resin and a powdered resin. They used the modified IAEA procedure with distilled water and with seawater. After 90 days in the distilled water tests, the bead resin had released 1.4% of the ^{137}Cs and about 0.1% of the ^{85}Sr. The powdered resin released about 18% of the ^{137}Cs and 24% of the ^{85}Sr. In the tests with seawater nearly all the radionuclides were released in 2 to 5 days from both the bead and powdered resins.

Neutron-activated nonfuel bearing components from the core of a reactor and sealed sources may contain an appreciable amount of the activity of radionuclides such as ^{60}Co. The radionuclides in these wastes are relatively immobile. If they are imbedded in concrete, the concrete must be chemically destroyed or dissolved before these wastes are exposed to the trench environment. If they are buried without a container or concrete, the radionuclides can be released only through the corrosion of the metal itself. Although the rate of corrosion will depend on the chemistry of the trench leachate, this should be a relatively slow process compared to the half-life of radionuclides such

Table 13
ENVIRONMENTAL MONITORING PROGRAMS AT THE U.S. COMMERCIAL BURIAL SITES

Disposal site	Water	Air	Vegetation	Soil	Other
Barnwell	10 onsite wells, semiannually; offsite water supplies, annually	Offsite, continuous	Offsite, annually	Offsite, weekly	Offsite, animals, annually
Beatty	1 onsite well, monthly; offsite wells, monthly	Continuous	Offsite, quarterly	Offsite, quarterly	None
Maxey Flats[a]	8 onsite wells, monthly; offsite water samples quarterly	Continuous	4 samples onsite, 4 offsite, quarterly	4 samples onsite, 4 offsite, quarterly	None
Richland	3 onsite wells, quarterly; offsite surface water, semiannually	Continuous	Onsite, quarterly	Onsite, quarterly	None
Sheffield[a]	8 onsite wells, quarterly; offsite surface water, quarterly	Continuous	Offsite, quarterly	Offsite, quarterly	None
West Valley[a]	2 onsite streams, quarterly; offsite surface water, weekly	Offsite, continuous	Offsite, annually	Offsite, quarterly	Offsite, animals and fish, semiannually; milk, weekly

[a] These are the reported monitoring activities when these sites were operational. Present monitoring may be different.

From *Improvements Needed in the Land Disposal of Radioactive Wastes — A Problem of Centuries,* Rep. RED-76-54, Office of the Comptroller General of the U.S., Washington, D.C., 1976.

as ^{60}Co (5.3 years) and ^{55}Fe (2.7 years). For longer-lived nuclides such as ^{63}Ni (100 years or ^{59}Ni (8×10^4 years), the metals may be completely corroded before significant decay has occurred.

Environmental Monitoring at Commercial Sites

As a condition of their license, the commercial burial sites are required to conduct routine monitoring for radionuclides. Table 13 shows the existing monitoring programs at the commercial sites.

Environmental monitoring programs should be designed to provide an early warning system to detect any migration of radionuclides so that corrective actions can be taken to minimize its impact. As a secondary purpose the program should adequately document the potential dose to people living adjacent to the burial site. The types of samples and sampling frequency should be determined by the site characteristics and the wastes accepted for burial.

For sites in humid climates an intensive effort must be placed on monitoring the ground and surface waters for radionuclides. Test wells need to be placed near the trenches to attempt to detect early movement of ^{3}H and other radionuclides. There should be additional wells near the site perimeter to document the presence or lack of radionuclides. Any wells in the vicinity of the site used for drinking water should also be routinely sampled. Except in the simplest cases of sites in unfractured, nearly homogeneous soils, there are no acceptable methods for determining the number or placement of these test wells. If the formations are fractured or have pockets or seams of permeable materials, water and radionuclides could flow between the near wells without detection.[6]

The surface runoff should be sampled to determine if radionuclides are being carried offsite as has already occurred at several sites. In addition to collecting surface runoff during storm events, continuous low flow samplers can be operated on nearby streams so that monitoring for radionuclide migration from runoff or discharge of groundwater is continuous.

In addition to radionuclide monitoring, basic hydrological data should be taken to understand and document the movement of water onto and off the site. At a minimum this should include total precipitation, temperature, pan evaporation, and the fluctuations of the water levels in wells on the site. Studies should be undertaken to document the surface runoff for various storm types for both the area over the trenches and the undisturbed land on the site. These hydrological data should be integrated to provide estimates of the net percolation of water through the trench caps and through undisturbed soil.

If water occurs in the trenches it should be sampled for radionuclides. Due to the anoxic nature of the trench water at Maxey Flats, special sampling procedures had to be developed to avoid precipitating the radionuclides from the water.[86] Chemical analysis of the water should be conducted to determine its pH, Eh, dissolved oxygen, organic and total carbon, and for the presence of organic complexing agents.

The air should be routinely monitored for both radioactive dusts that may be dispersed at the time of waste burial or suspended later and for radioactive gases that may emanate from the trenches. Samples of the gases in the trenches should be surveyed for radionuclides such as ^{3}H, ^{14}C, ^{85}Kr, ^{129}I, and ^{222}Rn.

The surface soil should be sampled to determine if it has been contaminated by spills or leaks from poorly packaged wastes or wastes damaged in shipment or burial. Soil samples should be routinely taken from the trench wall at or below the level of the trench bottom to determine if migration has occurred. Samples of the soil beneath the older trenches could be taken by boring at an angle from either the surface or from a newly dug trench adjacent to the older one. If radionuclides are detected, a series of samples at various distances from the trenches should be taken to determine the extent of migration as well as actual measurements of the sorptive capacity of the soil.

Since vegetation can take up radionuclides, routine samples of the onsite and offsite vegetation should be assayed for radionuclides.

In addition to the personal dosimeters worn by all site workers there is a need to survey all people and vehicles leaving the site to ensure that contamination has not occurred and will not be spread offsite.

ENVIRONMENTAL PROBLEMS AT LOW-LEVEL BURIAL SITES

Within the next decade there will be a need to expand the remaining commercial sites or to establish new sites in the U.S. To minimize transportation costs at least one site in the eastern half of the country would be desirable. Such a site would be in a humid climate and have a higher potential for the migration of radionuclides from the burial trenches than a site in an arid region. In light of the problems at Maxey Flats and West Valley, the closing of these sites and the Sheffield site, and because of a heightened public awareness concerning exposure to ionizing radiation and nuclear waste disposal, the siting, design, and operation of any new site must be done with great concern for the potential for migration of radionuclides. The following discussion examines factors that need to be considered for an environmental assessment of a site. Since the potential environmental impacts will depend on the site characteristics, trench design, and wastes buried, no estimates of their magnitude are presented.

Water-Borne Transport

The most recognized problem at burial grounds is the potential for radionuclide transport with water. In order to predict the potential for migration, the movement of water must be understood.

The local water budget starts with the input due to precipitation. Rain falling on the site will either run off or percolate down into the soil. Snow falling on the site must first melt before it seeps into the ground or runs off. Water that runs off the trench cap may percolate into the undisturbed soil adjacent to the trench. If either the cap or the site is uneven, water may temporarily collect in small pools before percolating downward or before being evaporated back to the atmosphere.

Water that enters the soil may continue to percolate down through the unsaturated zone to the saturated zone or into the trench itself. On the other hand, water in the unsaturated zone may be returned to the atmosphere by capillarity, plant uptake, and evaporation.

Water can enter the trench by percolation through the trench cap, by lateral transport through the trench walls, or by an increase in the height of the water table. In addition, water and other liquids are released from the wastes due to leaks in their containers or from biological decay of the wastes.

The infiltration of water through the trench cap will depend upon its permeability. To achieve a low permeability, the trench cap is frequently made with clayey materials. If this clay is allowed to become too dry, the clay will crack. Cracks may also be formed by uneven settling of the waste and slumping of the cap. If cracking occurs, large amounts of water can enter the trench with the next rainfall, as apparently occurred at the West Valley site.[64]

If the soil adjacent to the trench is more permeable than the trench cap, significant quantities of water can percolate downward and then laterally through the trench wall. If there is a nearly horizontal, impervious layer near the surface, water may be trapped or perched on this layer. This may form a permanent perched water table or may only occur during wet seasons or in the wettest years. Depending on the position of the perched water table and the lateral permeability of the soil, this water may flow laterally until it intersects the trench.

If the saturated zone or water table is near the trench bottom, an increase in the height of the water table due to increased precipitation could flood the trenches. At many locations, there is an annual fluctuation of the water table with the lowest levels at the end of a dry season and highest at the end of a rainy season. For example, Siple[87] reported that the water level in two wells at the Savannah River Plant showed annual fluctuations with the highest levels less than 1 m to annual lows of 5 to 6 m below the surface. Several seasons or years of unusually high precipitation could cause a dramatic increase in the level of a water table.

In addition to the water entering the trench, there will be small amounts of water and other liquids in the wastes. These can be present as uncombined water in solidified wastes, absorbed liquids, water in biological tissues and excreta, and water from wastes soaked by precipitation before burial. This water will be released as these wastes and their containers decay and corrode.

Water can leave the trench by percolation through the trench bottom and walls, by flowing through cracks, fissures, old root holes or permeable materials, by vapor diffusion through the soil, by evapotranspiration, and if the trench is flooded, by seepage up through the trench cap. At several sites water has been pumped from the trenches and treated to remove some radionuclides by evaporation[58] or by physical-chemical treatment before release to surface waters.[67]

Groundwater Hydrology

A major concern in the siting of low-level burial sites has been the fate of radionuclides that have percolated to the saturated zone or water table. In this saturated zone they can be carried by the water flow until it eventually seeps back to surface waters, is pumped from the ground at a well, or is taken up by deep-rooted vegetation.

The major processes involved in radionuclide transport in the saturated zone are convection by the bulk water flow, dispersion by variations in the soil's permeability, and sorption of radionuclides by the soil materials. A mathematical theory of the transport of sorbable radionuclides in relatively homogeneous soil materials without interfering or competing chemical agents has been developed and has been tested in laboratory experiments and in reasonably simple field situations.[88] The potential for difficulties arises when this theory is applied with blithe optimism to highly fractured formations, to relatively impermeable materials interbedded with layers of sand or coarse gravel, for water contaminated with chelating and complexing agents, or to the nonsorbable fraction of radionuclides.

An overly simplified view of groundwater transport that has been used in siting some burial sites is to obtain the average permeability of the soil from core samples taken at the site and the height of the water table from wells on the site. From the average permeability and the slope of the water table, the average speed and direction of groundwater flow can be estimated. This determination is used to estimate the minimum time for radionuclides to be transported back into the public domain. For those radionuclides that may be readily exchanged with the soil, an additional delay factor accounting for sorption is included. If the computed travel time is significantly longer than the half-life of the radionuclide, the decay time in the soil may be sufficient to render the radionuclide harmless.

If there are open fractures or thin layers of permeable materials, these methods can overestimate the travel time with a corresponding underestimate of the potential danger. In these cases a portion of the groundwater can take the path of least resistance through this fracture or porous layer. Even if there are no chemical agents inhibiting sorption, the sorptive capacity of this layer will be small and readily saturated. This may allow a fraction of the radionuclides that reach the saturated zone to be quickly transported back to surface waters. Such a pathway is one of several mechanisms proposed to explain the migration of radionuclides at Maxey Flats.[58]

Trench Leachate Characteristics

The wastes buried at a low-level radioactive disposal site contain a wide variety of organic and inorganic compounds. These include scintillation fluids, decontamination solutions, boric acid wastes, and laboratory chemicals. In addition, there is a significant quantity of organic material such as cardboard boxes, paper products, animal carcasses, and excreta that decompose to produce other organic compounds. These chemicals and the soil itself will affect the chemistry of any water in the trench.

The leachate produced may act to accelerate the decomposition or corrosion of other waste containers in the trench. If the leachate is mildly acidic, it may speed the dissolution of cements used in solidifying the wastes. Complexing agents in the waste may prevent the exchange of radionuclides to the surrounding soil. The leachate may have high concentrations of inorganic cations such as sodium, potassium, calcium, and magnesium or stable strontium and cesium that reduce the capacity of the soil to sorb the lower concentrations of radionuclides.

Water samples have been taken from several trenches at Maxey Flats[89] and from West Valley.[90] Table 14 shows a summary of the pH, dissolved organic carbon (DOC), specific conductance, and inorganic ions at these two sites and for typical values of sanitary landfill leachate.[91] With several exceptions the trench water from these two sites had dissolved organic carbon and inorganic ion concentrations similar to typical sanitary landfill leachate.

Table 14
WATER CHEMISTRY AT MAXEY FLATS, WEST VALLEY AND TYPICAL SANITARY LANDFILLS

	Maxey Flats[a]	West Valley[b]	Sanitary landfill[c]
pH	2.4—12.1	6.7—7.5	5.3—8.5
Specific conductance (micromhos/cm at 25°C)	2.3×10^3—9.4×10^3	3.9×10^3—8.8×10^3	
DOC[d]	7.3—5600	200—3,600	1,500—20,000
Calcium	44—650	72—300	200— 3,000
Magnesium	0.08—320	130—220	200—2,000
Potassium	4—280	120—340	200—2,000
Sodium	180—1,900	500—1,600	200—2,000
Iron	<0.01—1,200	13—260	50—600
Strontium	<0.1—7.0	0.9—8.3	
Cesium	<0.05—0.2	<0.1—0.5	
Chloride	140—3,900	230—2,100	100—3,000
Sulfate	<1—1,200	<5—75	100—1,500
Silica	1—130	6.8—26	

[a] Data compiled from Reference 87. Data represent extreme range of values for samples from seven trenches and one sample from an observation well adjacent to a trench.
[b] Data compiled from Reference 88. Data represent extreme range of values for samples from six trenches.
[c] Data compiled from Reference 89.
[d] Concentrations of dissolved organic carbon (DOC) and all ions are expressed in mg/ℓ.

Trench water samples from Maxey Flats and West Valley were analyzed using a gas chromatograph-mass spectrometer to identify specific organic compounds.[89,90] Dozens of compounds including toluene, xylene, tributyl phosphate, and many organic acids, alcohols, phenols, aldehydes, ketones, and amines were found. Microbial analysis of the Maxey Flats trench leachate was also performed.[89]

The water chemistry characteristics at low-level burial sites that have not had severe flooding of the trenches have not been reported. Because of differences in their wastes, soil chemistry, and quantity of water available, any leachate could be significantly different from the Maxey Flats or West Valley leachates.

Sorption of Radionuclides by the Soil

Radionuclides in the trench leachate or groundwater may be in a soluble or an insoluble form. The soluble forms can be subdivided into the sorbable and nonsorbable fractions. Most of the sorbable fraction exists in a charged or ionic state that can participate in ion exchange reactions with the clay minerals in the soil. The nonsorbable materials are probably in a complexed or polymerized state that is not readily adsorbed or ion exchanged to the soil. Due to chemical and biochemical reactions, the radionuclides may shift from one form to another.[92]

The principal sorption mechanism with clays is by cationic or anionic exchange. This sorption retards the movement of the radionuclides with respect to the bulk water flow. Under ideal conditions such as in laboratory tests, the migration velocity of the radionuclides may be a factor of 10^2 to 10^4 or more times slower than the groundwater velocity. Since these idealized laboratory tests rarely simulate actual field conditions, the direct transfer of these relative migration velocities to the siting of low-level burial sites can lead to an underestimate of the radionuclide transport. If this optimistic view of sorption is coupled with a hydrological model that ignores permeability anomalies, the predicted migration of radionuclides in the ground-water at some sites may be much lower than will actually be observed.

The ion exchange capacity of clay minerals varies with the radionuclide, the type of clay mineral, and the conditions used in the test. Many laboratory tests are conducted using distilled water with the addition of the radionuclide in an ionic form. The exchange capacity is expressed as milliequivalents per 100 g of soil. Typical laboratory values for cation exchange capacities range from 80 to 150 meq/100 g for minerals such as montmorillonite or vermiculite to 3 to 15 meq/100 g for kaolinite. Anion exchange capacities typically are less than or equal to the cationic exchange capacities.[93] The actual exchange capacity will depend on factors such as the pH, ionic strength, and concentrations of specific ions in the water.

In the siting of low-level burial grounds, an overly simplified approach considers sorption as an irreversible process with the exchange capacity based on laboratory measurements. This assumes that all radionuclides are in a sorbable form, that there is no competition for exchange from stable nuclides, and that the pH is the same as the laboratory conditions. For the leachates found at Maxey Flats and West Valley, these assumptions are not valid and this approach is incorrect.

A more proper view is to consider the sorption as a reversible process in which both sorption and desorption occur. If the groundwater velocities are slow compared to the sorption rate, equilibrium values can be used to predict the sorption. The equilibrium ratio of the radionuclide sorbed to the clay to the radionuclides in the water phase is called the distribution coefficient. For example, the distribution coefficient for strontium and a particular clay would be given by

$$K_d = \frac{[Sr\,(clay)_2]}{[Sr^{2+}]} \tag{2}$$

where the brackets indicate concentrations. The higher the distribution coefficient, the greater is the adsorption by the clay.

Since the actual ion exchange reactions are not well understood, a generalized approach based on overall exchange reactions is adopted. For example, consider a simple example from Tamura,[94] on strontium exchange on a sodium clay.

$$Sr^{2+} + 2\,Na - clay \rightleftarrows Sr\,(clay)_2 + 2Na^+ \tag{3}$$

The equilibrium constant or selectivity coefficient for this reaction is

$$K_{Na}^{Sr} = \frac{[Sr\,(clay)_2\,]\,[Na^+]^2}{[Sr^{2+}]\,\,[Na\,\,(clay)\,]} \tag{4}$$

If the strontium concentration is low and the clay is nearly saturated with sodium, the distribution coefficient can be expressed as

$$K_d = \frac{K^1}{[Na^+]^2} \tag{5}$$

where K^1 equals K_{Na}^{Sr} $[Na-(clay)]^2$. Tamura shows that K_d does decrease inversely with the square of the water sodium concentration for several clay minerals.

In a more realistic situation, the strontium would have to compete for exchange sites with other cations in the waters such as calcium, potassium, and magnesium. Also the strontium has opportunities to exchange with ions on the clay which are not sodium. Because of these factors, empirical distribution coefficients must be determined for each radionuclide. These tests should duplicate the conditions that will be found in the field.

If K_d is known, then the ratio of the velocity of the groundwater velocity, V, to the migration velocity of the radionuclide, V_R, is

$$\frac{V}{V_R} = 1 + \rho\left(\frac{1-f}{f}\right) K_d \qquad (6)$$

in which ϱ is the bulk soil density and f is the soil porosity.[88] For high values of K_d and low soil porosity, the radionuclide migration can occur at a substantially slower rate than the groundwater flow.

There is limited information on distribution coefficients for contaminated waters found at some low-level burial sites. In a review of the mobility of plutonium in soils, Francis[95] noted that its sorption was pH dependent, that high concentrations of salts caused a drastic reduction in plutonium sorption, that several organic compounds including tributyl phosphate were effective in leaching ^{85}Sr, ^{137}Cs, ^{239}Pu, and ^{241}Am from soils, and that laboratory measurements on intact soil cores may not give an accurate indication of radionuclide transport under field conditions. He cautioned that organic matter in the soil could play a significant role in the mobilization of plutonium. Cleveland and Rees[96] found that natural humic substances increased the solubilization of plutonium and americium.

As seen in Table 14, the trench waters at Maxey Flats and West Valley have high concentrations of inorganic salts and organic materials. The sodium, calcium, magnesium, and potassium are sufficiently high to decrease the distribution coefficient for radionuclides. The samples had stable cesium and strontium concentrations that will compete with radiocesium and radiostrontium for ion exchange. The organic compounds found in the water such as tributyl phosphate aid in leaching from the wastes or clay.

Colombo and Weiss[97] report preliminary data on distribution coefficients for ^{60}Co, ^{85}Sr, ^{134}Cs, and ^{137}Cs using West Valley leachate spiked with one of these radionuclides and West Valley soil. They conducted batch tests using the anoxic trench water, a 1:10 dilution of anoxic trench water, trench water exposed to air and then filtered to remove precipitates, and slightly acidified, de-ionized water. The K_d values for ^{134}Cs and^{137}Cs were greater than 1800 mℓ/g for the de-ionized water and about 30 mℓ/g for the anoxic trench water and 120 mℓ/g for the diluted trench water. The ^{60}Co had values greater than 900 mℓ/gm for the de-ionized water, about 20 mℓ/g for the anoxic trench water and about 115 mℓ/g for the diluted trench water. The tests with the air-exposed trench water had K_d values in the range of 20 to 30 mℓ/g for these three radionuclides. The tests using ^{85}Sr had a value of only 20 mℓ/g with the de-ionized trench water and around 10 mℓ/g for both the anoxic trench water and diluted anoxic trench water.

These investigations show that actual distribution coefficients are a complex function of the soil and water chemistry. If there are high concentrations of inorganic and organic compounds in the leachate, the distribution coefficients and exchange capacities will be much lower than those predicted from laboratory tests using inorganic salts in distilled water. At present there is no satisfactory method of predicting distribution coefficients and the transport of sorbable radionuclides in these situations. Also it must be assumed that the nonsorbable fraction will be transported with the groundwater.

Evapotranspiration and Radionuclide Transport

In addition to the downward and lateral transport of water and radionuclides, there can be upward movement in the soil due to capillarity, vapor diffusion, evaporation, plant uptake, and transpiration. Evapotranspirative movement can transport radionuclides; on the other hand, it reduces infiltration of surface water into the burial trenches.

In the unsaturated zone above the water table, the water movement in the soil is by capillary conductivity and vapor diffusion. Its direction is determined by the soil moisture gradient. If the surface soil is saturated by precipitation or local ponding of water, the flow will be downward. As evaporation dries out the surface, the soil moisture gradient will reverse and the water will flow upward. The rate of flow depends on the magnitude of the gradient and the soil properties. In addition to these processes, plants will carry moisture upward through their roots and transpire this water through their leaves.

The capillary conduction in the unsaturated zone can carry soluble radionuclides upward. The sorbable fraction of the radionuclides can be exchanged onto clay minerals as also occurs in the saturated zone. This retards the motion of the sorbed radionuclides with respect to the water movement. At very low soil moisture, capillary conductivity ceases. The remaining upward transport of water is by vapor diffusion.[98] In the vapor phase the only radionuclide transported is ^{3}H as tritiated water vapor (HTO). It is eventually lost to the atmosphere.

In arid regions the soil moisture is low and the water table may be 100 m or more deep. The only water-borne mechanism that can transport radionuclides a significant distance from the trenches is the vapor diffusion of ^{3}H. Although it is suspected that this is occurring at the Beatty, Richland, and Los Alamos sites, it has not yet been observed.[46] There have been no estimates of the potential concentrations of ^{3}H in the air above the site due to its gradual release from the trenches.

Plants take up water and radionuclides through their root systems. The plants discriminate against many radionuclides as the water passes through the plant tissues. The uptake by a plant is a function of the soil moisture, radionuclide concentration, and the concentration of stable ions in the soil. The presence of chelating agents in the soil increases the uptake of some ions by the plant.[95,99]

Evapotranspiration is an important element in the water balance at a burial site. If it is relatively high the infiltration of surface waters into the trenches can be reduced. It can be enhanced by careful selection of vegetation and soil materials for the trench cap to maximize evapotranspiration while being compatible with the goals of high surface runoff and low cap permeability.

Airborne Emissions of Radionuclides

In addition to the release of ^{3}H to the atmosphere by vapor diffusion and evaporation, there are other potential pathways for the release of radionuclides to the atmosphere including gaseous emanations, dust dispersal, fires, and emissions from evaporators used to treat trench water.[100] These releases can cause increased exposure to the site personnel and to those living near the site.

Radioactive gases can be released from the waste in the trench due to the decomposition of the waste, corrosion of cylinders containing radioactive gases, desorption of gases and vapors from the wastes, and the production of radioactive decay products. These gases can diffuse through the trench cap, flow to the surface through sump pipes or cracks in the trench cap, migrate laterally through cracks or permeable layers in the unsaturate zone or be absorbed by the trench waters.

Since a fraction of the low-level wastes are paper products and other organic, putrescible materials, they will eventually decompose or biologically decay. This should be similar to the decay of organic wastes in a sanitary landfill. Initially this should be aerobic decay producing mostly CO_2. As the oxygen supply in the trench is depleted, the anaerobic decay will take over to produce both CO_2 and CH_4 as well as smaller amounts of gases such as NH_3 and H_2S. As much as 0.7 m^3 gas can be generated from each kilogram of decomposable organic matter. The rate of gas generation will depend on the water content in the wastes. If water is kept from entering the trenches, the gas production will be low.[91] The gases generated will contain a fraction of any ^{14}C and ^{3}H in the wastes.

Another potential source of radioactive gases is the corrosion of cylinders containing radioactive gases. In the U.S. gaseous wastes acceptable for burial at commercial burial sites must be at a pressure of one and one half atmosphere or less.[101] The cylinders normally are sealed in a steel drum which is coated with tar.[46] If this cylinder and drum fail before the radioactivity of the gas has decayed, there will be a slow release of radioactive gas to the trench space.

Wastes containing large amounts of ^{3}H can pose special problems because its decay produces the gas ^{3}He. If the container is sealed, the helium produced will increase the pressure in the container and possibly cause its failure. Mershad et al.[102] calculate that 7×10^{4} Ci of ^{3}H as tritiated water solidified with concrete in a 115-ℓ drum will attain a pressure of 150 kPa (1.5) atmospheres) above atmospheric pressure after an 85-year decay period. If the container does leak, some ^{3}H as water vapor will be released to the trench.

The decay of ^{226}Ra produces gaseous ^{222}Rn which quickly decays to produce radioactive daughter products. The release of ^{222}Rn and its daughters will be limited by the total ^{226}Ra buried and the ^{226}Ra produced in the decay of uranium. Other radioactive gases that may be present include ^{85}Kr and the radioiodines.

The gases produced or released in the trench can diffuse through the soil or may flow along cracks or permeable layers or through sump pipes to the surface. Since little is known about gas production and its transport at low-level burial sites, analogy is made to two situations. The first is the diffusion of gases in ordinary soil. The second is the flow of gases from sanitary landfills.

In ordinary soil there is an exchange of gases between the atmosphere and the soil. Since growing plants take in some of their O_2 and respire CO_2 through their roots, there is a deficit of O_2 and excess of CO_2 in the soil air compared to the atmosphere. The gas exchange between the soil and the atmosphere is primarily due to diffusion. The rate of transfer is determined by the gradient and the diffusion coefficient which is an increasing function of free pore space in the soil. Changes in barometric pressure and temperature and the effects of the wind make only minor contributions to gas transfer in soil.[98]

If there are no sump pipes, observation wells, or cracks in trench cap, and no gas production, the trench gases will behave similarly to soil gases. They will diffuse slowly through the trench cap and the surrounding soil. If the trench cap is more impermeable than the trench wall materials, the gases may first diffuse laterally and then to the surface through more permeable materials.

In a sanitary landfill, the production of gases gives an added driving force to the movement of gases. Although most of the gases seep to the surface, they have been observed to migrate laterally more than 100 m from the waste cells. When well vents are installed in the landfill, the positive pressure can force out the gases.[91]

If there is significant gas generation at low-level burial sites, the gases should behave as they do in a sanitary landfill. They should flow through any sump pipes or observation wells installed in the trenches, through any cracks in the trench cap, or through the trench cap itself. Because of void space in the trench, changes in barometric pressure will cause the trenches to breathe in and out to balance the pressure. If the cap is impermeable, the gas will flow laterally.

Hawkins[103] describes an experiment in which Li-Al residues from a ^{3}H production process were buried in an open-top soil-filled lysimeter. The water percolating through the soil and gases diffusing through the cap were sampled. For these tests over 99% of the ^{3}H leached from the wastes was found in the water. Less than 1% was emitted to the air. Most of this was emitted as tritiated hydrogen (HT) and only small amounts as tritiated water vapor (HTO).

The CO_2 in the trench gases lowers the pH of any water present in the trench or in the surrounding soil.[91] This can increase the rate of leaching of radionuclides from the waste and the solubilization of minerals from the soil.

Radioactive dusts can be suspended by the wind and by the burial and earth moving operations. Although dusts may leak from packages damaged in shipment or in burial or from faulty packages , a more probable source of dust at some of the older sites is the contamination of the surface soil with any liquid spilled when solidifying liquid wastes onsite. This contaminated soil can later be suspended by the wind or burial operations.

Dusts can be suspended if the wastes are intentionally or accidentally exhumed. If wastes are intentionally exhumed, respirators may be required.[81] Although it is unlikely that wastes will be accidentally uncovered at a well-managed burial site during its operation, the digging of a new trench could expose and suspend soil contaminated by any radionuclide movement in the soil. Many years after the site is closed it is conceivable that the institutional safeguards will lapse and the site will be open to the general public. In that case the wastes could be exhumed during any earth-moving operations. Then long-lived radionuclides could be suspended and respired by the construction workers.[79]

There have been accidental fires at low-level burial trenches.[49,52,104] These have resulted in the suspension of radionuclides into the air and localized contamination of the soil. Since part of the wastes are combustible, sparks from vehicles, careless smoking, lightning, and spontaneous combustion can ignite them. The smoke can contain radionuclides that may be inhaled by site personnel and also spread radionuclides off the site. To prevent and limit damage due to fires, safety and emergency fire fighting programs are needed at each site. Daily covering of the wastes with soil will limit the volume of wastes that can be burned.

Another source of atmospheric emissions of radionuclides is the use of evaporators at low-level sites to treat leachate pumped from the trenches. Evaporators emit nearly all the ^{3}H and a small fraction of other nuclides. At Maxey Flats an evaporator has been used since 1973. It has evaporated over 10^{7} ℓ of water with an estimated ^{3}H emission of 10^{4} Ci. Blanchard et al.[63] made several emission tests for radionuclides. They found decontamination factors, the ratio of the activity of the influent waters to the activity of the airborne emissions, to range from 3 to 13 for ^{137}Cs, about 22 for ^{14}C, 11 to 41 for ^{60}Co, 1710 for ^{239}Pu, and 3670 for ^{238}Pu. Meyer[58] felt that the evaporator was a potential source of plutonium contamination of the soil. Although improved evaporators would have higher decontamination factors and lower emissions, a physical-chemical water treatment system incorporating ion exchange could be used alone or in conjunction with an evaporator to reduce atmospheric emissions. The ^{3}H would still be emitted to the atmosphere or discharged into surface waters.

Natural Events Affecting Low-Level Burial Sites

In addition to the waterborne and airborne problems at low-level burial sites, there are other problems that need to be considered in their siting and design. This review will consider the spreading of radionuclides by burrowing animals, the long term stability of the site, and the potential for problems caused by climatic change.

There have been several cases in which animals have spread radionuclides from radioactive disposal sites. At the Hanford Researvation some animals, possibly badgers, burrowed into a liquid waste disposal crib and exposed a salt layer.[52] Jackrabbits later used the layer as a salt lick and subsequently spread radionuclides further.[53,54] In an incident at Oak Ridge National Laboratories about 20 cotton rats lived in the bank of a liquid waste pond. The rodents were found to have ingested ^{137}Cs.[105]

At low-level burial sites deep burrowing animals or earthworms could similarly intrude on the waste and transport radionuclides away from the sites. In addition, a burrow provides a pathway for surface waters to drain into the trench. To prevent this from occurring, burial sites should have surveillance and control programs for any burrowing animals living in the surrounding area.

The integrity of the site can be affected by several geological processes. A severe earthquake could cause cracking of the trench caps and possible exposure or ejection of wastes. This would require immediate maintenance to repair the damage at the site. If the site is built on a slope there is the possibility for slope failure and exposure of the wastes. This may occur rapidly in an earthquake or over a long period of time due to either slope creep or the undercutting of the slope by streams. At the West Valley site there is concern that a steep slope near waste trenches could fail and expose a trench unless corrective actions are taken.[67]

A dramatic increase in precipitation could pose problems at burial sites. In the eastern U.S., hurricanes and tropical storms can flood partially filled burial trenches. At all locations a long-term increase in precipitation can cause many water-related problems such as an increase in the height of the water table, increased rates of erosion, and increased infiltration. For sites in humid areas these effects could cause flooding of the trenches. At locations in arid areas any dramatic short or long term increase in precipitation will cause an increase in infiltration of water due to the moderate permeability of the surficial soil materials at these sites.

Although it is known that extremely wet periods have occurred at various locations in recorded history, climatological records in most of the U.S. have only several hundred years of data. In many locations the records are considerably shorter. These records are inadequate to estimate the range of precipitation that may occur within the next several hundred to thousand years.

For sites in humid areas several precautions must be taken in siting future burial grounds. Since the water table level fluctuates with the average precipitation, it is unwise to rely on data taken on the water table level in either the season of the year that normally has the lowest level or in a year which has had significantly less rainfall than average. Also a site that has the water table near the bottom of the proposed trench should be considered to be marginal since it can be assumed that the water table will be higher in years of higher rainfall.

SITING AND DESIGN CRITERIA FOR LOW-LEVEL BURIAL SITES

When commercial low-level disposal sites were first opened in the U.S., the siting and design were dominated by the assumption that the natural soil barrier would be sufficient to contain the wastes and allow the radionuclides to decay. Siting procedures consisted primarily of a hydrogeological survey to determine the height of the water table, soil permeability, and exchange capacity. Using optimistic transport models, predictions were made of the travel time to the nearest well or surface waters. If this time was sufficiently long for decay to occur, the site was deemed adequate.

The past 15 years experience has shown that, at least in humid areas, this approach is inadequate. Three of the original six commercial sites are closed. There has been migration of radionuclides off the burial site at the Maxey Flats and West Valley sites. These environmental problems, the heightened public concern over nuclear wastes, and the controversy over the health effects of low-level radiation will make the siting and design of future burial sites a much more difficult task.

Criteria and Standards for Siting Low-Level Burial Grounds

Unlike the siting of nuclear power reactors and many non-nuclear facilities such as coal-fired power plants, oil refineries, and large industries, the siting of low-level burial

Table 15
PROPOSED CRITERIA FOR RADIOACTIVE WASTES

Materials Considered Radioactive Wastes

Radioactive materials should be considered radioactive wastes requiring control for environmental and public health protection if they have no designated product or resource value and:

1. Are human-produced by nuclear fission or activation, fabricated from naturally radioactive materials into discrete sources, or as a result of regulatory activities are prohibited from uncontrolled discharge to the environment; or
2. Contain diffuse naturally occurring radioactive materials that, if disposed into the biosphere, would increase exposure to humans above that which would occur normally in pathways due to the preexisting natural state of the area.

Control of Radioactive Wastes

The fundamental goal for controlling any type of radioactive waste should be complete isolation over its hazardous lifetime. Controls which are based on institutional functions should not be relied upon for longer than 100 years to provide such isolation; radioactive wastes with a hazardous lifetime longer than 100 years should be controlled by as many engineered and natural barriers as are necessary.

Risk Assessment

Radiation protection requirements for radioactive wastes should be based primarily on an assessment of risk to individuals and populations; such assessments should be based on predetermined models and should examine at least the following factors:

1. The amount and concentration of radioactive waste in a location and its physical, chemical, and radiological properties;
2. The projected effectiveness of alternative methods of control;
3. The potential adverse health effects on individuals and populations for a reasonable range of future population sizes and distributions, and of uses of land, air, water, and mineral resources for 1000 years, or any shorter period of hazard persistence;
4. Estimates of environmental effects using general parameters or of health effects based on generalized assumptions for as long as the wastes pose a hazard to humans, when such estimates could influence the choice of a control option;
5. The probabilities of releases of radioactive materials to the general environment due to failtures of natural or engineered barriers, loss of institutional controls, or intrusion; and
6. The uncertainties in the risk assessments and the models used for determining them.

Unacceptability of Risk

Any risks due to radioactive waste management or disposal activities should be deemed unacceptable unless it has been justified that the further reduction in risk that could be achieved by more complete isolation is impracticable on the basis of technical and social considerations; in addition, risks associated with any given method of control should be considered unacceptable if:

1. Risks to a future generation are greater than those acceptable to the current generation;
2. Probable events could result in adverse consequences greater than those of a comparable nature generally accepted by society; or
3. The probabilities of highly adverse consequences are more than a small fraction of the probabilities of high consequence events associated with productive technologies which are accepted by society.

Location and Waste Isolation

Locations for radioactive waste disposal should be chosen so as to avoid adverse environmental and human health impacts and, wherever practicable, to enhance isolation over time.

Table 15 (continued)
PROPOSED CRITERIA FOR RADIOACTIVE WASTES

Supplementary Protection Goals

Certain additional procedures and techniques should also be applied to waste disposal systems which otherwise satisfy these criteria if use of these additional procedures and techniques provide a net improvement in environmental and public health protection. Among these are:

1. Procedures or techniques designed to enhance the retrievability of the waste; and
2. Passive methods of communicating to future people the potential hazards which could result from an accidental or intentional disturbance of disposed radioactive wastes.

From Criteria for Radioactive Wastes, *U.S. Fed. Reg.*, 43, 53262—53268. November 15, 1978.

grounds is presently hampered by lack of objective standards and accepted procedures for their evaluation. Ideally, there should be general guidelines or criteria for developing environmental standards for waste disposal, objective standards based on these criteria, and well-accepted modeling techniques to determine if a particular site meets these standards. In the U.S. general criteria for all radioactive wastes have only recently been proposed.[12] There are no standards except for the maximum permissible concentrations for release to the environment.[106] There are no documented models to estimate the rates of release of radionuclides from the waste trenches. Finally, there are no field-tested models that can estimate the transport of radionuclides through the soil or release to the atmosphere. Without standards and accepted procedures the technical decisions on siting will remain subjective judgments.

The U.S. Environmental Protection Agency[12] has recently proposed criteria for radioactive wastes which are given in Table 15. If promulgated, these criteria will serve as the basis for developing standards for the disposal of various radioactive wastes. These guidelines recognize that the wastes should be completely isolated over their hazardous lifetime. This isolation can be achieved by institutional mechanisms, engineered barriers, and natural barriers. It is proposed that institutional controls, which include site boundaries, guards, land use policies, recordkeeping, and monitoring, must not be assumed to be dependable for more than 100 years. If the wastes are deemed hazardous for longer than 100 years, the wastes must be isolated by as many engineered and natural barriers as are necessary to ensure their isolation.

In the area of risk assessment the criteria state that assessments need to be made of the potential adverse health effects on present and future individuals and populations. These should include estimates of the effectiveness of alternative controls, probabilities of the failure of controls and barriers, and the health effects for a time period of the next 1000 years. To assess the unacceptability of risks, the criteria state that risks to future generations should not be greater than the current generation is willing to accept for itself and that any consequence leading to highly undesirable effects should have a probability of occurrence that is a small fraction of those accepted by a society for its present productive technologies.

The criteria state the locations for waste disposal sites be chosen to avoid health impacts and, when practicable, to enhance the isolation of the wastes over time. Finally, the criteria advocate that disposal technologies should be designed to enhance the retrievability of the wastes and to incorporate passive methods of communications with future generations such as markers, restricted land titles, and records to reduce the possibility of intrusion by future generations.

In 1979 the U.S. Nuclear Regulatory Commission issued a preliminary draft of proposed regulations on the licensing procedures, performance objectives, and technical

Table 16
HYDROGEOLOGICAL SITE CRITERIA PROPOSED BY CHERRY ET AL.

Characteristics of Sites for Intermediate Burial

1. "The land surface should be devoid of surface water, except during snowmelt runoff and exceptional periods of rainfall. In other words, the sites should not be located in swamps, bogs, or other types of very wet terrain.
2. The burial zone should be separated from fractured bedrock by an interval of geologic deposits sufficient to prevent migration of radionuclides into the fractured zone.
3. The predicted rate of radionuclide transport in the shallow . . . deposits at the site should be slow enough to provide many years or decades of delay time before radionuclides would be able to reach public waterways or any other area in the biosphere that might be considered hazardous. In other words, considerable time would be available for detection of contamination and for application of remedial measures if necessary.
4. The site should have sufficient depth to water table to permit all burial operations to occur above the water table, or as an alternative the site should be suitable for producing an adequate water table depth by flow-system manipulation.
5. The site should be well suited for effective monitoring and for containment by flow-system manipulation schemes."

Characteristics of Sites for Long-Term Burial

1. "The land should be generally devoid of surface water and be relatively stable geomorphically. In other words, erosion and weathering should not be proceeding at a rate that could significantly affect the position and character of the land surface during the next few hundred years.
2. The subsurface flow pattern in the area must be such that the flow lines from the burial zone do not lead to areas considered to be particularly undesirable, such as fractured bedrock, public waterways used by man, aquifers used for water supply, and others.
3. The predicted residence time of radionuclides within an acceptable part of the subsurface-flow system must be of the order of several hundred years. The hydrogeological conditions must be simple enough for reliable residence-time predictions to be made.
4. The natural water table should be below the burial zone by at least several metres, and the hydrogeological setting should be such that large water-table fluctuations are very unlikely. This condition would provide additional assurance that leaching of radionuclides would not occur quickly in the event of corrosion of the waste containers, or in the event that low-level wastes are put directly in the ground."

From Cherry, J. A., Crisak, G. E., and Jackson, P. E., Hydrogeological-factors in shallow subsurface radioactive waste management in Canada *Proc. Int. Conf. on Land for Waste Management,* Ottawa, October 1973, Agricultural Institute of Canada, Ottawa, 131—146, 1974.

criteria for low-level waste disposal sites. They proposed that the siting and application procedures would include consideration of alternative sites, state government and public participation in siting, assurances of sufficient funds to operate and decommission the site, and a detailed environmental and safety report. During the operation of the site, the proposed regulations would require that most wastes be in a dry, solidified, free-standing form and be in an approved package. The free liquid would be limited to the minimum of 0.5% by volume or 1 gal, and it must be noncorrosive. The void spaces between waste packages would be minimized to prevent the collapse of the trench cap. The wastes would need to be segregated so that waste containing potential complexing agents be separated from other wastes. Certain classes of chemicals would be banned and limits would be established on the concentration of activity suitable for shallow land burial. The decommissioning regulations would require a site stabilization plan such that no active maintenance is required, and a program of postclosure environmental monitoring.

There have been only a few guidelines proposed that can assist in siting shallow land burial sites. In Canada Mawson and Russell[104] gave general recommendations for an

Table 17
HYDROGEOLOGIC AND HYDROCHEMICAL DATA NEEDS FOR SITE EVALUATION

The types of hydrogeologic and hydrochemical data needed to determine whether proposed or existing sites meet the criteria stated earlier are listed below in approximate order of increasing difficulty and (or) cost of acquisition:

1. Depth to water table, including perched water tables, if present
2. Distance to nearest points of ground water, spring water, or surface water usage (includes well and spring inventory)
3. Ratio of pan evaporation to precipitation minus runoff (by month for period of at least 2 years)
4. Water table contour map
5. Magnitude of annual water table fluctuation
6. Stratigraphy and structure to base of shallowest confined aquifer
7. Baseflow data on perennial streams traversing or adjacent to storage site
8. Chemistry of water in aquifers and aquitards and of leachate from the waste trenches
9. Laboratory measurements of hydraulic conductivity, effective porosity, and mineralogy of core and grab samples (from trenches) of each lithology in unsaturated and saturated (to base of shallowest confined aquifer) zone—hydraulic conductivity to be measured at different water contents and suctions
10. Neutron moisture meter measurements of moisture content of unsaturated zone. Measurements to be made in especially constructed holes; at least 2 years' record needed.
11. *In situ* measurements of soil moisture tension in upper 15—30 feet (4.5—9.0 m) of unsaturated zone; at least 2 years' record necessary.
12. Three-dimensional distribution of head in all saturated hydrostratigraphic units to base of shallowest confined aquifer.
13. Pumping, bailing, or slug tests to determine transmissivity and storage coefficients.
14. Definition of recharge and discharge areas for unconfined and shallowest confined aquifers
15. Field measurements of dispersivity coefficients
16. Laboratory and field determination of the distribution coefficient (K_d) for movement of critical nuclides through all hydrostratigraphic units
17. Rates of denudation and (or) slope retreat

From Papadopulos, S. S. and Winograd, I. J., Storage of low-level radioactive wastes in the ground: Hydrogeologic and hydrochemical factors. With an appendix on the Maxey Flats, Ky. radioactive waste storage site: Current Knowledge and data needs for a quantitative hydrogeologic evaluation, Open-File Rep. 74—344, U.S. Geological Survey, 1974.

acceptable waste management site that included requirements that the site not drain into public waters used by man, no free standing water would accumulate, the soil would have a high cation exchange capacity, there be at least 5 m of unsaturated soil between the wastes and the water table and that the groundwater move at a rate of less than a few centimeters per day. They cautioned that some of these guidelines are almost contradictory. For example, soils with good exchange capacities are frequently poorly drained. They also recommended that the site be owned by the government in order to maintain responsible control over the site in the future.

As an extension of these Canadian guidelines, Cherry, et al.[2] proposed the hydrogeological criteria found in Table 16. They proposed different criteria for intermediate-term burial sites which accept wastes that will decay to innocuous levels in a few decades and long-term burial sites. For the intermediate-term wastes they felt that engineered containers could provide most of the protection. In the event that they failed, the soil should provide years to decades of delay to allow for decay. They proposed that groundwater flow manipulation could be used to keep water from the sites. This includes reduction of infiltration, subsurface drains, and pumping. A long-term site must be stable with respect to erosion and weathering and large water table fluctuations must be improbable. For both the intermediate- and long-term sites, they stress that the site must be separated from fractured deposits in which it is nearly impossible to predict the direction and velocity of the flow and the exchange capacity for radionuclides.

Papadopulos and Winograd[59] recommend the data requirements for a hydrogeologic and hydrochemical evaluation of a site. Their recommendations, shown in Table 17, require at least a 2-year laboratory and field study. Their complete program includes field measurements of the distribution coefficients for critical radionuclides, dispersivity coefficients, and water transmissivity.

A generic classification scheme for various physiographic regions of the U.S. has been given by the Energy Research and Development Administration.[46] It includes the advantages and inherent limitation of burial sites in each region.

Several simple schemes have been developed to numerically rank the suitability of sites for shallow burial. The International Atomic Energy Agency[107] proposed a point-ranking chart that rated potential sites with respect to the distance between the bottom of the trench and the water table, the soil permeability and sorption capacity, the hydraulic gradient, and the distance groundwater must travel to reach public waters. This chart is not applicable if over half the distance is in fractured rock or limestone.

Cherry et al.[2] gave two nomographs for hydrogeological evaluation of intermediate- and long-term burial sites. These are based on their guidelines and require subjective evaluations of characteristics such as suitability of the site for monitoring, depth to natural water table, and surface drainage characteristics.

Morisawa and Inoue[108] proposed a point-ranking system, similar to the IAEA chart, to evaluate the suitability of burial sites in Japan. This system considers 12 major variables. The relative points were determined with a numerical model. This system ranks potential sites with respect to a reference site. It is quite sensitive to the rate of flow of the groundwater and distribution coefficients of the specific radionuclides, but it appears to be anomalously insensitive to distance between the bottom of the trench and the groundwater, the infiltration rate of rain waters, and distance from the trenches to the nearest well.

Even though one of these systems may provide a convenient tool for preliminary evaluation or screening of potential sites, they can not be recommended as an absolute indication of site suitability. The charts rely too heavily on subjective judgments and each one ignores important factors in radionuclide transport.

Advanced Burial Site Design

In addition to greater care in selecting sites for low-level burial grounds, the release and migration of radionuclides can be reduced by improved trench design and waste packaging and by further restrictions on the type of wastes or their activities. These improvements generally will have their most significant impact on reducing migration in the first few decades to few centuries. Therefore they are most effective for shorter-lived radionuclides. In humid areas some of these engineered and administrative controls will be required to meet the proposed criteria for radioactive waste disposal.

For any site in humid areas the minimum design for the trenches should incorporate the features used at the commercial site at Barnwell, S.C. These include a gravel-filled drain sloping toward a sump at the low end of the trench, a sandy layer at the bottom to keep the wastes from direct contact with any small amount of water standing in the trench, a compacted clay cap, and a soil cover. If significant amounts of water are pumped from the trench, a water treatment system incorporating ion exchange resins should be used for decontamination.

Since common clays have a low hydraulic conductivity, a clay layer over the trench can significantly reduce the infiltration. Several potential problems exist with such a clay layer. If the wastes are not compacted, their subsidence can cause the clay to crack. If the clay dries out it will also crack. In either case surface water will be able to flow into the trenches and radioactive gas can flow out. To prevent the clay layer from drying out, it should be covered with soil. To minimize erosion the site has to be carefully graded and provided with ditches and diversion dams to control surface water. The site can be planted with a shallow-rooted grass to further decrease erosion and increase evapotranspiration. An alternative to grass for erosion control is to cover the site with riprap rock as is done to protect earth-filled dams. The rock would also discourage burrowing animals.[109]

Hawkins and Horton[110] showed the effectiveness of a layer of Wyoming bentonite clay to prevent infiltration. They buried 210-ℓ drums with open tops level with the surface. Sandy soil was placed in the bottom of the drums and covered with either 2.5 or 5-cm bentonite layers and 30- or 60-cm layers of soil. Over a 2-year period with a total of 259 cm of rainfall, no water infiltrated through the bentonite layers. On the basis of studies in smaller tubes they concluded that 60 cm of soil cover would be needed to prevent the bentonite from cracking during periods of drought. Since they found that some plant roots could penetrate 60 cm of soil and the bentonite layer, they concluded that the area over the site must be free from plant growth. They also demonstrated how bentonite could be applied with a pneumatic cement gun to cover the walls and top of a trench to prevent infiltration.

Synthetic covers can be used to reduce infiltration. Asphalt has an extremely low permeability but it does degrade and crack when exposed to sunlight and oxygen. Plastic liners or membranes can be used to cover the trench. They are easily torn and it is not known how long they will remain intact. To protect either the asphalt or the plastic membrane, they should be covered with soil. Although concrete can be used as a cover, leaks can develop at the expansion joints. It has been suggested that 0.3-cm thick stainless steel sheets could be welded together to form an impermeable cover.[107] To prevent buckling due to thermal expansion that could contribute to stress-induced failure of the welds, the sheet would also have to be covered with a layer of soil.

With all these methods the uneven subsidence of the wastes can cause the cover to crack, tear, or otherwise fail. Since the soil above the cover may be saturated with water, infiltration through a hole or tear into the trench could be high. With the clay, asphalt, or plastic membranes, uneven subsidence of the wastes can cause the soil cover to collapse into the trench. If the roots of the grass can temporarily hold the top of the soil from collapsing, the trench cap could appear to be intact. An unsuspecting person walking over this spot could drop into the waste trench as occasionally occurs with abandoned wells, cisterns, or septic tanks.

Although compaction of the wastes during their burial will aid in preventing uneven subsidence, it will crush many containers such as cardboard boxes and 210-ℓ steel drums. This can release any free liquids in the damaged packages. Some of the tritiated water in the wastes can evaporate before burial and other liquid wastes can seep into the soil. It is difficult to assess whether the possibility of immediate release of radionuclides due to compaction is a greater danger than those posed by subsidence.

In very well-drained soils where the trench is far above the saturated zone, water can be prevented from migrating laterally into the trench by surrounding the trench with coarse, well-graded gravel. The effective pore size of the gravel is so large that capillary conductivity is very low. This would have to be combined with an impermeable cover over the trench and gravel to prevent the gravel from forming a conduit for any surface waters.

A different approach to improving the acceptability of low-level waste burial is to use upgraded waste-packaging techniques. Waste containers using multiple barriers of steel, concrete, asphalt, fiberglass, and other materials have been designed to survive decades to centuries. Such containers are currently used for wastes of high activity or transuranically contaminated wastes.[85,102,111]

Improved packaging has its greatest effectiveness for shorter-lived wastes that may decay before the container fails and releases its wastes to the soil. For longer-lived radionuclides improved containers prevent contamination during burial and enhance the retrievability of the wastes if they must be exhumed during the first few years to decades. Since all containers will eventually fail, it must not be assumed that they will be able to provide protection for generations into the far future. This must be accomplished with natural barriers.

A chief drawback to improved packaging is the cost for the bulky wastes of low activity that comprise much of the wastes currently buried. Incineration of the combustible wastes and solidification of the ashes in concrete or in water-tight containers will provide a stable waste form, but incineration also poses technical and siting problems.

Other methods of improving low-level burial sites include waste segregation and the prohibition of certain wastes due to their activity, the presence of specific radionuclides, or their chemical nature. Waste segregation would entail the separation of different types of wastes for separate burial. For example, wastes containing decontamination solutions or organic chemicals that may serve as complexing or chelating agents can be buried separately from wastes containing potentially mobile radionuclides. This segregation requires alternative disposal techniques for these special wastes.

Certain wastes have been prohibited from being buried at commercial low-level burial sites. Transuranically contaminated wastes are currently banned. Certain sites have placed limits on certain wastes due to their high activity, chemical composition, or physical waste form. Each category of prohibitive materials requires an alternative disposal method or disposal site.

Perpetual Care of Low-Level Burial Sites

The problems of a burial site do not cease when the site is closed. Monitoring for radionuclide migration and maintenance of the site must continue. The site must be guarded to keep out unwanted visitors. These must be done for hundreds to thousands of years or longer depending on the wastes buried, their decay, and their containment by natural and engineered barriers.

In the U.S. five of the burial grounds are on state-owned lands and the sixth, the Richland site, is on federal lands leased to the State of Washington. The states have individually assumed the responsibility for the perpetual care of the sites in their state. Each state has a contract with the commercial operator that includes the payment of fees toward a fund for the long-term care. If these funds are not sufficient to meet the cost of maintenance and any unexpected problems, the balance must come from the state's general revenues. Since half of the original commercial sites in the U.S. have prematurely ceased burial, it is important that adequate funding arrangements be made for perpetual care with a contingency fund for any unanticipated problems.

Kentucky received 4% of the customer's charge for burial which netted about 5¢ for each cubic foot buried at Maxey Flats. In 1972 collection of fees was suspended in order to renegotiate the payment to increase revenue.[6] After the migration of radionuclides, the state legislature imposed a 10¢/lb surtax to try to raise funds to meet the costs if the site closed prematurely. This tax reduced the wastes buried to approximately 5% of normal prior to the site closing in 1977.[42]

Illinois received 5¢/ft^3 for wastes buried at Sheffield, and New York received 8¢/ft^3 from the West Valley site. Washington receives 5¢/ft^3 from the Richland site and Nevada receives 7¢/ft^3 from the Beatty site. Many states have attempted to renegotiate the fee because of problems at several sites.[6]

When the Barnwell site was opened, South Carolina negotiated an 8¢/ft^3 fee. The state later commissioned a study to examine the long-term funding arrangements.[112] A basic assumption of this study was that the monitoring and maintenance costs would be only approximately $52,000/year and that $130,000 (1974 dollars) would be an adequate contingency fund for any unanticipated problems. These estimates were made prior to the general knowledge of the extent of radionuclide migration at West Valley and Maxey Flats. The study concluded that a 14¢/ft^3 fee should be set, and a performance bond be posted by the operator in case of default. Based on this study, the fee was renegotiated to 16¢/ft^3 in 1976.

Since the closing of three other burial sites, the Barnwell site has received a substantial fraction of the nation's low-level wastes. To prevent this site from being filled too rapidly, the state has limited the annual volume of wastes that can be buried to about 68,000 m^3 [35] and set new fees to be paid to the state for wastes buried. In 1979 the fee was raised to 55¢/ft^3. It was to be raised to 75¢/ft^3 in 1980 and to $1/ft^3 in 1981.[113]

When a site is closed or if it is abandoned by the commercial operator, the state becomes responsible for the long-term care for as long as the site is deemed a potential hazard. Monitoring of the groundwaters, surface waters, air, and vegetation must continue to attempt to detect any radionuclide migration. In humid areas the level of the water table must routinely be measured to assess any long-term trends that may pose a danger to the site. The rainfall and pan evaporation should also be recorded to continue the hydrological record at the site.

The site will have to be maintained to continue the security of the site and to minimize the potential for radionuclide migration. This will include tasks like repairing fences, regrading and reseeding the site when necessary, and controlling burrowing animals. If water is found in the trenches, it must be pumped out and treated to remove many of the radionuclides. This treatment process will produce wastes that must be sent to an active disposal site.

The costs of the perpetual care will depend on the site characteristics and on any problems encountered. Because several sites are over 100 ha, it probably will be necessary to have a staff of one or more full-time caretakers to inspect, maintain, and secure the site. There will be a need for trucks and tractors and related equipment for site maintenance. In addition, there will have to be technicians and laboratory equipment for the monitoring program, as well as supervisory personnel.

An alternative to perpetual care is decommissioning the site for surface-only public use.[46] This is an attractive option because the costs of maintaining the site could be shared by the new user. For example, the site could be used as a public park or golf course as is done with some solid waste landfills. It is unlikely, however, that their requirements would be compatible with those of the disposal site. The need to maintain good control of surface waters with contouring and ditches would not make an attractive park or golf course. Since the sites are in sparsely populated areas, the population will not be sufficient to justify such a marginal park. Also the small, but finite, probability that the wastes will subside and trench cap fail and cause a person to drop into the waste cell is sufficient reason to restrict the usage of the site.

The use of the site for future nuclear or industrial development is probably incompatible with the need for stable foundation and sufficient water and sewerage. Also, there are potential problems of occupational exposure to low-level radiation. The use of the site for agriculture should be prohibited as long as there is any possibility of radionuclide uptake.

The only other alternative to perpetual care is exhumation of the wastes.[46] Except when dangers exist due to the burial of long-lived radionuclides at a site where migration is a certainty and health effects are a clear possibility, the risks of exhuming the randomly buried, poorly packaged wastes are potentially greater than attempting to construct barriers to minimize the hazards to the public.

Research in Shallow Land Burial

The premature closing of three burial sites has left the eastern half of the U.S. with only the Barnwell site for commercial radioactive wastes. Since the volume of wastes has been limited and certain types of wastes prohibited at this site, there is interest in the licensing of new sites. Because significant fractions of fuel- and nonfuel-cycle wastes are generated in the eastern half of the country, transportation costs could be minimized if a site can be located in this region. This raises the question of whether a new burial site should again be placed in a humid area. If one is sited there new regulations will be needed to prevent the difficulties that have plagued earlier sites.

To answer this question and to help formulate regulations, research is needed. At present there are research programs looking at various facets of shallow land burial such as the interactions among various soils and radionuclides, trench leachate chemistry of selected sites, packaging technologies, and biological uptake of radionuclides in soils. In addition to these focused studies, there have been intensive field investigations at the Maxey Flats and West Valley sites to determine the extent of migration of radionuclides and their pathways and to propose remedies to ameliorate their problems.

To complement these studies and aid in answering questions on future sitings, it is essential to initiate or continue research in several directions. The first involves comprehensive field studies at existing active burial sites in both humid and arid climates to determine how well their engineered and natural barriers are functioning in containing the radionuclides. Second, there is an urgent need for realistic radionuclide transport models to be developed and tested to be used in future site evaluations. Third, there is a need to continue studies on packaging technology and the integrity of wastes in actual trenches. Finally, there should be new surveys on the sources, waste volumes, the radionuclide content, and integrity of various wastes to understand the magnitude of potential problems in low-level waste disposal.

Although studies have been conducted at Maxey Flats and West Valley, there is a need to conduct comprehensive field investigations at active burial sites to determine how well they are containing the wastes. Such studies will give a better indication of whether their designs and burial practices are adequate than will laboratory studies or field investigations at the sites that have already closed. Studies at active sites will also have the advantage of allowing controlled *in situ* experiments on various waste forms and new burial techniques.

There should be a study at a site in a humid climate and one at a site in an arid climate to test the concept of shallow land burial. Although the Barnwell site is the only commercial site still operating in a humid area and is the logical choice, the study could also be carried out at the Savannah River Plant or at one of the better burial sites at Oak Ridge provided that the wastes they have and are burying are reasonably representative of those at commercial sites. The arid zone site could be the Beatty, Richland, or possibly the Hanford, Idaho, or Los Alamos sites.

A major portion of the study of the humid site will be a detailed water balance to determine the fate of precipitation on the site. For example, the trenches at the Barnwell and many of those at Savannah River have had no free standing water. It needs to be determined if this is due to the careful construction of an impermeable trench cap or if water that percolates downward or migrates laterally into the trench merely percolates through the trench bottom without detection.

To conduct such a study there is a need to account for all surface and groundwaters entering and leaving the site, including rainfall, surface runoff, evapotranspiration, and flow in both the saturated and unsaturated soil. To determine if water is percolating downward through the trench bottom, stainless steel pans could be placed in the soil beneath the trench floor. If these pans were filled with glass beads, gravel, or coarse sand, any water that flowed downward through the trench floor would collect in the bottom of the pan. By sloping the bottom of the pan toward a small well, even a small downward flux of water could be sampled. For example, 1mm of water over a 5-m diameter pan would eventually yield 20 ℓ of water. By placing typical wastes over these pans, the total water and its radionuclide and chemical composition could be routinely measured. The average total water collected in these pans should complete the water balance on the trenches. At the arid site there is a need to repeat this study on a modest scale to verify the present thought that there are few difficulties with liquid water at these sites.

To determine the rate of release of radionuclides from various wastes, open-top lysimeters can be filled with wastes and soil and placed in the trench cap. These could be 210-ℓ drums as used by Hawkins[103] or larger tanks that can accommodate a variety of wastes including cardboard boxes and 210-ℓ drums. The water collected from these lysimeters can be analyzed for the radionuclides present in the wastes.

Water samples from the trench, the collection pans, and the lysimeters can be chemically analyzed to determine their pH, inorganic, and organic composition, including concentrations of specific organic compounds capable of acting as complexing agents for radionuclides. The radionuclides can be analyzed to determine if they are in particulate or soluble form and whether the soluble fraction is sorbable on typical clays.

There should be a study of the gaseous emanations and vapor transport at these sites. This should include measurements of the concentration of radionuclides and composition of trench gases in both new and old trenches and their rates of transport through the soil. At the arid site, special attention should be paid to the vapor diffusion through the soil. These studies should determine if these problems are significant or inconsequential.

If in the course of these field investigations, migration of radionuclides in the soil is observed, there will be an opportunity to obtain field measurements of distribution coefficients for radionuclides and to relate them to actual conditions.

In addition to the field studies, there is a need to develop realistic transport models that can estimate the migration of radionuclides in both the saturated and unsaturated zones. These models must consider chemical interactions among the soil, trench water, and radionuclides for the range of conditions found at low-level sites. These models should also be able to predict water and radionuclide movement in fractured zones. These models must be verified with field tests at actual low-level sites or under very similar conditions. Without these models no objective evaluations of future sites can be made.

The research on integrity and leachability needs to be continued with an emphasis on simulating field conditions. This can be done in laboratory tests with actual or synthetic leachate or in field tests with small lysimeters. Tests should be done on actual wastes solidified at nuclear power plants to insure that they are chemically and physically similar to synthetic wastes presently used in these studies. Solidification agents for organic decontamination solutions and scintillation fluids need to be developed and tested to determine if it is safe to bury them with other wastes or if they should be buried elsewhere or incinerated.

A final research area that should be initiated involves new studies on the radionuclide composition, volume, and form of wastes from the fuel- and nonfuel-cycle sources. These are needed because of the questionable nature of some data presently available. A historical survey at various sites should be undertaken to document the specific sources of wastes buried and the radionuclide content and physical form of the wastes. Also, a survey of fuel-cycle waste generators and noninstitutional generators of nonfuel cycle wastes, similar to the existing institutional survey,[33,34] should be conducted to determine the present status of their actual waste handling practices for various types of wastes.

PERSPECTIVE ON LOW-LEVEL RADIOACTIVE WASTE DISPOSAL

Each year large volumes of low-level radioactive wastes are generated by both fuel-cycle and nonfuel-cycle sources. These wastes include a wide range of materials including solidified liquids, contaminated equipment, scintillation fluids, paper products, and animal carcasses. Some of these wastes have sufficient activity to require shielding and special handling to prevent unnecessary exposure to radiation. Other wastes have so little radioactive contamination that they could be treated as nonradioactive waste. At present, the disposal method practiced in the U.S. is shallow land burial at specially licensed facilities. Of the six commercial sites established, three are still operating.

At the time shallow land burial began it was assumed that radionuclides would be contained in their waste trenches or sorbed onto the soil adjacent to the trench. This assumption contributed to decisions that resulted in poor choices of burial sites, inadequate design of the burial trenches, and the acceptance of poorly packaged wastes and wastes containing complexing agents and decontamination solutions.

The migration of small amounts of radionuclides from several commercial sites has shown this assumption to be incorrect. Although the radionuclides released are not generally felt to pose a threat to public health, they led to the premature closing of two burial sites. These problems have brought greater public awareness of both existing sites and any proposed sites.

The U.S. Environmental Protection Agency and the U.S. Nuclear Regulatory Commission have proposed new criteria and regulations for low-level burial sites and have placed existing operations under greater scrutiny. These changes should bring about significant modifications in the practice of low-level waste management in this decade.

Due to the relatively low activity and short half-lives of most radionuclides in low-level waste, the problems of waste burial are not insurmountable. It will take research to determine what engineered containers and natural barriers are needed to ensure that radionuclides are contained until they decay to innocuous levels.

ACKNOWLEDGMENT

The support of Clemson University during the preparation of this review is gratefully acknowledged.

REFERENCES

1. **Holcomb, W. F.,** Inventory (1962—1978) and projections (to 2000) of shallow land burial of radioactive wastes at commercial sites, *Nucl. Saf.,* 21, 380—388, 1980.
2. **Cherry, J. A., Grisak, G. E., and Jackson, P. E.,** Hydrogeological factors in shallow subsurface radioactive waste management in Canada, *Proc. Int. Conf. on Land for Waste Management,* Ottawa, October, 1973, Agricultural Institute of Canada, Ottawa, 131—146, 1974.
3. *Low-Level Radioactive Waste Disposal,* Hearings before a subcommittee, Committee on Government Operations, U.S. House of Representatives, Washington, D.C., 433 pp., 1976.
4. *Nuclear Waste Disposal Costs (West Valley, New York),* Hearings before a subcommittee, Committee on Government Operations, U.S. House of Representatives, Washington, D.C., 302 pp. 1977.
5. *Nuclear Waste Burial Grounds and Storage Sites in Illinois,* Hearings before a subcommittee, Committee on Government Operations, U.S. House of Representatives, Washington, D.C., 453 pp., 1978.
6. *Improvements Needed in the Land Disposal of Radioactive Wastes — A Problem of Centuries,* Rep. RED-76-54, Offices of the Comptroller General of the U.S., Washington, D.C., 58 pp., 1976.
7. The Shallow Land Burial of Low-Level Radioactively Contaminated Solid Waste, Panel on Land Burial, National Research Council, National Academy of Sciences, Washington, D.C., 150 pp., 1976.

8. **Marshall, E.**, Radioactive waste backup threatens research, *Science,* 206, 431—433, 1979.
9. **Blake, E. M.**, Feeling the pinch, *Nucl. News,* 22, 12, 48—49, 1979.
10. *NRC Task Force Report on the Review of the Federal/State Program for the Regulation of Commercial Low-Level Radioactive Waste Burial Grounds,* Rep. NUREG-0217, U.S. Nuclear Regulatory Commission, Washington, D.C., 1977.
11. Disposal of Low-Level Radioactive Waste and Low-Activity Bulk Solid Waste, U.S. Nuclear Regulatory Commission, Washington, D.C., November 5, 1979 (Preliminary draft of 10 CFR Part 61).
12. Criteria for Radioactive Wastes, *U.S. Fed. Reg.,* 43, 53262—53268, November 15, 1979.
13. *The Shallow Land Burial at Low-Level Radioactively Contaminated Solid Waste,* Panel on Land Burial, National Research Council National Academy of Sciences, Washington, D.C., 143—150, 1976.
14. *Chart of the Nuclides,* 11th ed., General Electric, San Jose, Calif., 48 pp.
15. **Eisenbud, M.**, *Environmental Radioactivity,* 2nd ed., Academic Press, New York, 1973, 205—315.
16. *Alternatives for Managing Wastes from Reactors and Post-Fission Operations in the LWR Fuel Cycle,* Rep. ERDA-76-43, U.S. Energy Research and Development Administration, Vol. 1, 2.1—2.83, 1976.
17. APS Study Group, Report to the American Physical Society by the Study Group on Nuclear Fuel Cycles and Waste Management, *Rev. Mod. Phys.,* 50, S165—167, 1978.
18. **Mann, B. J., Goldberg, S. M., and Hendricks, W. D.**, Low-Level Solid Radioactive Waste in the Nuclear Fuel Cycle, American Nuclear Soc. Winter Meet., San Francisco, November 16—21, 1975.
19. **Kibby, A. H., Godbee, H. W., and Compere, E. L.**, A Review of Solid Radioactive Waste Practices in Light-Water-Cooled Nuclear Reactor Power Plants, *Nucl. Saf.,* 21, 193—205, 1980.
20. *Incineration of Radioactive Solid Wastes,* Rep. WASH-1168, U.S. Atomic Energy Commission, Washington, D.C., 142 pp., 1970.
21. **Drolet, T. S. and Sovka, J. A.**, An incinerator for power reactor low-level radioactive waste, Radwaste Management Workshop, New Orleans, January 12—14, 1977, Oak Ridge National Laboratories, 116—133.
22. **Kibbey, A. H.**, Summary of the ORNL-Sponsored Reactor Radwaste Management Workshop, ASME-IEEE Joint Power Conf., ASME Paper 77-JPGC-NE-14, Long Beach, California, September 18—21, 1977, 1977.
23. **Andrews, L. J.**, Engineered storage for the disposal of nonfuel bearing components from nuclear facilities and general radioactive waste, *Management of Radioactive Wastes from the Nuclear Fuel Cycle,* Proc. Symp., Vienna, March 22—26, 1976, International Atomic Energy Agency, Vienna, Vol. II, 373—382, 1976.
24. *Alternatives for Managing Wastes from Reactors and Post-Fission Operations in the LWR Fuel Cycle,* Rep. ERDA-76-43, U.S. Energy Research and Development Administration, Vol. 2, 12.1—12.29, 1976.
25. **Kraft, S. P.**, Notes on solidification workshop, Radwaste Management Workshop, New Orleans, January 12—14, 1977, Oak Ridge National Laboratories, 183—192.
26. Proposed standard for transuranic waste disposal, *U.S. Federal Register,* 79, 32921—32923, September 12, 1974.
27. *Barnwell Nuclear Fuel Plant Separation Facility Final Safety Analysis Report,* Allied-Gulf Nuclear Services, Barnwell, S.C., Vol. 3, 8.37—8.41, Amendment 8, 1976.
28. *Alternatives for Managing Wastes from Reactors and Post-Fission Operations in the LWR Fuel Cycle,* Rep. ERDA-76-43, U.S. Energy Research and Development Administration, Vol. 2, 15.1—15.27, 1976.
29. **La Guardia, T. S.**, Nuclear power-reactor decommissioning, *Nucl. Saf.,* 20, 15—23, 1979.
30. **McConnon, D. and Nemec, J. C.**, Experiences in decontamination/decommissioning of the Elk River reactor, *Proc. 2nd AEC Environmental Protection Conf.,* Albuquerque, April 16—19, 1974, Rep. WASH-1332 (74), U.S. Atomic Energy Commission, Washington, D.C., Vol. 2, 785—824, 1974.
31. *Cleaning Up the Remains of Nuclear Facilities — A Multibillion Dollar Problem,* Rep. EMD-77—46, Office of the Comptroller of the U.S., Washington, D.C., 33 pp., 1977.
32. **Schneider, J. J. and Jenkins, C. E.**, *Technology, Safety, and Costs of Decommissioning a Reference Nuclear Fuel Reprocessing Plant,* Rep. NUREG-0278, Battelle Pacific Northwest Laboratory for U.S. Nuclear Regulatory Commission, Vol. 1, 7—95, 1977.
33. **Andersen, R. L., Cooley, L. R., Beck, T. J., and Strauss, C. S.**, *Institutional Radioactive Wastes,* Rep. NUREG/CR-0028, U.S. Nuclear Regulatory Commission, University of Maryland (Baltimore), 97 pp., 1978.
34. **Beck, T. J., Cooley, L. R., and McCampbell, M. R.**, *Institutional Radioactive Waste — 1977,* Rep. NUREG/CR-1137, University of Maryland (Baltimore), 134 pp., 1979.
35. **Magarrell, J.**, Universities face new curbs on dumping radioactive wastes, *Chronicle on Higher Education,* 1, May 29, 1979.

36. **Straub, C. S.,** *Low-Level Radioactive Wastes — Their Handling, Treatment and Disposal,* U.S. Atomic Energy Commission, Washington, D.C., 315—338, 1964.
37. **Bradley, F. J.,** Radioactive waste disposal, *Handbook of Radioactive Nuclides,* Wang, Y., Ed., CRC Press, Cleveland, Ohio, 1969, 781—794.
38. **Roché-Farmer, L.,** *Study of Alternative Methods for the Management of Liquid Scintillation Counting Wastes,* Rep. NUREG-0656, U.S. Nuclear Regulatory Commission, 37 pp., 1980.
39. **Lee, P. K., Shotts, J. G., and Spate, D. L.,** Management and Surveillance of a University Radioactive Waste Burial Site, *Low-Level Radioactive Waste Management,* Proc. Health Physics Society 12th Midyear Topical Symp., February 11—15, 1979, Williamsburg, Va., Rep. EPA 502/3-79-002, U.S. Environmental Protection Agency, 141—150, 1979.
40. **Eng, J., Hendricks, D. W., Feldman, J., and Giardina, P. A.,** Low-Level Radioactive Waste from Rare Metals Processing Facilities, *Low-Level Radioactive Waste Managment,* Proc. Health Physics Society 12th Midyear Topical Symp. February 11—15, 1979, Williamsburg, Va., Rep. EPA 520/3-79-002, U.S. Environmental Protection Agency, 49—60, 1979.
41. *Regulation of Federal Radioactive Waste Activities,* Rep. NUREG-0527, U.S. Nuclear Regulatory Commission, 1979.
42. **Holcomb, W. F.,** A summary of shallow land burial of radioactive wastes at commercial sites between 1962 and 1976 with projections, *Nucl. Saf.,* 19, 50—59, 1978, Addendum, 19, 238, 1978.
43. **O'Connell, M. F. and Holcomb, W. F.,** A summary of low-level radioactive wastes buried at commercial sites between 1962—1973 with projections to the year 2000, *Radiat. Data Rep.,* 15, 759—767, 1974.
44. **Blomeke, J. O.,** Projections of future requirements in waste management, presented at the Workshop on Nuclear Waste Management, Health Physics Society Annu. Meet., New York, July, 1971.
45. *Alternatives for Managing Wastes from Reactors and Post-Fission Operations in the LWR Fuel Cycle,* Rep. ERDA-76-43, U.S. Energy Research and Development Administration Vol. 1, 3.1—3.23, 1976.
46. *Alternatives for Managing Wastes from Reactors and Post-Fission Operations in the LWR Fuel Cycle,* Rep. ERDA-76-43, U.S. Energy Research and Development Administration, Vol. 4, 24.1—24.49, 1976.
47. **Duguid, J. O.,** Groundwater transport of radionuclides from buried wastes: a case study at Oak Ridge National Laboratories, *Proc. 2nd AEC Environmental Protection Conf.,* Albuquerque, April 16—19, 1974, WASH-1332 (74), Vol. 1, 511—529, 1974.
48. **Means, J. L., Crenar, D. A., and Duguid, J. O.,** Migration of radioactive wastes: radionuclide mobilization by complexing agents, *Science,* 200, 1477—1480, 1978.
49. *Final Environmental Impact, Waste Management Operations, Savannah River Plant, Aiken, South Carolina,* ERDA-1537, U.S. Energy Research and Development Administration, (II) 116—126, (III) 19—20, (III) 121, September, 1977.
50. National Academy of Sciences, Radioactive Waste Management at the Hanford Reservation, *Nucl. Saf.,* 20, 434—445, 1979.
51. **Wegele, A. E.,** Comments on 'Radioactive Waste Management at the Hanford Reservation, *Nucl. Saf.,* 21, 214—216, 1980.
52. *Final Environmental Statement, Waste Management Operations, Hanford Reservation, Richland, Washington,* Rep. ERDA-1538, U.S. Energy Research and Development Administration, Vol. 1, (II) 1—2, (III) 1—26, (III) 2—21.
53. **O'Farrell, T. P. and Gilbert, R. O.,** Transport of radioactive materials by jackrabbits on the Hanford Reservation, *Health Phys.,* 29, 9—15, 1975.
54. **Springer, J. T.,** ^{90}Sr and ^{137}Cs in coyote scats from the Hanford Reservation, *Health Phys.,* 36, 31—33, 1978.
55. **Markham, O. D., Puphal, K. W., and Filer, T. D.,** Plutonium and americium contamination near a transuranic storage area in Southeastern Idaho, *J. Environ. Qual.,* 7, 422—428, 1978.
56. **Hendricks, D. W. and Fort, C. W., Jr.,** *Radiation Survey in Beatty, Nevada and Surrounding Area (March, 1976),* Tech. Note ORP/LV-76-1, U.S. Environmental Protection Agency, Office of Radiation Programs, Las Vegas Facility, 38 pp., April, 1976.
57. **Fry, R. M.,** Radioactive waste disposal, *Am. J. Public Health,* 59, 448—450, 1969.
58. **Meyer, G. L.,** Preliminary data on the occurrence of transuranic nuclides in the environment at the radioactive waste burial site Maxey Flats, Kentucky, Rep. EPA-520/3-75-021, U.S. Environmental Protection Agency, 72 pp., 1976.
59. **Papadopulos, S. S. and Winograd, I. J.,** Storage of low-level radioactive wastes in the ground: Hydrogeologic and hydrochemical factors. With an appendix on the Maxey Flats, Ky. radioactive waste storage site: Current knowledge and data needs for a quantitative hydrogeologic evaluation, Open-File Rep. 74—344, U.S. Geological Survey, 49 pp., 1974.
60. **Clark, D. T.,** A history and preliminary inventory report on the Kentucky radioactive waste disposal site, *Radiat. Data Rep.,* 14, 573—585, 1973.

61. Gat, U., Thomas, J. D., and Clark, D. T., Radioactive waste inventory at the Maxey Flats nuclear burial site, *Health Phys.*, 30, 281—289, 1976.
62. Meyer, G. L., Recent experience with land burial of solid low-level radioactive wastes, *Management of Radioactive Wastes from the Nuclear Fuel Cycle,* Proc. Symp. Vienna, March 22—26, 1976, International Atomic Energy Agency, Vienna, Vol. II, 384—395, 1976.
63. Blanchard, R. L., Montgomery, D. M., Kolde, H. E., and Gels, G. L., Supplementary radiological measurements at the Maxey Flats radioactive burial site, 1976—1977, Rep. EPA-520/5-78-011, U.S. Environmental Protection Agency, 33 pp., 1978.
64. Neel, J. N., Statement, *Low-Level Radioactive Waste Disposal,* Hearings before a Subcommittee, Committee on Government Operations, U.S. House of Representatives, Washington, D.C., 255—265, 1976.
65. Lester, R. K. and Rose, D. J., The nuclear wastes at West Valley, New York, *Technol. Rev.*, 79, 20—29, 1977.
66. Prudic, D. E. and Randall, A. D., Ground-water hydrology and subsurface migration of radioisotopes at a low-level radioactive disposal site, West Valley, N.Y., Open-File Rep. 77-566, U.S. Geological Survey, 27 pp., 1977.
67. Cashman, T. J., Statement, in *Decommissioning and Decontamination,* Hearings before the Subcommittee on the Environment and the Atmosphere, Committee on Science and Technology, U.S. House of Representatives, Washington, D.C., 217—226, 1977.
68. Terpilak, M. S. and Jorgensen, B. L., Environmental radiation effects of nuclear facilities in New York State, *Radiat. Data Rep.*, 15, 375—400, 1974.
69. Matuszek, J. M., Strnisa, F. V., and Baxter, C. F., Radionuclide dynamics and health implications for the New York Nuclear Service Center's radioactive waste burial site, *Management of Radioactive Wastes from the Nuclear Fuel Cycle,* Proc. Symp., Vienna, March 22—26, 1976, International Atomic Energy Agency, Vienna, Vol. II, 359—372, 1976.
70. Jump, M. J., Current practices for disposal of solid low-level radioactive waste, *Radioactive Wastes from the Nuclear Fuel Cycle,* AIChE Symp. Ser., Tomlinson, R. E., Ed., 154, Vol. 72, 65—68, 1976.
71. *Nuclear Waste Burial Grounds and Storage Sites in Illinois,* Hearings before a subcommittee, Committee on Government Operations, U.S. House of Representatives, Washington, D.C., 111, 415, 1978.
72. Report of the Subcommittee on Radioactive Waste Management of the Illinois Commission on Atomic Energy, 15 pp., February 1978 (reprinted in Reference 5).
73. Nuclear Waste Burial Grounds and Storage Sites in Illinois, Hearings before a subcommittee, Committee on Government Operations, U.S. House of Representatives, Washington, D.C., 210—212, 1978.
74. Wallace, J. R. and Fogle, G. H., *Report of Geologic and Hydrologic Studies near Snelling, South Carolina,* LETCO Job No. 6605, Law Engineering Testing Company, Atlanta, 1970.
75. Reichert, S. O., Radionuclides in ground water at the Savannah River Plant waste disposal facilities, *J. Geophys. Res.*, 67, 4363—4374, 1962.
76. Ebenhack, D. G., Operational Experience at Chem-Nuclear's Barnwell Facility, *Low-Level Radioactive Waste Management,* Proc. Health Physics Society 12th Midyear Topical Symp., February 11—15, 1979, Williamsburg, Va., Rep. EPA 520/3-79-002, U.S. Environmental Protection Agency, 133—140, 1979.
77. Shealy, H. G., Statement, *Low-Level Radioactive Waste Disposal,* Hearings before a Subcommittee, Committee on Government Operations, U.S. House of Representatives, Washington, D.C., 300—352, 1976.
78. Cohen, B. L. and Jow, H. N., A generic hazard evaluation of low-level waste burial grounds, *Nucl. Technol.*, 41, 381—388, 1978.
79. Adams, J. A. and Rogers, V. L., *A classification system for radioactive waste disposal — what goes where?,* Rep. NUREG-0456, U.S. Nuclear Regulatory Commission, Washington, D.C., 20—25, 1978.
80. Hickman, W. W., Plan for retrieval of solid low-level radioactive waste at NRTS, *Proc. 2nd Environmental Protection Conf.*, Albuquerque, April 16—19, 1974, Rep. 1332 (74), Vol. 2, 1007—1039, 1974.
81. The Shallow Land Burial of Low-level Radioactively Contaminated Solid Waste, Panel on Land Burial, National Research Council, National Academy of Sciences, Washington, D.C., 56—61, 1976.
82. Colombo, P. and Neilson, R. M., Jr., *Properties of Radioactive Wastes and Wastes and Waste Containers — First Topical Report,* Rep. BNL-NUREG-50957, NUREG/CR-0619, U.S. Nuclear Regulatory Commission, Brookhaven National Laboratory, 152 pp., 1979.
83. Lea, F. M., *The Chemistry of Cement and Concrete,* 3rd, ed., Edward Arnold, London, 1970, 338—358.

84. **Inoue, Y. and Morisawa, S.**, On the selection of a ground disposal site for radioactive wastes: an approach to its safety evaluation, *Health Phys.*, 26, 53—63, 1974.
85. **Colombo, P. and Neilson, R. M., Jr.**, Some techniques for the solidification of radioactive wastes in concrete, *Nucl. Technol.*, 32, 30—38, 1977.
86. **Colombo, P., Weiss, A. J., and Francis, A. J.**, Evaluation of isotope migration — land burial: Water chemistry at commercially operated low-level radioactive waste disposal sites, Q. Prog. Rep., October—December, 1976, Rep. BNL-NUREG-50670, U.S. Nuclear Regulatory Commission, Brookhaven National Laboratories, 26 pp., 1977.
87. **Siple, G. E.**, Geology and ground water of the Savannah River Plant and vicinity, U.S. Geological Water Survey Paper 1841, 71, 1967.
88. **Inoue, Y. and Kaufman, W. J.**, Prediction of movement of radionuclides in solution through porous media, *Health Phys.*, 9, 705—715, 1963.
89. **Colombo, P. and Weiss, A. J.**, Evaluation of isotope migration — land burial: water chemistry at commercially operated low-level radioactive waste disposal sites, Prog. Rep. No. 11, October—December, 1978, Rep. BNL-NUREG-51113, NUREG/CR-1167, U.S. Nuclear Regulatory Commission, Brookhaven National Laboratories, 53 pp., 1977.
90. **Colombo, P. and Weiss, A. J.**, Evaluation of isotope migration — land burial: water chemistry at commercially operated low-level radioactive waste disposal sites, Prog. Rep. No. 10, July—September 1978, Rep. BNL-NUREG-51083, NUREG/CR-1037, U.S. Nuclear Regulatory Commission, Brookhaven National Laboratories, 38 pp., 1979.
91. Tchobanoglous, G., Theisen, H., and Eliassen, R., *Solid Wastes — Engineering Principles and Management Issues,* McGraw-Hill, New York, 1977, 326—344.
92. **Polzer, W. L., Fowler, E. B., and Essington, E. H.**, Characterization of wastes and soils which affect transport of radionuclides through the soil and their relationship to waste management, Annu. Rep. FY78, Rep. LA-UR-79-1025, NUREG/CR-0842, U.S. Nuclear Regulatory Commission, Los Alamos Scientific Laboratories, 71 pp., 1979.
93. **Grim, R. E.**, *Applied Clay Mineralogy,* McGraw-Hill, New York, 1962, 29—34.
94. **Tamura, T.**, Sorption phenomena significant in radioactive-waste disposal, *Underground Waste Management and Environmental Implications,* Proc. Symp., Houston, December 6—9, 1971, Cook, T. D., Ed., American Association of Petroleum Geologists, Tulsa, Oklahoma, 318—330, 1972.
95. **Francis, C. W.**, Plutonium mobility in soil and uptake in plants: a review, *J. Environ. Qual.*, 2, 67—70, 1973.
96. **Cleveland, J. M. and Rees, T. F.**, Investigation of solubilization of plutonium and americium in soil by natural humic compounds, *Environ. Sci. Technol.*, 10, 802—806, 1976.
97. **Colombo, P. and Weiss, A. J.**, Evaluation of isotope migration — land burial: water chemistry at commercially operated low-level radioactive waste disposal sites, Prog. Rep. No. 9, April—June, 1978, Rep. BNL-NUREG-50965, NUREG/CR-0707, U.S. Nuclear Regulatory Commission, Brookhaven National Laboratories, 29 pp., 1979.
98. **Baver, L. D.**, *Soil Physics,* 3rd ed., John Wiley & Sons, New York, 1956, 199—303.
99. **Wallace, A.**, Increased uptake of americium 241 by plants caused by the chelating agent DTPA, *Health Phys.*, 22, 559—562, 1972.
100. *Radiological Impact Caused by Emission of Radionuclides into the Air of the United States — Preliminary Report,* Rep. EPA 520/7-79-006, U.S. Environmental Protection Agency, 2.7-1—2.7-8, 1979.
101. Environmental Assessment for Decontamination of the Three Mile Island Unit 2 Reactor Building Atmosphere, Rep. NUREG-0662 (Draft), U.S. Nuclear Regulatory Commission, 6—28, 1980.
102. **Mershad, E. A., Thomasson, W. W., and Dauby, J. J.**, Packaging of tritium-contaminated liquid waste, *Nucl. Technol.*, 32, 53—59, 1977.
103. **Hawkins, R. H.**, Migration of tritium from a nuclear waste burial site, *Proc. 3rd Environmental Protection Conf.*, Chicago, September 23—26, 1975, Rep. ERDA-92, CONF-750967, Energy Research and Development Administration, Washington, D.C., Vol. 2, 622—637, 1975.
104. **Mawson, C. A. and Russell, A. E.**, Canadian experience with a national waste-management facility, *Management of Low- and Intermediate-level Radioactive Wastes,* Proc. Symp. Aix-En-Provence, France, September 7—11, 1970, International Atomic Energy Agency, Vienna, 183—194, 1970.
105. **Garten, C. T., Jr.**, Radiocesium uptake by a population of cotton rats *(sigmodon hispidus)* inhabiting the banks of a radioactive liquid waste pond, *Health Phys.*, 36, 39—45, 1979.
106. Appendix B, Concentrations in air and water above natural background, in Title 10, Part 20, Code of Federal Regulations, Washington, D.C.,
107. *Radioactive Waste Disposal into the Ground,* International Atomic Energy Agency, Vienna, 41—43, 1965.
108. **Morisawa, S. and Inoue, Y.**, On the selection of a ground disposal site for radioactive wastes by means of a computer, *Health Phys.*, 27, 447—457, 1974.

109. **Macbeth, P. J., Wehmen, G., Thamer, B. J., and Card, D. H.**, Evaluation of alternative methods for the disposal of low-level radioactive wastes, Report NUREG/CR-0680, FBDU-209-03, U.S. Nuclear Regulatory Commission, Ford, Bacon & Davis Utah, 168 pp., 1979.
110. **Hawkins, R. H. and Horton, J. H.**, Bentonite as a protective cover for buried radioactive waste, *Health Phys.*, 13, 287—292, 1967.
111. **Wickland, C. E.**, Packaging Rocky Flats waste, *Nucl. Technol.*, 32, 25—29, 1977.
112. **Grant, C., Hite, J. C., and Shealy, H. G.**, Economic analysis of funding arrangements for maintenance, surveillance and contingency costs associated with burial of low-level radioactive wastes in South Carolina, Rep. AE 379, South Carolina Agric. Exp. Stn., Clemson University, 33 pp., 1974.
113. SC triples storage fee for n-wastes, *Charlotte Observer*, p. 6C, September 20, 1979.

HIGH-LEVEL RADIOACTIVE WASTE FROM LIGHT WATER REACTORS*

Bernard L. Cohen

In this section, the decay history of radioactive nuclei is presented as its production was traced during the operation of a light water reactor. As an example of the factors interacting in the evaluation of environment impacts by high-level waste, the potential environmental impacts are calculated as a function of time, including thermal effects, external gamma radiation, ingestion and inhalation pathways, and neutron emission; these potential hazards are compared with other man-made hazards. Various scenarios in which damage may occur are discussed, including the worst conceivable circumstances within reason and what are considered to be the most probable circumstances. A model for estimating the latter is developed and critiqued. The requirements for surveillance are discussed, and a comparison of risks from long-term buried wastes is made with the hazards from uranium mill tailings.

INTRODUCTION

In a light water reactor, uranium that is enriched to about 3.3% in ^{235}U is exposed to neutrons which induce fission and capture reactions. A great many of the products of these reactions are radioactive, and their radioactivity and that of their daughters, is a potential health hazard from a nuclear power industry. In a previous paper, this problem was explained in some details, and efforts were made to assess the hazards and place them in perspective. In this section, only problem-solving approaches, data, and references that may be useful in evaluating waste disposal proposals from the standpoint of plausibility and ultimate feasibility of enduring public safety will be presented. These methods of safety evaluation are not intended as a substitute for the detailed research, development, and design efforts required to provide specific waste disposal equipment or facilities. Also, this section does not deal with the methods for monitoring and securing waste disposal sites which are covered elsewhere in the handbook.

All calculations of isotopic inventories were carried out with the Oak Ridge National Laboratory computer program ORIGEN,[3] a highly versatile code which simultaneously solves the coupled differential equations for production and decay of a large number of isotopes. The program includes an extensive library of nuclear data, which was widely used.

Calculations were carried out for 1 t (1000 kg) of original fuel charged to the reactor, and many results are given on that basis. Frequent reference is also made to the total waste generated by 1 year of all nuclear power in the U.S. This is taken to be 400 million kw (400 gigawatt [GWe] electricity output) average power production, about 80% above current experience. This leaves allowances for growth and a factor of conservatism.

PHYSICAL CHARACTERISTICS AND COMPOSITION OF FUEL AND WASTES

Reactor Phase

In a typical design situation,[3] the reactor would produce an average of 30 Mw of

* A previous version of this section has been published in *Review of Modern Physics*.

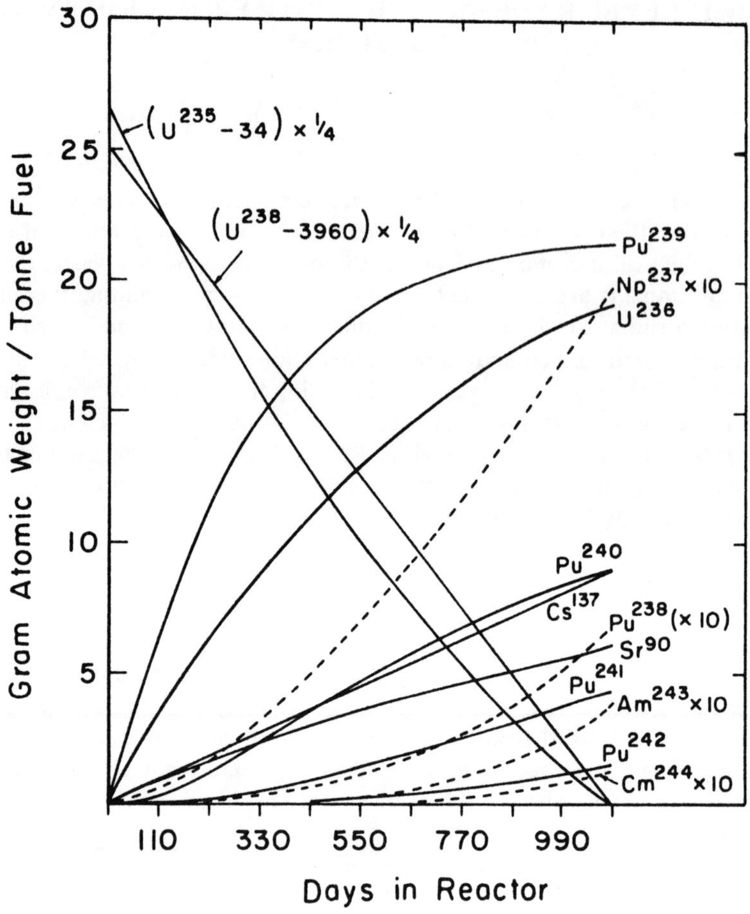

FIGURE 1. Quantities of various nuclei in reactor fuel as a function of their time in the reactor. Dashed curves have been multiplied by ten.

Table 1
CAPTURE AND FISSION CROSS SECTIONS FOR VARIOUS NUCLEI (IN BARNS)

Values are Averaged over the Neutron Spectrum in a Light Water Reactor[3]

Nucleus	σ(n,γ)	σ(n,f)	Nucleus	σ(n,γ)	σ(n,f)
^{238}U	8.4	0.60	^{235}U	105	409
^{239}Pu	443	1060	^{236}U	74	3.2
^{240}Pu	897	2.5	^{237}Np	359	2.5
^{241}Pu	394	1110	^{238}Pu	366	19
^{242}Pu	438	0.2	^{234}U	281	3.9
^{243}Am	566	0.8	^{90}Sr	1.23	—
^{244}Cm	223	4.9	^{137}Cs	0.17	—

thermal power per (metric) tonne of fuel.* The average neutron flux would be 2.9 × 10^{13} neutrons/cm^2-sec. Any given fuel rod would be replaced after about 1100 days in

* One metric tonne = 1000 kg.

the reactor, which means that 1 t of fuel produces 33,000 MW-days of thermal energy. The original fuel would contain an average of 3.3% ^{235}U and at discharge this would be reduced to 0.8%, a consumption of 24.9 kg/t of fuel. In the process, 2.4% of the ^{238}U which is 23.8 kg/t of fuel is also consumed. The fission reaction releases about 191 MeV of energy (exclusive of neutrino kinetic energy) — 168 MeV as fission kinetic energy, 5 MeV as neutron kinetic energy, 5 MeV as prompt gamma rays, 7 MeV as fission product beta particles, and 6 MeV as gamma rays accompanying beta decay. This total converts to 0.91 MW-days/g (910,000 MW days/t) undergoing fission, so the 33,000 MW-days /t yield implies that 3.6% of the original fuel undergoes fission.

The burn-up and build-up of various materials is shown as a function of time in Figure 1, and an understanding of it is aided by the list of cross sections given in Table 1. The ^{235}U is burned up exponentially, at a rate proportional to the quantity remaining, 80% by fission and 20% by capture to ^{236}U Because of its small cross section, only 10% of the ^{236}U becomes ^{237}Np which, with its large cross section, is more than 25% converted to ^{238}Pu. (We ignore short half-life beta decays needed to convert ^{237}U to ^{237}Np, ^{238}Np to ^{238}Pu, etc).

The ^{238}U is essentially burned up linearly with time (because of the small percentage consumption), 7% by fast neutron fission and 93% by neutron capture to produce ^{239}Pu; however, the latter, because of its large cross section, is largely destroyed, 71% by fission and 29% by capture. About 85 gram atoms of ^{239}Pu are produced but only 23 gram atoms survive; therefore, 0.71 (85—23) = 44 gram atoms of ^{239}Pu per tonne of fuel undergo fission as compared with 84 gram atoms of ^{235}U (from Figure 1, 105 g atoms of ^{235}U are consumed, and from Table 1, 409/514 of this undergoes fission). The ^{239}Pu that undergoes capture becomes ^{240}Pu, which has a very large cross section and thus is rapidly converted to ^{241}Pu. The latter has very large cross sections both for fission and for capture leading to ^{242}Pu, which may be followed by further neutron captures to produce ^{243}Am and ^{244}Cm. At the end of life, the fissile materials in gram atoms per tonne of fuel are ^{235}U-34, ^{239}Pu-23, and ^{241}Pu-4.4, so that after weighting by fission cross sections we see that the thermal fission reactions are occurring 32% in ^{235}U, 57% in ^{239}Pu, and 11% in ^{241}Pu.

The build-up of two important fission products, ^{90}Sr and ^{137}Cs, is also shown in Figure 1. Both of these have long half-lives and modest cross sections and, hence, build up almost linearly in time. On the whole, for each 1000 kg of uranium charged to the reactor, 44 kg of uranium is converted to 35 kg of fission products plus 9 kg of transuranics. In addition, this fuel contains 134 kg of oxygen (the material is UO_2) which is virutally unaffected. It is clad with 272 kg of a Zr alloy, containing 249 kg of Zr; 9.6 kg of Ni; 3.7 kg each of Fe, Cr, and Sn; and a few hundred grams of other materials of which the most significant is 54 g of cobalt, since 10% of it is converted into ^{60}Co, which is a potent gamma ray emitter with a 5.27-year half-life.

All of this material is sent to a fuel reprocessing plant where it is cut into pieces, dissolved in acid, and chemically processed to extract 99.5% of the uranium and plutonium to be used for fabrication of new fuel. In addition, the gases H, Kr, and Xe come off at this stage. The remains are what we refer to as "high level radioactive waste." In practice, cladding hulls do not dissolve and are handled separately, and 99.9% of the Br and I is removed for separate storage, but we treat these materials as though they are part of the waste. In our quantitative discussions, we will assume that the fuel is reprocessed 5 months after removal from the reactor. In general, our results are rather insensitive to this time interval, but if it is extended to several years, the decay of ^{241}Pu into ^{241}Am can increase the amount of the latter by an order of magnitude.

Waste Phase

The material in the waste continues to undergo radioactive decay, and while the

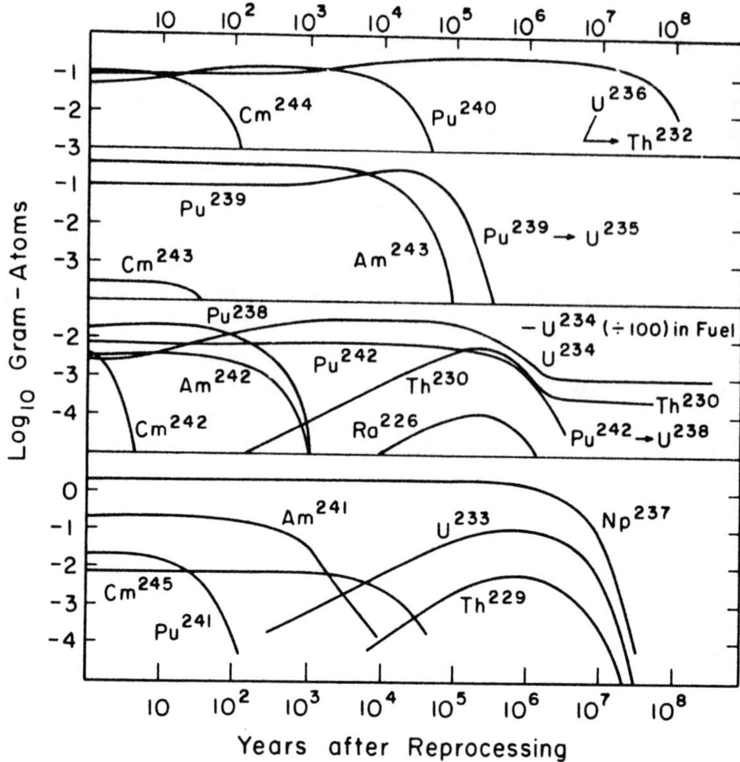

FIGURE 2. Quantities of various nuclei in waste as a function of time after reprocessing. The four parts of the figure are for the four radioactive decay series, (from top) A = 4n, (4n−1), (4n−2), and (4n−3) where A is the atomic weight and n is an integer.

decay chains are simple and straightforward for the fission products, the same is not true for the transuranics. The latter may be understood with the help of Figure 2 for each of the four decay chains, A = 4n, 4n − 1, 4n − 2, and 4n − 3 (where n is an integer). Pertinent half-lives and decay daughters are listed in Table 2. For A = 4n, initially there are nearly equal quantities of ^{244}Cm, ^{240}Pu (recall that 99.5% of the Pu is extracted in reprocessing), and ^{236}U. The ^{244}Cm decays rapidly into ^{240}Pu which eventually decays into ^{236}U, which, in turn, very slowly decays into ^{232}Th. (We skip over the decay chains of the naturally radioactive isotopes ^{232}Th, ^{235}U, and ^{238}U because their long half-lives make the hazards from them relatively unimportant. They are, however, included in all calculations.)

For A = 4n − 1, there is initially about four times as much ^{243}Am as ^{239}Pu and the former decays into the latter as does the small amount of ^{243}Cm present. The ^{239}Pu eventually decays into ^{235}U.

For A = 4n − 2, after 1 year where Figure 2 begins, there is a considerable amount of ^{242}Pu, ^{242}Cm, ^{242}Am, ^{238}Pu, and ^{234}U. The ^{234}U is carried over from the original fuel, since it is a naturally occurring isotope of uranium; most of the ^{238}Pu is derived from ^{242}Cm decay in the 1 year since reprocessing, as 99.5% of the original ^{238}Pu was removed in reprocessing. The ^{242}Pu decays into ^{238}U, but the ^{242}Cm and ^{242}Am by-pass ^{238}U by decaying into ^{238}Pu, which then decays directly to ^{234}U. The decay of ^{234}U to ^{230}Th, ^{226}Ra, and eventually to ^{210}Pb and ^{206}Pb is well-known, since ^{234}U is also a daughter of ^{238}U decay.

For A = 4n − 3, the decay is a straightforward chain, as ^{245}Cm → ^{241}Pu → ^{241}Am → ^{237}Np → ^{233}U → ^{229}Th → ^{207}Pb. The first three are not important contributors to the

Table 2
HALF-LIVES AND DECAY DAUGHTERS OF SELECTED NUCLEI (HALF-LIVES LESS THAN 1 YEAR ARE IGNORED IN FAVOR OF THEIR DECAY DAUGHTERS)

Nuclide	Half-life (years)	Daughters
^{244}Cm	18.1	^{240}Pu
^{240}Pu	6,760	^{236}U
^{236}U	2.39×10^{7}	^{232}Th
^{243}Cm	32	^{239}Pu
^{243}Am	7,650	^{239}Pu
^{239}Pu	24,000	^{235}U
^{242}Pu	3.79×10^{5}	^{238}U
^{242}Am	152	^{242}Cm
^{242}Cm	0.45	^{238}Pu
^{238}Pu	89	^{234}U
^{234}U	2.48×10^{5}	^{230}Th
^{230}Th	76,000	^{226}Ra
^{226}Ra	1,600	^{210}Pb
^{210}Pb	22	^{206}Pb
^{245}Cm	9,320	^{241}Pu
^{241}Pu	13	^{241}Am
^{241}Am	458	^{237}Np
^{237}Np	2.1×10^{6}	^{233}U
^{233}U	1.6×10^{5}	^{229}Th
^{229}Th	7,300	^{209}Bi

remainder of the chain, since ^{237}Np is initially present in such large quantities, but they have important potential environmental impacts during their lifetimes.

In summary, all four decay chains contribute important transuranics. There are important contributions in two chains from lower atomic number species, as ^{238}U gets by-passed in the $(4n - 2)$ series and there are no half-lives longer than 2.1 million years in the $(4n - 3)$ series.

The fission products with half-lives longer than 4 years are listed in Table 3. We see that with the unimportant exceptions of ^{151}Sm, ^{166m}Ho, and ^{79}Se, there are no half-lives between 30 and 10^5 years, a truly remarkable gap. Among the shorter lived group, ^{137}Cs and ^{90}Sr are of predominant importance, especially since ^{85}Kr is not included in the waste. From the sum of the figures in the last column, we see that 87% of the fission product atoms have half-lives shorter than 4 years or longer than 4×10^{10} years, and hence, are not of concern for long-term waste storage.

A ruling* has been published stating that nuclear waste be converted into a dry and stable solid within 5 years and shipped to a federal repository within 10 years. A commonly discussed plan is to incorporate the waste into glass in steel canisters about 10 ft long by 1 ft in diameter and bury it deep underground in some carefully chosen geological formation, with spacings of about 10 m between canisters. The dimensions are dictated largely by heat transfer problems. The thermal power in the waste due to various isotopes is shown in Figure 3. It may be noted that it decreases by nearly an order of magnitude between 1 and 10 years. As shown in Figure 4, calculations,[42] including thermal conductivity of the rock in which it is buried, indicate that this translates into nearly an order of magnitude reduction in maximum wall temperature if burial is delayed for 10 years. For the first 400 years after burial, the heat is due largely

* Code of Federal Regulations, Title 10, Part 50, Appendix F, available from office of Standards Development, U.S. Nuclear Regulatory Commission, Washington, D.C. 20555.

Table 3
LONG HALF-LIFE FISSION PRODUCTS[a]

Nucleus (Half-lives 10 to 100 years)	Half-life (years)	Percentage of gram atoms[b]
^{3}H	12.3	0.008
^{85}Kr	10.8	0.11
^{90}Sr	29	2.0
^{113m}Cd	14	0.0001
^{121m}Sn	25	10^{-7}
^{137}Cs	30	3.0
^{151}Sm	90	0.10
^{152}Eu	12	0.0001
^{154}Eu	16	0.10
Total		5.3
Half-lives 100 to 4×10^{10} years		
^{79}Se	7×10^{4}	0.01
^{93}Zr	9×10^{5}	2.7
^{99}Tc	2×10^{5}	2.9
^{107}Pd	7×10^{6}	0.74
^{126}Sn	1×10^{5}	0.05
^{129}I	1.6×10^{7}	0.61
^{135}Cs	2×10^{6}	0.81
^{166m}Ho	1.2×10^{3}	10^{-6}
Total		7.8

[a] For 30-mw 1100 days operating time, in 2.9×10^{13} n/cm²-sec, per metric tonne of fuel.

[b] This column is the percentage of all fission product atoms that are the designated isotope.

to ^{90}Sr, ^{137}Cs, and their daughters; it decreases by three orders of magnitude during this period. After 400 years, the dominant contributors for the next 100,000 years are plutonium and americium isotopes, and their decay daughters are dominant thereafter.

The reason for the choice of canister diameter and spacing is evident in Figure 5.[42] Larger diameters would be inconvenient for drilling and handling, and larger spacings would be more costly while contributing little to the heat dissipation problem. The height of the canister is chosen to minimize handling problems with due consideration for the total thermal power of the planar array. For a power of 250 KW/ha, corresponding to a square array with 11.8 m between rows of canisters and burial at 10 years, the temperature rise is shown in Figure 6[42] for various distances above and below the burial plane (assumed infinite in extent) and at various times after burial. It is seen that the maximum temperature does not occur until 40 years after burial. Also indicated in Figure 6 is one of the several advantages of burial in rock salt. Its thermal conductivity is about three times higher than that of average rock (1.24×10^{-2} vs. 4.1×10^{-3} cal/sec-cm².°C/cm) which results in a reduction of temperature rise in the burial plane from 145° to 85°C.

The wastes contained in a single waste canister are those from approximately 3 tons of original fuel, and represent about one tenth of the total waste produced annually by a 1000 MWe* reactor. A canister has a total volume of about 0.2 m³ and weighs

* MWe = megawatt electricity output, 1 GWe = 1000 MWe.

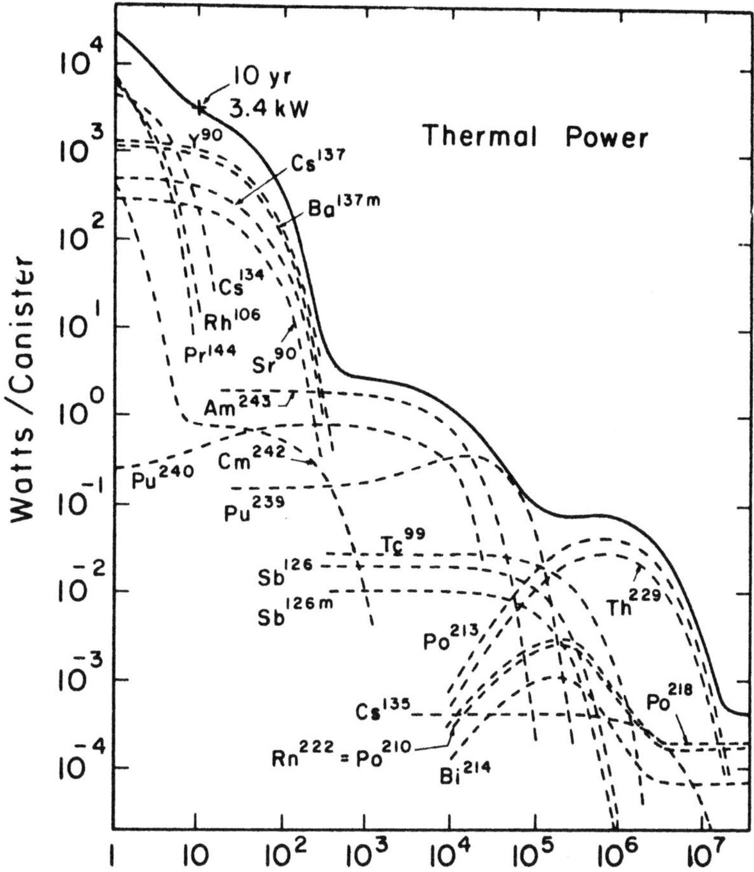

FIGURE 3. Thermal power released by the radioactivity in one waste canister. Such a canister contains the waste from 100 MWe-year; thus a typical large power plant would produce ten canisters of waste per year. Dashed curves are contributions from individual isotopes, and the solid curve is the sum of these contributions.

about 600 kg, including 86 kg of fission products, 14.4 kg of U, 1.44 kg of Np, and 0.66 kg of Pu, Am, and Cm combined. The steel casing contributes a great deal to safety in handling and transporting waste, but it is usually assumed that it corrodes away shortly after burial.

If all U.S. power were nuclear (400 GWe), about 4000 waste canisters per year would be generated. If they were buried in a square matrix with 10-m spacing between rows, they would occupy 0.4 km^2. A thousand years of waste so buried would, therefore, occupy 400 km,^{2} or an area of 12 mi.^{2}

POTENTIAL ENVIRONMENTAL IMPACTS OF HIGH-LEVEL WASTE

The potential environmental impacts of radioactivity considered here are those due to both external radiation, with gamma rays or with neutrons, and internal radiation, with material taken into the body by inhalation or ingestion. All of these effects are governed by the radiation emission rate which, apart from a generally well-known branching ratio, is equal to the disintegration rate, ordinarily expressed as "curies." The conversion from "gram atoms" used in Figures 1 and 2 to curies is shown at the left side of Figure 7 for several nuclei that turn out to be important; the slopes of the

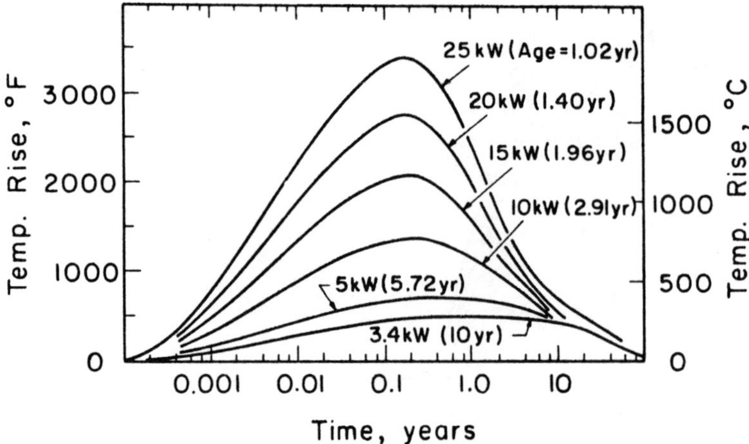

FIGURE 4. Effect of waste age at burial (labels attached to curves) on the wall temperature of a single buried waste canister, as a function of time after burial.[42] It is assumed that the surrounding rock has a thermal conductivity of 4.1×10^{-3} cal/cm²-sec/°C/cm, which is typical of crystalline rock.

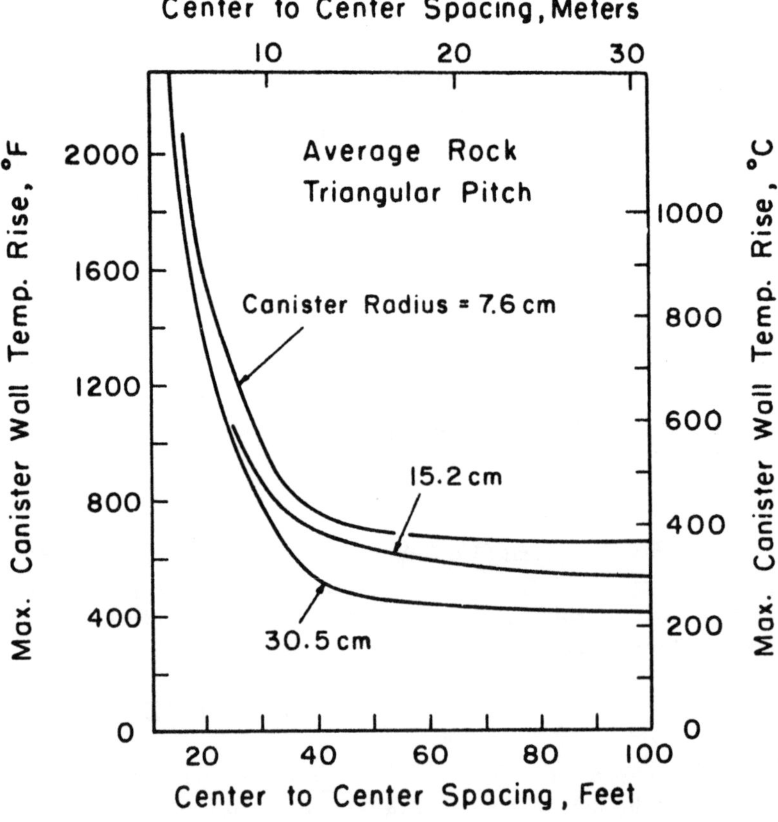

FIGURE 5. Effect of spacing and canister radius on maximum canister wall temperature.[42] It is assumed that each canister produces 3.4 kW of heat initially, decaying with a 30-year half-life.

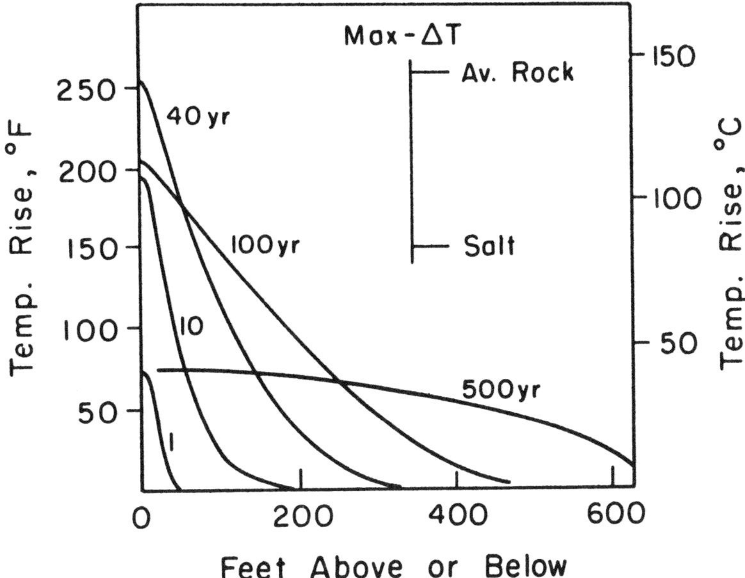

FIGURE 6. Rock temperature rise as a function of distance above or below the waste burial plane for various times after burial.[42] Thermal conductivity is as in Figure 4. The inset shows this temperature rise at the time when it is a maximum for burial in typical crystalline rock (assumed for curves) and in salt.

dashed lines are indicative of the half-life, with short half-lives sloping up to the right and long half-lives sloping down to the right.

The conversion from curies to thermal watts, used in constructing Figure 3, simply involves multiplying by the energies of the radiations emitted and converting from megaelectronvolts to joules. This is shown on the right side of Figure 7. All long half-life alpha emitters have about the same energy release; therefore, all dashed lines for these have about the same slope. The energy release from ^{90}Sr and ^{137}Cs decays is considerably lower, resulting in a lesser slope.

The effects of gamma radiation are roughly proportional to the gamma ray energy, and, thus, the pertinent quantity is gamma ray energy release per second, or just gamma ray power, expressed in watts. This is obtained by multiplying curies by the gamma ray energy release per disintegration and converting from megaelectronvolts per second to joules per second = watts. These conversions are not shown in Figure 7, but the results after reprocessing for each important isotope as a function of time are shown in Figure 8. The solid line in Figure 8 is the sum of all contributions. We see that ^{137}Cs is completely predominant from 10 to 400 years, after which ^{239}Np, ^{243}Am, and ^{126}Sb (a daughter of long-lived ^{126}Sn) predominate until Bi daughters of transuranics grow in and become important after 200,000 years.

The inhalation and ingestion hazards are much more complicated to calculate. For example, in calculating the risk of bone cancer per curie of a given ingested radioactive isotope, one must calculate the dose in rem to the bone and multiply it by the bone cancer risk per rem. The cancer risk per rem to various organs is obtained from the Committee on Biological Effects of Ionizing Radiation Report[48] and is listed in Table 4.

The calculation of dose to bone per curie ingested has been carried out using the International Commission on Radiological Protection (ICRP) procedure of considering only the organ giving the highest risk ("critical organ"). To ignore the others is to underestimate the risk somewhat, but this is more than compensated for by our as-

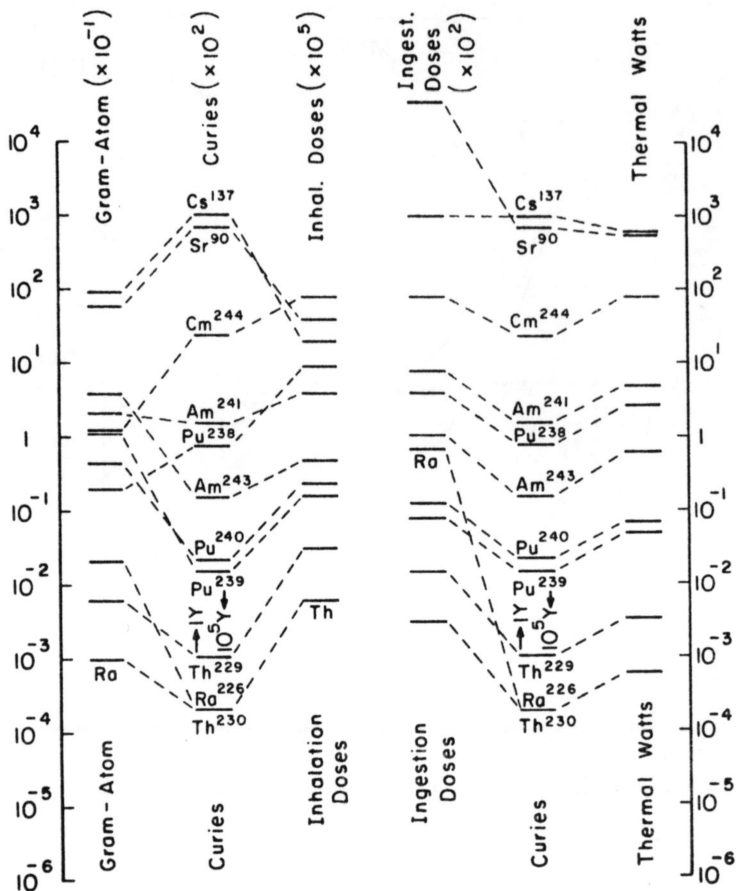

FIGURE 7. Conversions between curies and other interesting quantities for various radioactive isotopes that are important in the waste. Absolute values in the waste from 1 tonne of fuel may be read from the vertical scales after applying the indicated multipliers at a time 1 year after reprocessing (except for ^{226}Ra, ^{229}Th, and ^{230}Th which are for 10^5 years after reprocessing). Doses refers to number of cancer deaths expected if all of the material were to be taken into the bodies of humans, 10^2 inhalation doses ($\times 10^5$) means 10^7 inhalation doses. In this figure, all numbers as read from scales should be multiplied by the corresponding factors in parentheses.

sumption that all victims are of the most susceptible age (i.e., they have at least 45 years — 15 years latent period plus 30 years plateau period — life expectancy left and are not children less than age 10 from whom the risk is considerably lower) and by the general conservatism in ICRP estimates. In almost all important cases, the critical organ was the bone, with the only exceptions being ^{129}I (thyroid) and ^{99}Tc (G-I tract).

All the information needed for the above calculation is given in ICRP Publication Numbers 2 and 6.[24,25] Calculations were short-circuited by utilizing the relationships between the maximum permissible concentrations (MPC) given in tables in these publications and the maximum permissible organ dose rates. In particular, the MPC for a bone-seeking nuclide is the concentration of an isotope in water, which, if water is ingested at a rate of 2.2 1/day (0.8 m^3−W/year [where W refers to water]) would give a dose commitment of 30 rem to the bone (assuming that bone is the critical organ). Thus, a conversion from curies of a given radioactive nuclide produced per tonne of

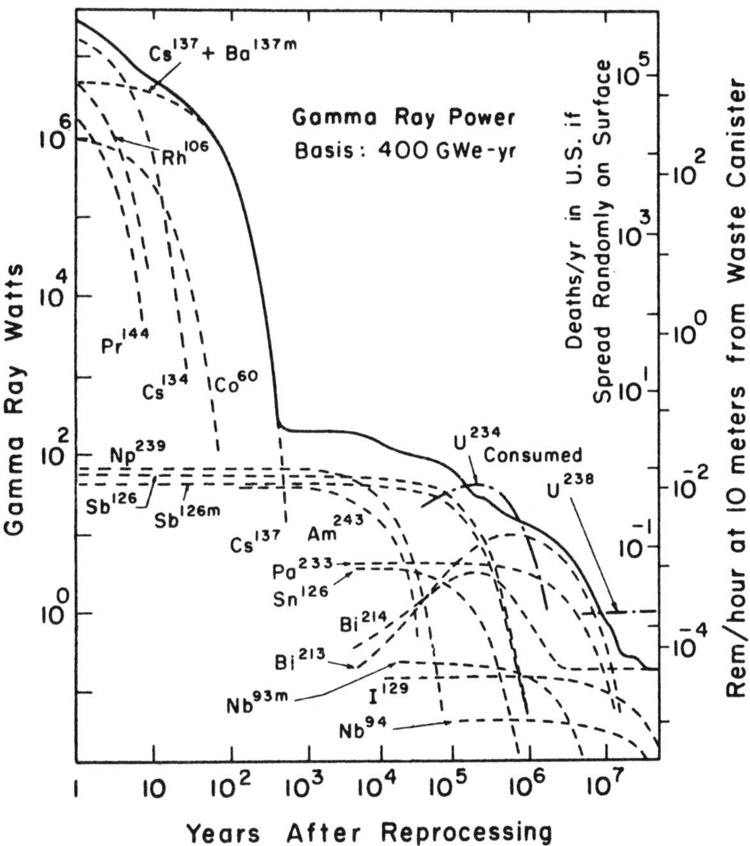

FIGURE 8. Gamma-ray power emitted by the waste from 400 GWe-year for nuclear electricity. Dashed curves are the contributions from various individual isotopes, and the solid curve is the total emitted power, which is the sum of these individual contributions. The dot-dash curves are what would be emitted by the uranium consumed by the operation. The scale inside the right margin shows the deaths per year expected from external gamma-ray-induced cancer if all of the waste were spread randomly (or uniformly) over the surface of the U.S. as a function of time when this is done. The scale on the outside of the right margin gives rem per hour exposure at a distance of 10 m from an unshielded waste canister (neglecting self-shielding by the canister material).

fuel to average "cancer dose"* per year in U.S. from that nuclide, if all our power were nuclear (requiring 1.2×10^4 t/year of fuel), is

$$\frac{\text{cancer doses}}{\text{year}} = \frac{\text{xCi}}{\text{tonne}} \times \frac{1 \text{ MPC}}{\text{y ci/m}^3\text{-W}} \times \frac{30 \text{ rem/MPC}}{0.8 \text{ m}^3\text{-W}} \times \frac{6 \times 10^{-6} \text{ deaths}}{\text{rem}} \times \frac{1.2 \times 10^4 \text{ t}}{\text{year}} = 2.7\,\text{x/y}$$

For example, after 10 years there is 6.0×10^4 Ci of ^{90}Sr per tonne of fuel ($x = 6.0 \times 10^4$), and the MPC is 4×10^{-6} Ci/m^3 ($y = 4 \times 10^{-6}$); therefore, the number of deaths expected if this were all ingested by people is $2.7 \times 6 \times 10^4/4 \times 10^{-6} = 4.0 \times 10^{10}$,** and we call this the number of "cancer doses." Note that in view of the linearity

* The term "cancer dose" is used for convenience in discussion and denotes an average estimated quantity which, if ingested by many persons, would eventually cause one cancer in the population under the conservative BEIR risk estimates. Later paragraphs will show how small a fraction of these "doses" is likely to enter the biosphere and have a chance to affect humans.

Table 4
RISK OF CANCER DEATH PER REM TO VARIOUS ORGANS — VALUES FROM THE BEIR REPORT[48] ASSUMING THE ABSOLUTE RISK MODEL WITH A 30-YEAR PLATEAU PERIOD (25 YEAR FOR LEUKEMIA) FOR A YOUNG ADULT

Type of cancer	Risk/rem($\times 10^6$)
Leukemia (bone marrow)	25
Breast	45
Lung	39
GI (including stomach)	30
Bone	6
Thyroid	6[a]
All other	24
Any one other	≤6[b]
Total	∿ 180

[a] Estimated from Reference 48, giving credit for the 90% cure rate.

[b] Estimated from fact that all others combined are less than 24.

hypothesis used here in estimating effects of radiation,* the way in which this ^{90}Sr is distributed among people and the number of people involved (as long as it is much larger than the number of deaths) are immaterial. These assumptions make the following calculations easier, but probably overestimate the actual cancer risks and thus set an upper limit to these risks.**

Up to this point, we have ignored the effect of radiation on bone marrow, causing leukemia. The ratios of doses to marrow and outer bone are ^{35}Sr, 0.26; Am, 1.8×10^{-3}; Pu, 1.7×10^{-3}; Np, 0.28. From Table 4, the effectiveness of marrow dose is 25/6 = 4.2 times that to bone. The risk of leukemia is thus about equal to that of bone cancer for ^{90}Sr and Np isotopes; therefore, the total risk from these as calculated above is doubled. For Am and Pu, the leukemia risk is negligible. There are no data for Ra in our reference, but from both human experience and animal experiments, radium causes bone cancer much more frequently than leukemia.

For inhalation, the calculation is similar. It was assumed that the material inhaled is in insoluble form, and, in all cases, this makes the lung the critical organ. The MPC in air is based on inhalation at a rate of 7300 m^3 of air per year, which gives a dose of 15 rem to the lung. The conversion is then

$$\frac{\text{cancer doses}}{\text{year}} = \frac{\text{xCi}}{\text{tonne}} \times \frac{1\ \text{MPC}}{\text{zCi/m}^3\text{-A}} \times \frac{15\ \text{rem/MPC}}{7300\ \text{m}^3\text{-A}} \times \frac{39 \times 10^{-6}\ \text{deaths}}{\text{rem}} \times \frac{1.2 \times 10^4\ \text{t}}{\text{year}}$$

$$= 1.0 \times 10^{-3}\ \text{x/z}$$

where m^3–A = cubic meters of air. For ^{90}Sr, $z = 2 \times 10^{-9}$ and $x = 6.0 \times 10^4$ as before;

* Editor's Note: This number of deaths from Sr-90 is obviously impossible, since the total quantity of Sr-90 could not by any imaginable process be divided and fed entirely to every person on earth. Thus, the sample calculation also indicates that the use of the term "cancer dose" merely means here that the risk factor (a probability) has been incorporated into calculations at an early stage for convenience.

** Editor's Note: Lower risk factors applicable to low linear energy transfer (LET) radiations at low doses and dose rates are under consideration by some agencies.

therefore, the number of deaths expected if this were all inhaled by people is 3.0×10^{10}.

The conversion from curie per tonne to inhalation and ingestion hazards is shown in Figure 7 for several important isotopes. The most dangerous materials shown per ingested curie are ^{90}Sr and ^{226}Ra because of their high transmission through the intestines into the bloodstream (30% for each), their high efficiency for concentration in bone (30 and 10%, respectively), and their long biological half-lives in bone (50 and 45 years, respectively). ^{226}Ra is considerably worse than ^{90}Sr because of the higher energy of its radiations and the relative biological effectiveness (RBE) of ten for alpha particles as opposed to one for electrons and gamma rays. The ingestion hazards for Am, Pu, and Th are relatively low because they are very poorly transmitted through the intestine walls and into the bloodstream (10^{-4}, 3×10^{-5}, and 10^{-4}, respectively). ^{137}Cs is relatively ineffective as it has a relatively short biological half-life (140 days in muscle and bone and less in other organs).

The principal reason for variations in the inhalation hazard among the actinides is the biological half-life in the lung, which is taken as 4 years for Th, 1 year for Pu and 120 days for all other elements. (It is well known that these biological half-lives vary considerably depending upon the physicochemical processing history of the material; the values chosen will provide conservative population risk estimates.) For ^{137}Cs and ^{90}Sr, the energy deposited in the lung and the RBE are each an order of magnitude lower than for the actinides, making them about 100 times less hazardous per curie.

In general, the MPC in air is lower for soluble than for insoluble actinides by approximately one order of magnitude; consequently, it may seem unconservative to consider only insoluble forms. A factor of 3.3 in this difference is made up by the fact that the critical organ for insolubles is the lung, for which the relative ratios of risk per MPC $= 39 \times 10^{-6}$/rem $\times$ 15 rem $= 5.9 \times 10^{-4}$, whereas the critical organ for solubles is the bone, for which the risk per MPC $= 6 \times 10^{-6}$/rem $\times$ 30 rem $= 1.8 \times 10^{-4}$. In addition, it was assumed in calculating MPCs that all soluble material deposited in the lung reaches the bone,[24] whereas more recent work shows this to be grossly in error. For example, only 10% of the soluble plutonium deposited in the lung reaches the bone.[26] Thus, the inhalation risk for insoluble material is generally greater than for soluble. Moreover, the waste is kept in insoluble form.

Although ICRP Publications 2 and 6 are not completely up to date, risks calculated from data and assumptions of these reports will generally be conservative within a factor of ten. Attempts to update dose calculations will be easier when ICRP publishes its current data on internal dose estimation. Other evaluations often use 10 Code of Federal Regulations (CFR) 20 values based on ICRP Publication 2 with modifications that make them less suitable[5,22] for purposes of this section.

The ingestion hazard from each isotope making an important contribution (expressed as the number of cancers to be expected if all the material could be ingested) is plotted against time after reprocessing in Figure 9; the solid line shows the sum of all contributions. ^{90}Sr is predominant for the first few hundred years, after which the isotopes of americium and plutonium dominate the problem for 20,000 years until ^{226}Ra grows in as the daughter of ^{234}U and ^{230}Th to dominate. After a few million years, the principal source of ^{226}Ra is ^{238}U decay, but it is still the most important hazard. The long half-life fission products are never predominant, but ^{129}I makes an appreciable contribution in the 1 to 20 million year range.

Figure 10 shows the same treatment applied to the inhalation hazard. Fission products never contribute as much as half of the total hazard. In the first hundred years, ^{244}Cm, ^{90}Sr, and ^{137}Cs are all important, and after that, the americium and plutonium isotopes determine the hazard until 100,000 years later when ^{229}Th grows in as a daugh-

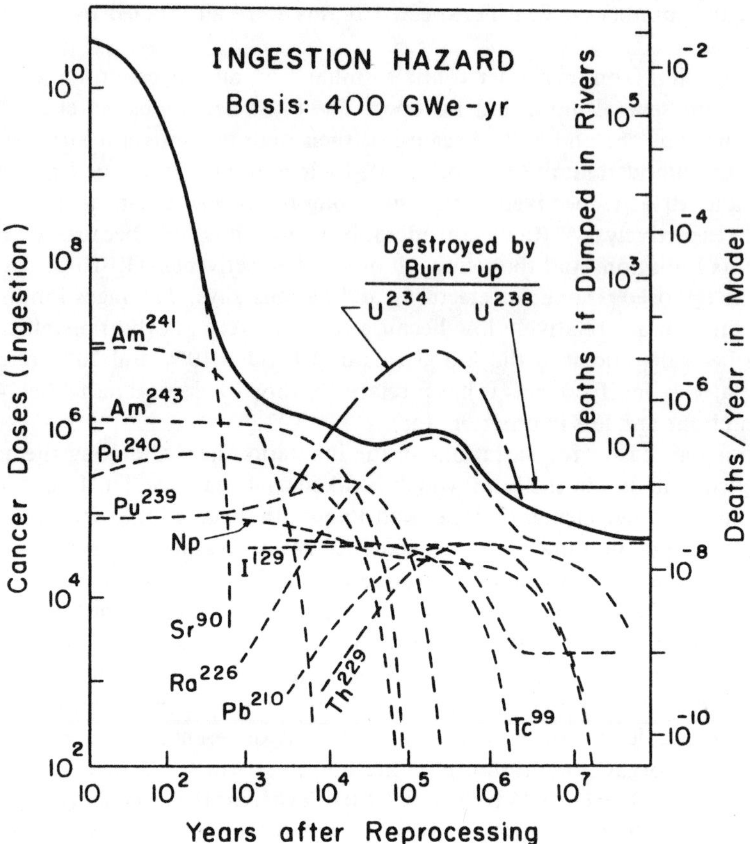

FIGURE 9. Number of cancer-causing doses in the waste from 400 GWe-year of nuclear electricity if all of the material could be ingested one time by humans in soluble, digestible form. See caption for Figure 8. The scale inside the right margin shows the number of cancers expected due to ingestion of this material if it were dumped randomly into U.S. rivers at the time indicated by the absclssa. The scale outside the right margin is developed and discussed in Section 21.2.7.

ter of ^{237}Np and ^{233}U to become predominant. After 15 million years, ^{230}Th from ^{238}U decay is the dominant hazard.

One other property of the waste that has some potential for environmental impact is the neutron emission. This arises from two sources, spontaneous fission and (α,n) reactions induced by alpha particles emitted from heavy nuclei. The calculation for spontaneous fission is straightforward as a product of curies, fractional decay by spontaneous fission, and neutrons per fission. The calculation for (α,n) uses an expression developed for alpha emitters in a UO_2 matrix[3] indicating reactions in oxygen.

$$\frac{\text{neutrons}}{\text{alpha distintegrations}} = 1.0 \times 10^{-10}\ E_{\alpha}^{\ 3.65}$$

While this is a crude approximation for use with waste, it should at least be valid as an order of magnitude estimate. The results are shown in Figure 11. We see that spontaneous fission of curium isotopes is the dominant source for the first few hundred thousand years, after which (α,n) from ^{237}Np daughters assumes importance until 5 million years later when spontaneous fission of ^{238}U takes over.

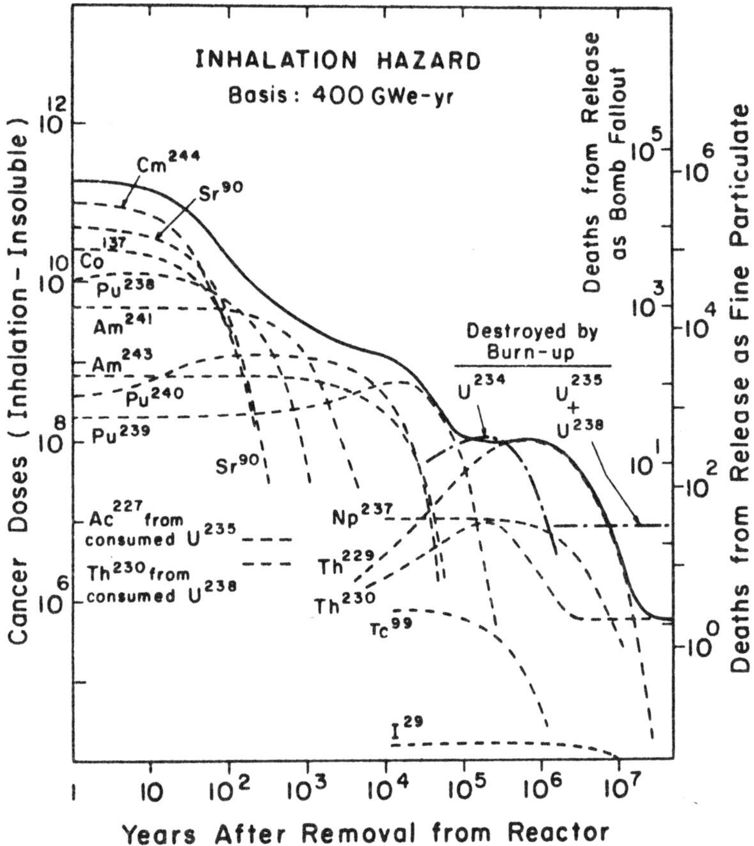

FIGURE 10. Number of cancer causing doses in the waste from 400 GWe-year of nuclear electricity if all of the material could be inhaled one time by humans as a fine, insoluble particulate. See caption for Figure 8. The scales on the right side give the effects of releasing the material as bomb fallout and as a fine particulate dispersed from a point source at ground level from a location in Illinois. The ^{227}Ac from ^{235}U and the ^{230}Th from ^{238}U are the principal components of the dot-dash line for ^{235}U plus ^{238}U burn-up.

Before closing this section, it should be recalled that 99.5% of the uranium and plutonium is assumed to have been removed in the reprocessing for burning in other reactors; therefore, the long-term equilibrium situations would be one in which plutonium is used as the fuel in a breeder reactor. After 500 years of decay, wastes from a breeder would have approximately one order of magnitude higher potential hazards than those discussed here. For example, the ratio of the amounts of a few important isotopes to those in present-day reactors are[2] ^{239}Pu, 10.8; ^{240}Pu, 9.0; ^{242}Pu, 9.4; ^{241}Am, 10.6; ^{243}Am, 2.7; but ^{237}Np, 0.27. On the other hand, we will find that ^{90}Sr is the most important contributor to waste hazards for the first 500 years and only 60% as much of it is produced in a breeder. We limit our discussion here to wastes from present-day reactors, but almost all aspects of the problem are readily translatable to breeder wastes. Plutonium recycle in light water reactors would give hazards intermediate between the two.

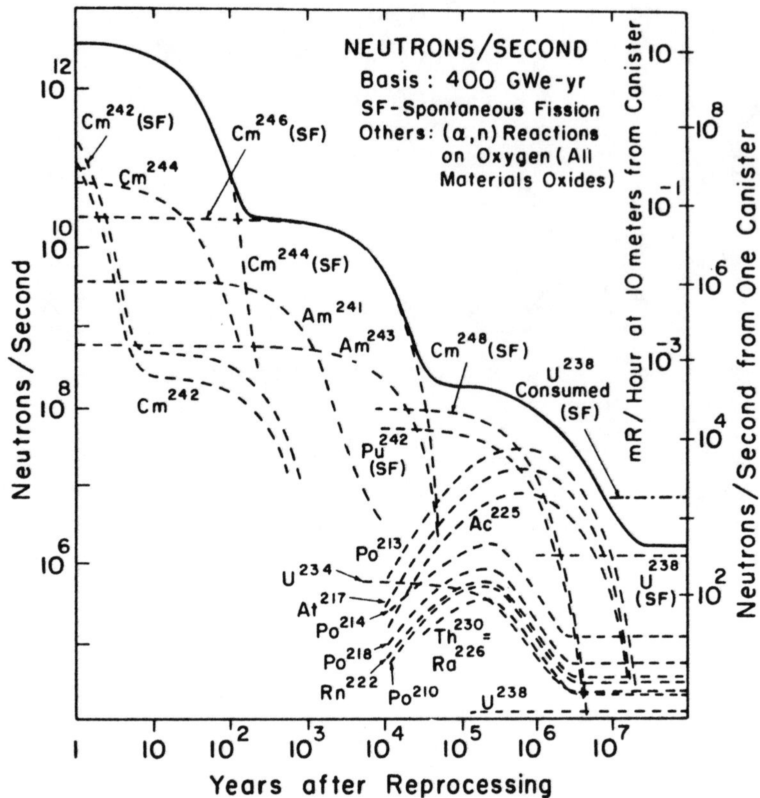

FIGURE 11. Neutrons per second emitted by the waste from 400 GWe-years of nuclear electricity. See caption for Figure 8. SF indicates spontaneous fission sources, and those not so marked are from (α,n) reactions induced by the alpha particles emitted by these nuclei striking oxygen nuclei. The scales on the right give the neutrons per second from a single waste canister and the mrem per hour at 10 m from an unshielded waste canister.

PERSPECTIVE ON RELATIVE QUANTITIES OF NUCLEAR POWER WASTES COMPARED TO OTHER INVENTORIES OF TOXIC MATERIALS

The relative hazards of nuclear wastes, as indicated in Figures 8 to 11, may be compared with other materials that can be taken into the body on the basis of approximate relative effects. The most obvious comparisons are with chemical poisons for which there is a great deal of information, mostly from animal studies but also including some human experience. Data on industrially produced chemicals are given in Table 5. The largest potential hazards occur if materials are administered in single large doses by inhalation. The chlorine gas produced annually in the U.S. (10^7 tons) is enough to administer an acute lethal dose (1000 part-per-million minutes (ppm-min) in air inhaled) to 4×10^{14} people if the total quantity available could be administered, and other gases such as phosgene, ammonia, and HCN are not very far behind.[45]

Poisoning by ingestion is somewhat less hazardous. To construct the entries in Table 5, we have used the values shown in Table 6 for the quantities of various elements that have a 50% chance of being lethal if ingested. The lethality in man was assumed to be derivable from that in animals by scaling in proportion to body weight. The toxicity of the waste is not much greater than that of other common materials, even after 10 years, and after 500 years, it is much less. The values in Table 6 are used in conjunction

Table 5
LETHAL DOSES PRODUCED OR CONSUMED PER YEAR IN U.S.

Inhalation[45]	
Chlorine	4×10^{14}
Phosgene	1.8×10^{13}
Ammonia	6×10^{12}
Hydrogen cyanide	6×10^{12}
Nuclear waste	10 years — 1.6×10^{11}
	500 years — 5×10^{9}
Ingestion[7]	
Barium	9×10^{10}
Copper	8×10^{10}
Arsenic	1×10^{10}
Nuclear waste	10 years — 8×10^{10}
	500 years — 10^{7}

Table 6
LETHAL QUANTITIES (LD_{50}) FOR VARIOUS ELEMENTS IF INGESTED ORALLY[7a]

Element	Compound	Average LD_{50} (mg/kg)	Animal	LD_{50} man (g)[a]
Selenium	Na_2SeO_3	5	Rabbit, mouse, rat, guinea pig	0.35
Cyanide	KCN	10	Rat	0.7
Mercury	$HgCl_2$	23	Rat, mouse	1.6
Arsenic	As_2O_3	45	Mouse, rat	3
Barium	$BaCl_2$,$Ba(NO_3)_2$	250	Rat	18
Copper	CuO,$CuCl_2$	300	Rat	21
Nickel	$Ni(NO_3)_2$	1620	Rat	110
Aluminum	$AlCl_3$	4000	Rat, mouse	280
Nuclear waste	$Al_2(SO_4)_3$			
−10 years				0.03
500 years				170

[a] Extrapolation to man assumes 70 kg body weight.

with annual U.S. production or consumption to derive the numbers of lethal ingestion doses in Table 5. For example, the barium compounds produced annually (1.6×10^6 tons) are enough to provide orally ingested lethal doses (18 g) to 9×10^{10} people. It may be argued that poisonous gases, such as chlorine, would have only a limited lifetime in our environment, but that is not true of barium, copper, and arsenic. It might be claimed that the barium compounds are present in the ground and, therfore, all we do is change their form. However, about half of our barium and arsenic and one fourth of our copper are imported; thus we are also introducing it artificially into our environment.

A potential hazard in our environment is the natural radioactivity in the ground, which is more similar to radioactive waste. If the waste is buried at a depth of 600 m (a typical plan), it might be reasonable to assume that the accessibility of waste to the biosphere is no larger than that from the uranium down to a depth of 600 m in the rock and soil in our country. There is 4×10^{16} g of ^{238}U in U.S. soil down to this depth,* and the 1.3×10^{10} g of ^{226}Ra in equilibrium with it is 3×10^{13} cancer doses by ingestion. This is 400 times more than the ingestion hazard in 1 year's waste at the time of burial. The waste, of course, decays away as shown in Figure 9, but the uranium and radium in the soil do not.

Using the same procedure Figure 8 indicates that the uranium in the top 600 m of our rock and soil contains 4×10^{14} cancer doses by inhalation, more than three orders of magnitude more than the waste at burial. It also emits 1.3×10^{8}W of gamma-ray power. In addition, the potassium-40 in this same soil emits about 2×10^{8}W of gamma-ray power; therefore, the two combined emit 50 times as much as 1 year's waste. The uranium in the ground emits 10^{15} neutrons per second from spontaneous fission, about 300 times more than the waste at burial. If we used nuclear power for hundreds of years, the combined waste would contain only 40 times more radioactivity than 1 year's waste at burial, because the hazard during this period is dominated by the 28-year half-life of ^{90}Sr.

If this argument were extended to include all the poisons in the top 600 m of the earth's crust, far higher potential hazards would be obtained. For example, the copper in the U.S. down to a depth of 600 m is 4×10^{16} lethal doses. Moreover, the toxicities of the Cr and Ni in the ground are quite comparable to that of the Cu and that of the aluminum (estimated as chloride or sulfate) is one order of magnitude higher.

The main purpose of the arguments presented in this section is not to compare the toxicity of the waste and that of other things but rather to counter the practice of emphasizing the potential hazards of the waste by showing that they are not of unprecedented, or even of unusual, magnitude in terms of the total quantities of material in units, expressed as lethal doses.

SOME APPROXIMATE ESTIMATES OF UPPER BOUNDS TO THE HAZARDS OF NUCLEAR WASTES DISPERSED TO THE ENVIRONMENT

The ordinates used on the left sides of Figures 8 to 11 are those derived from physical calculations, but they have no direct relevance to environmental impacts until some means of dispersal is postulated. This is obvious for the gamma-ray power and the neutron emission rate, but it is also true for the ingestion and inhalation hazards since there is no conceivable way in which all of the waste could be ingested or inhaled by people.

In order to give some scope to the potential environmental hazards, we consider here what the consequences would be if the waste were handled in the easiest and most careless manner conceivable. Scales corresponding to this are included on the right sides of the figures, and their origin will now be explained. For the gamma-ray hazard, we take this most careless handling to be uniform dispersal on the ground throughout the U.S. or what is completely equivalent in view of the linearity hypothesis used in dose-effect calculations, a random dispersal. We make the computation for ^{137}Cs, the most important single nuclide, but its 0.66-MeV energy is also typical of the other important nuclides. For ^{137}Cs, the gamma-ray power is 3.9×10^{-3} W/Ci; thus, 1 W spread evenly over the 8×10^{6} km^2 of the U.S. corresponds to 0.032 mCi/km^2. Using a dose rate[27] of 0.033 mrem/year to unshielded people per millicurie per square kilometer of ^{137}Cs on the ground and a factor for shielding by buildings of 0.4 then gives

* The area of the U.S. is 9×10^{12} m^2, so there are 5.4×10^{15} m^3 of rock down to a depth of 600 m. Its density is 2.7×10^{6} g rock per cubic meter and it contains 2.7×10^{-6} g U per gram rock;[15] the amount of uranium is then $5.4 \times 10^{15} \times 2.7 \times 2.7 = 4 \times 10^{16}$ g. The equilibrium ratio of Ra/U is the ratio of their half-lives, 1.6×10^{3} years/4.5×10^{9} years, times their mass ratio, 226/238, which gives 3.3×10^{-7}.

an average whole body dose of 0.44×10^{-6} rem/year. Multiplying by the 2×10^8 population and 180×10^{-6} cancers per man-rem of whole body radiation (from Table 4) then gives 0.016 deaths per year in the U.S. for each watt of gamma-ray power spread on the ground. This was used to generate the scale on the right of Figure 8.

Another scale located on the right side of Figure 8 is useful in assessing the problems in handling waste canisters. The radiation level at 10 m from a source emitting 1 W of gamma-ray power is about 1 rem/hr, ignoring shielding (the shielding by the waste itself reduces this by about a factor of 3). Without shielding, exposure anywhere near a fresh canister would result in a lethal dose in approximately 1 hr.

A scale similar to the one above is also included in Figure 11 for the hazard from neutron emission. It is based on the equivalence of 7.2 neutrons per square centimeter per second to 1 mrem/hr. A comparison of these scales for Figures 8 and 11 indicates that the neutrons are never as dangerous as the gamma rays, and in the early years when handling would be most common, the gamma rays are more dangerous by several orders of magnitude. We will, therefore, largely ignore the neutron hazard.

With regard to ingestion hazard, an index to the upper bound of any environmental impact would be obtained by dumping the material in soluble form randomly into rivers. The total annual runoff in the U.S. is 1.5×10^{15} ℓ/year, and the total water ingested is 1.6×10^{11} ℓ/year (2.2 ℓ/day × 365 days × 2 × 10^8 population). Therefore, the probability for human ingestion of a random sample of river water is about 10^{-4}. However, some fraction of the material would be removed by flocculation and filtering processes.[27] For example, rivers contain 0.2 pCi/ℓ of ^{226}Ra,[18] whereas tap water in U.S. cities typically contains 0.03 pCi/ℓ.[14] Therefore, no more than 1.5×10^{-5} of the Ra* in rivers may be assumed to be ingested by people. Since ^{226}Ra is one of the two most important radionuclides in the waste and the other (^{90}Sr) is chemically similar to it, the scale on the left in Figure 9 has been multiplied by 1.5×10^{-5} to obtain our rough scoping scale shown inside the right margin of Figure 9. One might think that dispersal as an aerosol and subsequent settling on vegetation would be the most important potential ingestion pathway to man — that is the pathway for ^{90}Sr from bomb fallout. However, only 1×10^{-5} of the ^{90}Sr from fallout is ingested by humans.**

We see from Figure 9 that if the material were randomly dumped in rivers shortly after reprocessing, almost a million deaths would result from the wastes generated by 1 year of all nuclear power due to ingesting radioactivity with drinking water. However, if the dumping were delayed for 500 years, the death toll would be reduced to 150. These consequences of dumping in rivers are five orders of magnitude larger than the consequences of dumping in oceans.[6]

From the standpoint of inhalation hazard, perhaps the most severe credible method of dispersal would be to release all the material as fine particulate from ground level. Calculations on this sort of release from a point in northern Illinois (upwind from the populous northeastern U.S.) indicate[30] that about 4×10^{-6} of the material released would be inhaled by people. One scale located on the right side of Figure 10 is calculated on that basis. Since the material would never actually exist as a fine powder, this estimate is, of course, somewhat unrealistic. Perhaps a more realistic basis would be to assume that the material might be dispersed by a very energetic explosion and thus be released in a manner similar to nuclear bomb fallout. An evaluation can then be made by use of plutonium data from fallout.[27] A typical integrated concentration-time

* Editor's Note: See also the estimates obtained later with this factor the net uptake of natural radium by people.

** From ICRP-1959,[24] the Ca in bone of a standard man is 1500 g. From UNSCEAR 1972,[27] the ^{90}Sr level in bone = 2 pCi/g Ca, so the content in standard man is 3000 pCi. From ICRP 1959,[24] 9% of ingested ^{90}Sr ends up in the bone, so the total ingested is 3.3×10^4 pCi. The total ^{90}Sr intake by all people is thus, $3 \times 3x\ 10^4 \times 3.5 \times 10^9 = 1.2 \times 10^{14}$ pCi = 120 Ci. In UNSCEAR 1972,[27] the ^{90}Sr released in bomb tests is 16×10^6 Ci, so that less than 10^{-5} of this has been ingested.

level of ^{239}Pu in the surface air of the temperate zone of the Northern Hemisphere is 4×10^{-15} Ci-year/m^3; therefore, the 2×10^9 people breathing 7300 m^3/year of this air have inhaled the product of these, or a total of 6×10^{-2} Ci. The total ^{239}Pu released in bomb tests is 3×10^5 Ci[30]; hence, the fraction of the release that has been inhaled is 2×10^{-7}.* This factor is used for the other scale on the right side of Figure 10.

BURIED WASTE — GENERAL CONSIDERATIONS AND TIME DELAYS

From the results of the last section, it is clear that the radioactive waste must be isolated from man's environment for at least a few hundred years. At first thought, this conclusion may appear to be a fearful one as few things in our experience have longevity of this magnitude. Typical time constants for change in structures and institutions in our society are of the order of a few tens of years, and even most natural formations undergo important changes with similar frequency. However, such time constants are typical only of the environment on the earth's surface; the situation is very different in a deep underground environment where time constants for change are of the order of tens of millions of years. The basic rationale for deep underground burial is to benefit from this difference in time constants. However, beyond such generalities, any analysis must delve into a study of detailed pathways by which the wastes, once buried deep underground, might be released.

The most widely considered scenario is that the waste might be contacted by ground water, leached into solution, travel through aquifers, and eventually reach surface waters from which it might get into food or drinking water supplies. In order to minimize the probability that ground water will reach the waste, great care should be exercised in choosing a burial site. Salt beds offer a measure of security in this regard, since their very existence over a time span of 250 million years is proof that water has not entered them, and in many situations all geological evidence indicates that this situation will continue far into the future.** There are several other types of rock that are known to be largely free of water and impervious to it,[42] including most intrusive igneous rocks such as granite; some volcanic rock such as tuff; some selected shales; and several types of low silica content metamorphic rocks, especially in the Precambrian shield (large deep mines in this shield rock operate without pumps). While generalities such as these are useful, the particular geology, lithology, and hydrology of an area must be thoroughly explored before it can be chosen for use as a burial site.

On the other hand, even if ground water does enter the geological formation in which the rock is buried, a disaster is not imminent. There are several important time delays before the waste can reach the surface. The nonporous material in which the waste is encased must be leached or dissolved away; the waste-containing glass must then be leached before the waste gets into the ground water. This water moves rather slowly and must travel long distances before coming into contact with surface waters. The radioactive materials are held up by ion-exchange and other absorption processes and, thus, move much more slowly than the water. We will now consider these time delay processes in some detail.

The first factor is most easily understood for burial in salt; the average time delay before the water reaches the waste is simply the time required to dissolve away half of the salt formation in which it is enclosed. In the site under consideration in New Mex-

* Editor's Note: There is obviously no direct relationship between the two situations, but this is the same fraction of AmO_2 powder material processed that was inhaled by a worker counted at the University of Pittsburgh in 1967 after 2 to 3 years of mixing powders under essentially open hood conditions.

** Evidence on this for the New Mexico site is reviewed by Claiborne and Gera;[8] the general rationale is discussed in NAS-1957, NAS-1961, NAS-1966, NAS-1970.[12,34,39,47]

ico, if all the ground water now flowing through aquifers above the salt were diverted to flow through the salt, this time delay would be at least 30,000 years, the time required to dissolve the salt enclosing the waste from 1 year of all nuclear power.* Even this would saturate the water with salt, making it incapable of further dissolution in downstream areas containing buried waste. Therefore, this is an unrealistically short time estimate for average waste.

If the burial is in a rock that is not self-sealing, such as salt, the repository would probably be backfilled with concrete or some similar impermeable and nonporous material. Moreover, the rock itself would also have these properties. It is difficult to visualize a scenario in which water could enter and have direct access to a large fraction of the waste without first having to leach away a great deal of this rock.

If the water should reach the waste, there is an important time delay in its leaching. The leach rate constant, L, is defined as the fraction of material leached per day divided by the ratio of surface area to mass of the material; alternatively, by multiplying both numerator and denominator by the mass, it is the mass leached per day divided by the surface area. In laboratory experiments, typical values of L for borosilicate glass are in the range 10^{-5} to 10^{-9} g/cm^2-day, and it seems reasonable to expect that current research will succeed in assuring a value not larger than 10^{-7}.[19] In a Canadian experiment with blocks of syanate glass incorprating ^{90}Sr buried below the water table, L was initially 2×10^{-8} g/cm^2-day; it decreased rapidly to 4×10^{-11} g/cm^2-day after 7 years and is still decreasing slowly after 15 years.[33] It would seem that glass buried in rock or soil saturated with water would leach more slowly than in a water tank.

For a long circular cylinder, the surface to mass ratio is 2 F/Rd where R is the radius, d is the density, and F is the factor by which the surface area is increased by fracturing. With L = 10^{-7} (fractional leaching per day/[surface/mass]), R = 15 cm, d = 3 g/cm^3, the fractional leaching, converted to an annual basis, is then 1.6×10^{-6} F per year. Experiments[31] indicate that F = 5 for slow cooling, F = 10 for free air convection cooling, and F = 20 for water quenching; therefore, a typical leach rate might be about 10^{-5} per year. If the glass temperature remains above 700°C for an appreciable length of time, devitrification occurs, increasing the leach rate by a factor of 4 to 10, but this would not be expected with normal handling.[41] Radiation apparently does not affect the leach rate, and this includes experience with glasses incorporating ^{244}Cm (alpha emitter), simulating a 2000-year radiation dose to the waste.[32] If the water temperature is 99°C, leach rates are about 100 times faster than at room temperature. This might be a serious problem during the first hundred years or so, when the temperatures are high; depending on the pressure release situation, water temperatures might substantially exceed 100°C. When temperatures are above the boiling point, water is repelled; thus the leach rate would go through a maximum just below the boiling point. If the latter is 100°C, the maximum leach rate is 0.1% per year.

These results on leaching, 10^{-5} per year at room temperature and 10^{-3} at 99°C, are probably conservatively high. An appreciable fraction of all rock within a kilometer or so of the surface is constantly saturated with water, but its leach rate is typically 10^{-7} to 10^{-8} per year. In laboratory tests, the waste glass is less leachable than most rock; in studies at Battelle Northwest Laboratory,[31] the following relative leachabilities

* The thickness of the salt formation is 600 m and the area covered by 1 year's waste is 0.4 km^2, thus, the volume of salt is 2.4×10^8 m^3, the density is 2.2×10^6 g/m^3, and, the mass involved in 5.3×10^{14}g. The solubility is 350 g/ℓ so dissolution would require $1.5 \times 10^{12} \ell$ of water. Ground water flow in the area is about 3.7×10^4 ℓ/year for each meter of width.[8] Therefore, if the burial area is square (i.e., 600 m wide), the water available is 2.3×10^7 ℓ/year, and the time required to dissolve it all would be $1/5 \times 10^{12}/2.3 \times 10^7 = 6 \times 10^4$ years.

were found: high-level waste glass, 0.7; granite, 1.1; marble, 2.9; clay slate, 4.1; and basalt, 6.1.

Once the material is leached, the water transport problem is encountered, and it introduces further important delays. A typical speed for water traveling through a deep aquifer is not more than 0.3 m/day (0.1 km/year) — more than 1 m/day is quite exceptional and velocities as low as 0.03 m/day are not unusual.*[16] Water from this depth would typically have to travel 100 km before reaching the surface (Galley[16] gives "tens or hundreds of kilometers"). Therefore, in typical situations, it would take the water, into which the waste is leached, many hundreds or even thousands of years to reach the surface.[13]

Denham et al.[11] list typical values for ion-exchange hold-up factors (the ratio of velocity of ions to velocity of the water) as 10^{-2} for Sr, 10^{-3} for Cs, 10^{-4} for Pu and Am, and 2×10^{-3} for Ra. In order to judge these values, let us look into the situation for Sr, which is held up the least. According to ion-exchange theory, this hold-up factor is $(1 + Kd/p)^{-1}$, where d is the rock density, typically about 2.5 g/mℓ (including a factor 1-p); p is the porosity (the fraction of the volume not occupied by solid material); and K is the distribution coefficient (in milliliters per gram). Values of K for Sr in various rock[21] are 100 to 3000 for tuff, 4 to 15 for granite, 5 to 12 for limestone and dolomite, 50 to 300 for basalt, and 12 to 12,000 for soils. If reasonable care is taken in choice of location, effective values of K should thus not be less than 4 mℓ/g for rock and 12 mℓ/g for soils. The most porous rock is sandstone for which p is typically 5 to 10%, while low-porosity rocks such as shale have p in the range 2 to 3%; thus, an effective p of 0.2 should be maximal.[46] For soils, typical porosities are 0.3 for sand, 0.4 for silt, and 0.5 for clay (which has high values of K); thus, 0.5 should be maximal. According to our formula then, a minimum hold-up factor for Sr should be $(1 + 4 \times 2.5/0.2)^{-1} = 1/50$ in rock and $(1 + 12 \times 2.5/0.5)^{-1} = 1/60$ in soils. The value of 10^{-2} given by Denham et al. therefore seems to be reasonably conservative.

Both the slow movement of water and the ion-exchange hold-up can be by-passed by cracks in the rock. However, cracks at great depth are largely sealed by the pressure and by cementing with ground-up rock. If the water is saturated with salt, as would be the case if the waste were buried in salt, ion-exchange hold-up would be substantially reduced.[28]

There are at least two situations in which ^{90}Sr has been released into aquifers. In a Canadian experiment,[33] the ^{99}Sr "front" moved 33 m in 11 years, or 3 m/year. Our typical rate was 0.3 m/day (water speed) × 0.01 (ion-exchange holdup for ^{90}Sr) × 365 day/year = 1 m/year. This is not necessarily inconsistent as the "front" presumably moves faster than the bulk of the material and with the shallow burial, cracks would be more important. The other situation is in the Idaho Chemical Processing Plant where ^{90}Sr was injected about 150 m below ground into the extraordinarily fast flowing (3.5 m/day) Snake River aquifer. About 1% of the ^{90}Sr migrated 1 km in 10 years,[1,40] an average of 100 m/year, as compared with our estimate for typical ion-exchange hold-up of $3.5 \times 0.01 \times 365 = 13$ m/year. Again, this is not inconsistent since it pertains to only 1% of the material and the burial depth is only 0.25 of the 600 m we have been considering; therefore, transmission through cracks would be more important.

It should be noted that two radionuclides of some importance, namely ^{99}Tc and ^{129}I, are not held up appreciably by ion exchange. Neither of these contributes as much as 1% to the hazard during the first 500 years, when time delays are most important. Iodine is physically separated from the other waste, making its handling a special problem, and ^{99}Tc never contributes more than 10% to the hazard.

* The flow rate in aquifers below the proposed New Mexico repository is 4 cm/year.[8]

In summary, there are three completely independent time-delay factors: burial in a formation expected to be free of water, the leaching time for the surrounding material and for the waste itself, and the travel time for the waste once it is dissolved in ground water. Any one would ordinarily be sufficient to prevent any appreciable fraction of the waste from reaching surface waters in the first few hundred years, when the potential hazards are so large. In fact, our discussions would lead one to believe that even if the waste were contacted by ground water and leached into solution, most of it would not reach man's environment for approximately 1 million years.

One final guarantee against disaster is the high detectability of radioactivity. There is routine radioactivity monitoring in many rivers now, and it would be extremely easy and cheap to maintain such monitoring in the region of the waste repository. It could, for example, be used as a continuing project for undergraduate students in a local college at a cost of perhaps $1000/year for covering an area in which a 1000-year waste accumulation is buried. In the event that appreciable quantities of radioactivity would escape, they would probably be detected in time to avert important health consequences (assuming a continued high level of technology).

If the dangers over the first 500 years can be discounted, it is interesting to put the residual dangers into perspective. From Figure 9, the waste from 1 year of all nuclear power in U.S. at this stage contains 10^7 "cancer doses." From Chapter 12.2, the mass of this waste is 600 kg per canister × 10 canisters/GWe × 400 GWe = 2.4×10^6 kg; thus, the mass per lethal dose is $2.4 \times 10^6/10^7 = 0.24$ kg. The LD_{50} for this material would then be about 170 g. From Table 6, we see that this makes it two orders of magnitude less toxic than materials commonly found in homes and one order of magnitude less toxic than common materials such as copper and barium. To have material of this toxicity buried deep underground in a low leachability form does not, intuitively, seem to be highly dangerous, but we will now quantify its hazard.

RELEASE THROUGH GROUND WATER — PROBABILITY ESTIMATES

Once the waste is buried underground, it seems reasonable to compare it with natural radioactivity in the ground, and, as shown earlier, such as comparison makes the hazards from the waste seem very mild indeed. A widespread reaction to such a comparison is to point out that the radioactivity in the waste is far more concentrated. However, this concentration is of no importance in estimating the average expected effects so long as the linear, no-threshold dose-effect relationship is maintained. The concentration does not increase the probability for any given radioactive atom to find its way into a person, and, with the linearity hypothesis, only the total number of radioactive atoms in people is relevant. Of course, the linear, no-threshold theory may be incorrect, but calculations based on it give at least a valid upper limit on effects to be expected.

In order to quantify the comparison of the waste with natural radioactivity in the soil, we introduce calculational models. Burial of the waste will probably be at a depth between 300 and 3000 m.[42] In the New Mexico salt bed now being considered for a waste repository, the depth would be 600 m, so we will use that number in our examples. We assume that the waste is buried at random locations throughout the U.S. but always at a depth of 600 m. We then assume that an atom of waste is no more likely to be released than an average atom of radium or uranium in the rock or soil above it.* The reason for the assumption of random burial is that it allows us to use the

* The choice of 600 m as the depth to which we average for the source of radium in the environment is the most unfavorable possibility here. If less than 600 m is used, it is clearly unfair to assume that the waste would escape as easily, and if more than 600 m is used, the probability for release of the waste would be reduced.

entire U.S. as our laboratory. In U.S. soil down to a depth of 600 m; as noted before, there is 4×10^{16} g of uranium and 1.3×10^{10} g of radium. The annual runoff water in the U.S. is $1.5 \times 10^{15} \ell$ and the radium content in rivers is typically 2×10^{-13} g/ℓ*[18] thus, about 300 g of radium is leached per year. The average probability of leaching is then 300 per $1.3 \times 10^{10} = 2.3 \times 10^{-8}$ per year; the average life of rock in the top 600 m is the inverse of that or 43 million years. As the radium to uranium ratio in rivers is also the equilibrium ratio, the leaching probability for uranium per year is also 2.3×10^{-8}. Therefore, we take this to be the leaching probability for the buried waste. The scale in Figure 9 for deaths per year if dumped in rivers is, therefore, multiplied by 2.3×10^{-8} to obtain an estimate of the deaths per year expected in our random burial model. This corresponds to multiplying the original scale of potential cancer doses by $2.3 \times 10^{-8} \times 1.5 \times 10^{-5}$ (transfer from rivers to people from earlier in this chapter) = 3.5×10^{-13}. This calculation could have been simplified by just noting that the ratio of the total Ra ingested in the U.S. annually with water (0.03×10^{-12} g/ℓ × 2.2 ℓ/day × 365 day/year × 2×10^8 population = 4.8×10^{-3} g) is 3.5×10^{-13} of the Ra in the top 600 m of the U.S. (1.3×10^{10}g).

There is some degree of question in this procedure. In the first place, it ignores the pathway through food, and, in the second place, it does not take into account the digestibility of the radium, which may vary from that assumed in estimating the number of cancer doses in Figure 9.** These difficulties may be by-passed if we go directly from the amount of radium in the soil to the amount of radium in human bone, as determined from measurements on corpses. The average bone dosage from ^{226}Ra is 10 mrem/year,***[29] which, combined with the U.S. population and the bone cancer risk from Table 4, gives an estimate of 12 bone cancers per year from this source. We have seen earlier in this chapter that the number of cancer doses from ^{226}Ra in the top 600 m of U.S. soil is 3×10^{13}, so the ratio between the actual hazard per year and the total potential hazard is $12/3 \times 10^{13} = 4 \times 10^{-13}$ per year, in agreement with our previous result. It may be viewed as the fraction of the radium in the top 600 m that is "effectively" ingested annually.

It is important to point out that this estimate obtained from our model is probably grossly exaggerated. Almost all erosion takes place near the surface of the earth, where water from rainfall penetrates readily, vegetation and freeze-thaw cycles break up the rock, and river currents and winds exert large mechanical forces. Material at 600 m depth is, thus, much less likely to be eroded than an average equal volume of material above it, which includes material near the surface. We, therefore, conclude that our model gives an *upper limit* estimate on deaths caused.

The total number of eventual deaths that may be expected, via the pathway under discussion, from 1 year of all nuclear power in the model can be obtained by integrating the curve in Figure 9, using the scale on the (outside) right. This integration is, of course, sensitive to its upper and lower limits. Figure 12 gives the integration for the first million years as a function of its lower limit, N_1, the number of years before waste first begins to reach man.

* It was assumed that 3% of ingested Ra ends up in the bone. This is in accordance with ICRP Publications 6 (1962) and 10 (1968), which give values for the most digestible form. Actually, about 1.5×10^{-12}Ci/day = 3.5×10^{-8} Ci/lifetime is ingested, but only 7×10^{-11}Ci ends up in the bone;[27] so transfer from ingestion to bone is only 0.2%, or 15 times less than assumed in these ICRP publications. For uranium, on the other hand, the ratio of that ingested to that in bone is roughly equal to estimates in the ICRP publications. (The reader should also refer to revised ICRP reports, expected in 1977.)

** This gives the average Ra content of rivers as 2×10^{-13} g/ℓ.[23,49]

***This number can also be calculated from the quantity in a human body, 36 pCi from UNSCEAR-1972.[27] Dosage to other organs from ^{226}Ra is relatively negligible. Other radionuclides giving appreciable internal dosage to the body reach man principally by inhalation.

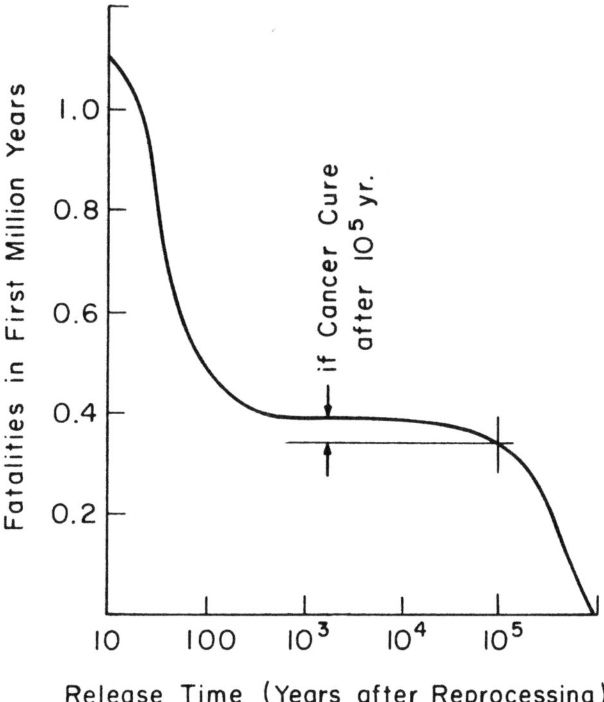

FIGURE 12. This is an integration of Figure 9 up to 10^6 years after reprocessing using the scale for our model (outside right margin) as a function of the initial time for the integration. If the discussion in the text of time delays is accepted as precluding release within the first few hundred years, about 0.4 eventual fatalities in one million years are expected from 400 GWe-years of nuclear power. If a cure for cancer is found at some time in the future (examples shown for 10^5 years), the fatalities obtained using that as the initial time should be subtracted off.

In view of our previous discussion of time delays, it would be most unlikely for much of the waste to reach the surface in less than 200 years; therefore, our result is 0.4 deaths in the first million years. In addition to the lower limit we have discussed, the integration in Figure 12 may also have an upper limit, based on finding a cure for cancer. Of course, if this cure is found in a number of years less than N_1, there will be no deaths from the wastes. If it is found in 10^5 years, the number of deaths is reduced by about one order of magnitude.

CRITIQUE OF PROBABILITY ESTIMATES

Use of 4×10^{-13} As Annual Transfer Rate From Rock to "Effective" Ingestion

The transfer per year from rock to actual ingestion for various elements is[10] Sr, 2.7×10^{-11}; I, 2.3×10^{-9}; U, 3.8×10^{-12}; Th, 1.5×10^{-12}; and Ra, 1.3×10^{-11}. An alternative reference[27] gives U as 2×10^{-12} and Ra as 5×10^{-12}.* The high values for Sr and I are due to their well-known concentration in the food chain, and these element should be

* The amounts in the top 600 m of the U.S. are given above as 4×10^{16} g of U and 1.3×10^{10} g of Ra. Average ingestion per person is 10^{-12} g/day for Ra and 1 μg/day for U.[27] The ratio of these numbers must be multiplied by the U.S. population (2×10^8) and the number of days per year. Thus, for Ra the transfer rate is $(10^{-12}/1.3 \times 10^{10}) \times 365 \times 2 \times 10^8 = 5 \times 10^{-12}$.

given special consideration. Therefore, our model should probably not be used in short time periods when ^{90}Sr is very important. Fortunately, ^{129}I is separated from the rest of the waste and handled separately, and this factor should be carefully considered in deciding on its disposal. However, for the pruposes of our integration leading to Figure 12, we are primarily concerned with Ra and actinides. For Ra and U, the correct transfer functions are known from measurements of quantities in bone to be 4×10^{-13} and 2×10^{-12}, respectively. Since Ra is the predominant contributor to the integration, it is important to use the correct value for it.

We might have used a higher value for the other materials, such as the uranium value for example, or something larger. If we had used 2×10^{-12}, it would have only increased our result from 0.4 fatalities to 0.8, because radium would still be the dominant contributor. If we had used the value for Sr, it would have increased it to about 10 fatalities. The reasons for not adopting these procedures are as follows.

First, our value of 4×10^{-13} was shown to be correct for ingestion with water, with all higher values coming from food intake. However, food intake is expected to be much less important, relative to water intake, for released waste than for natural elements in the soil. Plants take their materials from the soil above the water table, whereas the released waste would be largely confined to the water table. Indeed, this consideration would substantially reduce the effect of Ra, more than 90% of which is ingested with food, so that 4×10^{-13} may well be quite high and overconservative as our estimate of intake from buried wastes.

Second, the reason why the transfer rate for Ra from rock to "effective" ingestion is smaller than for actual ingestion is, as noted previously, due to overconservatism in ICRP estimates of how the human body transfers Ra from average food to bone and retains it there. Such overconservatism is more a rule than an exception in past ICRP estimates and may well be present for other isotopes. The purpose of ICRP is to set public health limits, and conservatism is clearly justified in that regard.

Burial Operations Introduce Release Mechanisms that Invalidate Comparisons with Undisturbed Rock

This question is really beyond the scope of this section; it is a problem for further research. However, we offer what information is available.

The problem has been studied mostly with regard to burial in salt. In fact one of the principal advantages of salt is that it flows plastically and seals cracks; therefore, the waste ends up sealed inside a gigantic crystal. This still leaves the problem of the vertical shaft through which the waste is brought in. This has a minuscule area in comparison with the area of the repository, and it is widely believed that if reasonable care is taken to assure good contact along the sides, this shaft can be satisfactorily plugged with concrete and cement. There is some work in progress on the possibility of using fused rock to better simulate the original geological situation.[20] In any case, since the shaft dead-ends in salt, water leaking in would become saturated, after which it would be incapable of further dissolution. Burial in rock other than salt would require considerable research, but it seems reasonable to expect that filling with concrete or some other material would handle the situation.

Implied Assumption that Radioactive Wastes is No More Leachable than Average Rock

Experimental evidence supporting this assumption was given in "Buried Waste — General Considerations and Time Delays" earlier in this chapter.

Ignoring the High Concentration of Radioactivity in the Waste

As noted earlier, the concentration of radioactivity does not affect the total number of fatalities so long as a linear, no-threshold dose-effect relationship is used. In fact, considerable dilution of this radioactivity must be assumed in order for it to be effectively dispersed to the population upon reaching the biosphere. The number of fatalities depends only on the total number of radioactive atoms, not on their concentration (assuming the low probability per person of cancer and the linearity hypothesis). However, the possible fluctuations about the average are, of course, greatly increased. If the average number of fatalities in the first million years is 0.4, there can still be a release causing 1000 fatalities, but its probability can be no more than 0.4 per 1000 for any 1 year's waste.

If the linear, no-threshold theory were abandoned, there might be an advantage in avoiding concentration. However, the total effect would be greatly decreased; therefore, if one accepts the very low total effects found in the last section of this chapter, it hardly seems to be worth the trouble and expense to undertake development of several different repositories.

Conservatism in the Probability Estimate

While considering criticism of our model, it is perhaps appropriate to recall some of its conservatism. We calculated that 1/43 millionth of the Ra in the top 600 m is leached away each year and assumed that this figure also applies to the waste. A more realistic procedure would be to recognize that the waste buried at 600 m depth should be compared with the average of radium down to 1200 m, for which the average leach rate is 1/86 million per year. If this rate is plotted against time, it would peak near 86 million years and in the first few million years would probably be at least one order of magnitude below the average. Thus, our model probably overestimates the release rate by at least a factor of 20.

It would seem that the random burial scenario used in the model should be considerably less favorable than what is planned for a waste repository. By carefully choosing a site, high permeability rocks, such as sandstone, conglomerate, limestone, dolomite, marble, etc., can be avoided, and areas with good ion-exchange properties can be favored. Low-strength rocks that tend to crack, such as most shales, quartzite, and many schists, can be avoided. The natural radium and uranium with which the waste is compared in the model does not enjoy these advantages. In fact, an appreciable fraction of the Ra and U is in rock permeated with circulating ground water.

COMPARISON OF HAZARDS FROM WASTE WITH HAZARDS OF URANIUM CONSUMED

In assessing effects of the radioactivity in the waste over very long periods of time, it seems reasonable to give credit for the fact that uranium, which also produces long-term effects from its radioactivity, is *consumed* in producing the waste. If it is assumed that this original uranium was as securely buried as the waste, the magnitude of this credit is shown by the dot-dash line for ^{238}U in Figure 9. This is based on the premise that the original uranium ore was as securely buried as the waste. The fact that all uranium is not so buried is evident from the natural radon, a uranium daughter, which pervades our atmosphere. This natural radon administers a dose of 150 mrem/year to the tracheo-bronchial tree of the average person.[27] Coupling this with the lung cancer dose from Table 4 and the U.S. population gives an estimated death toll of $0.15 \times 2 \times 10^8 \times 39 \times 10^{-6} = 1200$ per year. One year of all nuclear power would consume 2.9×10^8 g of ^{238}U, which is 4×10^{-8} of that in the top 100 m (we assume that the ore being mined is from depths uniformly distributed over the top 100 m); consuming this ^{238}U saves $4 \times 10^{-8} \times 1200$, or 48 lives per million years in the U.S.

If one accepts this treatment, it is difficult not to conclude that, on a long time scale, nuclear power is a device for *cleansing* the earth of radioactivity. While this may seem strange at first, the underlying logic is clear. Alpha-particle emitters are 100 times more dangerous than beta-gamma emitters where ingestion and inhalation are the principal pathways to man — they have typically 10 times higher energy and 10 times higher biological efficiency (50 times in bone) for doing damage — and every uranium nucleus is destined to decay with the emission of eight of these alphas. Instead, nuclear power converts it into two beta-gamma emitters (fission products), 87% of which has decayed away before they leave the reactor. We often hear proposals to burn up the actinides (principally the Pu, Am, etc. in the waste); however, on a long time scale, uranium is just as dangerous as the other actinides and its burn-up in reactors is a desirable end if radioactivity is to be avoided.

SPECIAL CONSIDERATIONS FOR BURIAL IN SALT FORMATIONS

The concept most favored at this time is burial in bedded salt formations. This has been recommended by each of four studies sponsored by the National Academy of Sciences,[12,34,39,47] for the following reasons:

1. The very existence of these salt beds indicates that there has been no ground water in them for hundreds of millions of years; therefore, in the absence of evidence for geological changes, no ground water would be expected in them for at least 1000 years and probably for very much longer.
2. Salt flows plastically under pressure and recrystallizes to heal cracks; therefore, the waste would be essentially sealed inside a gigantic rock crystal.
3. It has good thermal conductivity (see Figure 6).
4. It has high structural strength (similar to concrete).
5. Salt formations are generally located in tectonically stable sedimentary basins.
6. There is an established technology for mining the salt. Salt deposits are very widespread in this country, underlying 500,000 mi^2 in portions of 23 states, so there is no shortage of possible burial sites.

There are at least two potential disadvantages in salt: it is water soluble and ion-exchange hold-up is very much reduced if the water is highly saline.[28] The ion-exchange hold-up is important only as a time delay factor, and the time required to dissolve away the salt would seem to provide adequate protection in this regard. The most readily conceivable way for water to enter the salt formation in which the waste is buried would be as a result of severe faulting, opening a vertical crack through the salt bed,[8] or in an extreme situation, displacing the burial horizon vertically by more than 300 m to bring it into contact with circulating ground water. The probability for a significant fault to intersect the ½ km^2 area occupied by 1 year's waste in the New Mexico site has been estimated to be about 3×10^{-12} per year.[17] In most cases, fractures caused by such a fault would be healed by plastic flow. The water flow would not greatly impede this process, as it would become a saturated solution near the entry point and would be incapable of further dissolution over most of the path. The release probability through these processes is, thus, several orders of magnitude less than the 2.3×10^{-8} per year used in the "Release Through Ground Water" section of this chapter for a natural release rate.

Another possible disadvantage of burial in salt involves human intervention and will be evaluated later.

RELEASE AS AIRBORNE PARTICULATE

Since the potential hazards due to inhalation (Figure 10) are considerably larger and more persistent in time (if release should occur) than those due to ingestion (Figure 9), it is important to consider possible mechanisms for release of the buried waste as airborne particulate. The first thing that comes to mind is a nuclear bomb explosion; however, for the largest bombs yet exploded (50 Mton TNT-equivalent), the crater depth would be only 340 m and the fracture zone would reach only to 500 m.[8] Therefore, the waste buried at 600 m would not be affected. There are no publicly announced delivery systems for bombs larger than this size and no evident military reason to justify developing them. Release of the radioactive waste in this way would clearly not qualify as a justification, since far greater destruction could be wrought by using even a much smaller bomb on a city.

A natural event with the potential for releasing the waste would be the impact of a giant meteorite; one leaving a crater 2 km in diameter would be required to reach a depth of 600 m, and the probability of this has been estimated to be about 2×10^{-14}/km^2-yr.[8,17] Since 1 year's waste would occupy 0.5 km^2, the probability for its release in this manner is about 1×10^{-14} per year. Such an event would have many characteristics of a nuclear bomb explosion, including a fireball, and the release would be similar to nuclear fallout.

The average number of fatalities expected from such a release may be obtained by multiplying the integral over time of the solid curve in Figure 10 (read with the scale on the inside of the right margin) by the probability per year for such a release.* The integral works out to 4×10^7 in the first million years and 12×10^7 if extended to 10^8 years. Multiplying these by 10^{-14} gives an average fatality total of the order of 10^{-7} for each year of all nuclear power, millions of times lower than through the ground water-ingestion pathway. If there are worries about release through meteorite impact, it should be noted that the maximum number of fatalities from Figure 10 is 30,000 (read from inside right-base scale), whereas a direct impact on a city could easily kill millions, and an impact on water would form a tsunami that could easily kill hundreds of thousands.

Another natural release mechanism would be through volcanic action. Areas where volcanism may be expected are well known, and intrusive dykes give further evidence of the volcanic potential for any particular area. For the central plateau of the U.S. where the probability is minimal, the potential is estimated[4] to be of the order of 10^{-14} per km^2-year. Most of the magma comes up through "pipes" which break through the rock, but a few meters of rock around the circumference of these pipes may be melted and carried up. This cross-sectional area is estimated to be about 10^{-3} km^2, so the risk of particular rock being brought to the surface is of the order of 10^{-17} per year. This danger, therefore, is three orders of magnitude smaller than even the risk from meteorite impact.

Since these effects are so small, the principal mechanism for release as airborne particulate would probably be secondary effects from the 2.3×10^{-8} per year released into surface waters, resulting in some of the material ending up as a dry, finely divided powder on the surface that may be stirred up to become airborne particulate. Methods have been developed to calculate the resuspension of airborne particulate that has been deposited on the ground,[30] and they are used here. The resuspension coefficient K, defined as grams per cubic meters resuspended in air per grams per square meter deposited on the ground, is taken initially to be 10^{-5} m^{-1} and to decrease with a 50-day half-life until it reaches 10^{-9} m^{-1} after something less than 2 years, and thereafter to

* If p is the probability per year for release and E(t) is the effect of such a release, the average effect, E, is $\overline{E} = \int pE(t)dt = p\int E(t)dt$ since we take p to be constant.

decrease with a 10- to 100-year half-life* as the dust sinks into and becomes part of the soil. In this model, the exposure, integrated to infinity, is as though it were at the initial rate (K = 10^{-5} m^{-1}) and extended for 70 days (i.e., 50/ln 2). For each gram deposited randomly over the U.S. (area = 8×10^{12} m^2), the average surface deposit is 1.2×10^{-13} g/m^2 where the average concentration of dust initially suspended in air is 1.2×10^{-18} g/m^3. In 70 days, the average person inhales 1400 m^3 of air which then contains 1.6×10^{-15} g of dust; therefore, the 2×10^8 people in the U.S. inhale a total of 3×10^{-7} of the material initially deposited on the ground. Thus, the hazard in spreading material on the ground in readily suspendable form is essentially the same (according to the above model) as releasing it as bomb fallout (for which 2×10^{-7} is inhaled by people) and may be read on the scale inside the right margin of Figure 10.

Returning now to our original problem, let us assume that 4% of the material released to rivers ends up spread randomly over the surface of the U.S. as a readily suspendable dust; this is probably an overestimate as most of the material would sink into river bottoms or banks or be carried out to sea. That which does end up on land surfaces would generally be combined with mud or other sediments which would leave very little of the material in particle sizes less than about 5 μm, the maximum size for suspension in air and deposition in the lung on inhalation. With this assumption, the probability for waste to end up as a suspendable dust is 0.04 times the 2.3×10^{-8} per year probability for release into rivers, or 1×10^{-9} per year. To obtain the eventual resulting fatalities, this number must be multiplied by the integral of the curve in Figure 10 as read from the scale inside the right margin, which we have seen is 4×10^7 in the first million years. Via this pathway, the result is 0.04 eventual fatalities from the wastes generated by 1 year of all nuclear power, which is still one order of magnitude less than our estimate for the ingestion pathway. Factors discussed in the section entitled "Release Through Ground Water" that make the latter an upper limit would also be applicable here; thus inhalation would be much less important than the ingestion pathway.

EXTERNAL RADIATION RESULTING FROM RELEASE OF BURIED WASTE

If we assume, as in the last section, that 4% of the waste released via ground water ends up spread over the surface of the U.S. and remains there for T years, the effects of external gamma-ray exposure are 2.3×10^{-8} (fractional annual release) × 0.04 (fraction on surface) × T × the integral of the curve in Figure 8, using the scale on the right margin of that figure. This integral is 4×10^5 for the first million years, so the total number of deaths is $4T \times 10^{-4}$. Thus, if T is less than 1000 years, external radiation is less important than the ingestion pathway. If consideration is extended beyond one million years, the relative shapes of the curves in Figures 8 and 9 indicate that ingestion becomes, relatively, still more important.

Most people live in cities where radioactive materials on paved surfaces are rapidly washed away and where new construction frequently covers or replaces surfaces; therefore, T would be no more than a few tens of years and usually much less. In rural areas, radioactive material may be shielded by being washed deep into the soil or drained away, either of which would probably have time constants of 1000 years or less. The initial assumption of 4% being spread over the surface is probably pessimistic as explained in "Special Considerations for Burial in Salt Formations." For all these reasons, external radiation seems to be much less important than the ingestion pathway.

* The decrease below 10^{-9} was not used in AEC-1974,[30] but is implied by data given therein.

RELEASE THROUGH HUMAN INTRUSION

Once the repository is sealed, the waste would not be an attractive target for sabotage. It would take many days of effort with large machinery to remove it, and those working on the project would run grave risks of injury from the radiation. We therefore consider only release through inadvertent human intrusion. Even this possibility would be excluded without the collapse of civilization and social institutions. As long as these remain, the burial site would be remembered, retained in government ownership, and probably kept under surveillance. In addition there are plans for permanent markers explaining the dangers, which hopefully would outlast lapses in civilization.

Nevertheless, let us assume for the moment that all memory of the burial site is lost. The two most likely modes of intervention would be drilling or mining. Drilling for water to a depth of 600 m would be most unusual, and one of the criteria for selecting a repository is that it be in an area unattractive for oil or other mineral resources. Therefore, it seems reasonable to assume that the probability for a drill hole in the repository would not be larger than for an average location in the U.S. if the rate of exploratory drilling were equal to that of current "rank-wildcat" oil drilling. Averaged over the U.S., this is 3×10^{-4} drill holes per year per square kilometer.[43] An 18-in. diameter drill hole removes an area of 2×10^{-7} km^2, so the probability for an atom of waste to be brought to the surface by drilling is the product of 3×10^{-4} and 2×10^{-7}, or 6×10^{-11} per year. Its subsequent behavior in the environment would depend on a large number of imponderable factors, but a realistic guess might be that its effects are equivalent to those of release into rivers. This release mode would then be almost three orders of magnitude less probable than the natural release to rivers we have been assuming (2.3×10^{-8} per year). Another possibility is that it would be spread out over the ground in a form which allows some fraction of it to become suspended as airborne particulate but it was shown earlier that this leads to lesser consequences than release into rivers.*

If one considers future mining that might take place in the waste repository for unspecified minerals (presumably ones that are not now recognized to be economically interesting), it is difficult to conceive of operations more than 5% as extensive as our current coal mining operations. The latter annually involves 2×10^{-8} of the rock in the U.S. down to a depth of 1000 m,** so the probability of the waste being mined is not more than 10^{-9} per year. If the effect is equivalent to release into rivers, it is still 20 times less important than the natural release we have assumed.

An important exception to the above argument would be if the waste were buried in salt, which, after all, is a material we now recover by mining. There is enough salt underground in the U.S. to last about 25 million years at current rates of usage; hence, the probability for any particular small volume to be mined is 4×10^{-8} per year. Most of this (unless eaten, as evaluated below) would probably find its way eventually into rivers or other surface waters; therefore, this source would seem to be about equal to

* In addition to the effects of wastes brought to the surface, a drill hole would introduce a possible flow path connecting aquifers above and below the burial formation. If the latter is salt, this would cause its dissolution. If all the water normally flowing through a 1-m wide strip were to be diverted to this path, a 100-cm^2 cross section extending vertically through the formation could be dissolved away each year. At this rate, the salt enclosing 1 year's waste would be dissolved in 5×10^7 years; however, as soon as the cavity opened by the water became much larger than the hole through the impervious formation above the salt, dissolution would stop until plastic flow of the salt closes the hole. The process would thus take much longer than 5×10^7 years.

** About 3×10^8 tons/year is now obtained from underground coal mining. Assuming that half of the volume removed is coal, 1.5 tons of coal per cubic meter is mined; thus, 2×10^8 m^3 per year is excavated. The rock in U.S. to a depth of 1000 m occupies 10^{16} m^3, so 2×10^{-8} of this is mined for coal annually.

what we have assumed for natural releases into surface waters (2.3×10^{-8} per year). However, the waste released through salt mining would be in insoluble form, and insoluble radioactive material is at least an order of magnitude less dangerous if ingested than soluble material such as leached waste in natural releases — for the two most important nuclei in Figure 9, the ratio[24] is 20 for ^{90}Sr and 600 for ^{226}Ra — thus, release through salt mining is at least one order of magnitude less important than natural releases.

In reaching this conclusion, we have ignored the use of salt in food, which provides a direct pathway into man, thereby by-passing the 1.5×10^{-5} probability for materials in rivers to be ingested. However, only 1% of our salt is used for food. Moreover, it is purified by solution techniques allowing ample time for insolubles to settle out,[35] which should eliminate all but perhaps 10^{-3} of the waste (nearly all of the waste should be in large, glassy, highly insoluble lumps). These two factors reduce the importance of salt used for foods relative to other salt* by a factor of 10^5 (0.01×10^{-3}), making it of comparable importance and still one order of magnitude less important than what we have assumed for natural releases.

As further reinforcement for this conclusion, it should be noted that we have ignored sea water as a competing source for salt. In a low-technology civilization, sea water would seem to be a much more practical source than mining at 600 m depth, and, furthermore, such a civilization would not use salt at nearly the current rate. As radioactivity would undoubtedly be familiar in a high-technology society, there is an excellent chance that the problem would be discovered. Moreover, it should be recalled that there would be little difficulty with human intrusion if the burial site is not forgotten.

REQUIREMENTS FOR SURVEILLANCE

We will now consider the question of what type of surveillance would be desirable for a waste repository. While the technology is being developed, close surveillance would, of course, be important, but we will consider here the situation after the technology is established and the repository is sealed.

It is important to recognize that no surveillance was assumed in the model used to obtain our estimate of 0.4 eventual deaths from 1 year of all nuclear power. No one is watching to see that uranium ore is not getting into streams, and our estimate was based on a comparison with that process. Any effect of surveillance would then be to decrease the fatality toll below our estimate of 0.4.

If we are willing to place a dollar value on a random human life (average age 60, since cancers occur 15 to 45 years after exposure), we can use Figure 9 to estimate the maximum amount it is worth to watch 1 year's waste. It would be very difficult to justify a figure higher than $10 million per life saved.** Money spent on medical research, medical care, or public health could easily save one life for each $10 million

* In addition to factors discussed here, there are other reasons why mining salt for food is unlikely. As the process requires a great deal of water, mining in arid regions would be unlikely. Salt for food is mined only near population centers to minimize transport costs — the price of salt is so low that transport costs are an important factor.

** The U.S. Nuclear Regulatory Commission suggests that reduction of radiation exposure may warrant up to $1000 per man-rem of radiation exposure averted (Federal Register 40, 19441, 5/15/75). From Table 4, the cancer risk per man-rem is 180×10^{-6}, which corresponds to a value of life $= 1000/180 \times 10^{-6} =$ \$6 million.

spent, and there are countless examples* in which people submit their own lives to a 10^{-6} risk to save \$10, or to a 10^{-5} risk to save \$100.** If we accept the \$10 million figure and use Figure 9, we find that after 2000 years, watching might save 10^{-6} lives per year, so it would not pay to spend more than \$10 per year on the operation. Similarly, it would not pay to spend more than \$100 per year after 400 years, \$30 per year after 600 years, and \$1 per year after a half million years.

A realistic surveillance program might consist of periodic inspections to maintain warning markers and to prevent deep drilling or mining in the repository area and periodic water sample collections from nearby streams and wells for radioactivity measurements. A program of this type could easily maintain surveillance over 1000 years of waste (occupying an area of 500 km^2) with the part time service of a single employee.

Authors' Note

It is often said that watching our wastes will impose a great burden on our progeny. According to our model, the waste will increase their radiation exposure by one part in 10^{10} for each year of all nuclear power,*** which would be undetectable; our present exposures are not known to better than 10%. This is trivial in comparison with another burden we place on our progeny by consuming all the rich mineral resources of the earth, including most metals and the fossil fuels such as coal, oil, and gas. This will have a tremendous impact on their lives in denying them most of the benefits of technology. It is the author's opinion that we therefore owe our progeny a technology that will allow them to live in reasonable comfort without these resources. The key to such a technology is clearly cheap and abundant energy, and the only long-lasting source of this we can now guarantee is nuclear energy.

COMPARISON WITH URANIUM MILL TAILINGS

After being mined, the uranium ore is shipped to an ore processing mill where it is concentrated to produce "yellow cake," which is 80% U_3O_8. In this operation, the uranium decay daughters ^{230}Th, ^{226}Ra, ^{222}Rn, etc. are disposed of with the other rock and soil material in large piles referred to as "mill tailings." A typical pile of this sort, formed from producing fuel for 106 reactor-years of 1000 MWe light water reactor (LWR) operation, would cover about 250 acres.[43] It is of considerable interest to compare the hazards in these mill tailings and those in the waste.

In the isotopic enrichment process, the ^{235}U content is increased from 0.72% to 3.3%; therefore, if all of the ^{235}U were utilized, only 1/4.6 of the uranium would be converted into fuel rods. Actually, the depleted uranium from enrichment facilities contains about 0.3% ^{235}U, so only 58% of the ^{235}U is used and only 0.58/4.6 = 0.13 of all the uranium gets into the reactor. To account for other losses, we assume that for every tonne of fuel, 10 tonnes of uranium must pass through ore processing mills, leaving its daughters in the tailings piles. A convenient way to calculate the effects of

* For example, if a life is worth \$10 million, riding in an automobile which gives an average risk of 2 × 10^{-8} per mile costs 20 cents per passenger-mile. This is twice the cost of air travel which is considerably safer; therefore, if a family drives somewhere to save airline fare, they are effectively saying each of their lives is not worth \$5 million.

** Another approach is to recognize that \$10 million is equivalent to about 500 man-years of 40 hr/week labor or 100 man-years of around-the-clock labor. If this adds 20 years of life expectancy for the would-be victim, equivalently, five people are working around-the-clock to keep this person alive.

*** In our model, the waste causes 0.4 deaths per 10^6 years. From Reference 48 natural radioactivity causes about 3000 fatalities per year, so the waste increases average exposure to our progeny by $0.4 \times 10^{-6}/3000$ or 10^{-10} from 1 year of nuclear power.

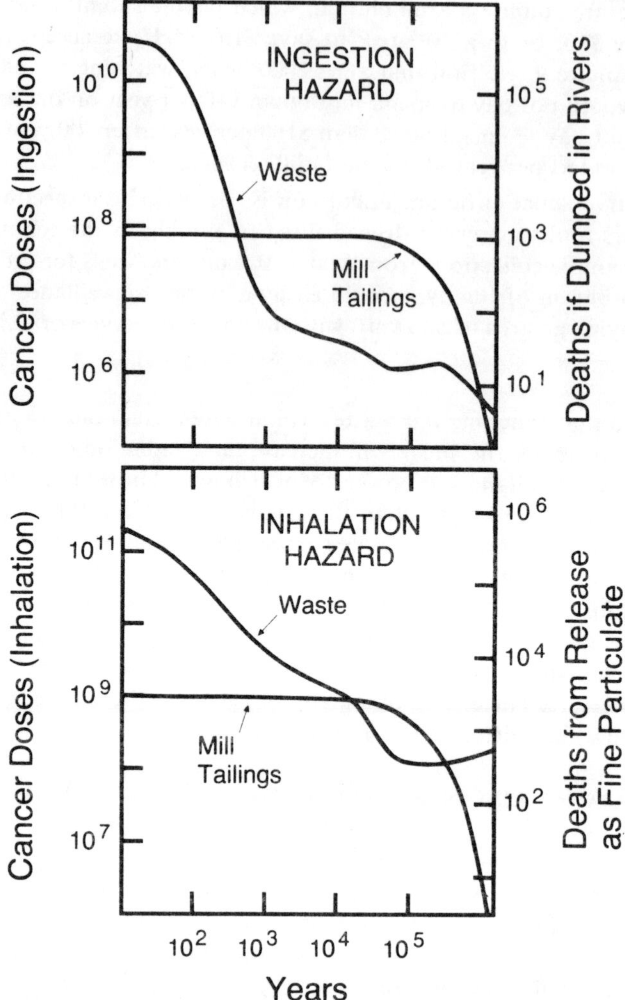

FIGURE 13. Comparison of hazards from high-level waste and from uranium ore processing mill tailings with respect to ingestion and inhalation. The curves for the waste are the solid curves from Figures 9 and 10.

this material is to compare it with this same material in the high-level wastes after all of their shorter half-life sources (e.g., ^{234}U) have decayed away (10^7 years) and they are in equilibrium with ^{238}U. Since 99.5% of the ^{238}U is removed in reprocessing, the amount in the nuclear power waste is 1/200 of that in the fuel and therefore 1/2000 of that originally mined; hence, the quantity of uranium daughters in the mill tailings is 2000 times that in the wastes after 10^7 years. From Figure 9, this represents an initial ingestion hazard (from ^{226}Ra) of $2000 \times 4 \times 10^4 = 8 \times 10^7$ cancer doses, and from Figure 8, it represents an initial inhalation hazard from ^{230}Th) of $2000 \times 5 \times 10^5 = 1 \times 10^9$ cancer doses. These potential hazards decay away with the 77,000-year half-life of ^{230}Th as shown in Figure 13, where they are compared with the hazards from the waste; we see that for the ingestion hazard, which we have found to be most important for the waste, the mill tailings surpass the waste as a hazard after only 250 years. Since the waste is much more securely buried than the mill tailings and is especially secure against release for the first several hundred years, it must be clearly evident that the mill tailings are a far larger potential hazard than the waste.

The rough scoping estimates from the section, "Some Appropriate Estimates of Upper Bounds to the Hazards of Nuclear Wastes Dispersed to the Environment" are included on the right side of the graphs in Figure 13. We see that if 0.1% of the tailings become suspended as airborne fine particulate over the next 100,000 years or so, we may expect about three lung cancers for each year of all nuclear power and if that amount is released to rivers, we may expect about one bone cancer from ingestion. It is, therefore, important that the mill tailings be handled so as to assure against releases greater than this, which may be a matter of some difficulty.

In this discussion, we have ignored the effects of the ^{222}Rn escaping from the tailings piles. This problem has been pointed out by others[37] and further emphasizes the fact that uranium mill tailings represent a far greater hazard than the high-level waste. Solutions to the mill tailings problem are discussed by Sears[44] and Cohen.[9]

ACKNOWLEDGMENTS

The author is greatly indebted to Charles Kee (Oak Ridge National Laboratory) for making available the ORIGEN code and helping in its use; to H. C. Claiborne, F. Gera, H. W. Godbee, D. G. Jacobs, J. O. Blomeke, and T. Lomenick (Oak Ridge National Laboratory); to J. W. Bartlett, G. Jansen, and J. E. Mendel (Battelle Pacific Northwest Laboratory); and to H. Soule (ERDA) for many helpful discussions.

REFERENCES

1. Barraclough, J. T. and Jensen, R. G., Open File Rep. 75-318, U.S. Geological Survey, Idaho Falls, Id., 1976; J. T. Barraclough, private communication, 1976.
2. Bell, M. J. and Dillon, R. S., Rep. ORNL-TM-3548, Oak Ridge Laboratory, Oak Ridge, Tenn., 1971.
3. Bell, M. J., *ORIGEN — The ORNL Isotope Generation and Depletion Code*, Report ORNL-4628, Oak Ridge National Laboratory, Oak Ridge, Tenn., 1973.
4. Bickerman, M., private communication, 1976.
5. Blomeke, J. O., Radioactive waste, *Phys. Today*, 26, 36, August 1973.
6. Burnett, T. W. T., Smith, C. F., and Kastenberg, W. E., unpublished report.
7. Christensen, H. E., Toxic Substance List, U.S. Department of Health, Education, and Welfare, Washington, D.C., 1974.
8. Claiborne, H. C. and Gera, F., *Potential Containmenta Failure Mechanisms and Their Consequences at a Radioactive Waste Repository in Bedded Salt in New Mexico*, Rep. ORNL-TM-4639, Oak Ridge National Laboratory, Oak Ridge, Tenn., 1974.
9. Cohen, B. L., Environmental impact of nuclear power from radioactive mill tailings, *Bull. At. Sci.*, 32, 61, February 1976.
10. Cook, J. E., private communication.
11. Denham, D. H. et al., Battelle Northwest Laboratory Rep. BNWL-1764, Richland, Wash., 1973, 29.
12. Committee on Radioactive Waste Management, Disposal of Solid Radioactive Wastes in Bedded Salt Deposits, National Academy of Sciences, Washington, D.C., 1970.
13. Ground water, *Encyclopedia Brittanica*, Vol. 10, 1970, 949.
14. Eisenbud, M., *Environmental Radioactivity*, Academic Press, New York, 1973, 1972.
15. Uranium, *Encyclopedia of Science*, McGraw-Hill, New York, 1971.
16. Galley, J. E., in *Underground Waste Management and Environmental Implications*, Cook, T. D., Ed., American Association of Petroleum Geologists, 1972, 122.
17. Gera, F. and Jacobs, D. G., *Considerations in the Long-term Management of High-level Radioactive Wastes*, Rep. ORNL-4762, Oak Ridge National Laboratory, Oak Ridge, Tenn., 1972.
18. Gera, F., Rep. ORNL-TM-4481, Oak Ridge National Laboratory, Oak Ridge, Tenn., 1975.
19. Godbee, H. W. and Joy, D. S., Rep. ORNL-TM-4333, Oak Ridge National Laboratory Oak Ridge, Tenn., 1974; Godbee, H. W., private communication.
20. Gormley, O., private communication.

21. **Grove, D. B.**, Rep. SC-CR-706139, Sandia Laboratory, Albuquerque, N.M., 1968.
22. **Hamstra, J.**, *Nucl. Saf.*, 16(2), 180, 1975.
23. **Heinreich, E. W.**, *Mineralogy and Geology of Radioactive Raw Materials*, McGraw-Hill, New York, 1958.
24. *International Commission on Radiation Protection Publ. No. 2*, Pergamon Press, New York, 1959.
25. *International Commission on Radiation Protection Publ. No. 6*, Pergamon Press, New York, 1962.
26. *International Commission on Radiation Protection Publ. No. 19*, Pergamon Press, New York, 1973.
27. *Ionizing Radiation: Levels and Effects*, United Nations Scientific Committee on Effects of Atomic Radiation, New York, 1972.
28. **Jansen, G. and Burkholder, H. C.**, Rep. BNWL-1876, Battelle Northwest Laboratory, Richland, Wash., 1975.
29. Rep. ORP/CSD 72-1, U.S. Environmental Protection Agency, 1972.
30. *LMFBR Program Environmental Statement*, Rep. WASH-1535, U.S. Atomic Energy Commission, Washington, D.C., 1974, p. II, G-16.
31. **McElroy, J. L.**, *The Expected Behavior of HLW Glass in Storage*, Rep. BNWL-SA-5581, Battelle Northwest Laboratory, Richland, Wash., 1976.
32. **Mendel, J. E. et. al.**, *Thermal and Radiation Effects on Borosilite Waste Glass*, IAEA-SM-207/100 and BNWL-SA-5534, Battelle Northwest Laboratory, Richaland, Wash., 1976.
33. **Merritt, W. F.**, *At. Energy Can. Ltd. AECL Rep.*, AECL-5317, 1976.
34. Minutes of the Meeting of December 7—8, Division of Earth Sciences Committee on Geologic Aspects of Radioactive Waste Disposal, National Academy of Sciences, Washington, D.C., 1961.
35. **Mulkey, J.**, private communications.
36. *Plutonium and other Actinides*, Rep. WASH-1539, U.S. Atomic Energy Commission, Washington, D.C., 1974.
37. **Pohl, R. O.**, unpublished manuscript, 1975.
38. *Reactor Safety Study*, Rep. WASH-1400, U.S. Nuclear Regulatory Commission, Washington, D.C., 1975.
39. Report to the Division of Reactor Development and Technology, Division of Earth Sciences Committee on Geologic Aspects of Radioactive Waste Disposal, National Academy of Sciences, Washington, D.C., 1966.
40. **Robertson, J. B. and Barraclough J. T.**, *Underground Waste Management and Artificial Recharge*, Vol. 1, 1973, 291.
41. **Ross, W.**, private communication, 1976.
42. **Schneider, K. J. and Platt, A. M.**, *High Level Radioactive Waste Management Alternatives*, Vol. 2, Rep. BNWL-1900, Battelle Northwest Laboratory, Richland, Wash., 1974.
43. **Searle, M.**, private communication.
44. **Sears, M. B., Blanco, R. E., Dahlman, R. C., Hill, R. S., Ryan, A. D., and Witherspoon, J. P.**, Rep. ORNL-TM-4903, Oak Ridge National Laboratory, Oak Ridge, Tenn., 1975.
45. **Simmons, J. A., Erdmann, R. C., and Naft, B. N.**, *The Risk of Catastrophic Spills of Toxic Chemicals*, UCLA-ENG-7425, University of California, Los Angeles, 1974.
46. **Tamura, T.**, private communication.
47. The Disposal of Radioactive Wastes on Land, Publ. 519, National Academy of Sciences, Washington, D.C., 1957.
48. *The Effects on Populations of Exposure to Low Levels of Ionizing Radiation*, National Academy of Sciences, National Research Council Committee on Biological Effects of Ionizing Radiation, Washington, D.C., 1972.
49. **Tokarev, A. N. and Sheherbakov, A. V.**, *Radiohydrology (Moscow)*, 1956 AEC-tr-4100, 1960.

Appendixes

APPENDIX I

CALCULATION OF ANNUAL DOSES TO MAN FROM ROUTINE RELEASES OF REACTOR EFFLUENTS FOR THE PURPOSE OF EVALUATING COMPLIANCE WITH 10 CFR PART 50, APPENDIX I†

A. INTRODUCTION

Appendix I, "Numerical Guides for Design Objectives and Limiting Conditions for Operation to Meet the Criterion 'As Low As Is Reasonably Achievable' for Radioactive Material in Light-Water-Cooled Nuclear Power Reactor Effluents," to 10 CFR Part 50 provides numerical guidance for radioactive effluent design objectives and technical specification requirements for limiting conditions of operation for light-water-cooled nuclear power plants.

To implement Appendix I, the NRC staff has developed a series of guides that provide methods acceptable to the staff for the calculation of preoperational estimates of effluent releases, dispersion of the effluent in the atmosphere and different water bodies, and estimation of the associated radiation doses* to man. This guide describes basic features of these calculational models and suggests parameters for the estimation of radiation doses to man from effluent releases. The methods used herein are general approaches that the NRC staff has developed for application in lieu of specific parameters for individual sites. The use of site-specific values by the applicant is encouraged. However, the assumptions and methods used to obtain these parameters should be fully described and documented.

Portions of this guide supersede Regulatory Guide 1.42, Revision 1, "Interim Licensing Policy on as Low as Practicable for Gaseous Radioiodine Releases from Light-Water-Cooled Nuclear Power Reactors," which has been withdrawn.

B. DISCUSSION

Appendix I to 10 CFR Part 50 provides guidance on the doses to members of the general public resulting from effluent releases that may be considered to be as low as is reasonably achievable. This guide describes basic features of the calculational models and assumptions in use by the NRC staff for the estimation of doses.

Appendix A of this guide describes suggested models and assumptions for calculating the estimated doses to man from discharges to the hydrosphere. Appendix B of this guide describes suggested models and assumptions for calculating doses from noble gases discharged to the atmosphere, and Appendix C gives models and assumptions for estimating doses from radioiodines and other radionuclides released to the atmosphere. Appendix D describes the models and assumptions for calculating population doses (man-rem and man-thyroid-rem) from radionuclide releases to the atmosphere and hydrosphere. Appendix E presents tabular data pertaining to two or more of the other appendices. Appendix F provides a discussion of, and derivation for, the I function used in computing gamma doses from elevated noble gas releases.

In providing guidance for implementing Section II of Appendix I, the NRC staff has made use of the maximum exposed individual approach. In this approach the numerical design objectives of Section II are compared to the calculated radiation exposures to maximum individuals in each of four age groups.

The population is considered to be made up of infants (0 to 1 year), children (1 to 11 years), teenagers (11 to 17 years), and adults (17 years and older). For the purpose of evaluating dose commitment, the maximum infant is assumed to be newborn, the maximum child is taken to be 4 years old, the maximum teenager is taken to be 14 years old, and the maximum adult is taken to be 17 years old.

Maximum individuals are characterized as "maximum" with regard to food consumption, occupancy, and other usage of the region in the vicinity of the plant site and as such represent individuals with habits representing reasonable deviations from the average for the population in general. In all physiological and metabolic respects the maximum exposed individuals are assumed to have those characteristics that represent the averages for their corresponding age group in the general

---

*In this guide, the term "dose," when applied to individuals, is used instead of the more precise term "dose equivalent," as defined by the International Commission on Radiological Units and Measurements (ICRU). When applied to the evaluation of internal deposition of radioactivity, the term "dose," as used here, includes the prospective dose component arising from retention in the body beyond the period of environmental exposure, i.e., the dose commitment. The dose commitment is evaluated over a period of 50 years.

† Regulatory Guide 1.109, Office of Standards Development, U. S. Nuclear Regulatory Commission, Washington, D.C., Rev. 1, October 1977.

population. Although specific individuals will almost certainly display dietary, recreational, and other living habits considerably different from those suggested here, and actual physiological and metabolic parameters may vary considerably, the NRC staff considers the maximum exposed individual to be a well-defined reference for implementation of Section II of Appendix I. The characterization of maximum exposed individuals is subject to continuing review by the NRC staff, and the applicant is encouraged to use information and data applicable to a specific region or site when possible. Where site-specific information and data is used, its justification should be documented for the NRC staff's review.

Since the radiation dose commitment per unit intake of a given radionuclide usually varies as a function of age, four sets of internal dose conversion factors have been calculated. These dose factors are appropriate for the four different age groups defined above. Specifically, these dose factors are based on continuous intake over a one-year environmental exposure period and an associated dose commitment extending over a 50-year period from initiation of intake.

The models and assumptions described in Appendices A, B, C, and D of this guide are acceptable to the NRC staff for calculating doses to individuals and populations. If other models are selected, they should include the same exposure pathways considered in the models described in this guide. The assumptions and methods used should be fully described and documented.

As discussed in Section III.A.2 of Appendix I to 10 CFR Part 50, the applicant may take into account any real phenomena or actual exposure conditions. Such conditions could include actual values for agricultural productivity, dietary habits, residence times, dose attenuation by structures, measured environmental transport factors (such as bioaccumulation factors), or similar values actually determined for a specific site. The applicant should provide enough information on the measurements or other methods used to derive these substitute values to enable the NRC staff to evaluate their validity.

C. REGULATORY POSITION

Equations are provided below by which the NRC staff will estimate radiation exposure for maximum individuals and the population within 50 miles. These equations are appropriate for the exposure pathways that the staff routinely considers in its evaluations. In addition, other exposure pathways that may arise due to unique conditions at a specific site should be considered if they are likely to provide a significant contribution to the total dose. A pathway is considered significant if a conservative evaluation yields an additional dose increment equal to or more than 10 percent of the total from all pathways considered in this guide.

1. Doses from Liquid Effluent Pathways

The NRC staff will calculate radiation doses from potable water, aquatic food, shoreline deposits, and irrigated food pathways by using the following equations, which are described in detail in Appendix A of this guide.

a. Potable Water

$$R_{apj} = 1100 \frac{U_{ap}M_p}{F} \sum_i Q_i D_{aipj} \exp(-\lambda_i t_p) \quad (1)$$

b. Aquatic Foods

$$R_{apj} = 1100 \frac{U_{ap}M_p}{F} \sum_i Q_i B_{ip} D_{aipj} \exp(-\lambda_i t_p) \quad (2)$$

c. Shoreline Deposits

$$R_{apj} = 110{,}000 \frac{U_{ap}M_pW}{F} \sum_i Q_i T_i D_{aipj} \, [\exp(-\lambda_i t_p)][1 - \exp(-\lambda_i t_b)] \quad (3)$$

d. Irrigated Foods

For all radionuclides except tritium:

$$R_{apj} = U_{ap}^{veg} \sum_i d_i \exp(-\lambda_i t_h) D_{aipj} \left[\frac{r[1 - \exp(-\lambda_{Ei} t_e)]}{Y_v \lambda_{Ei}} + \frac{f_I B_{iv}[1 - \exp(-\lambda_i t_b)]}{P\lambda_i} \right]$$
$$+ U_{ap}^{animal} \sum_i F_{iA} D_{aipj} \left\{ Q_F d_i \exp(-\lambda_i t_h) \left[\frac{r[1 - \exp(-\lambda_{Ei} t_e)]}{Y_v \lambda_{Ei}} + \frac{f_I B_{iv}[1 - \exp(-\lambda_i t_b)]}{P\lambda_I} \right] + C_{iAw} Q_{Aw} \right\} \quad (4)$$

For tritium:

$$R_{apj} = U_{ap}^{veg} C_v D_{apj} + U_{ap}^{animal} D_{apj} F_A (C_v Q_F + C_{Aw} Q_{Aw}) \quad (5)$$

where

B_{ip} is the equilibrium bioaccumulation factor for nuclide i in pathway p, expressed as the ratio of the concentration in biota (in pCi/kg) to the radionuclide concentration in water (in pCi/liter), in liters/kg;

B_{iv} is the concentration factor for uptake of radionuclide i from soil by edible parts of crops, in pCi/kg (wet weight) per pCi/kg dry soil;

C_{iAw} is the concentration of radionuclide i in water consumed by animals, in pCi/liter;

C_{iv} is the concentration of radionuclide i in vegetation, in pCi/kg;

D_{aipj} is the dose factor, specific to a given age group a, radionuclide i, pathway p, and organ j, which can be used to calculate the radiation dose from an intake of a radionuclide, in mrem/pCi, or from exposure to a given concentration of a radionuclide in sediment, expressed as a ratio of the dose rate (in mrem/hr) and the areal radionuclide concentration (in pCi/m^2);

d_i is the deposition rate of nuclide i, in pCi/m^2 per hr;

F is the flow rate of the liquid effluent, in ft^3/sec;

f_I is the fraction of the year crops are irrigated, dimensionless;

F_{iA} is the stable element transfer coefficient that relates the daily intake rate by an animal to the concentration in an edible portion of animal product, in pCi/liter (milk) per pCi/day or pCi/kg (animal product) per pCi/day;

M_p is the mixing ratio (reciprocal of the dilution factor) at the point of exposure (or the point of withdrawal of drinking water or point of harvest of aquatic food), dimensionless;

P is the effective "surface density" for soil, in kg(dry soil)/m^2;

Q_{Aw} is the consumption rate of contaminated water by an animal, in liters/day;

Q_F is the consumption rate of contaminated feed or forage by an animal, in kg/day (wet weight);

Q_i is the release rate of nuclide i, in Ci/yr;

r is the fraction of deposited activity retained on crops, dimensionless;

R_{apj} is the total annual dose to organ j of individuals of age group a from all of the nuclides i in pathway p, in mrem/yr;

t_b is the period of time for which sediment or soil is exposed to the contaminated water, in hours;

t_e is the time period that crops are exposed to contamination during the growing season, in hours;

t_h is a holdup time that represents the time interval between harvest and consumption of the food, in hours;

T_i is the radioactive half life of nuclide i, in days;

t_p is the average transit time required for nuclides to reach the point of exposure. For internal dose, t_p is the total time elapsed between release of the nuclides and ingestion of food or water, in hours;

U_{ap} is a usage factor that specifies the exposure time or intake rate for an individual of age group a associated with pathway p, in hr/yr, ℓ/yr, or kg/yr;

W is the shoreline width factor, dimensionless;

Y_v is the agricultural productivity (yield), in kg(wet weight)/m^2;

λ_{Ei} is the effective removal rate constant for radionuclide i from crops, in hr^{-1}, where $\lambda_{Ei} = \lambda_i + \lambda_w$, λ_i is the radioactive decay constant, and λ_w is the removal rate constant for physical loss by weathering (see Appendix E, Table E-15);

λ_i is the radioactive decay constant of nuclide i, in hr^{-1};

1100 is the factor to convert from (Ci/yr)/(ft^3/sec) to pCi/liter; and

110,000 is the factor to convert from (Ci/yr)/(ft^3/sec) to pCi/liter and to account for the proportionality constant used in the sediment radioactivity model.

These equations yield the dose rates to various organs of individuals from the exposure pathways mentioned above. Appendix I of 10 CFR Part 50 requires that the annual doses or dose commitments to the total body or any organ of any individual from the sum of the exposure pathways from liquid effluents associated with each reactor should not exceed 3 mrem and 10 mrem, respectively.

2. Gamma and Beta Doses from Noble Gases Discharged to the Atmosphere

The NRC staff will calculate radiation doses from noble gases using the following equations from Appendix B of this guide. Atmospheric dispersion models are found in Regulatory Guide 1.111, "Methods for Estimating Atmospheric Transport and Dispersion for Gaseous Effluents on Routine Releases from Light-Water-Cooled Reactors."

a. Annual Gamma Air Dose from Noble Gas Releases from Free-Standing Stacks More Than 80 Meters High

$$D^{\gamma}(r,\theta) = \frac{260}{r(\Delta\theta)} \sum_n \frac{1}{u_n} \sum_s f_{ns} \sum_k \mu_a(E_k)\, E_k I(H,u,s,\sigma_z,E_k) \sum_i Q^D_{ni} A_{ki} \quad (6)$$

where

A_{ki} is the photon yield for gamma-ray photons in energy group k from the decay of radionuclide i, in photons/disintegration;

$D^{\gamma}(r,\theta)$ is the annual gamma air dose at a distance r (meters) in the sector at angle θ, in mrad/yr;

E_k is the energy of the kth photon energy group, in MeV/photon;

f_{ns} is the joint frequency of occurrence of stability class s and wind speed class n for sector Θ, dimensionless;

$I(H,u,s,\sigma_z,E_k)$ is the dimensionless numerical integration constant accounting for the distribution of radioactivity according to meteorological conditions of wind speed (u) and atmospheric stability (s) which in part determine the effective stack height (H) and the vertical plume standard deviation (σ_z). In addition, I is a function of the photon energy E_k and is $\overline{I} = \overline{I}_1 + k\overline{I}_2$ as formulated in Slade (Appendix B, Reference 1);

Q_{ni}^D is the release rate of radionuclide i, corrected for decay during transit to the distance r under wind speed u_n, in Ci/yr;

u_n is the mean wind speed of wind speed class n, in m/sec;

$\Delta\Theta$ is the sector width over which atmospheric conditions are averaged, in radians;

$\mu_a(E_k)$ is the air energy absorption coefficient for the kth photon energy group, in m^{-1}; and

260 is the conversion factor to obtain $D^\gamma(r,\theta)$, in mrad/yr, and has the units of mrad-radians-m^3-disintegration/sec-MeV-Ci.

b. Annual Gamma Air Dose from All Other Noble Gas Releases; Annual Beta Air Dose from All Noble Gas Releases

$$D^\gamma(r,\Theta) \text{ or } D^\beta(r,\Theta) = 3.17 \times 10^4 \sum_i Q_i[\chi/Q]^D(r,\Theta)(DF_i^\gamma \text{ or } DF_i^\beta) \quad (7)$$

where

DF_i^γ, DF_i^β are the gamma and beta air dose factors for a uniform semi-infinite cloud of radionuclide i, in mrad-m^3/pCi-yr;

$D^\gamma(r,\Theta)$ or $D^\beta(r,\Theta)$ are the annual gamma and beta air doses at the distance r in the sector at angle Θ from the discharge point, in mrad/yr;

Q_i is the release rate of the radionuclide i, in Ci/yr;

$[\chi/Q]^D(r,\Theta)$ is the annual average gaseous dispersion factor (corrected for radioactive decay) at the distance r in sector Θ in sec/m^3 (see Regulatory Guide 1.111, "Methods for Estimating Atmospheric Transport and Dispersion of Gaseous Effluents in Routine Releases from Light-Water-Cooled Reactors," for methods to estimate χ/Q); and

3.17×10^4 is the number of pCi per Ci divided by the number of seconds per year.

c. Annual Total Body Dose from Noble Gas Releases from Free-Standing Stacks More Than 80 Meters High

$$D^T(r,\Theta) = 1.11\, S_F \sum_k D_k^\gamma(r,\Theta)\exp[-\mu_a^T(E_k)t_d] \quad (8)$$

where

$D^T(r,\Theta)$ is the annual total body dose at the distance r in sector Θ, in mrem/yr;

$D_k^\gamma(r,\Theta)$ is the annual gamma air dose associated with the kth photon energy group at the distance r in sector Θ, in mrad/yr;

S_F is the attenuation factor that accounts for the dose reduction due to shielding provided by residential structures, dimensionless;

t_d is the product of tissue density and depth used to determine a total body dose, in g/cm^2;

$\mu_a^T(E_k)$ is the tissue energy absorption coefficient, in cm^2/g; and

1.11 is the average ratio of tissue to air energy absorption coefficients.

d. Annual Skin Dose from Noble Gas Releases from Free-Standing Stacks More Than 80 Meters High

$$D^S(r,\theta) = 1.11 S_F D^\gamma(r,\theta) + 3.17 \times 10^4 \sum_i Q_i [\chi/Q]^D(r,\theta) DFS_i \qquad (9)$$

where

DFS_i is the beta skin dose factor for a semi-infinite cloud of radionuclide i, which includes the attenuation by the outer "dead" layer of the skin, in mrem-m^3/pCi-yr; and

$D^S(r,\theta)$ is the annual skin dose at the distance r in sector θ, in mrem/yr.

All other parameters are as defined in preceding paragraphs.

e. Annual Total Body Dose from All Other Noble Gas Releases

$$D_\infty^T(r,\theta) = S_F \sum_i \chi_i(r,\theta) DFB_i \qquad (10)$$

where

DFB_i is the total body dose factor for a semi-infinite cloud of the radionuclide i, which includes the attenuation of 5 g/cm^2 of tissue, in mrem-m^3/pCi-yr;

$D_\infty^T(r,\theta)$ is the annual total body dose due to immersion in a semi-infinite cloud at the distance r in sector θ, in mrem/yr; and

$\chi_i(r,\theta)$ is the annual average ground-level concentration of radionuclide i at the distance r in sector θ, in pCi/m^3.

All other parameters are as defined above.

f. Annual Skin Dose from All Other Noble Gas Releases

$$D_\infty^S(r,\theta) = 1.11\ S_F \sum_i \chi_i(r,\theta) DF_i^\gamma + \sum_i \chi_i(r,\theta) DFS_i \qquad (11)$$

where

$D_\infty^S(r,\theta)$ is the annual skin dose due to immersion in a semi-infinite cloud at the distance r in sector θ, in mrem/yr.

All other parameters are as defined above.

3. Doses from Radioiodines and Other Radionuclides* Released to the Atmosphere

The NRC staff will calculate radiation doses from radioiodines and other radionuclides released to the atmosphere using the following equations from Appendix C of this guide.

*Not including noble gases.

a. Annual Organ Dose from External Irradiation from Radionuclides Deposited onto the Ground Surface

$$D_j^G(r,\theta) = 8760\ S_F \sum_i C_i^G(r,\theta) DFG_{ij} \tag{12}$$

where

$C_i^G(r,\theta)$ is the ground plane concentration of radionuclide i at distance r in sector θ, in pCi/m^2;

DFG_{ij} is the open field ground plane dose conversion factor for organ j from radionuclide i, in mrem-m^2/pCi-hr;

$D_j^G(r,\theta)$ is the annual dose to the organ j at location (r,θ), in mrem/yr;

S_F is a shielding factor that accounts for the dose reduction due to shielding provided by residential structures during occupancy, dimensionless; and

8760 is the number of hours in a year.

b. Annual Organ Dose from Inhalation of Radionuclides in Air

$$D_{ja}^A(r,\theta) = R_a \sum_i \chi_i(r,\theta) DFA_{ija} \tag{13}$$

where

$D_{ja}^A(r,\theta)$ is the annual dose to organ j of an individual in the age group a at location (r,θ) due to inhalation, in mrem/yr;

DFA_{ija} is the inhalation dose factor for radionuclide i, organ j, and age group a, in mrem/pCi;

R_a is the annual air intake for individuals in the age group a, in m^3/yr; and

$\chi_i(r,\theta)$ is the annual average concentration of radionuclide i in air at location (r,θ), in pCi/m^3.

c. Annual Organ Dose from Ingestion of Atmospherically Released Radionuclides in Food

$$D_{ja}^D(r,\theta) = \sum_i DFI_{ija}\left[U_a^v f_g C_i^v(r,\theta) + U_a^m C_i^m(r,\theta) + U_a^F C_i^F(r,\theta) + U_a^L f_\ell C_i^L(r,\theta)\right] \tag{14}$$

where

$C_i^v(r,\theta)$, $C_i^m(r,\theta)$, $C_i^L(r,\theta)$, $C_i^F(r,\theta)$ are the concentrations of radionuclide i in produce (non-leafy-vegetables, fruits, and grains), milk, leafy vegetables, and meat, respectively, at location (r, θ), in pCi/kg or pCi/ℓ;

$D_{ja}^D(r,\theta)$ is the annual dose to the organ j of an individual in age group a from ingestion of produce, milk, leafy vegetables, and meat at location (r,θ), in mrem/yr;

DFI_{ija} is the ingestion dose factor for radionuclide i, organ j, and age group a, in mrem/pCi;

f_g, f_ℓ are the respective fractions of the ingestion rates of produce and leafy vegetables that are produced in the garden of interest; and

U_a^v, U_a^m, U_a^F, U_a^L are the annual intake (usage) of produce, milk, meat, and leafy vegetables, respectively, for individuals in the age group a, in kg/yr or ℓ/yr (equivalent to U_{ap}).

4. Integrated Doses to the Population

The NRC staff will calculate integrated doses to the local population from all pathways discussed in Sections C.1, 2, and 3. Because of the various conditions under which the equations in Appendix D are used, they are not presented in this section. It is recommended that Appendix D be read for a detailed discussion of the staff's models.

5. Summary of Staff Position

A brief summary of the staff position on methods of evaluating compliance with the numerical guides for design objectives of Appendix I is presented in Table 1. Methods of evaluating compliance with the cost-benefit provisions of Appendix I are addressed in Regulatory Guide 1.110, "Cost-Benefit Analysis for Radwaste Systems for Light-Water-Cooled Nuclear Power Reactors."

D. IMPLEMENTATION

The purpose of this section is to provide information to applicants and licensees regarding the NRC staff's plans for utilizing this regulatory guide.

This guide reflects current Nuclear Regulatory Commission practice. Therefore, except in those cases in which the license applicant or licensee proposes an acceptable alternative method, the method described herein for complying with specified portions of the Commission's regulations is being and will continue to be used in the evaluation of submittals for operating license or construction permit applications until the guide is revised as a result of suggestions from the public or additional staff review.

TABLE 1

SUMMARY OF STAFF POSITION -
METHODS OF EVALUATING COMPLIANCE WITH APPENDIX I

TYPE OF DOSE	APPENDIX I* DESIGN OBJECTIVES	RM-50-2 DESIGN OBJECTIVES*	POINT OF DOSE EVALUATION	EQUATIONS TO BE USED
Liquid Effluents				
Dose to total body from all pathways	3 mrem/yr per unit	5 mrem/yr per site	Location of the highest dose offsite.**	1, 2, 3, 4, & 5
Dose to any organ from all pathways	10 mrem/yr per unit	5 mrem/yr per site	Same as above.	1, 2, 3, 4, & 5
Non-tritium releases	- - - -	5 Ci/yr per unit	- - - -	- - - -
Gaseous Effluents***				
Gamma dose in air	10 mrad/yr per unit	10 mrad/yr per site	Location of the highest dose offsite.+	6 or 7, as appropriate
Beta dose in air	20 mrad/yr per unit	20 mrad/yr per site	Same as above.	7
Dose to total body of an individual	5 mrem/yr per unit	5 mrem/yr per site	Location of the highest dose offsite.**	8 or 10, as appropriate
Dose to skin of an individual	15 mrem/yr per unit	15 mrem/yr per site	Same as above.	9 or 11, as appropriate

See footnotes at end of table, on following page.

TABLE 1 (Continued)

SUMMARY OF STAFF POSITION -
METHODS OF EVALUATING COMPLIANCE WITH APPENDIX I

TYPE OF DOSE	APPENDIX I* DESIGN OBJECTIVES	RM-50-2 DESIGN OBJECTIVES*	POINT OF DOSE EVALUATION	EQUATIONS TO BE USED
Radioiodines and Particulates[††] Released to the Atmosphere				
Dose to any organ from all pathways	15 mrem/yr per unit	15 mrem/yr per site	Location of the highest dose offsite.[†††]	12, 13, & 14
I-131 releases	- - - -	1 Ci/yr per unit	- - - -	- - - -

[*] Evaluated for a maximum individual, as described in Section B of this guide.

[**] Evaluated at a location that is anticipated to be occupied during plant lifetime or evaluated with respect to such potential land and water usage and food pathways as could actually exist during the term of plant operation

[***] Calculated only for noble gases.

[†] Evaluated at a location that could be occupied during the term of plant operation.

[††] Doses due to carbon-14 and tritium intake from terrestrial food chains are included in this category.

[†††] Evaluated at a location where an exposure pathway and dose receptor actually exist at the time of licensing. However, if the applicant determines design objectives with respect to radioactive iodine on the basis of existing conditions and if potential changes in land and water usage and food pathways could result in exposures in excess of the guideline values given above, the applicant should provide reasonable assurance that a monitoring and surveillance program will be performed to determine: (1) the quantities of radioactive iodine actually released to the atmosphere and deposited relative to those estimated in the determination of design objectives; (2) whether changes in land and water usage and food pathways which would result in individual exposures greater than originally estimated have occurred; and (3) the content of radioactive iodine in foods involved in the changes, if and when they occur.

APPENDIX A

METHODS FOR CALCULATING DOSES TO MAN FROM LIQUID EFFLUENT PATHWAYS

The equations for estimating radiation exposure to man from four principal exposure pathways in the aquatic environment (potable water, aquatic foods, shoreline deposits, and irrigated foods) are listed in Section C, "Regulatory Position," of this guide.

1. Generalized Equation for Calculating Radiation Dose via Liquid Pathways

Equation (A-1) is the generalized equation for calculating the radiation dose to man via liquid effluent pathways.

$$R_{aipj} = C_{ip}U_{ap}D_{aipj} \qquad \text{(A-1)}$$

where

C_{ip} is the concentration of nuclide i in the media of pathway p, in pCi/ℓ, pCi/kg, or pCi/m^2;

D_{aipj} is the dose factor, specific to age group a, radionuclide i, pathway p, and organ j. It represents the dose due to the intake of a radionuclide, in mrem/pCi, or from exposure to a given concentration of a radionuclide in sediment, in mrem per hr/pCi per m^2;

R_{aipj} is the annual dose to organ j of an individual of age group a from nuclide i via pathway p, in mrem/yr; and

U_{ap} is the exposure time or intake rate (usage) associated with pathway p for age group a, in hr/yr, ℓ/yr or kg/yr (as appropriate).

The three factors making up Equation (A-1) are discussed in the following sections, most of which were taken directly from the WASH-1258 report (Ref. 1). (An updated version of the portion of the WASH-1258 report describing models and computer programs is contained in the BNWL-1754 report (Ref. 2).)

a. Radionuclide Concentration in Environmental Media (C_{ip})

The concentrations in environmental media of interest can be estimated from the mixing ratio M_p, the discharge flow F, the radionuclide release rate Q_i, and other terms presented in the pathway equations that appear later in this discussion.

b. Usage (U_{ap})

The second term of Equation (A-1) is the usage term U_{ap}. Usage is expressed as a consumption rate in kg/yr or liters/yr or as an exposure time in hr/yr, as appropriate for the pathway and age group under consideration.

The NRC staff encourages the use of site-specific data, whenever possible. Such data should be documented. In the absence of site-specific data, however, the usage values (consumption rates and exposure times) presented in Appendix E, Table E-5, are recommended.

c. Dose Factor (D_{aipj})

Dose factors for internal exposure via ingestion are provided in Appendix E, Tables E-11, 12, 13, and 14. Appendix E also provides further discussion of the data, models, and assumptions used.

Material deposited from sedimentation in an aquatic system represents a fairly large, nearly uniform thin sheet of contamination. The factors for converting surface contamination given in pCi/m^2 to the dose rate at one meter above a uniformly contaminated plane have been described by Soldat and others (Refs. 3 and 4). Dose factors for exposure to soil sediment have units of mrem/hr per pCi/m^2 and are presented in Appendix E, Table E-6.

2. Equations for Liquid Pathways

This section develops the equations required for the liquid pathway models. The principal difference between pathways is the manner in which the radionuclide concentrations are calculated. The doses from the four pathways should be added to determine the total dose.

a. Potable Water

The annual dose from ingestion of water is calculated from Equation (A-2) below:

$$R_{apj} = 1100 \frac{M_p U_{ap}}{F} \sum_i Q_i D_{aipj} \exp(-\lambda_i t_p) \tag{A-2}$$

Symbols for this equation were defined earlier, in Section C.1 of this guide.

The summation process adds the dose contribution from each nuclide to yield the total dose for the pathway-organ combination selected. The expression $(1100\ Q_i M_p/F)\exp(-\lambda_i t_p)$ yields the concentration of nuclide i at the time the water is consumed, in pCi/ℓ. This concentration is the term C_{ip} in Equation (A-1). As a minimum, the transit time t_p may be set equal to 12 hours to allow for radionuclide transport through the water purification plant and the water distribution system (Ref. 5). The transit time should be increased as appropriate to allow for travel from the point of effluent release to the water purification plant intake. Credit may be taken for radionuclide removal by water purification processes using techniques such as those outlined in Reference 3.

It should be noted that, depending on the hydrological dispersion model employed, the mixing ratio, M_p, or dilution factor may not be explicitly defined. In those instances (e.g., buildup of activity in a cooling pond), the relative concentration in the mixed stream (compared to the effluent concentration) may be supplied as a function of the radiological decay constant, with any potential effluent recycling taken into account. Suggested hydrological dispersion models are presented in Regulatory Guide 1.113, "Estimating Aquatic Dispersion of Effluents from Accidental and Routine Reactor Releases for the Purpose of Implementing Appendix I."

b. Aquatic Foods

The concentrations of radionuclides in aquatic foods are assumed to be directly related to the concentrations of the nuclides in water. Equilibrium ratios between the two concentrations, called bioaccumulation factors in this guide, can be found in the literature (Ref. 6). The inclusion of the bioaccumulation factor B_{ip} in Equation (A-2) yields Equation (A-3), which is suitable for calculating the internal dose from consumption of aquatic foods.

$$R_{apj} = 1100 \frac{U_{ap} M_p}{F} \sum_i Q_i B_{ip} D_{aipj} \exp(-\lambda_i t_p) \tag{A-3}$$

Values of B_{ip} are given in Table A-1; the other parameters have been previously defined. The methodology presented in Reference 7 for the development of site-specific freshwater bioaccumulation factors is considered to be acceptable by the NRC staff.

The transit time t_p may be set equal to 24 hours* to allow for radionuclide decay during transit through the food chain, as well as during food preparation.

c. Dose from Shoreline Deposits

The calculation of individual dose from shoreline deposits is complex since it involves estimation of sediment load, transport, and concentrations of radionuclides associated with

---

*Here, and in a number of other instances, the NRC staff has found it necessary to set forth guidance as to a parameter value in the absence of empirical data. In such instances judgments have been made after considering values assumed by others and model sensitivity to the parameter value in question. In this particular instance, the total body dose from fish ingestion, for a typical situation, was found to vary by less than a factor of two for a range of environmental transit times of from one to seven days.

TABLE A-1

BIOACCUMULATION FACTORS TO BE USED IN THE ABSENCE OF SITE-SPECIFIC DATA (pCi/kg per pCi/liter)*

ELEMENT	FRESHWATER FISH	FRESHWATER INVERTEBRATE	SALTWATER FISH	SALTWATER INVERTEBRATE
H	9.0E-01	9.0E-01	9.0E-01	9.3E-01
C	4.6E 03	9.1E 03	1.8E 03	1.4E 03
NA	1.0E 02	2.0E 02	6.7E-02	1.9E-01
P	1.0E 05	2.0E 04	2.9E 04	3.0E 04
CR	2.0E 02	2.0E 03	4.0E 02	2.0E 03
MN	4.0E 02	9.0E 04	5.5E 02	4.0E 02
FE	1.0E 02	3.2E 03	3.0E 03	2.0E 04
CO	5.0E 01	2.0E 02	1.0E 02	1.0E 03
NI	1.0E 02	1.0E 02	1.0E 02	2.5E 02
CU	5.0E 01	4.0E 02	6.7E 02	1.7E 03
ZN	2.0E 03	1.0E 04	2.0E 03	5.0E 04
BR	4.2E 02	3.3E 02	1.5E-02	3.1E 00
RB	2.0E 03	1.0E 03	8.3E 00	1.7E 01
SR	3.0E 01	1.0E 02	2.0E 00	2.0E 01
Y	2.5E 01	1.0E 03	2.5E 01	1.0E 03
ZR	3.3E 00	6.7E 00	2.0E 02	8.0E 01
NB	3.0E 04	1.0E 02	3.0E 04	1.0E 02
MO	1.0E 01	1.0E 01	1.0E 01	1.0E 01
TC	1.5E 01	5.0E 00	1.0E 01	5.0E 01
RU	1.0E 01	3.0E 02	3.0E 00	1.0E 03
RH	1.0E 01	3.0E 02	1.0E 01	2.0E 03
TE**	4.0E 02	6.1E 03	1.0E 01	1.0E 02
I	1.5E 01	5.0E 00	1.0E 01	5.0E 01
CS	2.0E 03	1.0E 03***	4.0E 01	2.5E 01
BA	4.0E 00	2.0E 02	1.0E 01	1.0E 02
LA	2.5E 01	1.0E 03	2.5E 01	1.0E 03
CE	1.0E 00	1.0E 03	1.0E 01	6.0E 02
PR	2.5E 01	1.0E 03	2.5E 01	1.0E 03
ND	2.5E 01	1.0E 03	2.5E 01	1.0E 03
W	1.2E 03	1.0E 01	3.0E 01	3.0E 01
NP	1.0E 01	4.0E 02	1.0E 01	1.0E 01

*Values in Table A-1 are taken from Reference 6 unless otherwise indicated.

**Data taken from Reference 8.

***Data taken from Reference 7.

suspended and deposited materials. One method of approaching this problem was presented in the Year 2000 Study (Ref. 3). Based on this model, an estimate of the radionuclide concentration in shoreline sediments can be obtained from the following expression:

$$C_{is} = K_c \frac{C_{iw}[1 - \exp(-\lambda_i t_b)]}{\lambda_i} \qquad \text{(A-4)}$$

where

- C_{is} is the concentration of nuclide i in sediment, in pCi/kg;
- C_{iw} is the concentration of nuclide i in water adjacent to the sediment, in pCi/liter;
- K_c is an assumed transfer constant from water to sediment, in liters/kg per hr;
- t_b is the length of time the sediment is exposed to the contaminated water, nominally 15 years (approximate midpoint of facility operating life), in hours; and
- λ_i is the decay constant* of nuclide i, in hours^{-1}. In the original evaluation of the equation, λ_i was chosen to be the radiological decay constant. The true value should include an as yet unknown "environmental" removal constant.

The value of K_c was derived for several radionuclides by using data from water and sediment samples collected over a period of several years in the Columbia River between Richland, Washington, and the river mouth and in Tillamook Bay, Oregon, 75 km south of the river mouth (Refs. 9 and 10). Since the primary use of the equation is to facilitate estimates of the exposure rate from gamma emitters one meter above the sediment, an effective surface contamination was estimated. This surface contamination was assumed to be contained within the top 2.5 cm (1 in.) of sediment (with a mass of 40 kg/m^2 of surface). The dose contribution from the radionuclides at depths below 2.5 cm was ignored. The resulting equation is

$$S_i = 100 T_i C_{iw} W[1 - \exp(-\lambda_i t_b)] \qquad \text{(A-5)}$$

where

- S_i is the "effective" surface contamination, in pCi/m^2, that is used in subsequent calculations;
- T_i is the radiological half-life of nuclide i, in days;
- W is a shore-width factor that describes the geometry of the exposure; and
- 100 is equal to $[K_c(\ell/\text{kg-hr})*40(\text{kg/m}^2)*\ 24(\text{hr/day})/0.693]$, in $\ell/\text{m}^2\text{-day}$.

Shore-width factors were derived from experimental data (Ref. 11) and are summarized in Table A-2. They represent the fraction of the dose from an infinite plane source that is estimated for these shoreline situations.

The combination of Equations (A-4) and (A-5) into the general Equation (A-1) leads to Equation (A-6) below for calculation of radiation dose from exposure to shoreline sediments.

$$R_{apj} = U_{ap} \sum_i S_i D_{aipj} = 100\ U_{ap} W \sum_i C_{iw} T_i D_{aipj} [1 - \exp(-\lambda_i t_b)] \qquad \text{(A-6)}$$

As in the development of Equation (A-2), the expression $(1100\ Q_i\ M_p/F)\exp(-\lambda_i t_p)$ may be substituted for C_{iw}. This results in the following relationship:

$$R_{apj} = 110{,}000 \frac{U_{ap} M_p W}{F} \sum_i Q_i T_i D_{aipj} [\exp(-\lambda_i t_p)][1 - \exp(-\lambda_i t_b)] \qquad \text{(A-7)}$$

---

*If the presence of a radionuclide in water and sediment is controlled primarily by radioactive equilibrium with its parent nuclide, the water concentration and decay constant of the parent should be used in Equations (A-4) and (A-5).

TABLE A-2

SHORE-WIDTH FACTORS FOR USE IN EQUATIONS (A-5), (A-6), AND (A-7)

EXPOSURE SITUATION	SHORE-WIDTH FACTOR, W
Discharge canal bank	0.1
River shoreline	0.2
Lake shore	0.3
Nominal ocean site	0.5
Tidal basin	1.0

d. Dose from Foods Grown on Land with Contaminated Water

The equations in the following paragraphs can be used to calculate doses from radionuclides released in liquid effluents but appearing in crops or animal products. Separate expressions are presented for tritium because of its unique environmental behavior.

(1) Vegetation

The concentration of radioactive material in vegetation results from deposition onto the plant foliage and from uptake from the soil of activity deposited on the ground. The model used for estimating the transfer of radionuclides from irrigation water to crops through water deposited on leaves and uptake from soil was derived for a study of the potential doses to people from a nuclear power complex in the year 2000 (Ref. 3).

The equation for the model (for radionuclides except tritium) is presented below in slightly modified form. The first term in brackets relates to the concentration derived from direct foliar deposition during the growing season. The second term relates to uptake from soil and reflects the long-term deposition during operation of the nuclear facility. Thus, for a uniform release rate, the concentration C_{iv} of radionuclide i in the edible portion of crop species v, in units of pCi/kg, is given by:

$$C_{iv} = d_i \left[\frac{r[1 - \exp(-\lambda_{Ei} t_e)]}{Y_v \lambda_{Ei}} + \frac{f_I B_{iv}[1 - \exp(-\lambda_i t_b)]}{P \lambda_i} \right] \exp(-\lambda_i t_h) \quad \text{(A-8)}$$

where the terms are defined in Section C, "Regulatory Position." Appendix E, Table E-15, presents suggested values for the parameters r, Y_v, t_e, P, and t_h. Values for B_{iv} are in Table E-1.

The deposition rate, d_i, from irrigated water is defined by the relation

$$d_i = C_{iw} I \text{ (water deposition)} \quad \text{(A-9)}$$

where

C_{iw} is the concentration of radionuclide i in water used for irrigation, in pCi/liter, and

I is the average irrigation rate, in liters/m^2/hr, during the growing season.

For a cow grazing on fresh forage, t_e in Equation (A-8) is set equal to 720 hours (30 days), the typical time for a cow to return to a particular portion of the grazing site (Refs. 3 and 12).

For tritium, the equation for estimating C_{iv} is (see Ref. 13):

$$C_v = C_w \quad \text{(A-10)}$$

(2) Animal Products

The radionuclide concentration in an animal product such as meat or milk is dependent on the amount of contaminated feed or forage eaten by the animal and its intake of contaminated water. The radionuclide concentration in animal products C_{iA} in terms of pCi/liter or pCi/kg is proportional to the animal's intake of the radionuclide in feed or forage (subscript F) and in water (subscript w):

$$C_{iA} = F_{iA}[C_{iF}Q_F + C_{iAw}Q_{Aw}] \qquad \text{(A-11)}$$

The second set of terms in the brackets in Equation (A-11) can be omitted if the animal does not drink contaminated water. Values for Q_F and Q_{Aw} are presented in Appendix E, Table E-3. Values for B_{iv} and F_{iA} are given in Appendix E, Table E-1.*

(3) Total Dose from Food Grown on Land

The total dose R_{apj} from irrigated foods and animal products (excluding tritium) is given by:

$$R_{apj} = U_{ap}^{veg} \sum_i C_{iv}D_{aipj} + U_{ap}^{animal} \sum_i C_{iA}D_{aipj} \qquad \text{(A-12)}$$

If values for C_{iv} from Equation (A-8) and C_{iA} from Equation (A-11) are substituted in Equation (A-12):

$$R_{apj} = U_{ap}^{veg} \sum_i d_i \exp(-\lambda_i t_h) D_{aipj} \left[\frac{r[1 - \exp(-\lambda_{Ei} t_e)]}{Y_v \lambda_{Ei}} + \frac{f_I B_{iv}[1 - \exp(-\lambda_i t_b)]}{P\lambda_i} \right]$$
$$+ U_{ap}^{animal} \sum_i F_{iA} D_{aipj} \left\{ Q_F d_i \exp(-\lambda_i t_h) \left[\frac{r[1 - \exp(-\lambda_{Ei} t_e)]}{Y_v \lambda_{Ei}} + \frac{f_I B_{iv}[1 - \exp(-\lambda_i t_b)]}{P\lambda_i} \right] + C_{iAw}Q_{Aw} \right\} \qquad \text{(A-13)}$$

where the terms are defined in Section C, "Regulatory Position."

It should be noted that the two components of Equation (A-12) imply that contributions from the individual vegetable and animal products have already been summed. In actual use, it will be necessary to compute separately the milk and meat portions of the dose due to animal products (also applicable to Equation (A-16)).

For tritium, the concentration in animal products (milk or meat) is given by the following equation:

$$C_A = F_a(C_v Q_F + C_{Aw}Q_{Aw}) \qquad \text{(A-14)}$$

where the terms are defined in Section C, "Regulatory Position."

Since by Equation (A-10) $C_v = C_w$, and since for all practical purposes $C_{Aw} = C_w$, Equation (A-14) can be restated as follows:

$$C_A = F_A C_w(Q_F + Q_{Aw}) \qquad \text{(A-15)}$$

---

*Values for F_{iA} appear as F_m and F_f in Table E-1.

Similarly, the above equations for tritium concentration can be combined with the general Equation (A-1):

$$R_{apj} = U_{ap}^{veg} C_v D_{apj} + U_{ap}^{animal} C_A D_{apj} \qquad \text{(A-16)}$$

REFERENCES FOR APPENDIX A

1. "Final Environmental Statement Concerning Proposed Rule Making Action: Numerical Guides for Design Objectives and Limiting Conditions for Operation to Meet the Criterion 'As Low As Practicable' for Radioactive Material in Light-Water-Cooled Power Reactor Effluents," USAEC Report WASH-1258, Washington, D.C., July 1973.

2. J. K. Soldat et al., "Models and Computer Codes for Evaluating Environmental Radiation Doses," USAEC Report BNWL-1754, Pacific Northwest Laboratories, February 1974.

3. J. F. Fletcher and W. L. Dotson (compilers), "HERMES - A Digital Computer Code for Estimating Regional Radiological Effects from the Nuclear Power Industry," USAEC Report HEDL-TME-71-168, Hanford Engineering Development Laboratory, 1971.

4. J. K. Soldat, "Conversion of Survey Meter Readings to Concentration ($\mu Ci/m^2$)," Item 04.3.4 in "Emergency Radiological Plans and Procedures," K. R. Heid (ed.), USAEC Report HW-70935, Hanford Laboratories, 1962.

5. D. H. Denham and J. K. Soldat, "A Study of Selected Parameters Affecting the Radiation Dose from Radionuclides in Drinking Water Downstream of the Hanford Project," Health Physics, Vol. 28, pp. 139-144, February 1975.

6. S. E. Thompson et al., "Concentration Factors of Chemical Elements in Edible Aquatic Organisms," USAEC Report UCRL-50564, Rev. 1, Lawrence Radiation Laboratory, October 1972.

7. H. A. Vanderploeg et al., "Bioaccumulation Factors for Radionuclides in Freshwater Biota," ORNL-5002, Oak Ridge, Tenn., November 1975.

8. G. G. Kilaugh and L. R. McKay, "A Methodology for Calculating Radiation Doses from Radioactivity Released to the Environment," ORNL-4992, Oak Ridge National Laboratory, Oak Ridge, Tenn., March 1976.

9. J. L. Nelson, "Distribution of Sediments and Associated Radionuclides in the Columbia River below Hanford," p. 3.80 in "Hanford Radiological Sciences Research and Development Annual Report for 1964," D. W. Pearce and J. K. Green (eds.), USAEC Report BNWL-36, Pacific Northwest Laboratories, 1965.

10. G. L. Toombs and P. B. Cutler (compilers), "Comprehensive Final Report for the Lower Columbia River Environmental Survey in Oregon June 5, 1961 - July 31, 1967," Oregon State Board of Health, Div. of Sanitation and Engineering, 1968.

11. "Handbook of Radiological Protection, Part I: Data," prepared by a panel of the Radioactivity Advisory Committee (H. J. Dunster, Chairman), Department of Employment, Department of Health and Social Security, Ministry of Health and Social Services, Northern Ireland, Number SNB 11-360079-8, Her Majesty's Stationery Office, London, England, 1971.

12. J. J. Koranda, "Agricultural Factors Affecting the Daily Intake of Fresh Fallout by Dairy Cows," USAEC Report UCRL-12479, 1965.

13. L. R. Anspaugh et al., "The Dose to Man via Food-Chain Transfer Resulting from Exposure to Tritiated Water Vapor," in Tritium (A. A. Moghissi and M. W. Carter, eds.), CONF-710809, 1973.

APPENDIX B

MODELS FOR CALCULATING DOSES FROM NOBLE GASES DISCHARGED TO THE ATMOSPHERE

The following analytical models are used for calculating doses from exposure to noble gases discharged to the atmosphere. Separate models are given for air and tissue doses due to gamma and beta rays. Except for the case of noble gas doses resulting from elevated releases, all models assume immersion in a semi-infinite cloud.

1. Annual Gamma Air Dose* from Noble Gas Releases from Free-Standing Stacks More Than 80 Meters High

Slade (Ref. 1) describes a derivation of equations for estimating annual air doses from photon emitters dispersed in the atmosphere. The following expression can be used for calculating annual doses:

$$D^{\gamma}(r,\theta) = \frac{260}{r(\Delta\theta)} \sum_n \frac{1}{u_n} \sum_s f_{ns} \sum_k \mu_a(E_k)E_k I(H,u,s,\sigma_z,E_k) \sum_i Q^D_{ni}A_{ki} \qquad \text{(B-1)}$$

Symbols for this equation were defined earlier, in Regulatory Position C.2.a of this guide. A discussion of, and derivation for, the I function are presented in Appendix F of this guide.

The photons are combined into energy groups, and each photon intensity within a group is weighted by its energy and energy absorption coefficient. Thus, the effective fraction of disintegrations of the nuclide i yielding photons corresponding to the photon energy group k, A_{ki}, is determined to be

$$A_{ki} = \sum_m [A_m E_m \mu_a(E_m)]/[E_k \mu_a(E_k)] \qquad \text{(B-2)}$$

where

A_m is the fraction of the disintegrations of nuclide i yielding photons of energy E_m;

E_m is the energy of the mth photon within the kth energy group, in MeV; and

$\mu_a(E_m)$ is the energy absorption coefficient in air associated with the photon energy E_m, in m^{-1}.

All other parameters are as previously defined. The summation is carried out over all photons within energy group k. Data for the photon energies and abundances for most of the noble gas nuclides were taken from Reference 2. For radionuclides not contained in Reference 2, data were obtained from Reference 3.

Decay during travel from the point of release to the receptor is

$$Q^D_{ni} = Q_i \exp(-\lambda_i r/u_n) \qquad \text{(B-3)}$$

*The term "gamma air dose" refers to the components of the air dose associated with photons emitted during nuclear and atomic transformations, i.e., gamma and x-rays. Annihilation and bremsstrahlung photon radiations are possible contributors to this component of the air dose.

where

Q_i is the initial release rate of nuclide i, in Ci/yr;

r is the distance from the source to the receptor, in m; and

λ_i is the decay constant of nuclide i, in sec^{-1}.

All other parameters are as previously defined.

2. <u>Annual Gamma Air Dose from All Other Noble Gas Releases and Annual Beta Air Dose* from All Noble Gas Releases</u>

Plumes of gaseous effluents are considered semi-infinite in the case of ground-level noble gas releases. The annual average ground-level concentration of radionuclide i at location (r,θ) is determined from

$$\chi_i(r,\theta) = 3.17 \times 10^4 Q_i [\chi/Q]^D(r,\theta) \quad \text{(B-4)}$$

where

$\chi_i(r,\theta)$ is the annual average ground-level concentration of nuclide i at the distance r in the sector at angle θ from the release point, in pCi/m^3, and

$[\chi/Q]^D(r,\theta)$ is the annual average gaseous dispersion factor (corrected for radioactive decay) in the sector at angle θ at the distance r from the release point, in sec/m^3. (See Regulatory Guide 1.111 for atmospheric dispersion models.)

All other parameters are as previously defined.

The associated annual gamma or beta air dose is then

$$D^\gamma(r,\theta) \text{ or } D^\beta(r,\theta) = \sum_i \chi_i(r,\theta)(DF_i^\gamma \text{ or } DF_i^\beta) \quad \text{(B-5)}$$

where the terms are as defined in Regulatory Position C.2.b.

Table B-1 presents a tabulation of the dose factors for the noble gases of interest.

3. <u>Annual Total Body and Skin Doses from Noble Gas Effluents</u>

It is also necessary to determine annual doses to real individuals in unrestricted areas. The staff computes the total body dose from external radiation at a depth of 5 cm into the body and the skin dose at a depth of 7 mg/cm^2 of tissue (Ref. 4).**

a. <u>Releases from Free-Standing Stacks More Than 80 Meters High</u>

The annual total body dose is computed as follows:

$$D^T(r,\theta) = 1.11 \times S_F \sum_k D_k^\gamma(r,\theta)\exp[-\mu_a^T(E_k)t_d] \quad \text{(B-6)}$$

---

*The term "beta air dose" refers to the component of the air dose associated with particle emissions during nuclear and atomic transformations, i.e., β+, β-, and conversion electrons.

**See discussion in Appendix E, Section 3.

TABLE B-1

DOSE FACTORS FOR EXPOSURE TO A SEMI-INFINITE CLOUD OF NOBLE GASES

Nuclide	β-air* (DF_i^{β})	β-Skin** (DFS_i)	γ-Air* (DF_i^{γ})	γ-Body** (DFB_i)
Kr-83m	2.88E-04***	---	1.93E-05	7.56E-08
Kr-85m	1.97E-03	1.46E-03	1.23E-03	1.17E-03
Kr-85	1.95E-03	1.34E-03	1.72E-05	1.61E-05
Kr-87	1.03E-02	9.73E-03	6.17E-03	5.92E-03
Kr-88	2.93E-03	2.37E-03	1.52E-02	1.47E-02
Kr-89	1.06E-02	1.01E-02	1.73E-02	1.66E-02
Kr-90	7.83E-03	7.29E-03	1.63E-02	1.56E-02
Xe-131m	1.11E-03	4.76E-04	1.56E-04	9.15E-05
Xe-133m	1.48E-03	9.94E-04	3.27E-04	2.51E-04
Xe-133	1.05E-03	3.06E-04	3.53E-04	2.94E-04
Xe-135m	7.39E-04	7.11E-04	3.36E-03	3.12E-03
Xe-135	2.46E-03	1.86E-03	1.92E-03	1.81E-03
Xe-137	1.27E-02	1.22E-02	1.51E-03	1.42E-03
Xe-138	4.75E-03	4.13E-03	9.21E-03	8.83E-03
Ar-41	3.28E-03	2.69E-03	9.30E-03	8.84E-03

* $\frac{\text{mrad-m}^3}{\text{pCi-yr}}$

** $\frac{\text{mrem-m}^3}{\text{pCi-yr}}$

*** 2.88E-04 = 2.88×10^{-4}

Symbols for this equation are defined in Regulatory Position C.2.c of this guide. The factor S_F accounts for the dose reduction provided by the shielding effect of typical residential structures (see Appendix E, Section 4 and Table E-15).

The skin dose has two components, the gamma and beta contributions. The skin dose rate is computed by

$$D^S(r,\theta) = 1.11 \times S_F D^\gamma(r,\theta) + 3.17 \times 10^4 \sum_i Q_i [\chi/Q]^D(r,\theta) DFS_i \qquad \text{(B-7)}$$

Symbols for this equation are defined in Regulatory Position C.2.d of this guide.

The skin beta dose factors DFS were determined using the decay scheme source documents cited above and the methods used in References 5, 6, and 7. They are presented in Table B-1.

b. <u>All Other Releases</u>

The annual total body dose is computed as follows:

$$D^T_\infty(r,\theta) = S_F \sum_i \chi_i(r,\theta) DFB_i \qquad \text{(B-8)}$$

Symbols for this equation are defined in Regulatory Position C.2.e of this guide.

The annual skin dose is computed as follows:

$$D^S_\infty(r,\theta) = 1.11 \times S_F \sum_i \chi_i(r,\theta) DF^\gamma_i + \sum_i \chi_i(r,\theta) DFS_i \qquad \text{(B-9)}$$

Symbols for this equation are defined in Regulatory Position C.2.f of this guide.

REFERENCES FOR APPENDIX B

1. "Meteorology and Atomic Energy 1968," D. H. Slade (ed.), USAEC Report TID-24190, 1968.

2. M. J. Martin, "Radioactive Atoms, Supplement I," USAEC Report ORNL-4923, November 1973.

3. M. E. Meek and R. S. Gilbert, "Summary of Gamma and Beta Energy and Intensity Data," NEDO-12037, 1970.

4. J. K. Soldat et al., "The Dosimetry of the Radioactive Noble Gases," The Noble Gases (A. A. Moghissi and R. E. Stanley, eds.), ERDA-CONF 730 915, U.S. Energy Research and Development Administration, 1975.

5. R. Loevinger et al., in Radiation Dosimetry (G. S. Hine and G. L. Brownell, eds.), Academic Press, New York, 1956.

6. M. J. Berger, "Improved Point Kernels for Electron and Beta-Ray Dosimetry," NBS Report NBSIR 73-107, 1973.

7. M. J. Berger, "Beta-Ray Dose in Tissue - Equivalent Material Immersed in a Radioactive Cloud," Health Physics, Vol. 26, pp. 1-12, January 1974.

APPENDIX C

MODELS FOR CALCULATING DOSES VIA ADDITIONAL PATHWAYS FROM RADIOIODINES AND OTHER RADIONUCLIDES* DISCHARGED TO THE ATMOSPHERE

1. Annual External Dose from Direct Exposure to Activity Deposited on the Ground Plane

The ground plane concentration of radionuclide i at the location (r,θ) with respect to the release point may be determined by

$$C_i^G(r,\theta) = \frac{[1.0 \times 10^{12}]\ [\delta_i(r,\theta)\ Q_i]}{\lambda_i} [1 - \exp(-\lambda_i t_b)] \qquad \text{(C-1)}$$

where

$C_i^G(r,\theta)$ is the ground plane concentration of the radionuclide i in the sector at angle θ at the distance r from the release point, in pCi/m^2;

Q_i is the annual release rate of nuclide i to the atmosphere, in Ci/yr;

t_b is the time period over which the accumulation is evaluated, which is 15 years (mid-point of plant operating life). This is a simplified method of approximating the average deposition over the operating lifetime of the facility;

$\delta_i(r,\theta)$ is the annual average relative deposition of effluent species i at location (r,θ), considering depletion of the plume during transport, in m^{-2};

λ_i is the radiological decay constant for nuclide i, in yr^{-1}; and

1.0×10^{12} is the number of pCi per Ci.

The annual dose resulting from direct exposure to the contaminated ground plane, from all radionuclides, is then

$$D_j^G(r,\theta) = 8760\ S_F \sum_i C_i^G(r,\theta) DFG_{ij} \qquad \text{(C-2)}$$

where the terms are defined in Regulatory Position C.3.a of this guide.

Values for the open field ground plane dose conversion factors for the skin and total body are given in Appendix E, Table E-6. The annual dose to all other organs is taken to be equivalent to the total body dose. The factor S_F is assumed to have a value of 0.7, dimensionless.

*Does not include noble gases.

2. Annual Dose from Inhalation of Radionuclides in Air

The annual average airborne concentration of radionuclide i at the location (r,θ) with respect to the release point may be determined as

$$\chi_i(r,\theta) = 3.17 \times 10^4 Q_i[\chi/Q]^D(r,\theta) \qquad \text{(C-3)}$$

where

Q_i	is the release rate of nuclide i to the atmosphere, in Ci/yr;
$\chi_i(r,\theta)$	is the annual average ground-level concentration of nuclide i in air in sector θ at distance r, in pCi/m^3;
$[\chi/Q]^D(r,\theta)$	is the annual average atmosphere dispersion factor, in sec/m^3 (see Regulatory Guide 1.111). This includes depletion (for radioiodines and particulates) and radioactive decay of the plume; and
3.17×10^4	is the number of pCi/Ci divided by the number of sec/yr.

The annual dose associated with inhalation of all radionuclides, to organ j of an individual in age group a, is then

$$D^A_{ja}(r,\theta) = R_a \sum_i \chi_i(r,\theta) DFA_{ija} \qquad \text{(C-4)}$$

Values for DFA_{ija} are given in Appendix E, Tables E-7 through E-10; values for R_a are given in Appendix E, Table E-5. All other symbols are as defined earlier in Regulatory Position C.3.b.

3. Concentrations of Airborne Radionuclides in Foods

The concentration of radioactive material in vegetation results from deposition onto the plant foliage and from uptake of activity initially deposited on the ground. The model used for estimating the transfer of radionuclides from the atmosphere to food products is similar to the model developed for estimating the transfer of radionuclides from irrigation water given in Appendix A of this guide.

a. Parameters for Calculating Nuclide Concentrations in Forage, Produce, and Leafy Vegetables

For all radioiodines and particulate radionuclides, except tritium and carbon-14, the concentration of nuclide i in and on vegetation at the location (r,θ) is estimated using

$$C^v_i(r,\theta) = d_i(r,\theta)\left\{\frac{r[1-\exp(-\lambda_{Ei}t_e)]}{Y_v\lambda_{Ei}} + \frac{B_{iv}[1-\exp(-\lambda_i t_b)]}{P\lambda_i}\right\}\exp(-\lambda_i t_h) \qquad \text{(C-5)}$$

See Regulatory Position C.1 of this guide for definitions of terms. Values for the parameters r, t_e, Y_v, P, and t_h are provided in Appendix E, Table E-15. For the parameters t_e, Y_v, and t_h, different values are given (in Appendix E) to allow the use of Equation (C-5) for different purposes: estimating concentrations in produce consumed by man; in leafy vegetables consumed by man; in forage consumed directly as pasture grass by dairy cows, beef cattle, or goats; and in forage consumed as stored feed by dairy cows, beef cattle, or goats.

The deposition rate from the plume is defined by

$$d_i(r,\theta) = 1.1 \times 10^8 \delta_i(r,\theta)Q_i \qquad \text{(C-6)}$$

where

$d_i(r,\theta)$ is the deposition rate of radionuclide i onto ground at location (r,θ), in pCi/m^2-hr;

$\delta_i(r,\theta)$ is the relative deposition of radionuclide i, considering depletion and decay in transit to location (r,θ), in m^{-2} (see Regulatory Guide 1.111); and

1.1×10^8 is the number of pCi per Ci (10^{12}) divided by the number of hours per year (8760).

For radioiodines, the model considers only the elemental fraction of the effluent. The deposition should be computed only for that fraction of the effluent that is estimated to be elemental iodine. Measurements at operating facilities indicate that about half the radioiodine emissions may be considered nonelemental (Ref. 1). With this consideration included, Equation (C-6) for radioiodine becomes

$$d_i(r,\theta) = 5.5 \times 10^7 \delta_i(r,\theta)Q_i \qquad \text{(C-7)}$$

where Q_i is the total (elemental and nonelemental) radioiodine emission rate. The retention factor r for elemental radioiodine on vegetation should be taken as unity, since the experimental measurements (Refs. 1, 2, and 3) used to evaluate this transfer mechanism consisted of direct comparison of the gross radioiodine concentration on vegetation and the concentration in air (Refs. 4 and 5).

For radioiodines, the deposition model is based only on the dry deposition process. Wet deposition, including "washout" of the organic and non-organic iodine fractions, should be considered at some sites depending on the meteorological conditions (see Regulatory Guide 1.111).

For particulates, the deposition model considers both wet and dry deposition. There is also a retention factor (r of Equation (C-5)) that accounts for the interception and capture of the deposited activity by the vegetative cover. A value of 0.2 is taken for this factor (Refs. 6 and 7). All nuclides except noble gases, tritium, carbon-14, and the iodines are treated as particulates.

Carbon-14 is assumed to be released in oxide form (CO or CO_2). The concentration of carbon-14 in vegetation is calculated by assuming that its ratio to the natural carbon in vegetation is the same as the ratio of carbon-14 to natural carbon in the atmosphere surrounding the vegetation (see Refs. 8 and 9). Also, in the case of intermittent releases, such as from gaseous waste decay tanks, the parameter p is employed to account for the fractional equilibrium ratio achieved. The parameter p is defined as the ratio of the total annual release time (for C-14 atmospheric releases) to the total annual time during which photosynthesis occurs (taken to be 4400 hrs), under the condition that the value of p should never exceed unity. For continuous C-14 releases, p is taken to be unity. These considerations yield the following relationship:

$$C^v_{14}(r,\theta) = 3.17 \times 10^7 pQ_{14}[\chi/Q](r,\theta)\ 0.11/0.16$$

$$= 2.2 \times 10^7 pQ_{14}[\chi/Q](r,\theta) \qquad \text{(C-8)}$$

where

$C^v_{14}(r,\theta)$ is the concentration of carbon-14 in vegetation grown at location (r,θ), in pCi/kg;

Q_{14} is the annual release rate of carbon-14, in Ci/yr;

p is the fractional equilibrium ratio, dimensionless;

0.11 is the fraction of total plant mass that is natural carbon, dimensionless;

0.16 is equal to the concentration of natural carbon in the atmosphere, in g/m^3; and

3.17×10^7 is equal to $(1.0 \times 10^{12} pCi/Ci)(1.0 \times 10^3\ g/kg)/(3.15 \times 10^7 sec/yr)$.

The concentration of tritium in vegetation is calculated from its concentration in the air surrounding the vegetation. Using the method described in Reference 10, the NRC staff derived the following equation:

$$C_T^v(r,\theta) = 3.17 \times 10^7 Q_T[\chi/Q](r,\theta)(0.75)(0.5/H)$$

$$= 1.2 \times 10^7 Q_T[\chi/Q](r,\theta)/H \qquad \text{(C-9)}$$

where

$C_T^v(r,\theta)$ is the concentration of tritium in vegetation grown at location (r,θ), in pCi/kg;

H is the absolute humidity of the atmosphere at location (r,θ), in g/m^3;

Q_T is the annual release rate of tritium, in Ci/yr;

0.5 is the ratio of tritium concentration in plant water to tritium concentration in atmospheric water, dimensionless; and

0.75 is the fraction of total plant mass that is water, dimensionless.

b. Parameters for Calculating Nuclide Concentrations in Milk

The radionuclide concentration in milk is dependent on the amount and contamination level of the feed consumed by the animal. The radionuclide concentration in milk is estimated as

$$C_i^m(r,\theta) = F_m C_i^v(r,\theta) Q_F \exp(-\lambda_i t_f) \qquad \text{(C-10)}$$

where

$C_i^m(r,\theta)$ is the concentration in milk of nuclide i, in pCi/liter;

$C_i^v(r,\theta)$ is the concentration of radionuclide i in the animal's feed, in pCi/kg;

F_m is the average fraction of the animal's daily intake of radionuclide i which appears in each liter of milk, in days/liter (see Appendix E, Tables E-1 and E-2 for cow and goat data, respectively; for nuclides not listed in Table E-2, use the values in Table E-1);

Q_F is the amount of feed consumed by the animal per day, in kg/day;

t_f is the average transport time of the activity from the feed into the milk and to the receptor (a value of 2 days is assumed); and

λ_i is the radiological decay constant of nuclide i, in $days^{-1}$.

The concentration of radionuclide i in the animal's feed is estimated as

$$C_i^v(r,\theta) = f_p f_s C_i^p(r,\theta) + (1 - f_p) C_i^s(r,\theta) + f_p(1 - f_s) C_i^s(r,\theta) \qquad \text{(C-11)}$$

where

$C_i^p(r,\theta)$ is the concentration of radionuclide i on pasture grass (calculated using Equation (C-5) with $t_h=0$), in pCi/kg;

$C_i^s(r,\theta)$ is the concentration of radionuclide i in stored feeds (calculated using Equation (C-5) with $t_h=90$ days), in pCi/kg;

f_p is the fraction of the year that animals graze on pasture; and

f_s is the fraction of daily feed that is pasture grass when the animal grazes on pasture.

The values of the parameters t_h, t_e, Y_v, and t_f that will be employed in evaluating the milk pathway, unless site-specific data is supplied, are provided in Appendix E, Table E-15.

c. Parameters for Calculating Nuclide Concentration in Meat

As in the milk pathway, the radionuclide concentration in meat is dependent on the amount and contamination level of the feed consumed by the animal. The radionuclide concentration in meat is estimated as

$$C_i^F(r,\theta) = F_f C_i^V(r,\theta) Q_F \exp(-\lambda_i t_s) \tag{C-12}$$

where

$C_i^F(r,\theta)$ is the concentration of nuclide i in animal flesh, in pCi/kg;

F_f is the fraction of the animal's daily intake of nuclide i which appears in each kilogram of flesh, in days/kg (see Appendix E, Table E-1 for values); and

t_s is the average time from slaughter to consumption (see Appendix E, Table E-15).

All the other symbols are as previously defined.

Beef cattle will be assumed to be on open pasture for the grazing periods outlined for milk cattle.

4. Annual Dose from Atmospherically Released Radionuclides in Foods

The annual dose to organ j of an individual in age group a resulting from ingestion of all radionuclides in produce, milk, meat, and leafy vegetables is given by

$$D_{ja}^D(r,\theta) = \sum_i DFI_{ija} [U_a^V f_g C_i^V(r,\theta) + U_a^m C_i^m(r,\theta) + U_a^F C_i^F(r,\theta) + U_a^L f_\ell C_i^L(r,\theta)] \tag{C-13}$$

where

$D_{ja}^D(r,\theta)$ is the annual dose to organ j of an individual in age group a from dietary intake of atmospherically released radionuclides, in mrem/yr;

DFI_{ija} is the dose conversion factor for the ingestion of nuclide i, organ j, and age group a, in mrem/pCi (from Tables E-11 through E-14 of Appendix E of this guide); and

U_a^V, U_a^m, U_a^F, U_a^L are the ingestion rates of produce (non-leafy vegetables, fruit, and grains), milk, meat, and leafy vegetables, respectively, for individuals in age group a (from Table E-5 of Appendix E of this guide).

All the other symbols are as previously defined. Values of f_g and f_ℓ to be assumed in the absence of site-specific information are given in Table E-15 of Appendix E as 0.76 and 1.0, respectively.

REFERENCES FOR APPENDIX C

1. B. H. Weiss et al., "Detailed Measurement of I-131 in Air, Vegetation and Milk Around Three Operating Reactor Sites," NUREG-75/021, U.S. Nuclear Regulatory Commission, Washington, D.C., March 1975.

2. D. F. Bunch (ed.), "Controlled Environmental Radioiodine Test, Progress Report Number Two," USAEC Report IDO-12063, January 1968.

3. J. D. Zimbrick and P. G. Voilleque, "Controlled Environmental Radioiodine Tests at the National Reactor Testing Station, Progress Report Number Four," USAEC Report IDO-12065, December 1968.

4. F. O. Hoffman, "Environmental Variables Involved with the Estimation of the Amount of ^{131}I in Milk and the Subsequent Dose to the Thyroid," Institute für Reaktorsicherheit, Cologne, West Germany, IRS-W-6, June 1973.

5. F. O. Hoffman, "A Reassessment of the Parameters Used To Predict the Environmental Transport of ^{131}I from Air to Milk," Institute für Reaktorsicherheit, IRS-W-13, April 1975.

6. C. A. Pelletier and P. G. Voilleque, "The Behavior of ^{137}Cs and Other Fallout Radionuclides on a Michigan Dairy Farm," Health Phys., Vol. 21, p. 777, 1971.

7. P. G. Voilleque and C. A. Pelletier, "Comparison of External Irradiation and Consumption of Cow's Milk as Critical Pathways for ^{137}Cs, ^{54}Mn and ^{144}Ce-^{144}Pr Released to the Atmosphere," Health Phys., Vol. 27, p. 189, 1974.

8. Y. C. Ng et al., "Prediction of the Maximum Dosage to Man from the Fallout of Nuclear Devices, IV Handbook for Estimating the Maximum Internal Dose from Radionuclides Released to the Biosphere," USAEC Report UCRL-50163, Part IV, 1968.

9. R. C. Weast (ed.), "Handbook of Chemistry and Physics," CRC Press, Cleveland, Ohio, 1970.

10. L. R. Anspaugh et al., "The Dose to Man via the Food-Chain Transfer Resulting from Exposure to Tritiated Water Vapor," USAEC Report UCRL-73195, Rev. 1, 1972.

APPENDIX D

MODELS FOR CALCULATING POPULATION DOSES FROM NUCLEAR POWER PLANT EFFLUENTS

Calculation of the annual population-integrated total body and thyroid doses* should be performed for the three effluent types identified in this guide. These doses should be evaluated for the population within a 50-mile radius of the site, as specified in paragraph D, Section II of Appendix I to 10 CFR Part 50.

For the purpose of calculating the annual population-integrated dose, the 50-mile region should be divided into a number of subregions consistent with the nature of the region. These subregions may represent, for example, the reaches of a river or land areas over which the appropriate dispersion factor is averaged. Dispersion factors, population data, and other information describing existing or planned uses of the subregions should be developed.

1. <u>General Expressions for Population Dose</u>

For pathways in which the permanent and transient population of the subregion can be considered to be exposed to the average radionuclide concentrations estimated for the subregion, the annual population-integrated dose is calculated as follows:

$$D_j^P = 0.001 \sum_d P_d \sum_a D_{jda} f_{da} \qquad \text{(D-1)}$$

where

D_{jda} is the annual dose to organ j (total body or thyroid) of an average individual of age group a in subregion d, in mrem/yr;

D_j^P is the annual population-integrated dose to organ j (total body or thyroid), in man-rems or thyroid man-rems;

f_{da} is the fraction of the population in subregion d that is in age group a;

P_d is the population associated with subregion d; and

0.001 is the conversion factor from mrem to rem.

The annual dose to the total body or thyroid of an average individual should be evaluated with the usage factors of Table E-4 of Appendix E. Models and equations for the detailed dose calculations are presented in Appendices A, B, and C of this guide. The annual population-integrated doses from ingestion of potable water, inhalation of airborne effluents, and external exposure to airborne or deposited radionuclides should be evaluated. In addition to the pathways for which equations are presented in Appendices A, B, and C, other exposure pathways should be evaluated if conditions at a specific site indicate that they might provide a significant contribution to the total population dose from all pathways. In this context, a significant contribution is defined as 10 percent or more.

For pathways that involve food products produced in the subregion, the food products may be distributed to other areas for consumption. For all the food that is produced within the 50-mile radius, the radioactivity concentrations are averaged over the entire area by weighting the concentrations in each subregion by the amount produced in each subregion. This average concentration is used in calculating the population doses. The 50-mile average concentration of nuclide i in food p is computed as

$$\bar{C}_{ip} = (1/V_p) \exp(-\lambda_i t_p) \sum_d C_{dip} v_{dp} \qquad \text{(D-2)}$$

---

*The population-integrated dose is the summation of the dose received by all individuals and has units of man-rem when applied to the total body dose and units of man-thyroid-rem when applied to the summation of thyroid dose.

where

C_{dip}	is the average concentration over subregion d of the nuclide i in pathway p, in pCi/kg or pCi/liter (see Appendices A and C of this guide for models and equations for calculation of pathway concentrations);
$\overline{C}_{ip}$	is the 50-mile average concentration of nuclide i in pathway p, in pCi/kg or pCi/liter;
t_p	is the transport time of the food medium p through the distribution system, in days (Table D-1 presents estimates of the transport times that may be used in lieu of site-specific data);
v_{dp}	is the annual mass or volume of food medium p produced in subregion d, in kg or liters;
V_p	is the mass or volume of the food medium p produced annually with the 50-mile radius about the site, in kg or liters; and
λ_i	is the radiological decay constant for nuclide i, in days^{-1}.

The population served by all the food produced within 50 miles of the site is estimated as

$$P_p^* = V_p / \sum_a U_{ap} f_a \tag{D-3}$$

where

f_a	is the fraction of the population within the age group a;
P_p^*	is the estimated population that can be served by the quantity of food p likely to be produced within 50 miles of the site;
U_{ap}	is the use or consumption factor of food medium p for the average individual in age group a, in kg/yr or liters/yr (taken from Table E-4); and
V_p	is the annual mass or volume of food medium p likely to be produced within a 50-mile radius about the site, in kg or liters.

The annual population-integrated dose is then calculated as

$$D_j^P = 0.001 \sum_p P_p \sum_i \sum_a f_a \overline{C}_{ip} U_{ap} DF_{ai} \tag{D-4}$$

where

$$P_p = \begin{cases} P_p^* & \text{if } P_p^* < P_{50} \\ P_{50} & \text{if } P_p^* \geq P_{50} \end{cases}$$

and

DF_{ai}	is the ingestion dose factor for age group a and nuclide i, in mrem/pCi (taken from Appendix E, Tables E-11 to E-14);

TABLE D-1

RECOMMENDED VALUES FOR THE TRANSPORT TIMES IN THE FOOD DISTRIBUTION SYSTEM*

FOOD MEDIUM	DISTRIBUTION TRANSPORT TIME (in days)
Fruits, grains, and vegetables	14
Milk	4
Meat and poultry	20
Sport fish	7
Commercial fish	10
Drinking water	1

*To be used in lieu of site-specific data on food distribution.

D_j^P is the annual population-integrated dose to organ j (total body or thyroid), in man-rem/yr or thyroid man-rem/yr;

P_p is the population consuming food medium p; and

P_{50} is the total population within 50 miles.

All other factors are as defined above.

Note that the above formulation limits the evaluation of the exposed population evaluation to the population residing within 50 miles as specified in paragraph D, Section II of Appendix I to 10 CFR Part 50. In calculating the annual population-integrated total body and thyroid doses, the age distribution of the population within 50 miles may be assumed to be the same as the age distribution of the U.S. population (Ref. 1). Reference 1 indicates the fractional breakdown to be as follows: children, 0.18; teenagers, 0.11; and adults, 0.71. Infants (0-1 year in age) are not projected to exceed 2% of the population (Ref. 1), and their population fraction has been included in that given above for children.

2. Use of the Models

a. Population-Integrated Doses from Liquid Effluents

The annual total body and thyroid population-integrated doses due to exposure to liquid effluents should be evaluated for the following principal pathways: potable water, aquatic food products, external irradiation from shoreline deposits, and terrestrial food products irrigated with water that has received the liquid effluent.

(1) Doses from Potable Water

The annual population-integrated total body and thyroid doses from water consumption are evaluated for all subregions that have water intakes existing or designated at the time of the license application. The products of the individual doses and the population exposed in each such subregion within 50 miles from the site are summed to obtain the total dose. The formulation expressed in Equation (D-1) may be used.

The total body and thyroid dose of the individuals should be evaluated using Equation (A-2) in Appendix A of this guide, together with the age-dependent usage factors U_{ap} obtained from Table D-1. The dilution from the discharge point to the usage point should be evaluated using appropriate hydrological models for the various subregions.

If the population served by a particular water supply system is not known, it can be estimated by the following:

$$P_w = v/c \tag{D-5}$$

where

c is the average daily usage of individuals on the system, in gal/day per person;

P_w is the estimated population served by the water system; and

v is the average daily intake of the water supply system, in gal/day.

If the industrial usage from the water supply system is known, it can be subtracted from the average daily intake of the system before this value is entered into Equation (D-5).

The population served by a water supply system whose intake is within the 50-mile radius may include individuals who reside outside the circle. This population may be pro-rated to include only the population within the 50-mile radius. Conversely, a water supply system with an intake beyond the 50-mile radius may serve the population within the 50-mile radius, whose exposure via drinking water should be included in the 50-mile population dose evaluation.

(2) Doses from Aquatic Food Products

The annual population-integrated total body and thyroid doses from consumption of aquatic food products are evaluated using the production of sport and commercial harvests in the various subregions. The mixing ratio (or dilution) should be evaluated for each subregion using an appropriate hydrological model. For sport harvests, the entire edible harvest is assumed to be ingested by the population within 50 miles. The formulation expressed by Equation (D-4) should be used with the population P_p given by the results of Equation (D-3). The age-specific ingestion rates of Table E-4 may be used in lieu of site-specific data.

For commercial harvests, the production within 50 miles from the site is considered as part of the total U.S. harvest. Equation (D-2) should be used to compute the average concentration, with V_p as the total estimated U.S. commercial harvest of the aquatic food medium p. The annual population-integrated dose is then computed using Equation (D-4) with $P_p = P_{50}$. The age-specific factors of Table E-4 may be used in lieu of site-specific data.

(3) Doses from Shoreline Deposits

The annual population-integrated total body and thyroid doses from recreational activities on the shoreline of the receiving water body are evaluated by summing the product of the individual doses in each subregion and the population exposed therein. All subregions within the 50-mile radius should be considered where existing or designated recreational facilities exist. If available, actual recreational usage in the vicinity of each facility should be used. The formulation of Equation (D-1) is appropriate.

(4) Doses from Consumption of Terrestrial Food Products Irrigated by Waters Receiving the Liquid Effluent

The annual population-integrated total body and thyroid doses from consumption of food irrigated with water from the body receiving the liquid effluent are evaluated following the procedures outlined in the development of Equation (D-4). Note that the term V_p of Equations (D-2) and (D-3) denotes the total production of food medium p within 50 miles, not just the total production of irrigated food medium p. The consumption rate data of Table D-1 may be used in lieu of site-specific data in the evaluation of Equation (D-4).

b. Population-Integrated Doses from Airborne Effluents

The annual total body and thyroid population-integrated doses should be evaluated for the following principal exposure pathways: noble gas submersion, inhalation of airborne effluents, ingestion of contaminated terrestrial foods (milk, meat, and produce), and external irradiation from activity deposited on the ground. Available state or county agricultural production data may be used for estimating the population-integrated doses from food consumption

For the evaluation of exposures from atmospheric releases, the 50-mile region should be divided into 160 subregions formed by sectors centered on the 16 compass points (N, NNE, NE, etc.) and annuli at distances of 1, 2, 3, 4, 5, 10, 20, 30, 40, and 50 miles from the center of the facility. The atmospheric dispersion factors (χ/Q) or similar factors should be evaluated at the radial midpoint for each of the subregions using appropriate atmospheric dispersion models such as those described in Regulatory Guide 1.111.

(1) Doses due to Exposure to Noble Gases

The annual population-integrated total body dose due to noble gas effluents should be evaluated by summing the products of the individual doses in each subregion and the population in each subregion. Equation (D-1) may be used. For external exposure, the model does not differentiate between age groups. A structural shielding factor of 0.5 should be applied in conjunction with the dose factor data of Table B-1.

(2) Doses due to Inhalation of Radioiodines and Particulates

The annual population-integrated total body and thyroid doses from inhalation of airborne effluents should be evaluated by summing the products of the individual doses received in each subregion and the population in each subregion. Equation (D-1) may be used. The age-specific inhalation rates of Table E-4 may be used with the data of Tables E-7 to E-10.

(3) Doses due to Ingestion of Terrestrial Food Products

The annual population-integrated total body and thyroid doses from ingestion of terrestrial food products should be evaluated using the production data for each subregion. For milk, meat, and commercial vegetables, the formulation of Equation (D-2) should be used to calculate the average concentrations in the foods. These concentrations are then used in Equation (D-4), along with the data of Tables D-1, E-4, and E-11 to E-14, to calculate population doses.

(4) Doses due to External Irradiation from Activity Deposited on the Ground

The annual population-integrated total body and thyroid doses from external exposure to surface deposition of the effluent should be evaluated using Equation (D-1). A household shielding and occupancy factor of 0.5 should be applied in conjunction with the dose factors of Table E-6.

REFERENCE FOR APPENDIX D

1. "Current Population Reports," Bureau of the Census, Series P-25, No. 541, U.S. Dept. of Commerce, 1975.

APPENDIX E

NUMERICAL DATA FOR THE CALCULATION OF ANNUAL DOSES TO MAN FROM ROUTINE RELEASES OF REACTOR EFFLUENTS

This appendix contains data for use in the equations presented in the Regulatory Position and in Appendices A, B, C, and D of this guide. The numerical values presented in this appendix are those routinely used by the NRC staff. In instances where more appropriate information of a site-specific nature has been developed and documented, that information should be used.

In a number of instances the staff has found it necessary to provide guidance as to the value of a particular parameter in the absence of substantial empirical data. In such instances the staff has exercised judgment and has considered values used by others and the sensitivity of the results to the value assumed.

Information is provided below under four broad categories: environmental data, human data, dose factors, and other parameters.

1. Environmental Data

Table E-1 provides values for the following stable element transfer coefficients:

a. B_{iv} for the estimation of produce, leafy vegetable, or pasture grass radioactivity from that in soil (pCi/kg in vegetation per pCi/kg in soil);

b. F_m for the estimation of cow milk activity from that in feed (pCi/ℓ in milk per pCi/day ingested by the animal); and

c. F_f for the estimation of meat activity from that in feed (pCi/kg in meat per pCi/day ingested by the animal).

The data are largely derived from Reference 1. The value of the cow milk transfer coefficient for radioiodine is based on the staff's review of the literature (Refs. 2-9).

Values of transfer coefficients for goat milk are presented in Table E-2 for a limited number of nuclides. For nuclides not listed in Table E-2, the milk transfer coefficient from Table E-1 should be used.

Various animal parameter values are presented in Table E-3 for use in estimating animal product activity levels as functions of the corresponding levels in feed and water supplies.

2. Human Data

Tables E-4 and E-5 present usage rates of various environmental media by average individuals and maximum individuals, respectively, according to age group. "Seafood" is used to indicate intake of aquatic invertebrates such as lobster, crab, clams, and oysters. Ingestion of aquatic plant material is not normally assumed.

3. Dose Factors

Dose factors for external irradiation from a uniformly contaminated ground plane are presented in Table E-6 (Refs. 10 and 11), in units of mrem/hr per pCi/m^2. These factors are applicable for surface contamination via deposition of liquid effluents on shoreline sediments or airborne effluents on ground surfaces. Dose factors are provided for the total body and skin only. Doses to other organs are assumed equal to the total body dose.

Dose factors provided in Table E-6 are derived from a consideration of the dose rate to air 1 meter above the ground plane and the penetration of the radiation into the body. The total body dose is computed at a penetration depth of 5 cm; the skin dose is computed at a depth of 7 mg/cm^2. These tissue depths are indicated by Reference 12, where it is suggested that, for

TABLE E-1

STABLE ELEMENT TRANSFER DATA*

Element	B_{iv} Veg/Soil	F_m(Cow) Milk (d/ℓ)	F_f Meat (d/kg)
H**	4.8E 00	1.0E-02	1.2E-02
C**	5.5E 00	1.2E-02	3.1E-02
Na	5.2E-02	4.0E-02***	3.0E-02
P	1.1E 00	2.5E-02	4.6E-02
Cr	2.5E-04	2.2E-03	2.4E-03
Mn	2.9E-02	2.5E-04	8.0E-04
Fe	6.6E-04	1.2E-03	4.0E-02
Co	9.4E-03	1.0E-03	1.3E-02
Ni	1.9E-02	6.7E-03	5.3E-02
Cu	1.2E-01	1.4E-02	8.0E-03
Zn	4.0E-01	3.9E-02	3.0E-02
Rb	1.3E-01	3.0E-02	3.1E-02
Sr	1.7E-02	8.0E-04***	6.0E-04
Y	2.6E-03	1.0E-05	4.6E-03
Zr	1.7E-04	5.0E-06	3.4E-02
Nb	9.4E-03	2.5E-03	2.8E-01
Mo	1.2E-01	7.5E-03	8.0E-03
Tc	2.5E-01	2.5E-02	4.0E-01
Ru	5.0E-02	1.0E-06	4.0E-01
Rh	1.3E 01	1.0E-02	1.5E-03
Ag	1.5E-01	5.0E-02	1.7E-02
Te	1.3E 00	1.0E-03	7.7E-02
I	2.0E-02	6.0E-03†	2.9E-03
Cs	1.0E-02	1.2E-02***	4.0E-03
Ba	5.0E-03	4.0E-04***	3.2E-03
La	2.5E-03	5.0E-06	2.0E-04
Ce	2.5E-03	1.0E-04***	1.2E-03
Pr	2.5E-03	5.0E-06	4.7E-03
Nd	2.4E-03	5.0E-06	3.3E-03
W	1.8E-02	5.0E-04	1.3E-03
Np	2.5E-03	5.0E-06	2.0E-04††

*Data presented in this table is from Reference 1 unless otherwise indicated.

**Meat and milk coefficients are based on specific activity considerations.

***From Reference 15.

†See text.

††From Reference 13.

TABLE E-2

NUCLIDE TRANSFER PARAMETERS FOR GOAT'S MILK*

Element	F_m (days/liter)
H	0.17
C	0.10
P	0.25
Fe	1.3E-04
Cu	0.013
Sr	0.014**
I	0.06**
Cs	0.30**

*Values in this table are from References 1 and 14 unless otherwise indicated.

**From Reference 15.

TABLE E-3

ANIMAL CONSUMPTION RATES

Animal	Q_F Feed or Forage (kg/day [wet weight])	Q_{Aw} Water (ℓ/day)
Milk cow	50 (Ref. 10)	60 (Ref. 16)
Beef cattle	50 (Ref. 10)	50 (Ref. 16)
Goats	6 (Ref. 17)	8 (Ref. 18)

TABLE E-4

RECOMMENDED VALUES FOR U_{ap} TO BE USED FOR THE AVERAGE INDIVIDUAL IN LIEU OF SITE-SPECIFIC DATA

Pathway	Child	Teen	Adult
Fruits, vegetables, & grain (kg/yr)*	200	240	190
Milk (ℓ/yr)*	170	200	110
Meat & poultry (kg/yr)*	37	59	95
Fish (kg/yr)*	2.2	5.2	6.9
Seafood (kg/yr)*	0.33	0.75	1.0
Drinking water (ℓ/yr)**	260	260	370
Shoreline recreation (hr/yr)**	9.5	47	8.3
Inhalation (m^3/yr)	3700***	8000***	8000†

*Consumption rate obtained from Reference 19 and age-prorated using techniques in Reference 10.

**Data obtained directly from Reference 10.

***Inhalation rate derived from data provided in Reference 20.

†Data obtained directly from Reference 20.

TABLE E-5

RECOMMENDED VALUES FOR U_{ap} TO BE USED FOR THE MAXIMUM EXPOSED INDIVIDUAL IN LIEU OF SITE-SPECIFIC DATA

Pathway	Infant	Child	Teen	Adult
Fruits, vegetables & grain (kg/yr)*,**	-	520	630	520
Leafy vegetables (kg/yr)*	-	26	42	64
Milk (ℓ/yr)*	330	330	400	310
Meat & poultry (kg/yr)*	-	41	65	110
Fish (fresh or salt) (kg/yr)***	-	6.9	16	21
Other seafood (kg/yr)*	-	1.7	3.8	5
Drinking water (ℓ/yr)†	330	510	510	730
Shoreline recreation (hr/yr)†	-	14	67	12
Inhalation (m^3/yr)	1400††	3700†††	8000†††	8000††

*Consumption rate obtained from Reference 19 for average individual and age-prorated and maximized using techniques contained in Reference 10.

**Consists of the following (on a mass basis): 22% fruit, 54% vegetables (including leafy vegetables), and 24% grain.

***Consumption rate for adult obtained by averaging data from References 10 and 21-24 and age-prorated using techniques contained in Reference 10.

†Data obtained directly from Reference 10.

††Data obtained directly from Reference 20.

†††Inhalation rate derived from data provided in Reference 20.

TABLE E-6

EXTERNAL DOSE FACTORS FOR STANDING ON CONTAMINATED GROUND

(mrem/hr per pCi/m^2)

Element	Total Body	Skin
H-3	0.0	0.0
C-14	0.0	0.0
NA-24	2.50E-08	2.90E-08
P-32	0.0	0.0
Cr-51	2.20E-10	2.60E-10
Mn-54	5.80E-09	6.80E-09
Mn-56	1.10E-08	1.30E-08
Fe-55	0.0	0.0
Fe-59	8.00E-09	9.40E-09
Co-58	7.00E-09	8.20E-09
Co-60	1.70E-08	2.00E-08
Ni-63	0.0	0.0
Nr-65	3.70E-09	4.30E-09
Cu-64	1.50E-09	1.70E-09
Zn-65	4.00E-09	4.60E-09
Zn-69	0.0	0.0
Br-83	6.40E-11	9.30E-11
Br-84	1.20E-08	1.40E-08
Br-85	0.0	0.0
Rb-86	6.30E-10	7.20E-10
Rb-88	3.50E-09	4.00E-09
Rb-89	1.50E-08	1.80E-08
Sr-89	5.60E-13	6.50E-13
Sr-91	7.10E-09	8.30E-09
Sr-92	9.00E-09	1.00E-08
Y-90	2.20E-12	2.60E-12
Y-91M	3.80E-09	4.40E-09
Y-91	2.40E-11	2.70E-11
Y-92	1.60E-09	1.90E-09
Y-93	5.70E-10	7.80E-10
Zr-95	5.00E-09	5.80E-09
Zr-97	5.50E-09	6.40E-09
Nb-95	5.10E-09	6.00E-09
Mo-99	1.90E-09	2.20E-09
Tc-99M	9.60E-10	1.10E-09
Tc-101	2.70E-09	3.00E-09
Ru-103	3.60E-09	4.20E-09
Ru-105	4.50E-09	5.10E-09
Ru-106	1.50E-09	1.80E-09
Ag-110M	1.80E-08	2.10E-08
Te-125M	3.50E-11	4.80E-11
Te-127M	1.10E-12	1.30E-12
Te-127	1.00E-11	1.10E-11
Te-129M	7.70E-10	9.00E-10
Te-129	7.10E-10	8.40E-10
Te-131M	8.40E-09	9.90E-09
Te-131	2.20E-09	2.60E-06
Te-132	1.70E-09	2.00E-09
I-130	1.40E-08	1.70E-08
I-131	2.80E-09	3.40E-09
I-132	1.70E-08	2.00E-08
I-133	3.70E-09	4.50E-09
I-134	1.60E-08	1.90E-08
I-135	1.20E-08	1.40E-08

TABLE E-6 (Continued)

Element	Total Body	Skin
Cs-134	1.20E-08	1.40E-08
Cs-136	1.50E-08	1.70E-08
Cs-137	4.20E-09	4.90E-09
Cs-138	2.10E-08	2.40E-08
Ba-139	2.40E-09	2.70E-09
Ba-140	2.10E-09	2.40E-09
Ba-141	4.30E-09	4.90E-09
Ba-142	7.90E-09	9.00E-09
La-140	1.50E-08	1.70E-08
La-142	1.50E-08	1.80E-08
Ce-141	5.50E-10	6.20E-10
Ce-143	2.20E-09	2.50E-09
Ce-144	3.20E-10	3.70E-10
Pr-143	0.0	0.0
Pr-144	2.00E-10	2.30E-10
Nd-147	1.00E-09	1.20E-09
W-187	3.10E-09	3.60E-09
Np-239	9.50E-10	1.10E-09

calculational purposes, the average depth of the blood-forming organs may be assumed to be 5 cm. Reference 12 also identifies the cells of the basal layer of epidermis as the tissue of interest in the computation of skin dose and states an average depth for these cells of 7 mg/cm^2. This guidance is reflected in the dose factors presented in Table E-6 and also in those presented in Appendix B, Table B-1, for use in calculating external doses from noble gases.

Dose factors for internal exposure are provided in Tables E-7 through E-14, in units of mrem per pCi intake (Ref. 25). Tables E-7 through E-10 are for inhalation (one table for each of the four age groups), while Tables E-11 through E-14 are for ingestion. Dose factors provided for the inhalation of H-3 include an increase of 50 percent to account for the additional amount of this isotope absorbed through the skin (Ref. 25).

As discussed in Section B, "Discussion," these dose factors are appropriate for continuous intake over a one-year period and include the dose commitment over a 50-year period. The calculational scheme by which these dose factors are derived includes elementary consideration of changing physical and metabolic characteristics during the period over which the dose commitment is evaluated. For example, environmental exposure of an infant over a one-year period is treated as follows: dose during the first year is computed based on infant physiological and metabolic characteristics considering both the buildup and decay of the appropriate organ burden; dose during years 1-10 is computed based on child physiological and metabolic data considering decay of the organ burden from its peak value at age 1; dose during years 11-16 is treated in a similar fashion using teenager characteristics; and dose during adulthood is computed based on the physiological and metabolic characteristics of an adult. Age-dependent parameters are changed in steps at the breaks between age groups.

4. Other Parameters

Table E-15 has been provided as a central location for the recommended values of many of the miscellaneous parameters appearing in equations in this guide. In some instances, a parameter's value or units is a function of the equation it is used in. Additionally, for some parameters used in calculating activities in vegetation, the value is also a function of the exposure pathway. Table E-15 has been organized to note these complications.

Values of the parameter S_F, a structural shielding and occupancy factor, are given in Table E-15 as 0.7 (for maximum individuals) and 0.5 (for the general population). Using the general approach given in Reference 26, the staff estimates an average structural shielding factor of 0.5 for typical reactor effluents. Assuming the maximum individual spends about 50 percent of the time indoors, the overall shielding and occupancy factor is then approximately 0.7. The factor of 0.5 is used directly for population dose calculations. These factors are applicable for external gamma exposure from noble gases and for external exposure from contaminated ground surfaces.

TABLE E-7

INHALATION DOSE DACTORS FOR ADULTS
(MREM PER PCI INHALED)

NUCLIDE	BONE	LIVER	T.BODY	THYROID	KIDNEY	LUNG	GI-LLI
H 3	NO DATA	1.58E-07	1.58E-07	1.58E-07	1.58E-07	1.58E-07	1.58E-07
C 14	2.27E-06	4.26E-07	4.26E-07	4.26E-07	4.26E-07	4.26E-07	4.26E-07
NA 24	1.28E-06	1.28E-06	1.28E-06	1.28E-06	1.28E-06	1.28E-06	1.28E-06
P 32	1.65E-04	9.64E-06	6.26E-06	NO DATA	NO DATA	NO DATA	1.08E-05
CR 51	NO DATA	NO DATA	1.25E-08	7.44E-09	2.85E-09	1.80E-06	4.15E-07
MN 54	NO DATA	4.95E-06	7.87E-07	NO DATA	1.23E-06	1.75E-04	9.67E-06
MN 56	NO DATA	1.55E-10	2.29E-11	NO DATA	1.63E-10	1.18E-06	2.53E-06
FE 55	3.07E-06	2.12E-06	4.93E-07	NO DATA	NO DATA	9.01E-06	7.54E-07
FE 59	1.47E-06	3.47E-06	1.32E-06	NO DATA	NO DATA	1.27E-04	2.35E-05
CO 58	NO DATA	1.98E-07	2.59E-07	NO DATA	NO DATA	1.16E-04	1.33E-05
CO 60	NO DATA	1.44E-06	1.85E-06	NO DATA	NO DATA	7.46E-04	3.56E-05
NI 63	5.40E-05	3.93E-06	1.81E-06	NO DATA	NO DATA	2.23E-05	1.67E-06
NI 65	1.92E-10	2.62E-11	1.14E-11	NO DATA	NO DATA	7.00E-07	1.54E-06
CU 64	NO DATA	1.83E-10	7.69E-11	NO DATA	5.78E-10	8.48E-07	6.12E-06
ZN 65	4.05E-06	1.29E-05	5.82E-06	NO DATA	8.62E-06	1.08E-04	6.68E-06
ZN 69	4.23E-12	8.14E-12	5.65E-13	NO DATA	5.27E-12	1.15E-07	2.04E-09
BR 83	NO DATA	NO DATA	3.01E-08	NO DATA	NO DATA	NO DATA	2.90E-08
BR 84	NO DATA	NO DATA	3.91E-08	NO DATA	NO DATA	NO DATA	2.05E-13
BR 85	NO DATA	NO DATA	1.60E-09	NO DATA	NO DATA	NO DATA	LT E-24
RB 86	NO DATA	1.69E-05	7.37E-06	NO DATA	NO DATA	NO DATA	2.08E-06
RB 88	NO DATA	4.84E-08	2.41E-08	NO DATA	NO DATA	NO DATA	4.18E-19
RB 89	NO DATA	3.20E-08	2.12E-08	NO DATA	NO DATA	NO DATA	1.16E-21
SR 89	3.80E-05	NO DATA	1.09E-06	NO DATA	NO DATA	1.75E-04	4.37E-05
SR 90	1.24E-02	NO DATA	7.62E-04	NO DATA	NO DATA	1.20E-03	9.02E-05
SR 91	7.74E-09	NO DATA	3.13E-10	NO DATA	NO DATA	4.56E-06	2.39E-05
SR 92	8.43E-10	NO DATA	3.64E-11	NO DATA	NO DATA	2.06E-06	5.38E-06
Y 90	2.61E-07	NO DATA	7.01E-09	NO DATA	NO DATA	2.12E-05	6.32E-05
Y 91M	3.26E-11	NO DATA	1.27E-12	NO DATA	NO DATA	2.40E-07	1.66E-10
Y 91	5.78E-05	NO DATA	1.55E-06	NO DATA	NO DATA	2.13E-04	4.81E-05
Y 92	1.29E-09	NO DATA	3.77E-11	NO DATA	NO DATA	1.96E-06	9.19E-06
Y 93	1.18E-08	NO DATA	3.26E-10	NO DATA	NO DATA	6.06E-06	5.27E-05
ZR 95	1.34E-05	4.30E-06	2.91E-06	NO DATA	6.77E-06	2.21E-04	1.88E-05
ZR 97	1.21E-08	2.45E-09	1.13E-09	NO DATA	3.71E-09	9.84E-06	6.45E-05
NB 95	1.76E-06	9.77E-07	5.26E-07	NO DATA	9.67E-07	6.31E-05	1.30E-05
MO 99	NO DATA	1.51E-08	2.87E-09	NO DATA	3.64E-08	1.14E-05	3.10E-05
TC 99M	1.29E-13	3.64E-13	4.63E-12	NO DATA	5.52E-12	9.55E-08	5.20E-07

TABLE E-7, CONT'D

INHALATION DOSE FACTORS FOR ADULTS
(MREM PER PCI INHALED)

NUCLIDE	BONE	LIVER	T.BODY	THYROID	KIDNEY	LUNG	GI-LLI
TC101	5.22E-15	7.52E-15	7.38E-14	NO DATA	1.35E-13	4.99E-08	1.36E-21
RU103	1.91E-07	NO DATA	8.23E-08	NO DATA	7.29E-07	6.31E-05	1.38E-05
RU105	9.88E-11	NO DATA	3.89E-11	NO DATA	1.27E-10	1.37E-06	6.02E-06
RU106	8.64E-06	NO DATA	1.09E-06	NO DATA	1.67E-05	1.17E-03	1.14E-04
AG110M	1.35E-06	1.25E-06	7.43E-07	NO DATA	2.46E-06	5.79E-04	3.78E-05
TE125M	4.27E-07	1.98E-07	5.84E-08	1.31E-07	1.55E-06	3.92E-05	8.83E-06
TE127M	1.58E-06	7.21E-07	1.96E-07	4.11E-07	5.72E-06	1.20E-04	1.87E-05
TE127	1.75E-10	8.03E-11	3.87E-11	1.32E-10	6.37E-10	8.14E-07	7.17E-06
TE129M	1.22E-06	5.84E-07	1.98E-07	4.30E-07	4.57E-06	1.45E-04	4.79E-05
TE129	6.22E-12	2.99E-12	1.55E-12	4.87E-12	2.34E-11	2.42E-07	1.96E-08
TE131M	8.74E-09	5.45E-09	3.63E-09	6.88E-09	3.86E-08	1.82E-05	6.95E-05
TE131	1.39E-12	7.44E-13	4.49E-13	1.17E-12	5.46E-12	1.74E-07	2.30E-09
TE132	3.25E-08	2.69E-08	2.02E-08	2.37E-08	1.82E-07	3.60E-05	6.37E-05
I 130	5.72E-07	1.68E-06	6.60E-07	1.42E-04	2.61E-06	NO DATA	9.61E-07
I 131	3.15E-06	4.47E-06	2.56E-06	1.49E-03	7.66E-06	NO DATA	7.85E-07
I 132	1.45E-07	4.07E-07	1.45E-07	1.43E-05	6.48E-07	NO DATA	5.08E-08
I 133	1.08E-06	1.85E-06	5.65E-07	2.69E-04	3.23E-06	NO DATA	1.11E-06
I 134	8.05E-08	2.16E-07	7.69E-08	3.73E-06	3.44E-07	NO DATA	1.26E-10
I 135	3.35E-07	8.73E-07	3.21E-07	5.60E-05	1.39E-06	NO DATA	6.56E-07
CS134	4.66E-05	1.06E-04	9.10E-05	NO DATA	3.59E-05	1.22E-05	1.30E-06
CS136	4.88E-06	1.83E-05	1.38E-05	NO DATA	1.07E-05	1.50E-06	1.46E-06
CS137	5.98E-05	7.76E-05	5.35E-05	NO DATA	2.78E-05	9.40E-06	1.05E-06
CS138	4.14E-08	7.76E-08	4.05E-08	NO DATA	6.00E-08	6.07E-09	2.33E-13
BA139	1.17E-10	8.32E-14	3.42E-12	NO DATA	7.78E-14	4.70E-07	1.12E-07
BA140	4.88E-06	6.13E-09	3.21E-07	NO DATA	2.09E-09	1.59E-04	2.73E-05
BA141	1.25E-11	9.41E-15	4.20E-13	NO DATA	8.75E-15	2.42E-07	1.45E-17
BA142	3.29E-12	3.38E-15	2.07E-13	NO DATA	2.86E-15	1.49E-07	1.96E-26
LA140	4.30E-08	2.17E-08	5.73E-09	NO DATA	NO DATA	1.70E-05	5.73E-05
LA142	8.54E-11	3.88E-11	9.65E-12	NO DATA	NO DATA	7.91E-07	2.64E-07
CE141	2.49E-06	1.69E-06	1.91E-07	NO DATA	7.83E-07	4.52E-05	1.50E-05
CE143	2.33E-08	1.72E-08	1.91E-09	NO DATA	7.60E-09	9.97E-06	2.83E-05
CE144	4.29E-04	1.79E-04	2.30E-05	NO DATA	1.06E-04	9.72E-04	1.02E-04
PR143	1.17E-06	4.69E-07	5.80E-08	NO DATA	2.70E-07	3.51E-05	2.50E-05
PR144	3.76E-12	1.56E-12	1.91E-13	NO DATA	8.81E-13	1.27E-07	2.69E-18
ND147	6.59E-07	7.62E-07	4.56E-08	NO DATA	4.45E-07	2.76E-05	2.16E-05
W 187	1.06E-09	8.85E-10	3.10E-10	NO DATA	NO DATA	3.63E-06	1.94E-05
NP239	2.87E-08	2.82E-09	1.55E-09	NO DATA	8.75E-09	4.70E-06	1.49E-05

TABLE E-8

INHALATION DOSE FACTORS FOR TEENAGER
(MREM PER PCI INHALED)

NUCLIDE	BONE	LIVER	T.BODY	THYROID	KIDNEY	LUNG	GI-LLI
H 3	NO DATA	1.59E-07	1.59E-07	1.59E-07	1.59E-07	1.59E-07	1.59E-07
C 14	3.25E-06	6.09E-07	6.09E-07	6.09E-07	6.09E-07	6.09E-07	6.09E-07
NA 24	1.72E-06	1.72E-06	1.72E-06	1.72E-06	1.72E-06	1.72E-06	1.72E-06
P 32	2.36E-04	1.37E-05	8.95E-06	NO DATA	NO DATA	NO DATA	1.16E-05
CR 51	NO DATA	NO DATA	1.69E-08	9.37E-09	3.84E-09	2.62E-06	3.75E-07
MN 54	NO DATA	6.39E-06	1.05E-06	NO DATA	1.59E-06	2.48E-04	8.35E-06
MN 56	NO DATA	2.12E-10	3.15E-11	NO DATA	2.24E-10	1.90E-06	7.18E-06
FE 55	4.18E-06	2.98E-06	6.93E-07	NO DATA	NO DATA	1.55E-05	7.99E-07
FE 59	1.99E-06	4.63E-06	1.79E-06	NO DATA	NO DATA	1.91E-04	2.23E-05
CO 58	NO DATA	2.59E-07	3.47E-07	NO DATA	NO DATA	1.68E-04	1.19E-05
CO 60	NO DATA	1.89E-06	2.48E-06	NO DATA	NO DATA	1.09E-03	3.24E-05
NI 63	7.25E-05	5.43E-06	2.47E-06	NO DATA	NO DATA	3.84E-05	1.77E-06
NI 65	2.73E-10	3.66E-11	1.59E-11	NO DATA	NO DATA	1.17E-06	4.59E-06
CU 64	NO DATA	2.54E-10	1.06E-10	NO DATA	8.01E-10	1.39E-06	7.68E-06
ZN 65	4.82E-06	1.67E-05	7.80E-06	NO DATA	1.08E-05	1.55E-04	5.83E-06
ZN 69	6.04E-12	1.15E-11	8.07E-13	NO DATA	7.53E-12	1.98E-07	3.56E-08
BR 83	NO DATA	NO DATA	4.30E-08	NO DATA	NO DATA	NO DATA	LT E-24
BR 84	NO DATA	NO DATA	5.41E-08	NO DATA	NO DATA	NO DATA	LT E-24
BR 85	NO DATA	NO DATA	2.29E-09	NO DATA	NO DATA	NO DATA	LT E-24
RB 86	NO DATA	2.38E-05	1.05E-05	NO DATA	NO DATA	NO DATA	2.21E-06
RB 88	NO DATA	6.82E-08	3.40E-08	NO DATA	NO DATA	NO DATA	3.65E-08
RB 89	NO DATA	4.40E-08	2.91E-08	NO DATA	NO DATA	NO DATA	4.22E-17
SR 89	5.43E-05	NO DATA	1.56E-06	NO DATA	NO DATA	3.02E-04	4.64E-05
SR 90	1.35E-02	NO DATA	8.35E-04	NO DATA	NO DATA	2.06E-03	9.56E-05
SR 91	1.10E-08	NO DATA	4.39E-10	NO DATA	NO DATA	7.59E-06	3.24E-05
SR 92	1.19E-09	NO DATA	5.08E-11	NO DATA	NO DATA	3.43E-06	1.49E-05
Y 90	3.73E-07	NO DATA	1.00E-08	NO DATA	NO DATA	3.66E-05	6.99E-05
Y 91M	4.63E-11	NO DATA	1.77E-12	NO DATA	NO DATA	4.00E-07	3.77E-09
Y 91	8.26E-05	NO DATA	2.21E-06	NO DATA	NO DATA	3.67E-04	5.11E-05
Y 92	1.84E-09	NO DATA	5.36E-11	NO DATA	NO DATA	3.35E-06	2.06E-05
Y 93	1.69E-08	NO DATA	4.65E-10	NO DATA	NO DATA	1.04E-05	7.24E-05
ZR 95	1.82E-05	5.73E-06	3.94E-06	NO DATA	8.42E-06	3.36E-04	1.86E-05
ZR 97	1.72E-08	3.40E-09	1.57E-09	NO DATA	5.15E-09	1.62E-05	7.88E-05
NB 95	3.32E-06	1.29E-06	7.08E-07	NO DATA	1.25E-06	9.39E-05	1.21E-05
MO 99	NO DATA	2.11E-08	4.03E-09	NO DATA	5.14E-08	1.92E-05	3.36E-05
TC 99	1.73E-13	4.83E-13	6.24E-12	NO DATA	7.20E-12	1.44E-07	7.66E-07

TABLE E-8, CONT'D

INHALATION DOSE FACTORS FOR TEENAGER
(MREM PER PCI INHALED)

NUCLIDE	BONE	LIVER	T.BODY	THYROID	KIDNEY	LUNG	GI-LLI
TC101	7.40E-15	1.05E-14	1.03E-13	NO DATA	1.90E-13	8.34E-08	1.09E-16
RU103	2.63E-07	NO DATA	1.12E-07	NO DATA	9.29E-07	9.79E-05	1.36E-05
RU105	1.40E-10	NO DATA	5.42E-11	NO DATA	1.76E-10	2.27E-06	1.13E-05
RU106	1.23E-05	NO DATA	1.55E-06	NO DATA	2.38E-05	2.01E-03	1.20E-04
AG110M	1.73E-06	1.64E-06	9.99E-07	NO DATA	3.13E-06	8.44E-04	3.41E-05
TE125M	6.10E-07	2.80E-07	8.34E-08	1.75E-07	NO DATA	6.70E-05	9.38E-06
TE127M	2.25E-06	1.02E-06	2.73E-07	5.48E-07	8.17E-06	2.07E-04	1.99E-05
TE127	2.51E-10	1.14E-10	5.52E-11	1.77E-10	9.10E-10	1.40E-06	1.01E-05
TE129M	1.74E-06	8.23E-07	2.81E-07	5.72E-07	6.49E-06	2.47E-04	5.06E-05
TE129	8.87E-12	4.22E-12	2.20E-12	6.48E-12	3.32E-11	4.12E-07	2.02E-07
TE131M	1.23E-08	7.51E-09	5.03E-09	9.06E-09	5.49E-08	2.97E-05	7.76E-05
TE131	1.97E-12	1.04E-12	6.30E-13	1.55E-12	7.72E-12	2.92E-07	1.89E-09
TE132	4.50E-08	3.63E-08	2.74E-08	3.07E-08	2.44E-07	5.61E-05	5.79E-05
I 130	4.50E-07	2.24E-06	8.96E-07	1.86E-04	3.44E-06	NO DATA	1.14E-06
I 131	4.43E-06	6.14E-06	3.30E-06	1.83E-03	1.05E-05	NO DATA	8.11E-07
I 132	1.99E-07	5.47E-07	1.97E-07	1.89E-05	8.65E-07	NO DATA	1.59E-07
I 133	1.52E-06	2.56E-06	7.78E-07	3.65E-04	4.49E-06	NO DATA	1.29E-06
I 134	1.11E-07	2.90E-07	1.05E-07	4.94E-06	4.58E-07	NO DATA	2.55E-09
I 135	4.62E-07	1.18E-06	4.36E-07	7.76E-05	1.86E-06	NO DATA	8.69E-07
CS134	4.62E-05	1.41E-04	6.86E-05	NO DATA	4.69E-05	1.83E-05	1.22E-06
CS136	6.44E-06	2.42E-05	1.71E-05	NO DATA	1.38E-05	2.22E-06	1.36E-06
CS137	8.38E-05	1.06E-04	3.89E-05	NO DATA	3.80E-05	1.51E-05	1.06E-06
CS138	5.82E-08	1.07E-07	5.58E-08	NO DATA	8.28E-08	9.84E-09	3.38E-11
BA139	1.67E-10	1.18E-13	4.87E-12	NO DATA	1.11E-13	8.08E-07	8.06E-07
BA140	6.84E-06	8.38E-09	4.40E-07	NO DATA	2.85E-09	2.54E-04	2.86E-05
BA141	1.78E-11	1.32E-14	5.93E-13	NO DATA	1.23E-14	4.11E-07	9.33E-14
BA142	4.62E-12	4.63E-15	2.84E-13	NO DATA	3.92E-15	2.39E-07	5.99E-20
LA140	5.99E-08	2.95E-08	7.82E-09	NO DATA	NO DATA	2.68E-05	6.09E-05
LA142	1.20E-10	5.31E-11	1.32E-11	NO DATA	NO DATA	1.27E-06	1.50E-06
CE141	3.55E-06	2.37E-06	2.71E-07	NO DATA	1.11E-06	7.67E-05	1.58E-05
CE143	3.32E-08	2.42E-08	2.70E-09	NO DATA	1.08E-08	1.63E-05	3.19E-05
CE144	6.11E-04	2.53E-04	3.28E-05	NO DATA	1.51E-04	1.67E-03	1.08E-04
PR143	1.67E-06	6.64E-07	8.28E-08	NO DATA	3.86E-07	6.04E-05	2.67E-05
PR144	5.37E-12	2.20E-12	2.72E-13	NO DATA	1.26E-12	2.19E-07	2.94E-14
ND147	9.83E-07	1.07E-06	6.41E-08	NO DATA	6.28E-07	4.65E-05	2.28E-05
W 187	1.50E-09	1.22E-09	4.29E-10	NO DATA	NO DATA	5.92E-06	2.21E-05
NP239	4.23E-08	3.99E-09	2.21E-09	NO DATA	1.25E-08	8.11E-06	1.65E-05

TABLE E-9

INHALATION DOSE FACTORS FOR CHILD
(MREM PER PCI INHALED)

NUCLIDE	BONE	LIVER	T.BODY	THYROID	KIDNEY	LUNG	GI-LLI
H 3	NO DATA	3.04E-07	3.04E-07	3.04E-07	3.04E-07	3.04E-07	3.04E-07
C 14	9.70E-06	1.82E-06	1.82E-06	1.82E-06	1.82E-06	1.82E-06	1.82E-06
NA 24	4.35E-06	4.35E-06	4.35E-06	4.35E-06	4.35E-06	4.35E-06	4.35E-06
P 32	7.04E-04	3.09E-05	2.67E-05	NO DATA	NO DATA	NO DATA	1.14E-07
CR 51	NO DATA	NO DATA	4.17E-08	2.31E-08	6.57E-09	4.59E-06	2.93E-07
MN 54	NO DATA	1.16E-05	2.57E-06	NO DATA	2.71E-06	4.26E-04	6.19E-06
MN 56	NO DATA	4.48E-10	8.43E-11	NO DATA	4.52E-10	3.55E-06	3.33E-05
FE 55	1.28E-05	6.80E-06	2.10E-06	NO DATA	NO DATA	3.00E-05	7.75E-07
FE 59	5.59E-06	9.04E-06	4.51E-06	NO DATA	NO DATA	3.43E-04	1.91E-05
CO 58	NO DATA	4.79E-07	8.55E-07	NO DATA	NO DATA	2.99E-04	9.29E-06
CO 60	NO DATA	3.55E-06	6.12E-06	NO DATA	NO DATA	1.91E-03	2.60E-05
NI 63	2.22E-04	1.25E-05	7.56E-06	NO DATA	NO DATA	7.43E-05	1.71E-06
NI 65	8.08E-10	7.99E-11	4.44E-11	NO DATA	NO DATA	2.21E-06	2.27E-05
CU 64	NO DATA	5.39E-10	2.90E-10	NO DATA	1.63E-09	2.59E-06	9.92E-06
ZN 65	1.15E-05	3.06E-05	1.90E-05	NO DATA	1.93E-05	2.69E-04	4.41E-06
ZN 69	1.81E-11	2.61E-11	2.41E-12	NO DATA	1.58E-11	3.84E-07	2.75E-06
BR 83	NO DATA	NO DATA	1.28E-07	NO DATA	NO DATA	NO DATA	LT E-24
BR 84	NO DATA	NO DATA	1.48E-07	NO DATA	NO DATA	NO DATA	LT E-24
BR 85	NO DATA	NO DATA	6.84E-09	NO DATA	NO DATA	NO DATA	LT E-24
RB 86	NO DATA	5.36E-05	3.09E-05	NO DATA	NO DATA	NO DATA	2.16E-06
RB 88	NO DATA	1.52E-07	9.90E-08	NO DATA	NO DATA	NO DATA	4.66E-09
RB 89	NO DATA	9.33E-08	7.83E=08	NO DATA	NO DATA	NO DATA	5.11E-10
SR 89	1.62E-04	NO DATA	4.66E-06	NO DATA	NO DATA	5.83E-04	4.52E-05
SR 90	2.73E-02	NO DATA	1.74E-03	NO DATA	NO DATA	3.99E-03	9.28E-05
SR 91	3.28E-08	NO DATA	1.24E-09	NO DATA	NO DATA	1.44E-05	4.70E-05
SR 92	3.54E-09	NO DATA	1.42E-10	NO DATA	NO DATA	6.49E-06	6.55E-05
Y 90	1.11E-06	NO DATA	2.99E-08	NO DATA	NO DATA	7.07E-05	7.24E-05
Y 91M	1.37E-10	NO DATA	4.98E-12	NO DATA	NO DATA	7.60E-07	4.64E-07
Y 91	2.47E-04	NO DATA	6.59E-06	NO DATA	NO DATA	7.10E-04	4.97E-05
Y 92	5.50E-09	NO DATA	1.57E-10	NO DATA	NO DATA	6.46E-06	6.46E-05
Y 93	5.04E-08	NO DATA	1.38E-09	NO DATA	NO DATA	2.01E-05	1.05E-04
ZR 95	5.13E-05	1.13E-05	1.00E-05	NO DATA	1.61E-05	6.03E-04	1.65E-05
ZR 97	5.07E-08	7.34E-09	4.32E-09	NO DATA	1.05E-08	3.06E-05	9.49E-05
NB 95	6.35E-06	2.48E-06	1.77E-06	NO DATA	2.33E-06	1.66E-04	1.00E-05
MO 99	NO DATA	4.66E-08	1.15E-08	NO DATA	1.06E-07	3.66E-05	3.42E-05
TC 99M	4.81E-13	9.41E-13	1.56E-11	NO DATA	1.37E-11	2.57E-07	1.30E-06

TABLE E-9, CONT'D

INHALATION DOSE FACTORS FOR CHILD
(MREM PER PCI INHALED)

NUCLIDE	BONE	LIVER	T.BODY	THYROID	KIDNEY	LUNG	GI-LLI
TC101	2.19E-14	2.30E-14	2.91E-13	NO DATA	3.92E-13	1.58E-07	4.41E-09
RU103	7.55E-07	NO DATA	2.90E-07	NO DATA	1.90E-06	1.79E-04	1.21E-05
RU105	4.13E-10	NO DATA	1.50E-10	NO DATA	3.63E-10	4.30E-06	2.69E-05
RU106	3.68E-05	NO DATA	4.57E-06	NO DATA	4.97E-05	3.87E-03	1.16E-04
AG110M	4.56E-06	3.08E-06	2.47E-06	NO DATA	5.74E-06	1.48E-03	2.71E-05
TE125M	1.82E-06	6.29E-07	2.47E-07	5.20E-07	NO DATA	1.29E-04	9.13E-06
TE127M	6.72E-06	2.31E-06	8.16E-07	1.64E-06	1.72E-05	4.00E-04	1.93E-05
TE127	7.49E-10	2.57E-10	1.65E-10	5.30E-10	1.91E-09	2.71E-06	1.52E-05
TE129M	5.19E-06	1.85E-06	8.22E-07	1.71E-06	1.36E-05	4.76E-04	4.91E-05
TE129	2.64E-11	9.45E-12	6.44E-12	1.93E-11	6.94E-11	7.93E-07	6.89E-06
TE131M	3.63E-08	1.60E-08	1.37E-08	2.64E-08	1.08E-07	5.56E-05	8.32E-05
TE131	5.87E-12	2.28E-12	1.78E-12	4.59E-12	1.59E-11	5.55E-07	3.60E-07
TE132	1.30E-07	7.36E-08	7.12E-08	8.58E-08	4.79E-07	1.02E-04	3.72E-05
I 130	2.21E-06	4.43E-06	2.28E-06	4.99E-04	6.61E-06	NO DATA	1.38E-06
I 131	1.30E-05	1.30E-05	7.37E-06	4.39E-03	2.13E-05	NO DATA	7.68E-07
I 132	5.72E-07	1.10E-06	5.07E-07	5.23E-05	1.69E-06	NO DATA	8.65E-07
I 133	4.48E-06	5.49E-06	2.08E-06	1.04E-03	9.13E-06	NO DATA	1.48E-06
I 134	3.17E-07	5.84E-07	2.69E-07	1.37E-05	8.92E-07	NO DATA	2.58E-07
I 135	1.33E-06	2.36E-06	1.12E-06	2.14E-04	3.62E-06	NO DATA	1.20E-06
CS134	1.76E-04	2.74E-04	6.07E-05	NO DATA	8.93E-05	3.27E-05	1.04E-06
CS136	1.76E-05	4.62E-05	3.14E-05	NO DATA	2.58E-05	3.93E-06	1.13E-06
CS137	2.45E-04	2.23E-04	3.47E-05	NO DATA	7.63E-05	2.81E-05	9.78E-07
CS138	1.71E-07	2.27E-07	1.50E-07	NO DATA	1.68E-07	1.84E-08	7.29E-08
BA139	4.98E-10	2.66E-13	1.45E-11	NO DATA	2.33E-13	1.56E-06	1.56E-05
BA140	2.00E-05	1.75E-08	1.17E-06	NO DATA	5.71E-09	4.71E-04	2.75E-05
BA141	5.29E-11	2.95E-14	1.72E-12	NO DATA	2.56E-14	7.89E-07	7.44E-08
BA142	1.35E-11	9.73E-15	7.54E-13	NO DATA	7.87E-15	4.44E-07	7.41E-10
LA140	1.74E-07	6.08E-08	2.04E-08	NO DATA	NO DATA	4.94E-05	6.10E-05
LA142	3.50E-10	1.11E-10	3.49E-11	NO DATA	NO DATA	2.35E-06	2.05E-05
CE141	1.06E-05	5.28E-06	7.83E-07	NO DATA	2.31E-06	1.47E-04	1.53E-05
CE143	9.89E-08	5.37E-08	7.77E-09	NO DATA	2.26E-08	3.12E-05	3.44E-05
CE144	1.83E-03	5.72E-04	9.77E-05	NO DATA	3.17E-04	3.23E-03	1.05E-04
PR143	4.99E-06	1.05E-06	2.47E-07	NO DATA	8.11E-07	1.17E-04	2.63E-05
PR144	1.61E-11	4.99E-12	8.10E-13	NO DATA	2.64E-12	4.23E-07	5.32E-08
ND147	2.92E-06	2.36E-06	1.84E-07	NO DATA	1.30E-06	8.87E-05	2.22E-05
W 187	4.41E-09	2.61E-09	1.17E-09	NO DATA	NO DATA	1.11E-05	2.46E-05
NP239	1.26E-07	9.04E-09	6.35E-09	NO DATA	2.63E-08	1.57E-05	1.73E-05

TABLE E-10

INHALATION DOSE FACTORS FOR INFANT
(MREM PER PCI INHALED)

NUCLIDE	BONE	LIVER	T.BODY	THYROID	KIDNEY	LUNG	GI-LLI
H 3	NO DATA	4.62E-07	4.62E-07	4.62E-07	4.62E-07	4.62E-07	4.62E-07
C 14	1.89E-05	3.79E-06	3.79E-06	3.79E-06	3.79E-06	3.79E-06	3.79E-06
NA 24	7.54E-06	7.54E-06	7.54E-06	7.54E-06	7.54E-06	7.54E-06	7.54E-06
P 32	1.45E-03	8.03E-05	5.53E-05	NO DATA	NO DATA	NO DATA	1.15E-05
CR 51	NO DATA	NO DATA	6.39E-08	4.11E-08	9.45E-09	9.17E-06	2.55E-07
MN 54	NO DATA	1.81E-05	3.56E-06	NO DATA	3.56E-06	7.14E-04	5.04E-06
MN 56	NO DATA	1.10E-09	1.58E-10	NO DATA	7.86E-10	8.95E-06	5.12E-05
FE 55	1.41E-05	8.39E-06	2.38E-06	NO DATA	NO DATA	6.21E-05	7.82E-07
FE 59	9.69E-06	1.68E-05	6.77E-06	NO DATA	NO DATA	7.25E-04	1.77E-05
CO 58	NO DATA	8.71E-07	1.30E-06	NO DATA	NO DATA	5.55E-04	7.95E-06
CO 60	NO DATA	5.73E-06	8.41E-06	NO DATA	NO DATA	3.22E-03	2.28E-05
NI 63	2.42E-04	1.46E-05	8.29E-06	NO DATA	NO DATA	1.49E-04	1.73E-06
NI 65	1.71E-09	2.03E-10	8.79E-11	NO DATA	NO DATA	5.80E-06	3.58E-05
CU 64	NO DATA	1.34E-09	5.53E-10	NO DATA	2.84E-09	6.64E-06	1.07E-05
ZN 65	1.38E-05	4.47E-05	2.22E-05	NO DATA	2.32E-05	4.62E-04	3.67E-05
ZN 69	3.85E-11	6.91E-11	5.13E-12	NO DATA	2.87E-11	1.05E-06	9.44E-06
BR 83	NO DATA	NO DATA	2.72E-07	NO DATA	NO DATA	NO DATA	LT E-24
BR 84	NO DATA	NO DATA	2.86E-07	NO DATA	NO DATA	NO DATA	LT E-24
BR 85	NO DATA	NO DATA	1.46E-08	NO DATA	NO DATA	NO DATA	LT E-24
RB 86	NO DATA	1.36E-04	6.30E-05	NO DATA	NO DATA	NO DATA	2.17E-06
RB 88	NO DATA	3.98E-07	2.05E-07	NO DATA	NO DATA	NO DATA	2.42E-07
RB 89	NO DATA	2.29E-07	1.47E-07	NO DATA	NO DATA	NO DATA	4.87E-08
SR 89	2.84E-04	NO DATA	8.15E-06	NO DATA	NO DATA	1.45E-03	4.57E-05
SR 90	2.92E-02	NO DATA	1.85E-03	NO DATA	NO DATA	8.03E-03	9.36E-05
SR 91	6.83E-08	NO DATA	2.47E-09	NO DATA	NO DATA	3.76E-05	5.24E-05
SR 92	7.50E-09	NO DATA	2.79E-10	NO DATA	NO DATA	1.70E-05	1.00E-04
Y 90	2.35E-06	NO DATA	6.30E-08	NO DARA	NO DATA	1.92E-04	7.43E-05
Y 91	2.91E-10	NO DATA	9.90E-12	NO DATA	NO DATA	1.99E-06	1.68E-06
Y 91	4.20E-04	NO DATA	1.12E-05	NO DATA	NO DATA	1.75E-03	5.02E-05
Y 92	1.17E-08	NO DATA	3.29E-10	NO DATA	NO DATA	1.75E-05	9.04E-05
Y 93	1.07E-07	NO DATA	2.91E-09	NO DATA	NO DATA	5.46E-05	1.19E-04
ZR 95	8.24E-05	1.99E-05	1.45E-05	NO DATA	2.22E-05	1.25E-03	1.55E-05
ZR 97	1.07E-07	1.83E-08	8.36E-09	NO DATA	1.85E-08	7.88E-05	1.00E-04
NB 95	1.12E-05	4.59E-06	2.70E-06	NO DATA	3.37E-06	3.42E-04	9.05E-06
MO 99	NO DATA	1.18E-07	2.31E-08	NO DATA	1.89E-07	9.63E-05	3.48E-05
TC 99M	9.98E-13	2.06E-12	2.66E-11	NO DATA	2.22E-11	5.79E-07	1.45E-06

TABLE E-10, CONT'D

INHALATION DOSE FACTORS FOR INFANT
(MREM PER PCI INHALED)

NUCLIDE	BONE	LIVER	T.BODY	THYROID	KIDNEY	LUNG	GI-LLI
TC101	4.65E-14	5.88E-14	5.80E-13	NO DATA	6.99E-13	4.17E-07	6.03E-07
RU103	1.44E-06	NO DATA	4.85E-07	NO DATA	3.03E-06	3.94E-04	1.15E-05
RU105	8.74E-10	NO DATA	2.93E-10	NO DATA	6.42E-10	1.12E-05	3.46E-05
RU106	6.20E-05	NO DATA	7.77E-06	NO DATA	7.61E-05	8.26E-03	1.17E-04
AG110M	7.13E-06	5.16E-06	3.57E-06	NO DATA	7.80E-06	2.62E-03	2.36E-05
TE125M	3.40E-06	1.42E-06	4.70E-07	1.16E-06	NO DATA	3.19E-04	9.22E-06
TE127M	1.19E-05	4.93E-06	1.48E-06	3.48E-06	2.68E-05	9.37E-04	1.95E-05
TE127	1.59E-09	6.81E-10	3.49E-10	1.32E-09	3.47E-09	7.39E-06	1.74E-05
TE129M	1.01E-05	4.35E-06	1.59E-06	3.91E-06	2.27E-05	1.20E-03	4.93E-05
TE129	5.63E-11	2.48E-11	1.34E-11	4.82E-11	1.25E-10	2.14E-06	1.88E-05
TE131M	7.62E-08	3.93E-08	2.59E-08	6.38E-08	1.89E-07	1.42E-04	8.51E-05
TE131	1.24E-11	5.87E-12	3.57E-12	1.13E-11	2.85E-11	1.47E-06	5.87E-06
TE132	2.66E-07	1.69E-07	1.26E-07	1.99E-07	7.39E-07	2.43E-04	3.15E-05
I 130	5.54E-06	9.91E-06	3.98E-06	1.14E-03	1.09E-05	NO DATA	1.42E-06
I 131	2.71E-05	3.17E-05	1.40E-05	1.06E-02	3.70E-05	NO DATA	7.56E-07
I 132	1.21E-06	2.53E-06	8.99E-07	1.21E-04	2.82E-06	NO DATA	1.36E-06
I 133	9.46E-06	1.37E-05	4.00E-06	2.54E-03	1.60E-05	NO DATA	1.54E-06
I 134	6.58E-07	1.34E-06	4.75E-07	3.18E-05	1.49E-06	NO DATA	9.21E-07
I 135	2.76E-06	5.43E-06	1.98E-06	4.97E-04	6.05E-06	NO DATA	1.31E-06
CS134	2.83E-04	5.02E-04	5.32E-05	NO DATA	1.36E-04	5.69E-05	9.53E-07
CS136	3.45E-05	9.61E-05	3.78E-05	NO DATA	4.03E-05	8.40E-06	1.02E-06
CS137	3.92E-04	4.37E-04	3.25E-05	NO DATA	1.23E-04	5.09E-05	9.53E-07
CS138	3.61E-07	5.58E-07	2.84E-07	NO DATA	2.93E-07	4.67E-08	6.26E-07
BA139	1.06E-09	7.03E-13	3.07E-11	NO DATA	4.23E-13	4.25E-06	3.64E-05
BA140	4.00E-05	4.00E-08	2.07E-06	NO DATA	9.59E-09	1.14E-03	2.74E-05
BA141	1.12E-10	7.70E-14	3.55E-12	NO DATA	4.64E-14	2.12E-06	3.39E-06
BA142	2.84E-11	2.36E-14	1.40E-12	NO DATA	1.36E-14	1.11E-06	4.95E-07
LA140	3.61E-07	1.43E-07	3.68E-08	NO DATA	NO DATA	1.20E-04	6.06E-05
LA142	7.36E-10	2.69E-10	6.46E-11	NO DATA	NO DATA	5.87E-06	4.25E-05
CE141	1.98E-05	1.19E-05	1.42E-06	NO DATA	3.75E-06	3.69E-04	1.54E-05
CE143	2.09E-07	1.38E-07	1.58E-08	NO DATA	4.03E-08	8.30E-05	3.55E-05
CE144	2.28E-03	8.65E-04	1.26E-04	NO DATA	3.84E-04	7.03E-03	1.06E-04
PR143	1.00E-05	3.74E-06	4.99E-07	NO DATA	1.41E-06	3.09E-04	2.66E-05
PR144	3.42E-11	1.32E-11	1.72E-12	NO DATA	4.80E-12	1.15E-06	3.06E-06
ND147	5.67E-06	5.81E-06	3.57E-07	NO DATA	2.25E-06	2.30E-04	2.23E-05
W187	9.26E-09	6.44E-09	2.23E-09	NO DATA	NO DATA	2.83E-05	2.54E-05
NP239	2.65E-07	2.37E-08	1.34E-08	NO DATA	4.73E-08	4.25E-05	1.78E-05

TABLE E-11

INGESTION DOSE FACTORS FOR ADULTS
(MREM PER PCI INGESTED)

NUCLIDE	BONE	LIVER	T.BODY	THYROID	KIDNEY	LUNG	GI-LLI
H 3	NO DATA	1.05E-07	1.05E-07	1.05E-07	1.05E-07	1.05E-07	1.05E-07
C 14	2.84E-06	5.68E-07	5.68E-07	5.68E-07	5.68E-07	5.68E-07	5.68E-07
NA 24	1.70E-06	1.70E-06	1.70E-06	1.70E-06	1.70E-06	1.70E-06	1.70E-06
P 32	1.93E-04	1.20E-05	7.46E-06	NO DATA	NO DATA	NO DATA	1.05E-05
CR 51	NO DATA	NO DATA	2.66E-09	1.59E-09	5.86E-10	3.53E-09	6.69E-07
MN 54	NO DATA	4.57E-06	8.72E-07	NO DATA	1.36E-06	NO DATA	1.40E-05
MN 56	NO DATA	1.15E-07	2.04E-08	NO DATA	1.46E-07	NO DATA	3.67E-06
FE 55	2.75E-06	1.90E-06	4.43E-07	NO DATA	NO DATA	1.06E-06	1.09E-06
FE 59	4.34E-06	1.02E-05	3.91E-06	NO DATA	NO DATA	2.85E-06	3.40E-05
CO 58	NO DATA	7.45E-07	1.67E-06	NO DATA	NO DATA	NO DATA	1.51E-05
CO 60	NO DATA	2.14E-06	4.72E-06	NO DATA	NO DATA	NO DATA	4.02E-05
NI 63	1.30E-04	9.01E-06	4.36E-06	NO DATA	NO DATA	NO DATA	1.88E-06
NI 65	5.28E-07	6.86E-08	3.13E-08	NO DATA	NO DATA	NO DATA	1.74E-06
CU 64	NO DATA	8.33E-08	3.91E-08	NO DATA	2.10E-07	NO DATA	7.10E-06
ZN 65	4.84E-06	1.54E-05	6.96E-06	NO DATA	1.03E-05	NO DATA	9.70E-06
ZN 69	1.03E-08	1.97E-08	1.37E-09	NO DATA	1.28E-08	NO DATA	2.96E-09
BR 83	NO DATA	NO DATA	4.02E-08	NO DATA	NO DATA	NO DATA	5.79E-08
BR 84	NO DATA	NO DATA	5.21E-08	NO DATA	NO DATA	NO DATA	4.09E-13
BR 85	NO DATA	NO DATA	2.14E-09	NO DATA	NO DATA	NO DATA	LT E-24
RB 86	NO DATA	2.11E-05	9.83E-06	NO DATA	NO DATA	NO DATA	4.16E-06
RB 88	NO DATA	6.05E-08	3.21E-08	NO DATA	NO DATA	NO DATA	8.36E-19
RB 89	NO DATA	4.01E-08	2.82E-08	NO DATA	NO DATA	NO DATA	2.33E-21
SR 89	3.08E-04	NO DATA	8.84E-06	NO DATA	NO DATA	NO DATA	4.94E-05
SR 90	7.58E-03	NO DATA	1.86E-03	NO DATA	NO DATA	NO DATA	2.19E-04
SR 91	5.67E-06	NO DATA	2.29E-07	NO DATA	NO DATA	NO DATA	2.70E-05
SR 92	2.15E-06	NO DATA	9.30E-08	NO DATA	NO DATA	NO DATA	4.26E-05
Y 90	9.62E-09	NO DATA	2.58E-10	NO DATA	NO DATA	NO DATA	1.02E-04
Y 91M	9.09E-11	NO DATA	3.52E-12	NO DATA	NO DATA	NO DATA	2.67E-10
Y 91	1.41E-07	NO DATA	3.77E-09	NO DATA	NO DATA	NO DATA	7.76E-05
Y 92	8.45E-10	NO DATA	2.47E-11	NO DATA	NO DATA	NO DATA	1.48E-05
Y 93	2.68E-09	NO DATA	7.40E-11	NO DATA	NO DATA	NO DATA	8.50E-05
ZR 95	3.04E-08	9.75E-09	6.60E-09	NO DATA	1.53E-08	NO DATA	3.09E-05
ZR 97	1.68E-09	3.39E-10	1.55E-10	NO DATA	5.12E-10	NO DATA	1.05E-04
NB 95	6.22E-09	3.46E-09	1.86E-09	NO DATA	3.42E-09	NO DATA	2.10E-05
MO 99	NO DATA	4.31E-06	8.20E-07	NO DATA	9.76E-06	NO DATA	9.99E-06
TC 99M	2.47E-10	6.98E-10	8.89E-09	NO DATA	1.06E-08	3.42E-10	4.13E-07

TABLE E-11, CONT'D

INGESTION DOSE FACTORS FOR ADULTS
(MREM PER PCI INGESTED)

NUCLIDE	BONE	LIVER	T.BODY	THYROID	KIDNEY	LUNG	GI-LLI
TC101	2.54E-10	3.66E-10	3.59E-09	NO DATA	6.59E-09	1.87E-10	1.10E-21
RU103	1.85E-07	NO DATA	7.97E-08	NO DATA	7.06E-07	NO DATA	2.16E-05
RU105	1.54E-08	NO DATA	6.08E-09	NO DATA	1.99E-07	NO DATA	9.42E-06
RU106	2.75E-06	NO DATA	3.48E-07	NO DATA	5.31E-06	NO DATA	1.78E-04
AG110M	1.60E-07	1.48E-07	8.79E-08	NO DATA	2.91E-07	NO DATA	6.04E-05
TE125M	2.69E-06	9.71E-07	3.59E-07	8.06E-07	1.09E-05	NO DATA	1.07E-05
TE127M	6.77E-06	2.42E-06	8.25E-07	1.73E-06	2.75E-05	NO DATA	2.27E-05
TE127	1.10E-07	3.95E-08	2.38E-08	8.15E-06	2.75E-05	NO DATA	8.68E-06
TE129M	1.15E-05	4.29E-06	1.82E-06	3.95E-06	4.80E-05	NO DATA	5.79E-05
TE129	3.14E-08	1.18E-08	7.65E-09	2.41E-08	1.32E-07	NO DATA	2.37E-08
TE131M	1.73E-06	8.46E-07	7.05E-07	1.34E-06	8.57E-06	NO DATA	8.40E-05
TE131	1.97E-08	8.23E-09	6.22E-09	1.62E-08	8.63E-08	NO DATA	2.79E-09
TE132	2.52E-06	1.63E-06	1.53E-06	1.80E-06	1.57E-05	NO DATA	7.71E-05
I 130	7.56E-07	2.23E-06	8.80E-07	1.89E-04	3.48E-06	NO DATA	1.92E-06
I 131	4.16E-06	5.95E-06	3.41E-06	1.95E-03	1.02E-05	NO DATA	1.57E-06
I 132	2.03E-07	5.43E-07	1.90E-07	1.90E-05	8.65E-07	NO DATA	1.02E-07
I 133	1.42E-06	2.47E-06	7.53E-07	3.63E-04	4.31E-06	NO DATA	2.22E-06
I 134	1.06E-07	2.88E-07	1.03E-07	4.99E-06	4.58E-07	NO DATA	2.51E-10
I 135	4.43E-07	1.16E-06	4.28E-07	7.65E-05	1.86E-06	NO DATA	1.31E-06
CS134	6.22E-05	1.48E-04	1.21E-04	NO DATA	4.79E-05	1.59E-05	2.59E-06
CS136	6.51E-06	2.57E-05	1.85E-05	NO DATA	1.43E-05	1.96E-06	2.92E-06
CS137	7.97E-05	1.09E-04	7.14E-05	NO DATA	3.70E-05	1.23E-05	2.11E-06
CS138	5.52E-08	1.09E-07	5.40E-08	NO DATA	8.01E-08	7.91E-09	4.65E-13
BA139	9.70E-08	6.91E-11	2.84E-09	NO DATA	6.46E-11	3.92E-11	1.72E-07
BA140	2.03E-05	2.55E-08	1.33E-06	NO DATA	8.67E-09	1.46E-08	4.18E-05
BA141	4.71E-08	3.56E-11	1.59E-09	NO DATA	3.31E-11	2.02E-11	2.22E-17
BA142	2.13E-08	2.19E-11	1.34E-09	NO DATA	1.85E-11	1.24E-11	3.00E-26
LA140	2.50E-09	1.26E-09	3.33E-10	NO DATA	NO DATA	NO DATA	9.25E-05
LA142	1.28E-10	5.82E-11	1.45E-11	NO DATA	NO DATA	NO DATA	4.25E-07
CE141	9.36E-09	6.33E-09	7.18E-10	NO DATA	2.94E-09	NO DATA	2.42E-05
CE143	1.65E-09	1.22E-06	1.35E-10	NO DATA	5.37E-10	NO DATA	4.56E-05
CE144	4.88E-07	2.04E-07	2.62E-08	NO DATA	1.21E-07	NO DATA	1.65E-04
PR143	9.20E-09	3.69E-09	4.56E-10	NO DATA	2.13E-09	NO DATA	4.03E-05
PR144	3.01E-11	1.25E-11	1.53E-12	NO DATA	7.05E-12	NO DATA	4.33E-18
ND147	6.29E-09	7.27E-09	4.35E-10	NO DATA	4.25E-09	NO DATA	3.49E-05
W 187	1.03E-07	8.61E-08	3.01E-08	NO DATA	NO DATA	NO DATA	2.82E-05
NP239	1.19E-09	1.17E-10	6.45E-11	NO DATA	3.65E-10	NO DATA	2.40E-05

TABLE E-12

INGESTION DOSE FACTORS FOR TEENAGER
(MREM PER PCI INGESTED)

NUCLIDE	BONE	LIVER	T.BODY	THYROID	KIDNEY	LUNG	GI-LLI
H 3	NO DATA	1.06E-07	1.06E-07	1.06E-07	1.06E-07	1.06E-07	1.06E-07
C 14	4.06E-06	8.12E-07	8.12E-07	8.12E-07	8.12E-07	8.12E-07	8.12E-07
NA 24	2.30E-06	2.30E-06	2.30E-06	2.30E-06	2.30E-06	2.30E-06	2.30E-06
P 32	2.76E-04	1.71E-05	1.07E-05	NO DATA	NO DATA	NO DATA	2.32E-05
CR 51	NO DATA	NO DATA	3.60E-09	2.00E-09	7.89E-10	5.14E-09	6.05E-07
MN 54	NO DATA	5.90E-06	1.17E-06	NO DATA	1.76E-06	NO DATA	1.21E-05
MN 56	NO DATA	1.58E-07	2.81E-08	NO DATA	2.00E-07	NO DATA	1.04E-05
FE 55	3.78E-06	2.68E-06	6.25E-07	NO DATA	NO DATA	1.70E-06	1.16E-06
FE 59	5.87E-06	1.37E-05	5.29E-06	NO DATA	NO DATA	4.32E-06	3.24E-05
CO 58	NO DATA	9.72E-07	2.24E-06	NO DATA	NO DATA	NO DATA	1.34E-05
CO 60	NO DATA	2.81E-06	6.33E-06	NO DATA	NO DATA	NO DATA	3.66E-05
NI 63	1.77E-04	1.25E-05	6.00E-06	NO DATA	NO DATA	NO DATA	1.99E-06
NI 65	7.49E-07	9.57E-08	4.36E-08	NO DATA	NO DATA	NO DATA	5.19E-06
CU 64	NO DATA	1.15E-07	5.41E-08	NO DATA	2.91E-07	NO DATA	8.92E-06
ZN 65	5.76E-06	2.00E-05	9.33E-06	NO DATA	1.28E-05	NO DATA	8.47E-06
ZN 69	1.47E-08	2.80E-08	1.96E-09	NO DATA	1.83E-08	NO DATA	5.16E-08
BR 83	NO DATA	NO DATA	5.74E-08	NO DATA	NO DATA	NO DATA	LT E-24
BR 84	NO DATA	NO DATA	7.22E-08	NO DATA	NO DATA	NO DATA	LT E-24
BR 85	NO DATA	NO DATA	3.05E-09	NO DATA	NO DATA	NO DATA	LT E-24
RB 86	NO DATA	2.98E-05	1.40E-05	NO DATA	NO DATA	NO DATA	4.41E-06
RB 88	NO DATA	8.52E-08	4.54E-08	NO DATA	NO DATA	NO DATA	7.30E-15
RB 89	NO DATA	5.50E-08	3.89E-08	NO DATA	NO DATA	NO DATA	8.43E-17
SR 89	4.40E-04	NO DATA	1.26E-05	NO DATA	NO DATA	NO DATA	5.24E-05
SR 90	8.30E-03	NO DATA	2.05E-03	NO DATA	NO DATA	NO DATA	2.33E-04
SR 91	8.07E-06	NO DATA	3.21E-07	NO DATA	NO DATA	NO DATA	3.66E-05
SR 92	3.05E-06	NO DATA	1.30E-07	NO DATA	NO DATA	NO DATA	7.77E-05
Y 90	1.37E-08	NO DATA	3.69E-10	NO DATA	NO DATA	NO DATA	1.13E-04
Y 91M	1.29E-10	NO DATA	4.93E-12	NO DATA	NO DATA	NO DATA	6.09E-09
Y 91	2.01E-07	NO DATA	5.39E-09	NO DATA	NO DATA	NO DATA	8.24E-05
Y 92	1.21E-09	NO DATA	3.50E-11	NO DATA	NO DATA	NO DATA	3.32E-05
Y 93	3.83E-09	NO DATA	1.05E-10	NO DATA	NO DATA	NO DATA	1.17E-04
ZR 95	4.12E-08	1.30E-08	8.94E-09	NO DATA	1.91E-08	NO DATA	3.00E-05
ZR 97	2.37E-09	4.69E-10	2.16E-10	NO DATA	7.11E-10	NO DATA	1.27E-04
NB 95	8.22E-09	4.56E-09	2.51E-09	NO DATA	4.42E-09	NO DATA	1.95E-05
MO 99	NO DATA	6.03E-06	1.15E-06	NO DATA	1.38E-05	NO DATA	1.08E-05
TC 99M	3.32E-10	9.26E-10	1.20E-08	NO DATA	1.38E-08	5.14E-10	6.08E-07

TABLE E-12, CONT'D

INGESTION DOSE FACTORS FOR TEENAGER
(MREM PER PCI INGESTED)

NUCLIDE	BONE	LIVER	T.BODY	THYROID	KIDNEY	LUNG	GI-LLI
TC101	3.60E-10	5.12E-10	5.03E-09	NO DATA	9.26E-09	3.12E-10	8.75E-17
RU103	2.55E-07	NO DATA	1.09E-07	NO DATA	8.99E-07	NO DATA	2.13E-05
RU105	2.18E-08	NO DATA	8.46E-09	NO DATA	2.75E-07	NO DATA	1.76E-05
RU106	3.02E-06	NO DATA	4.94E-07	NO DATA	7.56E-06	NO DATA	1.88E-04
AG110M	2.05E-07	1.94E-07	1.18E-07	NO DATA	3.70E-07	NO DATA	5.45E-05
TE125M	3.83E-06	1.38E-06	5.12E-07	1.07E-06	NO DATA	NO DATA	1.13E-05
TE127M	9.76E-06	3.43E-06	1.15E-06	2.30E-06	3.92E-05	NO DATA	2.41E-05
TE127	1.58E-07	5.60E-08	3.40E-08	1.09E-07	6.40E-07	NO DATA	1.22E-05
TE129M	1.63E-05	6.05E-06	2.58E-06	5.26E-06	6.82E-05	NO DATA	6.12E-05
TE129	4.48E-08	1.67E-08	1.09E-08	3.20E-08	1.88E-07	NO DATA	2.45E-07
TE131M	2.44E-06	1.17E-06	9.76E-07	1.76E-06	1.22E-05	NO DATA	9.39E-05
TE131	2.79E-08	1.15E-08	8.72E-09	2.15E-08	1.22E-07	NO DATA	2.29E-09
TE132	3.49E-06	2.21E-06	2.08E-06	2.33E-06	2.12E-05	NO DATA	7.00E-05
I 130	1.03E-06	2.98E-06	1.19E-06	2,43E-04	4.59E-06	NO DATA	2.29E-06
I 131	5.85E-06	8.19E-06	4.40E-06	2.39E-03	1.41E-05	NO DATA	1.62E-06
I 132	2.79E-07	7.30E-07	2.62E-07	2.46E-05	1.15E-06	NO DATA	3.18E-07
I 133	2.01E-06	3.41E-06	1.04E-06	4.76E-04	5.98E-06	NO DATA	2.58E-06
I 134	1.46E-07	3.87E-07	1.39E-07	6.45E-06	6.10E-07	NO DATA	5.10E-09
I 135	6.10E-07	1.57E-06	5.82E-07	1.01E-04	2.48E-06	NO DATA	1.74E-06
CS134	8.37E-05	1.97E-04	9.14E-05	NO DATA	6.26E-05	2.39E-05	2.45E-06
CS136	8.59E-06	3.38E-05	2.27E-05	NO DATA	1.84E-05	2.90E-06	2.72E-06
CS137	1.12E-04	1.49E-04	5.19E-05	NO DATA	5.07E-05	1.97E-05	2.12E-06
CS138	7.76E-08	1.49E-07	7.45E-08	NO DATA	1.10E-07	1.28E-08	6.76E-11
BA139	1.39E-07	9.78E-11	4.05E-09	NO DATA	9.22E-11	6.74E-11	1.24E-06
BA140	2.84E-05	3.48E-09	1.83E-06	NO DATA	1.18E-08	2.34E-08	4.38E-05
BA141	6.71E-08	5.01E-11	2.24E-09	NO DATA	4.65E-11	3.43E-11	1.43E-13
BA142	2.99E-08	2.99E-11	1.84E-09	NO DATA	2.53E-11	1.99E-11	9.18E-20
LA140	3.48E-09	1.71E-09	4.55E-10	NO DATA	NO DATA	NO DATA	9.82E-05
LA142	1.79E-10	7.95E-11	1.98E-11	NO DATA	NO DATA	NO DATA	2.42E-06
CE141	1.33E-08	8.88E-09	1.02E-09	NO DATA	4.18E-09	NO DATA	2.54E-05
CE143	2.35E-09	1.71E-06	1.91E-10	NO DATA	7.67E-10	NO DATA	5.14E-05
CE144	6.96E-07	2.88E-07	3.74E-08	NO DATA	1.72E-07	NO DATA	1.75E-04
PR143	1.31E-08	5.23E-09	6.52E-10	NO DATA	3.04E-09	NO DATA	4.31E-05
PR144	4.30E-11	1.76E-11	2.18E-12	NO DATA	1.01E-11	NO DATA	4.74E-14
ND147	9.38E-09	1.02E-08	6.11E-10	NO DATA	5.99E-09	NO DATA	3.68E-05
W 187	1.46E-07	1.19E-07	4.17E-08	NO DATA	NO DATA	NO DATA	3.22E-05
NP239	1.76E-09	1.66E-10	9.22E-11	NO DATA	5.21E-10	NO DATA	2.67E-05

TABLE E-13

INGESTION DOSE FACTORS FOR CHILD
(MREM PER PCI INGESTED)

NUCLIDE	BONE	LIVER	T.BODY	THYROID	KIDNEY	LUNG	GI-LLI
H 3	NO DATA	2.03E-07	2.03E-07	2.03E-07	2.03E-07	2.03E-07	2.03E-07
C 14	1.21E-05	2.42E-06	2.42E-06	2.42E-06	2.42E-06	2.42E-06	2.42E-06
NA 24	5.80E-06	5.80E-06	5.80E-06	5.80E-06	5.80E-06	5.80E-06	5.80E-06
P 32	8.25E-04	3.86E-05	3.18E-05	NO DATA	NO DATA	NO DATA	2.28E-05
CR 51	NO DATA	NO DATA	8.90E-09	4.94E-09	1.35E-09	9.02E-09	4.72E-07
MN 54	NO DATA	1.07E-05	2.85E-06	NO DATA	3.00E-06	NO DATA	8.98E-06
MN 56	NO DATA	3.34E-07	7.54E-08	NO DATA	4.04E-07	NO DATA	4.84E-05
FE 55	1.15E-05	6.10E-06	1.89E-06	NO DATA	NO DATA	3.45E-06	1.13E-06
FE 59	1.65E-05	2.67E-05	1.33E-05	NO DATA	NO DATA	7.74E-06	2.78E-05
CO 58	NO DATA	1.80E-06	5.51E-06	NO DATA	NO DATA	NO DATA	1.05E-05
CO 60	NO DATA	5.29E-06	1.56E-05	NO DATA	NO DATA	NO DATA	2.93E-05
NI 63	5.38E-04	2.88E-05	1.83E-05	NO DATA	NO DATA	NO DATA	1.94E-06
NI 65	2.22E-06	2.09E-07	1.22E-07	NO DATA	NO DATA	NO DATA	2.56E-05
CU 64	NO DATA	2.45E-07	1.48E-07	NO DATA	5.92E-07	NO DATA	1.15E-05
ZN 65	1.37E-05	3.65E-05	2.27E-05	NO DATA	2.30E-05	NO DATA	6.41E-06
ZN 69	4.38E-08	6.33E-08	5.85E-09	NO DATA	3.84E-08	NO DATA	3.99E-06
BR 83	NO DATA	NO DATA	1.71E-07	NO DATA	NO DATA	NO DATA	LT E-24
BR 84	NO DATA	NO DATA	1.98E-07	NO DATA	NO DATA	NO DATA	LT E-24
BR 85	NO DATA	NO DATA	9.12E-09	NO DATA	NO DATA	NO DATA	LT E-24
RB 86	NO DATA	6.70E-05	4.12E-05	NO DATA	NO DATA	NO DATA	4.31E-06
RB 88	NO DATA	1.90E-07	1.32E-07	NO DATA	NO DATA	NO DATA	9.32E-09
RB 89	NO DATA	1.17E-07	1.04E-07	NO DATA	NO DATA	NO DATA	1.02E-09
SR 89	1.32E-03	NO DATA	3.77E-05	NO DATA	NO DATA	NO DATA	5.11E-05
SR 90	1.70E-02	NO DATA	4.31E-03	NO DATA	NO DATA	NO DATA	2.29E-04
SR 91	2.40E-05	NO DATA	9.06E-07	NO DATA	NO DATA	NO DATA	5.30E-05
SR 92	9.03E-06	NO DATA	3.62E-07	NO DATA	NO DATA	NO DATA	1.71E-04
Y 90	4.11E-08	NO DATA	1.10E-09	NO DATA	NO DATA	NO DATA	1.17E-04
Y 91M	3.82E-10	NO DATA	1.39E-11	NO DATA	NO DATA	NO DATA	7.48E-07
Y 91	6.02E-07	NO DATA	1.61E-08	NO DATA	NO DATA	NO DATA	8.02E-05
Y 92	3.60E-09	NO DATA	1.03E-10	NO DATA	NO DATA	NO DATA	1.04E-04
Y 93	1.14E-08	NO DATA	3.13E-10	NO DATA	NO DATA	NO DATA	1.70E-04
ZR 95	1.16E-07	2.55E-08	2.27E-08	NO DATA	3.65E-08	NO DATA	2.66E-05
ZR 97	6.99E-09	1.01E-09	5.96E-10	NO DATA	1.45E-09	NO DATA	1.53E-04
NB 95	2.25E-08	8.76E-09	6.26E-09	NO DATA	8.23E-09	NO DATA	1.62E-05
MO 99	NO DATA	1.33E-05	3.29E-06	NO DATA	2.84E-05	NO DATA	1.10E-05
TC 99M	9.23E-10	1.81E-09	3.00E-08	NO DATA	2.63E-08	9.19E-10	1.03E-06

TABLE E-13, CONT'D

INGESTION DOSE FACTORS FOR CHILD
(MREM PER PCI INGESTED)

NUCLIDE	BONE	LIVER	T.BODY	THYROID	KIDNEY	LUNG	GI-LLI
TC101	1.07E-09	1.12E-09	1.42E-08	NO DATA	1.91E-08	5.92E-10	3.56E-09
RU103	7.31E-07	NO DATA	2.81E-07	NO DATA	1.84E-06	NO DATA	1.89E-05
RU105	6.45E-08	NO DATA	2.34E-08	NO DATA	5.67E-07	NO DATA	4.21E-05
RU106	1.17E-05	NO DATA	1.46E-06	NO DATA	1.58E-05	NO DATA	1.82E-04
AG110M	5.39E-07	3.64E-07	2.91E-07	NO DATA	6.78E-07	NO DATA	4.33E-05
TE125M	1.14E-05	3.09E-06	1.52E-06	3.20E-06	NO DATA	NO DATA	1.10E-05
TE127M	2.89E-05	7.78E-06	3.43E-06	6.91E-06	8.24E-05	NO DATA	2.34E-05
TE127	4.71E-07	1.27E-07	1.01E-07	3.26E-07	1.34E-06	NO DATA	1.84E-05
TE129M	4.87E-05	1.36E-05	7.56E-06	1.57E-05	1.43E-04	NO DATA	5.94E-05
TE129	1.34E-07	3.74E-08	3.18E-08	9.56E-08	3.92E-07	NO DATA	8.43E-06
TE131M	7.20E-06	2.49E-06	2.65E-06	5.12E-06	2.41E-05	NO DATA	1.01E-04
TE131	8.30E-08	2.53E-08	2.47E-08	6.35E-08	2.51E-07	NO DATA	4.36E-07
TE132	1.01E-05	4.47E-06	5.40E-06	6.51E-06	4.15E-05	NO DATA	4.50E-05
I 130	2.92E-06	5.90E-06	3.04E-06	6.50E-04	8.82E-06	NO DATA	2.76E-06
I 131	1.72E-05	1.73E-05	9.83E-06	5.72E-03	2.84E-05	NO DATA	1.54E-06
I 132	8.00E-07	1.47E-06	6.76E-07	6.82E-05	2.25E-06	NO DATA	1.73E-06
I 133	5.92E-06	7.32E-06	2.77E-06	1.36E-03	1.22E-05	NO DATA	2.95E-06
I 134	4.19E-07	7.78E-07	3.58E-07	1.79E-05	1.19E-06	NO DATA	5.16E-07
I 135	1.75E-06	3.15E-06	1.49E-06	2.79E-04	4.83E-06	NO DATA	2.40E-06
CS134	2.34E-04	3.84E-04	8.10E-05	NO DATA	1.19E-04	4.27E-05	2.07E-06
CS136	2.35E-05	6.46E-05	4.18E-05	NO DATA	3.44E-05	5.13E-05	2.27E-06
CS137	3.27E-04	3.13E-04	4.62E-05	NO DATA	1.02E-04	3.67E-05	1.96E-06
CS138	2.28E-07	3.17E-07	2.01E-07	NO DATA	2.23E-07	2.40E-08	1.46E-07
BA139	4.14E-07	2.21E-10	1.20E-08	NO DATA	1.93E-10	1.30E-10	2.39E-05
BA140	8.31E-05	7.28E-08	4.85E-06	NO DATA	2.37E-08	4.34E-08	4.21E-05
BA141	2.00E-07	1.12E-10	6.51E-09	NO DATA	9.69E-11	6.58E-10	1.14E-07
BA142	8.74E-08	6.29E-11	4.88E-09	NO DATA	5.09E-11	3.70E-11	1.14E-09
LA140	1.01E-08	3.53E-09	1.19E-09	NO DATA	NO DATA	NO DATA	9.84E-05
LA142	5.24E-10	1.67E-10	5.23E-11	NO DATA	NO DATA	NO DATA	3.31E-05
CE141	3.97E-08	1.98E-08	2.94E-09	NO DATA	8.68E-09	NO DATA	2.47E-05
CE143	6.99E-09	3.79E-06	5.49E-10	NO DATA	1.59E-09	NO DATA	5.55E-05
CE144	2.08E-06	6.52E-07	1.11E-07	NO DATA	3.61E-07	NO DATA	1.70E-04
PR143	3.93E-08	1.18E-08	1.95E-09	NO DATA	6.39E-09	NO DATA	4.24E-05
PR144	1.29E-10	3.99E-11	6.49E-12	NO DATA	2.11E-11	NO DATA	8.59E-08
ND147	2.79E-08	2.26E-08	1.75E-09	NO DATA	1.24E-08	NO DATA	3.58E-05
W 187	4.29E-07	2.54E-07	1.14E-07	NO DATA	NO DATA	NO DATA	3.57E-05
NP239	5.25E-09	3.77E-10	2.65E-10	NO DATA	1.09E-09	NO DATA	2.79E-05

TABLE E-14

INGESTION DOSE FACTORS FOR INFANT
(MREM PER PCI INGESTED)

NUCLIDE	BONE	LIVER	T.BODY	THYROID	KIDNEY	LUNG	GI-LLI
H 3	NO DATA	3.08E-07	3.08E-07	3.08E-07	3.08E-07	3.08E-07	3.08E-07
C 14	2.37E-05	5.06E-06	5.06E-06	5.06E-06	5.06E-06	5.06E-06	5.06E-06
NA 24	1.01E-05	1.01E-05	1.01E-05	1.01E-05	1.01E-05	1.01E-05	1.01E-05
P 32	1.70E-03	1.00E-04	6.59E-05	NO DATA	NO DATA	NO DATA	2.30E-05
CR 51	NO DATA	NO DATA	1.41E-08	9.20E-09	2.01E-09	1.79E-08	4.11E-07
MN 54	NO DATA	1.99E-05	4.51E-06	NO DATA	4.41E-06	NO DATA	7.31E-06
MN 56	NO DATA	8.18E-07	1.41E-07	NO DATA	7.03E-07	NO DATA	7.43E-05
FE 55	1.39E-05	8.98E-06	2.40E-06	NO DATA	NO DATA	4.39E-06	1.14E-06
FE 59	3.08E-05	5.38E-05	2.12E-05	NO DATA	NO DATA	1.59E-05	2.57E-05
CO 58	NO DATA	3.60E-06	8.98E-06	NO DATA	NO DATA	NO DATA	8.97E-06
CO 60	NO DATA	1.08E-05	2.55E-05	NO DATA	NO DATA	NO DATA	2.57E-05
NI 63	6.34E-06	3.92E-05	2.20E-05	NO DATA	NO DATA	NO DATA	1.95E-06
NI 65	4.70E-06	5.32E-07	2.42E-07	NO DATA	NO DATA	NO DATA	4.05E-05
CU 64	NO DATA	6.09E-07	2.82E-07	NO DATA	1.03E-06	NO DATA	1.25E-05
ZN 65	1.84E-05	6.31E-05	2.91E-05	NO DATA	3.06E-05	NO DATA	5.33E-05
ZN 69	9.33E-08	1.68E-07	1.25E-08	NO DATA	6.98E-08	NO DATA	1.37E-05
BR 83	NO DATA	NO DATA	3.63E-07	NO DATA	NO DATA	NO DATA	LT E-24
BR 84	NO DATA	NO DATA	3.82E-07	NO DATA	NO DATA	NO DATA	LT E-24
BR 85	NO DATA	NO DATA	1.94E-08	NO DATA	NO DATA	NO DATA	LT E-24
RB 86	NO DATA	1.70E-04	8.40E-05	NO DATA	NO DATA	NO DATA	4.35E-06
RB 88	NO DATA	4.98E-07	2.73E-07	NO DATA	NO DATA	NO DATA	4.85E-07
RB 89	NO DATA	2.86E-07	1.97E-07	NO DATA	NO DATA	NO DATA	9.74E-08
SR 89	2.51E-03	NO DATA	7.20E-05	NO DATA	NO DATA	NO DATA	5.16E-05
SR 90	1.85E-02	NO DATA	4.71E-03	NO DATA	NO DATA	NO DATA	2.31E-04
SR 91	5.00E-05	NO DATA	1.81E-06	NO DATA	NO DATA	NO DATA	5.92E-05
SR 92	1.92E-05	NO DATA	7.13E-07	NO DATA	NO DATA	NO DATA	2.07E-04
Y 90	8.69E-08	NO DATA	2.33E-09	NO DATA	NO DATA	NO DATA	1.20E-04
Y 91M	8.10E-10	NO DATA	2.76E-11	NO DATA	NO DATA	NO DATA	2.70E-06
Y 91	1.13E-06	NO DATA	3.01E-08	NO DATA	NO DATA	NO DATA	8.10E-05
Y 92	7.65E-09	NO DATA	2.15E-10	NO DATA	NO DATA	NO DATA	1.46E-04
Y 93	2.43E-08	NO DATA	6.62E-10	NO DATA	NO DATA	NO DATA	1.92E-04
ZR 95	2.06E-07	5.02E-08	3.56E-08	NO DATA	5.41E-08	NO DATA	2.50E-05
ZR 97	1.48E-08	2.54E-09	1.16E-09	NO DATA	2.56E-09	NO DATA	1.62E-04
NB 95	4.20E-08	1.73E-08	1.00E-08	NO DATA	1.24E-08	NO DATA	1.46E-05
MO 99	NO DATA	3.40E-05	6.63E-06	NO DATA	5.08E-05	NO DATA	1.12E-05
TC 99M	1.92E-09	3.96E-09	5.10E-08	NO DATA	4.26E-08	2.07E-09	1.15E-06

TABLE E-14, CONT'D

INGESTION DOSE FACTORS FOR INFANT
(MREM PER PCI INGESTED)

NUCLIDE	BONE	LIVER	T.BODY	THYROID	KIDNEY	LUNG	GI-LLI
TC101	2.27E-09	2.86E-09	2.83E-08	NO DATA	3.40E-08	1.56E-09	4.86E-07
RU103	1.48E-06	NO DATA	4.95E-07	NO DATA	3.08E-06	NO DATA	1.80E-05
RU105	1.36E-07	NO DATA	4.58E-08	NO DATA	1.00E-06	NO DATA	5.41E-05
RU106	2.41E-05	NO DATA	3.01E-06	NO DATA	2.85E-05	NO DATA	1.83E-04
AG110M	9.96E-07	7.27E-07	4.81E-07	NO DATA	1.04E-06	NO DATA	3.77E-05
TE125M	2.33E-05	7.79E-06	3.15E-06	7.84E-06	NO DATA	NO DATA	1.11E-05
TE127M	5.85E-05	1.94E-05	7.08E-06	1.69E-05	1.44E-04	NO DATA	2.36E-05
TE127	1.00E-06	3.35E-07	2.15E-07	8.14E-07	2.44E-06	NO DATA	2.10E-05
TE129M	1.00E-04	3.43E-05	1.54E-05	3.84E-05	2.50E-04	NO DATA	5.97E-05
TE129	2.84E-07	9.79E-08	6.63E-08	2.38E-07	7.07E-07	NO DATA	2.27E-05
TE131M	1.52E-05	6.12E-06	5.05E-06	1.24E-05	4.21E-05	NO DATA	1.03E-04
TE131	1.76E-07	6.50E-08	4.94E-08	1.57E-07	4.50E-07	NO DATA	7.11E-06
TE132	2.08E-05	1.03E-05	9.61E-06	1.52E-05	6.44E-05	NO DATA	3.81E-05
I 130	6.00E-06	1.32E-05	5.30E-06	1.48E-03	1.45E-05	NO DATA	2.83E-06
I 131	3.59E-05	4.23E-05	1.86E-05	1.39E-02	4.94E-05	NO DATA	1.51E-06
I 132	1.66E-06	3.37E-06	1.20E-06	1.58E-04	3.76E-06	NO DATA	2.73E-06
I 133	1.25E-05	1.82E-05	5.33E-06	3.31E-03	2.14E-05	NO DATA	3.08E-06
I 134	8.69E-07	1.78E-06	6.33E-07	4.15E-05	1.99E-06	NO DATA	1.84E-06
I 135	3.64E-06	7.24E-06	2.64E-06	6.49E-04	8.07E-06	NO DATA	2.62E-06
CS134	3.77E-04	7.03E-04	7.10E-05	NO DATA	1.81E-04	7.42E-05	1.91E-06
CS136	4.59E-05	1.35E-04	5.04E-05	NO DATA	5.38E-05	1.10E-05	2.05E-06
CS137	5.22E-04	6.11E-04	4.33E-05	NO DATA	1.64E-04	6.64E-05	1.91E-06
CS138	4.81E-07	7.82E-07	3.79E-07	NO DATA	3.90E-07	6.09E-08	1.25E-06
BA139	8.81E-07	5.84E-10	2.55E-08	NO DATA	3.51E-10	3.54E-10	5.58E-05
BA140	1.71E-04	1.71E-07	8.81E-06	NO DATA	4.06E-08	1.05E-07	4.20E-05
BA141	4.25E-07	2.91E-10	1.34E-08	NO DATA	1.75E-10	1.77E-10	5.19E-06
BA142	1.84E-07	1.53E-10	9.06E-09	NO DATA	8.81E-11	9.26E-11	7.59E-07
LA140	2.11E-08	8.32E-09	2.14E-09	NO DATA	NO DATA	NO DATA	9.77E-05
LA142	1.10E-09	4.04E-10	9.67E-11	NO DATA	NO DATA	NO DATA	6.86E-05
CE141	7.87E-08	4.80E-08	5.65E-09	NO DATA	1.48E-08	NO DATA	2.48E-05
CE143	1.48E-08	9.82E-06	1.12E-09	NO DATA	2.86E-09	NO DATA	5.73E-05
CE144	2.98E-06	1.22E-06	1.67E-07	NO DATA	4.93E-07	NO DATA	1.71E-04
PR143	8.13E-08	3.04E-08	4.03E-09	NO DATA	1.13E-08	NO DATA	4.29E-05
PR144	2.74E-10	1.06E-10	1.38E-11	NO DATA	3.84E-11	NO DATA	4.93E-06
ND147	5.53E-08	5.68E-08	3.48E-09	NO DATA	2.19E-08	NO DATA	3.60E-05
W 187	9.03E-07	6.28E-07	2.17E-07	NO DATA	NO DATA	NO DATA	3.69E-05
NP239	1.11E-08	9.93E-10	5.61E-10	NO DATA	1.98E-09	NO DATA	2.87E-05

TABLE E-15

RECOMMENDED VALUES FOR OTHER PARAMETERS

Parameter Symbol	Definition	Equation(s) Where Used	Values	Reference(s)*
f_g	Fraction of produce ingested grown in garden of interest	14 & C-13	0.76	--
f_ℓ	Fraction of leafy vegetables grown in garden of interest	14 & C-13	1.0	--
P	Effective surface density of soil (assumes a 15 cm plow layer, expressed in dry weight)	4, A-8, A-13, & C-5	240 kg/m^2	10
r	Fraction of deposited activity retained on crops, leafy vegetables, or pasture grass	4, A-8, & A-13 C-5	0.25 1.0 (for iodines) 0.2 (for other particulates)	27 2, 4, 13, 28-31
S_F	Attenuation factor accounting for shielding provided by residential structures	8, 9, 10, 11, 12, B-6, B-7, B-8, B-9, & C-2	0.7 (for maximum individual) 0.5 (for general population)	26 26
t_b	Period of long-term buildup for activity in sediment or soil (nominally 15 yr)	3, 4, A-4, A-5, A-6, A-7, A-8, A-13, & C-5	1.31 x 10^5 hr	--
t_e	Period of crop, leafy vegetable, or pasture grass exposure during growing season	4, A-8, A-13, & C-5	720 hrs (30 days, for grass-cow-milk-man pathway) 1440 hrs (60 days, for crop/vegetation-man pathway)	10 & 32
t_f	Transport time from animal feed-milk-man	C-10	2 days (for maximum individual) 4 days (for general population)	-- --

*Parameter values given without references are based on staff judgments.

TABLE E-15 (Continued)

Parameter Symbol	Definition	Equation(s) Where Used	Values	Reference(s)*
t_h	Time delay between harvest of vegetation or crops and ingestion			
	i) For ingestion of forage by animals	4, A-8, A-13, & C-5	Zero (for pasture grass) 2160 hr (90 days for stored feed)	--
	ii) For ingestion of crops by man	4, A-8, A-13, & C-5	24 hr (1 day, for leafy vegetables & maximum individual)	
			1440 hr (60 days, for produce & maximum individual) 336 hr (14 days, for general population)	--
t_p	Environmental transit time, release to receptor (add time from release to exposure point to minimums shown for distribution)	1 & A-2	12 hr (for maximum individual) 24 hr (for general population)	--
		2 & A-3	24 hr (for maximum individual) 168 hr (7 days for population sport fish doses) 240 hr (10 days for population commercial fish doses	--
		3 & A-7	Zero	
t_s	Average time from slaughter of meat animal to consumption	C-12	20 days	--
Y_v	Agricultural productivity by unit area (measured in wet weight)	4, A-8, A-13, & C-5	0.7 kg/m^2 (for grass-cow-milk-man pathway)	33
			2.0 kg/m^2 (for produce or leafy vegetables ingested by man)	34
λ_w	Rate constant for removal of activity on plant or leaf surfaces by weathering (corresponds to a 14-day half-life)	----	0.0021 hr^{-1}	--

*Parameter values given without references are based on staff judgments.

REFERENCES FOR APPENDIX E

1. Y. C. Ng et al., "Prediction of the Maximum Dosage to Man from the Fallout of Nuclear Devices, Handbook for Estimating the Maximum Internal Dose from Radionuclides Released to the Biosphere," USAEC Report UCRL-50163, Part IV, 1968.

2. B. H. Weiss et al., "Detailed Measurement of I-131 in Air, Vegetation and Milk around Three Operating Reactor Sites," Environmental Surveillance Around Nuclear Installations, International Atomic Energy Agency, IAEA/SM-180/44, Vienna, Austria, Vol. I: pp. 169-190, 1974.

3. F. O. Hoffman, "Environmental Variables Involved with the Estimation of the Amount of I-131 in Milk and the Subsequent Dose to the Thyroid," Institute für Reaktorsicherheit, Cologne, West Germany, IRS-W-6, June 1973.

4. F. O. Hoffman, "Parameters To Be Considered When Calculating the Age-Dependent I-131 Dose to the Thyroid," Institute für Reaktorsicherheit, Cologne, West Germany, IRS-W-5, April 1973.

5. F. O. Hoffman, "A Reassessment of the Parameters Used To Predict the Environmental Transport of I-131 from Air to Milk," Institute für Reaktorsicherheit, Cologne, West Germany, IRS-W-13, April 1975.

6. F. W. Lengemann, "Radioiodine in the Milk of Cows and Goats After Oral Administration of Radioiodate and Radioiodide," Health Phys., Vol. 17, pp. 565-9, 1969.

7. R. J. Garner and R. S. Russel, Radioactivity and Human Diet, R. Scott Russel (ed.), Pergamon Press, Oxford, England, 1966.

8. P. M. Bryant, "Data for Assessments Concerning Controlled and Accidental Releases of I-131 and Cs-137 to the Stratosphere," Health Phys., Vol. 17, p. 51, 1969.

9. J. D. Zimbrick and P. G. Voilleque (eds.), "1967 CERT Progress Report," USAEC Report IDO-12067, p. 36, 1968.

10. J. F. Fletcher and W. L. Dotson (compilers), "HERMES - A Digital Computer Code for Estimating Regional Radiological Effects from the Nuclear Power Industry," USAEC Report HEDL-TME-71-168, Hanford Engineering Development Laboratory, 1971.

11. J. K. Soldat, "Conversion of Survey Meter Readings to Concentration ($\mu Ci/m^2$)," Item 04.3.4 in "Emergency Radiological Plans and Procedures," K. R. Heid (ed.), USAEC Report HW-70935, Hanford Laboratories, 1962.

12. "Permissible Dose from External Sources of Ionizing Radiation," Handbook 59, U.S. Dept. of Commerce, 1954.

13. R. S. Booth et al., "A Systems Analysis Methodology for Predicting Dose to Man from a Radioactivity Contaminated Terrestrial Environment," Proceedings of the Third National Symposium on Radioecology, USAEC Report CONF-710501, Oak Ridge, Tenn., pp. 877-893, 1971.

14. D. S. Altman and P. L. Altman (eds.), "Metabolism," Federation of American Societies for Experimental Biology, Bethesda, Md., 1968.

15. R. J. Garner, "Transfer of Radioactive Materials from the Terrestrial Environment to Animals and Man," CRC Press, Cleveland, Ohio, 1972.

16. J. K. Soldat et al., "Models and Computer Codes for Evaluating Radiation Doses," USAEC Report BNWL-1754, Pacific Northwest Laboratories, February 1974.

17. A. L. Rogers, "Goat Keeping in the United States," International Dairy Goat Conference, London, July 1964.

18. R. G. Bond and C. P. Straub (eds.), Handbook of Environmental Control, Vol. III, "Water Supply and Treatment," CRC Press, Cleveland, Ohio, 1975.

19. "Food Consumption, Prices, and Expenditures," AER-138, U.S. Department of Agriculture, Washington, D.C., December 1974.

20. "Report of the Task Group on Reference Man," ICRP Publication 23, Pergamon Press, Oxford, England, 1975.

21. L. K. Bustad and J. L. Terry, "Basic Anatomical, Dietary, and Physiological Data for Radiological Calculations," HW-41638, General Electric Co., Richland, Wash., February 1956.

22. M. M. Miller and D. A. Nash, "Regional and Other Related Aspects of Shellfish Consumption - Some Preliminary Findings of the 1969 Consumer Panel Survey," NMFS Circular 361, USDC/NOAA, Seattle, Wash., June 1971.

23. "The Potential Radiological Implications of Nuclear Facilities in the Upper Mississippi River Basin in the Year 2000," USAEC Report WASH-1209, Washington, D.C., January 1973.

24. "Draft Environmental Statement - Waste Management Operations, Hanford Reservation, Richland, Washington," USAEC Report WASH-1528, Washington, D.C., September 1974.

25. G. R. Hoenes and J. K. Soldat, "Age-Specific Radiation Dose Commitment Factors for a One Year Chronic Intake," USNRC Report NUREG-0172, to be issued in 1977. A draft is available in the Public Document Room.

26. Z. G. Burson and A. E. Profio, "Structural Shielding from Cloud and Fallout Gamma Ray Sources for Assessing the Consequences of Reactor Accidents," EG&G-1183-1670, Las Vegas, Nev., 1975.

27. D. A. Baker et al., "FOOD - An Interactive Code to Calculate Internal Radiation Doses from Contaminated Food Products," BNWL-SA-5523, February 1976.

28. D. F. Bunch (ed.), "Controlled Environmental Radioiodine Test, Progress Report Number Two," USAEC Report IDO-12063, January 1968.

29. J. D. Zimbrick and P. G. Voilleque, "Controlled Environmental Radioiodine Tests at the National Reactor Testing Station, Progress Report Number Four," USAEC Report IDO-12065, December 1968.

30. C. A. Pelletier and P. G. Voilleque, "The Behavior of Cs-137 and Other Fallout Radionuclides on a Michigan Dairy Farm," Health Phys., Vol. 21, p. 777, 1971.

31. P. G. Voilleque and C. A. Pelletier, "Comparison of External Irradiation and Consumption of Cow's Milk as Critical Pathways for Cs-137, Mn-54 and Pr-144 Released to the Atmosphere," Health Phys., Vol. 27, p. 189, 1974.

32. J. J. Koranda, "Agricultural Factors Affecting the Daily Intake of Fresh Fallout by Dairy Cows," USAEC Report UCRL-12479, 1965.

33. M. E. Heath et al., Forages, the Iowa State University Press, Ames, Iowa, 1973.

34. "Statistical Abstract of the United States," U.S. Bureau of the Census, 93rd Edition, 1972.

APPENDIX F

METHODS FOR EVALUATING THE I FUNCTION

The NRC staff calculates ground-level gamma radiation doses from elevated noble gas releases using Equation (6) in Regulatory Position C.2.a of this guide. Equation (6) is based on the model presented in Slade (Ref. 1), which can be characterized as a vertically finite sector-averaged Gaussian plume model. Use of the model involves volume integration over a distributed source, resulting in certain integrals that define the I function, denoted by $\overline{I}_T$ in Reference 1.

1. Derivation of the I Function

The derivation of the I function presented below is taken directly from Reference 1, which should be consulted for further details.

The sector-average airborne radionuclide concentration resulting from a continuous release is given by the Gaussian plume model as (see Equation 7.60 of Ref. 1):

$$\overline{\chi}(R,z) = \frac{Q^D}{\sqrt{2\pi}\ \sigma_z \bar{u} R\theta}\left\{\exp\left[-\frac{(z-h)^2}{2\sigma_z^2}\right] + \exp\left[-\frac{(z+h)^2}{2\sigma_z^2}\right]\right\} \qquad \text{(F-1)}$$

where

h	is the effective release height, in meters;
Q^D	is the effective release rate, considering decay in transit, in Ci/sec;
R	is the downwind distance, in meters;
$\bar{u}$	is the average wind speed, in m/sec;
$\overline{\chi}(R,z)$	is the sector-average concentration at location (R,z), in Ci/m^3;
z	is the vertical distance above the ground plane, in meters;
θ	is the sector width, in radians; and
σ_z	is the vertical plume spread, in meters.

Equation (F-1) may be restated, for simplicity, as:

$$\overline{\chi}(R,z) = \frac{Q^D G(z)}{\sqrt{2\pi}\ \sigma_z \bar{u}\ R\theta} \qquad \text{(F-2)}$$

where

$$G(z) = \exp\left[-\frac{(z-h)^2}{2\sigma_z^2}\right] + \exp\left[-\frac{(z+h)^2}{2\sigma_z^2}\right] \qquad \text{(F-3)}$$

where the terms are as defined above.

The gamma dose rate to air at a distance of r meters from a point source of q curies is expressed by (see Equation 7.33 of Ref. 1):

$$D' = \frac{\mu_a q(3.7\times10^{10})E(1.6\times10^{-6})B(\mu,\mu_a,r)\exp(-\mu r)}{4\pi r^2(1293)(100)} \tag{F-4}$$

where

$B(\mu,\mu_a,r)$ is the buildup factor, dimensionless;

D' is the dose rate to air, in rad/sec;

E is the gamma ray energy per disintegration, in MeV;

q is the point source strength, in curies;

r is the distance, in meters;

μ is the attenuation coefficient for air, in m^{-1};

μ_a is the energy absorption coefficient for air, in m^{-1};

100 is the number of ergs per gram-rad;

1293 is the density of air at standard temperature and pressure, in g/m^3;

1.6×10^{-6} is the number of ergs per MeV; and

3.7×10^{10} is the number of disintegrations, per Ci-sec.

Equation (F-4) may be simplified as follows:

$$D' = \frac{K\mu_a qEB(\mu,\mu_a,r)\exp(-\mu r)}{4\pi r^2} \tag{F-5}$$

where

$$K = \frac{(3.7 \times 10^{10})(1.6 \times 10^{-6})}{(1293)(100)} = 0.46 \tag{F-6}$$

The next step is to incorporate Equation (F-2) into Equation (F-5) to arrive at an expression for the differential dose rate dD' from the differential volume dV containing the radionuclide concentration $\overline{\chi}(R,z)$. Consider a volume element of the plume located z meters above the ground and at a horizontal distance L meters from receptor location (R, 0) (see Figure 7.20 of Ref. 1). All such volume elements located at the horizontal distance L are included in the ring-shaped differential volume $2\pi LdLdz$. If R is sufficiently large that the concentration averaged over all such volume elements can be approximated by $\overline{\chi}(R,z)$, the contribution of the ring-shaped differential volume dV to the air dose rate at location (R,0) is given as

$$dD' = \frac{K\mu_a EB(\mu,\mu_a,r)\exp(-\mu r)}{4\pi r^2}\,\overline{\chi}(R,z)dV \tag{F-7}$$

where q has been replaced by $\overline{\chi}(R,z)dV$. Substituting $(L^2 + z^2)^{1/2}$ for r and $2\pi LdLdz$ for dV in Equation (F-7), and integrating, the following expression is obtained:

$$D' = \frac{K\mu_a EQ^D}{2\sqrt{2\pi}\,\overline{u}R\sigma_z\theta} \int_0^\infty \int_0^\infty \frac{B\left[\mu,\mu_a,(L^2 + z^2)^{1/2}\right] G(z) \exp\left[-\mu(L^2 + z^2)^{1/2}\right]}{L^2 + z^2} LdLdz \quad \text{(F-8)}$$

The I function, denoted by $\overline{I}_T$ in Reference 1, is defined as

$$I = \frac{1}{2^{3/2}\sigma_z} \int_0^\infty \int_0^\infty \frac{B\left[\mu,\mu_a,(L^2 + z^2)^{1/2}\right] G(z)\exp\left[-\mu(L^2 + z^2)^{1/2}\right]}{L^2 + z^2} LdLdz \quad \text{(F-9)}$$

which, when substituted into Equation (F-8), yields

$$D' = \frac{K\mu_a EQ^D}{\sqrt{\pi}\,\overline{u}R\theta} I \quad \text{(F-10)}$$

The constant K, equal to 0.46, when divided by $\sqrt{\pi}$ yields the factor 0.260, which is the same as the factor of 260 in Equation (6) of Regulatory Position C.2.a, after multiplying by the number of mrad per rad.

The buildup factor given in Reference 1 is of the form

$$B(\mu,\mu_a,r) = 1 + k\mu r \quad \text{(F-11)}$$

where

$$k = \frac{\mu - \mu_a}{\mu_a} \quad \text{(F-12)}$$

Substituting the above expression for the buildup factor into Equation (F-9), the I function is then given as

$$I = I_1 + kI_2 \quad \text{(F-13)}$$

where the I_1 and I_2 integrals can be written for this form of the buildup factor as

$$I_1 = \frac{1}{2^{3/2}\sigma_z} \int_0^\infty G(z)E_1(\mu z)dz \quad \text{(F-14)}$$

and

$$I_2 = \frac{1}{2^{3/2}\sigma_z} \int_0^\infty G(z)\exp(-\mu z)dz \quad \text{(F-15)}$$

where $E_1(\mu z)$ is the exponential integral defined by

$$E_1(\mu z) = \int_{\mu z}^\infty \frac{\exp(-\mu r)}{\mu r} d(\mu r) \quad \text{(F-16)}$$

2. Evaluation of the I Function

In Reference 1 the I_1 and I_2 integrals have been evaluated and the results presented graphically. Extraction of the data from these six-cycle log-log multicurve plots is a formidable task. A more satisfactory approach is to prepare a tabulation of the integrals as evaluated using numerical methods. These data can then be interpolated in implementing Equation (6) of Regulatory Position C.2.a.

The NRC staff has developed a computer routine that evaluates the I function as formulated in Equation (F-9). The I function as expressed in Equation (F-9) is independent of the buildup factor form. A listing of this routine is provided in Figure F-1. Communication with the routine is through the COMMON statement, which also communicates with the function subprogram BULDUP, which defines the dose buildup factor $B(\mu,\mu_a,r)$ desired by the user.

Also, Yankee Atomic Electric Company has supplied a routine written by Dr. John N. Hamawi of that company (Ref. 2). This routine evaluates the I_1 and I_2 integrals as formulated in Equations (F-14) and (F-15), respectively. A listing of the routine is providea in Figure F-2 (reproduced with the permission of Yankee Atomic Electric Company). With the exceptions of changes in the title, the addition of the COMMON statement, the computing of I from I_1 and I_2, and comment cards as to its authorship, the routine is reproduced as written by Dr. Hamawi. The staff has compared the two routines and found their results to be in excellent agreement. The routine supplied by the Yankee Atomic Electric Company was found to be considerably faster than the staff's routine.

```
      SUBROUTINE DINT
      COMMON/DATAIT/GMU,ZK,HS,SIGMZ,EBAR,DI,M
C**
C   DOSE INTEGRAL SUBROUTINE -K.F. ECKERMAN 11-24-74
C   SUBROUTINE EVALUATES THE DOSE INTEGRAL 'IT' AS DEFINED BY EQN 7.61
C   IN MET & AE-1968.  THE TWO DIMENSIONAL INTEGRATION IS EVALUATED
C   USING GAUSSIAN-LEGENDRE QUADRATURE OF ORDER 48.
C
C    COMMON INFO
C        GMU-MASS ATTENUATION COEFFICIENT (1/METERS)
C        ZK-BUILDUP FACTOR (MU-MUA)/MUA IF USED
C        HS-RELEASE POINT HEITH
C        RELEASE POINT HEIGHT (METERS)
C        SIGMZ-STANDARD DEVIATION OF PLUME (METERS)
C        EBAR-GAMMA RAY ENERGY (MEV)
C        DI-DOSE INTEGRAL
C        M-ENERGY GROUP INDEX IF NEEDED
C    NOTE-ZK,EBAR,& M ARE USED BY BULDUP
C**
      DIMENSION X(24),W(24)
      DATA NN/48/,A/2.828427125/
      DATA X/
     10.0323801709, 0.0970046992, 0.1612223560, 0.2247637903,
     20.2873624873, 0.3487558862, 0.4086864819, 0.4669029047,
     30.5231609747, 0.5772247260, 0.6288673967, 0.6778723796,
     40.7240341309, 0.7671590325, 0.8070662040, 0.8435882616,
     50.8765720202, 0.9058791367, 0.9313866907, 0.9529877031,
     60.9705915925, 0.9841245837, 0.9935301722, 0.9987710072/
      DATA W/
     10.0647376968, 0.0644661644, 0.0639242385, 0.0631141922,
     20.0620394231, 0.0607044391, 0.0591148396, 0.0572772921,
     30.0551995036, 0.0528901894, 0.0503590355, 0.0476166584,
     40.0446745608, 0.0415450829, 0.0382413510, 0.0347772225,
     50.0311672278, 0.0274265097, 0.0235707608, 0.0196161604,
     60.0155793157, 0.0114772345, 0.0073275539, 0.0031533460/
      SUM=0.
      B=0.5/(SIGMZ*SIGMZ)
      ZLB=HS-4.*SIGMZ
      ZUB=HS+4.*SIGMZ
      IF(ZLB.LT.0.)ZLB=0.
      YUB=15./GMU
      C=0.5*(ZUB-ZLB)
      G=0.5*(ZUB+ZLB)
      E=0.5*YUB
      DO 70 II=1,NN
      I=II-II/2
      F=1.
      EX=0.
      IF(MOD(II,2).EQ.0)F=-1.
      ZZ=F*X(I)*C+G
      ARGU=B*(ZZ-HS)*(ZZ-HS)
      IF(ARGU.GT.20.)GO TO 55
      EX=EXP(-ARGU)
   55 ARGU=B*(ZZ+HS)*(ZZ+HS)
      IF(ARGU.GT.20.)GO TO 58
      EX=EX+EXP(-ARGU)
   58 IF(EX.EQ.0.)GO TO 70
      DO 60 KK=1,NN
      K=KK-KK/2
      F=1.
      IF(MOD(KK,2).EQ.0)F=-1.
```

Figure F-1. Staff-Written Computer Listing

```
      YY=F*X(K)*E+E
      D1=YY*YY+ZZ*ZZ
      ARGU=GMU*SQRT(D1)
      IF(ARGU.GT.20.)GO TO 60
      EX1=EX*EXP(-ARGU)*BULDUP(ARGU)*YY/D1
      SUM=SUM+W(I)*W(K)*EX1
   60 CONTINUE
   70 CONTINUE
      DI=SUM*C*E/(A*SIGMZ)
      RETURN
      END
```

Figure F-1 (continued)

```
      SUBROUTINE DINT
      REAL MU
      COMMON/DATAIT/MU,ZK,H,SIGZ,DI,L
C**
C   DOSE INTEGRAL ROUTINE WRITTEN BY
C               DR. JOHN N. HAMAWI
C         YANKEE ATOMIC ELECTRIC COMPANY
C           NUCLEAR SERVICES DIVISION
C               20 TURNPIKE ROAD
C        WESTBOROUGH, MASSACHUSETTS 01581
C   YAEC REPORT NO. 1105
C
C   COMMON INFO
C     MU-MASS ATTENUATION COEFFICIENT (1/METERS)
C     ZK-BUILDUP FACTOR (MU-MUA)/MUA
C     SIGZ-STANDARD DEVIATION OF PLUME (METERS)
C     DI-DOSE INTEGRAL -I TOTAL
C     L- DETERMINES NUMBER OF INTERVALS USED IN INTEGRATION
C**
      DIMENSION CDATA(5),E(49),B(49),P(49)
      DATA M/9/,CDATA/5.0D+3,1.0D+4,2.0D+4,5.0D+4,1.0D+5/
      DATA A0,A1,A2,A3,A4,A5/ -0.57721566, 0.99999193, - 0.24991055,
     C  0.05519968,-0.00976004, 0.00107857/
      DATA B0,B1,B2,B3/ 0.2677737343, 8.6347608925, 18.0590169730,
     C  8.5733287401/
      DATA C0,C1,C2,C3/ 3.9584969228, 21.0996530827, 25.6329561486,
     C  9.5733223454/
      DATA D,D1,D2,D3,D4,D5,D6,D7,D8,D9/
     C  3543.75,989.,5888.,-928.,10496.,-4540.,10496.,-928.,5888.,989./
C**** COMPUTE LIMITS OF INTEGRATION ZMIN AND ZMAX, AND INTERVAL WIDTH
      IF(L.LT.2.OR.L.GT.6) L = 6
      C = CDATA(L-1)
      N = L*(M-1) + 1
      SIGZ2 = SIGZ*SIGZ
      ALFA = H - MU*SIGZ2
      BETA = SIGZ* SQRT(2.0*ALOG(C))
      IF(ALFA.GT.0.0) GO TO 150
      ZMIN = 0.0
      ZMAX = ALFA +  SQRT(ALFA*ALFA + BETA*BETA)
      GO TO 200
  150 ZMIN = ALFA - BETA
      IF(ZMIN.LT.0.0) ZMIN = 0.0
      ZMAX = ALFA + BETA
  200 DZ = (ZMAX-ZMIN)/(N-1)
C**** COMPUTE EXPONENTIAL INTEGRAL TERMS E(I) (SPECIAL PROCED. FOR E(1))
      E(1) = 2.18907-ALOG(MU*DZ)
      DO 250 I = 1, N
      Z = ZMIN + (I-1)*DZ
      X = MU*Z
      IF(X.LE.0.0) GO TO 250
      X2 = X*X
      X3 = X*X2
      X4 = X*X3
      X5 = X*X4
      IF(X.LE.1.0) E(I) = -ALOG(X) + A0+A1*X+A2*X2+A3*X3+A4*X4+A5*X5
      IF(X.GT.1.0) E(I) = (B0+B1*X+B2*X2+B3*X3+X4)/
     C                    (C0+C1*X+C2*X2+C3*X3+X4)/(X* EXP(X))
  250 CONTINUE
C**** COMPUTE INTEGRAND TERMS B(I) AND P(I)
      DO 300 I = 1, N
      Z = ZMIN + (I-1)*DZ
```

Figure F-2. Hamawi-Written Computer Listing

```
      G= EXP(-(Z+H)*(Z+H)/(2.0*SIGZ2)) +  EXP (-(Z-H)*(Z-H)/(2.0*SIGZ2))
      B(I) = G*E(I)
  300 P(I) = G* EXP(-MU*Z)
C**** PERFORM NUMERICAL INTEGRATION USING 9-POINT NEWTON-COTES FORMULA
      SUMB = 0.0
      SUMP = 0.0
      MM = M - 1
      KM = N - M + 1
      DO 350 K = 1,KM,MM
      SUMB = SUMB + D1*B(K)+D2*B(K+1)+D3*B(K+2)+D4*B(K+3)+D5*B(K+4)
     C                  +D6*B(K+5)+D7*B(K+6)+D8*B(K+7)+D9*B(K+8)
      SUMP = SUMP + D1*P(K)+D2*P(K+1)+D3*P(K+2)+D4*P(K+3)+D5*P(K+4)
     C                  +D6*P(K+5)+D7*P(K+6)+D8*P(K+7)+D9*P(K+8)
  350 CONTINUE
      DI=DZ*(SUMB+SUMP*ZK)/(D*2.828427*SIGZ)
      RETURN
      END
```

Figure F-2 (continued)

REFERENCES FOR APPENDIX F

1. "Meteorology and Atomic Energy 1968," D. H. Slade (ed.), USAEC Report TID-241090, 1968.

2. J. N. Hamawi, "A Method for Computing the Gamma-Dose Integrals $\overline{I}_1$ and $\overline{I}_2$ for the Finite-Cloud Sector-Average Model," Yankee Atomic Electric Company Report YAEC-1105, 1976.

APPENDIX II

METHODS FOR ESTIMATING ATMOSPHERIC TRANSPORT AND DISPERSION OF GASEOUS EFFLUENTS IN ROUTINE RELEASES FROM LIGHT-WATER-COOLED REACTORS†

A. INTRODUCTION

Section 20.106, "Radioactivity in Effluents to Unrestricted Areas," of 10 CFR Part 20, "Standards for Protection Against Radiation," establishes limits on concentrations of radioactive material in effluents to unrestricted areas. Paragraph 20.1(c) of 10 CFR Part 20 states that licensees should, in addition to complying with the limits set forth in that part, make every reasonable effort to maintain radiation exposures, and releases of radioactive materials in effluents to unrestricted areas, as far below the limits specified in that part as is reasonably achievable.

Section 50.34a, "Design Objectives for Equipment to Control Releases of Radioactive Material in Effluents - Nuclear Power Reactors," of 10 CFR Part 50, "Licensing of Production and Utilization Facilities," sets forth design objectives for equipment to control releases of radioactive material in effluents from nuclear power reactors. Section 50.36a, "Technical Specifications on Effluents from Nuclear Power Reactors," of 10 CFR Part 50 further provides that, in order to keep power reactor effluent releases as low as is reasonably achievable, each license authorizing operation of such a facility will include technical specifications that require establishment of operating procedures for effluent control, installation and maintenance of effluent control equipment, and reporting of actual releases.

Appendix I, "Numerical Guides for Design Objectives and Limiting Conditions for Operation to Meet the Criterion 'As Low As Is Reasonably Achievable' for Radioactive Material in Light-Water-Cooled Nuclear Power Reactor Effluents," to 10 CFR Part 50 provides numerical guidance for those design objectives and limiting conditions for operation for light-water-cooled nuclear power plants. To implement Appendix I, the NRC staff has developed a series of guides providing acceptable methods for the calculation of effluent releases, dispersion of the effluent in the atmosphere and water bodies, and associated radiation doses to man. This guide describes basic features of calculational models and assumptions for the estimation of atmospheric transport and dispersion of gaseous effluents in routine releases from land-based light-water-cooled reactors.

The procedures and models provided in this guide will be subject to continuing review by the staff with the aim of providing greater flexibility to the applicant in meeting the requirements of Appendix I. As a result of such review, it is expected that alternative acceptable methods for calculation will be made available to applicants and that calculational procedures found to be unnecessary will be eliminated.

This guide supersedes portions of Regulatory Guide 1.42, Revision 1, "Interim Licensing Policy on As Low As Practicable for Gaseous Radioiodine Releases from Light-Water-Cooled Nuclear Power Reactors," which has been withdrawn (see 41 FR 11891, 3/22/76). | *

B. DISCUSSION

The transport and dilution of radioactive materials in the form of aerosols, vapors, or gases released into the atmosphere from a nuclear power station are a function of the state of the atmosphere along the plume path, the topography of the region, and the characteristics of the effluents themselves. For a routine airborne release, the concentration of radioactive material in the surrounding region depends on the amount of effluent released; the height of the release; the momentum and buoyancy of the emitted plume; the windspeed, atmospheric stability, and airflow patterns of the site; and various effluent removal mechanisms. Geographic features such as hills, valleys, and large bodies of water greatly influence dispersion and airflow patterns. Surface roughness, including vegetative cover, affects the degree of turbulent mixing. Sites with similar topographical and climatological features can have similar dispersion and airflow patterns, but detailed dispersion patterns are usually unique for each site.

Most gaseous effluents are released from nuclear power plants through tall stacks or vents near the tops of buildings. Certain plant designs can result in other release pathways. For example, auxiliary equipment and major components such as turbines may be housed outside buildings; releases from these components could occur near ground level.

1. Diffusion Models

Atmospheric diffusion modeling has developed along two basic approaches: gradient-transport theory and statistical theory. Gradient-transport theory holds that diffusion at a fixed point

*Lines indicate substantive changes from previous issue.

† Regulatory Guide 1.111, Office of Standards Development, U. S. Nuclear Regulatory Commission, Washington, D.C., Rev. 1, July 1977 (Errata January 1977 incorporated). (For Comment).

in the atmosphere is proportional to the local concentration gradient; this theory attempts to determine momentum or material fluxes at fixed points. The statistical (e.g., Gaussian) approach attempts to determine the histories of individual particles and the statistical properties necessary to represent diffusion. Input data for models based on either approach include windspeed, atmospheric stability, and airflow patterns in the region of interest. Several basic models have been developed using these approaches. These models vary according to their treatment of the spatial changes of input data and the consideration of either a variable trajectory model or a constant mean wind direction model.

a. Variable Trajectory Models

Variable trajectory models allow conditions to vary spatially and temporally over the region of interest; thus, they require regional data. The number of sampling locations needed to approximate the regional airflow depends on the meteorological and topographical characteristics of that region.

The particle-in-cell model is a variable trajectory model based on the gradient-transport approach. In this model, "particles" representing the effluent mass are released in groups over the time period of interest. The particles move at the effective transport velocity of the windflow field into which the effluent is released. The effective velocity is determined by the mean and turbulent windflows within the field. The number of particles located at any given time in each cell (volume) of a fixed coordinate grid determines the effluent concentration. Concentration averages are determined from the total number of particles that pass through a cell during the time of interest.

The plume element models, another class of variable trajectory models, are based on the statistical approach to diffusion. These models approximate a continuous release by dividing a plume into a sufficient number of plume elements to represent a continuous plume. These elements are released at specified intervals and are tracked over the region of interest. The advective transport of these elements and the diffusion of the elements about their individual centers cause the dispersion of the plume effluent. Concentration averages are calculated by determining the contribution each element makes to the grid of points over which it passes.

b. Constant Mean Wind Direction Models

Constant mean wind direction models assume that a constant mean wind transports and diffuses effluents, within the entire region of interest, in the direction of airflow at the release point. A commonly used version of this model is the Gaussian straight-line trajectory model. In this model, the windspeed and atmospheric stability at the release point are assumed to determine the atmospheric dispersion characteristics in the direction of the mean wind at all distances.

These basic models can be modified to account for various modes of effluent release and for effluent removal mechanisms.

2. Release Mode

At ground-level locations beyond several miles from the plant, the annual average concentrations of effluents are essentially independent of the release mode; however, for ground-level concentrations within a few miles, the release mode is very important.

For a typical nuclear power plant, gaseous effluents released from tall stacks generally produce peak ground-level air concentrations near or beyond the site boundary; near-ground-level releases usually produce concentrations that monotonically decrease from the release point to all locations downwind. Under certain conditions, the effluent plume may become entrained in the aerodynamic wake of the building and mix rapidly down to ground level; under other conditions, the full effect of the elevation of the release may be realized.

Methods have been developed to estimate the effective release height for calculations of effluent concentrations at all downwind locations. The important parameters in these methods include the initial release height, the location of the release point in relation to obstructions, the size and shape of the release point, the initial vertical velocity of the effluent, the heat content of the effluent, ambient windspeed and temperature, and atmospheric stability.

For those effluents that are entrained into the aerodynamic wake of a building, mixing of the effluent into the wake is usually assumed. This mixing zone can constitute a plume with an initial cross section of one-half or more of the cross-sectional area of the building.

3. Removal Mechanisms

As the effluent travels from its release point, several mechanisms can work to reduce its concentration beyond that achieved by diffusion alone. Such removal mechanisms include radioactive decay and dry and wet deposition.

Radioactive decay is dependent on the half-life and the travel time of the radioactive effluent. All effluents can undergo dry deposition by sorption onto the ground surface; however, the dry deposition rate for noble gases, tritium, carbon-14, and nonelemental radioiodines is so slow that depletion is negligible within 50 miles of the release point. Elemental radioiodines and other particulates are much more readily deposited. The transfer of elemental radioiodines and particulates to a surface can be quantified as a transfer velocity (where concentration x transfer velocity = deposition rate). There is evidence that the transfer velocity is directly proportional to windspeed and, as a consequence, the rate of deposition is independent of windspeed since concentration in air is inversely proportional to windspeed.

Dry deposition is a continuous process while wet deposition only occurs during periods of precipitation. However, the dry removal process is not as efficient as the wet removal process. At most sites, precipitation occurs during a small percentage of the hours in a year so that, despite the greater efficiency of the wet removal process, dose calculations for long-term averages considering only dry deposition should not be significantly changed by the consideration of wet deposition. However, wet deposition can be a significant factor in dose calculations for releases from stacks at sites where a well-defined rainy season corresponds to the local grazing season.

Deposition of radionuclides over large bodies of water is not considered in this guide. Such deposition will be analyzed on a case-by-case basis.

C. REGULATORY POSITION

This section identifies types of atmospheric transport and diffusion models, source configuration and removal mechanism modifications, and input data that are acceptable to the NRC staff for use in providing assessments of potential annual radiation doses to the public resulting from routine releases of radioactive materials in gaseous effluents.

The listing of the atmospheric transport and diffusion models below is presented in order of decreasing model complexity and should not be construed as indicating the preference of any one type of model over another. The preferred model is that which best simulates atmospheric transport and diffusion in the region of interest from source to the receptor location, considering the meteorological characteristics of the region, the topography, the characteristics of the effluent source and the effluent as well as the receptor, the availability and representativeness of input data, the distance from source to receptor, and the ease of application.

Models proposed by the applicant and accepted by the NRC staff will be used by the staff in determining environmental technical specifications.

1. Atmospheric Transport and Diffusion Models

The following types of atmospheric transport and diffusion models can be modified for elevated sources and for effective area sources created when effluent is trapped in the building wake cavity in accordance with the source configuration considerations presented in regulatory position 2. Plume rise due to momentum or buoyancy effects can also be incorporated into the calculations. Radiological decay and dry and wet deposition, consistent with the guidelines presented in regulatory position 3, should also be considered.

a. Particle-in-Cell (PIC) Model

The basic equation for each "particle" group in this variable trajectory model, modified from Sklarew (Ref. 1), is:

$$\delta(\overline{\chi})/\delta t + \nabla \cdot V(\overline{\chi}) = 0 \quad (1)$$

where

t is the travel time;

V is the velocity vector for effective mean wind transport, which includes the mean flow component, $\overline{V}$, and the turbulent flow component, V', such that $V = \overline{V}+V'$; and

$(\overline{\chi})$ is the average atmospheric concentration produced by a group of particles.

Concentration averages for long time intervals are obtained by summing all "particles" passing through each grid cell during the period of interest.

The PIC model uses spatial and temporal variations of wind direction, windspeed, atmospheric stability, and topography as input parameters to define airflow and atmospheric diffusion rates. The representativeness of the input data determines the accuracy of estimates (i.e., fewer data acquisition locations tend to increase the uncertainty of the estimates); therefore, detailed discussion of the applicability and accuracy of the model and input data used should be provided.

b. Plume Element Models

In these types of models, the transport and dispersion of an effluent plume are determined by using a horizontal wind field that can vary in time and space. The diffusion of individual plume elements, according to Gifford (Ref. 2), can be determined from the general Gaussian diffusion model. Commonly used plume segment elements are vertical "disk" segments and three-dimensional "puffs." In using the "puff" version, if it is assumed that the plume spread within a puff along the direction of flow is equal to the spread in the lateral direction, the "disk segment" and "puff" versions of this model would be expected to yield similar results.

An equation for a "puff" version of a fluctuating plume model, as presented by Start and Wendel (Ref. 3), is:

$$\chi/Q = 2[(2\pi)^{3/2}\sigma_H^2\sigma_z]^{-1}\exp[-1/2(r^2/\sigma_H^2 + h_e^2/\sigma_z^2)] \quad (2)$$

where

$$r^2 = (x - \bar{u}t)^2 + y^2 \text{ and}$$

$$\sigma_H = \sigma_y = \sigma_x$$

and where

h_e is the effective release height;

Q is the effluent emission over the time interval;

t is the travel time;

$\bar{u}$ is the mean windspeed at the height of the effective release point;

x is the distance from center of puff along the direction of flow;

y is the distance from center of puff in the crossflow direction;

σ_x is the plume spread along the direction of flow;

σ_y is the lateral plume spread;

σ_z is the vertical plume spread; and

χ is the atmospheric concentration of effluent in a puff at ground level and at distance x from the puff center.

Concentration averages for long time intervals should be calculated by summing the concentrations of individual elements for the grid of points over which they pass.

The number of elements and the plume spread parameters (σ_x, σ_y, and σ_z) should be selected such that the resulting concentration estimate is representative of the concentration from a continuous point source release. Elements should be followed in the computational scheme until they are beyond the region of interest or until their peak concentration falls below a specified value.

The plume segment model uses spatial and temporal variations of wind direction, windspeed, and atmospheric stability as input parameters to define the transport and diffusion rate of each element. The effectiveness of the meteorological input data in defining atmospheric transport and diffusion conditions is dependent on the representativeness of these data and the complexity of the topography in the site region; therefore, a detailed discussion of the applicability and accuracy of the model and input data used should be provided.

c. Constant Mean Wind Direction Models

The equation for this model, as presented by Sagendorf (Ref. 4), is:

$$(\overline{\chi/Q'})_D = 2.032 \sum_{ij} n_{ij}[N X \bar{u}_i \Sigma_{zj}(X)]^{-1} \exp[-h_e^2/2\sigma_{zj}^2(X)] \quad (3)$$

where

h_e is the effective release height (see regulatory position 2);

n_{ij} is the length of time (hours of valid data) weather conditions are observed to be at a given wind direction, windspeed class, i, and atmospheric stability class, j;

N is the total hours of valid data;

$\bar{u}_i$ is the midpoint of windspeed class, i, at a height representative of release;

X is the distance downwind of the source;

$\sigma_{zj}(X)$ is the vertical plume spread without volumetric correction at distance, X, for stability class, j (see Figure 1);

$\Sigma_{zj}(X)$ is the vertical plume spread with a volumetric correction (see regulatory position 2.c) for a release within the building wake cavity, at a distance, X, for stability class, j; otherwise $\Sigma_{zj}(X) = \sigma_{zj}(X)$;

$(\overline{\chi/Q'})_D$ is the average effluent concentration, χ, normalized by source strength, Q', at distance, X, in a given downwind direction, D; and

2.032 is $(2/\pi)^{1/2}$ divided by the width in radians of a 22.5° sector.

Effects of spatial and temporal variations in airflow in the region of the site are not described by the constant mean wind direction model. Unlike the variable trajectory models, the constant mean wind direction model can only use meteorological data from a single station to represent diffusion conditions within the region of interest. For Appendix I considerations, the region of interest can extend to a distance of 50 miles from the site. Therefore, if the constant mean wind direction model is to be used, airflow characteristics in the vicinity of any site should be examined to determine the spatial and temporal variations of atmospheric transport and diffusion conditions and the applicability of single station meteorological data to represent:

(1) Conditions between the site and the nearest receptors (generally within 5 miles) and

(2) Conditions out to a distance of 50 miles from the site.

Examples of spatial and temporal variations of airflow to consider for three basic categories of topography are:

(1) At inland sites in open terrain, including gently rolling hills, with airflow dominated almost entirely by large-scale weather patterns, recirculation of airflow and directional biases during periods of prolonged atmospheric stagnation;

(2) At sites in pronounced river valleys, with airflow patterns largely dominated by terrain, restrictions to lateral and vertical spread of the effluent plume, and the diurnal distributions of downvalley and upvalley circulation, with particular attention to the period of flow reversal; and

(3) At sites along and near coasts of large bodies of water, with significant land-water boundary layer effects on airflow, sea (or lake) land breeze circulation (including

distance of penetration, vertical development, temporal variations of wind direction, and conditions during periods of flow reversal), variation of the mixing layer height with time and distance from the shore (e.g., fumigation and plume trapping), and the effects of shoreline bluffs and dunes.

Therefore, adjustments to Equation (3) may be necessary to prevent misrepresentation of actual atmospheric transport and diffusion characteristics that could result in substantial underestimates of actual exposure to an individual or population. Adjustments to Equation (3) should be based on data (e.g., comparison to other sites in the region) or studies that characterize airflow patterns in the region of the site out to a distance of 50 miles.

For all sites, a detailed discussion of the applicability and accuracy of the model and input data should be provided. Use of Equation (3) will be acceptable only if a well-documented and substantiated discussion of the effects of spatial and temporal variations in airflow in the region of the site out to a distance of 50 miles is provided.

2. Source Configuration Considerations

The actual height above ground of the gaseous effluent plume should be considered in making estimates of average effluent concentrations downwind from the release points. An acceptable method to determine the effective plume height is described below. In addition, for effluent plumes traversing irregular terrain under stable or neutral atmospheric conditions, the model described by Egan (Ref. 5) may be used. On the other hand, the model described by Burt (Ref. 6) may be used when stable atmospheric conditions exist.

Source configuration evaluations may consider the effluent release point(s) and adjacent or nearby solid structure(s) in conjunction with the individual direction sector (as described in regulatory position 4) in which the downwind receptor of interest is located.

a. Elevated Releases

For effluents exhausted from release points that are higher than twice the height of adjacent solid structures, the effective release height (h_e) is determined (Ref. 4) from:

$$h_e = h_s + h_{pr} - h_t - c \qquad (4)$$

where

- c is the correction for low relative exit velocity (see below);
- h_e is the effective release height;
- h_{pr} is the rise of the plume above the release point, according to Sagendorf (Ref. 4), whose treatment is based on Briggs (Ref. 7);
- h_s is the physical height of the release point (the elevation of the stack base should be assumed to be zero); and
- h_t is the maximum terrain height (above the stack base) between the release point and the point for which the calculation is made (h_t must be greater than or equal to zero).

Note that the effective release height is a function of the distance between the release point and the location where the concentration is being calculated.

When the vertical exit velocity is less than 1.5 times the horizontal windspeed, a correction for downwash is subtracted from Equation (4), according to Gifford (Ref. 8):

$$c = 3(1.5 - W_0/\bar{u})d \qquad (5)$$

where

- c is the downwash correction;
- d is the inside diameter of the stack or other release point;
- $\bar{u}$ is the mean windspeed at the height of release; and
- W_0 is the vertical exit velocity of the plume.

b. Releases Other Than Elevated

For effluents released from points less than the height of adjacent solid structures, a ground-level release should be assumed ($h_e = 0$).

For effluents released from vents or other points at the level of or above adjacent solid structures, but lower than elevated release points, the effluent plume should be considered as an elevated release whenever the vertical exit velocity of the plume, W_o, is at least five times the horizontal windspeed, $\bar{u}$, at the height of release; i.e., as modified from Johnson et al. (Ref. 9):

$$W_o/\bar{u} \geq 5.0 \tag{6}$$

In this case, the release should be evaluated as described in regulatory position 2.a.

If $W_o/\bar{u}$ is less than 1.0 or unknown, a ground-level release should be assumed ($h_e = 0$)

For cases where the ratio of plume exit velocity to horizontal windspeed is between one and five, a mixed release mode should be assumed, in which the plume is considered as an elevated release during a part of the time and as a ground-level release ($h_e = 0$) during the remainder of the time. An entrainment coefficient, E_t, modified from Reference 9, is determined for those cases in which $W_o/\bar{u}$ is between one and five:

$$E_t = 2.58 - 1.58(W_o/\bar{u}) \text{ for } 1 < W_o/\bar{u} \leq 1.5 \tag{7}$$

and

$$E_t = 0.3 - 0.06(W_o/\bar{u}) \text{ for } 1.5 < W_o/\bar{u} \leq 5.0 \tag{8}$$

The release should be considered to occur as an elevated release $100(1 - E_t)$ percent of the time and as a ground release $100E_t$ percent of the time. Each of these cases should then be evaluated separately and the concentration calculated according to the fraction of time each type of release occurs. Windspeeds representative of conditions at the actual release heights should be used for the times when the release is considered to be elevated. Windspeeds measured at the 10-meter level should be used for those times when the effluent plume is considered to be a ground release. If Equation (3) is used, the adjustment described in regulatory position 2.c may be made for the ground release portion of the calculation.

c. Building Wake Correction

For ground-level releases only ($h_e = 0$), an adjustment may be made in Equation (3) that takes into consideration initial mixing of the effluent plume within the building wake. This adjustment, according to Yanskey et al. (Ref. 10), should be in the form of:

$$\Sigma_{zj}(X) = (\sigma_{zj}^2(X) + 0.5D_z^2/\pi)^{1/2} \leq \sqrt{3}\sigma_{zj}(X) \tag{9}$$

where

D_z is the maximum adjacent building height either up- or downwind from the release point;

X is the distance from the release point to the receptor, measured from the lee edge of the complex of adjacent buildings;

$\sigma_{zj}(X)$ is the vertical standard deviation of the materials in the plume at distance, X, for atmospheric stability class, j; and

$\Sigma_{zj}(X)$ is the vertical standard deviation of plume material as above, with the correction for additional dispersion within the building wake cavity, restricted by the condition that

$$\Sigma_{zj}(X) = \sqrt{3}\sigma_{zj}(X)$$

when

$$(\sigma_{zj}^2(X) + 0.5D_z^2/\pi)^{1/2} > \sqrt{3}\sigma_{zj}(X).$$

3. Removal Mechanism Considerations

Radioactive decay and dry and wet deposition should be considered in radiological impact evaluations. Acceptable methods of considering these removal mechanisms are described below.

a. Radioactive Decay

For conservative estimates of radioactive decay, an overall half-life of 2.26 days is acceptable for short-lived noble gases and of 8 days for all iodines released to the atmosphere. Alternatively, the actual half-life of each radionuclide may be used. The decay time used should be the calculated time of travel between the source and receptor based on the airflow model used.

b. Dry Deposition

Dry deposition of elemental radioiodines and other particulates and attendant plume depletion should be considered for all releases.

Acceptable plume depletion correction factors and relative deposition rates are presented in Figures 2 through 9. These figures are based on measurements of deposition velocity as a function of windspeed as presented in Reference 11 and on a diffusion-deposition model as presented in Reference 12.

Figures 2 through 5 illustrate an acceptable method for considering plume depletion effects for all distances from the source and atmospheric stability classes for ground and elevated release modes. After a given concentration is calculated by using the models in regulatory position 1, the concentration should be corrected by multiplying by the fraction remaining in the plume, as determined from these figures.

Figures 6 through 9 show acceptable values of relative deposition rate (meters^{-1}) as a function of distance from the source and atmospheric stability for ground and elevated release modes. The relative deposition rate is the deposition rate per unit downwind distance (Ci/sec per meter) divided by the source strength (Ci/sec).

To obtain the relative deposition per unit area (meters^{-2}) at a given point in a given sector, the relative deposition rate must be (1) multiplied by the fraction of the release transported into the sector, determined according to the distribution of wind direction and (2) divided by an appropriate crosswind distance (meters), as discussed below.

Figures 6 through 9 are based on the assumption that the effluent concentration in a given sector is uniform across the sector at a given distance. Therefore, for the straight-line trajectory model, or for any model that assumes uniform concentration across the sector at a given distance, the relative deposition rate should be divided by the arc length of the sector at the point being considered. In addition, for the straight-line trajectory model, the relative deposition rate should be multiplied by the appropriate correction factor discussed in regulatory position 1.c.

For models where concentration at a given distance is not uniform across the sector, the relative deposition at a given point should be calculated as above, but then multiplied by the ratio of the maximum effluent concentration in the sector at the distance being considered to the average concentration across the sector at the same distance.

c. Wet Deposition

For long-term averages, dose calculations considering dry deposition only are not usually changed significantly by the consideration of wet deposition. However, the effects of wet deposition and attendant plume depletion should be considered for plants with predominantly elevated releases and at sites that have a well-defined rainy season corresponding to the grazing season. Consideration of wet deposition effects should include examination of total precipitation, number of hours of precipitation, rainfall rate distributions, and the precipitation wind rose. If the precipitation data indicate that wet deposition may be significant, washout rates and attendant plume depletion should be calculated in accordance with the relationships identified by Engelmann (Ref. 13).

d. Deposition Over Water

For dispersion over small bodies of water, deposition may be assumed to occur at the same rate as over land. For calculations involving radionuclide transport over large bodies of water, deposition should be considered on a case-by-case basis.

4. Meteorological Data for Models

Sufficient meteorological information should be obtained to characterize transport processes (i.e., airflow trajectory, diffusion conditions, deposition characteristics) out to a distance of 50 miles (approximately 80,000 meters) from the plant. The primary source of meteorological information should be the onsite meteorological program (see Regulatory Guide 1.23, Ref. 14). Other sources should include nearby National Weather Service (NWS) stations, other well-maintained meteorological facilities (e.g., other nuclear facilities, universities, or private meteorological programs), and satellite facilities.

Adequate characterization of transport processes within 50 miles of the plant may include examination of meteorological data from stations further than 50 miles when this information can provide additional clarification of the mesoscale transport processes. To augment the assessment of atmospheric transport to distances of 50 miles from the plant, the following regional meteorological data, based on periods of record specified in Regulatory Guide 4.2 (Ref. 15), from as many relevant stations as practicable should be used:

a. Windspeed

b. Wind direction

c. Atmospheric stability

d. Mixing height

e. Precipitation

For input to variable trajectory atmospheric transport models, measured hourly values of windspeed should be used. Calms* should be assigned a windspeed of one-half of the appropriate starting speed, as described in the footnote, for instruments conforming to the recommendations or intent of Regulatory Guide 1.23 (Ref. 14). Otherwise, a windspeed of 0.1 meter/second should be assigned to calms. Hourly wind directions should be classed into at least the 16 compass point sectors (i.e., 22.5-degree sectors, centered on true north, north-northeast, etc.) according to measured values averaged over the time interval.

For input to the constant mean wind direction model, windspeed data should be presented as (1) hourly measured values or (2) windspeed classes divided in accordance with the Beaufort wind scale or other suitable class division (e.g., a greater number of light windspeed classes should be used for sites with high frequencies of light winds). Wind directions should be divided into the 16 compass directions (22.5-degree sectors, centered on true north, north-northeast, etc.). If joint frequency distributions of wind direction and speed by atmospheric stability class, rather than hourly values, are used in this model, calms* should be assigned to wind directions in proportion to the directional distribution within an atmospheric stability class of the lowest noncalm windspeed class. If hourly data are used, calms should be assigned to the recorded wind direction averaged over the time interval. The windspeed to be assumed for calms is one-half of the starting speed of the vane or anemometer, whichever is higher, for instruments conforming to the recommendations or intent of Regulatory Guide 1.23. Otherwise, the windspeed to be assumed for calms is 0.1 meter/second.

Atmospheric stability should be determined by vertical temperature difference (ΔT) between the release point and the 10-meter level, or by other well-documented parameters that have been substantiated by diffusion data. Acceptable stability classes are given in Reference 14.

Appropriate time periods for meteorological data utilization should be based on constancy of the source term (rate of release) and potential availability of the receptor (e.g., man or cow). If emissions are continuous, annual data summaries should be used. If releases are intermittent, consideration should be given to frequency and duration of release. If emissions are

---

*Calms are defined as hourly average windspeeds below the starting speed of the vane or anemometer, whichever is higher.

infrequent and of short duration, atmospheric dispersion models and meteorological data applicable to the time of release should be considered. Use of annual average conditions for consideration of intermittent releases will be acceptable only if it is established that releases will be random in time. Otherwise the method of evaluation of intermittent releases should follow the methodology outlined in Section 2.3.4 of NUREG-75/087 (Ref. 16). This method uses an appropriate χ/Q probability level, as well as the annual average χ/Q, for the direction and point of interest being evaluated to provide the basis for adjustments reflecting more adverse diffusion conditions than indicated by the annual average. These adjustments are applied to the annual average χ/Q and D/Q for the total number of hours associated with intermittent releases per year. Detailed information for this calculation is given by Sagendorf and Goll (Ref. 17). However, if intermittent releases are limited by technical specifications to periods when atmospheric conditions are more favorable than average for the site, annual average data and annual average dispersion models could be used. For calculations of doses through ingestion pathways, particularly through the cow-milk pathway, meteorological data for only the grazing or growing season should be used.

D. IMPLEMENTATION

The purpose of this section is to provide information to license applicants and licensees regarding the NRC staff's plans for implementing this regulatory guide.

This guide reflects current NRC staff practice. Therefore, except in those cases in which the license applicant or licensee proposes an acceptable alternative method, the method described herein for complying with specified portions of the Commission's regulations will continue to be used in the evaluation of submittals for operating license or construction permit applications until this guide is revised as a result of suggestions from the public or additional staff review.

REFERENCES

1. R. C. Sklarew et al., "A Particle-in-Cell Method for Numerical Solution of the Atmospheric Diffusion Equation and Applications to Air Pollution Problems," Final Report 3SR-844, Vol. 1, EPA Contract 68-02-0006, 1971.

2. F. A. Gifford, "Statistical Properties of a Fluctuating Plume Dispersion Model," in Advances in Geophysics, Vol. 6, F. N. Frankiel and P. A. Sheppard, Editors, Academic Press, Inc., New York, pp. 117-138, 1959.

3. G. E. Start and L. L. Wendell, "Regional Effluent Dispersion Calculations Considering Spatial and Temporal Meteorological Variations," NOAA Tech Memo ERL-ARL-44, 1974.

4. J. F. Sagendorf, "A Program for Evaluating Atmospheric Dispersion From a Nuclear Power Station," NOAA Tech Memo ERL-ARL-42, 1974.

5. B. A. Egan, "Turbulent Diffusion in Complex Terrain" in Lectures on Air Pollution and Environmental Impact Analyses - AMS Workshop on Meteorology and Environmental Assessment, Boston 1975, Dwayne Haugen, Workshop Coordinator, American Meteorological Society, Boston, MA, pp. 123-124, 1975.

6. E. W. Burt, "Description of Valley Model-Version C9M3D," U.S. Environmental Protection Agency Dispersion Program, available from the United States Environmental Protection Agency, Office of Air Quality Planning and Standards, Research Triangle Park, NC 27711, pp. 4-6.

7. G. A. Briggs, "Plume Rise," AEC Critical Review Series, TID-25075, 1969.

8. F. A. Gifford, "Atmospheric Transport and Dispersion Over Cities," Nuclear Safety, Vol. 13, pp. 391-402, Sept.-Oct. 1972.

9. W. B. Johnson et al., "Gas Tracer Study of Roof-Vent Effluent Diffusion at Millstone Nuclear Power Station," AIF/NESP-007b, Atomic Industrial Forum, Inc., 1975.

10. G. R. Yanskey et al., "Climatography of National Reactor Testing Station," Idaho Operations Office, USAEC, IDO-12048, 1966.

11. E. H. Markee, Jr., "A Parametric Study of Gaseous Plume Depletion by Ground Surface Adsorption," in Proceedings of USAEC Meteorological Information Meeting, C. A. Mawson, Editor, AECL-2787, pp. 602-613, 1967.

12. C. A. Pelletier and J. D. Zimbrick, "Kinetics of Environmental Radioiodine Transport Through the Milk-Food Chain," in Environmental Surveillance in the Vicinity of Nuclear Facilities, W. C. Reinig, Editor, Charles C. Thomas Publishers, Springfield, Ill., 1970.

13. R. J. Englemann, "The Calculation of Precipitation Scavenging," in Meteorology and Atomic Energy-1968, D. H. Slade, Editor, USAEC TID-24190, pp. 208-221, 1968.

14. Regulatory Guide 1.23 (Safety Guide 23), "Onsite Meteorological Programs," U. S. Nuclear Regulatory Commission, Washington, D.C.

15. Regulatory Guide 4.2, "Preparation of Environmental Reports for Nuclear Power Stations," U.S. Nuclear Regulatory Commission, Washington, D.C.

16. "Standard Review Plan for the Review of Safety Analysis Reports for Nuclear Power Plants," NUREG-75/087, September 1975, Office of Nuclear Reactor Regulation, U.S. Nuclear Regulatory Commission, Washington, D.C.

17. J. Sagendorf and J. Goll, "XOQDOQ-Program for the Meteorological Evaluation of Routine Effluent Releases at Nuclear Power Stations," Draft, U.S. Nuclear Regulatory Commission, Washington, D.C., 1976.

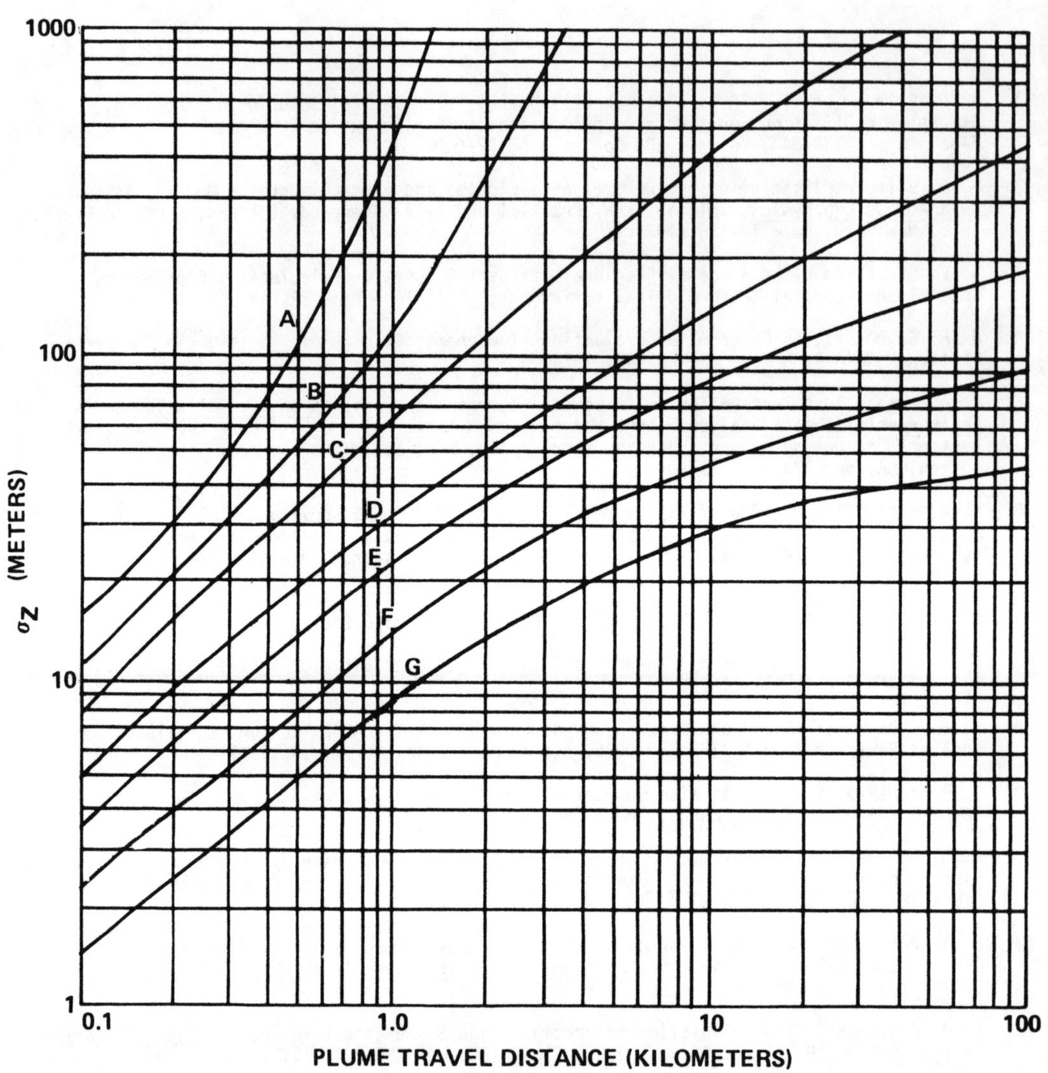

Figure 1. Vertical Standard Deviation of Material in a Plume (Letters denote Pasquill Stability Class)

NOTE: THESE ARE STANDARD RELATIONSHIPS AND MAY HAVE TO BE MODIFIED FOR CERTAIN TYPES OF TERRAIN AND/OR CLIMATIC CONDITIONS (E.G., VALLEY, DESERT, OVER WATER).

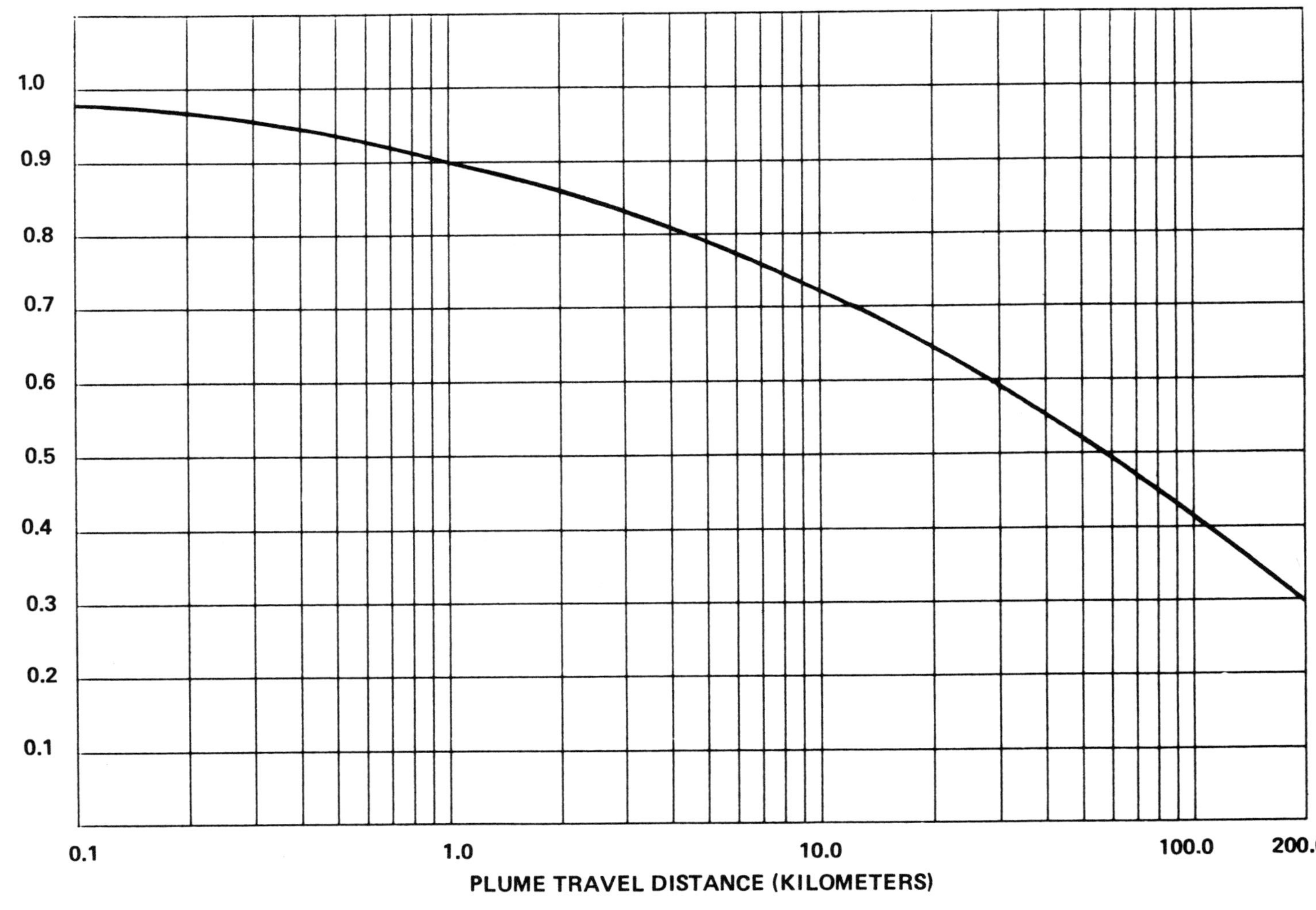

Figure 2. Plume Depletion Effect for Ground-Level Releases (All Atmospheric Stability Classes)

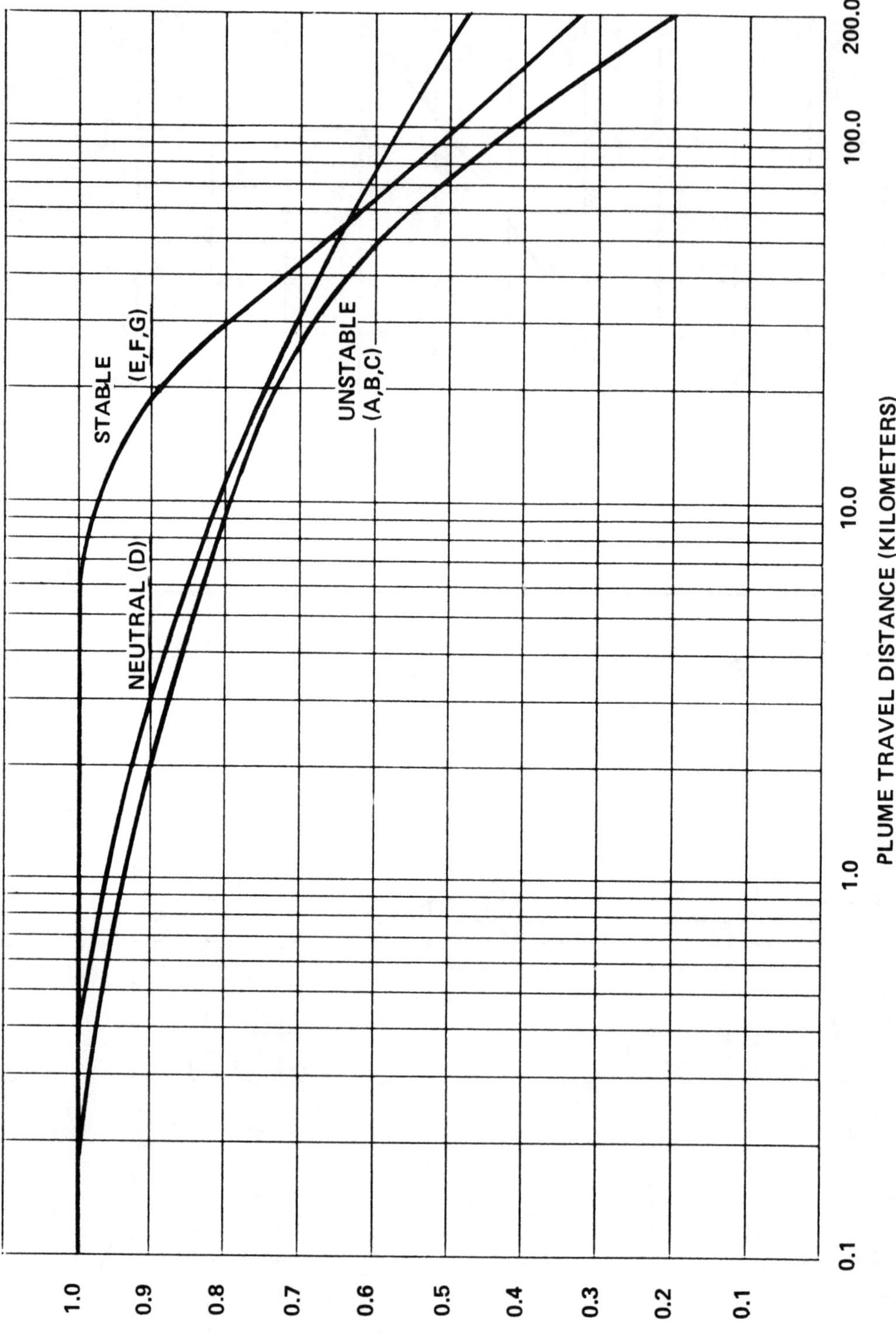

Figure 3. Plume Depletion Effect for 30-m Releases (Letters denote Pasquill Stability Class)

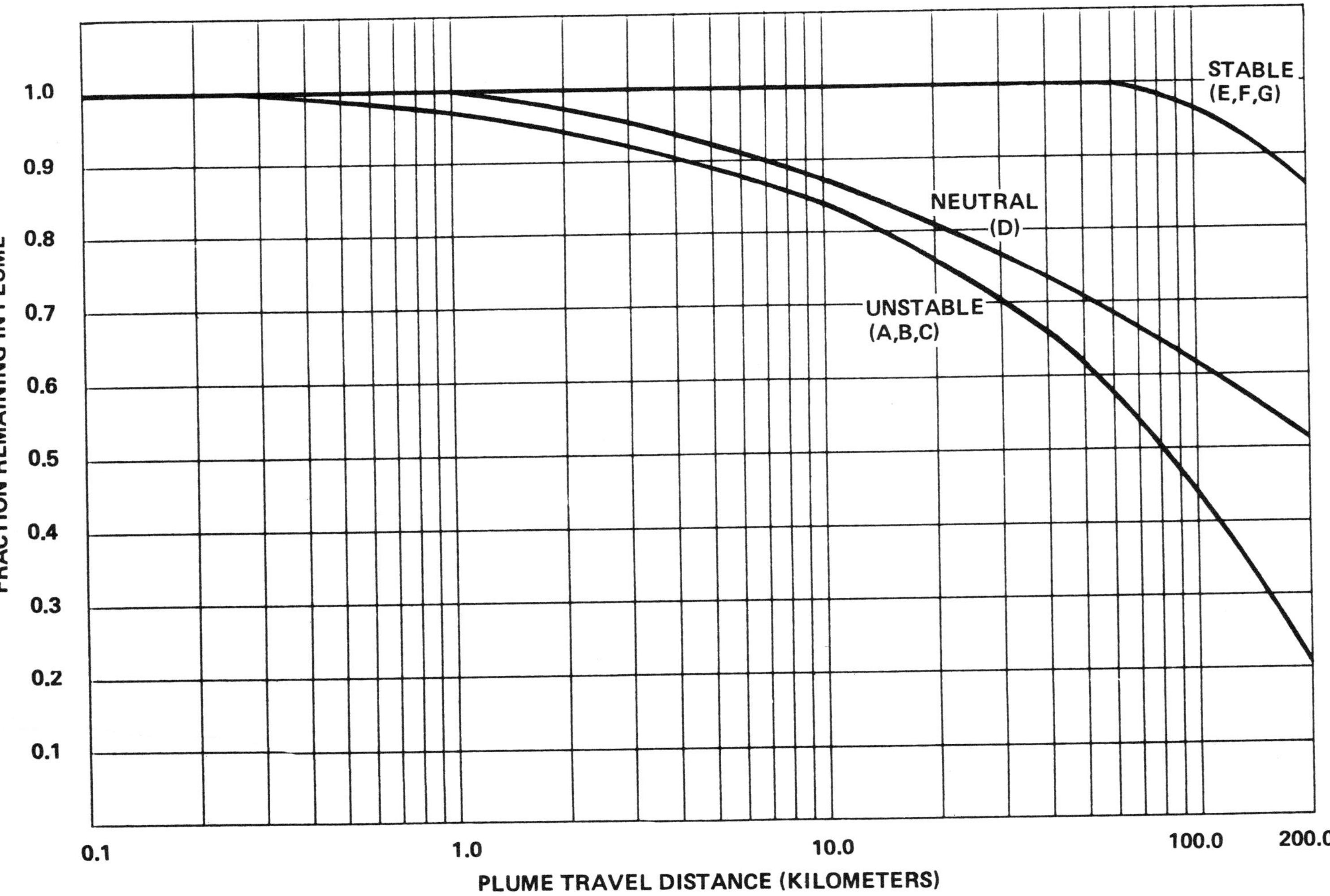

Figure 4. Plume Depletion Effect for 60-m Releases (Letters denote Pasquill Stability Class)

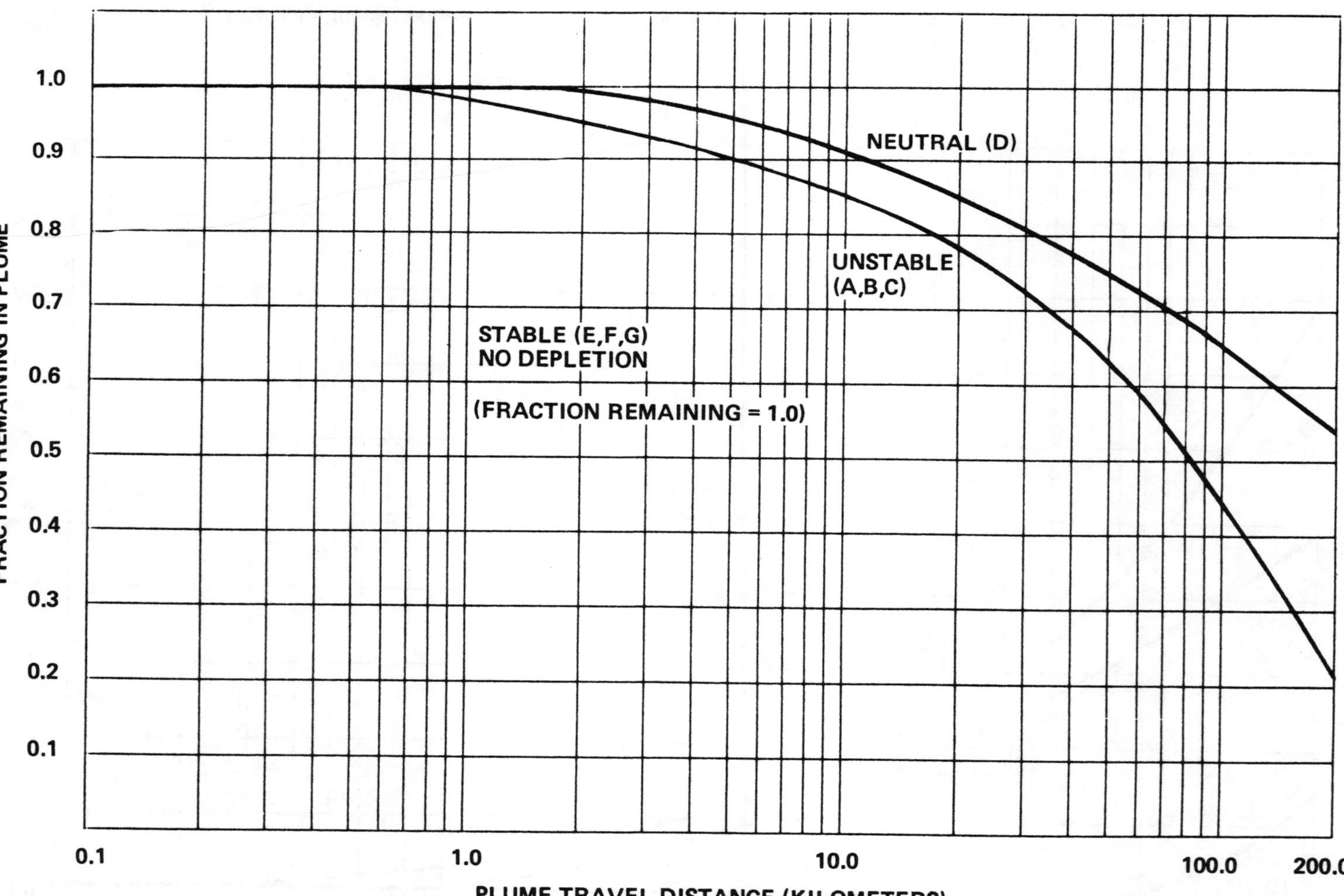

Figure 5. Plume Depletion Effect for 100-m Releases (Letters denote Pasquill Stability Class)

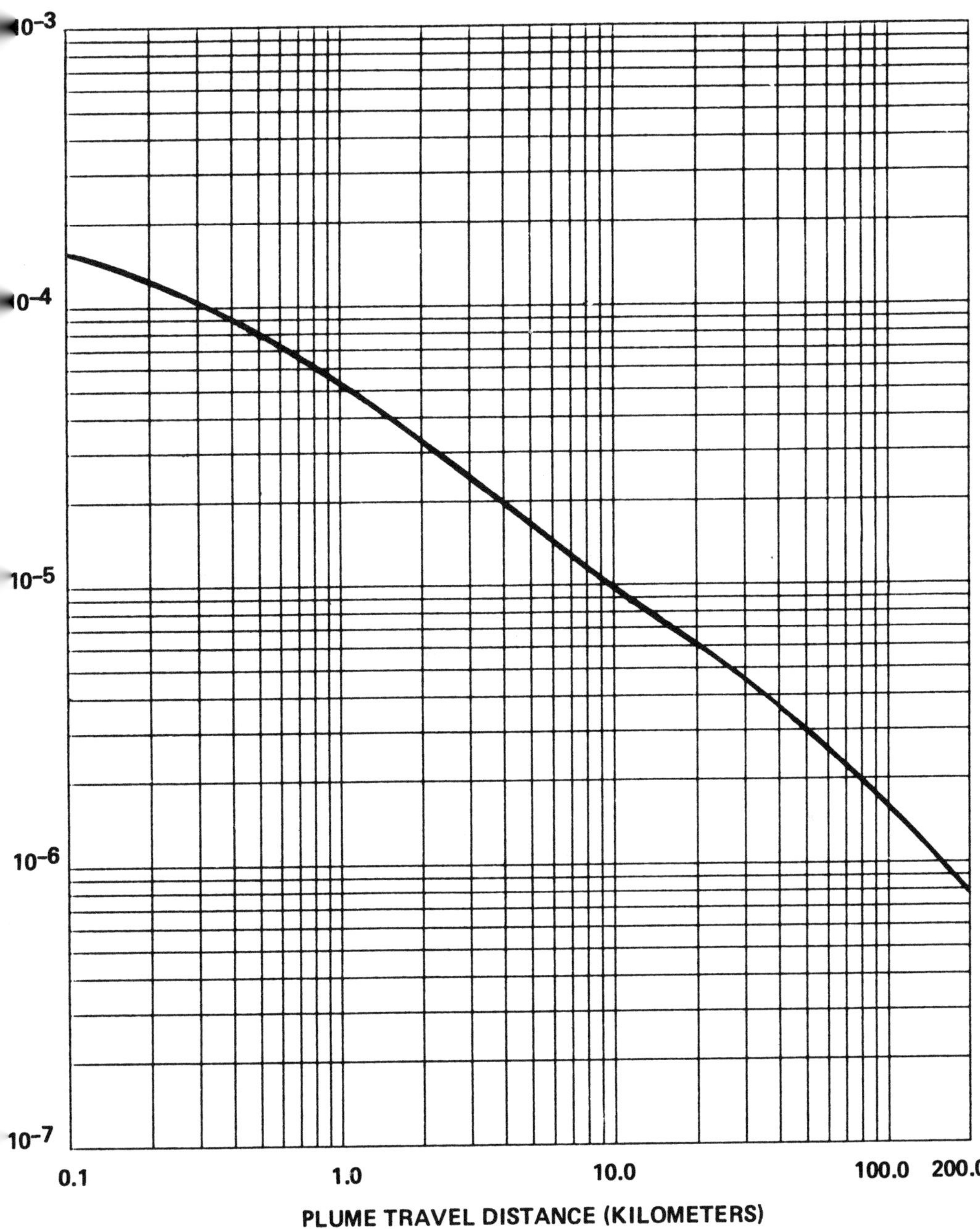

Figure 6. Relative Deposition for Ground-Level Releases (All Atmospheric Stability Classes)

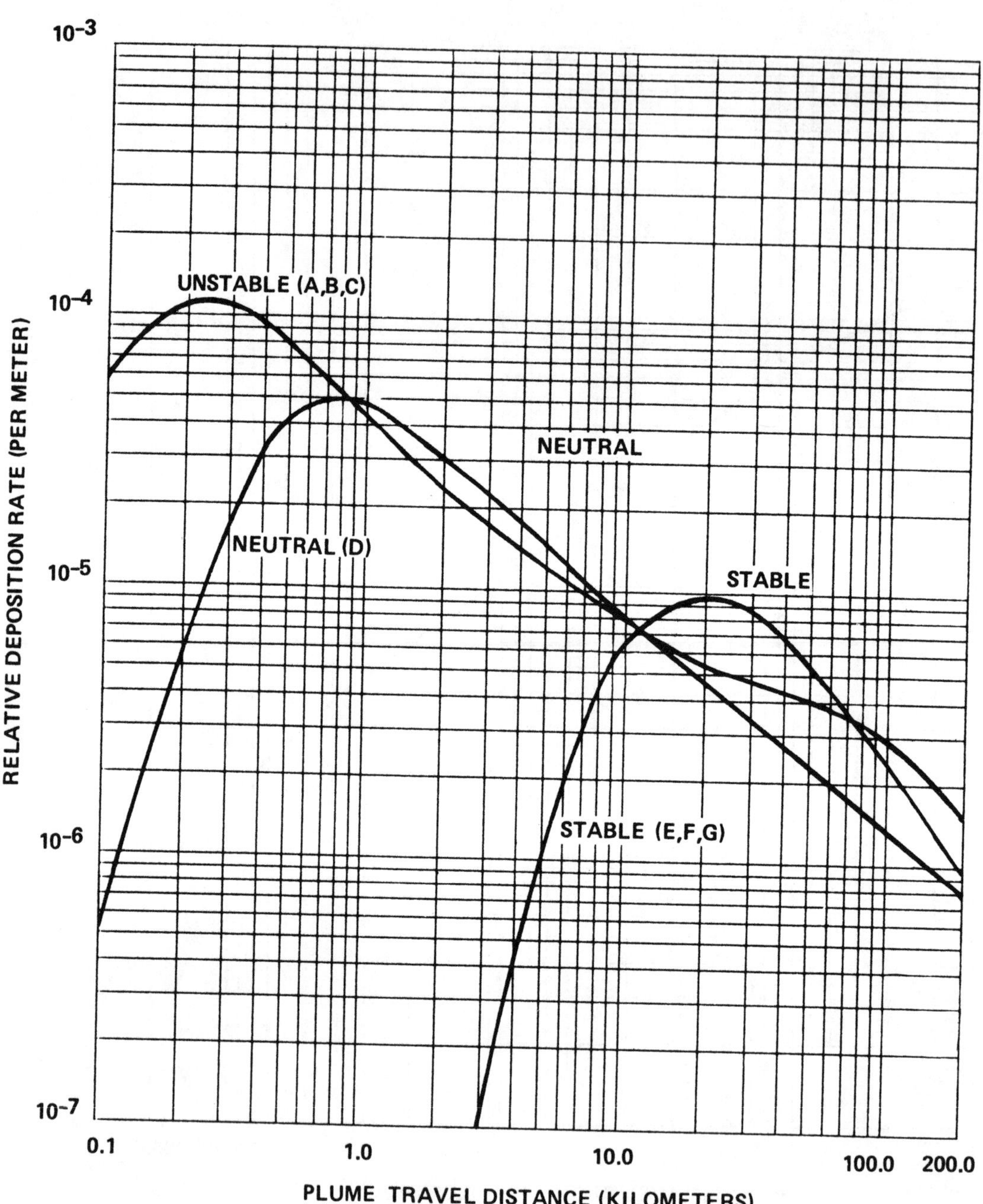

Figure 7. Relative Deposition for 30-m Releases (Letters denote Pasquill Stability Class)

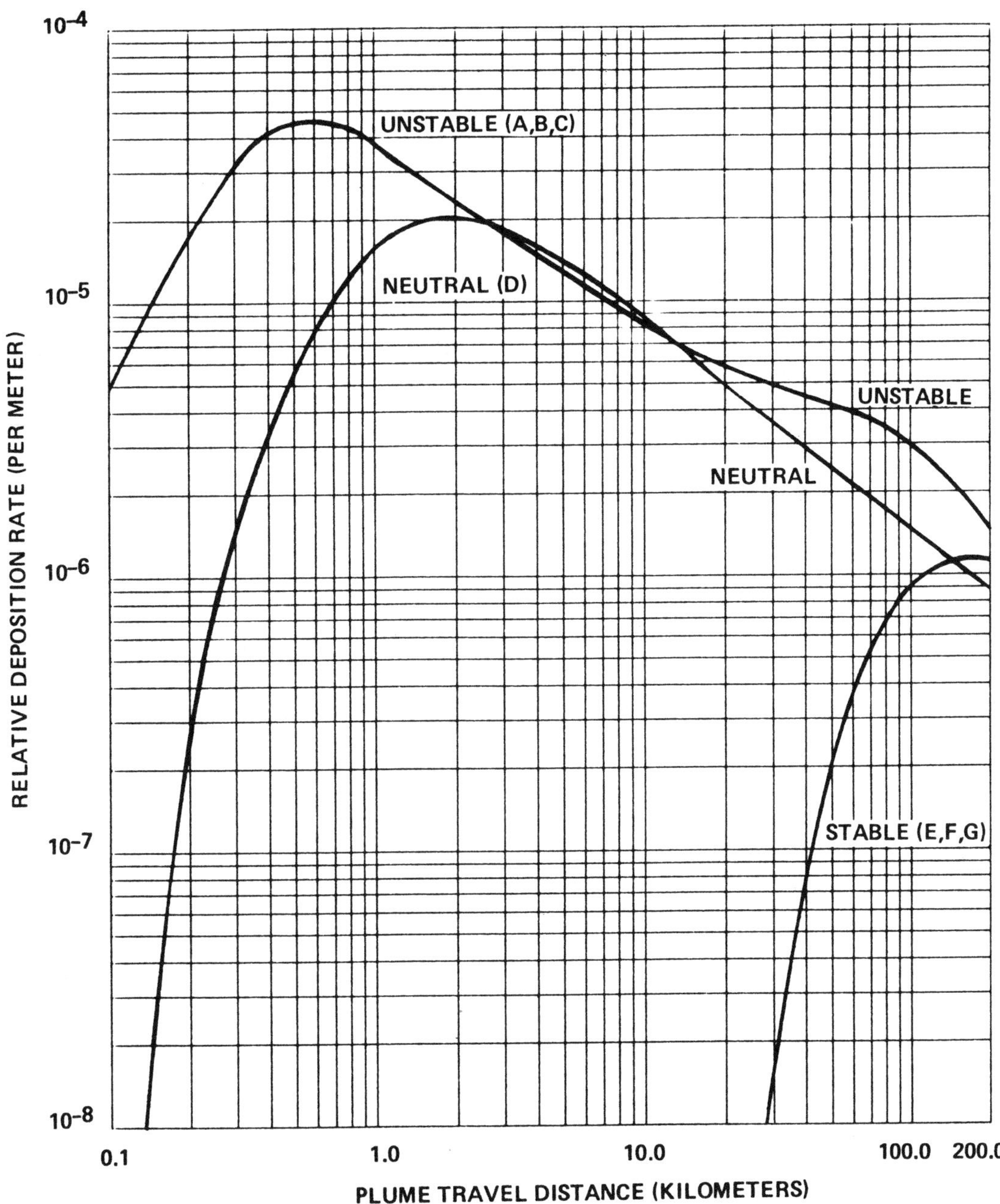

Figure 8. Relative Deposition for 60-m Releases (Letters denote Pasquill Stability Class)

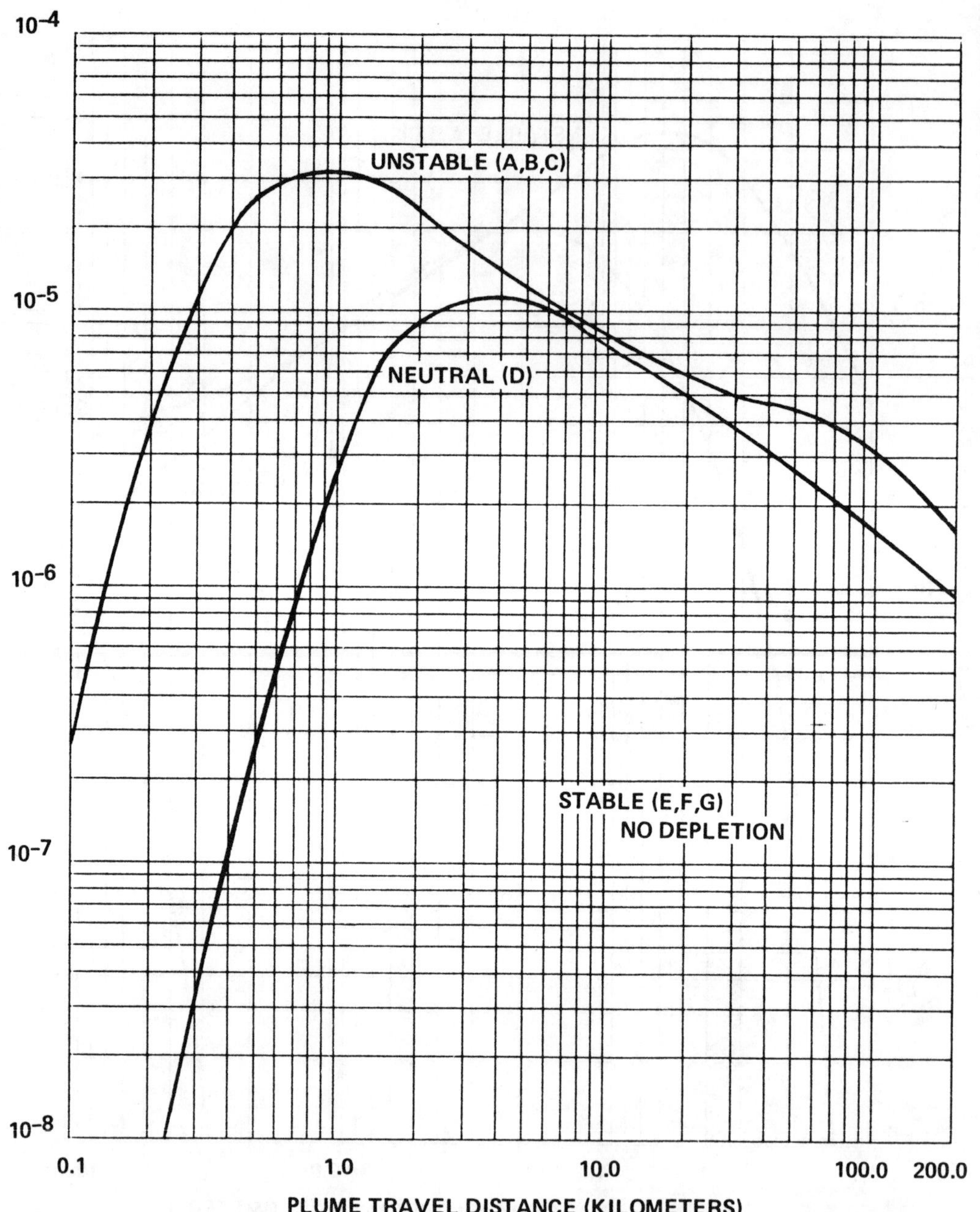

Figure 9. Relative Deposition for 100-m Releases (Letters denote Pasquill Stability Class)

APPENDIX III

ESTIMATING AQUATIC DISPERSION OF EFFLUENTS FROM ACCIDENTAL AND ROUTINE REACTOR RELEASES FOR THE PURPOSE OF IMPLEMENTING APPENDIX I†

A. INTRODUCTION

Section 20.106, "Radioactivity in Effluents to Unrestricted Areas," of the Commission's regulations in 10 CFR Part 20, "Standards for Protection Against Radiation," establishes limits on concentrations of radioactive material in effluents to unrestricted areas. Paragraph 20.1(c) of 10 CFR Part 20 states that, in addition to complying with the limits set forth in that part, licensees should make every reasonable effort to maintain releases of radioactive materials in effluents to unrestricted areas as far below the limits specified as is reasonably achievable (ALARA).

Section 50.34a, "Design Objectives for Equipment to Control Releases of Radioactive Material in Effluents - Nuclear Power Reactors," of 10 CFR Part 50, "Licensing of Production and Utilization Facilities," sets forth design objectives for equipment to control releases of radioactive effluents from light-water-cooled nuclear power reactors. Section 50.36a, "Technical Specifications on Effluents from Nuclear Reactors," of 10 CFR Part 50 further provides that, in order to keep power reactor effluent releases as low as is reasonably achievable, each operating license will include technical specifications on effluent discharge limits, operating procedures for installation, use, and maintenance of effluent control equipment, and requirements for reporting measured releases of radionuclides to the environment.

Appendix I, "Numerical Guides for Design Objectives and Limiting Conditions for Operation to Meet the Criterion 'As Low As Is Reasonably Achievable' for Radioactive Material in Light-Water-Cooled Nuclear Power Reactor Effluents," to 10 CFR Part 50 provides numerical guidance for radioactive effluent design objectives and technical specification requirements for limiting conditions of operation for light-water-cooled nuclear power plants.

To implement Appendix I, the staff has developed a series of guides that present methods acceptable to the staff for calculating preoperational estimates of effluent releases, dispersion of the effluent in the atmosphere and different water bodies, and the associated radiation doses* to man. This guide describes basic features of calculational models and suggests methods of determining values of model parameters for the estimation of aquatic dispersion of both routine and accidental releases of liquid effluents. The methods described herein are general approaches that the NRC staff has adopted for the analysis of routine and accidental releases into various types of surface water bodies. Models for the ground-water pathway are not covered in this guide. Those few cases where the ground-water pathway makes a significant contribution to the dose estimates will be analyzed on a case-by-case basis. Standards for analysis of releases to ground water are currently being developed by the American Nuclear Society and will be published by the American National Standards Institute.

B. DISCUSSION

Radioactive material in aqueous effluents may be released from nuclear power stations, either routinely or accidentally, into a variety of receiving surface water bodies, including nontidal rivers, lakes, reservoirs, cooling ponds, estuaries, and open coastal waters. This material is dispersed by turbulent mixing and by streamflow in rivers, by tidal or nontidal coastal currents in estuaries and coastal waters, and by internal circulation or flow-through in lakes, reservoirs, and cooling ponds. Parameters influencing the dispersion patterns and concentration reduction near a site include the direction and speed of flow of currents, both natural and plant-induced, in the receiving water; the intensity of turbulent mixing; the size, geometry, and bottom topography of the water body; the location of effluent discharge in relation to the receiving water surface and shoreline; the amount of recirculation of previously discharged effluent; the characteristics of suspended and bottom sediments; the sediment sorption properties; and radioactive decay.

This guide describes calculational models acceptable to the NRC staff for estimating aquatic dispersion of routine or accidental releases of radioactive material from a nuclear power station to a surface water body. The models discussed include both simplified models having straightforward analytical solutions and more complex models requiring numerical solution. In general,

*In this guide, the term "dose," when applied to individuals, is used instead of the more precise term, "dose equivalent," as defined by the International Commission on Radiological Units and Measurements (ICRUM).

† Regulatory Guide 1.113, Office of Standards Development, U. S. Nuclear Regulatory Commission, Washington, D.C., Rev. 1, April 1977.

the modeling techniques discussed represent adaptations of work currently available in the literature. Because of increasing environmental concerns during the past decade, considerable effort has been expended in advancing the state of the art of water quality simulation and thermal plume modeling. The models discussed herein draw heavily from this body of information.

Although specific models are considered, they are intended to represent specific classes of models. Furthermore, discussions of particular techniques for determining model parameters are intended to provide guidance and to stress the desirability of determining these parameters from physical principles or measurements. Applicants may, however, use modeling techniques other *than those considered herein. In particular, physical hydraulic models that may have been constructed for hydrothermal studies or other purposes may often be used as reliable predictive tools for radionuclide dispersion. Tracer release studies conducted *in situ* can provide accurate predictions without need for a model.

The degree of realism inherent in each model described in this guide depends on the ability of that model to account for the physical processes involved and the validity of model coefficients and assumed future flow fields. As a general rule, more complex models are capable of yielding more realistic results. However, a realistic model requires realistic input data, and little is gained by using highly sophisticated calculational models when the input parameters are ill-defined. The simplest models are closed-form analytical solutions of the governing transport equations. Such solutions are possible only for simplified cases. It is seldom possible to obtain analytical solutions for time-dependent flow fields or for complex receiving-water geometry. Consequently, any analytical solution should be carefully assessed by the applicant to ascertain the conditions under which the model might be a valid predictive tool. Simplified models do not necessarily produce conservative results. If such models are used, it is the applicant's responsibility to demonstrate their degree of conservatism. The staff's position on such demonstration is presented in Section C of this guide.

In identifying liquid pathways to man, applicants should identify the location of water users, the types of uses, and the usage estimated out to a distance of 50 miles from the site. Because of high usage rates along many streams and estuaries, the effects of water usage on the spatial and temporal distribution of flows should be estimated. In addition, water usage upstream of a nuclear plant can alter flows at or downstream of the plant. This guide presents an acceptable methodology for evaluating water usage and the consequences thereof on streams and estuaries receiving routine or accidental releases of radionuclides from nuclear power plants.

The ability of suspended and bottom sediments to absorb and adsorb radioactive nuclides from solution, thereby concentrating otherwise dilute species of ions, may create a significant pathway to man. Sorption by sediment is also an important mechanism for reducing the area of influence of plant releases. Unfortunately, the state of the art in evaluating sediment-related effects is less advanced than in other engineering disciplines. Consequently, the transport models discussed in this guide do not explicitly include sediment uptake mechanisms. Until reliable generalized sediment uptake and transport models become available, the NRC staff will rely on existing field studies and the staff's and consultants' experience to determine the level of conservatism or realism of the applicant's estimates. If the applicant elects to take credit for removal of certain ions from the surface waters by the process of sediment uptake, verification using site-related field data will be necessary.

C. REGULATORY POSITION

1. The transport and water use models described in Appendix A of this guide are acceptable to the NRC staff for use in calculating the potential annual average radiation doses to the public that may result from radioactive material in liquid effluents routinely released to surface water bodies. No general models for transport in ground water are included, as such analyses are considered to be site-specific. The models in Appendix A are also acceptable to the staff for analyzing the dispersion and dilution of accidental spills of radioactive material in liquids to surface water bodies. Standards for ground-water analysis, currently being prepared by the American Nuclear Society for publication by the American National Standards Institute, will be evaluated for acceptability by the NRC staff when completed.

2. Although specific models are cited in Appendix A of this guide, the citations are intended to provide guidance in the selection of model types rather than to specify models. Applicants may use models other than those described in Appendix A, but should justify fully the analytical techniques, assumptions, and level of conservatism of the model ultimately chosen.

---

*Lines indicate substantive change from previous issuance.

3. The choice of a specific model, values of input parameters, and assumed future flow fields is the responsibility of the applicant. The NRC staff recognizes that the applicant may choose initially to use simplified models employing demonstrably conservative assumptions. The most conservative assumption would be no dilution of the radwaste discharge and a travel time of zero. In some cases, this extreme approach may be acceptable for calculation of dose to man. Should the results of this initial analysis support a conclusion of compliance with Appendix I of 10 CFR Part 50, no further effort is indicated. However, if compliance is not demonstrated by the simplified analysis, more refined and more realistic analyses of liquid transport may be undertaken. The NRC staff will also consider such analyses acceptable provided the applicant establishes the realism of the model, coefficients, parameters, and flow field.

D. IMPLEMENTATION

The purpose of this section is to provide information to license applicants and licensees regarding the NRC staff's plans for implementing this regulatory guide.

This guide reflects current Nuclear Regulatory Commission practice. Therefore, except in those cases in which the license applicant or licensee proposes an acceptable alternative method, the method described herein for complying with specified portions of the Commission's regulations is being and will continue to be used in the evaluation of submittals for operating license or construction permit applications until this guide is revised as a result of suggestions from the public or additional staff review.

APPENDIX A

LIQUID EFFLUENT TRANSPORT AND WATER USE MODELS

This appendix describes transport and water use models for calculating the radiation doses to the public that may result from radioactive material in liquid effluents released to surface water bodies. Symbols used in this description are defined in the "List of Symbols" following the appendix.

1. INITIAL DILUTION

Initial dilution of liquid radioactive effluents (e.g., dilution upon discharge to the receiving water body) is often accomplished by using relatively high-velocity surface or submerged jets or multiport diffusers. Mathematical modeling of such discharges requires solution of the conservation equations applicable to buoyant jets. These equations are solved routinely as a part of the near-field analysis for thermal discharges. Initial dilution rates for waterborne radionuclides should be obtained directly as an integral part of the thermal analysis.

Applicable near-field models are in common usage throughout the industry and are not discussed in detail herein. Jirka et al. (Ref. 1) and Dunn et al. (Ref. 2) discuss in detail the theory and ranges of applicability of near-field models. These references should be consulted for guidance in determining the modeling approach to be used for a specific problem. General remarks on surface and submerged jet discharges are presented below.

For surface discharges, acceptable initial dilution analyses may be obtained from the models of Stolzenbach and Harleman (Ref. 3), Stolzenbach et al. (Ref. 4), Prych (Ref. 5), Shirazi and Davis (Ref. 6), and Pritchard (Refs. 7 and 8). Dilution estimates for surface discharges require a careful assessment of the adverse effects of shoreline and bottom interference. Methods for estimating the magnitude of these boundary effects under given receiving water conditions are discussed in detail in Reference 1.

Estimates of dilution from submerged discharges require careful analysis of the flow conditions in the immediate vicinity of the discharge. The two possible flow conditions, stable or unstable, depend on the discharge and receiving water characteristics. Under stable conditions the discharge, upon reaching the free surface, spreads laterally in the form of a stable density current. As a result, there is little re-entrainment of previously discharged water. Such stable discharges can be characterized as "deep-water." Unstable or "shallow-water" discharges are characterized by counterflow which causes re-entrainment of previously mixed effluent into the discharge jet. Application of deep-water jet models to shallow-water discharges can result in serious overestimation of initial dilution. References 1, 9, and 10 discuss in detail the behavior of stable and unstable discharges and stability criteria for various types of submerged discharges. In practice, the results of a stability analysis will determine whether a "deep-water" or "shallow-water" model should be used for a given discharge-receiving water system.

For deep-water (stable) conditions the commonly used submerged jet models of Koh and Fan (Ref. 11) and Hirst (Ref. 12) and similar models are applicable provided the thickness of the buoyant surface layer is taken into account.

For shallow-water (unstable) conditions the above models (and other similar deep-water models) are not applicable and their use will result in predicting excessively high dilution. The models of Lee et al. (Ref. 10) and Jirka and Harleman (Ref. 9), with appropriate stability analyses, are directly applicable to either deep- or shallow-water discharges.

2. NONTIDAL RIVERS

a. Model Formulations

(1) Steady-State Stream Tube Model

Application of the models herein is restricted to those portions of the river removed from influences of the discharge. Initial dilution near the point of discharge is usually controlled by turbulent mixing induced by momentum effects of the discharge jet. Techniques for the determination of initial dilution were discussed in Section 1 of this appendix.

For nontidal rivers the flow is assumed to be uniform and approximately steady. Under these conditions, the diffusive transport in the flow direction may be neglected compared with the advective transport (Ref. 13). It has been shown that far-field transport of dissolved constituents in rivers can be satisfactorily treated by a two-dimensional model in which vertical variations of velocity and concentration are averaged out (Refs. 14, 15, and 16). Such a model, however, retains transverse variations of river bottom topography and velocity.

Consider a section of a steady natural stream as shown in Figure 1. The origin of the coordinate system is placed on the near shore. The x-axis is taken positive in the downstream direction, the z-axis is directed vertically downward from the water surface, and the y-axis is directed across the stream. The steady-state mass balance equation for a vertically mixed radionuclide concentration may be written (Ref. 14) as follows:

$$ud\,\frac{\partial C}{\partial x} = \frac{\partial}{\partial y}\left(K_y d\frac{\partial C}{\partial y}\right) - (\lambda d)C \qquad (1)$$

where

- C is the radionuclide concentration (activity/volume);
- d is the stream depth;
- K_y is the lateral turbulent diffusion coefficient (vertically averaged, two dimensional);
- u is the stream velocity; and
- λ is the decay coefficient and is = (ln 2)/half life.

Since, for a real stream, u and d will be functions of the transverse coordinate y, Equation (1) will generally not have a closed-form analytical solution. A more tractable form of the equation is obtained through introduction of a new independent variable q, defined by

$$q = \int_0^y (ud)dy \qquad (2)$$

The quantity q is the cumulative discharge measured from the near shore. Hence, as $y \to B$, $q \to Q$, where B is the river width and Q is the total river flow.

Substitution of Equation (2) into Equation (1) yields the following transport equation:

$$\frac{\partial C}{\partial x} = \frac{\partial}{\partial q}\left[(K_y ud^2)\frac{\partial C}{\partial q}\right] - \frac{\lambda}{u}C \qquad (3)$$

In the decay term, the velocity u may be replaced, to a good approximation, by the sectional mean value $\bar{u}$. If this is done, the decay term may be removed through the transformation

$$C(x,q) = \chi(x,q)e^{-\frac{\lambda x}{\bar{u}}} \qquad (4)$$

The result is the following transport equation for the nondecaying concentration χ:

$$\frac{\partial \chi}{\partial x} = \frac{\partial}{\partial q}\left[(K_y ud^2)\frac{\partial \chi}{\partial q}\right] \qquad (5)$$

The quantity $K_y ud^2$ is known as the "diffusion factor." Yotsukura and Cobb (Ref. 14) have shown that the variable diffusion factor may be replaced by a constant factor $\overline{K_y ud^2}$, where

$$\overline{K_y ud^2} = \frac{1}{Q}\int_0^Q K_y ud^2 dq$$

is the discharge-weighted mean value. Equation (5) may now be written

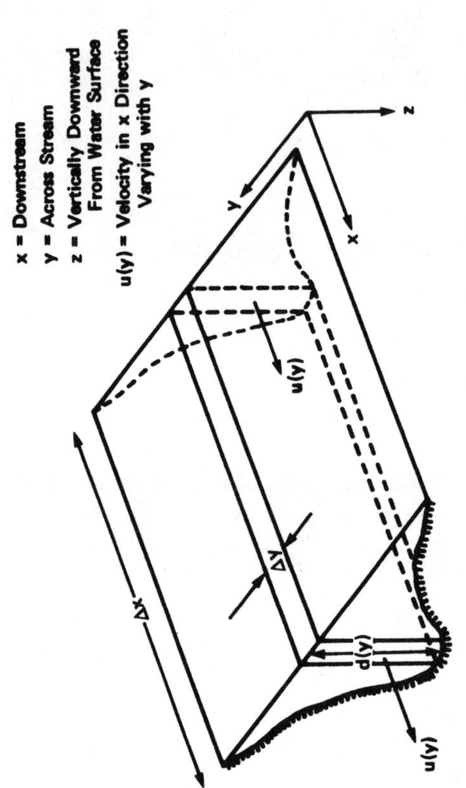

FIGURE 1. MODEL OF AN INFINITESIMAL STREAM TUBE IN A NATURAL STREAM (Redrawn from Yotsukura and Cobb, Ref. 14.)

$$\frac{\partial \chi}{\partial x} = D \frac{\partial^2 \chi}{\partial q^2} \qquad (6)$$

where

$$D = \overline{K_y u d^2} = \text{constant diffusion factor}$$

Equation (6) is a standard diffusion equation which has a closed-form analytical solution.

Assume a steady vertical line source discharge emitting a constant W Ci/sec is located at $x = 0$, $y = y_s$. Since there is a one-to-one correspondence between the transverse distance y and the cumulative discharge q, the vertical line source discharge may be located at $x = 0$, $q = q_s$. A closed-form solution to Equation (6) that satisfies the condition that there be no flux of material across the bounding surfaces is given by

$$\chi = \frac{W}{Q}\left[1 + 2 \sum_{n=1}^{\infty} e^{-\frac{n^2\pi^2 Dx}{Q^2}} \cos\frac{n\pi q_s}{Q} \cos\frac{n\pi q}{Q}\right] \qquad (7)$$

This expression, although of different form, is equivalent to Equation (14) of Reference 14.

If the liquid effluent is injected as an area source perpendicular to the river flow, the solution may be obtained by integration of Equation (7) over the source dimensions. If the source is located in the river between distances y_{s1} and y_{s2} (cumulative discharges q_{s1} and q_{s2}), the area source solution may be obtained from Equation (7) by integration with respect to q_s between the limits $q_{s1} < q_s \leq q_{s2}$.

$$\chi_{Area(\perp)} = \frac{W}{Q}\left[1 + 2 \sum_{n=1}^{\infty} e^{-\frac{n^2\pi^2 Dx}{Q^2}} \frac{\sin n\alpha}{n\alpha} \cos\frac{n\pi}{2}\left(\frac{q_{s2} + q_{s1}}{Q}\right) \cos\frac{n\pi q}{Q}\right] \qquad (8)$$

where

$$\alpha = \frac{\pi}{2}\left(\frac{q_{s2} - q_{s1}}{Q}\right)$$

Note that the more familiar solutions for the concentration, as a function of x and y in a uniform, straight, rectangular channel of constant velocity U, can be obtained immediately from Equations (7) and (8) through the transformation of the terms within the brackets:

$$\begin{Bmatrix} D/Q^2 \\ q \\ Q \end{Bmatrix} \longrightarrow \begin{Bmatrix} K_y/UB^2 \\ y \\ B \end{Bmatrix}$$

The more general forms given by Equations (7) and (8), however, are preferable, since they are applicable to irregularly shaped channels. Yotsukura and Sayre (Ref. 16) have recently generalized Equations (5) and (6) so that these can be applied to any nonuniform channel with a minor modification to the diffusion factor.

(2) Transient Release Model

In many cases, routine releases of radioactive effluents are batched and infrequent, rather than continuous. In such cases, it may be important to calculate concentrations as a function of both time and space. The concentration in a straight, rectangular channel corresponding to the instantaneous release of a finite quantity of material from a vertical line source at $x = 0$ and $y = y_s$ is:

$$C = \frac{M}{(4\pi K_x t)^{1/2} A} \exp\left\{-\frac{[x - ut]^2}{4K_x t} - \lambda t\right\}\left[1 + 2 \sum_{n=1}^{\infty} \exp\left(-\frac{n^2\pi^2 K_y t}{B^2}\right) \cos n\pi\frac{y_s}{B} \cos n\pi\frac{y}{B}\right] \qquad (9)$$

where

- A is the cross-sectional area;
- B is the channel width;
- K_x is the longitudinal turbulent transport coefficient (vertically averaged, two dimensional);
- M is the amount of activity released (in curies);
- t is the time after the release;

and the other terms are as previously defined.

Note that this solution accounts for turbulent diffusion in the direction of flow, which may be important for short-duration releases.

The case of a more general time-dependent release may be obtained by integrating Equation (9) with respect to time:

$$C = \int_0^t \frac{Wf(\tau)}{(4\pi K_x)^{1/2} A(t-\tau)^{1/2}} \exp\left\{-\frac{[x - u(t-\tau)]^2}{4K_x(t-\tau)} - \lambda(t-\tau)\right\}$$

$$\left[1 + 2\sum_{n=1}^{\infty} \exp\left(-\frac{n^2\pi^2 K_y(t-\tau)}{B^2}\right) \cos n\pi\frac{y_s}{B} \cos n\pi\frac{y}{B}\right] d\tau \qquad (10)$$

where the release rate is $Wf(\tau)$ curies/sec. In general, Equation (10) must be solved by numerical quadrature.

Near the source, convergence of the Fourier series terms in Equations (9) and (10) may be extremely slow. However, in this region, the effects of the far shore are not usually important, and the series solution may be replaced by a single image source at the near shore (see the transient lake solution, Equations (19) and (20), Section 3.a.(2)(b) of this appendix). In this case, the solutions do not involve infinite series and present no convergence problems.

b. Model Applications

(1) Steady-State Stream Tube Model

Application of the model requires determination of stream channel geometry, the cross-stream distribution of flow, and the diffusion factor at representative river cross-sections downstream of the effluent discharge. In addition, definition of stream discharge is necessary (see Section 6 of this appendix).

The preferred method of determining the flow cross-sectional distribution is by current-meter measurements using standard stream-gaging techniques. Because it is not always practical to obtain velocity measurements at every river cross-section at which concentration distributions are desired, transverse velocity distributions may be estimated from observed stream bottom profiles and the application of steady-state flow equations such as Manning's formula to channels of compound cross-section (Refs. 17 and 18).

Evaluation of the diffusion factor $\overline{K_y u d^2}$ requires a separate determination of the diffusion coefficient K_y. For steady open-channel flow, K_y can be determined from hydrodynamic properties of the channel by using Elder's empirical formula (Ref. 19):

$$K_y = \beta u^* d \qquad (11)$$

where

- d is the river depth;
- u^* is the shear velocity; and

β is a dimensionless constant.

(The user is not restricted to this formula. A number of alternative approaches have been published.)

For straight natural stream channels β has a value of approximately 0.23 (Refs. 14 and 16). For curved channels, however, secondary flows can lead to increased lateral mixing and the value of β is larger (Refs. 20-22). Fischer (Ref. 20), for example, has shown that the lateral mixing coefficient is increased in bending streams, varying inversely as the square of the radius of curvature. In general, to obtain realistic transport estimates, values of the lateral mixing coefficient should be determined by onsite tracer studies. Although transverse variations of K_y have not been adequately confirmed in field tests, longitudinal variation of K_y in a sharp bend has been reported by Sayre and Yeh (Ref. 22). Equations (7) and (8) may be modified as follows to account for a diffusion factor that varies in the direction of flow:

$$\overline{D}x \rightarrow \int_0^x D(x)dx$$

If the diffusion factor is known for each river cross-section of concern, the integral can be evaluated by simple numerical integration. If the variation in D(x) is small over the river stretch under consideration, then Equations (7) and (8) may be used directly, with the quantity D being interpreted as the mean value over the river reach.

It is useful to write Equation (7) in dimensionless form.

$$\tilde{\chi} = 1 + 2 \sum_{n=1}^{\infty} e^{-n^2\pi^2\tilde{x}} \cos n\pi\tilde{q}_s \cos n\pi\tilde{q} \qquad (12)$$

where

$\tilde{q} = q/Q$ is the dimensionless cumulative discharge;

$\tilde{\chi} = \chi/\frac{W}{Q}$ is the dimensionless concentration relative to the fully mixed value; and

$\tilde{x} = \frac{Dx}{Q^2}$ is the dimensionless downstream distance.

The utility of the dimensionless form is illustrated in Figure 2, which shows near- and far-shore concentrations resulting from a near-shore point discharge. For a given downstream location and given flow parameters, the dimensionless concentration for either shoreline may be obtained directly from the two curves. The near-shore concentration exhibits the expected $x^{-1/2}$ dependence for two-dimensional mixing until the influence of the far shore is felt. Both curves in Figure 2 approach unity (complete sectional mixing) for large values of $\tilde{x}$. Hence, for a given set of flow parameters, the downstream distance to sectional homogeneity ("mixing distance") can be estimated directly. (Note that the mixing distance for a shoreline discharge is four times the mixing distance for a centerline discharge.)

(2) Transient Release Model

The transient release model is formulated in this guide only for the case of a vertical line source in a straight rectangular channel, since its primary purpose is to furnish information on the time-dependent behavior of non-continuous releases. However, the model can be extended to treat other source configurations in stream tube coordinates as employed in Section 2.a.(1) of this appendix.

Application of the model requires the determination of the longitudinal turbulent diffusion coefficient K_x, in addition to the parameters necessary for the steady-state model in the previous section. The longitudinal dispersion coefficient should be obtained by site-specific tracer experiments. However, crude estimates of K_x may be obtained from the following formula, which is similar to that for the lateral diffusion coefficient (Ref. 19):

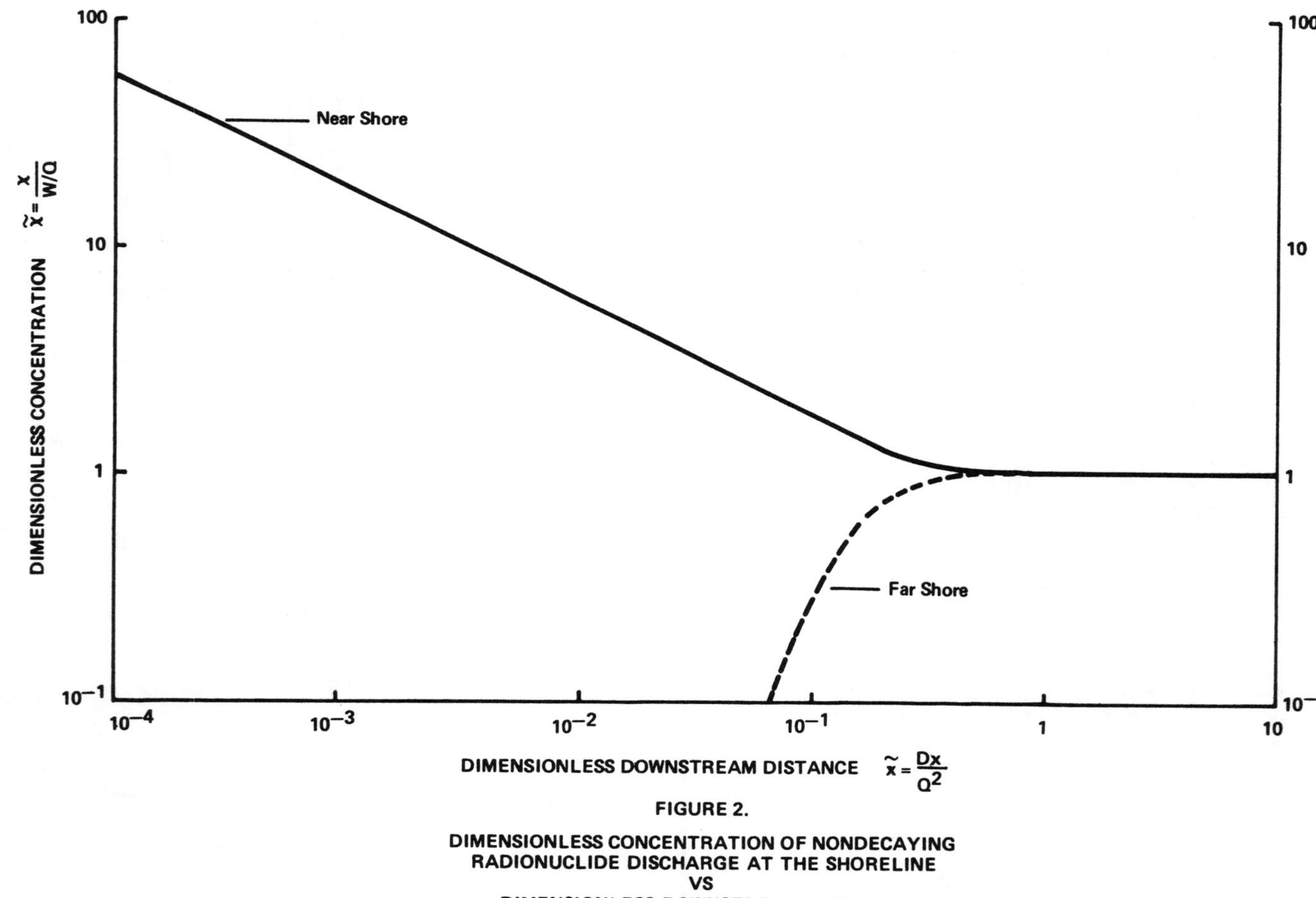

FIGURE 2.

DIMENSIONLESS CONCENTRATION OF NONDECAYING RADIONUCLIDE DISCHARGE AT THE SHORELINE VS DIMENSIONLESS DOWNSTREAM DISTANCE

$$K_x = \beta u^* d, \tag{13}$$

where

d is the river depth;

u^* is the shear velocity; and

β is a dimensionless constant.

(Again, the user is not restricted to the use of this formula. A number of alternative approaches have been published.)

For straight rectangular stream channels, β has a value of about 5.93. The value of β, however, increases in curved channels and in general must be determined by field studies (Refs. 20-22). The two-dimensional coefficient, K_x, is usually much smaller in magnitude than the one-dimensional coefficient, E, as described later.

The usefulness of the transient model, even for simplified rectangular geometry, is that it allows analysis of the dispersion of material released in a realistic fashion. In the case of short-duration batch releases, spreading in the direction of flow may be an important mechanism for effluent dispersion, which is not included in the steady-state continuous release model.

3. OPEN COASTS

a. Great Lakes

(1) Discussion

Field studies in the Great Lakes have shown that coastal currents are predominantly parallel to the shore and have typical speeds of 10 to 20 cm/sec (0.2 to 0.4 knots). These currents usually persist in one direction for several days. Then, in direct response to wind shifts, they quickly reverse and persist in the opposite direction for several days. The stagnation time at reversal seldom exceeds a few hours (Refs. 23 and 24).

The studies further suggest that each reversal of the coastal current is accompanied by a large-scale mass exchange with offshore waters that effectively removes pollutants from the shore zone. Possible physical mechanisms responsible for this behavior are discussed by Csanady (Refs. 25 and 26). Observations near pollutant discharges have shown a well-defined pollutant plume hugging the shoreline for several days, then relatively quick dispersal offshore, followed by redevelopment of the plume in the opposite direction. Throughout this sequence, the buildup of pollutant concentration in the vicinity of the discharge is small (Refs. 23 and 27). A stable coastal current of, say, 10 cm/sec that persists for about three days before reversal causes an upcoast or downcoast excursion of an effluent plume which is of the order of 25 km (about 16 miles).

In view of the above findings, it is possible to construct a quasi-steady-state model valid for distances of about 25 km and time scales on the order of a few days. For those cases in which lateral mixing and mass exchange occur during flow stagnation periods, extension of the model beyond these limits should provide conservative results. It should be emphasized, however, that knowledge of Great Lakes coastal circulation patterns is far from complete. The existing data base is inadequate to conclude that the behavior described above is applicable to the entire Great Lakes system. A general knowledge of near-shore current climatology is needed. It is therefore recommended that modeling efforts be accompanied by time series current measurements at the site. Such measurements should be of sufficient duration to resolve the important time scales of flow variability. Of particular importance are field studies to define the extent and frequency of near-shore fumigation occurring at a given site.

(2) Analytical Models

(a) Steady-State Model

Analytical models of routine releases of liquid effluents along open coasts are usually based on Gaussian-like solutions to the steady-state diffusion equation. The form of each solution may differ in detail, depending on the number of dimensions retained, the location of the bounding surfaces, and the discharge configuration.

A simple diffusion model for a steady point-source discharge into a lake having a known steady longshore current, u, may be formulated by neglecting the longitudinal diffusion and time dependence in the dissolved constituent transport equation as follows:

$$u \frac{\partial C}{\partial x} = \varepsilon_y \frac{\partial^2 C}{\partial y^2} + \varepsilon_z \frac{\partial^2 C}{\partial z^2} - \lambda C \tag{14}$$

where ε_y and ε_z are the lateral and vertical turbulent diffusion coefficients, respectively. The remaining symbols are as defined in Section 2.

The decay term may again be removed through the transformation

$$C(x,y,z) = \chi(x,y,z)e^{-\lambda x/u} \tag{15}$$

resulting in the following equation for the nondecaying concentration χ:

$$u \frac{\partial \chi}{\partial x} = \varepsilon_y \frac{\partial^2 \chi}{\partial y^2} + \varepsilon_z \frac{\partial^2 \chi}{\partial z^2} \tag{16}$$

It is assumed that the discharge is located at the point $(0,y_s,z_s)$, i.e., at the origin of the x-axis and a distance y_s from the shoreline and z_s beneath the water surface. For a large lake of constant depth d and straight shoreline the solution is

$$\chi = \frac{W}{2\pi u \sigma_y \sigma_z} f(\sigma_z,z,z_s,d) f(\sigma_y,y,y_s) \tag{17}$$

where

$$f(\sigma_z,z,z_s,d) = \sum_{m=-\infty}^{\infty} \left\{ \exp\left[-\frac{(2md + z_s - z)^2}{2\sigma_z^2}\right] + \exp\left[-\frac{(2md - z_s - z)^2}{2\sigma_z^2}\right] \right\}$$

$$f(\sigma_y,y,y_s) = \exp\left[-\frac{(y_s - y)^2}{2\sigma_y^2}\right] + \exp\left[-\frac{(y_s + y)^2}{2\sigma_y^2}\right]$$

$$\sigma_y = \sqrt{\frac{2\varepsilon_y x}{u}}, \quad \sigma_z = \sqrt{\frac{2\varepsilon_z x}{u}}$$

This model may be used for curved shorelines by substituting, for y and y_s, the corresponding distances normal to the shoreline.

In Equation (17), the condition that there be no flux of material through the bounding surfaces is ensured by placement of an image source of strength W (Ci/sec) at $y = -y_s$ and an infinite series of image sources along the z-axis.

Equation (17) is a basic expression that can be modified to yield solutions for a variety of discharge configurations into bounded water bodies. For the sake of simplicity, the present discussion is limited to point discharges. However, if W is interpreted as source strength per unit length, or per unit area, line and plane sources, respectively, may be treated by integration of Equation (17) over the source dimensions.

The predictive capabilities of this model are limited because of the spatial variations in the flow field under actual conditions and because there are large uncertainties in the diffusion coefficients ε_y and ε_z (or, equivalently, in the standard deviations σ_y and σ_z). Studies in the Great Lakes and other large lakes suggest that "representative" near-shore values of ε_y are roughly in the range of 500 to 1000 cm^2/sec (0.5 to 1.1 ft^2/sec) and that ε_z is in the range 1 to 30 cm^2/sec (0.001 to 0.030 ft^2/sec) (Refs. 23 and 28). These values are typical only of the near-shore zone. Furthermore, there is evidence to suggest that the ε_y is reasonably constant for discharge plume widths exceeding about 50 m (~ 165 ft) (Ref. 23). Hence Richardson's "four-thirds power law" should not be used to describe the lateral diffusion coefficient without justification on the basis of site-specific tracer studies.

Figure 3 shows centerline and shoreline values of χ/W calculated from Equation (17) for the case of a point source discharging at the surface 500 m (1640 ft) offshore into a 10 cm/sec (0.3 ft/sec) current. The horizontal and vertical mixing coefficients are 1000 cm^2/sec (1.1 ft^2/sec) and 5 cm^2/sec (0.005 ft^2/sec), respectively. The depth is 10 m. The centerline concentrations decrease inversely with distance from the source, x^{-1}, for about the first 10 km (6 miles), beyond which the concentration decrease is approximately $x^{-1/2}$. The dilution factor, D_F, is given by

$$D_F = W/(\chi q_p) \tag{18}$$

where q_p is the volumetric discharge rate of the effluent.

The dilution factor, for example, at 10 km (6 miles) downcurrent is approximately 7 for a 52 m^3/sec (1,830 ft^3/sec) discharge.

This result suggests that, for a nondecaying substance, the downstream concentration reduction in lake plumes parallel to the shore is rather small. This is consistent with observations reported for several of the Great Lakes (Ref. 23). It should be kept in mind that the dilution calculated above is for the far field and does not include possible additional dilution arising from initial mixing in the near field.

For a given location, the presence of a plume might be periodic. Therefore, long-term average dilution factors can be estimated from the above model by multiplying the solution by an appropriate flow-field frequency function. As discussed previously, observations suggest that the directional distribution of Great Lakes coastal currents is approximately bimodal. In such a case, long-term dilution factors would be about twice those calculated from Equation (17). It is emphasized, however, that the presence of reversing currents at a given site should be demonstrated by field observations of flow patterns before credit is taken for concentration reduction attributable to intermittent plume behavior.

(b) Transient Source Model

For other than a continuous source, the transient form of the constituent transport equation must be solved. In this case, diffusive transport in the direction of flow may be important, especially for short-duration releases, whereas it is unimportant in the case of continuous releases.

For an instantaneous release of a finite quantity of material from a vertical line source at x = 0, $y = y_s$, into a lake of known steady longshore current u, a simple transient model can be formulated:

$$C = \frac{M}{4\pi\sqrt{K_x K_y}\ td} \exp\left\{-\left(\frac{[x - Ut]^2}{4K_x t} + \lambda t\right)\right\}\left\{\exp\left(\frac{-[y - y_s]^2}{4K_y t}\right) + \exp\left(\frac{-[y + y_s]^2}{4K_y t}\right)\right\} \tag{19}$$

where

d is the depth;

M is the amount of activity released (in curies);

t is the time after the release;

and the other terms are as previously defined.

The case of a more general time-dependent release may be obtained by integrating Equation (19) with respect to time:

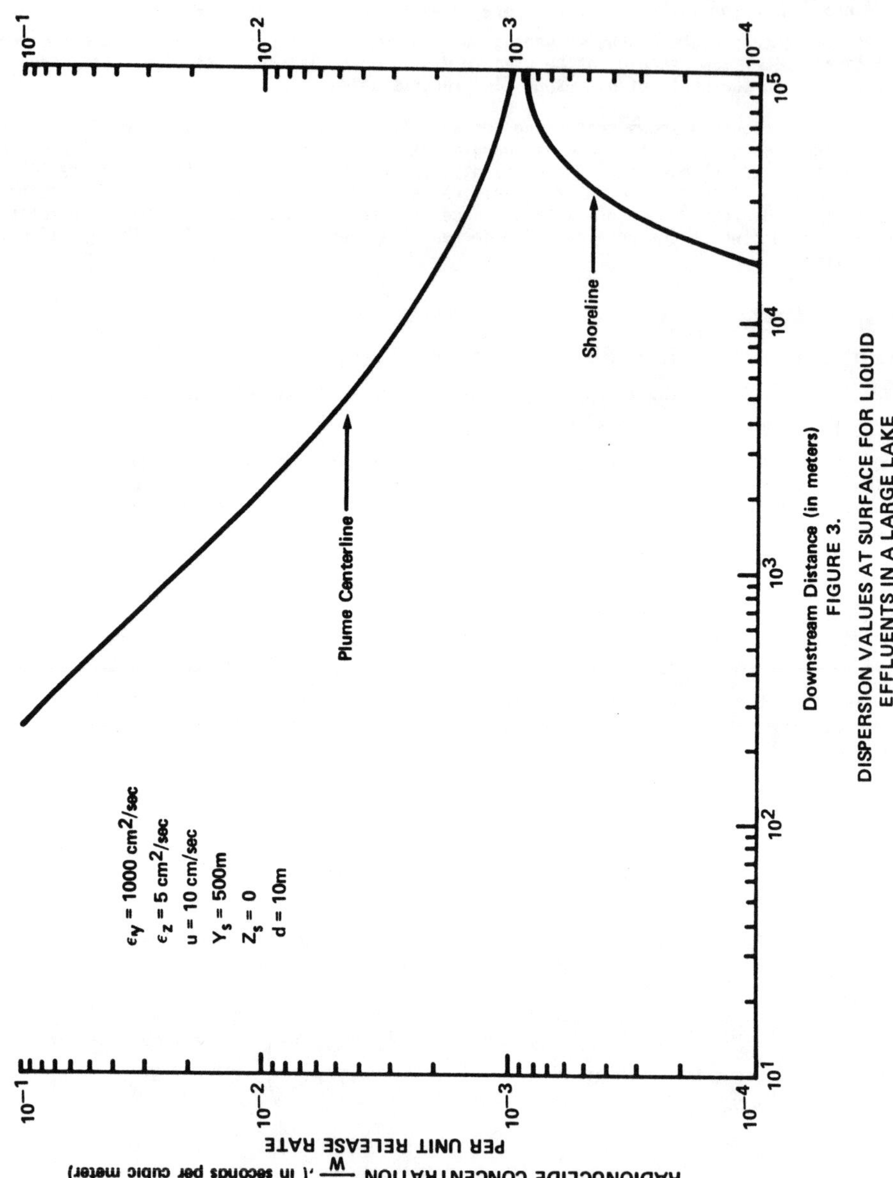

FIGURE 3.
DISPERSION VALUES AT SURFACE FOR LIQUID EFFLUENTS IN A LARGE LAKE

$$C = \int_0^t \frac{Wf(\tau)}{4\pi\sqrt{K_x K_y}\, d(t - \tau)} \exp\left\{-\left(\frac{(x-u(t - \tau))^2}{4K_x(t - \tau)} + \lambda(t - \tau)\right)\right\}\left\{\exp\left(\frac{-(y - y_s)^2}{4K_y(t - \tau)}\right) + \exp\left(\frac{-(y + y_s)^2}{4K_y(t - \tau)}\right)\right\}d\tau \quad (20)$$

where the release rate is $Wf(\tau)$ curies/sec. In general, Equation (20) must be solved using numerical quadrature.

Equations (19) and (20) are also useful for releases into rivers in the region near the source, where the effects of the far shore are unimportant.

(3) Numerical Models

Analytical solutions to the diffusion equation are strictly applicable only to cases of steady uniform flow. In coastal regions having complex geometry and time-dependent nonuniform flow, analytical models might not be adequate for predicting realistic concentration values. In such cases multi-dimensional numerical models are more suitable. The use of such models is becoming increasingly common in water-quality simulation.

Typical acceptable numerical models are the two-dimensional, vertically integrated models developed by Leendertse and co-workers (Refs. 29-34), Codell (Ref. 35), Loziuk et al. (Ref. 36), and Eraslan (Ref. 37).

These and other numerical models fall into two broad categories, depending on the method in which the advective velocity field is obtained. The Leendertse, Codell, and Loziuk models, for example, compute the velocity field from the following vertically integrated two-dimensional equations of mass and momentum conservation:

$$\left.\begin{aligned}
&\frac{\partial U}{\partial t} + U\frac{\partial U}{\partial x} + V\frac{\partial U}{\partial y} - fV = -g\,\frac{\partial \zeta}{\partial x} + \frac{\tau_x^s}{H} - \frac{gU(U^2 + V^2)^{1/2}}{C_h^2 H}\\
&\frac{\partial V}{\partial t} + U\frac{\partial V}{\partial x} + V\frac{\partial V}{\partial y} + fU = -g\,\frac{\partial \zeta}{\partial y} + \frac{\tau_y^s}{H} - \frac{gV(U^2 + V^2)^{1/2}}{C_h^2 H}\\
&\frac{\partial \zeta}{\partial t} + \frac{\partial}{\partial x}(HU) + \frac{\partial}{\partial y}(HV) = 0
\end{aligned}\right\} \quad (21)$$

where

C_h is the Chezy coefficient;

f is the Coriolis parameter;

H is the depth from water surface to bottom;

(U,V) are the vertically averaged x and y component velocities;

ζ is the water surface location above an undisturbed level datum; and

τ_x^s, τ_y^s are the x and y component surface stresses.

The resulting velocity field then becomes the advective mechanism in the following vertically averaged conservation equation for the dissolved constituent concentration C:

$$\frac{\partial}{\partial t}(HC) + \frac{\partial}{\partial x}(HUC) + \frac{\partial}{\partial y}(HVC) = \frac{\partial}{\partial x}\left(HK_x\frac{\partial C}{\partial x}\right) + \frac{\partial}{\partial y}\left(HK_y\frac{\partial C}{\partial y}\right) - H\lambda C \quad (22)$$

where K_x and K_y are the dispersion coefficients in the indicated directions.

The Eraslan model, on the other hand, requires synthesis of the flow field from current measurements. Use of this technique requires a careful analysis of the flow data to ensure that the resulting velocity field conserves mass. The velocity field is then applied to the integral form of the conservation equation for the dissolved constituent in question (donor cell method) (Ref. 37).

b. Oceans

Modeling techniques for estimating radionuclide transport in ocean coastal waters are similar to those applicable to near-shore waters in the Great Lakes. The primary differences in behavior between the two systems results from the greater temporal and spatial variability in flow occurring in ocean coastal waters. This variability results primarily from two factors. The first and more readily defined factor is the major influence of astronomical tidal currents, which are negligibly small in the Great Lakes. The second factor, whose effects are important but much more difficult to quantify, is the influence of meteorological driving forces. These forces include the direct effects of both meso-scale and synoptic-scale wind systems and the indirect effects of seasonal variations in heating or cooling and coastal river discharges. As a result of these factors, the flow variability in oceanic coastal waters contains components having magnitudes and characteristic time scales greater than those of the near-shore waters of the Great Lakes.

In practice, the choice of transport modeling techniques applicable to a given ocean coastal region depends, to a large extent, on the level of knowledge of local near-shore current climatology. A particular model choice and range of model parameters should be demonstrated to include, to the extent practical, the effects of the important scales of flow variability. For synoptic scale fluctuations in flow patterns, it will often be necessary to perform transport calculations for conditions "typical" of various seasons or wind patterns.

For a given set of conditions, however, the choice of modeling techniques is further determined by the interpretation of the role of tidal currents in the mixing process. The interpretation depends on the averaging period used to define the velocity field. If the averaging time is long compared to the tidal period, tidal currents cannot contribute to the advective transport, since their contributions to the mean flow field have been removed by the averaging. Tidal effects would be contained solely in "tidally averaged" turbulent diffusion coefficients. This result is largely a mathematical artifact that assigns the actual advective effects of tidal currents to large-scale turbulent diffusion. Nevertheless, if detailed descriptions of the field of radionuclide concentrations are not required, it is possible to construct quasi-steady-state transport models that are valid for time scales larger than the tidal period and smaller than those associated with major nontidal fluctuations in flow.

For regular shoreline geometry, or discharges removed from the shoreline, steady-state Gaussian models based on Equation (17) may be used (Refs. 38-41). The results based on these models require careful interpretation, however, because of the large uncertainty in input parameter values, particularly the turbulent diffusion coefficients. Since these coefficients arise from time averaging, their values for any given case will depend on the averaging period used to define the mean velocity field. Furthermore, there is evidence to indicate that in the ocean the rate of spread of a contaminant plume depends upon the plume age. Hence, in general, turbulent diffusion coefficients will be time and space dependent. The methodology for obtaining reasonable estimates for these coefficients is based primarily on the interpretation of the results of tracer studies in the light of modern turbulence theory (Refs. 38-45).

More realistic detailed descriptions of radionuclide transport in ocean coastal waters will require the use of numerical models. The advantage of such models is that they are applicable to fully time-dependent flow fields in receiving waters having complex geometry. In particular, these models have the capability of treating tidal currents as advective rather than diffusive mechanisms ("real-time" models), hence removing a large element of uncertainty in the determination of turbulent diffusion coefficients.

Typical acceptable numerical models (Ref. 29-37) were discussed in Section 3.a.(3). In the "real-time" modeling approach, tidal currents are explicitly included as advective transport mechanisms. Leendertse and co-workers (Refs. 29-34) have shown that in this case, reasonable estimates of longitudinal and lateral turbulent dispersion coefficients may be based on Elder's (Ref. 19) formulas for steady open-channel flow.

The applicability of numerical models and the techniques for establishing horizontal mixing coefficients are discussed further in Sections 4.c and 4.d.

4. ESTUARIES

Transport of contaminants in estuaries differs from that in rivers because of oscillatory tidal advection and the nontidal gravitational circulation induced by salinity differences. An important consequence of these differences is that there is transport of material upstream from the discharge point in estuaries, the maximum upstream penetration being limited to the general region of oceanic salt intrusion.

a. One-Dimensional Models

For purposes of radionuclide transport prediction, reduction of the estuarine problem to a single dimension (longitudinal) produces satisfactory results, except in the lower reaches of the estuary, where circulation is clearly two or three dimensional. The one-dimensional simplification is accomplished by averaging over the estuary cross-section. The resulting constituent transport equation is

$$\frac{1}{A}\frac{\partial}{\partial t}(AC) + \frac{1}{A}\frac{\partial}{\partial x}(A\overline{U}C) = \frac{1}{A}\frac{\partial}{\partial x}\left(AE\frac{\partial C}{\partial x}\right) - \lambda C \qquad (23)$$

where

$A(x,t)$ is the cross-sectional area;

$E(x)$ is the sectionally averaged, one-dimensional longitudinal dispersion coefficient; and

$\overline{U}(x,t)$ is the sectionally averaged longitudinal velocity.

Both simple and elaborate methods of solving Equation (23) exist.

The simplest models depend on the "tidally averaged" approximation, in which the tidal oscillations are not included explicitly, but are considered to be responsible for large-scale longitudinal diffusion. The more elaborate "real-time" models consider the actual tidal flow to be advective, with longitudinal diffusion occurring through motions having time scales considerably shorter than a tidal cycle. Each type of model is discussed below.

(1) Analytical Model (Steady State)

The least elaborate one-dimensional model assumes a constant cross-sectional area A, a constant (tidally and sectionally averaged) longitudinal dispersion coefficient E_L, and a constant fresh water velocity U_f. For this case Equation (23) reduces to

$$E_L \frac{d^2C}{dx^2} - U_f \frac{dC}{dx} - \lambda C = 0 \qquad (24)$$

where C is the time and sectionally averaged concentration. The solution (Ref. 46) to Equation (24) for a source at x = 0 and the boundary conditions C = 0 at $x = \pm\infty$ is

$$C = \frac{W}{AU_f\sqrt{1 + \frac{4\lambda E_L}{U_f^2}}} \exp\left(\frac{U_f}{2E_L}\left[1 \pm \sqrt{1 + \frac{4\lambda E_L}{U_f^2}}\right]x\right) \qquad (25)$$

The sign within the exponential is negative downstream from the source (x positive) and positive upstream from the source (x negative).

In terms of dimensionless variables, Equation (25) reduces to

$$\Gamma = \Gamma_{max} \exp\left(\frac{N \pm \sqrt{N^2+4}}{2}\,\xi\right) \qquad (26)$$

where

$$N = \frac{U_f}{\sqrt{\lambda E_L}}$$

$$\Gamma = \frac{A\sqrt{\lambda E_L}}{W} C$$

$$\Gamma_{max} = \left(\frac{\lambda E_L}{U_f^2 + 4\lambda E_L}\right)^{1/2}$$

$$\xi = \sqrt{\frac{\lambda}{E_L}}\, x$$

Figure 4 illustrates this dimensionless equation evaluated for ξ and N.

Several features of Equation (26) are evident from Figure 4. The dimensionless source concentration Γ_{max} depends not only on the source strength and freshwater flow, but also on the diffusivity E_L and the decay constant λ. This dependency is explained by the fact that a steady concentration is maintained by a balance between the discharge source, the net advective-diffusive transport away from the source, and a local sink due to radioactive decay.

The upstream and downstream curves have equal but opposite slopes for N = 0, since there is no nontidal advection where the net freshwater flow is zero. The curves become skewed in the downstream direction for increasing values of U_f because of the nontidal advection downstream.

(2) Releases of Short Duration

For releases of short duration, the preceding steady-state model does not apply. In the case of a time-dependent source term, the transport equation is given by

$$\frac{\partial C}{\partial t} + U_f \frac{\partial C}{\partial x} = E_L \frac{\partial^2 C}{\partial x^2} - \lambda C \tag{27}$$

The solution to Equation (27) for a time-dependent release may be obtained from the solution corresponding to the instantaneous release of a finite quantity of effluent uniformly over the flow cross-section (unit impulse function) (Ref. 47).

The unit impulse solution is given by

$$C = \frac{M}{A\sqrt{4\pi E_L t}} \exp\left(-\frac{(x - U_f t)^2}{4E_L t} - \lambda t\right) \tag{28}$$

where M is the amount of activity introduced (Ci).

For a more general time-dependent release, results may be obtained by time integration of Equation (28). Assume that, instead of the instantaneous introduction of a finite quantity at x = 0 and t = 0, effluent is continuously discharged at the rate $\frac{dM}{dt} = Wf(t)$ Ci/sec. The concentration distribution resulting from a continuous discharge in the time interval $0<\tau<t$ is given by

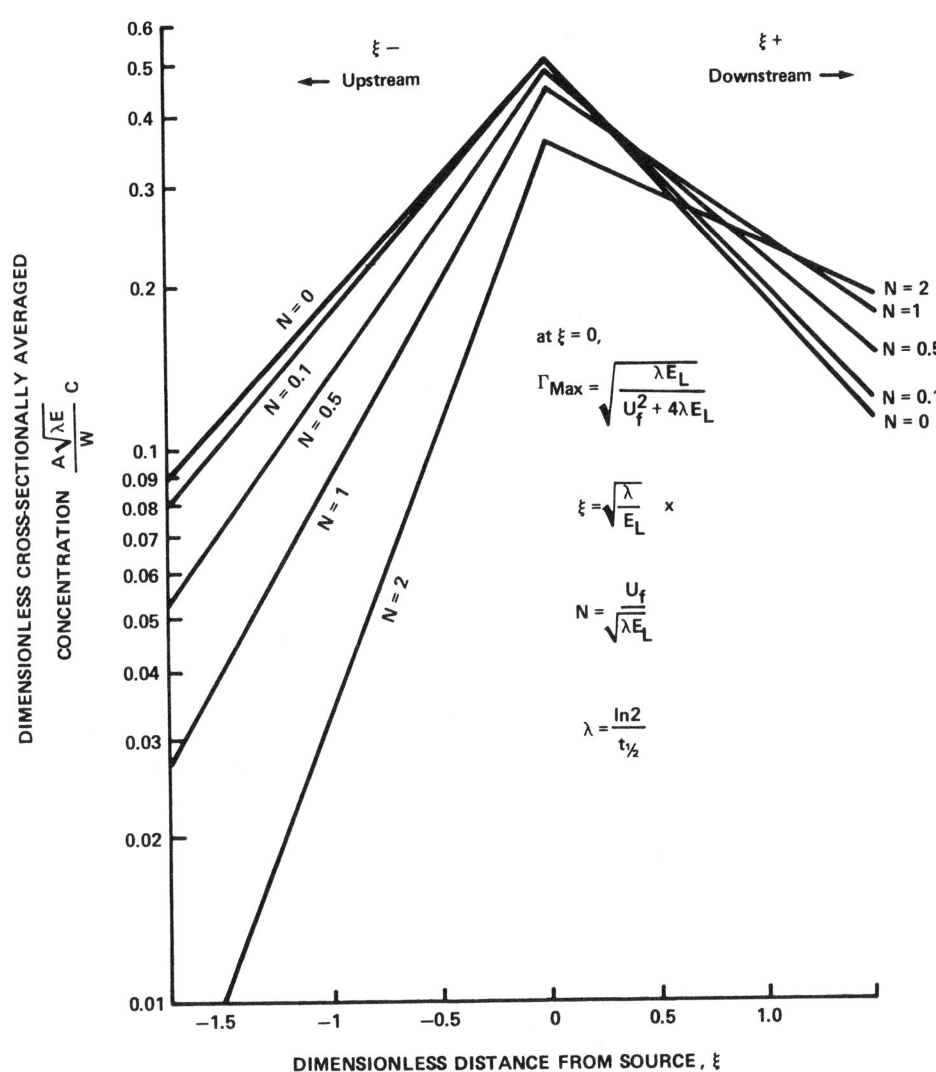

FIGURE 4.
DIMENSIONLESS PLOT OF CONTAMINANT CONCENTRATION VS DISTANCE FROM SOURCE (FROM O'CONNER ET AL., REF. 46)

$$C = \frac{W}{A\sqrt{4\pi E_L}} \int_0^t \frac{f(\tau)}{\sqrt{t - \tau}} \exp\left\{- \frac{[x - U_f(t - \tau)]^2}{4E_L(t - \tau)} - \lambda(t - \tau)\right\} d\tau \tag{29}$$

From Equation (29) the concentration distribution corresponding to a square pulse release of amplitude W and duration t_D is

$$C = \frac{W}{A\sqrt{4\pi E_L}} \int_0^{t_D} \frac{1}{\sqrt{t - \tau}} \exp\left\{- \frac{[x - U_f(t - \tau)]^2}{4E_L(t - \tau)} - \lambda(t - \tau)\right\} d\tau \tag{30}$$

Equation (30) may be integrated to give the following solution in terms of exponentials and error functions:

$$\left.\begin{aligned} C &= \frac{W}{2A\Omega} \exp\left(\frac{Ux}{2E_L}\right) g(x,t) \text{ for } 0 < t < t_D \\ C &= \frac{W}{2A\Omega} \exp\left(\frac{Ux}{2E_L}\right) [g(x,t) - g(x,t - t_D)] \text{ for } t > t_D \end{aligned}\right\} \tag{31}$$

where

$$g(x,t) = \left[\text{erf}\left\{\frac{x + \Omega t}{\sqrt{4E_L t}}\right\} \pm 1\right] \exp\left(\frac{\Omega x}{2E_L}\right) - \left[\text{erf}\left\{\frac{x - \Omega t}{\sqrt{4E_L t}}\right\} \pm 1\right] \exp\left(- \frac{\Omega x}{2E_L}\right)$$

$$\Omega = \sqrt{U^2 + 4\lambda E_L}$$

The function $g(x,t - t_D)$ has the same form as $g(x,t)$, with $(t - t_D)$ replacing t. The sign within the brackets is chosen negative downstream of the source (positive x) and positive upstream of the source (negative x).

Equation (31) holds for any pulse duration t_D. In the limit as $(t,t_D) \rightarrow \infty$, the solution reduces to the steady-state solution given by Equation (25).

Release rates other than square pulses are most easily computed by solving Equation (29) directly, using numerical quadrature. (See Sections 2.a.(2) and 3.a.(2) of this appendix.)

(3) Tidally Averaged Numerical Models

To simulate constituent transport in many types of estuaries, it is necessary to include detail beyond the capabilities of analytical models. For example, the distribution of sources and sinks (both man-made and natural) may be important.

Additionally, the estuary may have a nonuniform cross-section and tidal mixing properties that vary along its length.

The next level of sophistication above the analytical models are one-dimensional numerical models, which can account for variable cross-sections, inputs, withdrawals, and tidally averaged longitudinal diffusion. These models solve what is essentially the finite difference equivalent of Equation (23) in either the steady-state or transient (but tidally averaged) form. Models similar to the EPA AUTOSS and AUTOQD models fall into this category (Ref. 48).

The estuary is considered to be divided into variable-length segments. Each segment is coupled to the next upstream and downstream segment, as well as to external sources and sinks. Typically, the boundary conditions are chosen so that the concentrations of the first and last segments are known constants. This is the most realistic assumption for this model, provided the model is extended to the headwaters of the estuary and to the ocean. In practice, the model can easily be extended from the headwaters to the ocean by fine grid spacing in the area near the discharge and by coarse spacing farther away--in the regions of less interest.

A useful application of this model occurs where there are recycle streams such as municipal water withdrawal and return. The recirculation with partial or total removal of certain radionuclides could be important for heavily used tidal and nontidal waterways.

(4) Intratidal Numerical Models

The tidally averaged models are often subject to error because of uncertainty in the longitudinal dispersion coefficient. A more acceptable approach is the intratidal model, in which velocity, water level, and concentration in the estuary are simultaneously solved for, the tidal velocity being retained explicitly as an advective transport mechanism. In such a model, the longitudinal diffusion coefficient is better defined on the basis of physical principles and is less important than in the tidally averaged case. The model solutions are suitable for digital computation and do not require excessive computer resources.

Included are models such as the Dailey-Harleman (Ref. 49) one-dimensional finite element model, the Lee-Harleman (Ref. 50) finite difference model, and the Eraslan (Ref. 51) one-dimensional donor cell model. Basically, these models solve the one-dimensional equations of mass, momentum, and constituent conservation,

$$b\frac{\partial \zeta}{\partial t} + \frac{\partial Q}{\partial x} - \text{Source} = 0 \tag{32}$$

$$\frac{\partial Q}{\partial t} + \bar{U}\frac{\partial Q}{\partial x} + Q\frac{\partial \bar{U}}{\partial x} + g\frac{\partial \zeta}{\partial x}A + \frac{gQ|Q|}{AC_h^2R_h} = 0 \tag{33}$$

$$\frac{1}{A}\frac{\partial}{\partial t}(AC) + \frac{1}{A}\frac{\partial}{\partial x}(A\bar{U}C) = \frac{1}{A}\frac{\partial}{\partial x}\left(AE\frac{\partial C}{\partial x}\right) - \lambda C \tag{34}$$

where

b is the width of the estuary at the water surface;

C_h is the Chezy coefficient;

R_h is the hydraulic radius; and

ζ is the water surface location above an undisturbed level datum.

Concentration boundary conditions can be treated realistically in the intratidal formulation. The upstream boundary is usually the concentration at the head of the tide. The downstream boundary, however, usually differs according to whether the tide is flooding or ebbing. During ebb tide, the downstream boundary is chosen so that all constituents leave by advection. During flood tide, the entering concentration must be specified. This is determined by the physical situation assumed. If the downstream boundary is the ocean, the concentration of constituents in ocean water can be the input. If the downstream boundary is a bay or other water body where a discharged constituent can accumulate, an approximation of this concentration must be made.

An advantage of the intratidal model is its ability to simulate releases coordinated with the tide. If the source of contaminant is close to the mouth of the estuary, it may be advantageous to discharge only during ebb tide to flush the contaminant rapidly out of the estuary. Such operation could not be simulated with a tidally averaged model.

b. Multi-Dimensional Models

In very wide estuaries and embayments, the one-dimensional assumption is not realistic. For such conditions, both transverse and longitudinal velocity components are important, and concentration gradients across the channel approach those along the channel. To simulate this case with one-dimensional models, unreasonably large longitudinal dispersion coefficients must be used.

Two-dimensional vertically averaged numerical models are more suitable for these situations. Typical acceptable models were discussed in Section 3 of this appendix.

In some cases, numerical models which simulate vertical concentration variations rather than horizontal variations may be more appropriate, for instance, in the salinity intrusion region of an estuary, or a highly stratified reservoir.

Although three-dimensional numerical models are currently being developed, their complexity and relatively high cost of observation are rarely warranted for the purpose of computations under Appendix I.

c. Exchange Coefficients

The sectionally averaged, one-dimensional longitudinal dispersion coefficient, E, includes a combination of several individual processes. In the prototype, these processes include molecular exchange and flow- and wind-induced turbulent exchange. In most cases, these processes make a relatively minor contribution to the overall dispersion, which is in part an artifact resulting from the temporal and spatial averaging of the three-dimensional transport equations. In general, the greater the simplification of the model, the larger the exchange coefficient must be to simulate the prototype.

The simplest model is the tidally averaged one-dimensional model. The actual three-dimensional oscillating flow is drastically simplified into a one-dimensional system in which the advective transport is determined by the fresh water flow rate. The diffusive transport includes the effects of deviations from sectional homogeneity and "turbulence" components of time scales on the order of the tidal period or less.

In the intratidal models, the true oscillating or unidirectional flow is simulated and is treated as part of the advective process. The diffusive term includes the effects of deviations from sectional homogeneity of the concentration and velocity fields. However, in this case, tidal effects are no longer included in the turbulence field.

In the case of two-dimensional intratidal models, it is, in general, only necessary to include deviations of velocity and concentration in the vertical direction since, with sufficient resolution, the lateral flow field is simulated correctly.

In all cases, the most acceptable procedure for choosing the diffusion coefficient is to adjust the model to match observed prototype conditions, usually through tracer study results. In general, the more refined the model, the less empirical tuning is necessary because the turbulent transport coefficients are more firmly based on physical principles.

(1) Tidally Averaged Models

If the tidally averaged model is used, the determination of the diffusion coefficient is empirical and must be based on the observed dispersion of a known tracer, with prototype and model constituent concentrations being matched. The tidally averaged longitudinal dispersion coefficient E_L may be determined from Equations (25), (28), or (29) by a trial and error procedure where E_L is changed until the model concentrations match observed values of the tracer.

In the case of tidally averaged numerical models covered under paragraph 4.a(3), it is possible to restructure the finite difference equations to solve for E_L with input of observed concentration of the tracer. The calculated values of E_L may then be used for subsequent concentration computations.

As a rough approximation to the dispersion coefficient, lacking any field data, a formula by Hetling and O'Connell (Ref. 52) based on data in the salinity intrusion region of the Potomac River estuary may be used:

$$E_L = 1680\, V_{max}^{4/3} \tag{35}$$

where

E_L is the sectionally and tidally averaged, one-dimensional longitudinal dispersion coefficient (in ft^2/sec), and

V_{max} is the maximum tidal velocity (in knots).

It must be cautioned that this equation can only be relied upon for order of magnitude estimates and is not necessarily conservative.

(2) One-Dimensional Real-Time Models

Less "tuning" is necessary for real-time models than for the tidally averaged models. In the well-mixed region of the estuary, Taylor's formula (Ref. 53) for dispersion is acceptable for reasons discussed in Section 4.d of this appendix.

The salinity intrusion region of the estuary is still poorly defined on physical grounds. Since the presence of gravitational circulation casts doubts on the applicability of sectional averaging, it is this region for which tuning is most important.

An approximation for the longitudinal dispersion coefficient that is applicable to the whole length of the estuary is based on the work of Thatcher and Harleman (Ref. 54). This approach is based on a combination of Taylor's dispersion formula applicable to the well-mixed portion of the estuary combined with an empirical correlation for mixing in the salinity intrusion region based on observed salinity distributions. The dispersion coefficient is

$$E(x,t) = K\left|\frac{d(\frac{S}{S_o})}{d(\frac{x}{L})}\right| + 77nU_tR_h^{5/6} \qquad (36)$$

where

- L is the length of estuary;
- n is Manning's coefficient (local);
- R_h is the hydraulic radius (local);
- S is the salinity (local);
- S_o is the salinity at mouth;
- U_t is the RMS velocity (local); and
- x is the distance from mouth.

The factor K is given by

$$K = 0.00215V_{max}LE_D^{-0.25} \qquad (37)$$

and is shown in Figure 5.

The quantity E_D is the so-called "estuary number" and is given by

$$E_D = \frac{P_TF_D^2}{Q_fT} \qquad (38)$$

where

- F_D is the densimetric Froude number evaluated at the estuary mouth;
- P_T is the tidal prism, in ft^3;
- Q_f is the freshwater flow rate; and
- T is the tidal period.

The dispersion formula given in Equation (36) may be used with good results as a first approximation in the tuning of a real-time model.

In an oscillatory flow such as a hydroelectric or pump storage reservoir where there is no salinity intrusion region, the Taylor formula alone may be used as a first approximation:

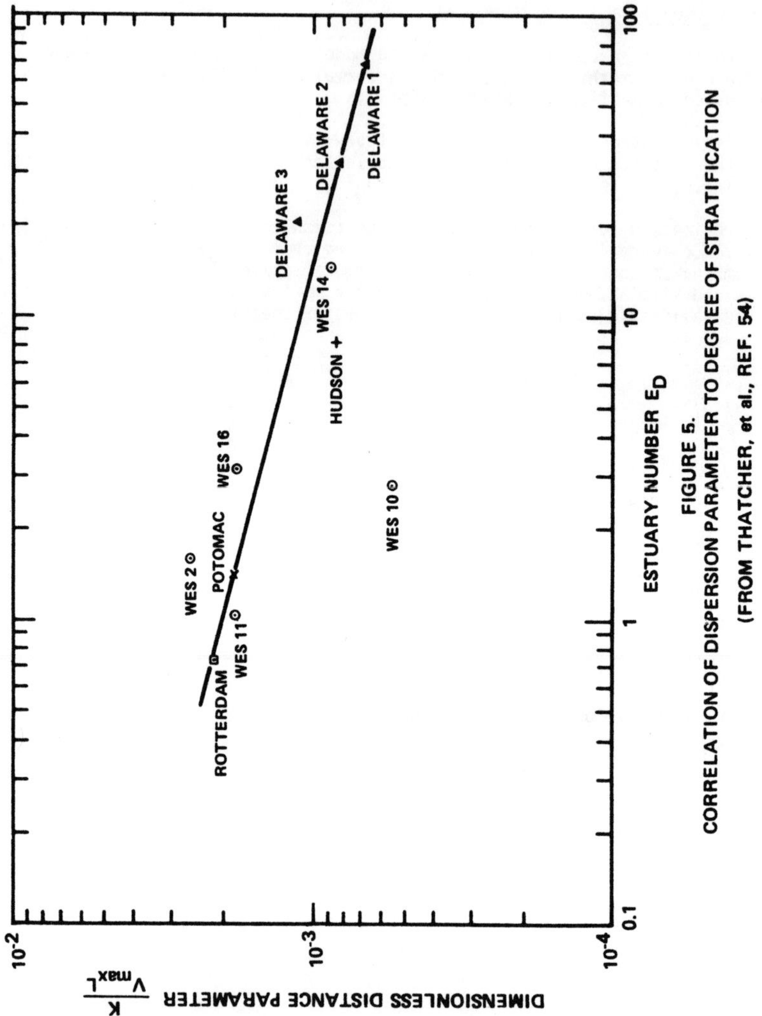

FIGURE 5.
CORRELATION OF DISPERSION PARAMETER TO DEGREE OF STRATIFICATION
(FROM THATCHER, et al., REF. 54)

$$E(x,t) = 77nU_tR_h^{5/6} \quad (39)$$

These approximations are suitable only for periodic oscillating flows and not necessarily for unidirectional flows (as will be further explained in Section 4.d of this appendix). Tuning of the dispersion coefficient should be performed after the friction coefficients are adjusted to simulate the observed flows, since Equation (39) is a function of Manning's coefficient.

(3) Two-Dimensional Models

The best approximation for the dispersion coefficients in the two-dimensional estuary model appears to be the one adapted for the one-dimensional real-time model discussed above. For example, as a first approximation in the simulation of Jamaica Bay, which can be classified as a well-mixed two-dimensional estuary, Leendertse (Ref. 29) used Elder's formula with an additional factor for the effect of wind-induced turbulence.

As with the one-dimensional models, tuning is necessary to match prototype observations and should be performed after roughness factors in the hydraulic part of the model have been established. In the salinity intrusion regions of the estuary, initial estimates based on the method described in Thatcher and Harleman (Ref. 54) should be adequate.

d. Applicability of Models

Choice of one of the above models involves several factors. Although these models are classified as estuary models, they may be used for other types of water bodies, such as reservoirs with hydroelectric power generation flow reversals and, in most cases, unidirectional rivers. However, the assumptions implicit in one-dimensional models may be invalid in some cases, as explained below.

Fischer (Ref. 55) analyzed the mechanics of dispersion in nontidal rivers and concluded that Elder's formula yielded dispersion coefficients that were low by as much as two orders of magnitude. He concluded that longitudinal dispersion in rivers is primarily due to velocity variations in the lateral direction, while Elder's formula accounts only for velocity variations in the vertical direction. An approximate diffusion coefficient for unidirectional rivers derived by Fischer (Ref. 55) is

$$E \simeq 0.3\ \overline{u'^2}\ \frac{\ell^2}{R_h u^*} \quad (40)$$

where

ℓ is approximately the cross-sectional distance from the point of maximum velocity to the further bank;

R_h is the hydraulic radius;

u'^2 is the mean squared deviation of the river flow from the sectional mean velocity $\bar{u}$; and

u^* is the shear velocity.

The one-dimensional model is valid only for downstream distances corresponding to travel times greater than the so-called "Taylor period":

$$t \geq 1.8\ \frac{\ell^2}{R_h u^*} \quad (41)$$

at which point the constituent introduced at t = 0 is sufficiently well mixed in the cross-section for the transport to be considered one-dimensional.

In an oscillating tidal flow in a wide, shallow estuary, however, the tidal period is large compared to the vertical mixing time scale, but small compared to the lateral mixing time scale. In this case, velocity variations in the lateral direction add little to the longitudinal mixing, and Equation (39) is appropriate.

5. IMPOUNDMENTS

There are two basic types of cooling ponds. The first is a closed-loop system in which the thermal effluent is cooled in the pond and recirculated through the power plant condensers. Some water ("blowdown") must be removed from the pond to limit the dissolved solids concentration to an acceptable level. Fresh water ("make-up") must be added to the pond to compensate for evaporation and blowdown.

The second type of cooling pond is a flow-through system in which there is little or no recirculation of effluent through the power plant. The effluent is discharged to the pond which, in turn, discharges to a larger body of receiving water. The pond serves as a holding reservoir, allowing effluent to cool before entering the receiving water.

The source of radionuclides may either be located on the impoundment or upstream on a tributary of the impoundment. For the simplest models, this distinction is irrelevant because concentration is based on flow through the impoundment and does not depend on the placement of the input. In the case of the upstream plant, the source term W is the rate of radionuclide entering with the flow at the boundary of the reservoir.

Figure 6 illustrates a closed-loop cooling pond. Water for cooling is drawn through the intake, circulated through condensers, and returned to the pond via the discharge. There are two important hydrological parameters of this system. The first is the internal recirculation time constant associated with the flushing of the pond by the makeup and blowdown streams. The second is the time constant associated with the decay of radioisotopes.

Figure 7 illustrates the flow-through pond. The hydraulics of this pond are simpler than the closed-loop pond, since no recirculation occurs between intake and discharge. In this case, the only hydraulic time constant is that associated with the travel time from the plant discharge to the receiving water.

a. Simple Analytical Models

Simple models may be used to obtain conservative estimates of the radioisotope concentrations. Four models can be used to describe all cooling ponds: the completely mixed model, the plug-flow model, the partially mixed model, and the stratified model. In each case, the effect of evaporation is neglected.

(1) Completely Mixed Model

Figure 8 shows the first case (the closed loop), in which the pond is represented as a completely mixed tank. All inputs of material makeup are instantaneously mixed throughout the tank, so that the concentration is homogeneous.

By performing a mass balance on the volume of the pond, a solution for concentration is obtained, assuming zero initial concentration and complete mixing:

$$\frac{C}{C_o} = \frac{\frac{q_b}{V_T\lambda}}{\frac{q_b}{V_T\lambda} + 1}\left[1 - \exp\left(-\frac{q_b}{V_T\lambda} - 1\right)\lambda t\right] \tag{42}$$

where

q_b is the pond blowdown rate and

V_T is the volume of the pond.

The concentration C_o is the steady-state concentration that would exist for a nondecaying substance and is given by

$$C_o = \frac{W}{q_b}$$

where W is the rate of addition of radioactivity (in Ci/sec).

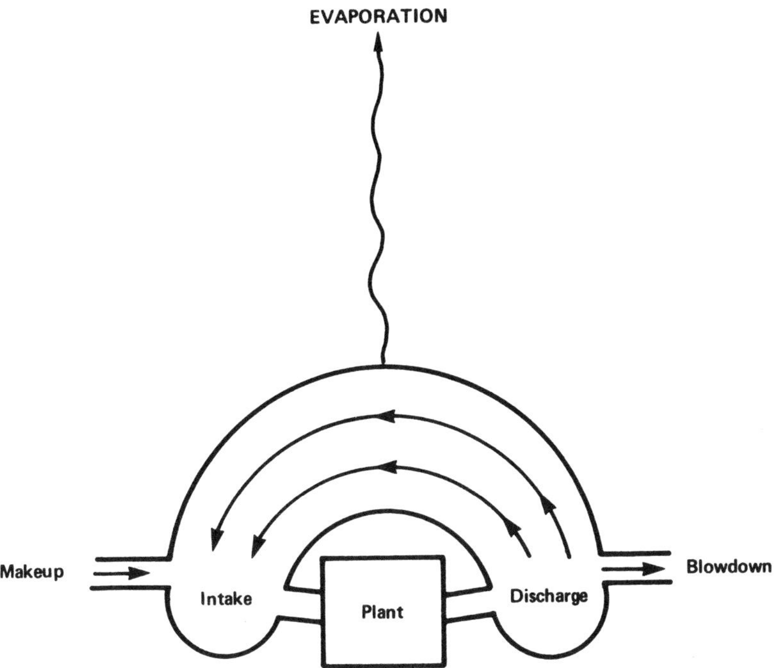

FIGURE 6.
CLOSED-LOOP COOLING POND

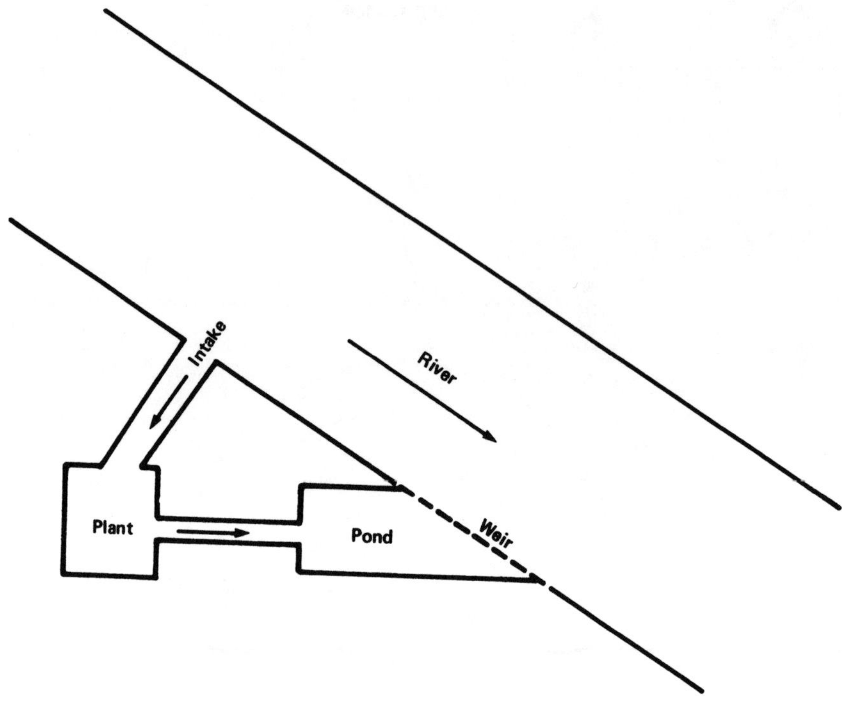

FIGURE 7.
FLOW-THROUGH COOLING POND

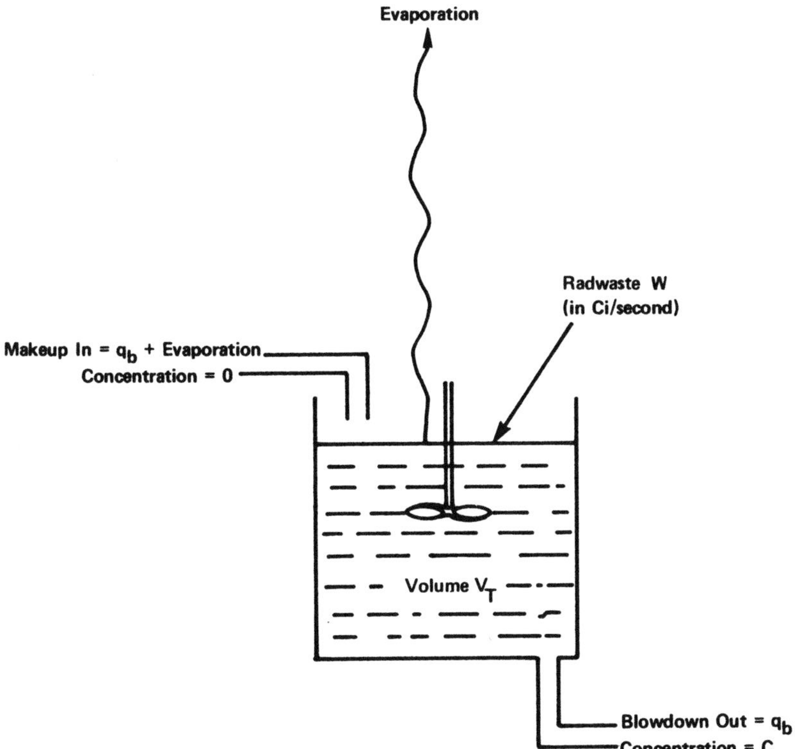

FIGURE 8..
COMPLETELY MIXED MODEL

For the steady-state concentration of a decaying substance, Equation (42) reduces to

$$\frac{C}{C_o} = \frac{\frac{q_b}{V_T\lambda}}{\frac{q_b}{V_T\lambda} + 1} \tag{43}$$

In terms of the half-life, $t_{1/2}$, of the added radioactivity, Equations (42) and (43) reduce to

$$\frac{C}{C_o} = \frac{\tau}{\tau + \ln 2}\left(1 - \exp\left\{-[\tau + \ln 2]\frac{t}{t_{1/2}}\right\}\right) \tag{44}$$

(at steady state) $$\frac{C}{C_o} = \frac{\tau}{\tau + \ln 2} \tag{45}$$

where

$$\tau = \frac{t_{1/2}\, q_b}{V_T} \quad \text{and}$$

$$t_{1/2} = (\ln 2)/\lambda$$

The dimensionless variable τ is the radioisotope half-life expressed in multiples of the flushing time (V_T/q_b). Figure 9 illustrates the steady-state concentration defined by Equation (45) as a function of τ. This figure shows that for small half-lives (compared with the flushing time, V_T/q_b), the concentration depends strongly on half-life, but for long half-lives, this dependence diminishes.

The completely mixed tank model (see Figure 8) is adequate for substances with long half-lives, where the internal circulation time is short compared with the half-life. In this case, the concentration in the pond is fairly homogeneous, satisfying the "completely mixed" limitation of this model.

(2) Plug-Flow Model

For the flow-through cooling pond, the plug-flow model illustrated in Figure 10 may be adequate if it is presumed that there is no recirculation. The concentration is expressed as

$$C = C_o \exp(-\lambda V_T/q_b) = C_o \exp(-\ln 2/\tau) \tag{46}$$

where q_b is now the flow rate through the pond.

This expression is evaluated in Figure 9 and compared with the completely mixed case. Agreement is best for large τ. Although not easily seen in Figure 9, the models deviate for small τ.

(3) Partially Mixed Model

Where a significant part of the flow is due to both blowdown and plant pumping, neither of the above models is adequate. A suitable model that includes both the plant pumping rate q_p and blowdown rate q_b is illustrated in Figure 11. The recirculation factor R is defined as

$$R = \frac{q_b}{q_p}$$

The steady-state concentration is then defined as

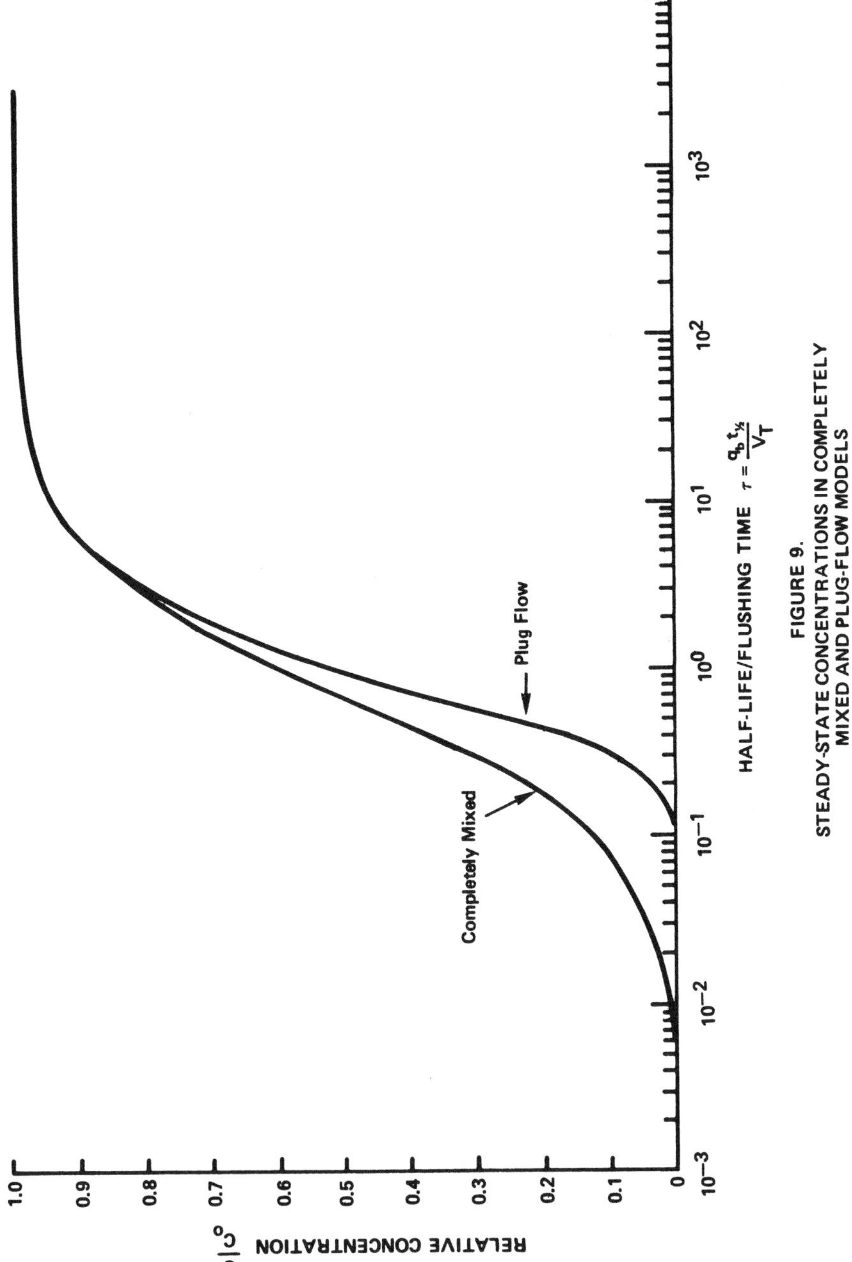

FIGURE 9.
STEADY-STATE CONCENTRATIONS IN COMPLETELY MIXED AND PLUG-FLOW MODELS

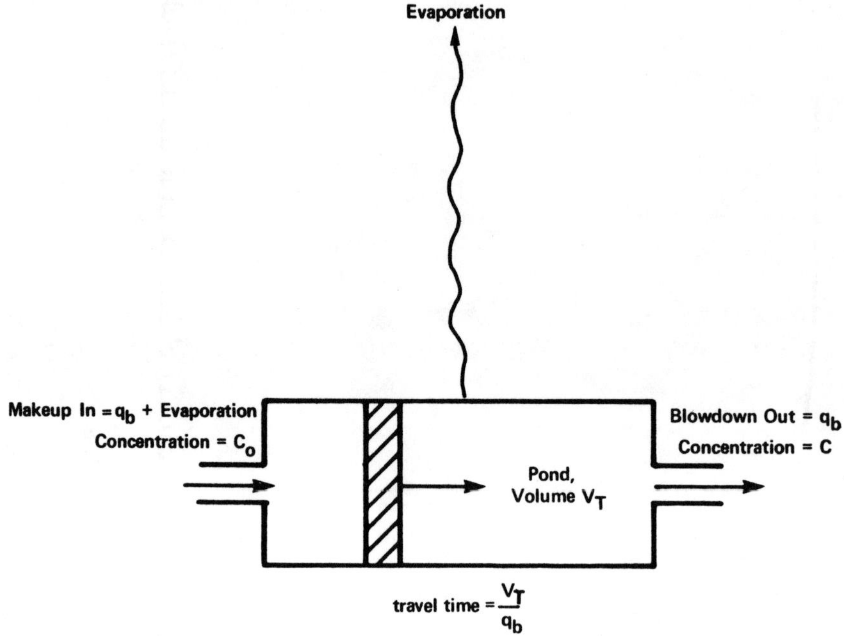

FIGURE 10.
PLUG-FLOW MODEL

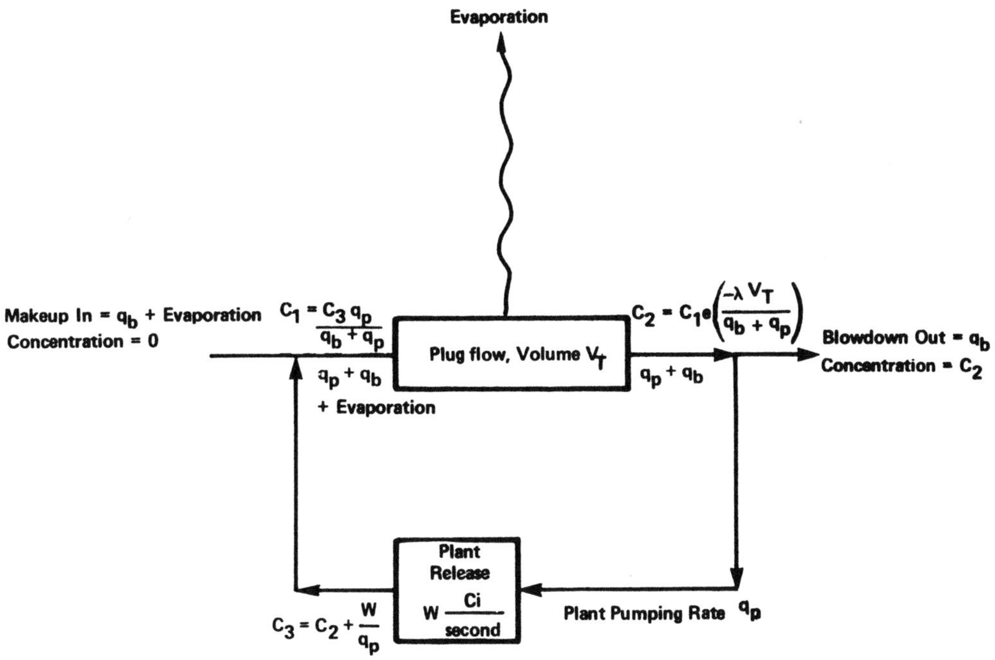

FIGURE 11.
PARTIALLY MIXED MODEL

$$\frac{C}{C_o} = \frac{R}{(R + 1)\exp\left[\frac{R}{\tau(R + 1)} \ln 2\right] - 1} \tag{47}$$

Figure 12 shows the relative concentration C/C_0 as a function of τ and R. Notice that the asymptotic forms of Equation (47) for R = 0 reduce to the completely mixed case:

$$\frac{C}{C_0} = \frac{\tau}{\tau + \ln 2} \tag{45}$$

and for R = ∞ to the plug-flow case:

$$\frac{C}{C_0} = \exp(-\ln 2/\tau) \tag{46}$$

(4) Stratified Reservoir Lumped Parameter Model

A simple model based on an approach of Trent (Ref. 56) is useful for a gross approximation of the mixing processes in stratified reservoirs that have seasonal turnover. The lake is assumed to have two layers, each totally mixed (Figure 13). Water can flow into and be withdrawn from either layer, but the layers do not mix during stratified flow periods. The volume of each layer is assumed constant during the period of stratification or during unstratified flow. Turnover is assumed to mix the two layers totally and instantaneously. This assumption is reasonable for systems in which the turnover time is small compared to the residence time.

Input data needed for this model are as follows:

Stratified Period

1. Length of stratified period
2. Volume of epilimnion and hypolimnion (constant over period)
3. Inflow and withdrawal (same), either layer
4. Concentration in inflow
5. Half-life of constituent

Unstratified Period

1. Length of unstratified period
2. Total volume of reservoir (constant over period)
3. Inflow and withdrawal (same)
4. Concentration in inflow
5. Half-life of constituent

The model is initialized with concentration C(o) at time t = 0. The first period, $(0<t<t_1)$, corresponds to stratified conditions. Concentration in the epilimnion during this period is

$$C_E = \frac{a - [a - b\,C(o)]e^{-bt}}{b} \tag{48}$$

$$a = \frac{C_i q_i}{V_E}, \quad b = \frac{q_i}{V_E} + \lambda$$

where

C_i is the input concentration in the upper layer;

q_i is the inflow to the upper layer;

V_E is the volume of epilimnion; and

λ is the decay constant and is $= \ln 2/t_{1/2}$.

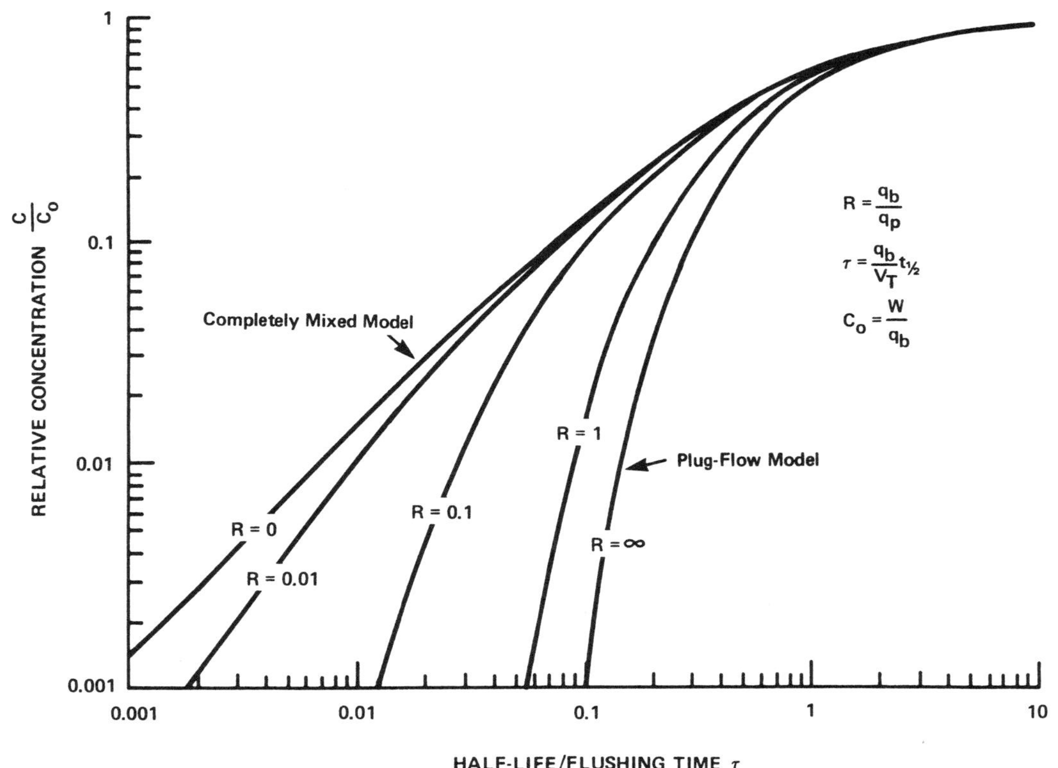

FIGURE 12.
CONCENTRATION IN PARTIALLY MIXED CASE

a. Stratified

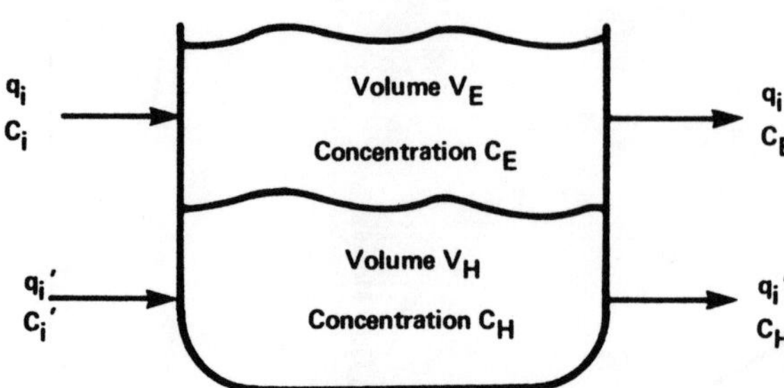

b. Unstratified

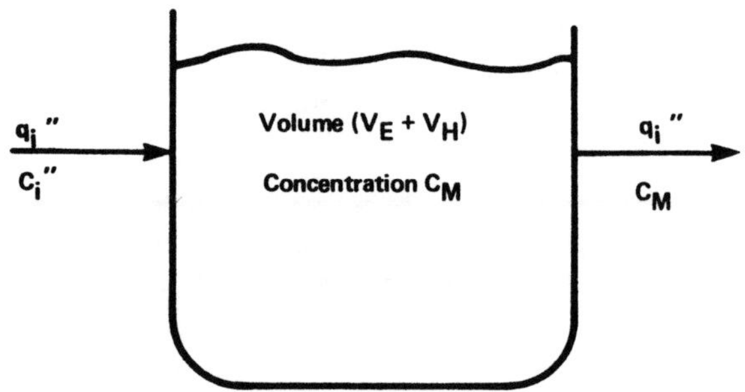

FIGURE 13.

LUMPED PARAMETER STRATIFIED RESERVOIR MODEL

The concentration in the lower layer during this period is

$$C_H = \frac{a' - [a' - b'C(o)]e^{-b't}}{b'} \qquad (49)$$

$$a' = \frac{C_i'q_i'}{V_H}$$

$$b' = \frac{q_i'}{V_H} + \lambda$$

where

C_i' is the input concentration to the lower layer;

q_i' is the inflow to the lower layer; and

V_H is the volume of hypolimnion.

During turnover, instantaneous mixing of the two layers is assumed as

$$C_T = \frac{C_E V_E + C_H V_H}{V_E + V_H} \qquad (50)$$

During the unstratified flow period, $(t_1<t<t_2)$, the concentration is

$$C_M = \frac{a''-(a''-b''C_T)e^{-b''(t - t_1)}}{b''} \qquad (51)$$

$$a'' = \frac{C_i''q_i''}{V_T}, \quad b'' = \frac{q_i''}{V_T} + \lambda$$

where

C_i'' is the input concentration for the total pond;

q_i'' is the inflow; and

V_T is the total volume.

Subsequent seasonal stratification cycles repeat with Equation (48), but with the latest fully mixed concentration substituted for C(o).

Simple methods such as the well mixed, partially mixed, and stratified models covered in this and the previous section are most suitable for estimating concentrations in reservoirs, ponds, and lakes that are downstream of the radionuclide discharge and consequently already partially mixed. In such a case, the hydraulics of the pond are less important and simple methods may suffice.

More elaborate models may be required, however, for a direct radionuclide discharge to the reservoir. In this case, the hydraulics of the reservoir may strongly affect the way in which the radionuclide releases disperse.

(5) Buildup of Isotopes Using Simple Models

For large cooling ponds with relatively small blowdown rates, the concentrations of the longer-lived isotopes may build up over a period of several years (exclusive of sediment uptake effects). It may be desirable to know the rate of this buildup, since the flushing time would be a significant fraction of the useful life of the plant.

Since the only concern is long-lived isotopes, the completely mixed model is analyzed for transient conditions.

If the concentration in the pond is initially zero, then

$$\frac{C}{C_o} = \frac{\tau}{\tau + \ln 2}\left(1 - \exp\{-[\tau + \ln 2]t/t_{1/2}\}\right) \qquad (44)$$

Figure 14 shows the buildup to steady-state concentration C_{SS} as a function of dimensionless time θ (time/flushing time) for several values of τ. Notice that Equation (44) becomes fairly insensitive to τ for large τ. This fact is illustrated more clearly by observing the time to reach some arbitrary fraction, say 99% of steady state:

$$1 - \exp\left[-(\tau + \ln 2)\frac{t}{t_{1/2}}\right] = 0.99 \text{ and} \qquad (52)$$

$$\theta_{99} = \left(\frac{tq_b}{V_T}\right)_{99} = -\tau\left(\frac{\ln 0.01}{\tau + \ln 2}\right)$$

Figure 15 illustrates the 99% buildup time as a function of τ, clearly showing how, for very long half-lives compared with pond flushing times, the time depends only on the flushing time of the pond.

(6) Hydraulics of Ponds Using Simple Models

The simple models presented here must be used with caution for several reasons. Large portions of a pond may be unused for dilution if the pond is unstratified and irregularly shaped. If the same pond becomes stratified during certain times of the year, however, previously unused sections may become useful because of density flows (Ref. 57) and because of the strong mixing induced by seasonal turnover.

In a flow-through cooling pond without recirculation, stratification may be detrimental because the thermal effluent and the radioisotopes may be confined to the upper layer, thereby reducing the effective volume of the pond. Thus, definition of the effective volume of a pond may be difficult.

It should be possible, however, to pick a conservative volume for a "worst case" calculation. Calculation of the steady-state concentration of isotopes whose half-lives are long should cause little error because the concentrations approach that of a conservative substance

$$C_o = \frac{W}{q_b}$$

regardless of pond hydraulics.

b. Numerical Models

Stratified reservoir models are in most cases numerical evaluations of the one- or two-dimensional equations describing convection and diffusion in stratified flow. The simplest numerical models are the one-dimensional diffusion models, such as the MIT deep reservoir model (Ref. 57). In such models, concentration is assumed to be horizontally uniform. Vertical diffusion and advection are modeled. The flow field is calculated by the equation of continuity and by accounting for inflows and outflows such as dams, tributaries, and outfalls to and from the different layers of the reservoir. Such models are useful where there is strong stratification, especially where the reservoir is used for direct condenser cooling. In such cases, the stratification is reinforced by the additional heat, discharge is usually to the surface, withdrawal is from the hypolimnion, and vertical gradients are more pronounced than horizontal gradients. These models are less accurate for reservoirs that have seasonal turnover and subsequent unstratified periods. Furthermore, these models are incapable of simulating certain important effects, such as horizontal mixing in the vicinity of a power plant discharge.

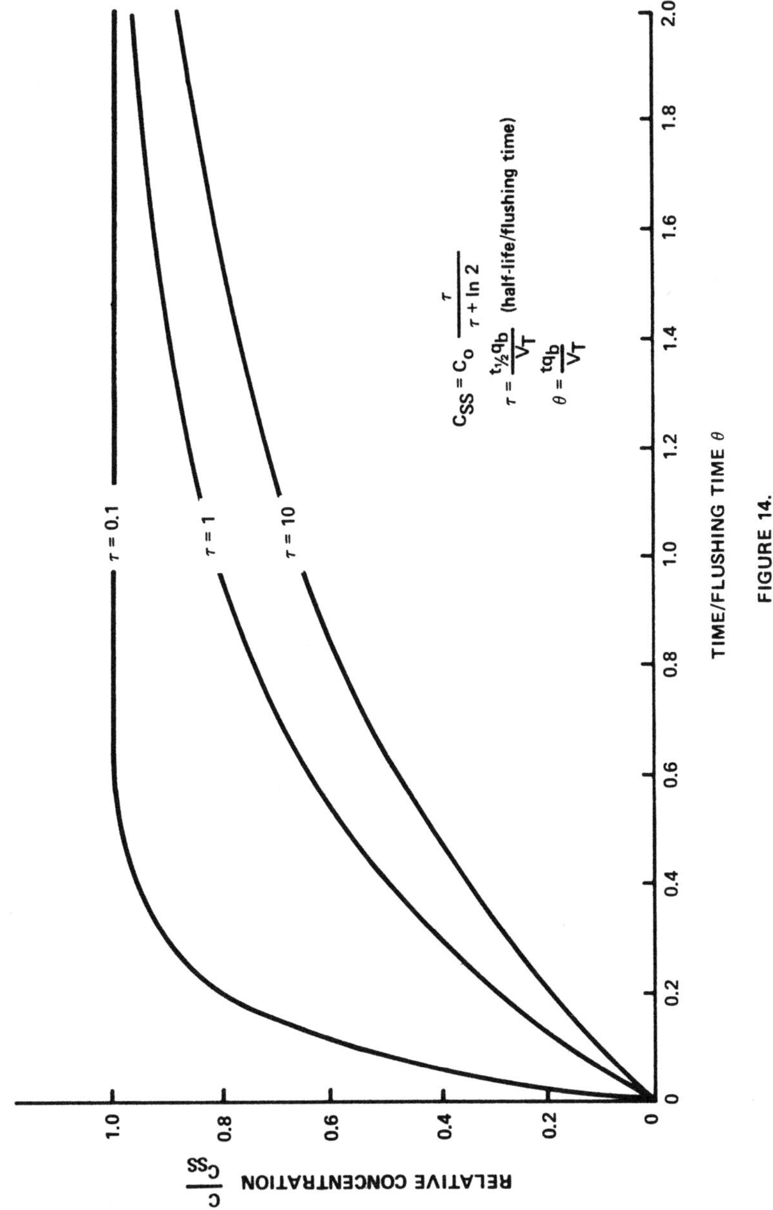

FIGURE 14.
BUILDUP OF RADIOISOTOPES IN COMPLETELY MIXED MODEL (NORMALIZED)

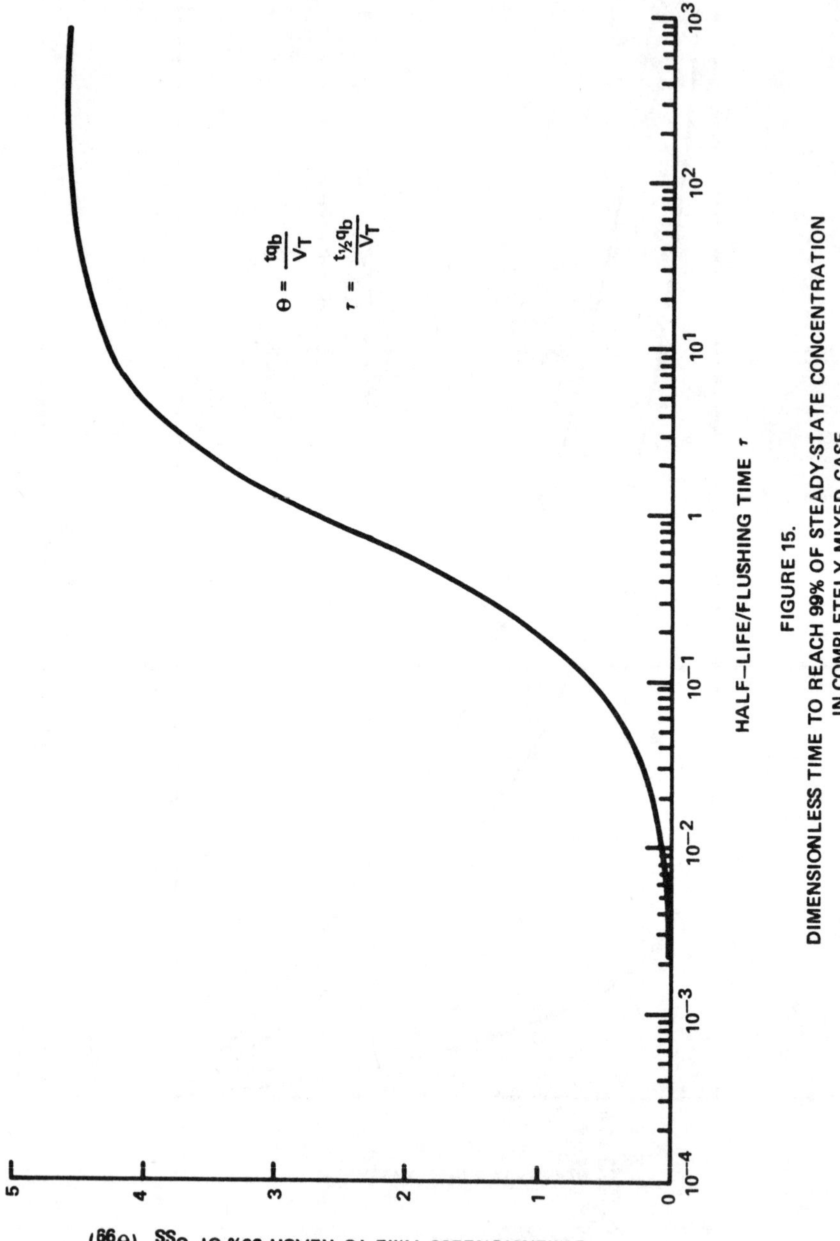

FIGURE 15.
DIMENSIONLESS TIME TO REACH 99% OF STEADY-STATE CONCENTRATION IN COMPLETELY MIXED CASE

Where both vertical and horizontal effects are important, more complicated models are warranted. For example, the EPA Reservoir Model (Ref. 58) allows for the horizontal segmentation of the reservoir. Each reservoir segment is solved in the vertical direction. Inputs from upstream and downstream segments are coupled empirically to account for density flows.

Another useful model is the reservoir model of Ryan and Harleman (Ref. 59). In this model, the one-dimensional horizontal solution in the surface layer is coupled with a one-dimensional solution in the vertical direction. Effects of discharge mixing, surface cooling, and lateral gradients are calculated in the surface layer solution. Vertically stratified flows and selective withdrawals are handled by the vertical solution. The model is most useful for cooling reservoirs where stratification is strong.

6. WATER USE

For identifying liquid pathways to man for realistic evaluations of the doses from normal releases from nuclear power plants, it is necessary to locate water users, identify types of uses, and estimate usage to a distance of 50 miles from a site. Because of high usage rates along many streams and estuaries, it is also necessary to identify the effects of water usage on the spatial and temporal distribution of flows. In addition, water usage upstream of a nuclear power plant can alter flows at or downstream of the plant. The following is an acceptable methodology to evaluate water usage and the consequences thereof on streamflows. This methodology provides a realistic evaluation of the liquid transport of normal releases of radionuclides from nuclear power plants along streams and estuaries.

a. Users

A schematic diagram of the river basin that locates the following features in relation to the plant site should be prepared: (1) surface water uses* upstream and downstream of the plant site, (2) major tributaries and their junctions, (3) streamflow gaging stations (including their period of record), and (4) major reservoirs and diversions upstream and downstream of the plant site. Approximate contributing drainage areas and types of water use for all points identified should be shown on the diagram or tabulated separately. An example schematic diagram is shown in Figure 16.

From the diagram, key diversion and streamflow stations should be selected to provide the basis for establishing reasonable spatial and temporal distributions of runoff patterns, upstream and downstream of nuclear power plant sites. Historical streamflows at major mainstem and tributary locations should be adjusted for historical diversions and reservoir effects to produce "natural" flows (e.g., flows independent of reservoir and diversion effects). Missing streamflow data (i.e., gaps in records) at critical stations may subsequently be synthesized by direct correlation with nearby streamflow stations or by statistical correlation with many stations using models such as "HEC-4, River Flow Simulation" (Ref. 60). In general, a period of at least 20 to 30 years of record, including the historical drought of record in the region, should be used.

Monthly durations have been found (Refs. 61 and 62) to describe adequately the fluctuations in streamflow without introducing significant errors in long-term estimates of reservoir yields. Similarly, estimates of average annual radionuclide concentrations along a river, based on monthly streamflow averages, produced acceptable values when compared with longer flow periods (see Figure 17). Flow periods for multidirectional estuaries, lakes, and ocean sites were discussed in Sections 3 and 4 of this appendix.

b. Usage

The effects on streamflows at and downstream of a site caused by reservoirs or diversions should be identified. Reservoirs may cause significant changes in the distribution of seasonal runoff. Operating constraints on reservoir storage, outflow, and diversions should be established on a monthly basis for existing conditions of basin development and water demand and for anticipated future conditions throughout the lifetime of the plant. Where proposed reservoirs may significantly affect flow conditions, their effects should be considered by simulating their operation using models such as "HEC-3, Reservoir Analysis" (Ref. 63).

*Use types include drinking water, irrigation, process water (consumed by such users as breweries and soft drink manufacturers), recreation areas, and fisheries. Ground water users with wells whose zones of influence extend to streams should also be included.

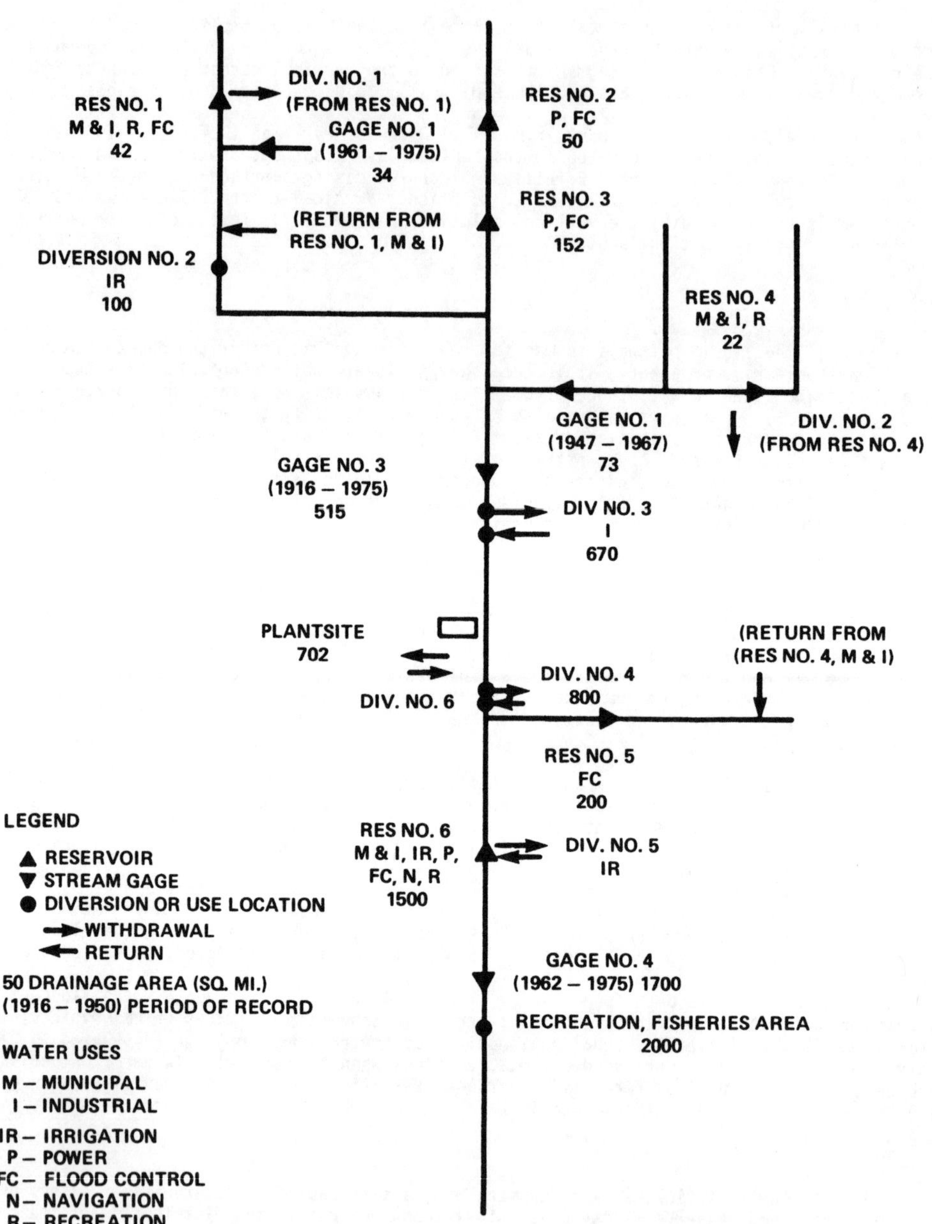

FIGURE 16. TYPICAL SCHEMATIC DIAGRAM OF A RIVER BASIN

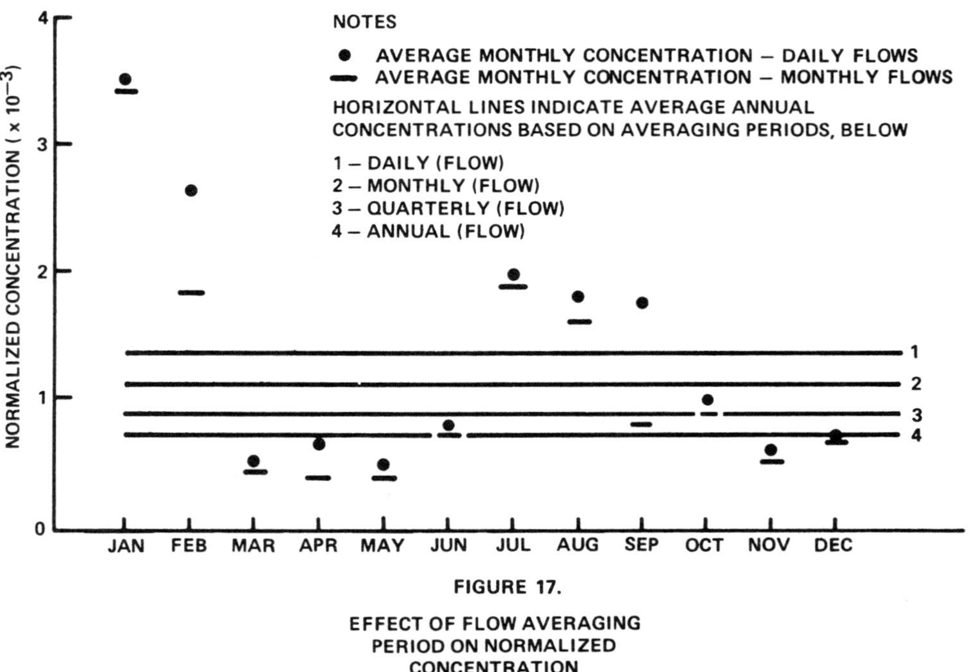

FIGURE 17.

EFFECT OF FLOW AVERAGING PERIOD ON NORMALIZED CONCENTRATION

(DATA – KANKAKEE RIVER 1961)

Many alternative schemes for developing water resources may have been proposed in a particular region, and it is difficult to conclude which, if any, are likely to be constructed. The evaluation described herein should consider any Federal, state or locally authorized projects; any projects adopted by local river basin commissions; or any other projects whose chances of being constructed are considered likely.

The locations of fisheries and recreation areas that will be exposed to normal releases of radionuclides within 50 radial miles of a plant should be identified. Present and projected future contact by humans and fish should be estimated.

The use of river system simulation models such as HEC-3 to adjust historic streamflows and to synthesize existing and potential future water use can provide acceptable estimates of the spatial and temporal distributions of streamflows at the locations for which estimates of average radionuclide concentrations are required. Two basic assumptions are required. First, it is assumed that the period of recorded historical streamflow selected for simulation is representative of conditions to be expected in the future. Secondly, it is assumed that it is necessary to adjust historical streamflows for the effects of reservoirs and diversions. If both of these assumptions are not supported by historical basin water usage, no adjustments are necessary. Furthermore, if projected water use cannot be expected to alter streamflows in a way such as to require basin simulation, no flow adjustments are necessary.

Water use should be estimated, on a monthly basis, for present and projected future conditions. Local, state, or regional agencies often maintain records of such use, and such information should be summarized and appropriately annotated. These same agencies have in many cases made projections of future usage; these projections should be summarized and annotated.

Where existing records or locally projected usage information is not available or is considered unreliable, conservative estimates may be made from population projections and forecasted per capita usage estimates of agencies such as the U.S. Geological Survey or the Water Resources Council. Where population or water use forecasts are at variance with other forecasts submitted by the applicant, the bases for the differences should be provided.

Although conservative estimates are sometimes required to ensure that the consequences of accidents are acceptable, realistic estimates will be adequate for the normal effluent release evaluations required by 10 CFR Part 50, Appendix I.

c. Existing Studies

Many studies of the effects of water resource development schemes have been completed in great detail. For example, many large river basins have been studied by the Corps of Engineers and others. These existing studies, with only minor modifications for plant water use, may be used directly.

7. SEDIMENT UPTAKE AND TRANSPORT MODELS

The ability of suspended and bottom sediments to absorb and adsorb radioactive nuclides from solution is recognized as contributing to important pathways to man through the sediment's ability to concentrate otherwise dilute species of ions. The pathways are by direct contact with the populace and by transfer to the aquatic food chain. Sorption by sediments is also an important mechanism for reducing the area of influence of plant releases.

The state of the art in sediment-related effects is not as advanced as in other engineering disciplines. For this reason, and until reliable models become available, the staff will rely on existing field studies and the staff's and consultants' experience to determine the conservatism or reasonableness of the applicant's analyses and results.

If the applicant elects to take credit for the removal of certain ions from the surface waters by sediment uptake, extensive verification of the techniques used will be necessary because of the lack of existing verified generalized models. The applicant's models will be evaluated based on their adherence to physical principles and their proven reliability in simulating prototype data. Models will be compared, in terms of physical principles, to those listed in the references, in accordance with the classification of receiving water. However, the staff does not accept these models *a priori*. Because most existing sediment uptake and transport modeling techniques are crude, the applicant should demonstrate that the model is conservative or realistically simulates the prototype. The model verification will be accepted based on the quality of comparison with measurements for water bodies having characteristics similar to those at the site. Actual measurements of sorption characteristics for pertinent radionuclides should be presented for areas of the water body within the influence of the plant. These measurements should reflect seasonal variations of sources and sinks (spatial and grain size) and the physical and chemical properties of the receiving water.

Estimates of sediment movement should be supported by actual field measurements (by the applicant or others). Events and processes affecting sediment movement and deposition (e.g., floods, storms, wave activity, and estuarine stratification) should be considered. Changes in the character of the receiving water that would influence sediment transport (e.g., dams, jetties, groins, and shoreline changes) should be considered.

LIST OF SYMBOLS

Symbol	Description
A	Cross-sectional area of river or estuary
b	Width of estuary at water surface
B	Width of river
C	Concentration of constituent in water
C_E	Concentration in epilimnion of stratified impoundment
C_h	Chezy resistance coefficient
C_H	Concentration in hypolimnion of stratified impoundment
C_i	Input concentration in the upper layer of a stratified impoundment
C_i'	Input concentration to the lower layer of a stratified impoundment
C_i''	Input concentration for the total impoundment
C_o	Steady-state concentration of a nondecaying substance
C_T	Concentration in total impoundment at time of turnover
C_{SS}	Steady-state concentration of a decaying substance
d	Depth of river
D	Diffusion factor
D_F	Dilution factor
E	Sectionally averaged, one-dimensional longitudinal dispersion coefficient
E_L	Estuarine, sectionally and tidally averaged, one-dimensional longitudinal dispersion coefficient
E_D	Estuary number (dimensionless coefficient)
f	Coriolis parameter
F_D	Densimetric Froude number at downstream boundary of estuary
g	Acceleration of gravity
H	Depth in estuary or open coast measured from water surface to bottom
K	Empirical coefficient used in description of mixing in salinity intrusion region of an estuary
K_x, K_y	Vertically averaged, two-dimensional turbulent diffusion coefficients in x and y directions, respectively
ℓ	Distance from point of maximum velocity to further bank in river flow
L	Length of estuary

LIST OF SYMBOLS (Continued)

Symbol	Description
M	Quantity of radioactivity released in a pulse discharge
n	Manning's coefficient
N	Dimensionless estuarine freshwater velocity
P_T	Tidal prism
q	Cumulative river discharge measured from near shore
Q	Total river discharge
$\tilde{q}$	Dimensionless cumulative river discharge
q_b	Flow rate of blowdown through the pond
Q_f	Freshwater volumetric discharge rate in estuary
q_i	Inflow to the upper layer of a reservoir
q_i'	Inflow to the lower layer of a reservoir
q_i''	Inflow to the total reservoir
q_p	Plant pumping rate
q_s	Cumulative river discharge rate at position of point source
$\tilde{q}_s$	Dimensionless cumulative river discharge rate at position of point source
q_{s1}, q_{s2}	Cumulative river discharges at beginning and end of line source, respectively
R	Recirculation factor for impoundments
R_h	Hydraulic radius
S	Salinity in estuary
S_o	Salinity at downstream boundary of estuary
t	Time
t_d	Duration of pulse discharge
T	Tidal period
$t_{1/2}$	Half-life of radionuclide
u	Velocity in x direction
$\bar{u}$	Sectional mean velocity in x direction
u'	Deviation from sectional mean velocity $\bar{u}$
U	Vertically averaged velocity in x direction
$\bar{U}$	Sectionally averaged longitudinal velocity in river or estuary
U_f	Sectionally averaged fresh water velocity in estuary
U_t	RMS velocity in an oscillating flow
u^*	Shear velocity

LIST OF SYMBOLS (Continued)

Symbol	Description
v	Velocity in y direction
V	Vertically averaged velocity in y direction
V_E	Volume of epilimnion in stratified impoundment
V_H	Volume of hypolimnion in stratified impoundment
V_{max}	Maximum local tidal velocity
V_T	Total volume of impoundment
W	Rate of radioactivity addition, in Ci/sec
x	Longitudinal coordinate
$\tilde{x}$	Dimensionless longitudinal coordinate
y	Lateral coordinate
y_s	Lateral position of a point source
y_{s1}, y_{s2}	Lateral positions of beginning and end of line source in cartesian coordinates
z	Vertical coordinate
z_s	Vertical position of a point source
α	Dimensionless coefficient
β	Dimensionless coefficient
Γ	Dimensionless cross-sectionally averaged concentration
Γ_{max}	Γ at the source position
ε_y	Lateral turbulent diffusion coefficient
ε_z	Vertical turbulent diffusion coefficient
ζ	Water surface elevation above undisturbed datum
θ	Dimensionless time (ratio of time to flushing time)
λ	Radioactive decay coefficient ($\ln 2/t_{\frac{1}{2}}$)
ξ	Dimensionless longitudinal distance from source in a one-dimensional estuary
σ_y, σ_z	Standard deviations of radionuclide concentrations in y- and z-directions, respectively
τ	Ratio of the half-life to the impoundment flushing time
τ_x^s, τ_y^s	x and y components of surface wind stress
χ	Nondecaying concentration
$\tilde{\chi}$	Dimensionless nondecaying concentration

CITED REFERENCES

1. G. H. Jirka, G. Abraham, and D. R. F. Harleman, Massachusetts Institute of Technology, "An Assessment of Techniques for Hydrothermal Prediction," U.S. Nuclear Regulatory Commission, NUREG-0044, 1976. (Copies may be obtained from the National Technical Information Service, Springfield, Va.)

2. W. E. Dunn, A. J. Policastro, and R. A. Paddock, "Surface Thermal Plumes: Evaluation of Mathematical Models for the Near and Complete Field," Parts One and Two, Argonne National Laboratory, Energy and Environmental Systems Division, ANL/WR-75-3, 1975.

3. K. D. Stolzenbach and D. R. F. Harleman, "An Analytical and Experimental Investigation of Surface Discharges of Heated Water," Ralph M. Parsons Laboratory for Water Resources and Hydrodynamics, Massachusetts Institute of Technology, Rep. No. 135, 1971.

4. K. D. Stolzenbach, E. E. Adams, and D. R. F. Harleman, "A User's Manual for Three-Dimensional Heated Surface Discharge Conditions," Ralph M. Parsons Laboratory for Water Resources and Hydrodynamics, Massachusetts Institute of Technology, Rep. No. 156, 1972.

5. E. A. Prych, "A Warm Water Effluent Analyzed as a Buoyant Surface Jet," Sveriges Meteorologiska och Hydrologiska Institut, Serie Hydrologi, nr 21, Stockholm, Sweden, 1972.

6. M. A. Shirazi and L. R. Davis, "Workbook of Thermal Plume Prediction Vol. 2 - Surface Discharge," U.S. Environmental Protection Agency, National Environmental Research Center, Environmental Protection Technology Series, Rep. No. EPA-R2-72-005b, Corvallis, Ore., 1974.

7. D. W. Pritchard, "Design and Siting Criteria for Once-Through Cooling Systems," presented at American Institute of Chemical Engineers, 68th Annual Meeting, Houston, Tex., 1971.

8. D. W. Pritchard, "Fate of and Effect of Excess Heat Discharged into Lake Michigan with Specific Application to the Condenser Cooling Water Discharge from the Zion Nuclear Power Station," Testimony at the AEC Licensing Hearings for the Zion Nuclear Power Station Operating Permit, Chicago, Ill., 1973.

9. G. H. Jirka and D. R. F. Harleman, "The Mechanics of Submerged Multiport Diffusers for Buoyant Discharges in Shallow Water," Ralph M. Parsons Laboratory for Water Resources and Hydrodynamics, Massachusetts Institute of Technology, Rep. No. 169, 1973.

10. J. H. W. Lee, G. H. Jirka, and D. R. F. Harleman, "Stability and Mixing of a Vertical Round Buoyant Jet in Shallow Water," Ralph M. Parsons Laboratory for Water Resources and Hydrodynamics, Massachusetts Institute of Technology, Rep. No. 195, 1974.

11. R. C. Y. Koh and L. N. Fan, "Mathematical Models for the Prediction of Temperature Distributions Resulting from the Discharge of Heated Water in Large Bodies of Water," Water Pollution Control Research Series, Rep. No. 16130DW010/70, 1970.

12. E. Hirst, "Analysis of Round, Turbulent, Buoyant Jet Discharged to Flowing Stratified Ambients," Oak Ridge National Laboratory, Rep. No. 4685, 1971.

13. W. W. Sayre and F. M. Chang, "A Laboratory Investigation of Open-Channel Dispersion Processes for Dissolved, Suspended, and Floating Dispersants," U.S. Geological Survey, Professional Paper 433-E, 1968.

14. N. Yotsukura and E. D. Cobb, "Transverse Diffusion of Solutes in Natural Streams," U.S. Geological Survey, Professional Paper 582-C, 1972.

15. N. Yotsukura, "A Two-Dimensional Temperature Model for a Thermally Loaded River with Steady Discharge," Proceedings, 11th Annual Environmental and Water Resources Engineering Conference, Vanderbilt University, Nashville, Tenn., 1972.

16. N. Yotsukura and W. W. Sayre, "Transverse Mixing in Natural Channels," Water Resources Research, Vol. 12, No. 4, August 1976.

17. F. M. Henderson, Open Channel Flow, New York: Macmillan Company, 1959.

18. V. T. Chow, Open Channel Hydraulics, New York: McGraw-Hill Book Company, 1959.

19. J. W. Elder, "The Dispersion of Marked Fluid in Turbulent Shear Flow," Journal of Fluid Mechanics, No. 5, 1959, pp. 544-60.

20. H. B. Fischer, "The Effects of Bends on Dispersion in Streams," Water Resources Research 5(2), 1969, pp. 496-506.

21. N. Yotsukura, H. B. Fischer, and W. W. Sayre, "Measurement of Mixing Characteristics of the Missouri River Between Sioux City, Iowa, and Plattsmouth, Nebraska," U.S. Geological Survey, Water-Supply Paper 1899-G, 1970.

22. W. W. Sayre and T. P. Yeh, "Transverse Mixing Characteristics of the Missouri River Downstream from the Cooper Nuclear Station," University of Iowa, Iowa Institute of Hydraulic Research, Rep. No. 145, Iowa City, Iowa, 1973.

23. G. T. Csanady, "Dispersal of Effluents in the Great Lakes," Water Research, vol. 4, 1970, pp. 79-114.

24. Stone and Webster, "1970 Lake Temperature and Current Studies," Report to Power Authority, State of New York, AEC Docket No. 50-333, 1971.

25. G. T. Csanady, "Response of Large Stratified Lakes to Wind," Journal of Physical Oceanography, vol. 2, no. 1, 1972, pp. 3-13.

26. G. T. Csanady, "The Coastal Boundary Layer in Lake Ontario: Part II. The Summer-Fall Regime," Journal of Physical Oceanography, vol. 2, no. 2, 1972, pp. 168-176.

27. C. R. Murthy and G. T. Csanady, "Experimental Studies of Relative Diffusion in Lake Huron," Journal of Physical Oceanography, vol. 1, 1971, pp. 77-24.

28. T. R. Sundaram and R. G. Rehm, "The Seasonal Thermal Structure of Deep Temperate Lakes," Tellus, vol. 25, 1973, pp. 157-168.

29. J. J. Leendertse, "A Water-Quality Simulation Model for Well-Mixed Estuaries and Coastal Seas: Volume I, Principles of Computation," The Rand Corporation, No. RM-6230-RC, 1970.

30. J. J. Leendertse and E. C. Gritton, "A Water-Quality Simulation Model for Well-Mixed Estuaries and Coastal Seas: Volume II, Computation Procedures," The Rand Corporation, No. R-708-NYC, 1971.

31. J. J. Leendertse and E. C. Gritton, "A Water-Quality Simulation Model for Well-Mixed Estuaries and Coastal Seas: Volume III, Jamaica Bay Simulation," The Rand Corporation, No. R-709-NYC, 1971.

32. J. J. Leendertse, "A Water-Quality Simulation Model for Well-Mixed Estuaries and Coastal Seas: Volume IV, Jamaica Bay Tidal Flows," The Rand Corporation, No. R-1009-NYC, 1972.

33. E. C. Gritton, "A Water-Quality Simulation Model for Well-Mixed Estuaries and Coastal Seas: Volume V, Jamaica Bay Rainstorms," The Rand Corporation, No. R-1010-NYC, 1972.

34. J. J. Leendertse and S. K. Liu, "A Water-Quality Simulation Model for Well-Mixed Estuaries and Coastal Seas: Volume VI, Simulation, Observation, and State Estimation," The Rand Corporation, No. R-1586-NYC, 1974.

35. R. B. Codell, "Digital Simulation of Thermal Effluent Dispersion in Rivers, Lakes, and Estuaries," Ph.D. Dissertation, Lehigh University, 1973.

36. L. A. Loziuk, J. C. Anderson, and T. Belytschko, "Hydrothermal Analysis by Finite Element Method," Proceedings of the American Society of Civil Engineers, Journal of the Hydraulics Division, vol. 98 (HY11), 1972.

37. A. H. Eraslan, "Two-Dimensional, Discrete Element, Far Field Model for Thermal Impact Analysis of Power Plant Discharges in Coastal and Offshore Regions," Oak Ridge National Laboratory, Rep. No. 4940, 1975.

38. N. H. Brooks, "Diffusion of Sewage Effluent in an Ocean Current," Proceedings, 1st International Conference on Waste Disposal in the Marine Environment, Pergamon Press, 1960.

39. J. E. Foxworthy, "Eddy Diffusivity and the Four-Thirds Law in Near-Shore (Coastal Waters)," The Allan Hancock Foundation, University of Southern California, Report 68-1, 1969.

40. J. E. Foxworthy, "Eddy Diffusion and Bacterial Reduction in Waste Fields in the Ocean," The Allan Hancock Foundation, University of Southern California, Report 69-1, 1969.

41. R. E. Stewart, H. D. Putnam, R. H. Jones, and T. N. Lee, "Diffusion of Sewage Effluent from Ocean Outfall," Proceedings of the American Society of Civil Engineers, Journal of the Sanitary Engineering Division, vol. 97, SA4, 1971.

42. H. H. Carter and A. Okubo, "A Study of the Physical Processes of Movement and Dispersion in the Cape Kennedy Area," Chesapeake Bay Institute, The Johns Hopkins University, Report No. NYO-2973-1, 1965.

43. G. Kullenberg, "Vertical Diffusion in Shallow Waters," Tellus, vol. 23, 1971, pp. 129-135.

44. G. Kullenberg, "Results of Diffusion Experiments in the Upper Reaches of the Sea," Institute of Physical Oceanography, University of Copenhagen, Rep. No. 12, 1971.

45. A. Okubo, "Oceanic Mixing," Chesapeake Bay Institute, Johns Hopkins University, Tech. Rep. 62, Docket No. NYO-3109-49, 1970.

46. D. J. O'Conner and J. P. Lawler, "Mathematical Analysis of Estuarine Pollution," 55th National Meeting, American Institute of Chemical Engineers, Reprint No. 31a, Houston, Tex., 1965.

47. TRACOR, Inc., "Estuarine Modeling, An Assessment," Environmental Protection Agency, Project No. 16070OZV, Contract 14-12-551, 1971.

48. R. L. Crim and N. L. Lovelace, "Auto-Qual Modeling System," U.S. Environmental Protection Agency, EPA-440/9-73-003, Washington, D.C., March 1973.

49. J. E. Dailey and D. R. F. Harleman, "Numerical Model for the Prediction of Transient Water Quality in Estuary Networks," Ralph M. Parsons Laboratory for Water Resources and Hydrodynamics, Massachusetts Institute of Technology, Tech. Rep. 158, 1972.

50. C. H. Lee and D. R. F. Harleman, "One-Dimensional Real Time Model for Estuarine Water Quality Prediction," Water Quality Office, Environmental Protection Agency, Report 16070DGW, Washington, D.C., 1971.

51. A. H. Eraslan, unpublished users manual, "One Dimensional Model," Oak Ridge National Laboratories, 1975.

52. L. J. Hetling and R. L. O'Connell, "Estimating Diffusion Characteristics of Tidal Waters," Department of the Interior, Federal Water Pollution Control Administration, Middle Atlantic Region, CB-SRBP Technical Paper No. 4, 1967.

53. G. I. Taylor, "The Dispersion of Matter in Turbulent Flow in a Pipe," Proc. Royal Society London (A), vol. 223, May 1954.

54. M. L. Thatcher and D. R. F. Harleman, "A Mathematical Model for the Prediction of Unsteady Salinity Intrusion in Estuaries," R. M. Parsons Laboratory, Massachusetts Institute of Technology, Technical Report No. 144, February 1972.

55. H. B. Fischer, "The Mechanics of Dispersion in Natural Streams," Proceedings of the American Society of Civil Engineers, Journal of the Hydraulics Division, No. 93 (HY6), 1967, pp. 187-216.

56. D. S. Trent, "Mathematical Modeling of Transport Processes in Aquatic Systems," Battelle-Pacific Northwest Laboratories, BNWL-SA-5379, Richland, Wash., April 1975.

57. P. J. Ryan and D. R. F. Harleman, "Prediction of the Annual Cycle of Temperature Changes in a Stratified Lake or Reservoir - Mathematical Model and User's Manual," R. M. Parsons Laboratory, Massachusetts Institute of Technology, Report No. 137, 1971.

58. Water Resources Engineers, Inc., "Mathematical Models for the Prediction of Thermal Energy Changes in Impoundments," Walnut Creek, Calif., prepared for the Water Quality Office, Environmental Protection Agency, December 1969.

59. P. J. Ryan and D. R. F. Harleman, "An Analytical and Experimental Study of Transient Cooling Pond Behavior," R. M. Parsons Laboratory, Massachusetts Institute of Technology, Report No. 161, January 1973.

60. U.S. Army Corps of Engineers, "HEC-4, River Flow Simulation," Hydrologic Engineering Center, Davis, Calif., 1971.

61. L. G. Hulman, "Regional Water Supply Systems Analysis for a Megalopolis," paper presented at the August 1971 ASCE Hydraulics Division Specialty Conference, Iowa City, Iowa, 1971.

62. L. G. Hulman and D. D. Erickson, "Delaware River Basin Modeling," presented at the 17th Annual ASCE Specialty Conference, Logan, Utah, August 1969.

63. U. S. Army Corps of Engineers, "HEC-3, Reservoir Analysis," Hydrologic Engineering Center, Davis, Calif., 1971.

ADDITIONAL REFERENCES

SEDIMENT UPTAKE MODELS

Selected Mathematical Models and Theoretical Development

1. Oak Ridge National Laboratories, ORNL-TM-4751, "A System Analysis Model for Calculating Radionuclide Transport Between Receiving Waters and Bottom Sediments," R. S. Booth, Oak Ridge, Tenn., April 1975.

2. E. K. Duursma and C. J. Bosch, "Theoretical, Experimental, and Field Studies Concerning Diffusion of Radioisotopes in Sediments and Suspended Particles of the Sea," Netherlands Journal of Sea Research, vol. 4, no. 4, 1970, pp. 395-469.

3. D. E. Fields, "Modification of the Unified Transport Model to Allow for Sediment Transport and Chemical Exchange," Proceedings of the Second Annual NSF-RANN Trace Contaminants Conference, Asilomar, Calif., August 1974.

4. J. F. Fletcher and W. L. Dotson, "HERMES - A Digital Computer Code for Estimating Regional Radiological Effects from the Nuclear Power Industry," Hanford Engineering Development Lab., Hanford, Wash., December 1971.

5. E. F. Gloyna, A. A. Yousef, and T. J. Padden, "Radionuclide Transport and Responses to Organic Stress in a Research Flume," Advances in Water Pollution Research, vol. 1, no. 1, Pergamon Press, Great Britain, 1971.

6. Geological Survey Professional Paper 433-F, "Role of Certain Stream Sediment Components in Radioion Sorption," E. A. Jenne and J. S. Wahlberg, U.S. Government Printing Office, 1968.

7. Oak Ridge National Laboratories, ORNL-NSF-EATC-7, "A User's Manual for the FORTRAN IV Version of the Wisconsin Hydrologic Transport Model," M. R. Patterson et al., Oak Ridge, Tenn., October 1974.

8. R. J. Raridon et al., "Computer Model for Chemical Exchange in the Stream System," Proceedings of the First Annual NSF Trace Contaminant Conference, Conf-730802, 1973.

9. Geological Survey Professional Paper 433-A, "Uptake and Transport of Radionuclides by Stream Sediments," W. W. Sayre, H. P. Guy, and A. R. Chamberlain, U. S. Government Printing Office, 1963.

10. Center for Research in Water Resources, Technical Report 19, "Radioactivity Transport in Water, Summary Report," Y. A. Yousef, A. Kudo, and E. F. Gloyna, University of Texas, Austin, Texas, 1970.

Selected Field Studies, Surveillance Programs, and Data

1. Oak Ridge National Laboratories, ORNL-3721, TID4500, "Concentrations, Total Stream Loads, and Mass Transport in the Clinch and Tennessee Rivers," M. A. Churchill et al., (and others in this series), Oak Ridge National Laboratories, August 1965.

2. C. Collison and N. F. Shimp, "Trace Elements in Bottom Sediments from Upper Peoria Lake, Middle Illinois River," Environmental Geology Notes, Illinois State Geological Survey, No. 56, September 1972.

3. S. Davies, F. Cosolito, and M. Eisenbud, "Radioactivity in the Hudson River," Proceedings First Symposium on Hudson River Ecology, Hudson River Valley Commission of New York, 1966, p. 289.

4. National Academy of Sciences, "Marine Sediments and Radioactivity," Chapter Six of "Radioactivity in the Marine Environment," E. K. Duursma and M. G. Gross, National Academy of Sciences, Washington, D.C., 1971, pp. 147-160.

5. U. S. Environmental Protection Agency, RD No. 71-1, "Radiological Surveillance Studies at a Pressurized Water Nuclear Power Reactor," B. Kahn et al., National Environmental Research Center, Cincinnati, Ohio, August 1971.

6. A. Lerman, "Time to Chemical Steady-States in Lakes and Oceans," Nonequilibrium Systems in Natural Water Chemistry: Symposium of the American Chemical Society, Houston, Texas, February 24-25, 1970, Advances in Chemistry Series 106, American Chemical Society, Washington, D.C., 1971.

7. A. Lerman and G. J. Brunskill, "Migration of Major Constituents from Lake Sediments into Lake Water and Its Bearing on Lake Water Composition," Limnology and Oceanography, vol. 16, no. 6, November 1971, pp. 880-890.

8. A. Lerman and R. R. Weiler, "Diffusion and Accumulation of Chloride and Sodium in Lake Ontario Sediments," Earth and Planetary Science Letter, vol. 10, 1970, pp. 150-156.

9. T. F. Lomenick and T. Tamura, "Naturally Occurring Fixation of Cesium-137 on Sediments of Lacustrine Origin," Soil Science Society of America Proceedings, vol. 29, no. 4, July-August 1965, pp. 383-387.

10. F. T. Manheim, "The Diffusion of Ions in Unconsolidated Sediments," Earth and Planetary Science Letter, vol. 9, 1970, pp. 307-309.

11. D. K. Phelps, "Partitioning of the Stable Elements Fe, Zn, Se, and Sm Within a Benthic Community, Anasco Bay, Puerto Rico," Proceedings of the Symposium on Radioecological Concentration Processes, April 22-29, 1966, Stockholm, ed. by B. Aberg and F. P. Hungate, Pergamon Press, pp. 721-733.

12. G. K. Riel, "Radioactive Cesium in Estuaries," Radiological Health Data and Reports, December 1970, pp. 659-665.

13. N. I. Sax et al, "Radioecological Surveillance of the Waterways Around a Nuclear Fuels Reprocessing Plant," Radiological Health Data and Reports, vol. 10, no. 7, July 1969, pp. 289-296.

14. U. S. Environmental Protection Agency, Radiological Health Data and Reports, (published monthly 1959-74), Washington, D.C.

15. U. S. Atomic Energy Reports, BNWL-1341, and 1341-Appended. "Evaluation of Radiological Conditions in the Vicinity of Hanford for 1968," C. B. Wilson (ed.), Pacific Northwest Labs, Richland, Wash. (and others in this series back to 1961), 1970.

16. G. K. Riel, "Distribution of Fallout of Cesium 137 in the Chesapeake Bay," Second International Symposium on Natural Radiation Environment, Houston, Texas, August 1972.

Selected Sediment Transport Methodology

Sedimentation Committee, Hydraulics Division

1. American Society of Civil Engineers, "Sediment Discharge Formulas," Journal of the Hydraulics Division, ASCE, vol. 97, no. HY4, April 1971.

2. U. S. Army Coastal Engineering Research Center, "Shore Protection Manual," 1973.

3. U. S. Geological Survey, "Quality of Surface Waters of the United States," U.S. Government Printing Office, all years.

Selected Symposia

1. Proceedings, Symposium on Disposal of Radioactive Wastes into Seas, Oceans, and Surface Waters, International Atomic Energy Agency, Vienna, Austria, 1966.

2. Proceedings, Second National Symposium on Radio Ecology, Ann Arbor, Mich., 1967.

3. Proceedings, Symposium on Environmental Surveillance in the Vicinity of Nuclear Facilities, W. C. Reinig (ed), Charles Thomas Corp., Springfield, Ill., 1968.

4. Proceedings, Fifth Annual Health Physics Society Midyear Topical Symposium, "Health Physics Aspects of Nuclear Facility Siting," Idaho Falls, Idaho, 1970.

5. Proceedings, Third National Symposium, Radioecology, Oak Ridge, Tennessee, May 10-12, 1971.

6. Proceedings, International Symposium, Radioecology Applied to the Protection of Man and the Environment, Rome, Sept. 1971, EUR 4800-d-f-i-e, Luxembourg, May 1972.

Index

INDEX

A

B

C

D

E

F

G

H

I

J

K

L

M

N

Q

R

S

T

U

V

W

X

Y

Z